Harden's

London Restaurants

2019

Survey driven reviews of 1,700 restaurants

28th edition

Put us in your pocket!

Download our app for iPhone or Android

© **Harden's Limited 2018**

ISBN 978-0-9929408-1-2

British Library Cataloguing-in-Publication data:
a catalogue record for this book is available from
the British Library.

Printed in Italy by Legoprint

Assistant editors: Bruce Millar, Antonia Russell

Harden's Limited
Beta Space, 25 Holywell Row, London, EC2A 4XE

Would restaurateurs (and PRs) please address
communications to 'Editorial' at the above address,
or ideally by email to: editorial@hardens.com

CONTENTS

RATINGS & PRICES

Ratings

Our rating system does not tell you – as most guides do – that expensive restaurants are often better than cheap ones! What we do is compare each restaurant's performance – as judged by the average ratings awarded by reporters in the survey – with other similarly-priced restaurants. This approach has the advantage that it helps you find – whatever your budget for any particular meal – where you will get the best 'bang for your buck'.

The following qualities are assessed:

F — Food
S — Service
A — Ambience

The rating indicates that, *in comparison with other restaurants in the same price-bracket,* performance is…

5 — Exceptional
4 — Very good
3 — Good
2 — Average
1 — Poor

Prices

The price shown for each restaurant is the cost for one (1) person of an average three-course dinner with half a bottle of house wine and coffee, any cover charge, service and VAT. Lunch is often cheaper. With BYO restaurants, we have assumed that two people share a £7 bottle of off-licence wine.

Telephone number – all numbers are '020' numbers.

Map reference – shown immediately after the telephone number.

Full postcodes – for non-group restaurants, the first entry in the 'small print' at the end of each listing, so you can set your sat-nav.

Website and Twitter – shown in the small print, where applicable.

Last orders time – listed after the website (if applicable); Sunday may be up to 90 minutes earlier.

Opening hours – unless otherwise stated, restaurants are open for lunch and dinner seven days a week.

Credit and debit cards – unless otherwise stated, Mastercard, Visa, Amex and Maestro are accepted.

Dress – where appropriate, the management's preferences concerning patrons' dress are given.

Food Made Good Star Rating – the sustainability index, as calculated by the Sustainable Restaurant Association – see page 8 for more information.

HOW THIS GUIDE IS WRITTEN

Nearly 30 years of the Harden's survey

This guide is based on our 28th annual survey of what 'ordinary' diners-out think of London's restaurants.

This year, the total number of reporters in our combined London/UK survey, conducted mainly online, numbered 8,000, and, between them, they contributed 50,000 individual reports.

At a time when a recent study suggested that as many as 1/3 of the reviews on TripAdvisor are paid for by the restaurants they cover, we believe there is an ever-greater need for trusted sources such as the Harden's annual diner survey. For while obviously folks can attempt to stuff the Harden's ballot too, the high degree of editorial oversight plus the historical data we have both about the restaurants and also about those commenting makes it much harder to succeed. In this way Harden's can socially source restaurant feedback, but – vitally – curate it fully as we do so. It is this careful curation which provides extra 'value-added' for diners.

How we determine the ratings

In the great majority of cases, ratings are arrived at statistically. This essentially involves 'ranking' the average survey rating each restaurant achieves in the survey – for food, service and ambience – against the average ratings of the other establishments in the same price-bracket.

(This is essentially like football leagues, with the most expensive restaurants going in the top league and the cheaper ones in lower leagues. The restaurant's ranking *within its own particular league* determines its ratings.)

How we write the reviews

The tone of each review and the ratings are largely determined by the ranking of the establishment concerned, which we derive as described above.

At the margin, we may also pay some regard to the proportion of positive nominations (such as for 'favourite restaurant') compared to negative nominations (such as for 'most overpriced').

To explain why a restaurant has been rated as it has, we extract snippets from survey comments ("enclosed in double quotes"). On well-known restaurants, we receive several hundred reports, and a short summary cannot possibly do individual justice to all of them.

What we seek to do – *without any regard to our own personal opinions* – is to illustrate the key themes which have emerged in our analysis of the collective view.

A sea change is taking place in our attitude towards what and how we eat and it's unlikely the tide will turn any time soon. The catalyst? Sir David Attenborough's Blue Planet II series in which he revealed the devastating scale of destruction plastic is wreaking on our precious oceans.

thesra.org

SUSTAINABLE RESTAURANT ASSOCIATION

Chefs, restaurateurs and crucially the dining public have responded. In a survey of Harden's diners in January 2018, less than one in five said they were satisfied with the efforts of the restaurants they ate in to protect the environment.

As well as the giant wave of restaurants and bars removing millions of plastic straws, many have gone much further, taking the opportunity to review what single-use plastic items they really need and are on the way to using more sustainable alternatives.

The shift away from stereotypical, meat-centric offerings continues apace too. Record numbers of participants in events like Veganuary have seen a general move towards more dishes celebrating the joys of veg. In that same survey, almost nine out of ten said they wanted restaurants to focus on creating menus that help them to make sustainable choices.

Faced with a full menu of dishes to choose from, it can be hard to use the power of your appetite wisely. That's why, in 2018 the SRA launched One Planet Plate, a movement to put sustainability on the menu. A One Planet Plate is effectively the chef's sustainable special – his or her recommendation whether it celebrates local produce, features more veg, has a lower carbon footprint, includes better meat, showcases sustainably sourced seafood, or wastes no food. More than 2,000 restaurants offering these dishes and their recipes can be found at www.oneplanetplate.org.

We've supported the SRA since soon after their launch in 2010 because, like them, we believe in helping diners vote with their forks for a better food future.

Look out for those restaurants in the guide with an SRA Sustainability Rating, either One, Two or Three Stars, achieved by proving they are doing these ten things:

Support Global Farmers	Source Fish Responsibly
Value Natural Resources	Serve More Veg & Better Meat
Treat People Fairly	Reduce Reuse Recycle
Feed Children Well	Waste no Food
Celebrate Local	Support the Community

w: thesra.org
Twitter: @the_SRA
Instagram: @foodmadegood

SURVEY FAQs

Q. How do you find your reporters?
A. Anyone can take part. Simply register at
www.hardens.com. Actually, we find that many people who
complete our survey each year have taken part before.
So it's really more a question of a very large and ever-
evolving panel, or jury, than a random 'poll'.

Q. Wouldn't a random sample be better?
A. That's really a theoretical question, as there is no
obvious way, still less a cost-efficient one, by which one
could identify a random sample of the guests at each of, say,
5,000 establishments across the UK, and get them to take
part in any sort of survey. And anyway, which is likely to be
more useful: a sample of the views of everyone who's been
to a particular place, or the views of people who are
interested enough in eating-out to have volunteered their
feedback?

Q. What sort of people take part?
A. A roughly 60/40 male/female split, from all adult age-
groups. As you might expect – as eating out is not the
cheapest activity – reporters tend to have white collar jobs
(some at very senior levels). By no means, however, is that
always the case.

Q. Do people ever try to stuff the ballot?
A. Of course they do! A rising number of efforts are
weeded out every year. But stuffing the ballot is not as
trivial a task as some people seem to think: the survey
results throw up clear natural voting patterns against which
'campaigns' tend to stand out.

Q. Aren't inspections the best way to run a guide?
A. It is often assumed – even by commentators who ought
to know better – that inspections are some sort of 'gold
standard'. There is no doubt that the inspection model
clearly has potential strengths, but one of its prime
weaknesses is that it is incredibly expensive. Take the most
famous practitioner of the 'inspection model', Michelin. It
doesn't claim to visit each and every entry listed in its guide
annually. Even once! And who are the inspectors? Often
they are catering professionals, whose likes and dislikes may
be very different from the establishment's natural customer
base. On any restaurant of note, however, Harden's typically
has somewhere between dozens and hundreds of reports
each and every year from exactly the type of people the
restaurant relies upon to stay in business. We believe that
such feedback, carefully analysed, is far more revealing and
accurate than an occasional 'professional' inspection.

SURVEY MOST MENTIONED

These are the restaurants which were most frequently mentioned by reporters. (Last year's position is given in brackets.) An asterisk* indicates the first appearance in the list of a recently opened restaurant.

1   J Sheekey (1)
2   Clos Maggiore (2)
3   Chez Bruce (3)
4   Le Gavroche (5)
5   Scott's (4)
6   The Ledbury (6)
7   Gymkhana (8)
8   Gauthier Soho (9)
9   La Trompette (12)
10 The Wolseley (7)

11 Brasserie Zédel (10)
12 The River Café (15)
13 Core by Clare Smyth (-)
14 The Ivy (-)
15 A Wong (34)
16 The Delaunay (11)
17 Andrew Edmunds (13)
18 Trinity (23)
19 Le Caprice (26)
20 Jamavar (-)

21 The Cinnamon Club (16)
22 La Poule au Pot (22)
23 Pollen Street Social (20)
24 Bocca Di Lupo (17)
25 The Five Fields (32)
26 Enoteca Turi (40)
27 Benares (21)
28 Bleeding Heart Restaurant (31)
29 Noble Rot (29)
30 Elystan Street (-)

31 Bentley's (33)
32 Mere (-)
33 Pied À Terre (37)
34 Moro (38)
35 Marcus, The Berkeley (-)
36 Dinner, Mandarin Oriental (18)
37 Gordon Ramsay (24)
38 Fera at Claridge's (14)
39 Oxo Tower (-)
40 The Ritz (-)

SURVEY NOMINATIONS

Top gastronomic experience

1   The Ledbury (1)
2   Le Gavroche (3)
3   Chez Bruce (2)
4   La Trompette (8)
5   Gauthier Soho (4)
6   Core by Clare Smyth (-)
7   Trinity (-)
8   Pied À Terre (-)
9   The Frog (-)
10 The Five Fields (7)

Favourite

1   Chez Bruce (1)
2   Barrafina (-)
3   The Ledbury (8)
4   Gauthier Soho (10)
5   The Wolseley (6)
6   Le Caprice (-)
7   Le Gavroche (4)
8   La Trompette (3)
9   J Sheekey (2)
10 The Ivy (-)

Best for business

1   The Wolseley (1)
2   The Delaunay (2)
3   Hawksmoor (Group) (9)
4   Scott's (4)
5   Bleeding Heart Restaurant (3)
6   Ivy Grills & Brasseries (-)
7   The Don (10)
8   Côte (-)
9   Savoy Grill (7)
10 The Ivy (-)

Best for romance

1   Clos Maggiore (1)
2   La Poule au Pot (2)
3   Andrew Edmunds (3)
4   Bleeding Heart Restaurant (5)
5   Le Gavroche (7)
6   Gauthier Soho (4)
7   Chez Bruce (10)
8   Café du Marché (-)
9   Galvin at Windows (-)
10 Galvin La Chapelle (-)

Best breakfast/brunch

1   The Wolseley (1)
2   The Delaunay (2)
3   Ivy Grills & Brasseries (3)
4   Granger & Co (6)
5   Dishoom (-)
6   Caravan (5)
7   Breakfast Club (10)
8   Côte (Group) (-)
9   The Ivy Café (-)
10 Cecconi's (-)

Best bar/pub food

1   Harwood Arms (2)
2   The Anchor & Hope (1)
3   Bull & Last (3)
4   The Anglesea Arms (4)
5   The Ladbroke Arms (10)
5= The Wells Tavern (-)
7   The Marksman (9)
7= Canton Arms (-)
9   Churchill Arms (-)
10 The Cow (-)

Most disappointing cooking

1   Ivy Grills & Brasseries (-)
2   Oxo Tower (1)
3   The Ivy (-)
4   Jamie's Italian (-)
5   Alain Ducasse (3)
6   Brasserie Blanc (-)
7   Gordon Ramsay (-)
8   Sexy Fish (2)
9   Chiltern Firehouse (4)
10 Polpo (-)

Most overpriced restaurant

1   The River Café (1)
2   Sexy Fish (2)
3   Oxo Tower (4)
4   Gordon Ramsay (3)
5   The Chiltern Firehouse (6)
6   Ivy Grills & Brasseries (-)
7   Alain Ducasse (7)
8   Le Gavroche (8)
9   Sushisamba (-)
10 Dinner, Mandarin Oriental (5)

SURVEY HIGHEST RATINGS

FOOD

SERVICE

£100+

	FOOD		SERVICE
1	Texture	1	The Five Fields
2	The Araki	2	The Araki
3	The Ledbury	3	Le Gavroche
4	La Dame de Pic London	4	Marianne
5	Core by Clare Smyth	5	Core by Clare Smyth

£75–£99

1	Sushi Tetsu	1	Noizé
2	Zuma	2	Chez Bruce
3	Trinity	3	Trinity
4	La Trompette	4	Wiltons
5	Chez Bruce	5	Hide

£60–£74

1	Brat	1	Brat
2	Quilon	2	Cabotte
3	Pidgin	3	Oslo Court
4	Jikoni	4	Quilon
5	Anglo	5	The Game Bird

£45–£59

1	A Wong	1	Babur
2	Som Saa	2	The Anglesea Arms
3	Jin Kichi	3	The Oystermen
4	Babur	4	Lemonia
5	José	5	Six Portland Road

£44 or less

1	Padella	1	Department of Coffee
2	Kiln	2	Paradise Hampstead
3	Farang	3	Toffs
4	Department of Coffee	4	Padella
5	Tayyabs	5	Ma Goa

SURVEY HIGHEST RATINGS

AMBIENCE

1	The Ritz
2	Sketch (Lecture Rm)
3	Le Gavroche
4	Pied À Terre
5	Club Gascon

1	L'Escargot
2	Clos Maggiore
3	Duck & Waffle
4	Bob Bob Ricard
5	Min Jiang

1	La Poule au Pot
2	Brat
3	The Wolseley
4	Fredericks
5	Quo Vadis

1	The Anglesea Arms
2	Andrew Edmunds
3	José
4	The Wigmore
5	Babur

1	Brasserie Zédel
2	Padella
3	Churchill Arms
4	Kiln
5	Paradise Hampstead

OVERALL

1	The Ledbury
2	The Five Fields
3	The Araki
4	Le Gavroche
5	Core by Clare Smyth

1	Chez Bruce
2	Sushi Tetsu
3	Noizé
4	Trinity
5	Roux at the Landau

1	Brat
2	Cabotte
3	Jikoni
4	Quo Vadis
5	Smith's Wapping

1	Babur
2	The Anglesea Arms
3	José
4	Som Saa
5	A Wong

1	Padella
2	Department of Coffee
3	Paradise Hampstead
4	Kiln
5	Brasserie Zédel

SURVEY BEST BY CUISINE

These are the restaurants which received the best average food ratings (excluding establishments with a small or notably local following).

Where the most common types of cuisine are concerned, we present the results in two price-brackets. For less common cuisines, we list the top three, regardless of price.

For further information about restaurants which are particularly notable for their food, see the cuisine lists starting on page 244. These indicate, using an asterisk*, restaurants which offer exceptional or very good food.

British, Modern

£60 and over
1 The Ledbury
2 Core by Clare Smyth
3 The Five Fields
4 Trinity
5 The Frog

Under £60
1 Brat
2 The Anglesea Arms
3 Lupins
4 The Dairy
5 Six Portland Road

French

£60 and over
1 La Dame de Pic London
2 La Trompette
3 Le Gavroche
4 Club Gascon
5 The Square

Under £60
1 Cigalon
2 The Wells Tavern
3 Casse-Croute
4 The Coach
5 Café du Marché

Italian/Mediterranean

£60 and over
1 Clarkes
2 Murano
3 The River Café
4 Olivomare
5 Sartoria

Under £60
1 Padella
2 L'Amorosa
3 Margot
4 Oak
5 San Carlo Cicchetti

Indian & Pakistani

£60 and over
1 Quilon
2 Indian Accent
3 Jikoni
4 Chutney Mary
5 Gymkhana

Under £60
1 Dastaan
2 Lahore Kebab House
3 Babur
4 Ragam
5 Darjeeling Express

Chinese

£60 and over

1. Min Jiang
2. Hunan
3. Yauatcha
4. Hakkasan
5. Park Chinois

Under £60

1. A Wong
2. The Four Seasons
3. Singapore Garden
4. Yming
5. Royal China

Japanese

£60 and over

1. The Araki
2. Sushi Tetsu
3. Dinings
4. Zuma
5. Roka

Under £60

1. Takahashi
2. Atari-Ya
3. Jin Kichi
4. Tsunami
5. Pham Sushi

British, Traditional

1. St John Smithfield
2. Wiltons
3. Scott's

Vegetarian

1. Vanilla Black
2. Gate
3. Ceremony

Burgers, etc

1. Bleecker Burger
2. Patty and Bun
3. Honest Burgers

Pizza

1. Yard Sale Pizza
2. Pizza East
3. Homeslice

Fish & Chips

1. Bradys
2. Toffs
3. North Sea Fish

Thai

1. Som Saa
2. Kiln
3. Sukho Fine Thai

Steaks & Grills

1. Blacklock
2. Goodman
3. Zelman Meats

Fish & Seafood

1. Texture
2. Angler
3. Outlaws at the Capital

Fusion

1. Twist
2. Bubbledogs (KT)
3. 108 Garage

Spanish

1. Barrafina
2. José
3. Cambio de Tercio

Turkish

1. Mangal 1
2. Oklava
3. Le Bab

Lebanese

1. Crocker's Folly
2. Maroush
3. Meza

THE RESTAURANT SCENE

Record closures and 'churn'

There are 167 newcomers in this year's guide. Although this is the fourth-best year we have recorded, it is lower than for all three preceding years: significantly down from 2017's record of 200, and taking openings back to pre-2016 levels.

Closures, by contrast, are at a record level. At 117, they are the highest-ever recorded since we started keeping count in 1992, just exceeding the previous record closure-level of 113 in calendar 2003 (recorded in the 2004 guide).

Net openings (openings minus closures) slipped to 50: less than half last year's figure of 115. Since the financial crash of 2008, only one year has seen a weaker level of net openings (2012 at 36).

A further sense of turmoil in the market comes from the ratio of openings to closures. At 1.43:1, only one year has seen a worse performance than this, which was, as above, in 2003/4 (1.2:1) a time when for nearly every restaurant that opened another one closed.

Because Harden's focuses on listing 'indies' over restaurant groups, the above figures almost certainly understate how tough the market is. Although we do rate some bigger groups, we have never sought to track them in our statistics. After a chain becomes more numerous than a couple of spin-offs, it is excluded from our tally. Thus, none of the well-publicised closures of London branches of Jamie's Italian or Byron, for example, are included in our figures.

What's more, the last year saw a significant number of recently opened restaurants (that had been short-listed for inclusion) come and go before we had a chance to write about them. Allowing for these factors would almost certainly paint a picture of the weakest state of growth in the London restaurant sector in the history of the guide.

This time it's different

It is easy to forget how dire conditions were in 2003. The double whammy of the second gulf war in March and the SARS epidemic in May of that year saw London hotel occupancy rates dive to their lowest levels in recent decades. The knock-on hit to dining out was sufficiently strong to wipe out growth in the restaurant trade.

This time it is not weakness of demand that is hitting the sector, as consumer surveys (for example from Visa) show like-for-like consumer spending on dining-out continuing to increase year-on-year. No, the trade is being squeezed by a large overhang of supply from the restaurant opening boom of the last three years. On top of that it is struggling with huge rates increases. And, as if these challenges were not enough, restaurateurs are also adapting to the cost pressures from Brexit-induced inflation on imported foodstuffs, and Brexit-induced pressures on attracting quality staff.

However, as the numbers above show, openings have far from collapsed and the 'animal spirits' of London's new generation of restaurant entrepreneurs are proving remarkably resilient in the face of this storm system of economic headwinds.

Where and what's hot

After Central London (with 65), North London (30) was for the first time the hottest point of the compass for new openings, just ahead of East London (29). The strength of North London openings however is largely accounted for by debuts in the hipster hinterlands of N1, which accounted for just over half of North London openings. So although the restaurant frontier has shifted slightly to the north, the hipster-heavy areas of East and inner North London remain the restaurant hot zone for the time being.

South London only performed marginally less strongly than the other non-central areas (with 27 launches). Yet another particularly dismal performance from West London – historically the strongest point of the compass – yet again made it the least interesting area (with just 16 openings).

Modern British and Italian cuisines remain the most popular for launching a new restaurant, but Japanese newcomers made a stronger showing this year to be the third-most-represented cuisine for new arrivals.

Unless you include chicken shops, the shift away from meat-based formulae continued for a second year, with too many cuisines to list ranking higher than those with a primarily steak-led or burger-led offering. In fact – highlighting the increasing popularity of veganism and all things plant-based – purely vegetarian openings were as numerous this year as for those two red meat categories combined.

The hottest of the hot

Every year, we do an editors' pick of the ten most significant openings of the year. This year our selection is as follows:

Aulis London	Indian Accent
Beck at Brown's	Kettners
Brat	Kerridge's Bar & Grill
Cornerstone	Mãos
Hide	Parsons

Prices

The average price of dinner for one at establishments listed in this guide is £55.76 (compared to £53.20 last year). Prices have risen by 4.8% in the past 12 months (up on 3.6% in the preceding 12 months). This rate compares with a general annual inflation rate of 2.4% for the 12 months to August 2018, yet further accelerating the trend seen in the last two years by which restaurant bills have seen price rises running significantly higher than inflation generally.

OPENINGS AND CLOSURES

Openings (167)

Abd El Wahab
Akira at Japan House
Amber
L'Ami Malo
L'Antica Pizzeria da Michele
Ardiciocca
Arlo's *(SW11)*
Aulis London
Authentique Epicerie & Bar
Babel House
Bagatelle
Bánh Bánh *(SW9)*
Baptist Grill, L'Oscar Hotel
Beck at Browns
Beef & Brew *(N1)*
Belmond Cadogan Hotel
Berenjak
Bergen House
Bistro Mirey
Blacklock *(EC2)*
Bluebird Café White City
Bombay Bustle
Brat
Bryn Williams at Somerset House
Bucket
Buongiorno e Buonasera
Butchies
Caractère
Casa Pastór
Ceremony
Chick 'n' Sours *(N1)*
Chilly Katz
Chimis
The Chipping Forecast *(W1)*
Chokhi Dhani London
Chucs Serpentine *(W2)*
Claw Carnaby
The Coach
Coal Office
Cora Pearl
Cornerstone
Cub
Cut + Grind
Daddy Bao
Delamina *(W1)*
Din Tai Fung
Dip in Brilliant
Dozo *(SW7)*
The Drop
The Drunken Butler
The Duke of Richmond

Dynamo *(SW17)*
Eccleston Place by Tart London
Enoteca Rosso
Essence Cuisine
Evelyns Table at The Blue Posts
Fannys Kebabs
Fayre Share
La Ferme *(NW1)*
Forest Bar & Kitchen
Freak Scene
The Frog Hoxton *(N1)*
Gazelle
Genesis
La Goccia
The Good Egg *(W1)*
Good Neighbour
Granary Square Brasserie
The Greyhound Cafe
Gunpowder *(SE1)*
Ham
Hans Bar & Grill
The Harlot
Harry's Bar
Harrys Dolce Vita
Hatched (formerly Darwin)
Hicce
Hide
Home SW15
Hovarda
Icco Pizza *(NW1)*
Ichi Buns
Inko Nito
Ippudo London *(WC2)*
Jidori *(WC2)*
Jolene
Jollibee
The Jones Family Kitchen
K10 *(EC4)*
Kahani
Kanada-Ya *(N1)*
Kaosarn *(SW17)*
Kazu
Kerridges Bar & Grill
Kettners
Kudu
Kutir
Kym's by Andrew Wong
Kyseri
Lahpet
Laurent at Cafe Royal

Leroy
Levan
Lina Stores
Linden Stores
Llerena
Lokhandwala
Londrino
Maison Bab
Mamarosa
Mãos
Market Hall Fulham
Melange *(NW3)*
La Mia Mamma
Mien Tay *(SW6)*
Native
Neptune, The Principal
Nuala
Nusr-Et Steakhouse
Omars Place
On the Dak
Oval Restaurant
Paladar
Parsons
Passo
Peckham Levels
Purezza
Red Farm
ROVI
Ruya
Sacro Cuore *(N8)*
Sam's Riverside
San Carlo
San Pietro
Santa Maria *(W1)*
Sapling
Sargeants Mess
Scarlett Green
Schmaltz Truck
Scully
Sea Garden & Grill
Shu Xiangge Chinatown
Soutine
The Spread Eagle
St Leonards
Stem
Stockwell Continental
Street Pizza
Tell Your Friends
temper *(WC2)*
Terroirs *(SE22)*
Three Cranes
Tish
a

Titu
The Trafalgar Dining Rooms
1251
24 The Oval
Two Lights
Vermuteria
Via Emilia
Wahlburgers
Wander
Wellbourne
Wulf & Lamb
Yamabahce
Yen
Zela

Closures (117)
Albion *(SE1, E2)*
L'Anima
L'Anima Café
Assunta Madre
Aurora
Babaji Pide
Babylon
Barbecoa Piccadilly *(W1)*
Belpassi Bros
Bó Drake
Brindisa Food Rooms
Bronte
Brown's Hotel, HIX Mayfair
Bukowski Grill *(W1, SW9, E1)*
Bumpkin *(SW3)*
Burger & Lobster *(WC1)*
Cah-Chi *(SW18, SW20)*
Camino Blackfriars *(EC4)*
Cau *(SE3, SW19, E1)*
Cellar Gascon
Charlottes Place
Cheyne Walk Brasserie
Chriskitch *(N1)*
Cinnamon Soho
Como Lario
Counter Vauxhall Arches
Dandy
Darbaar
The Dock Kitchen
Duckroad
Dukes Brew & Que
Ebury Restaurant
8 Hoxton Square

Closures (continued)

Ellory, Netil House
Encant
L'Etranger
Eyre Brothers
Falafel King
Flavour Bastard
The Frog E1 *(E1)*
Gallipoli *(N1)*
Gay Hussar
Geales Chelsea Green *(SW3)*
The Gowlett Arms
The Grand Imperial
The Greek Larder
Gul and Sepoy
Hardys Brasserie
HKK
Hush *(WC1)*
James Cochran N1 *(N1)*
JAN
Jar Kitchen
Jules
Juniper Tree
Kerbisher & Malt *(W5)*
Killer Tomato *(W12, W10)*
Lahore Kebab House *(SW16)*
Lahpet
Latium
Legs
Lutyens
Madame D's
Marianne
The Magazine Restaurant
The Manor
Massimo, Corinthia Hotel
May The Fifteenth
The Modern Pantry *(EC2)*
Native
New World
Nirvana Kitchen
Nordic Bakery *(W1 x2)*
Oliver Maki
One-O-One
The Painted Heron
Paradise Garage
Pizza Metro *(W11)*
Pizzastorm
Platform1
Pomaio
Popeseye *(SW15)*
La Porchetta Pizzeria *(N1)*

La Porte des Indes
QP LDN
Raouls Café & Deli *(W11)*
Rasa Maricham *(WC1)*
Rök *(EC2)*
Royal Exchange Grand Café
Sardo
Sauterelle
Savini at Criterion
Smoking Goat *(WC2)*
Sosharu
Sree Krishna
Star of India
Summers
Taberna do Mercado
Taiwan Village
Temple & Sons
Test Kitchen
Trawler Trash
Typing Room
Veneta
Villandry *(W1, SW1)*
Vineet Bhatia London
Walnut Cafe and Dining
Winemakers Deptford
Yalla Yalla *(SE10)*

DIRECTORY

Comments in "double quotation marks" were made by reporters.

A Cena TW1 £50 **3**2**3**

418 Richmond Rd 020 8288 0108 1–4A

This upmarket Italian, just over the bridge from Richmond in St Margaret's, continues to earn solid local praise for its "good food" and "excellent value"; and is also useful for rugby fans from further afield who want to make a full day of a game at nearby Twickenham. / TW1 2EB; www.acena.co.uk; @acenarestaurant; 11 pm, Sun 10 pm; closed Mon L & Sun D; booking max 6 may apply.

A Wong SW1 £47 **553**

70 Wilton Rd 020 7828 8931 2–4B

"It's hard to get a table, but persevere, you're in for some of the best Chinese cooking in town" at Andrew Wong's Pimlico HQ, which "doesn't look very distinguished, but once the food starts coming, you know you're somewhere special". "Incredible dim sum offers lots of choice and unusual combinations" and – like the "amazing" evening tasting menu – delivers "a taste explosion with every dish". And while the "mind-blowing" cuisine seems "different and contemporary, it still feels authentic in terms of its flavours". "Upstairs feels a bit canteen-like" (and is "noisy and clattery") – you can also eat "in the tucked-away little bar downstairs". As of September 2018, he has also opened a new spin-off City outlet within the Bloomberg HQ (see Kym's). / SW1V 1DE; www.awong.co.uk; @awongSW1; 10 pm; closed Mon L, closed Sun; credit card required to book.

Abd El Wahab SW1 NEW £50 **333**

1-3 Pont St 020 7235 0005 6–1D

On a well-known Belgravia site that's seen lots of swanky places come and go over the years (including the US steakhouse Palms in recent times), this swish Lebanese is the first non-Middle Eastern branch of a Beirut-based chain that's since spread its wings to Dubai and beyond. Early feedback is up-and-down, but with more positives than negatives. / SW1X 9EJ; www.abdelwahab.restaurant.

The Abingdon W8 £65 **334**

54 Abingdon Rd 020 7937 3339 6–2A

"Always a winner" – this "comfortable" neighbourhood gastropub stalwart in a chichi Kensington backstreet is a case study in consistency. "Very accommodating" staff serve "ever-dependable food" in "agreeable surroundings". "Great for Sunday lunch with children" too. / W8 6AP; www.theabingdon.co.uk; @theabingdonw8; 10.30 pm, Sun & Mon 10 pm.

About Thyme SW1 £56 **233**

82 Wilton Rd 020 7821 7504 2–4B

A "thriving local delight" for many years, this Pimlico stalwart provides "well above average" Spanish food under the eye of popular host Issy ("you never feel rushed out here"). / SW1V 1DL; www.aboutthyme.co.uk; 10.30 pm, Sun & Mon 10 pm; closed Sun.

L'Absinthe NW1 £49 **233**

40 Chalcot Rd 020 7483 4848 9–3B

This "friendly and cheerful" little double-decker bistro on a Primrose Hill corner is "always a good local to go to for steak frites". "The menu doesn't change" and the food is "OK", not more, but that hardly matters: "the place is made by the maître d' and owner, JC" (Burgundian, Jean-Christophe Slowik). / NW1 8LS; www.labsinthe.co.uk; @absinthe07jc; 10 pm, Sun 9 pm; closed Mon, Tue L, Wed L & Thu L.

Abu Zaad W12　　　　　　　　£23　　　3 3 2
29 Uxbridge Rd　020 8749 5107　8–1C
"Looks a bit cheesy from the outside, but more than makes up once you're in" – this *"authentic"* Syrian near the top of Shepherd's Bush Market, provides *"freshly prepared, generous and delicious Middle Eastern specialities"* with *"courteous and pleasant service"*, all at prices that are *"excellent value"*. / W12 8LH; www.abuzaad.co.uk; Mon-Fri 11 pm, Sat & Sun midnight; no Amex.

Adams Café W12　　　　　　　£35　　　3 5 3
77 Askew Rd　020 8743 0572　8–1B
"A gem for North African food", *"off the beaten track"* in deepest Shepherd's Bush, this is a *"lovely family-run restaurant with super, authentic Tunisian and Moroccan food by night"* and *"greasy-spoon fare by day"*. *"The hosts epitomise hospitality"* and have *"maintained high standards for over 25 years"*. It's *"good value, too"*, with *"the bonus of being able to BYO"* (although they are now licensed). / W12 9AH; www.adamscafe.co.uk; @adamscafe; 10 pm; closed Mon-Sat L, closed Sun.

Addie's Thai Café SW5　　　　£35　　　3 3 3
121 Earl's Court Rd　020 7259 2620　6–2A
"Very authentic" Thai street food – *"excellently spiced and at a very reasonable price"* – again wins a big thumbs up for this basic canteen in Earl's Court. *"It's very cheap, and we're always cheerful after we've eaten there!"*. No wonder the place is *"increasingly packed, but I guess that's part of the (winning) formula"*. / SW5 9RL; www.addiesthai.co.uk; 11 pm, Sun 10.30 pm; no Amex.

Addomme SW2　　　　　　　　£53　　　4 3 2
17-21 Sternhold Avenue　020 8678 8496　11–2C
A *"tiny, friendly family run pizzeria"* next to Streatham Hill station, where *"fantastic welcoming owners"* Stefano and Nadia are from Capri, and provide *"superb Neapolitan style pizzas and bread, plus great pasta dishes"* from *"very high quality ingredients and dough"*. / SW2 4PA; www.addomme.co.uk; @PizzAddomme; 11 pm.

The Admiral Codrington SW3　　£58　　　3 3 4
17 Mossop St　020 7581 0005　6–2C
A Chelsea mainstay since the days of the Sloane Ranger Handbook, this backstreet gastroboozer is *"fantastic for business lunches but also brilliant for fun socialising"*. Its food scores are up again this year. / SW3 2LY; www.theadmiralcodrington.co.uk; @TheAdCod; Mon & Tue 11 pm, Wed & Thu midnight, Fri & Sat 1 am, Sun 10.30 pm; No trainers.

Afghan Kitchen N1　　　　　　£28　　　4 2 2
35 Islington Grn　020 7359 8019　9–3D
"Still there, still serving excellent food" – this *"cheap 'n' cheerful"*, Islington canteen has seen many of its neighbours come and go. The secret of its success? – a very affordable limited selection of yummy curries. *"Easier for take-away than for sit-down as the place is tiny with slightly harassed staff"*. / N1 8DU; 11 pm; closed Sun & Mon; cash only; no booking.

Aglio e Olio SW10　　　　　　£54　　　3 3 2
194 Fulham Rd　020 7351 0070　6–3B
This *"canteen-style Italian"* near Chelsea & Westminster Hospital *"always hits the spot"* with its *"simple, peasant-style cooking"* – *"excellent antipasti and pasta, and a fine selection of secondi if you want one"* – although it can get *"very noisy"*. *"Always welcoming with kids."* Top Menu Tip: *"proper fresh zabaglione made to order"*. / SW10 9PN; www.aglioeolio.co.uk; 10.30 pm.

Akira at Japan House W8 NEW £56
101-111 Kensington High St   020 3971 4646   6–1A
The Japanese Government's meticulously designed new cultural centre and store – Japan House in Kensington's old Derry & Toms department store – opened in June 2018 and is one of three globally aiming to showcase Nipponese heritage and craft. Its robatayaki and sushi restaurant is brought to us by Akira Shimizu, former chef of Engawa. It's far from being a showcase for budget Japanese dining however! / W8 5SA; www.japanhouselondon.uk; @japanhouseldn; 10.30 pm, Sun 4 pm; closed Sun D.

Al Duca SW1 £57   2 2 2
4-5 Duke of York St   020 7839 3090   3–3D
Low-key St James's Italian that's worth knowing about in this posh location. The harsh would say that the food quality is merely "fairly ordinary" or "reliable", but "given its position in the very heart of London, it delivers on value better than some of its central competitors". / SW1Y 6LA; www.alduca-restaurant.co.uk; 11 pm; closed Sun.

Al Forno £46   2 3 4
349 Upper Richmond Rd, SW15   020 8878 7522   11–2A
2a King's Rd, SW19   020 8540 5710   11–2B
"Family focused fun" ("expect noise, kids and even old people dancing") is on the menu at these "loud and bubbly" local Italians across south west London. "They can't do enough for you, and the food is pretty good too": a "perfectly respectable selection of standard traditional dishes", led by pasta and particularly pizza. / 10 pm-11 pm.

Alain Ducasse at The Dorchester W1 £134   2 2 3
53 Park Ln   020 7629 8866   3–3A
"I still do not understand why this above other amazing restaurants is one of only three Michelin three-star establishments in London!" The world-famous Gallic chef's luxurious Mayfair outpost is not without a significant number of advocates who hail it as "the best of the best!", with "truly first-class cuisine", "staff who seemingly glide around the floor" and "stunning surroundings". Even they can find it "stupidly expensive" however, and for far too many critics the cooking here is terribly "overrated" and the overall experience "underwhelming compared to other offerings". Top Tip: the best seats in the house are on the 'Table Lumière', surrounded by 4,500 fibre optic cables. / W1K 1QA; www.alainducasse-dorchester.com; 9.30 pm; closed Sat L, closed Sun & Mon; Jacket required.

Albertine W12 £56   4 4 5
1 Wood Ln   020 8743 9593   8–1C
This "very buzzy wine bar and bistro" is a "breath of fresh air" in Shepherd's Bush, with "clever, original and inexpensive food" by "the amazing Allegra (McEvedy), who is constantly popping out from the kitchen to check all is well with the world". A refuge from the nearby Westfield shopping centre, it was set up by McEvedy's mother in 1978, and she has retained the charming interior. There's a "huge range of wines from Greece to Morocco, with very strong French selection". / W12 7DP; www.albertinewinebar.co.uk; @AlbertineWine; closed Sat L & Sun; no Amex.

Alcedo N7 £44   3 4 3
237 Holloway Rd   020 7998 7672   9–2D
"Wonderful service from the friendly owner" drives the experience at this bright spark in Holloway – a "decent albeit not outstanding British bistro-style" venue. / N7 8HG; 10 pm.

Aleion N10 £45 3️⃣3️⃣3️⃣
346 Muswell Hill Broadway 020 8883 9207 1–1B
"A find in a part of London which has been poorly served by quality restaurants for a long time" – this year-old "small café with a short menu" in Muswell Hill serves "delicious", "fresh" food (from brunch and light lunches to more ambitious fare in the evening) and service is "helpful and friendly" too. / N10 1DJ; www.aleion.co.uk; @Aleion346; Mon-Thu 10 pm, Fri 11 pm, Sat 11.30 pm, Sun 4 pm; closed Sun D.

The Alfred Tennyson SW1 £62 2️⃣2️⃣3️⃣
10 Motcomb St 020 7730 6074 6–1D
"Craft ales, excellent wines and an interesting menu" are the offer at this plush Belgravia pub. Formerly known as The Pantechnicon Dining Rooms, it has become "much more approachable since its reincarnation". "Upstairs the atmosphere is more gentle for an intimate meal". / SW1X 8LA; thealfredtennyson.co.uk; @TheTennysonSW1; Mon-Fri 10 pm; closed Sat & Sun.

Ali Baba NW1 £26 3️⃣2️⃣2️⃣
32 Ivor Pl 020 7723 5805 2–1A
"Idiosyncratic, different and engaging"; if you're happy to chance it a bit and like Middle Eastern food, this family-run Egyptian – a simple room behind a take-away off Baker Street – is worth a trip and it's not a huge investment: "I have always liked the food even if the ambience is a bit caff-style, but recently for a dinner party I went there, ordered the food, and half an hour later was on my way home with a magnificent spread for the same price as a pizza delivery!" / NW1 6DA; alibabarestaurant.co.uk; @alibabalondon; midnight; cash only.

Alounak £26 3️⃣3️⃣3️⃣
10 Russell Gdns, W14 020 7603 1130 8–1D
44 Westbourne Grove, W2 020 7229 0416 7–1B
Now in their 21st year, this pair of "bustling, tightly packed" BYO Persian cafés in Bayswater and Olympia knock out "cheap but tasty kebabs and other typical Iranian dishes". Not bad for a business that started in a Portakabin next to Olympia Station. / 11.30 pm; no Amex.

Alyn Williams, Westbury Hotel W1 £104 5️⃣5️⃣3️⃣
37 Conduit St 020 7183 6426 3–2C
"What a find!". Alyn Williams's "outstanding" dining room hidden away at the back of a luxury Mayfair hotel is "one of the very best restaurants in London" ("and bizarrely underrated"). "It's hard to fault the cooking and staff" – accolades reflected in this year's high ratings – "and there's even plenty of space between the tables". / W1S 2YF; www.alynwilliams.com; @Alyn_Williams; 10.30 pm; closed Sun & Mon; Jacket required.

Amaya SW1 £85 4️⃣2️⃣3️⃣
Halkin Arcade, 19 Motcomb St 020 7823 1166 6–1D
"Treat yourself – you won't be sorry!" This "dark and luxurious", "fusion-Indian" has a "surprisingly different tapas-style approach that just works". "Subtly-spiced", "wonderfully fragrant" small dishes (many of them from the grill) are prepared in the open kitchen, providing "contemporary food at its best… if at Belgravia prices". "Don't let the staff cajole you into more dishes than you need!". / SW1X 8JT; www.amaya.biz; @theamaya_; 11.30 pm, Sun 10.30 pm; closed Sun L

Amber E1 NEW £39
21 Piazza Walk 020 7702 0700 12–1A
This bright, attractively decorated, new Middle Eastern café opened in Whitechapel in early 2018. No survey feedback yet, but its modern take on Moorish cuisine looks promising. / E1 8FU; www.thisisamber.co.uk; @ldn.amber.

The American Bar SW1 £76 2 5 3
16 - 18 Saint James's Place   020 7493 0111   3–4C
"Benoit's team provide perfect service" in this "very attractive room" –
part of a luxurious St James's hideaway at the end of a cute mews – serving
upscale brasserie fare from breakfast on. Top Tip: "the lunchtime food
served 'on your lap' is a great partner for the wines on special offer".
/ SW1A 1NJ; thestaffordlondon.com/the-american-bar; @StaffordLondon; 10 pm;
booking L only.

Ametsa with Arzak Instruction,
Halkin Hotel SW1 £103 3 4 2
5 Halkin St   020 7333 1234   2–3A
"Very experimental", "highly creative and fun tasting menus" win high praise
for this "high-end Basque eatery", and although one or two reporters
"expected more given its association with the fabulous Arzak in San
Sebastian", most are dazzled by its "skilful and dramatic" cuisine. The very
'boutique-hotel-y' dining room is "clinical", but "what the space lacks
in ambience is more than made up for by the terrific attitude of the staff!"
/ SW1X 7DJ; www.comohotels.com/thehalkin/dining/ametsa; @AmetsaArzak; 10 pm;
closed Sun & Mon.

L'Ami Malo E1 NEW £42 5 4 4
14 Artillery Lane   020 7247 8595   13–2B
"What a refreshing addition to the City restaurant scene!" – "simple but
beautifully prepared dishes with wonderful flavours" inspire gushing
feedback on this Brêton newcomer: a modern interpretation of a classic
French crêperie in the byways just south of Old Spitalfield Market (there's
also a 'speakeasy-style' bar at the back, Le Moulin, serving calvados-based
cocktails and craft cidres). "Staff seem like they really enjoy working there,
and prices are reasonable; I don't want to share my knowledge in the fear
that once others discover this gem it'll become over-run!" / E1 7LJ;
www.lamimalo.com; @lamimalo; Tue-Thu 9.30 pm, Fri & Sat 10 pm; closed
Sun & Mon.

L'Amorosa W6 £54 4 4 3
278 King St   020 8563 0300   8–2B
"Andy Needham has the right formula" at his "top Italian local with very
reasonable prices" near Ravenscourt Park, which is "well worth a detour".
"Fine cooking from a limited menu, shows real care given to each dish",
and is delivered by "particularly friendly" staff who help foster "a pleasing
and lively atmosphere". "If I lived close, I would happily go every week!"
/ W6 0SP; www.lamorosa.co.uk; @LamorosaLondon; 10 pm; closed Mon & Sun D.

Anarkali W6 £37 3 4 3
303-305 King St   020 8748 1760   8–2B
This "favourite" fixture of the Hammersmith strip (which opened in 1972)
sports a brighter, more modern look than once it did (the '70s-tastic dark
glazed frontage is long gone). Praise remains steady for chef Rafiq's deft
curries (including "the best bhuna lamb ever"). / W6 9NH;
www.anarkalifinedining.com; @anarkalidining; midnight; closed Mon-Sun L; no Amex.

The Anchor & Hope SE1 £53 4 3 3
36 The Cut   020 7928 9898   10–4A
By a single vote, this "amazing" South Bank boozer finally lost its crown this
year as London's No.1 pub (to Fulham's Harwood Arms), but it still remains
"the ultimate gastropub" for its huge fan club. It's "cramped", "busy" and
"difficult to get a seat" (you can only book for Sunday lunch) but "worth the
gamble" thanks to its "changing but always interesting menu at very keen
prices", with an emphasis on game, offal and other "thoughtful", hearty
British dishes. / SE1 8LP; www.anchorandhopepub.co.uk; @AnchorHopeCut;
10.30 pm, Mon 11 pm, Sun 3 pm; closed Mon L closed Sun D; no Amex; no booking.

Andi's N16 £47 **3****3****4**
176 Stoke Newington Church St   020 7241 6919   1–1C
"The energy bowl is simply gorgeous!" – Great British Menu judge,
Andi Oliver's "relaxed and friendly" neighbourhood haunt has proved
"a brilliant addition to Stoke Newington Church Street", and is most popular
for a "delicious brunch", particularly of the healthy variety. / N16 0JL;
www.andis.london; @andisrestaurant; 11.30 pm, Sun 10.30 pm; closed weekday L.

Andina £51 **3****3****3**
31 Great Windmill St, W1   020 3327 9464   4–3D
157 Westbourne Grove, W11   020 3327 9465   7–1B
1 Redchurch St, E2   020 7920 6499   13–1B
"Bustling, friendly, full of colour and fresh tastes, with lots of fascinating
choices (including a whole section of the menu devoted to ceviche)" – these
trendily located Peruvians win many upbeat reviews and the general feeling
is "they're not a case of style over substance – flavour combinations work
well". They are "pricey" though – "while the food was very good, I'm not
sure it was great value, probably thanks to the prime location, so I won't
rush back". Notting Hill is the latest site with a 'panaderia' (bakery) as well
as the 'picanteria'.

The Andover Arms W6 £51 **2****3****4**
57 Aldensey Rd   020 8748 2155   8–1B
"A proper boozer", lost in the backstreets of Hammersmith, with a
quintessentially "cosy and friendly atmosphere, open fireplace, large portions
and a great Sunday roast". Fuller's closed it for a refurb and change
in management from which it emerged in late September 2018 – we've
rated it on the assumption of plus ça change... / W6 0DL;
www.theandoverarms.com; @theandoverarms; 10 pm, Sun 9 pm; no Amex.

Andrew Edmunds W1 £57 **3****4****5**
46 Lexington St   020 7437 5708   4–2C
"Even the plainest of dining partners seems to take on a glow" at this
"utterly charming" and amazingly popular veteran – a "Bohemian" old
town-house which is "refreshingly constant in the chopping and changing
Soho scene" and whose straightforward, notably affordable dishes are
perennially "prepared with passion and care". "For a candle-lit supper"
it has few equals, as most reporters feel "the cramped conditions only add
to the cosy ambience" (although not everyone is wowed by the basement).
Top billing goes to the "fantastic wine" – "because of the generosity of the
owner, the markups on wines are minimal and it is a very interesting list":
"anything on the blackboard deserves attention and, nearly always,
consumption!" / W1F 0LP; www.andrewedmunds.com; 10.30 pm; no Amex; booking
max 6 may apply.

Angelus W2 £75 **3****4****2**
4 Bathurst St   020 7402 0083   7–2D
"An oasis in a part of London ill-served by good restaurants", this attractive
Lancaster Gate venue is a "pub converted into an art nouveau bistro" by ex-
Gavroche sommelier, Thierry Tomasin "with a wine cellar to match".
Tomasin's team provide "great old-fashioned service" ("they welcome you
like a regular even if you've never been before") and "though you eat cheek
by jowl" the Gallic cuisine "makes it worthwhile". / W2 2SD;
www.angelusrestaurant.co.uk; @AngelusLondon; 11 pm, Sun 8 pm.

Angie's Little Food Shop W4 £36 **3****3****3**
114 Chiswick High Rd   020 8994 3931   8–2A
"Freshly made divine salads each day, and amazing brunch dishes" (not all
of them virtuous) at "reasonable prices" (for Chiswick) make Angie Steele's
tightly packed, shabby-chic café "great for snacks and coffee", particularly
at weekends. / W4 1PU; www.angieslittlefoodshop.com; 7 pm, Sun 6 pm; L only.

Angler,
South Place Hotel EC2   £95   4 3 3
3 South Pl   020 3215 1260   13–2A

"One of the best places for lunch in the City" (with "nicely spaced tables
so conversations are not overheard") – this "terrific" D&D London operation
is the best culinary performer in the group nowadays. "Gary Foulkes is a
brilliant fish chef" and tears up the rulebook which says there's no decent
cooking in the Square Mile, especially at places with "great views", such as
you get at this penthouse perch. "The entrance through the South Place
Hotel limits expectations for what lies ahead" and although "it does feel like
you're in a hotel" the dining room itself is a "lovely", "light and airy" space.
"Get a table on the terrace on a sunny day and enjoy the delicious seafood."
/ EC2M 2AF; www.anglerrestaurant.com; @Angler_London; 11.30 pm, Sun 10 pm;
closed Sat L; may need 8+ to book.

The Anglesea Arms W6   £57   4 4 4
35 Wingate Rd   020 8749 1291   8–1B

"The kitchen is on song" at this "brilliant gastropub" in a side-street near
Ravenscourt Park, long known as one of the capital's best, thanks to its
"proper" cooking and characterful interior, complete with "roaring fire"
in winter, and small outside terrace. Service – historically a weak point –
is "attentive and accommodating" too. / W6 0UR; www.angleseaarmspub.co.uk;
@_AngleseaArmsW6; Mon-Thu, Sat 10 pm, Sun 9 pm; closed Mon-Thu L, closed Fri;
no booking.

Anglo EC1   £69   5 4 2
30 St Cross St   020 7430 1503   10–1A

"If I could give it ten stars I would!" – "Forget the shopfront and the
concrete floor" and the "cramped premises" of this Hatton Garden two-
year-old. Mark Jarvis's cuisine here is "brilliantly conceived, superbly
prepared and keenly priced" and complemented by a "superb wine pairing".
Service is "knowledgeable and friendly" and the overall style "relaxed". That
it holds no Michelin star is bizarre. / EC1N 8UH; www.anglorestaurant.com;
@AngloFarringdon; Tue-Sat, Mon 9.15 pm; closed Mon L, closed Sun; booking max 4
may apply.

Anima e Cuore NW1   £48   5 3 1
129 Kentish Town Rd   020 7267 2410   9–2B

"A hidden gem in Kentish Town" – "don't be put off by the transport caff
surroundings, this is Italian cooking at its very best", "prepared with great
care in a tiny kitchen by young chefs who work their socks off to produce
excellent food". "BYO is the icing on the cake!". There's a Catch 22:
"they never answer the phone so it's almost impossible to book, but booking
is essential". Top Tip: "strangolapreti (or priest stranglers), gnocchi made
from stale bread rather than potatoes". / NW1 8PB; @animaecuoreuk; 9 pm,
Sun 2.30 pm.

Anjanaas NW6   £35   4 4 3
57-59 Willesden Lane   020 7624 1713   1–1B

"The food has finesse and is consistently superb at this humble family-run
restaurant" – "an excellent Keralan local" that shines even brighter in the
still-underprovided 'burb of Kilburn. / NW6 7RL; www.anjanaas.com; Mon-Thu
10.30 pm, Fri & Sat 11 pm, Sun 10 pm.

Annies   £53   2 3 4
162 Thames Rd, W4   020 8994 9080   1–3A
36-38 White Hart Ln, SW13   020 8878 2020   11–1A

This pair of "super-reliable locals" near the Thames in Barnes and Strand-
on-the-Green, are "just all-round great places for lazy lunch and intimate
dinner". "Top service from a very friendly crew" ensures that you "feel very
welcome", and "portions are large and full of flavour".
/ www.anniesrestaurant.co.uk; 10 pm, Sun 9.30 pm.

The Anthologist EC2 £54   2 3 3
58 Gresham St 0845 468 0101 10–2C
Well-known bar/café/restaurant, near the Guildhall, whose versatile menu (from breakfast on), attractive interior and handy location make it an ideal City rendezvous. Critics dismiss it as too "average", but, "even when it's heaving, service is efficient, and it continues to produce reliable food day after day". / EC2V 7BB; www.theanthologistbar.co.uk; @theanthologist; 10.30 pm; closed Sat & Sun.

L'Antica Pizzeria NW3 £39   4 5 3
66 Heath St 020 7431 8516 9–1A
"This tiny authentic pizzeria in Hampstead is simply fantastic!". "Cheerful and good service from the Italian owners ensures a lively atmosphere", while locals rate their wood-fired pizza "among the best in town". / NW3 1DN; www.anticapizzeria.co.uk; @AnticaHamp; 7 pm; Mon-Thu D only, Fri-Sun open L & D.

L'Antica Pizzeria da Michele NW1 NEW £20
199 Baker St 020 7935 6458 2–1A
The original London outpost of the famous Naples pizzeria (est 1870, it featured in the film 'Eat, Pray, Love') ceased to trade under this name this year (in Stoke Newington) leaving a single, tourist-friendly outlet on Baker Street. The pizzas in Stokey were generally reckoned "fabulously authentic", but this is a franchise so similarities between locations are looser than might otherwise be the case (hence we've left it unrated). / NW1 6UY; anticapizzeriadamichele.co.uk; @DaMicheleNapoli.

Antidote Wine Bar W1 £59   2 2 3
12a Newburgh St 020 7287 8488 4–1B
Quirky, French-run wine-bar (plus upstairs dining room) tucked away just off Carnaby Street, which has dropped on and off the foodie radar in recent years. Scores currently are well off their highs of a few years ago, but it's still tipped for its wine list and reasonable selection of accompanying nibbles (which incorporate some fairly substantial options). / W1F 7RR; www.antidotewinebar.com; @AntidoteWineBar; 10.30 pm; closed Sun.

Applebee's Fish SE1 £62   4 2 2
5 Stoney St 020 7407 5777 10–4C
"Fresh off the boats", "simply" and "beautifully cooked" – some of the best seafood in town for a very "reasonable price" is to be found at this "little gem" at Borough Market. "It's bit crowded but the cooking makes up for it". / SE1 9AA; www.applebeesfish.com; @applebeesfish; Mon-Wed 10 pm, Thu-Sat 11 pm; closed Sun; no Amex.

Apulia EC1 £52   3 3 2
50 Long Ln 020 7600 8107 10–2B
"The sort of little local you want around the corner" – this southern Italian near Smithfield Market serves "satisfying and appetising Puglian food" at "very sensible prices" – including "fresh homemade pasta in the evenings" and "family dishes using grandmother's recipes". "Freshly made cakes for dessert and a terrific Puglian wine list, too". / EC1A 9EJ; www.apuliarestaurant.co.uk; 11 pm; closed Sun D.

aqua kyoto W1 £63   3 3 4
240 Regent St (entrance 30 Argyll St) 020 7478 0540 4–1A
The "beautiful top-floor setting in the West End with big outside terrace" creates a vibey environment – "reminiscent of a nightclub" – at this branch of the Hong Kong chain. For somewhere so central (seconds from Oxford Circus), feedback historically has been surprisingly limited and variable, but those who did make the trip this year report "high quality" Japanese sushi and other fare "with an interesting twist on standard dishes". See also Aqua Nueva. / W1B 3BR; www.aqua-london.com; @aqualondon; Mon-Wed 10.30 pm, Thu-Sat 11 pm, Sun 6 pm; closed Sun D.

Aqua Nueva W1 £68 3 2 4
240 Regent Street (entrance 30 Argyll St)   020 7478 0540   4–1A
The Spanish neighbour to Aqua Kyoto shares all the characteristics of this roof-top operation – terraces, clubby decor, dazzlingly central location – and generates even less feedback that its sibling! Such as there is however paints it in a good light this year. / W1B 3BR; www.aqua-london.com; @aquanueva; 1 am, Sun 8 pm.

Aqua Shard SE1 £104 1 1 3
Level 31, 31 St Thomas St   020 3011 1256   10–4C
"You can't beat the view" from the 31st floor of Western Europe's tallest building: "sitting up in the heavens, overlooking the twinkling lights of London" puts it high on some diners' lists "for a special occasion". Prices at this Hong Kong-owned landmark venture are appropriately "astronomical", but the food is definitely not out-of-this-world and for too many reporters the overall package "can seem poor value for money (even with the special deal!)" / SE1 9RY; www.aquashard.co.uk; @aquashard; 10.45 pm.

Aquavit SW1 £77 2 2 2
St James's Market, 1 Carlton St   020 7024 9848   4–4D
"A bit of a goldfish bowl with big windows" – this "awesome-looking" St James's yearling (sibling to one of NYC's most famous restaurants) has yet to reach its full potential. To fans it's "a big, bustling, brassy brasserie with really well-executed Scandi food (and cracking Aquavit)" that's "an excellent place to impress"; to sceptics, it "somehow lacks something" – "it looks beautiful, but feels cold and clinical" and the food is "quite sophisticated, but a bit soulless, mixed in realisation, and not a patch on the one in Manhattan". / SW1Y 4QQ; www.aquavitrestaurants.com; @aquavitlondon.

Arabica Bar and Kitchen SE1 £52 3 3 3
3 Rochester Walk   020 3011 5151   10–4C
"The flavours are amazing" at this modern Levantine outfit on the edge of foodie Borough Market – it has a "real buzz about it" and is "good value" too. / SE1 9AF; www.arabicabarandkitchen.com; @ArabicaLondon; 11 pm, Sun 9 pm; closed Sun D.

The Araki W1 £380 5 5 3
Unit 4 12 New Burlington St   020 7287 2481   4–3A
"Hands down most memorable restaurant experience of our lives" – Mitsuhiro Araki's Mayfair import from Tokyo (where, as with here, he also held three Michelin stars) offers "the pinnacle of Japanese cuisine": "mind-blowing, mouthwatering food" ("too many amazing dishes to mention") "lovingly handmade in front of you at a tiny 9 seater bar", where "Mr Araki makes you feel like guests in his living room". Is it expensive? Flippin' 'eck it is. But "ignore the price: it's a complete cultural immersion and should be compared to a night in top seats at the opera, not a mere meal!", is the view most folks seem content, nay, ecstatic to take. They say "If you can afford to splash-out, this is a must-try". At the margin are slightly more sceptical types (or maybe just non-billionaires) who find the prices "galling" but ultimately feel it's a Faustian pact that works for them: "It's utterly brilliant and I loved going; but my goodness, it's expensive, at about £40 a mouthful with the same for a modest glass of wine. But I'm so glad I experienced it. One to save for…" / W1S 3BH; www.the-araki.com; seatings only at 6 pm and 8.30 pm; closed Tue-Sun L, closed Mon.

Ardiciocca SW6 NEW £46
461-465 North End Rd   020 3848 6830   6–4A
Gluten-free pizza and pasta is the promise at this coeliac-friendly, dairy-free, sugar-free Italian on the site near Fulham Broadway vacated by Hanger (RIP). Too few reports as yet for a rating, but such as we have are upbeat: "hope they succeed in a location that's had many failures!" / SW6 1NZ; www.ardiciocca.com; 11 pm.

Ariana II NW6 £20 3|3|2
241 Kilburn High Rd   020 3490 6709   1–2B
"For the money (and the ability to BYO) this place cannot be beat!" –
this family-run Afghani in Kilburn provides good *"cheap 'n' cheerful"* scoff
and *"particularly good service from the owner"*; handy for the Tricycle
Theatre. / NW6 7JN; www.ariana2restaurant.co.uk; @Ariana2kilburn; Mon-Thu
11.30 pm, Fri-Sun midnight.

Ark Fish E18 £39 3|4|2
142 Hermon Hill   020 8989 5345   1–1D
"Shame you can't book" – this South Woodford chippy – it's *"a good
reliable, casual fish place"* that's one of the best options in the area. Owners
Mark and Liz Farrell have in their time run legendary chippies (including
Lisson Grove's famous Seashell, and Dalston's Faulkners). / E18 1QH;
www.arkfishrestaurant.co.uk; 10.30 pm; closed Mon; no Amex; no booking.

Arlo's £50 3|3|3
47 Northcote Rd, SW11   awaiting tel   11–2C **NEW**
1 Ramsden Rd, SW12   020 3019 6590   11–2C
This two-year-old Balham steakhouse, now joined by a branch in Clapham's
Northcote Road, is *"a must for serious steak fans"* – and *"the salads are
good too"*. *"Friendly, helpful staff and decent wine"* contribute to the appeal,
and there's an *"exceptional value set lunch"*. What's more, the *"light and
airy"* décor makes a *"nice change from exposed brickwork!"*

Arthur Hooper's SE1 £63 4|4|3
8 Stoney St   020 7940 0169   10–4C
"A great new addition to Borough Market" – this *"really enjoyable"*
contemporary wine bar (named for the now-defunct greengrocer's premises
that it occupies) wins very consistent praise for its *"interesting"*
Mediterranean dishes and *"equally good wine list"*, with an excellent range
by the glass. / SE1 9AA; www.arthurhoopers.co.uk; @arthurhoopers; Mon-Thu
11 pm, Fri & Sat midnight; closed Sun; booking max 6 may apply.

L'Artista NW11 £42 3|5|3
917 Finchley Rd   020 8731 7501   1–1B
*"Buzzy pizzeria under the railway arches opposite Golders Green station
that's been serving pasta and pizza (mostly pizza) to the locals since
forever, and which is always busy, so they must be doing something right!"*
It's *"extremely noisy and cramped"*, but they are *"especially great with
children"*. / NW11 7PE; www.lartistapizzeria.com; 11 pm.

L'Artiste Musclé W1 £48 2|2|5
1 Shepherd Mkt   020 7493 6150   3–4B
For a taste of 'la vie en rose', head to this atmospheric Shepherd Market
bolthole – *"a reminder of bistros in small French towns years ago"*.
"The cooking is simple traditional French, with some depth of flavour", while
"the wine is very reasonably priced, especially for Mayfair". / W1J 7PA;
@lartistemuscle; 10 pm.

Artusi SE15 £48 4|3|3
161 Bellenden Rd   020 3302 8200   1–4D
An excellent *"cheap 'n' cheerful choice"* – this *"small neighbourhood place
in gentrified Peckham"* has won more-than-local renown for its *"wonderful
modern Italian food, executed with style and elegance"*. There's a *"very good
if limited menu (three choices each of starter, main and pudding)"* and
"lovely staff who are attentive in the right way". / SE15 4DH; www.artusi.co.uk;
@artusipeckham; Mon-Wed 11 pm, Thu-Sat midnight, Sun 9.30 pm; closed Mon L.

Asakusa NW1 £36 5 2 2
265 Eversholt St 020 7388 8533 9–3C
"Top-notch sashimi, tempura and sushi at reasonable prices" inspire the highest praise for this offbeat operation near Mornington Crescent, whose "mock-Tudor-cum-Tyrolean decor is bizarre but doesn't detract from the authentic Japanese cooking". "I'm trying, and failing miserably, to keep it a secret from my friends!". / NW1 1BA; 11.30 pm, Sat 11 pm; closed Mon-Sat L, closed Sun.

Asia de Cuba,
St Martin's Lane Hotel WC2 £82 2 2 3
45 St Martin's Ln 020 7300 5588 5–4C
This glitzy Cuban-Chinese restaurant and cocktail bar in a boutique hotel near the Coliseum has a "great location" and groovy decor. Verdicts on the main food offering, though, are variable: "first time I've been back for more than a decade, when it first opened: still lovely looking, starters were tasty, mains very ordinary and it was certainly overpriced". Top Tip: "afternoon tea with an original twist". / WC2N 4HX; www.morganshotelgroup.com; @asiadecuba; Mon-Fri 9 pm, Sat 9.30 pm, Sun 3 pm.

Assaggi W2 £76 3 4 2
39 Chepstow Pl 020 7792 5501 7–1B
On the plus-side, this quirky first-floor of a Bayswater pub – "an old favourite" that was re-launched by one of its original owners a couple of years ago – still mostly 'walks the walk', with the "exceptional" cooking and "wonderful personal service" that established it in times gone by as "one of the best Italians in London". Even some fans, though, are losing patience with the "outrageous" pricing nowadays: "very good, but doesn't justify the see-how-much-we-can-get-away-with approach". / W2 4TS; www.assaggi.co.uk; Fri & Sat, Wed & Thu 9.30 pm; closed Sun; no Amex.

Assaggi Bar & Pizzeria W2 £64 4 3 2
39 Chepstow Place 020 7792 5501 7–1B
"Quite exceptional pizzas" and a small menu "that changes to reflect seasonal ingredients" are proving a big hit at the street-level bar of this former pub on the Notting Hill-Bayswater border, taken over in recent times by the team who resurrected Assaggi above (see also). Unlike upstairs, here ratings are rock-solid – maybe this is where their focus increasingly lies? / W2 4TS; www.assaggi.co.uk; 10 pm; closed Sun; no booking.

Aster Restaurant SW1 £58 3 2 3
150 Victoria St 020 3875 5555 2–4B
Neither D&D London nor the Nova development are known for their unswerving commitment to interesting cuisine, which makes Helena Puolakka's "unusual", "Scandi-French fusion" venture – "arguably the best new eatery in all these concrete Victoria canyons" – all the more unexpected; and "while it's a bit of a Curate's Egg, it's got a lot going for it" too. On the downside, the design is "a bit soulless", "service can be slow" and "prices are just a bit higher than they should be". But on the bright side, the "roomy" space is "light and airy", and "there's always something interesting on the menu to try". / SW1E 5LB; www.aster-restaurant.com; @AsterVictoria; 10 pm; closed Sun.

L'Atelier de Joel Robuchon WC2   £117   2 2 2
13-15 West St   020 7010 8600   5–2B

August 6 2018 saw the passing of Michelin's most fêted chef ever, and where that leaves the London outpost of his global luxury chain – whose "small plates of taste bombs are a little piece of food theatre" – muddies an already-unclear outlook. For most of its lifetime, the assessment of his "intimate" and opulent two-floor venue (plus cocktail bar with roof terrace) in Covent Garden has been that the experience it provides is "an always-exceptional delight" (if a nose-bleedingly expensive one). But "the food has worsened" in the last 2-3 years, and service at times can be "diabolical", while the sense that the place is "horrendously overpriced" has magnified. In the year prior to M Robuchon's death its ratings had staged something of a comeback on all fronts, so all is by no means lost for whoever takes the business forwards from now on. / WC2H 9NE; www.joelrobuchon.co.uk; @latelierlondon; Sun & Mon 10.30 pm, Tue-Thu 11 pm, Fri & Sat midnight; No trainers.

The Atlas SW6   £50   4 4 4
16 Seagrave Rd   020 7385 9129   6–3A

"If only all pubs were like this" gastroboozer near West Brompton tube, whose "Med-led" menu "punches over its weight" and which also provides "fabulous wine" and "some of the finest real ale in London". "Now in its 20th year", it finds itself increasingly surrounded by the burgeoning Lillie Square development, but is "still the best place in the area". "The new secluded garden terrace" (much bigger and smarter than the old one) is another reason to visit. / SW6 1RX; www.theatlaspub.co.uk; @theatlasfulham; 10.30 pm, Mon 11 pm, Sun 3 pm.

Augustine Kitchen SW11   £52   3 4 3
63 Battersea Bridge Rd   020 7978 7085   6–4C

«Dix points!» – This "honest local bistro, serving excellent Savoyard fare" has made itself at home just south of Battersea Bridge. Locals value it for "good, reliable, reasonably priced French food, well served in pleasant surroundings". / SW11 3AU; www.augustine-kitchen.co.uk; @augustinekitchen; closed Mon & Sun D.

Aulis London W1 NEW   £195   5 5 4
Soho - address on booking   020 3948 9665

"Simon Rogan's development kitchen offers a unique and unforgettable experience" that's "even better than his Claridge's iteration". Its secret location is revealed only on booking, with pre-payment expected (for food and wine pairings). Despite an entry level cost for the evening – wherein two chefs cook for 8 diners in a relatively small room around a chef's table – of upwards of £200 per head, all reporters agree, it's "an all-round exceptional performance". On the menu: new dishes, before they are potentially served at Roganic. / W1; aulis.london; @AulisSimonRogan; Mon-Fri 10 pm, Sat & Sun 9 pm.

Authentique Epicerie & Bar NW5 NEW   £42
114-116 Fortess Rd   020 3609 6602   9–2C

A Tufnell Park wine bar, restaurant, grocery and wine store all rolled into one, featuring a rotating roster of guest chefs and winemakers, which opened in Spring 2018. Alongside food and wine evenings in the wine bar, the attached grocery store offers French delicacies, cheeses and charcuterie, over 400 different vintages and 50 craft beers. / NW5 5HL; authentique-epicerie.com; Tue-Thu, Sun 11 pm, Fri & Sat midnight; closed Mon.

L'Aventure NW8   £67   3 4 5
3 Blenheim Terrace   020 7624 6232   9–3A

"Madame Catherine reigns as always with French charm" ("although at times she can be a little touchy") at her St John's Wood stalwart, whose superbly atmospheric quarters are particularly "perfect for an intimate and romantic meal for two". She "keeps high standards" including very "dependable" cuisine bourgeoise (but "some new additions on the menu" might not go amiss). / NW8 0EH; www.laventure.co.uk; 11 pm; closed Sat L.

The Avenue SW1   £71   2 2 2
7-9 St James's St   020 7321 2111   3–4D

This "stylish" if "cavernous" modern brasserie – nowadays part of D&D London – trades largely on its Manhattan-esque looks and St James's address, and wins its highest praise from expense-accounters. For folks spending their own cash, the food's not distinguished but not bad, but service can be awful, and management's attempts to pep up the big interior ("blaring muzak", "singer wasn't enough to lift the ambience") don't always go down well. / SW1A 1EE; www.avenue-restaurant.co.uk; @avenuestjames; 10.30 pm, Sun 6 pm; closed Sun D.

Aviary EC2   £57   2 2 3
10th Floor, 22-25 Finsbury Square   020 3873 4060   13–2A

"The rooftop views are amazing" from this 10th floor perch on Finsbury Square, which boasts a big outside terrace. Critics feel "you pay for it" when it comes to food though, and argue "it's better as a bar" or for quieter mealtimes like breakfast. / EC2A 1DX; aviarylondon.com; @AviaryLDN; 9.30 pm.

Awesome Thai SW13   £26   3 4 2
68 Church Rd   020 8563 7027   11–1A

"All the classics are nicely done" at this "excellent", "professionally run Thai local" in Barnes, whose brilliant location opposite the popular Olympic Studios cinema ensures that it is "always crowded". / SW13 0DQ; www.awesomethai.co.uk; 10.30 pm, Sun 10 pm; Mon-Thu D only, Fri-Sun open L & D.

Le Bab W1   £44   4 3 3
2nd Floor, Kingly Ct   020 7439 9222   4–2B

"Kebabs but not as we know them" – this "fantastic concept" in Kingly Court off Carnaby Street has pimped up the humble skewer to great acclaim. "Good quality fancy kebabs, run by a bunch of public school boys – weird, but enjoyable". / W1B 5PW; www.eatlebab.com; @EatLeBab; 10 pm, Sun 7 pm; booking max 6 may apply.

Babel House W1 NEW   £83
26-28 Bruton Place   020 7629 5613   3–2B

Inspired by the cuisine of countries bordering the Black Sea – and with a particular focus on the food of Odessa (it's named for that city's famous writer, Isaac Babel, and fresh fish is flown in from Odessa's Pryvoz market), this swanky-looking newcomer set up shop in a super-chichi Mayfair mews in May 2018, just as the survey was coming to a close. Feedback was too sparse for a rating, but the first report is encouraging – "ate just after opening with Ukrainian friends; excellent food; good wine list; will work well once it gets going properly". / W1J 6NG; www.babelhouse.co.uk; @BabelHouseLDN; 12.30 am, Sun 11.30 pm.

Babette SE15   £39   3 3 4
57 Nunhead Lane   020 3172 2450   1–4D

"Welcome to the big plate phenomenon!" – practically the only options are imaginative sharing boards from the blackboard menu at this "excellent French-run neighbourhood spot" – a revamped Old Truman pub in Nunhead. / SE15 3TR; www.babettenunhead.com; @babettenunhead; Wed & Thu 11 pm, Fri & Sat midnight, Sun 7 pm; closed Wed & Thu L, closed Mon & Tue.

Babur SE23 £57 5 5 4
119 Brockley Rise 020 8291 2400 1–4D
"A marvel in a suburban desert" – this Forest Hill "jewel" takes "South London Indian cuisine to a new level and puts it equal with the best in the West End and City". "The cooking is refined and inventive, beautifully spiced and seasoned, and looks as good as it tastes, while service is amiable rather than expert and the decor rather smart". "I've been going there for over 20 years and it remains relevant and delicious with a constantly evolving menu and drinks list". "If you live anywhere remotely within striking distance, you have to try it out!" / SE23 1JP; www.babur.info; @BaburRestaurant; 11.30 pm; closed Sun L.

Bacco TW9 £58 2 2 2
39-41 Kew Rd 020 8332 0348 1–4A
"An excellent local Italian with gracious service" that's "very convenient to the Orange Tree and Richmond Theatres" – that's how fans think of this "comfortable" and well-established Richmond mainstay. Even they, however, admit "there aren't many good places in the vicinity", and sceptics say it's "OK but nothing special, with food that's presentable but expensive for what it is". / TW9 2NQ; www.bacco-restaurant.co.uk; @BaccoRichmond; 11 pm; closed Sun D.

Bagatelle W1 NEW
34 Dover St 020 3972 7000 3–3C
On the former site of Quattro Passi (RIP) – an opening from a swish, well-established international chain with 'clubstaurants' from Dubai to Rio de Janeiro – arrived in Mayfair in Spring 2018. Culinarily speaking it takes its lead from the South of France, with a Provençal-inspired menu. / W1S 4NG; www.bistrotbagatelle.com; @bebagatelle.

Bageriet WC2 £12 4 3 3
24 Rose St 020 7240 0000 5–3C
"Cinnamon buns, full of spice and crunchy sugar topping (but not oily) and great for dunking in a coffee" are a highpoint at this "tiny" ("ten people and the place is full") but "welcoming" slice of Sweden, hidden down a Covent Garden alleyway. / WC2E 9EA; www.bageriet.co.uk; @BagerietLondon; 7 pm; closed Sun; no booking.

Bala Baya SE1 £60 4 2 2
Old Union Yard Arches, 229 Union St 020 8001 7015 10–4B
A flavour of Tel Aviv café culture is to be found in a railway arch in Southwark – the first venture of Israeli-born chef Eran Tibi, formerly of Ottolenghi: "great sharing dishes that look as amazing as they taste". Top Tip: "an astonishing cauliflower dish changed my perception of this vegetable". / SE1 0LR; balabaya.co.uk; @bala_baya; 11 pm, Sun 5 pm; closed Sun D.

The Balcon,
Sofitel St James SW1 £69 2 3 3
8 Pall Mall 020 7968 2900 2–3C
A "very classy set-up" – certainly for a hotel by Trafalgar Square – this all-day Gallic brasserie offers "good-value set menus" and "attentive service in surprisingly comfortable surroundings", which make it a "great West End location for lunch or pre-theatre". Afternoon tea is also a feature here. / SW1Y 5NG; www.thebalconlondon.com; @TheBalcon; 11 pm, Sun 10 pm.

Balthazar WC2 £70 2 2 4
4 - 6 Russell St 020 3301 1155 5–3D
A "terrific buzz" helps justify the presence of Keith McNally's "bustling"
NYC import, as does its "handiness for Covent Garden". Opinions differ over
its performance relative to the Manhattan original, but there's some
agreement that here in WC2 "the service is only just OK,
the bistro/brasserie food is very average, but it's the ambience which makes
it bearable". Brunch is a good way to give it a whirl. / WC2B 5HZ;
www.balthazarlondon.com; @balthazarlondon; Mon-Thu 11.30 pm, Fri & Sat
midnight, Sun 11 pm.

Baltic SE1 £57 3 4 3
74 Blackfriars Rd 020 7928 1111 10–4A
It's "always fun" to pay a visit to this "interesting" venue – a converted
Georgian factory near The Cut, which provides a "buzzy" ("very noisy when
full") if slightly "cavernous" backdrop to a meal. On the menu, "hearty,
reasonably authentic Mittel-European food" but it's "the amazing
list of vodkas" that really gets the party started… / SE1 8HA;
www.balticrestaurant.co.uk; @balticlondon; 11.30 pm, Sun 10.30 pm; closed Mon L.

Baluchi,
Lalit Hotel London SE1 £77 3 2 4
181 Tooley St 020 3765 0000 10–4D
The "lovely room" is a highpoint at this former school hall near Tower Bridge
(nowadays part of the first European opening from an Indian luxury
boutique hotel chain). The food (with inspirations from across India) is on all
accounts "beautiful" and "imaginative" too, but "pricey" (some would say
"ridiculously expensive") for what it is, especially given service that can prove
"lethargic". / SE1 2JR; www.thelalit.com/the-lalit-london/eat-and-drink/baluchi;
@TheLalitLondon; 9.30 pm.

Bang Bang Oriental NW9 £37 3 2 3
399 Edgware Rd no tel 1–1A
A "fantastic choice of different Asian cuisines" including "all sorts of street
food" is available at this vast oriental food court in Colindale: "from Indian
and traditional Chinese and Thai to Korean, Filipino, Japanese, Indonesian
and more". "Some is toned down for the London market", but the "number
of Asian diners is a testament to the authenticity and quality of the food".
"Fight for a seat and enjoy the buzz." / NW9 0AS; www.bangbangoriental.com;
@bangbangofh; Mon-Thu 10 pm, Fri & Sat 10.30 pm, Sun 9.30 pm.

Bánh Bánh £41 3 4 3
46 Peckham Rye, SE15 020 7207 2935 1–4D
326 Coldharbour Lane, SW9 020 7737 5888 11–2D **NEW**
"Go for the pho and the other Vietnamese specialties… not to mention the
spectacular cocktails" – reasons to visit the Nguyen family's "fun, cool, well-
priced local" in Peckham Rye. It's only been open a couple of years,
and they've already opened a new Brixton sibling too. / www.banhbanh.com;
@BanhBanhHQ.

Banners N8 £51 3 2 4
21 Park Rd 020 8348 2930 9–1C
Founded by Juliette Banner nearly 30 years ago, this community-minded
Crouch End diner offers an all-day world-food menu and is a local hero for
its "great breakfasts" (less so for a visit at other times). / N8 8TE;
www.bannersrestaurant.com; 10.30 pm, Mon 11 pm, Sun 3 pm; no Amex.

Bao £37 ▮4▮3▮3

31 Windmill St, W1   020 3011 1632   5–1A
53 Lexington St, W1   07769 627811   4–2C
13 - 23 Westgate St, E8   no tel   14–2B

"Oriental steamed buns to die for" explain the "perpetual queue" at these "tiny", "fast 'n' furious" cafés in Soho and Fitzrovia, whose "reinvented Taiwanese street food" ("complex, apparently simple, always daring") includes other intriguing dishes ("like beef cheek and tendon nuggets"), as well as "interesting Taiwanese teas". / W1F Mon-Wed 10 pm, Thu-Sat 10.30 pm, W1T Mon-Sat 10 pm, E8 Sat 4 pm; W1F & W1T closed Sun, E8 open Sat L only; W1 no bookings, E8 takeout only.

The Baptist Grill,
L'Oscar Hotel WC1 **NEW**

2-6 Southampton Row   020 7405 5555   2–1D

Occupying a once derelict Grade II-listed building by Holborn station (a former HQ of the Baptist Church), this new 39-bedroom luxury hotel opened in mid-summer 2018 and also boasts a mezzanine restaurant & bar (Baptist Bar); and cafe (Café Oscar). The main restaurant, overseen by former Angler chef Tony Fleming, aims for 'a contemporary approach to the traditional grill room'. / WC1B 4AA; www.loscar.com/dining; 11.30 pm.

Bar Boulud,
Mandarin Oriental SW1 £69 ▮3▮2▮3

66 Knightsbridge   020 7201 3899   6–1D

"A good balance between being casual and fine dining" – this deluxe Knightsbridge diner under the name of the famous NYC chef could be thought of as where the rich go "if you are in the mood for burgers but want the restaurant experience and a good glass of wine" (although the overall menu includes some "seriously accomplished", more 'culinary' options). The space feels like the hotel basement it is, but can develop "a great buzz". / SW1X 7LA; www.barboulud.com; @barbouludlondon; 1 am, Sun midnight; No trainers.

Bar Douro SE1 £53 ▮4▮4▮3

Arch 25b Flat Iron Square, Union St   020 7378 0524   10–4B

With its "authentic Portuguese small plates" and "fab list of Portuguese wines", this small blue-and-white-tiled bar near Borough Market "manages, unbelievably, to bring something new to London". It's "a bit hard to find" in the new Flat Iron Square food development – "but worth the search". / SE1 1TD; www.bardouro.co.uk; @BarDouro; 11.30 pm; booking max 4 may apply.

Bar Esteban N8 £48 ▮3▮3▮3

29 Park Rd   020 8340 3090   1–1C

"Definitely a few cuts above your typical tapas", this popular Crouch End spot is "always a joy, with relaxed, affable and attentive staff". Ratings would be even higher but "the food does wobble from time to time". / N8 8TE; www.baresteban.com; @barestebanN8; Mon-Wed 11 pm, Thu-Sat midnight, Sun 9.30 pm; closed weekday L; booking max 8 may apply.

Bar Italia W1 £32 ▮3▮3▮5

22 Frith St   020 7437 4520   5–2A

"Still the best espresso in the capital", say fans of this 24/7 veteran, now in its 70th year and little changed, and where posing elbow-to-elbow with other late night denizens of Soho, or squeezing in to watch Italian footie, is a London rite of passage. There are light bites, but they aren't the point. / W1D 4RF; www.baritaliasoho.co.uk; @TheBaristas; 11.30 pm, Sun 10.30 pm; no Amex; no booking.

The Barbary WC2 £50 **5** **5** **4**

16 Neal's Yard   no tel   5–2C

"Believe the hype!" – Palomar's younger sibling in Neal's Yard rocks, from its *"exceptional, tasty and distinctive Eastern Mediterranean small plates"* to its *"exciting atmosphere"*. Eating is *"buzzy, counter-style only"* – *"get there early if you cannot bear to queue!"* / WC2H 9DP; www.thebarbary.co.uk; @barbarylondon; 10 pm, Sun 9.30 pm; no booking.

Barbecoa EC4 £75 **2** **2** **2**

20 New Change Pas   020 3005 8555   10–2B

"The setting overlooking St Paul's is fantastic" but even some praising *"decent" cooking at Jamie Oliver's remaining luxury grill leave "feeling like you're being ripped off"* and to critics the dishes here are just plain *"mediocre and badly served"*. In addition, the swish-looking setting is *"just unbelievably noisy – I've been at gigs that were quieter!"*. Its plush sister venue in Piccadilly closed its doors (after just a year) in February. / EC4M 9AG; www.barbecoa.com; @Barbecoa_london; 9.30 pm.

Barrafina £50 **5** **5** **5**

26-27 Dean St, W1   020 7813 8016   4–1D
10 Adelaide St, WC2   020 7440 1456   5–4C
43 Drury Ln, WC2   020 7440 1456   5–2D
Coal Drops Yard, N1   awaiting tel   9–3C **NEW**

"The perfect alternative to a trip to Spain!" – in fact *"the food is better than in Barcelona"* in the branches of the Hart Bros' small chain, which pays homage to that city's Cal Pep with its small (no more than 30 covers) bars in Soho and Covent Garden (and – arriving in autumn 2018, in the trendy new Coal Drops Yard development in King's Cross, alongside a covered and heated terrace separately branded as 'Parrillan'). Confidently 'surfing the Zeitgeist' – no other individual restaurant, never mind group, has ever achieved such an outstanding and consistent level of support in the survey, over many years. There's *"no booking and no fuss"* – *"you often have to queue"* (though drinks and nibbles enliven the experience) and seating is *"counter-stye"* at the bar (*"which works less well for any kind of group, but for couples is ideal"*). With its *"bold Spanish flavours"* the tapas selection is *"arguably some of London's best food at any price, and remarkable value"* (while by the same token *"watching the chefs at work is brilliant"* – *"there's nothing theatrical, but it's mesmerising seeing experts so engrossed in their stations"*). *"The wine list is short, punchy and perfectly complements the food"*, *"staff seem to be having as good a time as the clientele"* and the overall effect is properly *"effervescent"*. Top Tip: *"always go for the daily blackboard specials, especially the fish"*, which is *"cooked to a tee and beautifully seasoned"*. / www.barrafina.co.uk; 11 pm, Sun 10 pm; no booking, max group 4.

Barrica W1 £55 **3** **3** **2**

62 Goodge St   020 7436 9448   2–1B

"Really great tapas and a good list of sherries" fit the bill at this *"lively if a little cramped"* venue in Goodge Street that *"feels just like being in Spain"*. *"Everyone we take here adores it."* *"Can get very busy, so booking is important."* / W1T 4NE; www.barrica.co.uk; @barricatapas; Tue-Thu 10 pm, Fri & Sat 10.30 pm, Mon 9.30 pm, Sun 9 pm; closed Sun.

Barshu W1 £58 **4** **2** **2**

28 Frith St   020 7287 6688   5–3A

"One of Soho's best" – the Sichuan food in this well-known café is *"first-rate"* – *"really spicy and delicious"*. Much of the menu is not for the faint-hearted, but *"it's always possible to avoid overly hot dishes with the aid of the helpful staff"*. / W1D 5LF; www.barshurestaurant.co.uk; @BarshuLondon; Sun-Thu 11 pm, Fri & Sat 11.30 pm.

Bean & Wheat EC1 £29 4|3|3
321 Old St 020 3802 2190 10–2D

High marks (if from a small fan club) for Adam Handling's new deli-cafe, featuring coffee from independent roasters; and where locally produced bread, and offerings in Kilner jars made from by-products from the kitchen at The Frog help underpin its sustainable aims. Reports were for the original Spitalfields location: it's now moved to this new larger site in Hoxton. / EC1V 9LE; www.beanandwheat.co.uk; @beanandwheat; closed Sat & Sun.

Bears Ice Cream W12 £7 3|3|3
244 Goldhawk Rd 020 3441 4982 8–1B

Yummy sprinkles and a mind-numbing array of toppings to decorate the single flavour of Icelandic ice cream draw families to this cute little ice cream parlour on the busy gyratory north of Ravenscourt Park. / W12 9PE; www.bearsicecream.co.uk; @bears_icecream; 8.30 pm; L & early evening only; no booking.

Bea's Cake Boutique WC1 £43 3|3|3
44 Theobalds Rd 020 7242 8330 2–1D

"Fabulously busy… in a good way (as it feels like you have come to the right place)" – this cute tea rooms near Holborn Library spawned a chain of the same name on the back of its inviting-looking cakes and "tasty lunches and snacks" that are "worth a little waiting for". / WC1X 8NW; www.beas.london; @beas_bloomsbury; 7 pm; L & early evening only.

Beast W1 £117 1|2|2
3 Chapel Pl 020 7495 1816 3–1B

Most reporters are left speechless by the stratospheric prices at this candle-lit surf 'n' turf experience off Oxford Street (part of the Goodman group), where huge portions of Norwegian king crab, Canadian lobster and Nebraskan beef are the building blocks of the small menu. / W1G 0BG; www.beastrestaurant.co.uk; @beastrestaurant; 10.30 pm; closed Sun; may need 7+ to book.

Beck at Browns, Browns Hotel W1 NEW £97 3|4|4
Browns Hotel, Albemarle St 020 7518 4004 3–3C

"Definitely one of London's top Italian restaurants" – Heinz Beck (who has three stars for La Pergola, in Rome, and whose last London venture was at Apsleys, RIP) has achieved a much better showcase for his classic Italian approach at this new incarnation for the main dining room at Mayfair's grand Brown's Hotel. Until recently it traded as Hix Mayfair (now RIP), and the spacious room itself now has a much more "stylish and comfortable" atmosphere than formerly, with bold floral wallpaper above its traditional wood panelling, and feels "so relaxed and convivial". The opening has achieved mixed newspaper reviews and accusations of being over-engineered, but our feedback is much more upbeat. Even fans acknowledge that it's "not cheap", but – by the same token – even the one disappointed reporter who thought the high cost made it "incredibly bad value" acknowledged the food is good. All-in-all, the majority view is that the experience is to be "very highly recommended", not least owning to "a simply scrumptious menu (with plenty of pasta, fish and meat options)", which delivers dishes that are "apparently simple but very skilfully produced, and presented in a stylish yet unfussy manner". A thumbs-up to the "efficient and friendly staff" too, including the "well-informed and helpful sommelier" who presides over an "interesting and long wine list". / W1S 4BP; www.roccofortehotels.com/hotels-and-resorts/browns-hotel/restaurants-and-bars/beck-at-browns; @Browns_Hotel.

Beef & Brew £46 **3** **4** **3**

33 Downham Rd, N1   020 7254 7858   14–2A **NEW**
323 Kentish Town Rd, NW5   020 7998 1511   9–2B

"Fantastic beef at affordable prices" and nifty craft beers have carved
a local reputation for this *"great neighbourhood steak and chips joint"*
in Kentish Town – it's *"friendly and not too pricey"*, and with *"cool music
and vibes"*. In summer 2018, it opened a new Haggerston spin-off too.
/ www.beef-and-brew.co.uk; @BeefandBrewLDN.

The Begging Bowl SE15 £45 **4** **2** **2**

168 Bellenden Rd   020 7635 2627   1–4D

"As close to the food in Thailand as you're likely to get in London",
this *"good value"* Peckham café has invigorated the southeast London
culinary scene in recent years. *"Go for the food"* even if the no-bookings
policy – which irritates some reporters – *"can mean a long wait in The
Victoria opposite"*. / SE15 4BW; www.thebeggingbowl.co.uk; @thebeggingbowl;
9.45 pm, Sun 9.15 pm; no booking.

Beijing Dumpling WC2 £33 **4** **3** **2**

23 Lisle St   020 7287 6888   5–3A

"An impressive choice of dumplings" and other *"surprisingly good"*, *"un-
gloopy and fresh"* dishes make it well worth discovering this small, simple
Chinatown café. / WC2H 7BA; 11.30 pm, Sun 10.30 pm.

Bellamy's W1 £62 **3** **4** **4**

18-18a Bruton Pl   020 7491 2727   3–2B

Proprietor Gavin Rankin (ex-MD of Annabel's) *"is much in evidence"* at this
"very discreet and efficient" Mayfair fixture – *"a comfortable English take
on a Parisian brasserie"* that's one of a tiny handful of restaurants ever
visited by The Queen (and, fair to say, *"a safe place to entertain"*). For its
traditional following, *"this is the sort of restaurant you aspire to go to once
a week, for the rest of your life"* – a *"properly grown-up and elegant"* venue,
with *"impeccable service"*, offering *"good interpretations"* of *"Anglo-French
classic dishes"* and *"a well-chosen and fairly-priced all-French wine list"*.
/ W1J 6LY; www.bellamysrestaurant.co.uk; 10.30 pm; closed Sat L, closed Sun.

Bellanger N1 £60 **2** **2** **3**

9 Islington Grn   020 7226 2555   9–3D

"Pretty much the only 'grown-up' restaurant on Upper Street" – Corbin
& King's *"elegant"* Islington outpost is a *"spacious"*, *"clubby and wood
lined"* operation that makes *"a classy destination for anyone at any time –
be it for a drink, a snack or a meal"* (and is kid- and dog-friendly too). The
"unusual and interesting" cuisine – schnitzels, *"good tartes flambées, hearty
sausages (try the aligot mash), steaks"* – aims to recreate that of an
Alsatian brasserie and is *"decent, if a bit uneven"* (ditto the service). *"Great
range of breakfast options, too, and the atmosphere makes it feel special,
whether it's a business meeting or you're lingering at the weekend"*.
/ N1 2XH; www.bellanger.co.uk; @BellangerN1; Mon & Tue, Sun 10 pm, Wed-Sat
11 pm.

Belmond Cadogan Hotel SW1 **NEW**

75 Sloane St   020 3117 1505   6–2D

Luxury hotel group Belmond (as in Belmond Le Manoir Aux Quat' Saisons)
has taken on The Cadogan Hotel, Knightsbridge. A multi-million pound
refurb' is in the works, and when it reopens in December 2018 the 54-room
hotel will also boast a restaurant with views of Cadogan Place Gardens and
wunderkind chef, Adam Handling at the stoves (known as Adam Handling
Chelsea, with its own street entrance, and open from breakfast on).
Afternoon tea in The Tea Lounge will be another option. / SW1X 9SG;
www.belmond.com/hotels/europe/uk/london/belmond-cadogan-hotel; @belmond;
11.30 pm, Sun 10 pm.

Belvedere Restaurant W8 £69 3 3 5

off Abbotsbury Rd in Holland Park   020 7602 1238   8–1D
"Difficult to beat for romance" – this "beautiful and elegant" 17th-century
ballroom inside Holland Park (with outside terrace) provides one of London's
most "delightful and secluded" settings for dinner on a summer's evening
or Sunday lunch. Perennially the not-particularly-modern British cuisine
is "pretty ordinary", but its ratings batted well above their normal average
this year, amidst reports that it was found to be "much better than
expected". / W8 6LU; www.belvedererestaurant.co.uk; @BelvedereW8; 11 pm,
Sun 3.30 pm; closed Sun D.

Benares W1 £110 3 2 3

12a Berkeley Square House,   020 7629 8886   3–3B
"Modern Indian done with style!" Atul Kochhar's swish Mayfair destination
in very contemporary, first-floor Berkeley Square premises put in a much
stronger showing than in last year's survey. True, "when the dining room
is quiet the atmosphere can feel a little strained", but when it fills up it's
"much more vibrant", and at its best the cuisine here is "really stunning and
beautifully presented". STOP PRESS – in August 2018, Kochhar left the
restaurant which he founded, whose cuisine will now be led by Executive
Chef Brinder Narula, who has been with the group controlling Benares for
three years. / W1J 6BS; www.benaresrestaurant.co.uk; @benaresofficial; 10.45 pm,
Sun 9.45 pm; closed Sun L; booking max 10 may apply.

Bentley's W1 £84 3 4 3

11-15 Swallow St   020 7734 4756   4–4B
"Top up my bubbles and bring on the gorgeous succulent oysters!" – Richard
Corrigan's celebrated, 100-year-old veteran, near Piccadilly Circus, is "an all-
time favourite" for many reporters – particularly the "bustling" ground-floor
bar – thanks to its "barking fresh seafood" ("a wide variety" incorporating
"superbly shucked oysters", an "exceptional seafood platter", dressed crab,
and so on). "Downstairs is cosier" and the upstairs dining room can seem
"bland" by comparison, but "ideal if you want it to be easier to talk in a
bigger group". / W1B 4DG; www.bentleys.org; @bentleys_london; 10.30 pm,
Sun 10 pm; No shorts; booking max 8 may apply.

Berber & Q E8 £48 5 3 5

Arch 338 Acton Mews   020 7923 0829   14–2A
"Hearty... well-seasoned and flavoured... YUMMM!" – "The most delicious
selection of smoky grilled meats" can be "a revelation" at Josh Katz's North
African-style grill in a funky Haggerstone railway arch... and "the veggie
dishes are actually even better (the roast beetroot with whipped feta is to
die for!"). "The menu evolves enough to keep things interesting and bring
you back for more" and there's "fabulous wine" and spicy cocktails too.
/ E8 4EA; www.berberandq.com; @berberandq; 11 pm, Sun 9 pm; D only, closed Mon;
May need 6+ to book.

Berber & Q Shawarma Bar EC1 £51 4 3 3

Exmouth Market   020 7837 1726   10–1A
The Tel Aviv-style spit-roasted chicken and lamb, mezze and hummus
is "cheap, but very tasty" at this excellent two-year-old Exmouth Market
offshoot of Josh Katz's Berber & Q. Primarily walk-in, but you can book for
bigger groups. / EC1R 4QL; shawarmabar.co.uk; @berberandq; Mon-Thu 11 pm,
Fri & Sat 11.30 pm, Sun 10 pm; closed Mon; no booking.

Berenjak W1 NEW

27 Romilly St   awaiting tel   5–2A
In conjunction with the successful JKS restaurant empire, Iranian chef Kian
Samyani will open this Persian restaurant in Soho in October 2018; named
for the toasted rice snack eaten at fairs in Iran, the restaurant will replicate
the street food and hole-in-the-wall kebab shop cuisine of the chef's
homeland. / W1D 5AL; berenjaklondon.com.

Bergen House N16 NEW   £45
47 Newington Green   020 7226 2779   1–1C
Joining a growing number of restaurants in Newington Green, this bar-bistro opened in early 2018 and serves steak 'n' chips plus a big selection of hearty sharing plates. Not much feedback yet (hence we've left it unrated) but all positive. / N16 9PX; www.bergenhouse.co.uk; Mon & Tue 9 pm, Fri & Sat 11.30 pm, Wed 10 pm, Thu 11 pm, Sun 5 pm.

Bernardi's W1   £64   3 3 3
62 Seymour St   020 3826 7940   2–2A
"Stylish and cool", this modern Italian on the Marylebone-Bayswater border "surprises with the quality of the food". "There's always a buzz" as well – too much for some, who find "the noise level is unbearable" – and prices are West End-high. / W1H 5BN; www.bernardis.co.uk; @BernardisLondon; 10.30 pm, Sun 9.30 pm.

The Berners Tavern W1   £75   2 3 5
10 Berners St   020 7908 7979   3–1D
The "awesome" setting of its "beautiful" interior provides one of London's most impressive backdrops for a meal at this grand dining room, north of Oxford Street (recommended for romance, but especially for business). Most reports give a thumbs-up to the "pricey-but-solid" cuisine overseen by Jason Atherton, but – especially at the price – results can be "rather forgettable" (and there were a couple of disastrous meals reported this year). Afternoon teas and Sunday roasts are a recent innovation. / W1T 3NP; www.bernerstavern.com; @bernersTavern; 10.30 pm.

Best Mangal   £38   4 3 3
619 Fulham Rd, SW6   020 7610 0009   6–4A
104 North End Rd, W14   020 7610 1050   8–2D
66 North End Rd, W14   020 7602 0212   8–2D
"Magic, hearty things are done to all things meaty" at this trio of "glorious" Turkish grills, which have established a strong local following in Fulham over 22 years. "Great kebabs are cooked before your eyes", and there's a "warm welcome". / www.bestmangal.com; midnight, Sat 1 am; no Amex.

Bibendum SW3   £132   3 3 4
81 Fulham Rd   020 7581 5817   6–2C
After a year at the stoves, ex-Hibiscus patron, Claude Bosi, is getting more into his stride in this "perennially wonderful dining room", within "the iconic setting of the Michelin building". True, there are still many reporters who are not persuaded by his new regime ("Come back Sir Terence Conran, all is forgiven…") and also many who feel that the "results from the classic French high-falutin' menu are dangerously close to ordinary at this price point" ("only an expense accounter could stomach the stratospheric bill"). Ratings have risen sharply since last year's faltering debut, however, amidst accounts of "a return to form", with "smiling staff gliding about smoothly as though on coasters" and "stunningly crafted dishes with fabulous flavours". / SW3 6RD; www.bibendum.co.uk; @bibendumltd; Wed-Fri 9.45 pm, Sat 10 pm, Sun 9 pm; closed Mon & Tue; booking max 12 may apply.

Bibendum Oyster Bar SW3   £53   3 3 3
Michelin House, 81 Fulham Rd   020 7581 5817   6–2C
(Mostly) upbeat reports again this year on this luxurious café in the beautiful, if echoey tiled foyer of the Michelin Building, where Claude Bosi has added hot items to its traditional offering of cold seafood platters. / SW3 6RD; www.bibendum.co.uk; @bibendumrestaurant; 9.30 pm, Sun 8.30 pm; closed Sun D; no booking.

Bibimbap £24 3 2 2
10 Charlotte St, W1   020 7287 3434   2–1C
11 Greek St, W1   020 7287 3434   5–2A
39 Leadenhall Mkt, EC3   020 72839165   10–2D
You can find "some of the tastiest street food ever" at these modern Korean
canteens in Soho and Fitzrovia. It also has takeaway outlets; three in the City
and another in Oxford Street. / 11pm, EC3 3 pm; W1 Sun, EC3 Sat & Sun;
no bookings.

Big Easy £62 2 2 3
12 Maiden Ln, WC2   020 3728 4888   5–3D
332-334 King's Rd, SW3   020 7352 4071   6–3C
Crossrail Pl, E14   020 3841 8844   12–1C
"Guilty-pleasure comfort food" served in a "crowded but fun atmosphere"
have made this "so authentically American" BBQ and crabshack a King's
Road fixture for 27 years (and it underwent a major upgrade in 2018). Now
with offshoots in Covent Garden and Canary Wharf, the outfit can seem
"very corporate" and is "probably best for large groups or office parties".
/ www.bigeasy.co.uk; @bigeasytweet; Mon-Thu 11 pm, Fri & Sat 11.30 pm,
Sun 10.30 pm.

The Bingham TW10 £69 3 4 5
61-63 Petersham Rd   020 8940 0902   1–4A
"A breathtaking panorama overlooking the Thames" helps makes the
restaurant of this small boutique hotel "an exceptional choice in Richmond".
The cuisine is very "reliable" too, using "fine ingredients", but there's
a recurring complaint: "the portions are very small" ("the dining room was
full of ladies-who-lunch, and judging by their figures they don't eat that
much!"). Top Tip: "the market menu is good value". / TW10 6UT;
www.thebingham.co.uk; @thebingham; 11 pm, Sun 10.30 pm; closed Sun D;
No trainers.

The Bird in Hand W14 £63 3 2 3
88 Masbro Rd   020 7371 2721   8–1C
"A pub with better pizza than most pizzerias!" sums up the appeal of this
converted boozer in the backstreets of Olympia. "Stick to the excellent
pizzas", though, "the rest of the food is not amazing and the little tapas
never quite hit the mark". Sibling to the Oaks in W2 and W12. / W14 0LR;
www.thebirdinhandlondon.com; @TBIHLondon; Mon-Wed 10 pm, Thu-Sat 11 pm;
booking weekdays only.

Bird of Smithfield EC1 £59 3 3 3
26 Smithfield St   020 7559 5100   10–2B
"A fine Georgian townhouse in Smithfield with interesting art and a lovely
upstairs dining room" hosts Tommy Boland's five-storey venture
(with summer roof terrace). Yet again it only inspires limited feedback,
but all of it positive for its British fare of some ambition. / EC1A 9LB;
www.birdofsmithfield.com; @BirdoSmithfield; Mon-Fri midnight; closed Sat & Sun.

Bistro Aix N8 £56 2 2 3
54 Topsfield Pde, Tottenham Ln   020 8340 6346   9–1C
A "friendly, retro French bistro sticking unswervingly to the provincial
classics" – chef-proprietor Lynne Sanders's smart little venue in Crouch End
is "like stepping back in time 30 years". Mixed reports have knocked its
ratings this year. Fans reckon it is "always reliable and consistently good",
but for a fair few critics, "the quality has been slipping a bit lately"
("variable, and on our last visit, poor"). / N8 8PT; www.bistroaix.co.uk;
@bistroaixlondon; Sun-Thu 11 pm, Fri & Sat midnight; closed Mon-Fri L; no Amex.

Bistro Mirey SW6 NEW £55 443

98 Lillie Rd   020 3092 6969   8–2D

Gerald Mirey and Ko Ito have put down permanent roots in Fulham at this cute little modern bistro, near the top of North End Road's market. Dig beyond the weekend brunch, and the à la carte here is distinctive and very competitively priced, offering fusion dishes underpinned by classic French cuisine with Japanese notes. Alongside the inventive food menu is a list of French wines and Japanese sake (as well as London craft sake Kanpai). / SW6 7SR; www.bistromirey.com; @bistromirey; Wed & Thu 9 pm, Fri & Sat 9.30 pm.

Bistro Union SW4 £58 333

40 Abbeville Rd   020 7042 6400   11–2D

Adam Byatt's "nice local" in Abbeville Road doesn't aim for the culinary fireworks of its stablemate Trinity, but generally delivers enjoyable modern bistro cuisine in a "relaxed" setting. There are a few reporters this year, however, who are "hoping for a return to form" saying that of late it "didn't deliver" as hoped – perhaps a blip. Top Tip: "kids-eat-free Sunday Supper Club". / SW4 9NG; www.bistrounion.co.uk; @BistroUnion; 10 pm, Sun 9 pm; closed Sun L; booking max 8 may apply.

Bistro Vadouvan (French & Spice) SW15 £57 443

30 Brewhouse Lane   020 3475 3776   11–2B

"A brilliant combination of flavours" – "predominantly Western but with subtle, Asian-influenced (but not Asian-dominated) spicing" – helps make this "original" yearling "a welcome addition to SW15"; although it has "a great riverside location near Putney Bridge" too. It's the brainchild of Durga Misra and Uttam Tripathy, who both hail from the same town in India (but only met years later at college). / SW15 2JX; bistrovadouvan.co.uk; @BistroVadouvan; 11 pm, Sun 5 pm.

Bistrotheque E2 £64 324

23-27 Wadeson St   020 8983 7900   14–2B

Occupying "a great open space", this hip warehouse-conversion in Cambridge Heath has been a "lively" East End feature – particularly for brunch – since 'cool', 'East End' and 'restaurant' first appeared in the same sentence; live music is a regular feature. / E2 9DR; www.bistrotheque.com; @bistrotheque; midnight, Sun 11 pm; closed Mon-Fri L

Black Axe Mangal N1 £46 432

156 Canonbury Rd   no tel   9–2D

"What can you say? Offal flatbread, blaring hard rock and lurid genitalia painted on the floor – but the food is great" at Lee Tiernan's tiny heavy-metal kebab joint, still taking no prisoners in its third year at Highbury Corner. "Painful seating, but just incredible, confident, stunning cooking". And for those who reckon "Queens of the Stone Age at full volume ruins everything" – Top Tip: "take away!". / N1 \N; www.blackaxemangal.com; @blackaxemangal; 10.30 pm, Sun 3 pm; D only Mon-Fri, Sat L & D, Sun L only; no booking.

Black Prince SE11 £38 332

6 Black Prince Rd   020 7582 2818   2–4D

"Superior pub food (with an outstanding Sunday lunch)" makes it worth remembering this classic Kennington boozer. / SE11 6HS; www.theblackprincepub.co.uk; Sun-Thu midnight, Fri & Sat 1 am.

Black Roe W1 £74 323

4 Mill St   020 3794 8448   3–2C

It's "something unique" to its fans, but this Hawaiian-inspired Mayfair three-year-old (speciality poké and other fish dishes) inspires little in the way of feedback. Fans say it can be "outstanding", but toppish prices give rise to some complaint. / W1S 2AX; www.blackroe.com; @blackroe; 11 pm; closed Sun.

Blacklock £44 444

24 Great Windmill St, W1   020 3441 6996   4–2D
28 Rivington St, EC2   020 7739 2148   13–1B **NEW**
13 Philpot Lane, EC3   020 7998 7676   10–3D

"Simply mouthwatering plates" of "succulent and well-seasoned chops" reward a trip to these "fun" haunts, which in September 2018 added a Shoreditch branch to initial ventures in Soho and the City. It's a case of "simple food but done extremely well" and "if you like meat, this is a good place to share lots of it with friends, and at a very good price too". "OK, so I was sceptical: yet another beards and tatts place, I thought – but the quality is such that I (and my meat-loving wife) discuss little else but when to go next!" / theblacklock.com; @BlacklockChops.

Blanchette £57 223

9 D'Arblay St, W1   020 7439 8100   4–1C
204 Brick Lane, E1   020 7729 7939   13–1C

"Specialising in Gallic small plates, cheeses and charcuterie" plus dry-aged beef – and with "portions somewhere between tapas and a full plate" – this French-owned duo in Soho (2013) and Brick Lane (2016) have earned quite a culinary reputation, and – though "cramped" and "very noisy" – have a "fun atmosphere". Although praised by their many fans as a "reliable" option, their ratings slipped this year, with various gripes about the tapas-y format: either that it's "expensive", "un-relaxing" or just "doesn't suit this kind of French food". / 11 pm, Sun 9 pm.

Blandford Comptoir W1 £60 333

1 Blandford St   020 7935 4626   2–1A

As befits a well-known wine expert, Xavier Rousset's "buzzy" Marylebone bar has a "superbly curated selection of vintages by the glass", but also "excellent", straightforward Mediterranean (primarily Italian) cooking. Top Tip: "very good value set lunch for £20". / W1U 3DA; blandford-comptoir.co.uk; @BlandfordCompt; 10 pm; no Amex.

Bleecker Burger £22 522

205 Victoria St, SW1   no tel   2–4B
Unit B Pavilion Building, Spitalfields Mkt, E1   07712 540501   13–2B
Bloomberg Arcade, Queen Victoria St, EC4   020 7929 3785   10–3C

"The best burgers in London" – that's the survey verdict on Zan Kaufman's permanent-now-pop-up chain, now with four outlets including the new Bloomberg arcade and a (May-Sep only) South Bank stall. "Consistently juicy and perfectly cooked burgers and fries are served by friendly, helpful staff who always make you feel welcome". "I eat there any chance I get, they are epic and every bite makes me happy!"

Bleeding Heart Restaurant EC1 £75 335

Bleeding Heart Yd, Greville St   020 7242 8238   10–2A

That "it's a bit of a maze" adds to the "cosy" and "charming" atmosphere of this intriguing and immensely popular Dickensian cellar, in a "secluded courtyard" on the fringes of the City. Done out in a "conservative", traditional style (with some panelled rooms), it's "a great place to strike a business deal", but likewise smoochy couples also "have a romantic time tucked away in a delightful nook or cranny, somehow isolated from the hubbub and well looked after by the staff". "The French menu is wide-ranging" and quite "traditional". To critics, results can "lack spark", but for most reporters "they get the classics just right". Arguably a bigger deal is the "excellent French-based wine list", also including "interesting choices from the owners' own New Zealand vineyard". / EC1N 8SJ; bleedingheart.co.uk; @bleedingheartyd; 10.30 pm; closed Sat & Sun.

Blixen E1 £47 333
65a Brushfield St 020 7101 0093 13–2C
This elegant all-day venue in a former bank by Spitalfields Market is inspired by European grand cafés and serves "really good" modern brasserie food. It also has a plant-filled conservatory with a "lovely, nicely cool ambience". / E1 6AA; www.blixen.co.uk; @BlixenLondon; 11 pm, Sun 9 pm.

Bluebird SW3 £74 233
350 King's Rd 020 7559 1000 6–3C
With its "buzzy ambience" and "stylish interior", this D&D London bar/restaurant prominently situated in a large and elegant building (built in 1923 as a car garage) on the King's Road attracts feedback that's far more good than bad. On the downside, the food is no better than "OK", and the atmosphere can seem "lacking something… perhaps the room is too large". / SW3 5UU; www.bluebird-restaurant.co.uk; @bluebirdchelsea; Wed-Sat 9.30 pm, Sun 3 pm.

Bluebird Café White City W12 NEW £49
2 Television Centre, 101 Wood Lane 020 3940 0700 1–2B
D&D London are rolling out the Bluebird Café concept with this sibling in the former TV Centre at White City: the first eatery to open in the shiny new development. Initial feedback on the food is mostly positive, but its best feature is probably the outside terrace. / W12 7FR; bluebirdcafe.co.uk; @bluebirdcafew12; 10 pm, Sun 9 pm.

Blueprint Café SE1 £48 224
28 Shad Thames, Butler's Wharf 020 7378 7031 10–4D
Spectacular first-floor views over the Thames are the primary (some would say only) motivation to visit this D&D London venue on the first floor of the former Design Museum near Tower Bridge. The venue has always tended to score indifferently for its food – even when big name Jeremy Lee was at the stoves – and this profile has persisted since his departure years ago. Heralded chef-patron Mini Patel stepped down in August 2018 having lasted only six months in the role. / SE1 2YD; www.blueprintcafe.co.uk; @BlueprintCafe; 10.30 pm; closed Mon & Sun; no booking.

Bob Bob Cité EC3
122 Leadenhall St 020 3145 1000 10–2D
Tomorrow and tomorrow and tomorrow; we've been billing the arrival of 'BBC' – sibling to Soho's glam Bob Bob Ricard – for over a year now as its opening is pushed back and back. Set to occupy the entire third floor of 'The Cheesegrater', more 'press for Champagne' buttons are promised, alongside a menu provided by Eric Chavot. When it finally arrives, one thing is certain: it won't be subtle! STOP PRESS: a new, new opening date of January 2019 has been announced. / EC3V 4PE; www.bobbobricard.com; @bobbobcite; Wed-Sat 10 pm, Sun 5 pm.

Bob Bob Ricard W1 £85 335
1 Upper James St 020 3145 1000 4–2C
"Who doesn't love a button by the table that is exclusively for ordering Champagne?" And the "matchless", fantasy-plush interior of Leonid Shutov's lavish Soho 'diner' creates a "gorgeous" setting, especially "for a fun date". Eric Chavot's menu of "luxury staples" delivers some "pretty good food", and – while the fact that it's certainly "not a bargain" is a sticking point for a few reporters – most "don't begrudge a penny". / W1F 9DF; www.bobbobricard.com; @BobBobRicard; 11.15 pm, Sat midnight, Sun 11.15 pm; closed Sat L; Jacket required.

Bocca Di Lupo W1 £62 **4 4 3**

12 Archer St   020 7734 2223   4–3D

"Paradise for Italian food lovers" – Jacob Kenedy's *"easygoing"* yet *"well-run"* and immensely popular operation, a short walk from Piccadilly Circus, is one of the most culinarily interesting destinations in town (especially of the *"reasonably priced"* variety). *"It's not just your standard Italian trat fayre, yet neither is it merely über-trendy small plates"*. Instead, an *"unrivalled selection of vigorous and distinctive dishes are labelled by region and available in two sizes"* (tapas-style or 'main'). *"Dishes are from all over Italy, change regularly"* and *"are often unusual (for example fried calf's foot)"*. There's also *"a terrific Italian wine list (available by the carafe), with knowledgeable advice available at all price levels"*. *"Go early if possible, as it can get too buzzy"* and *"vibrant"* and *"is quite packed-in"* (although most reporters feel that *"the food justifies any lack of comfort"*). *"Sit at the counter for a bird's-eye-view of the chefs"* (although these perches in particular can feel *"high, cramped and noisy"*). *"I think I have eaten over 75 times at Bocca and the food and team there remain at the top of their game – the food is always different and amazingly authentic to its origins"*. Top Menu Tip: *"great puddings including the signature sanguinaccio (blood, pistachio, chocolate)"*. / W1D 7BB; www.boccadilupo.com; @boccadilupo; 11 pm, Sun 9.30 pm; booking max 10 may apply.

Bocconcino W1 £93 **3 2 2**

19 Berkeley St   020 7499 4510   3–3C

A modern take on classic Italian cuisine, this Russian-owned joint in a glossy corner of Mayfair is *"glitzy and noisy"*, but the cooking, from fish to pizza, is *"credible if overpriced"*. / W1J 8ED; www.bocconcinorestaurant.co.uk; @BocconcinoUK; 12.30 am, Sun 10.30 pm.

Al Boccon di'vino TW9 £66 **4 4 5**

14 Red Lion St   020 8940 9060   1–4A

"You never know what you're going to eat" at this no-choice Italian feast in Richmond, which has built a loyal following over the last decade. *"More than a restaurant, it feels like a holiday in Italy, where you're eating at Nonna's home"*. Chef Riccardo Grigolo and his team *"are so welcoming"* and deliver a lengthy Venetian-style meal – *"fantastic food that just keeps on coming"* and where *"every course is delicious"*. / TW9 1RW; www.nonsolovinoltd.co.uk; @alboccondivino; Tue-Sun 11 pm; closed Tue, Wed L, closed Mon; no Amex.

Bodeans £50 **3 2 3**

10 Poland St, W1   020 7287 7575   4–1C
25 Catherine St, WC2   020 7257 2790   5–3D
4 Broadway Chambers, SW6   020 7610 0440   6–4A
348 Muswell Hill Broadway, N10   020 8883 3089   1–1C
225 Balham High St, SW17   020 8682 4650   11–2C
169 Clapham High St, SW4   020 7622 4248   11–2D
201 City Rd, EC1   020 7608 7230   13–1A
16 Byward St, EC3   020 7488 3883   10–3D

"If you want a pile of BBQ meat, you won't be disappointed" by these *"laid back"*, *"typically American and un-subtle"* Kansas City-style BBQs. *"No frills"*, *"tender and tasty"* food at *"decent"* prices has proved a recipe for longevity for the group, an early pioneer of London's flesh-plus-fire dining scene. Top Tip: *"the pulled pork and burnt ends combo is not to be sniffed at"*. / www.bodeansbbq.com; 11 pm, Sun 10.30 pm, NW10 10 pm, Fri & Sat 11 pm; booking: min 8.

Boisdale of Belgravia SW1 £68 2️⃣2️⃣3️⃣

15 Eccleston St 020 7730 6922 2–4B

*With its "plush Jockinese decor" and "traditional, meaty Scottish fare" –
Ranald Macdonald's long-established Belgravia haunt has become
synonymous in some quarters with a very masculine style of dining, buoyed
by fine wines and whiskies, plus a cigar terrace and "good jazz". This wasn't
a vintage year for its ratings, however – "staff are friendly but can struggle
to handle a packed house" and the experience can seem "expensive
if you're not booked on a deal". / SW1W 9LX; www.boisdale.co.uk/belgravia;
@boisdale; 1 am; closed Sat L, closed Sun.*

Boisdale of Bishopsgate EC2 £73 3️⃣2️⃣3️⃣

Swedeland Court, 202 Bishopsgate 020 7283 1763 10–2D

*Just off Bishopsgate, this bar (ground floor) and restaurant (basement) is a
chip off the original Belgravia block, with plush Caledonian styling and
a menu of meaty Scottish fare. Not all reporters are upbeat,
but most acclaim it for its "good location" and "food that's good if not
cheap". / EC2M 4NR; www.boisdale.co.uk; @Boisdale; 11 pm; closed Sat & Sun.*

Boisdale of Canary Wharf E14 £68 2️⃣2️⃣3️⃣

Cabot Place 020 7715 5818 12–1C

*This Boisdale spin-off in Canary Wharf (for a drink, try to grab a seat on the
terrace) aims to replicate the Caledonian styling of the Belgravia original,
down to the live music and focus on wines and whiskies. When it comes
to its traditional, meaty fare, no culinary fireworks were reported this year,
but it was consistently well-supported. / E14 4QT;
www.boisdale.co.uk/canary-wharf; @boisdaleCW; Mon & Tue 11 pm, Wed-Sat
midnight, Sun 4 pm; closed Sat L closed Sun D.*

Bokan E14 £70 3️⃣3️⃣3️⃣

40 Marsh Wall 020 3530 0550 12–2C

*"On a clear day the sights across London are wonderful" on the 37th floor
of the recently opened Novotel Canary Wharf. This 65-cover venue still
inspires limited feedback, but such as we have praises "beautifully presented
dishes, tasty drinks and a great atmosphere". / E14 9TP; bokanlondon.co.uk;
@BokanLondon; 10 pm, Sun 9 pm; closed Mon-Thu L.*

Bombay Brasserie SW7 £65 4️⃣3️⃣3️⃣

Courtfield Rd 020 7370 4040 6–2B

*"Looking very smart" again nowadays, this upmarket "institution" in South
Kensington has been run in recent times by luxury Indian chain Taj Hotels
and is winning more consistent praise for its "helpful staff and delicious
food". It's yet to step back properly onto London's culinary map, however,
and even some fans feel "it's still to some extent relying on past glories".
/ SW7 4QH; www.bombayb.co.uk; @bbsw7; Mon-Fri 11.30 pm, Sat 11 pm,
Sun 10.30 pm; closed Mon L.*

Bombay Bustle W1 NEW £68 4️⃣4️⃣3️⃣

29 Maddox St 020 7290 4470 4–2A

*"The spicing is fantastic – very authentic", at Samyukta Nair and Rohit
Ghai's Mayfair newcomer, on the former site of Hibiscus (RIP), which takes
the Mumbai institution of tiffin (and the trains the dabbawalas use to deliver
it) as its theme. Many "wonderful" meals are reported in feedback that
includes nothing but praise. / W1S 2PA; www.bombaybustle.com; @BombayBustle;
Mon-Fri 10 pm, Sat & Sun 9 pm.*

Bombay Palace W2 £47 4️⃣3️⃣2️⃣

50 Connaught St 020 7723 8855 7–1D

*"The cooking is back on form after a year or two off" (during which the
restaurant was closed following a fire), say fans of this Bayswater old-timer,
hailing its "excellent food, with fresh spices and not messed about as at
many of the newer nouvelle Indians". The interior is a little "dull" but
"at least you can hear yourself talk". / W2 2AA; www.bombay-palace.co.uk;
@bombaypalaceW2; 1 am.*

Bon Vivant WC1 £57 ☒☒☒
75-77 Marchmont St 020 7713 6111 9–4C
*"A brave and ambitious attempt to lift culinary standards in a corner
of Bloomsbury otherwise only well-served with mid-range chains"* –
this *"very authentic French bistro"* is a *"very pleasing neighbourhood
restaurant"*. / WC1N 1AP; www.bonvivantrestaurant.co.uk; 10.30 pm.

Bone Daddies £42 ☒☒☒
Nova, Victoria St, SW1 no tel 2–4B
14a, Old Compton St, W1 020 7734 7492 5–2A
30-31 Peter St, W1 020 7287 8581 4–2D
46-48 James St, W1 020 3019 7140 3–1A
Whole Foods, Kensington High St, W8 020 7287 8581 6–1A
The Bower, Baldwin St, EC1 020 7439 9299 13–1A
The *"perfect westernised Japanese food"* at former Zuma and Nobu chef
Ross Shonhan's *"hip"* ramen-bar chain *"shows how to do fusion"*: *"the soup
stock is wonderfully thick and full of flavour, not watery like other places"*.
Top Tip: *"soft shell crab ramen"*. / www.bonedaddies.com; 10 pm, Thu-Sat 11 pm,
Sun 9.30 pm; W1 no bookings.

Bonhams Restaurant,
Bonhams Auction House W1 £77 ☒☒☒
101 New Bond St 020 7468 5868 3–2B
Chef Tom Kemble's *"excellent cooking"* has been blessed by the Tyre Men,
and professional service to match makes eating in this *"calm and perfect"*
dining room, at the back of a Mayfair auctioneer, *"like a private dining
experience"* and an excellent business choice. *"But the wine is the key
factor"*: the auction house has access to a *"fast-changing list"* that offers
some of the best value in town. / W1K 5ES; www.bonhamsrestaurant.com;
@dineatbonhams; 10 pm; L only, Fri L & D, closed Sat & Sun.

Bonnie Gull £58 ☒☒☒
22 Bateman St, W1D 020 7436 0921 5–2A
21a Foley St, W1 020 7436 0921 2–1B
"The perfect seafood restaurant… in Fitzrovia!" – this *"tiny"*, *"casual"* and
"cramped" dining room has won a major following thanks
to *"straightforward"* cooking showing *"great attention to detail"* – *"fish can
be tricky in London, but here it works"*. *"The newer shack in Soho is great
for a quick bite"*, too. / www.bonniegull.com; @BonnieGull.

Bonoo NW2 £39 ☒☒☒
675 Finchley Rd 020 7794 8899 1–1B
"It looks nothing from the modest outside", but this *"excellent newcomer"*
in the *"gastronomic desert of Childs Hill"* is *"always packed"* – its *"unusual
Indian tapas dishes are absolutely superb"*: *"beautifully spiced street food
that outstrips more fashionable eateries"*. / NW2 2JP; www.bonoo.co.uk;
@bonoohampstead; 10.30 pm, Sun 9.30 pm.

The Booking Office,
St Pancras Renaissance Hotel NW1 £67 ☒☒☒
Euston Rd 020 7841 3566 9–3C
The *"lovely location"* of this all-day operation in the former ticket office
at St Pancras station makes it an attractive option for breakfast or afternoon
tea (*"the pastries are truly exquisite"*). For a more substantial meal,
feedback is more limited (and mixed). / NW1 2AR;
www.bookingofficerestaurant.com; @StPancrasRen; Sun-Wed midnight, Thu-Sat 1 am.

Booma SW9 £34 4 3 2
244 Brixton Road 020 7737 4999 11–2D
"Lots of small, tapas-y dishes to share, accompanied by a glass of craft beer" is the formula at this modern Indian café on the northern fringes of Brixton, which delivers "accurate, well-spiced cooking to a higher standard than one might expect". / SW9 6AH; booma-brixton.co.uk; @boomabrixton; Mon-Thu 11 pm, Fri & Sat 11.30 pm, Sun 10 pm; closed Mon-Fri L.

Boqueria £49 4 3 3
192 Acre Ln, SW2 020 7733 4408 11–2D
278 Queenstown Rd, SW8 020 7498 8427 11–1C
"Different and delicious tapas" is bolstered by a "great specials board and cocktails" to win consistent esteem for this Hispanic duo, close together in Battersea and Clapham, where regulars are full of praise for the "welcoming staff" and "buzzy" (if authentically "noisy") atmosphere.

Il Bordello E1 £64 3 4 4
81 Wapping High St 020 7481 9950 12–1A
This "enduringly appealing", "family-run Italian in fashionable Wapping is always packed, so you have to book well ahead". It's "so noisy the children can't be heard", and the "old-style cooking (good pizzas and pasta) means no one leaves hungry — in fact, "the only fault is that the servings are too large!". / E1W 2YN; www.ilbordello.com; 9.30 pm, Sun 8.30 pm; closed Sat L.

Boro Bistro SE1 £44 3 3 3
Montague Cl, 6-10 Borough High St 020 7378 0788 10–3C
"A real find" in a "lovely setting on the edge of Borough Market", and with "an attractive outside eating area" – this contemporary bistro is "well worth discovering" for its "great sharing boards and tapas" and a "good selection of beers". / SE1 9QQ; www.borobistro.co.uk; @borobistro; 10.30 pm, Mon & Sun 9 pm; closed Mon & Sun; booking max 6 may apply.

The Botanist £66 2 2 2
7 Sloane Sq, SW1 020 7730 0077 6–2D
Broadgate Circle, EC2 020 3058 9888 13–2B
Opinions divide on these "spacious" and well-located all-day brasseries in Chelsea (right on Sloane Square) and the City (in Broadgate). Fans vaunt them as "very pleasant" for many occasions, and particularly for a business lunch or "excellent breakfast/brunch". Critics, though, rate them for being "so noisy" and dismiss the food as "overpriced and disappointing". / thebotanist.uk.com; @thebotanistuk; SW1 breakfast 8, Sat & Sun 9, SW1 & EC2 11 pm.

Boudin Blanc W1 £65 3 2 3
5 Trebeck St 020 7499 3292 3–4B
Crowded and charming, long-established bistro, which creates a "proper Gallic buzz" in Mayfair's picturesque Shepherd Market. With its "lovely" main dining room and attractive outdoor seating in summer, it used to be a higher profile destination, but its ratings have slightly come off the boil in recent years. It's still pretty popular though, particularly as a business lunching choice. / W1J 7LT; www.boudinblanc.co.uk; Mon & Tue 11 pm, Wed-Sat midnight, Sun 4 pm.

Boulestin SW1 £72 2 3 2
5 St James's St 020 7930 2030 3–4D
A revival of a venerable name from the 1920s on a classic St James's site (once L'Oranger, RIP), Joel Kissin's bistro rates well for "excellent breakfasts". Beyond that it is "just about OK" but there's an issue: "there's no need to charge their prices". Its trump card is "the courtyard – a hidden joy for al fresco dining in the summer". / SW1A 1EF; www.boulestin.com; @BoulestinLondon; 10 pm; closed Sun; No trainers.

Bowling Bird EC1 £34 **4 4 3**
44 Cloth Fair 020 7324 7742 10–2B
Excellent but limited feedback on this cute yearling – a straightforward looking operation tucked away down a Smithfield alleyway in a quaint old townhouse that was once Sir John Betjeman's home (and which some older reporters may remember as Betjeman's Restaurant, very long RIP). The small menu, complemented by daily specials, is of diverse inspiration, but the stand-outs are the meat dishes, reflecting chef Emiliano Gallegos's experience at La Pulperia, an Argentinian steakhouse in Paris. / EC1A 7JQ; bowlingbird.com; closed Mon, Sat & Sun.

Boxcar Butcher & Grill W1 £50 **4 4 3**
23 New Quebec St 020 3006 7000 2–2A
From Barry Hirst's Cubitt House group, this Marylebone yearling combines butcher, deli and steakhouse and serves from breakfast onwards. "It does what it says on the tin!" – a short selection of steaks, burgers and other fare offering "top quality meat at a decent price": "given the location, this is great value, fun and quick". / W1H 7SD; boxcar.co.uk; @BoxcarLondon; 10.30 pm, Sun 10 pm.

Boyds Grill & Wine Bar WC2 £58 **3 3 3**
8 Northumberland Ave 020 7808 3344 2–3C
The potentially "lovely room", just off Trafalgar Square – part of a monumental, much-marbled Victorian hotel (which spent most of the 20th century as part of the MoD) – and "good-value set menu" can make this an "excellent central London location", although its "rather cavernous" nature can mean there's "not a great ambience"; "very nice wine list". / WC2N 5BY; www.boydsbrasserie.co.uk; 10 pm, Sun 12 pm; closed Sun D.

The Brackenbury W6 £58 **4 4 4**
129-131 Brackenbury Rd 020 8741 4928 8–1C
One of London's more accomplished backstreet haunts – this long-established Hammersmith stalwart, buried deep in 'Brackenbury Village', has a convivial style founded in a superior basic formula comprising "a seasonal, well-executed menu, good wine list and knowledgeable staff". The layout is quirky – a u-shaped space with a newish bar area on one side, with the remaining space dedicated to dining; superb summer terrace too. / W6 0BQ; www.brackenburyrestaurant.co.uk; @BrackenburyRest; 10.30 pm; closed Mon & Sun D.

Brackenbury Wine Rooms W6 £58 **2 2 3**
Hammersmith Grove 020 3696 8240 8–1C
"A good range of wines" (served by the glass as well as by the bottle) helps win praise for this attractive Hammersmith corner spot, with deli and wine shop attached (part of a small west London group), and with lovely outside tables in summer. No-one makes exaggerated claims for the cuisine, but for the most part it's well-rated. / W6 0NQ; winerooms.london/brackenbury; @Wine_Rooms; midnight, Sun 11 pm.

Bradley's NW3 £64 **2 2 2**
25 Winchester Rd 020 7722 3457 9–2A
This "friendly neighbourhood restaurant" in Swiss Cottage, now closing in on its 30th anniversary, is "good if not brilliant… probably the best in the area". OK, you might not cross town for it, but it's very handy for the Hampstead Theatre, with a "great pre-theatre menu". / NW3 3NR; www.bradleysnw3.co.uk; 10 pm, Sun 2.30 pm; closed Sun D.

Brady's SW18 £40 **3** **4** **3**

39 Jews Row   020 8877 9599   11–2B

"The formula of fish 'n' chips and daily fish specials has worked for years and years" for the Brady family's restaurant, which nowadays has *"a great location on the river"* with *"a lovely atmosphere"*, near Wandsworth Bridge – *"less frantic than its original location"* which it left behind a few years ago. Top Menu Tip: *"everyone comes for the fish but most have a dessert as well!"* / SW18 1DG; www.bradysfish.co.uk; @Bradyfish; 9.30 pm, Sun 3.30 pm; closed Tue-Thu L closed Sun D, closed Mon; no booking.

Brasserie Blanc £56 **2** **2** **2**

Even if it's not *"the most gastronomic option"*, Raymond Blanc's contemporary brasserie chain does have fans who laud its *"pleasant"* branches, and *"reliable, routine French cuisine"*. Critics take a similar view but from a glass-half-empty standpoint: *"no big complaints, but the value-for-money is low and service so-so"*. / www.brasserieblanc.com; most branches close between 10 pm & 11 pm; SE1 closed Sun D, City branches closed Sat & Sun.

Brasserie Toulouse-Lautrec SE11 £62 **3** **3** **3**

140 Newington Butts   020 7582 6800   1–3C

Solid all-round ratings (if on limited feedback) for this bravely located Gallic brasserie (and live music venue) convenient for Kennington's cinema museum. / SE11 4RN; www.btlrestaurant.co.uk; @btlrestaurant; Tue-Thu 10 pm, Fri & Sat 10.30 pm, Mon 9.30 pm, Sun 9 pm.

Brasserie Zédel W1 £41 **1** **3** **5**

20 Sherwood St   020 7734 4888   4–3C

"Worth a visit just to look at the main salon" – Corbin & King's *"improbably glamorous and huge"*, Grade I-listed, Art Deco basement is *"an extraordinary space that dazzles every newcomer"*; and *"so handy, being just by Piccadilly Circus tube"*. *"It was a great concept of C & K to try and re-create a proper Parisian brasserie, with menu to match"*, and by and large they've succeeded. But even some of its greatest fans (of which there are bazillions) would admit that the trade-off is mightily *"indifferent"* traditional fare and service – which though improved this year – can still be *"patchy"*. Don't be put off though: especially if you're counting the pennies, its low, low prices make it a total *"bargain"* in the heart of the West End. Top Tips – the set menu is *"limited"* but *"excellent value"*. Also, *"the amazing '30s-style American Bar, and small nightclub called 'The Crazy Coqs'!"* (Final note for style anoraks: if you want to be pernickety, *"while the basement is genuine Art Deco, the main dining room itself is actually more flamboyant neo-classical. Its only 'real' Art Deco elements are the splendid ceiling lights, added during the last refurbishment."*) / W1F 7ED; www.brasseriezedel.com; @brasseriezedel; midnight, Sun 11 pm.

Brat E1 NEW £61 **5** **4** **4**

First Floor, 4 Redchurch St   no tel   13–1B

"I just loved everything about it!" – Behind an inconspicuous side-door in Shoreditch, on the panelled first-floor of a converted pub (a pre-gentrification strip club, whose ground floor is nowadays Smoking Goat), chef Tomos Parry (ex-head-chef of Kitty Fishers) *"exceeds high expectations"* and has a smash hit on his hands, with this *"terrific"* launch – the survey's highest rated newcomer. The *"open plan kitchen approach works well"*, with the focus on the large grill which produces most of the Basque-influenced cuisine here. *"So, obviously you're going to order the turbot"* – for which the restaurant is named (look it up) – which is presented whole and *"utterly delicious"*. But *"the food is superb throughout and well priced considering its quality and the chef's pedigree"*. *"Very happy staff"*, *"a lovely atmosphere"* and thoughtful wine list complete the picture. / E1 6JJ; www.bratrestaurant.com; @bratrestaurant; Mon-Fri 10 pm, Sat & Sun 9 pm.

Bravas E1 £55 3 4 4
St Katharine Docks 020 7481 1464 10–3D
Overlooking the marina at St Katharine Docks, this "cosy and romantic" modern Basque venture serves "brilliant tapas, including some unusual items". "Often busy", it "recently expanded by taking over the sushi bar next door". / E1W 1AT; www.bravasrestaurant.com; @Bravas_Tapas; 11 pm.

Brawn E2 £63 4 3 3
49 Columbia Rd 020 7729 5692 14–2A
"Put on yer skinnies and wax that beard for this cool-crowd place in hipster central." Ed Wilson's enduring foodie mecca in Bethnal Green is part of the original Terroirs stable that brought natural and biodynamic wines into vogue, and continues to win praise for its "always interesting and well-prepared" dishes and "a great wine list that alone makes it worth a visit". One or two refuseniks feel it falls short, however: "I was expecting / hoping for more". / E2 7RG; www.brawn.co; @brawn49; Mon-Thu 10.30 pm, Fri & Sat 11 pm; closed Mon L, closed Sun; no Amex.

Bread Street Kitchen EC4 £64 2 2 3
10 Bread St 020 3030 4050 10–2B
"Huge" Gordon Ramsay Group operation in a City mall by St Paul's that wins more enthusiasm for its "buzzing setting" and "really nice warehouse-style modern décor" than for its food, which is at a "reliably good" level for a business lunch, but can otherwise seem "mind-numbingly middle-of-the-road". / EC4M 9AJ; www.breadstreetkitchen.com; @breadstreet; Mon-Wed, Sat midnight, Thu & Fri 1 am, Sun 10 pm.

Breakfast Club £41 3 3 3
33 D'Arblay St, W1 020 7434 2571 4–1C
2-4 Rufus St, N1 020 7729 5252 13–1B
31 Camden Pas, N1 020 7226 5454 9–3D
12-16 Artillery Ln, E1 020 7078 9633 13–2B
"Breakfast for lunch, breakfast for dinner – and anywhere in between" is the offer – with "really interesting choices" backed up by "speakeasy-style" cocktails – at these "buzzy" cafés which attract "queues out of the door". "I've never been a fan of breakfast but this place has made me think again!" / www.thebreakfastclubcafes.com; @thebrekkyclub; SRA-Food Made Good – 3 stars.

Breddos Tacos £48 3 3 3
26 Kingly Street, W1 4–2B
82 Goswell Rd, EC1 020 3535 8301 10–1B
"Brilliant" Mexican-inspired tacos using top-quality British ingredients have taken this operation from a shack in a Hackney car park to a permanent site in Clerkenwell (with a second in Soho). But its marks took a knock across the board this year amid complaints from erstwhile fans that the food nowadays "lacks a bit of the zing of the street food stall". / breddostacos.com; @breddostacos.

Brew House Café,
Kenwood House NW3 £31 2 2 3
Hampstead Heath 020 8348 1286 9–1A
For "homemade cakes with good tea and coffee" – or breakfast which "is also excellent" – stroll to the top of Hampstead Heath, to the self-service café within the stable blocks of this English Heritage property: best in summer when you can sit in the marvellous garden. / NW3 7JR; searcyskenwoodhouse.co.uk; @Searcys; closed Mon-Sun D.

Briciole W1 £50 3 2 2
20 Homer St 020 7723 0040 7–1D
"Wonderful, genuine Italian food" justifies a visit to this Marylebone deli-trattoria (an offshoot of Latium, RIP), but at peak times "you have to put up with cramped and noisy surroundings". / W1H 4NA; www.briciole.co.uk; @briciolelondon; Tue-Thu 10 pm, Fri & Sat 10.30 pm, Mon 9.30 pm, Sun 9 pm.

Brick Lane Beigel Bake E1 £6 3 1 1
159 Brick Ln   020 7729 0616   13–1C
"Salt beef and salmon – what more could you ask for?" say fans of the epic filled beigels, sold at prices seemingly unchanged from the 1980s, at this famous, if dead grungy, 24/7 East End bakery. Service is of the unsmiling, Soviet-era variety. / E1 6SB; www.beigelbake.com; @BeigelBake; open 24 hours; cash only; no booking.

Brigadiers EC2 £52 5 4 4
Bloomberg Arcade, Queen Victoria St   020 3319 8140   10–3C
Very early feedback is adulatory for the massive menu of flavour-packed Indian BBQ dishes served at this JKS Restaurants (Gymkhana, Hoppers) newcomer (opened in June 2018), which occupies the largest restaurant space in the City's Bloomberg Arcade. A sizeable operation inspired by traditional Indian Army mess halls (well, that's what the press release said) it comprises multiple spaces including several bars (The Tap Room, Blighters) and private rooms (the biggest, The Pot Luck, has its own entrance). / EC2R; www.jksrestaurants.com; @brigadiersldn; 9 pm, Sun 5 pm.

The Bright Courtyard W1 £69 4 2 2
43-45 Baker St   020 7486 6998   2–1A
"Ignore the departure lounge setting (especially if you get exiled to the office block atrium)" – this "new-wave Chinese" in Marylebone is "one of the leading Chinese restaurants in London". Top of the bill is its "unusual dim sum" of "Hong Kong standard". / W1U 8EW; www.lifefashiongroup.com; @BrightCourtyard; 11.30 pm, Sun 10.30 pm.

Brilliant UB2 £53 4 4 3
72-76 Western Rd   020 8574 1928   1–3A
"Straightforward Indian cuisine doesn't come much better" that at this large, legendary, Punjabi venture – lost deep in the 'burbs of Southall – which feels very "unpretentious", but "still maintains its high standards". / UB2 5DZ; www.brilliantrestaurant.com; @brilliantrst; 10.30 pm; closed Mon, Sat L & Sun L.

Brinkley's SW10 £63 2 2 3
47 Hollywood Rd   020 7351 1683   6–3B
A "good", "well-priced" wine list and an "excellent atmosphere" are key to the enduring success of John Brinkley's "neighbourhood stand-by" in a sidestreet near Chelsea & Westminster Hospital. Despite "pretty average cooking" and "pleasant if slow service", it "serves its Chelsea fanbase well (mostly ageing roués on the pull, and with a strong leaning to Eurotrash!)" / SW10 9HX; www.brinkleys.com/brinkleys-restaurant.html; @BrinkleysR; 11 pm, Sun 10.30 pm; closed Mon-Fri L.

Brookmill SE8 £54 3 3 3
65 Cranbrook Rd   020 8333 0899   1–4D
Gentrified a couple of years ago, this "lively" Deptford gastropub is thriving on its "excellent pub food and great ambience"; cute garden too. / SE8 4EJ; www.thebrookmill.co.uk; @thebrookmillpub; 11 pm, Sun 10.30 pm.

The Brown Dog SW13 £46 3 3 3
28 Cross St   020 8392 2200   11–1A
You'll need to book for the "great Sunday lunch" at this cute gastropub with a "convivial atmosphere" in the tangle of backstreets comprising Barnes's gorgeous 'Little Chelsea'. "The beef in their Sunday roast is always really tasty", and "my favourite ever roast beef sandwich" also cuts the mustard. A favourite for dog walkers and local families. / SW13 0AP; www.thebrowndog.co.uk; @browndogbarnes; Mon-Thu 10.30 pm, Fri & Sat 11 pm.

Brown's Hotel,
The English Tea Room W1 £76 **3** **4** **4**
Albemarle St 020 7493 6020 3–3C
"Home to one of the foremost traditional afternoon teas in London" –
this plush hotel lounge wins many nominations as providing one of the
finest teatime spreads in town, "boasting an extensive array of teas,
plus traditional-with-a-twist sandwiches, scones and cakes that really do melt
in the mouth!"; "a thoroughly enjoyable experience". / W1S 4BP;
www.roccofortehotels.com; No trainers.

Brunswick House Café SW8 £56 **3** **3** **5**
30 Wandsworth Rd 020 7720 2926 11–1D
The "bizarrely brilliant location" of an architectural salvage shop in a grand
Georgian mansion on the Vauxhall Cross gyratory provides a "quirky setting
for inventive seasonal cooking and cocktails". The food is "unexpectedly
lovely": "lunch a bargain and dinner a treat" – "in a unique ambience
surrounded by reclaimed chandeliers". ("It's always fun to spot the new
arrivals and mentally fit out your dream house!") / SW8 2LG;
www.brunswickhouse.co; Mon-Wed 10 pm, Thu-Sat 11 pm; closed Sun D.

Bryn Williams at Somerset House WC2 NEW £60 **4** **4** **3**
Somerset House 020 7845 464 2–2D
Welsh chef, Bryn Williams (of Odette's, in NW3 and in North Wales
at Porth Eirias) makes a foray into a more central location, in a stately
chamber within Somerset House. There's nothing but praise for the
"personable" service and "very imaginatively conceived and carefully
prepared dishes", but the way it promotes its 'flexitarian' credentials (putting
fruit and veg front and centre) can grate – "the menu can seem irritating
owing to placing the protein after the veg" and, more seriously, more than
one veggie luncher has bizarrely encountered a set menu with
no satisfactory veggie alternative ("unheard of in modern veg-friendly
civilisation?"). / WC2; www.bryn-somersethouse.co.uk; @bwsomersethouse; 10 pm,
Sun 4 pm; closed Sun D.

Bubbledogs W1 £51 **3** **4** **4**
70 Charlotte St 020 7637 7770 2–1C
Sandia Chang's "buzzy if slightly cramped" Fitzrovia haunt (a unique double
act with husband, James Knappett's fine-dining Kitchen Table, see also) is an
unlikely success. As concepts go, hot dogs and Champagne make
an "odd couple" – "the dogs are great" "but the real star is the range
of fizz – lots of small producers and excellent variety, at good prices".
/ W1T 4QG; www.bubbledogs.co.uk; @bubbledogsUK; 11 pm; closed Sun & Mon.

Bucket W2 NEW £46
107 Westbourne Grove 020 3146 1156 7–1B
On the Bayswater/Notting Hill border, this seafood café opened in May
2018, too late in the day to receive survey feedback. If you fancy sustainably
sourced seafood served by the bucket-load (literally, it seems) then it looks
worth a try. / W2 4UW; www.bucketrestaurant.com; 11.30 pm, Sun 10.30 pm.

Buen Ayre E8 £68 **4** **3** **2**
50 Broadway Market 020 7275 9900 14–2B
"The best steak ever" (well, nearly) continues to draw enthusiastic fans
to this popular little Argentinian parrilla, which is one of the longest standing
foodie destinations on Hackney's thriving Broadway Market. / E8 4QJ;
www.buenayre.co.uk; Sun-Thu 10 pm, Fri & Sat 10.30 pm; no Amex.

The Builders Arms SW3 £55 **2** **2** **4**
13 Britten St 020 7349 9040 6–2C
A super-cute Chelsea backstreet location boosts the attractions of this
Geronimo Inns property, whose "reliable pub grub" gives no cause for
complaint. Top Tip: "grab a table near the fire" in winter. / SW3 3TY;
www.thebuildersarmschelsea.co.uk; @BuildersChelsea; 10 pm, Sun 9 pm; no booking.

The Bull N6 £53 **3** **4** **4**
13 North Hill 020 8341 0510 9–1B
"Always of high quality", say fans of the dependable gastrofare at this popular microbrewery-cum-gastropub in Highgate. It's "good with families" too. / N6 4AB; thebullhighgate.co.uk; @Bull_Highgate; 10.30 pm, Mon 11 pm, Sun 3 pm.

Bull & Last NW5 £65 **3** **3** **3**
168 Highgate Rd 020 7267 3641 9–1B
"Still setting the standard" for north London gastropubs (amongst which it generates the highest amount of survey feedback) – this "ever-reliable" Kentish Town fixture "has a lovely cosy interior, plus friendly staff" and "a delicious and varied menu". Top Tip: "they produce excellent picnic baskets for taking advantage of a lunch on Hampstead Heath on those warm days". / NW5 1QS; www.thebullandlast.co.uk; @thebullandlast; 10 pm, Sun 9 pm.

Bumpkin £57 **2** **2** **3**
102 Old Brompton Rd, SW7 020 7341 0802 6–2B
Westfield Stratford City, The St, E20 020 8221 9900 14–1D
"Buzzy and informal", this pair of farm-to-fork brasseries in South Kensington and Westfield Stratford (shrunk from a mini-chain) "have some interesting English dishes on the menu" which "can be good". But they are "still unbelievably variable", and "can be rather noisy and chaotic". / www.bumpkinuk.com; 11 pm; closed Mon.

Bun House W1 £14 **4** **4** **4**
24 Greek St 020 8017 9888 5–2A
"Fantastic bao buns" win praise from the small but super-enthusiastic fan club of this year-old Cantonese Soho café on corner of Greek and Old Compton Streets; and "it's such a cute little space" too. Downstairs is a bar, Tea Room, complete with late licence. / W1D 4DZ; www.bun.house; @8unhouse; closed Mon-Sun L.

Buongiorno e Buonasera W1 NEW £35
58 Baker St 020 7935 4223 2–1A
Early 2018 opening – a new pizzeria with two branches already in Oxford arrives in Marylebone on Baker Street, serving light, Roman-style pizzas using organic, non-GMO wheat, soy and rice flour. / W1U 7DD; www.buongiornoebuonasera.com; @buongiornoebuonasera.

Burger & Lobster £59 **3** **3** **3**
Harvey Nichols, 109-125 Knightsbridge, SW1 020 7235 5000 6–1D
26 Binney St, W1 020 3637 5972 3–2A
29 Clarges St, W1 020 7409 1699 3–4B
36 Dean St, W1 020 7432 4800 5–2A
6 Little Portland St, W1 020 7907 7760 3–1C
18 Hertsmere Rd, E14 020 3637 6709 12–1C
40 St John St, EC1 020 7490 9230 10–1B
Bow Bells Hs, 1 Bread St, EC4 020 7248 1789 10–2B
"Does what it says on the tin" – these bustling upscale diners no longer seem quite as novel as they once did but continue to offer "a winning combination of burger and lobster served at a reasonable price point". Under the same ownership as the Goodman steak chain – from autumn 2018, the owners plan a new, more informal spin-off brand, 'Shack by Burger & Lobster', to be launched in Camden. / www.burgerandlobster.com; @Londonlobster; 10.30 pm-11pm, where open Sun 8 pm-10 pm; WC1 & EC2 closed Sun; booking: min 6.

Busaba Eathai £46 2 1 2

*For a "reliable cheap 'n' cheerful meal, with attractive decor", these Thai
canteens still have a big fan club thanks to their well-styled communal
interiors and "perhaps-not-wholly-authentic, but tasty" fare ("a good choice,
from mild to pretty spicy"). Ratings were more than usually mixed this year,
however, especially regarding "chaotic", "disinterested" or even "awful"
service. / www.busaba.co.uk; @busabaeathai; 11 pm, Fri & Sat 11.30 pm,
Sun 10 pm; W1 no booking; WC1 booking: min 10.*

Butchies EC2 NEW £24 3 2 2

22 Rivington St no tel 13–1B
*Garrett and Emer FitzGerald launched their first permanent venture on the
former site of Santo Remedio (RIP) in Shoreditch: a take-away (ground floor)
and jammed-in diner upstairs serves premium fried chicken; fair value,
but food takes its time coming. / EC2A 3DY; www.butchies.co.uk;
@Butchies_London; Mon-Fri 10 pm, Sat & Sun 9 pm.*

**Butler's Restaurant,
The Chesterfield Mayfair W1** £84 2 4 3

35 Charles St 020 7958 7729 3–3B
*"Like an old London club", this traditional Mayfair dining room is "spacious"
and "there is absolutely no rush to serve you and get you out". In a similar
vein, "you wouldn't necessarily go there for the food", except for the
afternoon tea in the adjoining 'Conservatory', go for the classic or novelty-
themed version (it's currently 'The Original Sweetshop'). / W1J 5EB;
www.chesterfieldmayfair.com; @chesterfield_MF; 12.30 am, Sun 10.30 pm; Jacket
required; booking max 8 may apply.*

Butlers Wharf Chop House SE1 £70 3 2 4

36e Shad Thames 020 7403 3403 10–4D
*Created by Sir Terence Conran as part of his '90s 'gastrodrome' overlooking
Tower Bridge, this D&D London venue is valued for its "splendid location,
especially at night". "Attentive service" makes it business-friendly, and it
"lends itself to group bookings with good table sizes". Its wide menu,
incorporating lots of steak and grill options, doesn't set the world on fire,
but was well-rated this year. / SE1 2YE; www.chophouse-restaurant.co.uk;
@BWChophouse; 11 pm.*

La Buvette TW9 £48 3 2 3

6 Church Walk 020 8940 6264 1–4A
*"A feeling of smart cosiness is the best thing" about this "quiet and secluded
bistro in central Richmond" (peacefully tucked away beside a churchyard),
which makes it "a lovely place for a lunchtime date". If there's a gripe, it is
that the "traditional French fare" is "consistent" but, some feel, "not very
memorable". / TW9 1SN; www.labuvette.co.uk; @labuvettebistro; 10 pm, Sun 9 pm;
booking max 8 may apply.*

by Chloe WC2

34-43 Russell St 020 3883 3273 5–2D
*The first branch from this US-based vegan chain (a 70-seater, also with
'grab and go') arrived in Covent Garden in Spring 2018, with a big menu
from fish 'n' chips developed specially for the UK, to salads, sarnies, burgers
and brunch fare. Too little feedback for a rating as yet, although fans say it's
"amazing", with service that's "on it". They're already onto number two with
a second site near Tower Bridge (at 6 Duchess Walk, One Tower Bridge).
/ WC2B 5HA; www.eatbychloe.com; @eatbychloe; Sun-Wed 10 pm, Thu-Sat 11 pm;
no booking.*

Byron £36 2 2 2
"Once upon a time this chain of posh burger joints stood out from the pack", but – in an ever-moving and competitive market – its troubles in Spring 2018 were well publicised, with five of its 39 restaurants within the M25 (and a total of 16 nationally) having closed. That said, while the view that it is "OK but nothing special" has become widespread nowadays, it still remains one of the most talked-about brands in the survey; ratings improved a smidgeon this year; and a fair few reporters feel that "the business may be in trouble, but the burgers are still the real deal". Top Tip: "love the courgette fries". / www.byronhamburgers.com; most branches 11 pm.

C&R Cafe £30 4 2 2
3-4 Rupert Ct, W1   020 7434 1128   4–3D
52 Westbourne Grove, W2   020 7221 7979   7–1B
"Cheap, cheerful and authentic" cafés in Chinatown and Bayswater "popular with Malaysian expats". Most order the "superb noodles", while the "aggressive ginger drinks" offer another blast of southeast Asian flavour. "Not as inexpensive as they used to be, but worth it". / www.cnrrestaurant.com; W1 10 pm, Fri & Sat 11 pm; W2 10.30 pm, Fri & Sat 11 pm, Sun 10 pm; W2 closed Tue.

Cabotte EC2 £68 4 5 4
48 Gresham St   020 7600 1616   10–2C
"If you like Burgundy and are based in the City, it's your Holy Grail!" This year-old, "still relatively undiscovered gem" near the Guildhall ("not traditionally an area which has been over-served with good, regional French food!!") provides "an oasis in the Square Mile", with its combination of "excellent food with a modern twist on classic Burgundian dishes, and a wine list that's heaven for the connoisseur (with plenty on offer for every wallet, City bonus or none)". It's "extremely professionally run, very friendly and authentic". / EC2V 7AY; www.cabotte.co.uk; @Cabotte_; 9.30 pm; closed Sat & Sun.

Cacio & Pepe SW1 £56 3 3 2
46 Churton St   020 7630 7588   2–4B
This "friendly and stylish Italian in Pimlico" with "very good pasta dishes" was launched two years ago by Florentine Enrica Della Martira as her first restaurant project. It's rated a "sound choice" with a "menu that changes frequently". Top Tip: "the signature cacio e pepe (pasta with cheese and pepper), served in a parmesan basket". / SW1V 2LP; www.cacioepepe.co.uk; Mon-Thu 10.30 pm, Fri & Sat 11 pm, Sun 10 pm.

Café Below EC2 £44 3 2 2
St Mary-le-Bow, Cheapside   020 7329 0789   10–2B
The thousand-year-old crypt of the Bow Bells church provides a "great location" for breakfast and lunch – "you feel so far from the City". It has a "short but excellent menu of hot meals and salads" that are "cheap, tasty, and major on the vegetarian". (Weather permitting, you can eat al fresco in the churchyard here.) / EC2 6AU; www.cafebelow.co.uk; 9.30 pm, Sun 3.30 pm; L only.

Café del Parc N19 £50 4 5 3
167 Junction Rd   020 7281 5684   9–1C
"A splendid array of fusion tapas" combining Spanish and North African flavours makes this "fun" Archway destination an "absolute north London gem". "The no-choice format of successive dishes works superbly" ("they just bring you a selection, but you can make requests"). / N19 5PZ; www.delparc.com; 10.30 pm; open D only, Wed-Sun; no Amex; booking D only.

Café du Marché EC1 £58 **3** 3 **5**

22 Charterhouse Sq   020 7608 1609   10–1B

"A slice of Paris in a City cobbled lane"; this long-established, "hidden-away gem" – "an attractive, rustic-style dining room with regular live piano music" – has a classic, "very Gallic", "cosy, candlelit, and romantic" ambience of a kind "it's so rare to find nowadays". "The seasonal and all-French menu is packed with classics that are easy choices" and "always well-executed" ("great steaks" in particular). / EC1M 6DX; www.cafedumarche.co.uk; @cafedumarche; 10 pm; closed Sat L, closed Sun.

Café East SE16 £16 **5** 2 2

100 Redriff Rd   020 7252 1212   12–2B

Possibly "the best pho in London" and "must-have summer rolls" set the standard at this "no frills" Vietnamese canteen in Bermondsey. "There's so much to choose between, all so appetising and delicious" – "there's always a quick turnaround" and it's "great value". / SE16 7LH; www.cafeeastpho.co.uk; @cafeeastpho; Mon, Wed-Sat 10.30 pm, Sun 10 pm; closed Tue; no Amex; no booking.

Café in the Crypt, St Martin in the Fields WC2 £30 **2** 1 **4**

Duncannon St   020 7766 1158   2–2C

"Plain but well-cooked food at a reasonable price" – "in the beautiful crypt" of St Martin-in-the-Fields – makes this self-service café a useful option for a snack "in the midst of tourist-land". It's right on Trafalgar Square, so "ideal for the National Gallery" – "and the cakes are delicious". / WC2N 4JJ; stmartin-in-the-fields.org/cafe-in-the-crypt; @smitf_london; Mon & Tue 8 pm, Thu-Sat 9 pm, Wed 10.30 pm, Sun 6 pm; L & early evening only; no Amex; may need 5+ to book.

Café Monico W1 £62 **2** 3 **4**

39-45 Shaftesbury Avenue   020 3727 6161   5–3A

"Slap bang in the middle of Theatreland, this agreeable brasserie is not without a bit of theatre itself" – inspired by an 1877 café of the same name in the area, it has a carefully curated retro vibe and a menu of Franco-Italian classics assembled by Rowley Leigh for the Soho House group, which are "well-priced" ("invaluable given the area") if ultimately rather forgettable. / W1D 6LA; www.cafemonico.com; @cafemonico; Mon-Thu midnight, Fri & Sat 1 am; closed Sun.

Cafe Murano £69 **2** 3 2

33 St James's St, SW1   020 3371 5559   3–3C
34 Tavistock St, WC2   020 3535 7884   5–3D
36 Tavistock St, WC2   020 3371 5559   5–3D

"For a handy pre-theatre option, light lunch or mid-afternoon snack; meeting someone for a coffee or glass of bubbles; or for an informal, relaxed business rendezvous", Angela Hartnett's massively popular "relatively casual" spin-offs provide conveniently located venues, which – at their best – deliver a "lovely, regional Italian menu" and "a well-priced, exclusively Italian wine list" in a "pleasantly vibrant" atmosphere. Ratings dipped this year though, with increasing gripes about food that's "decent but lacking that extra sparkle", or decor that's "slightly cramped and nothing special". Higher marks though for the "charming and engaging service". / www.cafemurano.co.uk; 11 pm, Sun 4 pm, Pastificio 9 pm, Sun closed.

Café Spice Namaste E1 £56 `4` `4` `3`

16 Prescot St   020 7488 9242   12–1A

"In an unlikely location" east of the City, Cyrus Todiwala's brightly decorated HQ delivers "time and time again". "No ordinary Indian, the varied food is prepared with panache and extraordinarily skilled mixes of subtle flavours". Service is "excellent" too, and the worst complaint amongst the many reports we receive is that "it's a bit pricey". Events are a regular feature here, and "Cyrus is very informative and entertaining throughout". / E1 8AZ; www.cafespice.co.uk; @cafespicenamast; Wed & Thu 10.30 pm, Fri & Sat 11 pm; closed Mon & Tue & Sun.

Caffè Caldesi W1 £73 `3` `3` `2`

118 Marylebone Ln   020 7487 0754   2–1A

"Real Italian food" – and "not a giant pepper-grinder in sight" – is on the menu at this "reliably enjoyable" old-school venture in Marylebone ("not too starched, but certainly smart and formal enough"). Downstairs is a wine bar with antipasti, while the upstairs dining room specialises in Tuscan dishes. / W1U 2QF; www.caldesi.com; 10.30 pm; closed Sat L, closed Sun.

La Cage Imaginaire NW3 £48 `2` `3` `4`

16 Flask Walk   020 7794 6674   9–1A

Few restaurants enjoy such a picture-book location as this little French restaurant in a gorgeous-looking Hampstead backwater. Over many years, it has never provoked huge feedback, and on occasion the cuisine can seem "tired and unimaginative" but, so long as you go with moderate expectations foodwise, it can provide a "charming" experience. / NW3 1HE; www.la-cage-imaginaire.co.uk; 10.30 pm, Sun 6 pm.

The Camberwell Arms SE5 £54 `5` `3` `3`

65 Camberwell Church St   020 7358 4364   1–3C

"Exactly what a good gastropub should be" – Camberwell's sibling to the acclaimed Anchor & Hope offers "outstanding cooking with very fresh ingredients" and "oomph and umami galore". "An upgrade to the interior has kept its neighbourhood boozer charm", and locals are "thankful it's open for lunch once more (if with a somewhat restricted menu)". It gets very busy: be prepared for "noise" and a bit of "jostling". / SE5 8TR; www.thecamberwellarms.co.uk; @camberwellarms; Mon-Wed 11 pm, Thu-Sat midnight, Sun 9.30 pm; closed Mon L & Sun D.

Cambio de Tercio SW5 £70 `4` `3` `3`

161-163 Old Brompton Rd   020 7244 8970   6–2B

"Surely among the best Spanish restaurants in London", Abel Lusa's well-regarded (if "pricey") Earl's Court outfit "is getting better and better" – a judgement that is reflected in higher ratings this year. "Very high-class food", including "imaginative, innovative tapas" and an "exceptional tasting menu", is accompanied by an "astonishing range of Spanish wines". / SW5 0LJ; www.cambiodetercio.co.uk; @CambiodTercio; 11.30 pm, Sun & Mon 11 pm.

Cambridge Street Kitchen SW1 £66 `2` `3` `3`

52 Cambridge St   020 3019 8622   2–4B

"A lovely, surprising find" in a Pimlico side street, this "cheerful local" filled with art is a great place to hang out socially – a "real benefit" in an area where most restaurants are "designed just for tourists". / SW1V 4QQ; www.cambridgestreetcafe.co.uk; @TheCambridgeSt; Mon-Wed 5 pm, Thu-Sat 10 pm, Sun 6 pm.

Camino £52   3 3 2
3 Varnishers Yd, Regent Quarter, N1   020 7841 7330   9–3C
The Blue Fin Building, 5 Canvey St, SE1   020 3617 3169   10–4A
2 Curtain Rd, EC2   020 3948 5003   13–2B **NEW**
15 Mincing Ln, EC3   020 7841 7335   10–3D
A small group of "buzzy" tapas joints "full of culinary delights" – "and it's possible to eat well without breaking the bank". It caters to a business crowd during the week and families at weekends – "there's always plenty of things on the menu that the kids love". The Blackfriars, Notting Hill and Canary Wharf branches have closed, but a new spot in Shoreditch opened this year. / www.camino.uk.com; 11pm, EC3 Sat 10 pm, Sun 10pm; EC3 closed Sun, EC4 closed Sat & Sun.

Campania & Jones E2 £18   4 3 4
23 Ezra St   020 7613 0015   14–2A
"It feels like home… and I want to eat everything on the menu!" – Columbia Road's Campania Gastronomia moved around the corner a year ago into this brilliantly characterful former cowshed, which serves "wonderful and slightly unusual Italian food" (including fresh, homemade pasta) in a supremely "relaxed" atmosphere. / E2 7RH; www.campaniaandjones.com; 11 pm, Sun 6 pm; closed Mon.

**Cannizaro House,
Hotel du Vin SW19** £56   1 1 4
West Side, Wimbledon Common   0871 943 0345   11–2A
A "wonderful orangery" with "lovely views over Wimbledon Common" is let down by "dreadful food" and "indifferent service" at this Hotel du Vin venue. "What a shame to ruin this beautiful location" is typical of many complaints. / SW19 4UE; www.hotelduvin.com/locations/wimbledon; @HotelduVinBrand; Mon-Wed, Sat midnight, Thu & Fri 1 am, Sun 10 pm.

Cantina Laredo WC2 £58   2 2 2
10 Upper St Martin's Lane   020 7420 0630   5–3C
This Theatreland Mexican, part of a US chain, "manages to be both big and stylish" and is a "pretty good option for vegetarians". "The food is very fresh" and "satisfactory without being inspiring", but everyone loves the "fun guacamole made at the table". / WC2H 9FB; www.cantinalaredo.co.uk; @CantinaLaredoUK; Mon-Thu 11.30 pm, Fri & Sat midnight, Sun 10.30 pm.

Canto Corvino E1 £78   3 2 3
21 Artillery Lane   020 7655 0390   13–2B
This "new-style Italian" by Spitalfields Market features "superb pasta", "first-class ingredients" and a menu that "changes with the seasons". "Maybe a bit 'suits'-dominated, but food, service and style are excellent". Top Tip: "great for Italian brunch". / E1 7HA; www.cantocorvino.co.uk; @cantocorvinoE1; 10 pm; closed Sun.

Canton Arms SW8 £51   4 3 4
177 South Lambeth Rd   020 7582 8710   11–1D
"Still one of the best gastropubs", and Stockwell sibling to the famous Anchor & Hope, "this place has nailed it: it's excellent as a pub and brilliant as a bistro". "Innovative dishes of consistent quality" deliver "punchy and intense flavours" and there's "proper drinking ales and pints of quality bitter". Top Tip: "a favourite for Sunday pub lunch". / SW8 1XP; www.cantonarms.com; @cantonarms; 10.30 pm; closed Mon L & Sun D; no Amex; no booking.

Capricci SE1 £55   3 3 2
72 Holland St   020 7021 0703   10–3B
"Don't be put off by the rows of olive oil and Italian delicacies that line the walls of this family-run bistro, just across the road from Tate Modern." "If you're in the vicinity, it serves good, simple Italian food in a small but pleasant location." / SE1 9NX; www.capricciforlondon.co.uk; 10 pm.

Le Caprice SW1 £75 2 4 4
20 Arlington St   020 7629 2239   3–4C
"Professional, charming and fun" – this "always elegant and welcoming" stalwart near The Ritz "never fails to turn a meal into a special occasion" and remains one of London's foremost "old favourite" destinations, including for expense accounters (it helps it's "chav-free, unlike The Ivy"). Perhaps it's "not quite what it was" before it was absorbed into Richard Caring's empire, but few would notice given its "polished and discreet" staff and "great buzz". The posh brasserie fare? "predictable but sound". (In 2019, Richard Caring's group is to launch a new spin-off brand, Caprice Café, the first of which will occupy the Mayfair space that's currently trading as Mayfair Garden at 8-10 North Audley Street). / SW1A 1RJ; www.le-caprice.co.uk; @CapriceHoldings; 11 pm; may need 6+ to book.

Caractère W11 NEW
209 Westbourne Park Rd   awaiting tel   7–1B
The Notting Hill site that was formerly Bumpkin (RIP) has had a change of fortune: Emily Roux (yes, daughter of Michel) and her husband Diego Ferrari (currently head chef at Le Gavroche) have taken it over with a view to creating this October 2018 newcomer with its own, er, character (geddit!). A blend of French and Italian cuisines is promised, but the style is to be simple and seasonal rather than 'fayne dayning'. / W11 1EA; Wed-Fri 11 pm, Sat & Sun midnight.

Caraffini SW1 £62 3 5 4
61-63 Lower Sloane St   020 7259 0235   6–2D
"A great local stalwart that never seems to change" – this "traditional and welcoming" trattoria near Sloane Square particularly benefits from "wonderful" long-serving staff, who provide "the best welcome of any restaurant in London" to regular patrons (including junior members of the party). The fairly old-fashioned cooking is "consistent", if not especially 'foodie'. / SW1W 8DH; www.caraffini.co.uk; 11 pm; closed Sun.

Caravaggio EC3 £62 3 2 2
107-112 Leadenhall St   020 7626 6206   10–2D
"Ideally located in the City and ideal for business" – a "quality Italian" near Leadenhall Market that thrives as "a good venue for entertaining clients", even if "service is a bit mixed". / EC3A 4DP; www.etruscarestaurants.com; 10 pm; closed Sat & Sun.

Caravan £57 3 3 3
152 Great Portland St, W1   020 3963 8500   2–1B NEW
1 Granary Sq, N1   020 7101 7661   9–3C
30 Great Guildford St, SE1   020 7101 1190   10–4B
11-13 Exmouth Mkt, EC1   020 7833 8115   10–1A
Bloomberg Arcade, EC4   020 3957 5555   10–3C
A "brilliant option" for brunch – which can be "excitingly different, or traditionally comforting as you choose" – these "vibey", "extremely busy" ("you may have to wait for a table") haunts are "just the job if you're feeling a bit jaded" and "hard to fault" generally. The menu has its wild and wacky moments which are usually "interesting and super-delicious" and "the freshly roasted-on-site coffee is some of the best in London". All its branches are strong performers – especially the Exmouth Market original and well-known Granary Square outlet – and in July 2018 the brand finally reached the West End, in a striking space near Oxford Circus that once housed BBC Radio 1. / www.caravanonexmouth.co.uk; @CaravanResto; 10.30 pm, Sun 8 pm ; closed Sun.

Carob Tree NW5 £41 3 4 2
15 Highgate Rd 020 7267 9880 9–1B
"They won't let anyone go hungry!", say fans of this "always crowded"
Greek local in Dartmouth Park, where "you're treated as a long lost friend",
and which is praised for its "excellent fish and mezze". (One terrible meal
was reported here this year – so far it seems like just a blip.) / NW5 1QX;
www.carobtree.in; Tue-Fri 11 pm, Sat midnight, Sun 10.30 pm; closed Mon; no Amex.

Carousel W1 £58 4 3 4
71 Blandford St 020 7487 5564 3–1A
"A great concept", this Marylebone venue invites a never-ending roster
of top chefs from around the world to prepare their greatest hits at single-
sitting dinners. The "always interesting" and "typically high quality" results
justify regular visits as "an excellent way to try different food experiences
and unusual cuisines". Meanwhile, the versatile in-house kitchen team
knock out excellent small plates at lunch times. The gallery upstairs rotates
the artists, too. / W1U 8AB; www.carousel-london.com; @Carousel_LDN; Sun-Thu
midnight, Fri & Sat 1 am; closed Mon L & Sun L.

Casa Brindisa SW7 £50 3 3 2
7-9 Exhibition Rd 020 7590 0008 6–2C
From the Spanish food importer of the same name, this Brindisa operation
has a very attractive location – near South Kensington tube, with a big
outside terrace – "go on a summer's day and watch the world go by". The
press of tourists means it doesn't have to try as hard as it might, but its
tapas-and-more offering is consistently rated a good "cheap 'n' cheerful"
choice. / SW7 2HE; www.brindisatapaskitchens.com/casa-brindisa; @TapasKitchens;
11.30 pm, Sun 10.30 pm; booking max 8 may apply.

Casa Cruz W11 £80 1 1 3
123 Clarendon Rd 020 3321 5400 7–2A
It still seems "very popular", but Juan Santa Cruz's "very bling-y"
Argentinian hangout on the edge of Notting Hill saw ratings plummet this
year. "Starters were great, but main courses slightly disappointing" is about
as good as it gets. Others reckon it's "the worst value for money" – "snotty,
overpriced, Euroflash with dreadful service". / W11 4JG; www.casacruz.london;
@CasaCruzrest; 11 pm, Sun 10.30 pm; closed Mon.

Casa Pastór N1 NEW
Coal Drops Yard awaiting tel 9–3C
A larger sister restaurant to the Hart Bros' Borough Market taqueria
El Pastór arrives, complete with large outside heated terrace (to be known
separately as Plaza Pastór), at new canal-side retail development Coal Drops
Yard in King's Cross in October 2018. / N1C 4AB.

Casa Tua WC1 £40 4 3 3
106 Cromer St 020 7833 1483 9–4C
"A lovely, small, cheap 'n' cheerful Italian restaurant" which preserves
"a neighbourhood feel" despite being "walking distance from King's Cross".
The "authentic food is very fresh", the atmosphere is "relaxed" and "even if
service is not fast (Italian) it's invariably friendly". / WC1H 8BZ;
www.casatuacamden.com/kings-cross; @casatuagastro.

Casse-Croute SE1 £55 4 4 4
109 Bermondsey St 020 7407 2140 10–4D
"So French you can hardly find it in France!" – you "walk straight into Paris"
when you visit this "authentic" Bermondsey bistro south of Tower Bridge,
where "everything: wine, waiters, menu, decoration, ambience, whatever –
it's all very Gallic". "Simple-but-delicious classics" at "sensible prices" are
served by "the friendliest staff" in a "cosy" interior, but, "while squashed,
somehow you aren't disturbed by the conversations at adjacent tables".
/ SE1 3XB; www.cassecroute.co.uk; @CasseCroute109; 10 pm, Sun 4 pm; closed
Sun D.

Catford Constitutional Club SE6 £39 **3** **4** **4**
Catford Broadway   020 8613 7188   1–4D
"Formerly the local Conservative Club and maintaining its 1950s decor",
this "vintage-looking" gastropub (run by Antic Pubs) is "a shabby,
but charming if cavernous place". "They do a great burger, and other decent
grub, and it has a lovely vibe, plus a suntrap garden". / SE6 4SP;
catfordconstitutionalclub.com; @CatfordCClub; Tue-Thu midnight, Fri & Sat 1 am,
Mon 11 pm; closed Mon-Fri L, closed Sun.

Cây Tre £43 **3** **2** **2**
42-43 Dean St, W1   020 7317 9118   5–2A
301 Old St, EC1   020 7729 8662   13–1B
"Vibrant, fresh Vietnamese cooking" is the hallmark of these "buzzy" but
basic canteens in Hoxton and Soho. / www.vietnamesekitchen.co.uk; 11 pm, Fri &
Sat 11.30 pm, Sun 10.30 pm; booking: min 8.

Cecconi's £78 **2** **2** **3**
19-21 Old Compton St, W1   020 7734 5656   5–2A
5a Burlington Gdns, W1   020 7434 1500   4–4A
58-60 Redchurch St, E2   awaiting tel   13–1C **NEW**
The Ned, 27 Poultry, EC2   020 3828 2000   10–2C
"Brash but fun" Italian bar and brasserie in Mayfair where "the people
watching is good", and where "a window table, especially when the front
is open in summer, is the best place to be". Service can be "slightly
dismissive" and "it's not the greatest food, but it's worth it for the buzz",
and particularly popular for business entertaining, notably as "a go-to venue
for breakfast with clients". Owned by Soho House, it has been rolled out
as a global brand, but how well its expansion goes within London remains
to be seen. The year-old venture in The Ned (see also) is a bit of a non-
event ("a business Italian with City prices, but nothing exceptional in the
food"); and it's still early days for its 'Pizza Bar' in Soho, or its September
2018 opening in Redchurch Street, Shoreditch.

Cecconi's at The Ned EC2 £55 **2** **2** **3**
27 Poultry   020 3828 2000   10–2C
"In the magnificent surroundings of the Lutyens-designed banking hall of the
old Midland Bank building", this 3,000 square metre food hall houses seven
different restaurants each with about 100 covers. It's easy to feel
lost in such a big interior though and these spaces are actually "not that
ambient", but are nonetheless very handy for a City rendezvous with
OK fare. The top tips are Kaia (Asian-Pacific: "perfect for a quick lunch time
meeting"); Malibu Kitchen (Californian: "some unusual and excellent brunch
choices"); and Zobler's ('NYC'-Jewish: "comfort food that's easy to eat").
Millie's Lounge (British) also rates mention. Less so Cecconi's, except
on business. In each case, go with realistic expectations – otherwise you
may sense "too much hype". / EC2R 8AJ; www.thened.com/restaurants/cecconis;
@TheNedLondon; 11 pm, Sun 5 pm.

The Cedar Restaurant £40 **3** **3** **2**
65 Fernhead Rd, W9   020 8964 2011   1–2B
81 Boundary Rd, NW8   020 3204 0030   9–3A
Good all-round standards again win solid ratings for this low-key Lebanese
chain in Hampstead, Maida Vale and St John's Wood – open from
breakfast on, and "a good place to take the family of a weekend".

Celeste at The Lanesborough SW1   £133   2 2 **4**

Hyde Park Corner   020 7259 5599   2–3A

This "elegant" dining room with "large and well-spaced tables" and "amazing decor" is the flagship eatery of one of the capital's most luxurious hotels, by Hyde Park Corner, yet it has struggled to catch London's gastronomic imagination. The latest regime, overseen from Paris by multi-Michelin-starred chef Eric Fréchon, continues the trend, but those reporters who have made the trip report an "expensive but well-constructed" menu that "straddles the modern and the traditional". / SW1X 7TA; www.oetkercollection.com/destinations/the-lanesborough/restaurants-bars/restaurants/celeste; @TheLanesborough; 10.30 pm.

Cepages W2   £51   **4** 3 **4**

69 Westbourne Park Rd   020 3602 8890   7–1B

"A fabulous little local French restaurant/bistro/wine bar" on the borders of Bayswater and Notting Hill that's "always busy". "There's a great wine list which you can sit and work your way through with a selection of good, reasonably priced light dishes or more substantial fare." / W2 5QH; www.cepages.co.uk; @cepagesWPR; 11 pm, Sun 10 pm; closed Mon-Fri L.

Ceremony NW5 NEW   £53   3 **4** 3

131 Fortess Rd   020 3302 4242   9–1C

"A wonderful new opening that happens to be vegetarian, with cracking cocktails, all in Tufnell Park!"; a "hip" formula that's helped this brick-walled ("noisy") newcomer earn stonking reviews from reporters (and many newspaper reviewers) for its "exceptional veggie food (even for meat lovers who need a big feed)", served by "staff who seem to enjoy what they do". Not quite everyone agrees though, depriving it of a higher rating: niggles include "small portions" or "bland dishes" all at "fine dining prices". / NW5 2HR; www.ceremonyrestaurant.london; Tue-Thu 11 pm, Fri & Sat 11.30 pm, Sun 10 pm; closed Tue-Sat L, closed Mon.

Ceru SW7   £34   **4** 3 2

7-9 Bute St   020 3195 3001   6–2C

A "different and very refreshing" formula combining "helpful service" and "consistently delicious and inventive Levantine food" all at affordable prices for the area wins enthusiasm for this "cheerful" café in the heart of South Kensington's French quarter. (A second branch has just opened in Soho at 11 D'Arblay Street, W1.) / SW7 3EY; www.cerurestaurants.com; @cerulondon; 2 am, Sun midnight.

Ceviche   £59   **5** 3 **4**

17 Frith St, W1   020 7292 2040   5–2A

Alexandra Trust, Baldwin St, EC1   020 3327 9463   13–1A

"The flavours are like being stood on Lake Titicaca" – Martin Morales's Peruvian operation with venues in Soho and Old Street "delivers a gastronomical explosion on the palate", with "really flavoursome and unusual combinations of ingredients" including "fish like no other". They "may not have a Michelin star, but can't be beaten although others try". Top Tip: pisco sour cocktails. / www.cevicheuk.com; @cevicheuk; W1D 11.30 pm, Sun 10.15 pm, EC1V 10.45 pm, Fri & Sat 11.30 pm, Sun 9.30 pm.

Chai Thali NW1   £34   3 3 3

Centro 3, 19 Mandela St   020 7383 2030   9–3C

"Cute and cheerful" pan-Indian street food and bar operation in a new development near Mornington Crescent. All reports are upbeat, if with a caution that you should "pick your way through the menu carefully to have a better-than-standard curry house experience". / NW1 0DU; chaithali.com; @ChaiThaliCamden; 11 pm.

Champor-Champor SE1 £54 3️⃣3️⃣3️⃣
62 Weston St   020 7403 4600   10–4C

"Thai-Malaysian cooking with a twist" (the name means 'mix 'n' match') results in "seriously tasty food" at this "charming", if "unprepossessing-looking" little outfit, tucked away behind the Shard and near Guy's Hospital. Scores have ebbed and flowed here over many years, but for the most part "the quality is still high". / SE1 3QJ; www.champor-champor.com; @ChamporChampor; 10 pm; D only.

Charlotte's £56 3️⃣3️⃣3️⃣
6 Turnham Green Ter, W4   020 8742 3590   8–2A

"Smart and reliable bistro" (with a cosy, little gin bar) near Turnham Green tube that offers "a menu of crowd-pleasers, cooked with care and a little flair". Part of the Ealing-based Charlotte's Place group, it is "far better than expected from a neighbourhood warhorse". / www.charlottes.co.uk; W4 midnight, Sun 11 pm, W53 10 pm, W5 11.30 pm.

Chelsea Cellar SW10 £41 4️⃣4️⃣4️⃣
9 Park Walk   020 7351 4933   6–3B

"A small, very welcoming Southern Italian" near the Chelsea & Westminster Hospital, which has become an "absolute local favourite" thanks to its "very appealing and romantic" interior; a very good menu of antipasti plates, home made pasta and daily specials; plus "a selection of good and inexpensive wines from Puglia chosen by the two charming owners". / SW10 0AJ; www.thechelseacellar.co.uk; midnight; closed Tue-Sat L, closed Sun & Mon.

Chettinad W1 £38 4️⃣2️⃣2️⃣
16 Percy St   020 3556 1229   2–1C

"Don't be deceived by its average curry house appearance" – "excellent southern Indian food" is to be found at this Fitzrovia fixture. "Dhosas are as good as can be found in Kerala" and "there is (fortunately) little sign of adulteration to suit British tastes". / W1T 1DT; www.chettinadrestaurant.com; @chettinadlondon; Mon & Tue 8 pm, Thu-Sat 9 pm, Wed 10.30 pm, Sun 6 pm; no Amex.

Chez Abir W14 £41 3️⃣4️⃣2️⃣
34 Blythe Rd   020 7603 3241   8–1D

Small Lebanese café lost in the backstreets immediately behind Olympia. Known mainly to a faithful local crowd since the days of its redoubtable but endearingly chaotic former owner, "it maintains the standards set by Marcelle: the big difference is in the improved reliability of the service!" / W14 0HA; www.chezabir.co.uk; Mon-Thu 10 pm, Fri & Sat 10.30 pm, Sun 9.30 pm; closed Mon.

Chez Bruce SW17 £83 5️⃣5️⃣4️⃣
2 Bellevue Rd   020 8672 0114   11–2C

"The perfect neighbourhood restaurant... I just wish it was actually in my neighbourhood!" – Bruce Poole's "consistently exceptional" legend by Wandsworth Common is, for the 14th year, the survey's No. 1 favourite: "it simply never lets you down". "The attention to detail is wonderful", but "there is nothing flashy or pretentious" about the place. Service is "delightful, chatty enough and knowledgeable", "without ever verging on the fussy or obsequious"; and "there are always gorgeous surprises from the regularly changing, seasonal menu" of "flawless modern European cooking" ("filled with delicate flavours, but also packing a punch!"). Save a little space for the "epic cheese board", which is arguably "the best in town". There is little but a hymn of praise in the huge volume of reports we receive: "on our visit Gordon Ramsay was dining and even he found nothing to complain about!" / SW17 7EG; www.chezbruce.co.uk; @ChezBruce; Sun-Thu 9.30 pm, Fri & Sat 10.30 pm.

Chez Elles E1   £54   4 4 5

45 Brick Ln   020 7247 9699   13–2C

"So you're in Paris and the food's great, the wine yummy and it feels intimate but not too packed. No you're not: you're in Brick Lane, and at half the cost!" – that's the gist of all feedback on this *"lovely"*, *"very friendly"*, *"very quaint and authentic"* East End bistro. / E1 6PU; www.chezellesbistroquet.co.uk; 10.30 pm; closed Tue, Wed L, closed Sun & Mon.

Chicama SW10   £65   4 2 4

383 King's Rd   020 3874 2000   6–3C

"Fantastic Peruvian fish, both raw and cooked" – prepared *"either incredibly simply or with great imagination"* – is the draw to this King's Road yearling from the team behind Pachamama. It's *"fun"*, if *"sometimes very noisy"*, and you really have to like fish! – *"otherwise the choice is oddly limited"*. / SW10 0LP; www.chicamalondon.com; @chicamalondon; midnight; closed Sun.

Chick 'n' Sours   £42   4 3 3

1 Earlham St, WC2   020 3198 4814   5–2B
62 Upper St, N1   020 7704 9013   9–3D **NEW**
390 Kingsland Rd, E8   020 3620 8728   14–2D

"Sublimely juicy chicken with absurdly crunchy coating" – *"like KFC pimped to the max"* with *"must-have dips such as Kewpie mayo and Sriracha sour cream"* – have won high ratings for this free-range chicken and sour cocktails duo in Haggerston and Covent Garden (and from September 2018 in Islington too). *"It's so good I can't stop going back!"*. / www.chicknsours.co.uk; @chicknsours.

Chik'n W1   £37   3 2 2

134 Baker St   020 7935 6648   2–1A

"Not in the least bit healthy, but love the Korean BBQ and 'hot chick' sandwiches in particular" – this diner-style, grab-and-go yearling near Baker Street scores an enthusiastic thumbs-up (if from quite a small fan club). / W1U 6SH; www.chikn.com; @lovechikn; Mon-Thu 11 pm, Fri & Sat midnight; no booking.

Chilli Cool WC1   £34   4 2 1

15 Leigh St   020 7383 3135   2–1D

"Wonderful, spicy" Sichuan cooking, *"shabby"* surroundings and *"authentic service-without-a-smile"* – make an outing to this *"very low dive"* in Bloomsbury a *"fun"* culinary treat. *"The unremarkable exterior does not prepare you for some of the most genuine food ever"* and *"you'll leave with perfectly tingling pepper-and-chilli lips"*. / WC1H 9EW; www.chillicool.co.uk; 10.15 pm; no Amex.

Chilly Katz W6 **NEW**

Lyric Square   no tel   8–2C

Chef Phil Harrison and fashion designer Vera Thordardottir, the team behind Goldhawk Road's 'Bears Ice Cream', launched this funky-looking hole-in-the-wall on Hammersmith's Lyric Square in spring 2018, serving weird-sounding hot dogs (From Reykjavik with Love, Truffle Dog...) / W6 0NB; chillykatz.co.uk; @chillykatz; no booking.

The Chiltern Firehouse W1   £99   1 1 3

1 Chiltern St   020 7073 7676   2–1A

Fans still "love, love, love" this beautiful-crowd Marylebone haunt which occupies a gorgeous building, complete with "lovely terrace" ("it makes me feel like I'm on holiday... perhaps New England... or in the South of France"). Critics, though (and, oh boy, there are bazoodles of 'em) deride it as "a place for poseurs", whose "churned-out, style-over substance food", "snooty service" and "joke prices" ("it makes The River Café look like a walk in the park") "mark it out as a stand-out place to avoid". / W1U 7PA; www.chilternfirehouse.com; 10.30 pm.

Chimis SE1 NEW   **£50**
132 Southwark Bridge Rd   020 7928 7414   10–4B
In a no-man's-land stretch of Southwark, this Spring 2018 opening is an Argentinian/Chilean parrilla majoring in meaty and fish grills. It is brought to us by Nicolas Modad (previously head chef at Brindisa) and Federico Fugazza (founder of Porteña at Borough Market). / SE1 0DG; www.chimichurris.co.uk; @ChimichurrisUK.

China Tang,
Dorchester Hotel W1   **£84**   **4** **4** **4**
53 Park Ln   020 7629 9988   3–3A
Modelled after 1930s Shanghai by the late Sir David Tang, this opulent and gorgeous-looking Mayfair basement perennially seemed "expensive for what it is" in the food department. Scores have improved across the board in the past couple of years though, and it's winning more consistent praise for "excellent" cuisine (Peking duck the speciality) and gluggable cocktails. / W1K 1QA; www.chinatanglondon.co.uk; @ChinaTangLondon; Fri & Sat, Wed & Thu 9.30 pm.

The Chipping Forecast   **£46**   **3** **2** **2**
58 Greek St, W1   020 7851 6688   5–2A **NEW**
29 All Saints Rd, W11   020 7460 2745   7–1B
"Quirky and obliging" (if slightly "expensive") new-wave Notting Hill chippy on the characterful All Saints Road, that's won a reputation for its "proper fish 'n' chips" using sustainable fresh fish from Cornwall and "the friendliest staff". It started out with a stall on Berwick Market, and it's going back to its Soho roots, with the opening of a new branch in autumn 2018.

Chisou   **£63**   **4** **3** **2**
4 Princes St, W1   020 7629 3931   4–1A
31 Beauchamp Pl, SW3   020 3155 0005   6–1D
"Classic Japanese – not trendy but lovely and with good-quality food" sums up the appeal of this pair in Mayfair (long-established) and off Knightsbridge (quite new). The "awesome sushi and very good cooked dishes" are accompanied by "great sake" ("do try the sake flights"). They're "not cheap, and like many Japanese restaurants the ambience is functional rather than funky". / www.chisourestaurant.com; Mon-Sat 10.30 pm, Sun 9.30 pm.

Chit Chaat Chai SW18   **£33**   **3** **3** **3**
356 Old York Rd   020 8480 2364   11–2B
"Deliciously different", "sensibly priced" Indian street food café near Wandsworth Town station that makes a "good addition to an increasingly foodie street". / SW18 1SS; chitchaatchai.com; @ChitChaatChai; 11 pm, Sun 10.30 pm.

Chokhi Dhani London SW11 NEW   **£57**   **4** **4** **3**
Unit 2, 2 Riverlight Quay, Nine Elms Lane   020 3795 9000   11–1D
A household name in India, this group of luxury hotels and resorts expands internationally for the first time with this expensively decorated newcomer on the ground floor of a block amidst the new riverside developments of Vauxhall. "It's different from a typical London offering" and fans say "the Rajasthani Royal cuisine alone justifies the trip". / SW11 8AW; www.chokhidhani.co.uk; @cdgchokhidhani; 10.30 pm, Sun 9.30 pm.

Chotto Matte W1   **£60**   **3** **2** **4**
11-13 Frith St   020 7042 7171   5–2A
"A noisy nightclub vibe" boosts the appeal of this funkily decorated (big colourful murals and architectural furniture) Japanese-Peruvian fusion joint in Soho, but for a stylish scene the food's no after thought, and on all feedback "very good". / W1D 4RB; www.chotto-matte.com; @ChottoMatteSoho; 1.30 am, Sun midnight.

Chriskitch N10 £48 **4** **3** **3**
7 Tetherdown 020 8411 0051 1–1C
"The food all looks so irresistible" at this "lovely neighbourhood spot"
in Muswell Hill, serving "delicious salads, breakfasts and lunches";
"the cakes are to die for" too; its short-lived Hoxton spin-off is no more.
/ N10 1ND; www.chriskitch.com; @ChrisKitch_; Sun-Wed midnight, Thu-Sat 1 am;
L & early evening only; may need 3+ to book.

Christopher's WC2 £78 **2** **2** **3**
18 Wellington St 020 7240 4222 5–3D
The "stunning interiors", "great cocktails" and "wonderful central location"
have made this smart American outfit, in a gorgeous and grand Covent
Garden townhouse, a key destination for more than 25 years. Diners are
divided over the quality of the food, although the "excellent sirloin steak"
is recommended. Another plus: "it's never too busy at lunchtime, so good for
business". / WC2E 7DD; www.christophersgrill.com; @christopherswc2; 11 pm,
Sun 10.30 pm; may need 6+ to book.

Chucs £82 **3** **3** **3**
Harrods, 87-135 Brompton Rd, SW1 020 7298 7552 6–1D **NEW**
31 Dover St, W1 020 3763 2013 3–3C
226 Westbourne Grove, W11 020 7243 9136 7–1B
Serpentine Sackler Gallery, W2 020 7298 7552 7–2D **NEW**
"A chic take on Italian cooking" makes these in-store deluxe cafés – run by
a luxury clotheswear brand of the same name – a popular option "for a
quiet and unassuming" (but fairly loaded) Mayfair, Notting Hill and Chelsea
clientele, who often choose it for business. The sceptical view is that it's
"perfectly nice, but why all the fuss – should they stick to frocks?" They
must be doing something right though, with new branches this year
in Harrods and – most notably – their takeover of Zaha Hadid's magnificent
restaurant space (formerly The Magazine, RIP) at the Serpentine Sackler
Gallery. / www.chucsrestaurants.com; W1 11.30 pm, Sat midnight, Sun 4.30 pm;
W11 11 pm, Sun 10 pm ; W1 closed Sun D.

Churchill Arms W8 £35 **3** **2** **5**
119 Kensington Church St 020 7792 1246 7–2B
"Stunningly good-value, cheap 'n' cheerful" Thai food is served in "portions
which might prove a challenge even for the very hungry" at this one-of-a-
kind boozer near Notting Hill Gate. The whole set-up can seem "as mad
as a box of frogs" but is "always a fun night out" – you eat in a "a cute,
butterfly garden conservatory at the back of a totally normal Irish pub".
"You only get an hour at the table but service is very fast." / W8 7LN;
www.churchillarmskensington.co.uk; @ChurchilArmsW8; Mon-Wed 11 pm, Thu-Sat
midnight; closed Sun.

Chutney Mary SW1 £87 **4** **4** **4**
73 St James's St 020 7629 6688 3–4D
"Top-of-the-range, expensive but memorable… nice cocktails too!";
this "beautiful and intimate" stalwart is very well-established now in its
swanky St James's location, and "better all-round than when it was located
in Chelsea". "A great variety of spices are used very subtly and with
first class ingredients" to create some "divine" dishes. / SW1A 1PH;
www.chutneymary.com; @thechutneymary; 10.30 pm; closed Sat L & Sun; Cash &
cards; booking max 4 may apply.

Chutneys NW1 £27 **3** **2** **2**
124 Drummond St 020 7388 0604 9–4C
"You can't beat Chutney's on taste and price" – this age-old vegetarian
Indian is "a firm favourite among its Drummond Street competitors"
by Euston station. "The ground-floor dining room is attractive enough –
the basement less so." / NW1 2PA; www.chutneyseuston.uk; 11 pm; no Amex;
may need 5+ to book.

Ciao Bella WC1 £44 2 3 4
86-90 Lamb's Conduit St   020 7242 4119   2–1D
This "ever bustling traditional Italian" has brought an affordable taste
of 'la dolce vita' to Bloomsbury for 35 years. The "standard" food "is pretty
good for the reasonable price", "but is not really the point": it's
"very cheerful" with a "superb buzz". "Perfect for a family get-together with
children." / WC1N 3LZ; www.ciaobellarestaurant.co.uk; @CiaobellaLondon;
10.30 pm, Sun 6 pm.

Cibo W14 £58 4 5 3
3 Russell Gdns   020 7371 6271   8–1D
"A proper Italian restaurant, like being in Rome" – this stalwart between
Olympia and Holland Park serves "consistently great food", with an
emphasis on "fresh fish and seafood". A favourite of the late Michael
Winner, it has fallen off the foodie radar in recent years but still scores
highly, not least thanks to its "welcoming" and sympathetic staff. / W14 8EZ;
www.ciborestaurant.net; 10.30 pm; closed Sat L, closed Sun.

Cigala WC1 £65 3 2 2
54 Lamb's Conduit St   020 7405 1717   2–1D
With its "old-fashioned style" and "authentic Spanish tapas", this Iberian
haunt in one of Bloomsbury's more attractive streets is a "neighbourhood
favourite that's always fun to go to" – if with decor that's a little "lacking
in character". / WC1N 3LW; www.cigala.co.uk; 10.45 pm, Sun 9.45 pm.

Cigalon WC2 £58 4 4 4
115 Chancery Lane   020 7242 8373   2–2D
Eating the "lovely fresh Provençal food in this attractive airy room
on Chancery Lane" is "a very satisfying experience". Housed in a light-filled
former book auction room with a huge glass rooflight, it has the "trademark
quirks and innovation of the Club Gascon team" that is behind it,
and "the prices are fair". / WC2A 1PP; www.cigalon.co.uk; @cigalon_london;
10 pm; closed Sat & Sun.

Cinnamon Bazaar WC2 £38 3 3 3
28 Maiden Lane   020 7395 1400   5–4D
"Fun decor" helps breathe life into this two-floor Covent Garden venture,
which can get "noisy". Its Indian fusion-esque menu "is different to other
Cinnamon eateries", and most reports acclaim its "fantastic dishes at a
great price". / WC2E 7NA; www.cinnamon-bazaar.com; @Cinnamon_Bazaar;
Tue-Thu 9 pm.

The Cinnamon Club SW1 £84 3 2 3
Old Westminster Library, Great Smith St   020 7222 2555   2–4C
"It's been around a long time and is perhaps now overshadowed
by newcomers like Gymkhana", but this posh nouvelle Indian remains one
of London's most popular grand restaurants (and still features in our Top
40 most mentioned ranking) and many folks' "go-to fancy Indian". Set
in Westminster's "fantastic" old Public Library it has "a lovely club-like feel,
with the bookshelves reaching to the ceiling" – an incongruous but somehow
fitting backdrop for Vivek Singh's "beautiful, innovative, nouvelle-Indian food"
("lots of complex flavours and some bite"). This was not a vintage year for
its survey results, however, with gripes about "variable food, and service that
ebbs and flows, which just isn't acceptable at these prices". / SW1P 3BU;
www.cinnamonclub.com; @cinnamonclub; 11 pm, Sun 3.30 pm; closed Sun;
No trainers; booking max 14 may apply; SRA-Food Made Good – 2 stars.

Cinnamon Kitchen EC2 £62 **4**|**3**|**3**

9 Devonshire Sq 020 7626 5000 10–2D

"Indian favourites imaginatively recreated" and "fusion food such as steak with masala chips" comprise a "superb menu that is hard to choose from" at the Cinnamon Club's offshoot in the City. The setting – a large atrium near Liverpool Street – is a real bonus, because "you can sit outside in a covered courtyard in virtually all weathers". / EC2M 4YL;
www.cinnamon-kitchen.com; @cinnamonkitchen; 10.30 pm; closed Sat L, closed Sun.

Cinnamon Kitchen Battersea SW11 £55 **4**|**3**|**3**

Battersea Power Station 020 3955 5480 11–1C

A "new restaurant that has much promise" – this yearling in a railway arch that's part of the redevelopment of Battersea Power Station is the latest offspring of Westminster's plush Cinnamon Club, and its "refined Indian cooking under the care of Vivek Singh" is by early accounts "both interesting and delicious". / SW11 8EZ; @CinnamonKitchen.

City Barge W4 £51 **3**|**3**|**3**

27 Strand-on-the-Green 020 8994 2148 1–3A

"A great location on a sunny day", this riverside gastropub at Chiswick's Strand-on-the-Green (smartened up in recent times) delivers "unpretentious good food with a bit more finesse than most pubs". "The perfect end to a walk along the Thames." / W4 3PH; www.citybargechiswick.com; @citybargew4; Tue-Thu 10 pm, Fri & Sat 10.30 pm.

City Càphê EC2 £10 **3**|**3**|**2**

17 Ironmonger St no tel 10–2C

"Superb Vietnamese street food" draws a hungry City crowd to this pitstop near Bank. It's "super-busy at lunchtime – better to take away than sit at the tiny tables". / EC2V 8EY; www.citycaphe.com; @CityCaphe; closed Mon-Fri D, closed Sat & Sun; no Amex; no booking.

City Social EC2 £92 **3**|**3**|**3**

Tower 42 25 Old Broad St 020 7877 7703 10–2C

"On the 24th-floor of Tower 42, looking across at the Gherkin and Heron Tower, you enjoy some of the most spectacular views of the City" at Jason Atherton's "sleek, swish and professional" eyrie: a natural favourite for wining and dining in the Square Mile. On most accounts the "fantastic" cuisine is almost as stunning as the panorama, but there is also a school of thought that it's "average for such excessive prices". / EC2N 1HQ;
www.citysociallondon.com; @CitySocial_T42; 10.30 pm; closed Sat L, closed Sun; booking max 4 may apply.

Clarette W1 £81 **3**|**3**|**3**

44 Blandford St 020 3019 7750 3–1A

This year-old Marylebone wine bar, owned in part by a scion of the family who own Château Margaux, has yet to win a huge fan base amongst reporters – those who have discovered it however award high ratings to its wine list and its menu of Mediterranean small plates. / W1U 7HS; www.clarettelondon.com; @ClaretteLondon; 10.15 pm, Sun 8.45 pm.

Clarke's W8 £76 **4 5 4**

124 Kensington Church St 020 7221 9225 7–2B

"There's no messing around by chefs trying to be clever: just first class ingredients allowed to speak for themselves" alongside a "fabulous wine list" and "so-gracious" service at Sally Clarke's California-inspired institution – a Kensington stalwart that "isn't content to rest on its laurels", and whose "fresh-flavoured dishes" are "some of the best seasonal food in London". "The main room's elegant decor makes it feel more like a private dining room than a restaurant and the tables are set far enough apart to allow for quiet conversation" making it a favourite for romance (of the silver-haired variety). "A warm welcome from Sally each and every visit sets the tone for a great evening" ("she must have some clones of herself, as she always seems to be around!"). / W8 4BH; www.sallyclarke.com; @SallyClarkeLtd; 10 pm; closed Sun; booking max 14 may apply.

Claude's Kitchen, Amuse Bouche SW6 £60 **3 3 4**

51 Parsons Green Lane 020 7371 8517 11–1B

Claude Compton has won an enthusiastic following for his "excellent and inventive" cooking, deployed in a quirky dining room above the Amuse Bouche fizz bar opposite Parsons Green station. But the food level has dropped a notch this year – "sometimes it misses, and when it does it misses badly". / SW6 4JA; www.amusebouchelondon.com/claudes-kitchen; @AmuseBoucheLDN; 11 pm; D only, closed Sun.

Claw Carnaby W1 NEW £40 **3 3 2**

21 Kingly St 020 7287 5742 4–2B

"Crab specialist that's a welcome addition" – that's the general verdict on this "buzzy" Soho newcomer, which is the first permanent home of a sustainable seafood pop-up, food truck and City takeaway outlet. There are caveats though – "it's sort of street food but at restaurant or pub prices…" – "couldn't taste the crab because the fries were covered in spices as well as salt". / W1B 5QA; claw.co.uk; @CLAWfood; Mon-Fri 10.30 pm, Sat 11 pm, Sun 10 pm.

Clerkenwell Cafe £36 **3 3 3**

80a Mortimer St, W1 020 7253 5754 10–1A
St Christopher's Place, W1 020 7253 5754 3–1A
27 Clerkenwell Rd, EC1 020 7253 5754 10–1A
60a Holborn Viaduct, EC1 no tel 10–2A

"Better roasted, better brewed, better poured – just better" agree fans of the coffee at this small chain with its own roastery. They also sell simple snacks, coffee-making equipment and their own beans – "so take some home!". / workshopcoffee.com; @workshopcoffee; EC1M 6 pm, Tue-Fri 7 pm; W1U & W1W 7 pm, Sat & Sun 6 pm; EC1A 6 pm; EC1 closed Sat & Sun; no bookings.

The Clifton NW8 £51 **3 3 5**

96 Clifton Hill 020 7625 5010 9–3A

"Wonderful local pub", hidden-away in St John's Wood (where, back in the day, Edward VII used to conduct his affair with Lillie Langtry). Rescued from the developers, and relaunched last year, it still has yet to attract a big following amongst reporters, but food ratings are fair, and it's worth a go for its marvellous interior (enhanced by the addition of a new conservatory). / NW8 0JT; www.thecliftonnw8.com; @thecliftonnw8; 10 pm, Sun 8 pm.

Clipstone W1 £82 **3** **3** **2**

5 Clipstone St   020 7637 0871   2–1B

"Still punching above its weight", Will Lander & Daniel Morgenthau's "tiny", "somewhat hipster" Fitzrovia haunt (sibling to Portland) "has dispensed with its small plates concept and now provides proper starters and main courses". Fans applaud its "imaginative take on a simple range of ingredients (with results that can be superlative)"; its "limited but intriguing wine list"; and feel that even if it's "packed" and "noisy" ("lots of hard surfaces") "that's not the point" for a "relaxed" and "lovely" place. Overall ratings are blunted, however, by a minority who feel "it's not terrible, but I hoped for more…" / W1W 6BB; www.clipstonerestaurant.co.uk; @clipstonerestaurant; 11 pm; closed Sun.

Clos Maggiore WC2 £77 **3** **3** **5**

33 King St   020 7379 9696   5–3C

"Deserving its accolade as London's most romantic restaurant" – this "special and luxuriant" venue is an unexpected haven of "peace and tranquility", despite being bang smack in the centre of touristy Covent Garden, and "just has that certain 'je ne sais quoi' to create vibes with your significant other". "Try to get a table in the extraordinary conservatory" ("where the glass roof opens on summer days and a warming fire is lit in the winter") as "that is how the magic happens" but NB – "it needs to be booked many months in advance". The numerous other sections can be "memorable" and "cosseting" too, but there's no hiding the fact that they do play second fiddle to the "headline event". Given the emphasis on atmosphere, the surprise here has always been the high standards generally: the "professional" service, "classic and well-presented" French-inspired cuisine and the "immense wine list (you could get lost in it, look up, and find your partner gone!)". But the formerly high proportion of reports of seriously good cooking here fell off sharply this year, and a few regulars have concerns: "Once I'd have overlooked a decidedly average meal here, but two similar experiences have left me wondering: is it starting to live off a great room and stellar reputation?" / WC2E 8JD; www.closmaggiore.com; @closmaggiorewc2; 11 pm, Sun 9.30 pm.

The Clove Club EC1 £147 **4** **3** **3**

Shoreditch Town Hall, 380 Old St   020 7729 6496   13–1B

"Top-end, creative dining without pretensions" has carved a global reputation for Daniel Willis, Isaac Mchale and Johnny Smith's "relaxed" blue-tiled chamber within Shoreditch's fine old town hall (whose renown is sealed by achieving the UK's highest position in the 'World's 50 Best', ranking at 33). The results from the open kitchen via a five-course or ten-course tasting menu focus on British-sourced produce and are "phenomenally good, exceptionally interesting and always innovative". As well as "inspired wine pairings", the forward-thinking approach is shown by "(surprisingly) good non-alcoholic pairings" too. "Staff have amazing knowledge of the food and wine" and their "real care" adds a lot to the experience ("my veggie boyfriend never feels like he's an inconvenience here like at so many other restaurants"). Gripes? The setting is quite "Spartan". More significantly, whereas most reports say it "exceeded our sky-high expectations", ratings here softened this year, with the chief complaint being a feeling that it's becoming "hugely overpriced": "even if the food's a wow, it's so expensive", and some feel "it's beginning to rival the River Café for non-value!" / EC1V 9LT; www.thecloveclub.com; @thecloveclub; 10.30 pm; closed Mon L, closed Sun.

Club Gascon EC1 £106 4 4 4
57 West Smithfield   020 7600 6144   10–2B
Pascal Aussignac and Vincent Labyrie's "magnificent and innovative" temple
to the cuisine of southwest France (and famously foie gras) has "upped its
game" following a complete makeover that marked their 20 years beside
Smithfield Market. There's now "more space and an expanded menu",
and although one or two long-term fans are "not sure about the refurb",
the ambience rating has improved dramatically and the food remains
"first class". / EC1A 9DS; www.clubgascon.com; @club_gascon; Tue-Fri 10 pm;
closed Mon, Sat & Sun.

The Coach EC1 NEW £59 4 3 3
26-28 Ray St   020 3954 1595   10–1A
"So good to have Henry Harris back again!" – this "great revamped
gastropub in Clerkenwell is under his gastronomic tutelage" (one of four,
where he is collaborating with James McCulloch, including The Hero
of Maida, The Three Cranes and The Harlot). "The downstairs is still
recognisable as a pub at the front and has a light and airy dining area at the
back, while upstairs is a more formal dining area with lovely original
features". Ultimately there's the risk he may move on or spread himself too
thinly, but for the present "keenly priced French food" – "more fine dining
than pub grub" and reminiscent of his Racine days – is the pay-off here
(some dishes are "incredible", not least "knockout roasts"). / EC1R 3DJ;
www.thecoachclerkenwell.co.uk; @thecoachldn; Mon & Tue 9 pm, Fri & Sat 11.30 pm,
Wed 10 pm, Thu 11 pm, Sun 5 pm.

Coal Office N1 NEW
2 Bagley Walk   020 3848 6085   9–3C
Assaf Granit, chef and co-owner of The Palomar and The Barbary, is behind
this early autumn 2018 Mediterranean/Middle Eastern-inspired opening in a
big, Victorian, ex-industrial brick pile by the canal in King's Cross: a 160-
cover space split over three floors, with a rooftop terrace and al fresco
dining area, complete with panoramic views over Granary Square. Designer
Tom Dixon, whose practice is nearby, is also involved creating, for example,
tableware which is for sale. / N1C 4PQ; coaloffice.com.

Coal Rooms SE15 £53 4 3 3
11a Station Way   020 7635 6699   1–4D
The tastefully restored, Grade II listed, former ticket office of Peckham Rye
station is the venue for this year-old venture, named for its 'live fire' mode
of cooking from the large smoker and robata grills which are central to the
open kitchen. Open from breakfast on – and serving a flatbread menu
at lunch – fans hail its "amazing and interesting food" ("I daren't rate it too
highly for fear we won't be able to get a table!"), although other feedback
say it's good but not outstanding. / SE15 4RX; www.coalrooms.com; @coalrooms;
10 pm, Sun 5 pm; closed Sun D.

The Coal Shed SE1 £65 3 3 3
One Tower Bridge   020 3384 7272   10–4D
"A great addition to the SE1 restaurant scene" – this import from Brighton
has a "sleek and contemporary design" within one of the new units of the
development near Tower Bridge incorporating London's newest theatre,
The Bridge. Although there are one or two dissenting voices for whom the
venue fell short, most reports say it's a "meat-lovers dream", with "superb
and personal service too". Top Menu Tips – numerous dishes are
recommended: "the smoked goat is an absolute revelation", there's
"exceptionally good steak", "fabulous grilled octopus" and "really pleasing
sweets". / SE1 2AA; www.coalshed-restaurant.co.uk; @TheCoalShed1; 10.15 pm,
Sun 8.45 pm.

CôBa N7 £23 4 3 2

244 York Way 07495 963336 9–2C

"Mouth-wateringly good" Vietnamese BBQ tucker comes with an Aussie accent at Damon Bui's former pub north of King's Cross, which is "pleasant if not that comfortable". / N7 9AG; www.cobarestaurant.co.uk; @cobafood; midnight; booking D only.

Cocotte £51 4 4 3

95 Westbourne Grove, W2 020 3220 0076 7–1B
8 Hoxton Square, N1 020 7033 4277 13–1B

"If you like chicken this is your place" say fans of this affordable Gallic two-year-old, on the fringes of Notting Hill and Bayswater: "simple mission (rotisserie chicken), well delivered; chicken itself good quality, tasty and wholesome". In April 2018, the French owners opened a new branch in Hoxton Square.

Colbert SW1 £63 1 1 3

51 Sloane Sq 020 7730 2804 6–2D

"A magnificent location on the corner of Sloane Square" is the crown jewel feature of this "bustling" Parisian-style brasserie, whose "position right near the tube makes it so easy for a business appointment"; and where breakfasting marks "a civilised start to the day". This is still the weakest runner in the Corbin & King stable however, with Gallic brasserie fare that can be of "Cafe Rouge/airport lounge quality", and sometimes "snooty" service. Fans are un-moved though: "formulaic it may be, but it's still the best people watching site in London and a great local hangout!" / SW1W 8AX; www.colbertchelsea.com; @ColbertChelsea; Mon-Wed midnight, Thu & Fri 1am, Sat & Sun 12 pm.

La Collina NW1 £55 3 3 2

17 Princess Rd 020 7483 0192 9–3B

Tucked away below Primrose Hill, this "boutique Italian" specialises in "delicious, uncomplicated" Piedmontese cuisine. "Simple, quiet and sophisticated", its "unpretentious food surpasses expectations" – and is "great value". Top Tip: "the garden is a delight in the summer". / NW1 8JR; www.lacollinarestaurant.co.uk; @LacollinaR; Wed-Sat 10 pm, Tue 9.30 pm, Sun 9 pm; closed Tue L, closed Mon; booking max 8 may apply.

The Collins Room,
The Berkeley Hotel SW1 £101 2 3 4

Wilton Place 020 7107 8866 6–1D

"The famous Pret-a-Portea is a treat for the eyes as well as the palette" when you take tea in this refined chamber, which is part of Maybourne's super-swanky Belgravia hotel, just off Knightsbridge. The miniature cakes are inspired by catwalk creations and are a "stunning and very quirky" assortment in fab-u-lous designs. Admittedly the experience is "not exactly cheap" – "you could have a Michelin-starred lunch with wine for less money!" / SW1X 7RL; www.the-berkeley.co.uk; @TheBerkeley; 10.45 pm, Sun 10.15 pm.

Le Colombier SW3 £70 3 5 4

145 Dovehouse St 020 7351 1155 6–2C

"A little slice of France in Chelsea which never fails to please" – Didier Garnier's "tucked-away, corner-restaurant" is in the style of a "classic Gallic brasserie" and particularly benefits from its "hands-on owner" and "enthusiastic and charming" service. For its (older) "very loyal clientele", "the greatest virtue is that, as all around it changes, everything here remains the same", not least the dependable "traditional" fare. What's more "M Garnier knows his wine and has a superb list that's sensibly priced and imaginative". It's "the perfect place to take your grand aunt" – "the fact that so many regulars keep coming back in an area where there is so much top-notch competition speaks for itself!" / SW3 6LB; www.le-colombier-restaurant.co.uk; 10.30 pm, Sun 10 pm.

Colony Grill Room, Beaumont Hotel W1 £78 2️⃣3️⃣4️⃣

8 Balderton Street, Brown Hart Gardens   020 7499 9499   3–2A

Corbin & King's "terrific 1920s New York-style grill room in the stunning art deco Beaumont Hotel is a stone's throw away from Selfridges, yet impossible to come across by chance". According to most reports, a visit is "a luxurious treat", on account of its "comfortable and plush" style and "typical American fare, from hot dogs to chicken pot pie". To some tastes though, the pricey food is so "straightforward" as to seem "a little uninspired." Top Tips – "the breakfast hashes are superb" and "design-your-own ice cream sundae with an amazing selection of flavours, toppings and sauces is great fun for kids and adults alike". / W1K 6TF; www.colonygrillroom.com; @ColonyGrillRoom; 10.30 pm.

The Colton Arms W14 £52 2️⃣3️⃣4️⃣

187 Greyhound Rd   020 3757 8050   8–2C

"Excellent for some comfort food and a decent drink at the end of the day" – this year-old rejuvenated old tavern (nowadays owned by Hippo Inns) is set deep in the backstreets of Barons Court. A brilliant back garden is a big draw. / W14 9SD; www.thecoltonarms.co.uk; @thecoltonarms; 10 pm, Sun 8 pm.

Comptoir Gascon EC1 £57 2️⃣2️⃣2️⃣

63 Charterhouse St   020 7608 0851   10–1A

"The duck fat chips are worth the potential coronary", say fans of this "slightly cramped" Smithfield bistro – offshoot of nearby Club Gascon – which has some renown as "a high quality eating experience at a very reasonable price". Doubts are creeping in, though: "is this place starting to lose its flair?" – "the choices have become more limited and seem less creative", and at worse "banal". / EC1M 6HJ; www.comptoirgascon.com; @ComptoirGascon; 10 pm, Sun 9 pm; closed Mon & Sun.

Comptoir Libanais £39 2️⃣2️⃣2️⃣

As a "decent enough pit stop" (or "a great introduction to Lebanese food") these brightly decorated venues are well-located, "not bad for the price" and "a solid option for a quick bite". Expect "reliable Middle Eastern food" combined with a "nice level of hustle & bustle". / www.lecomptoir.co.uk; 10 pm (SW 8 pm), W1C & E20 Sun 8 pm; W12 closed Sun D; no bookings.

Con Gusto SE18 £52 3️⃣4️⃣4️⃣

No 1 St   020 8465 7452   12–2D

"A tiny (only 9 tables), really quirky restaurant in a fun, former military building" near the waterside in the historic setting of the Woolwich Arsenal. "A small menu of authentic Italian food" is served up "by genuine Italian chefs all from a tiny 300-year-old guard room which holds the open kitchen and restaurant". / SE18 6GH; www.congusto.co.uk; 9.30 pm, Sun 9 pm; closed Tue-Fri L, closed Mon.

Il Convivio SW1 £76 3️⃣3️⃣3️⃣

143 Ebury St   020 7730 4099   2–4A

"A real old favourite which seems to have new life with its current chef" (Cedric Neri) – this converted Georgian townhouse in Belgravia is "a secret gem", with "some very fine Italian cooking". It's "smart", "very friendly", and "the prices are fairly modest considering the quality". / SW1W 9QN; www.etruscarestaurants.com/il-convivio; 10.45 pm; closed Sun.

Coopers Restaurant & Bar WC2 £49 2 3 3
49 Lincoln's Inn Fields 020 7831 6211 2–2D
*"The restaurant's regulars are a mix of LSE professors and barristers from
Lincoln's Inn, resulting in a lively, argumentative atmosphere!" at this legal-
land staple, which "hardly has any competition nearby" and which some
regulars feel "could benefit from more inspiration". That said, "it's a really
reliable spot where service is always welcoming and the staff attentive and
helpful; and meat, sourced each day from Smithfield, is always a good
choice". / WC2A 3PF; www.coopersrestaurant.co.uk; @coopers_bistro; 10.30 pm;
closed Sat & Sun; no booking.*

Coppa Club Tower Bridge EC3 £44 2 3 4
Three Quays Walk, Lower Thames St 020 7993 3827 10–3D
*There's a "lovely atmosphere and buzz" at this all-day 'club without
membership' comprising a restaurant, bar and lounge, whose outside
'igloos', with stunning views of nearby Tower Bridge, have become famous
for their celebratory yuletide potential. It's the first London outpost of an
operation which began in gorgeous Sonning on Thames (there's now another
in St Paul's) – ratings are solid the board although "the food is a bit
gastropub cliché..." / EC3R 6AH; www.coppaclub.co.uk; @wearecoppaclub;
Mon-Thu 11 pm, Fri & Sat midnight, Sun 10.30 pm; booking max 6 may apply.*

Coq d'Argent EC2 £95 2 3 3
1 Poultry 020 7395 5000 10–2C
*"Fantastic in the summer, with amazing views over the City" – D&D's
London's stalwart rooftop brasserie is still, after all these years, a striking
venue, complete with gardens and adjoining bar, and its classic Gallic fare
is "reliable" if "not cheap". Despite its handy location right by Bank,
it's perhaps "no longer the business must-do it used to be", but nevertheless
still a regular choice for legions of Square Mile expense-accounters.
/ EC2R 8EJ; www.coqdargent.co.uk; @coqdargent1; 11 pm; closed Sun; booking
max 10 may apply.*

Cora Pearl WC2 NEW
30 Henrietta St 020 7324 7722 5–3D
*The trio behind Shepherd Market's quirky hit Kitty Fisher's (Tom Mullion,
Tim Steel and Oliver Milburn) backed up their Mayfair success with this
mid-Summer 2018 opening in Covent Garden, which – like its sister –
is named for a well-known British-born courtesan. / WC2E 8NA;
www.corapearl.co.uk; @CoraPearlCG; Mon & Tue 9 pm, Fri & Sat 11.30 pm,
Wed 10 pm, Thu 11 pm, Sun 5 pm.*

Corazón W1 £44 2 4 3
29 Poland St 020 3813 1430 4–1C
*"Part of a new wave finally bringing authentic Mexican cuisine to the
capital", Laura Sheffield's "cosy and buzzing" taqueria off Oxford Street
benefits from "friendly service" and "reasonable prices", and its tacos are
"fresh and piquant" – "compares well with the Mexican food I sampled
in LA recently". / W1F 8QN; www.corazonlondon.co.uk; @corazon_uk; 10 pm,
Sun 9 pm.*

Core by Clare Smyth W11 £115 **5 5 4**
92 Kensington Park Rd   020 3937 5086   7–2B
"A flying start from the former head chef at Gordon Ramsay" – in this "unmissable" yearling, Clare Smyth "has finally created a fabulous restaurant on this difficult site" (most recently Notting Hill Kitchen, RIP, and in days of yore, Leith's). "If she doesn't get at least two Michelin stars this year, it will be astounding!" given the "ethereal cuisine she delivers with confidence, exuberance and pleasure". "Outstanding produce is allowed to really sing in the dishes" – with the emphasis on two tasting menu options – and "seasonal ingredients (really – not just the lip service you sometimes hear) are centre stage, with an interesting and rare focus on vegetables": "I mean, how on earth can you make a humble potato so attractive and so tasty? It's magic!" .The "light and sophisticated" room "has a relaxed feel, no tablecloths or hushed tones" and – with the "faultless", "friendly" service – the overall effect is "a pleasant, unusually relaxed and unpompous atmosphere". "Attention to detail is amazing, and watching the kitchen staff quietly gliding between stations behind the pass, overseen by Clare, is like watching a theatre production" STOP PRESS: Having won the 'Top Gastronomic' award at the Harden's London Restaurant awards, on October 1 Michelin followed suit with the award of two stars. / W11 2PN; www.corebyclaresmyth.com; @CorebyClare; 10.30 pm; closed Tue, Wed L, closed Sun & Mon.

Cork & Bottle WC2 £57 **2 3 4**
44-46 Cranbourn St   020 7734 7807   5–3B
"An eclectic mix of stunning wines from around the globe" makes this legendary 47-year-old basement wine bar "a great oasis to escape the hustle and bustle of Leicester Square". "The food is incidental", mostly "good bistro dishes from the 1980s", and they've sold nearly a million portions of the house ham & cheese pie in the past 40 years. (Nowadays owned by Will Clayton, it has a spin-off no-one's ever heard of in Bayswater and another opening in Hampstead in September 2018). Top Tip: "the cheese selection is pretty special". / WC2H 7AN; www.thecorkandbottle.co.uk; @corkbottle1971; midnight, Sun 11 pm; no booking D.

Cornerstone E9 NEW
3 Prince Edward Road,   020 8986 3922   14–1C
Tom Brown (formerly behind the stoves at Nathan Outlaw at The Capital), has branched out on his own with this minimalist Hackney Wick newcomer, where the kitchen is centre-stage in the room, putting the focus even more firmly on the predominantly fishy fare from this native Cornishman. It opened in May 2018, just too late for survey feedback – Giles Coren went overboard for it in his early press review, while our jungle telegraph says it's a brilliant addition to east London, but that the earth doesn't always move, and that it's priced for somewhere more central. / E9 5LX; cornerstonehackney.com; @Cornerstone_h_w; Mon-Wed 9 pm, Thu-Sat 9.30 pm, Sun 3.30 pm.

Corrigan's Mayfair W1 £102 **3 3 3**
28 Upper Grosvenor St   020 7499 9943   3–3A
Richard Corrigan's "understated", "comfortable" and "well-spaced" Mayfair HQ is a "perfect place for business", particularly of a slightly traditionalist nature, given its high quality, luxurious British cuisine (available à la carte, or with a tasting option). To the extent that it draws criticism, it's, perhaps predictably, primarily for being "too expensive for what it is" – take the company's plastic. Top Tip: "set lunch is exceptional value". / W1K 7EH; www.corrigansmayfair.com; @CorriganMayfair; 10.30 pm; closed Sat L, closed Sun; booking max 12 may apply.

Côte £52 2 2 2

These "accurate imitations of a well-run French brasserie" have become the survey's most-mentioned chain, on the strength of the huge army of fans who find them an "always-dependable" standby. The "perfectly acceptable" food "is quite good when you factor in the price": "stick to their basic menus and you get a quite a good-value meal (although stray onto the more expensive dishes and you are better off going elsewhere)". The wide range of options – including breakfast and prix-fixe pre-theatre – means there's "plenty of choice for different appetites". Unlike some chains there's no effort to make outlets individual: "every branch is cut from the same cloth, but that's no bad thing". / www.cote-restaurants.co.uk; 11 pm.

Counter Culture SW4 £54 3 4 2

16 The Pavement 020 8191 7960 11–2D
"It's cramped – 16 covers (stools) in a small space – but the food can be tremendous" at this two-year-old offshoot from Robin Gill's Dairy in Clapham Common (and even though it didn't score quite as highly as next door this year, the ability to BYO for £10 corkage can make it a very decent overall bargain). / SW4 0HY; www.countercultureclapham.co.uk; @culturesnax; no booking.

The Cow W2 £59 3 3 5

89 Westbourne Park Rd 020 7221 0021 7–1B
"Fish stew and oysters to die for", washed down by a pint of Guinness, makes Tom Conran's Irish-style pub on the Notting Hill-Bayswater border an enduring favourite. "The food is always delicious, with a great emphasis on seafood". / W2 5QH; www.thecowlondon.co.uk; @TheCowLondon; Mon-Thu 11 pm, Fri & Sat midnight, Sun 10.30 pm; no Amex.

Coya £83 3 2 3

118 Piccadilly, W1 020 7042 7118 3–4B
Angel Court, 31-33 Throgmorton St, EC2 020 7042 7118 10–2C
"Good fun and great food is an easy mix" and it's one this Mayfair fixture carries off with its "wonderful, well-executed Peruvian fare" ("delicious ceviche"), copious Pisco sours and an "ever-buzzy" ("intolerably noisy") setting. "A decent meal is seldom enhanced by astronomical pricing" however, which can dampen enthusiasm for the experience. Comments on its year-old City sibling near Bank are in a similar vein – "a welcome addition" if a pricey one, with "crowd pleasing food that's perfect for sharing". Top Tip: Sommelier Mondays at the City branch with 50% off wine.

Craft London SE10 £61 3 4 2

Peninsula Square 020 8465 5910 12–1D
"Delicious pizzas with unusual toppings, plus great coffee and salads too" win praise for the ground floor café of Stevie Parle's outpost at the O2. There's also a more stylish first-floor bar and restaurant serving more ambitious, locally sourced fare. / SE10 0SQ; www.craft-london.co.uk; @CraftLDN; 10.30 pm; closed Tue-Fri L, closed Sun & Mon.

Crate Brewery and Pizzeria E9 £24 4 3 4

7, The White Building, Queens Yard 020 8533 3331 14–1C
"Great pizzas with a brilliant thin crispy base" reward a stroll through the Olympic Park to this engagingly grungy craft brewery and pizzeria, a short walk from Hackney Wick station: "the venue always has a great atmosphere... and lovely beer". / E9 5EN; www.cratebrewery.com; @cratebrewery; Sun-Thu 10 pm, Fri & Sat 11 pm.

Crocker's Folly NW8 £64 3 2 4
23-24 Aberdeen Pl 020 7289 9898 9–4A
The "ornate surroundings" – "one of the country's most spectacular pub interiors", in St John's Wood – make an "eccentric" setting in which to enjoy "above average Lebanese specialities". Owned by Maroush, the group have successfully ditched the more traditional British formula they trialled initially, to focus on what they do best. Irrespective of eating, the place is worth a visit "just for the building" alone. Crocker, a Victorian entrepreneur, built his epic gin palace here – in what seems like the middle of nowhere – in the misguided expectation that it would become a major railway terminus. / NW8 8JR; www.crockersfolly.com; @Crockers_Folly; Sun-Thu 11 pm, Fri & Sat 11.30 pm.

The Crooked Well SE5 £48 3 2 3
16 Grove Ln 020 7252 7798 1–3C
Limited feedback on this elegantly updated neighbourhood pub in the heart of Camberwell, but all of it is positive regarding its gastrofare ("excellent Sunday roast"), and a setting that's "full of atmosphere". / SE5 8SY; www.thecrookedwell.com; @crookedwell; 10.30 pm; closed Mon L; no Amex; booking max 6 may apply.

The Cross Keys SW3 £60 3 4 4
1 Lawrence St 020 7351 0686 6–3C
The oldest boozer in Chelsea is now a gastropub with an "awesome new chef" who turns out "great pub food". Under the same ownership as the Sands End in Fulham, it's "always welcoming" and "excellent value". / SW3 5NB; www.thecrosskeyschelsea.co.uk; @CrossKeys_PH; 9.30 pm, Sun 3.30 pm.

Cub N1 NEW £77 4 4 3
153-155 Hoxton St 020 3693 3202 14–2A
Feedback is limited but impressed by this offbeat Shoreditch newcomer – a collaboration between Ryan Chetiyawardana and chef Doug McMaster of Brighton's acclaimed zero-waste restaurant Silo, and with a similarly eco-zealous approach. A multi-course tasting menu is served from a tiny open kitchen in an "intimate" room with a counter and yellow leather banquette seating. The Sunday Times's Marina O'Loughlin left intellectually exhilarated but hungry: our reporters describe "one of the most innovative meals in a long time" – "thoughtful, sensitive, sometimes genius food served by passionate staff" and "a wonderful way to spend a couple of hours over a tasting menu". / N1 6PJ; closed Thu-Sat L, closed Mon-Wed & Sun; Online only.

The Culpeper E1 £58 3 3 4
40 Commercial St 020 7247 5371 13–2C
"Always buzzing" Spitalfields gastropub, with the rare option to eat (in summer) "in the rooftop garden where they grow veg and herbs". Cleverly converted from an old corner boozer three years ago, it inspired mixed feedback in its second year but scores have recovered their mojo of late, with some reports of "very good" cooking. / E1 6LP; www.theculpeper.com; @TheCulpeper; 10 pm, Sun 9 pm; SRA-Food Made Good – 1 star.

Cumberland Arms W14 £47 3 3 3
29 North End Rd 020 7371 6806 8–2D
"A pub which does a first-class risotto!" – this Olympia gastroboozer is "under same ownership as The Atlas in Earl's Court, and with a similarly delicious and quick Med-inspired menu". "If you have to go to the nearby Olympia exhibition halls, it's like Médecins sans Frontières provided a nearby life-line!" / W14 8SZ; www.thecumberlandarmspub.co.uk; @thecumberland; Mon-Wed 10 pm, Thu-Sat 11 pm.

Cut,
45 Park Lane W1 £124 3 2 2
45 Park Ln 020 7493 4545 3–4A
"Other patrons put on a glamorous show" at this "stylish and expensive"
London outpost of Los Angeles-based celeb chef, Wolfgang Puck's Cut brand,
in a Park Lane hotel. For its most ardent fans, it has "the best steak
in London", but it has always had such kick-in-the-crotch prices that it has
never attracted a significant following amongst reporters. / W1K 1PN;
www.45parklane.com; @45ParkLaneUK; 10.30 pm; closed Sun L.

Cut + Grind N1 NEW £33 4 3 2
The Urbanest Building, 25-27 Canal Reach 020 3668 7683 9–3C
"Outstanding burgers" ("very tasty and not too greasy") are "served with
charm and no little panache" (alongside local ale from Shoreditch brewery
Redchurch) at this new operation, at the foot of a King's Cross tower block
(and which won the National Burger Awards 2018). Top Tip: the vegan
burger here gets a shout out. / N1C 4DD; www.cutandgrindburgers.com;
@cngburgers; Mon-Fri 10 pm, Sat & Sun 9 pm.

Cut The Mustard SW16 £24 3 3 3
68 Moyser Rd 07725 034101 11–2D
"Top brunch, top coffee and top sourdough bread" all win praise for this
little café down Streatham way. / SW16 6SQ; cutthemustardcafe.com;
@WeCutTheMustard; 5.30 pm, Sun 4 pm; closed Mon-Sun D.

Cyprus Mangal SW1 £41 3 3 2
45 Warwick Way 020 7828 5940 2–4B
Consistently rated for some of the "best kebabs around", this popular
Turkish grill is a good "cheap 'n' cheerful" option in Pimlico. / SW1V 1QS;
www.cyprusmangal.co.uk; Sun-Thu midnight, Fri & Sat 1 am.

Da Mario SW7 £45 3 3 3
15 Gloucester Rd 020 7584 9078 6–1B
"For pizza lovers", this "very friendly local Italian" near the Royal Albert Hall
is "brilliant for a family meal". "The food – nice, not spectacular –
is just a small part of an excellent dining experience." / SW7 4PP;
www.damario.co.uk; 11.30 pm.

Da Mario WC2 £55 3 4 3
63 Endell St 020 7240 3632 5–1C
"Busy, fun and great value for money" – this "typical family-run Italian"
(and there aren't many of them left in Covent Garden) serves "really good
classics, not just pasta"; but "the real bonus is the friendly service and buzz
– when so many customers seem to be regulars, you know they
must be doing something right!". / WC2H 9AJ; www.da-mario.co.uk; 10.30 pm,
Mon 11 pm, Sun 3 pm; closed Sun.

Daddy Bao SW17 NEW £42 4 3 3
113 Mitcham Rd 020 3601 3232 11–2C
"A local gem of a Taiwanese kitchen specialising in bao" (steamed buns) –
this cosy Tooting spin-off from Peckham's Mr Bao opened in January 2018,
and if anything is more popular than the original. Attractions include
a bottomless brunch: "loving their pancakes". / SW17 9PE; www.daddybao.com;
11 pm, Sun 10.30 pm.

The Dairy SW4 £50 4 4 4
15 The Pavement 020 7622 4165 11–2D
Irish chef Robin Gill's "really excellent and clever (but not too clever!) food"
has carved a major reputation for his "vibrant" small-plates venture
by Clapham Common, where the "combination of culinary skill and
boundary-pushing ideas make it really special". / SW4 0HY;
www.the-dairy.co.uk; @thedairyclapham; 10 pm, Sun 3.30 pm; closed Sun D,
closed Mon.

Dalloway Terrace,
Bloomsbury Hotel WC1 £56 | 3 | 2 | 4 |
16-22 Great Russell St   020 7347 1221   2–1C
Breakfast and brunch get top billing at this marvellous al fresco eating space, whose gorgeous greenery and attractive design (complete with retractable roof) are all the more remarkable in the un-lovely area around Centre Point. Its general food service throughout the day inspires little feedback, but this would be a great spot for a drink, coffee or light bite. / WC1B 3NN; www.dallowayterrace.com; @DallowayTerrace; 10.30 pm.

La Dame de Pic London EC3 £119 | 4 | 3 | 2 |
10 Trinity Square   020 7297 3799   10–3D
"Amazing food with amazing attention to detail", backed up by a formidable wine list, have made this "glossy" yearling, within the palatial ex-HQ of the Port of London Authority (by the Tower of London), a "superb addition to London's top-rank restaurants" and a feather-in-the-cap for the Pic family (from Valence, in SE France) who run it. As an imposing backdrop to a business meal it's particularly well-suited, but other diners are a bit unsure about the design: "it can seem a little disjointed with different styles and spaces, one part modern with white tiles, another Art Deco with black mirrors and banquettes – this doesn't spoil the experience but could have enhanced it further". / EC3N 4AJ; ladamedepiclondon.co.uk; @FSTenTrinity; closed Sun; No shorts.

Daphne's SW3 £80 | 2 | 2 | 2 |
112 Draycott Ave   020 7589 4257   6–2C
To a "smart Chelsea crowd" this delightful-looking stalwart is a "perennial favourite" (as it was for Princess Di when she was alive) with Italian cooking they say is "always good". It's pricey though, and the overall value equation for those without deep pockets is questionable. It inspires less and less feedback – perhaps Richard Caring's Caprice group have forgotten they own it? / SW3 3AE; www.daphnes-restaurant.co.uk; @DaphnesLondon/; 11 pm, Sun 10 pm.

Daquise SW7 £49 | 2 | 2 | 2 |
20 Thurloe St   020 7589 6117   6–2C
This "old-fashioned", "homely" institution has been knocking out "huge portions of solid Polish food" washed down with "potato vodka" in "ancient surroundings" near South Ken station for 70-odd years. "Like meeting a friend from the distant past and discovering there's still something special" – "I'm just glad it's still there!" / SW7 2LT; www.daquise.co.uk; @GesslerDaquise; 10.30 pm, Mon 11 pm, Sun 3 pm; no Amex.

Darjeeling Express W1 £52 | 5 | 3 | 3 |
6-8 Kingly St   020 7287 2828   4–2B
"On the top floor of Kingly Court and less frantic than the more happening places below" – "Asma Khan has a winner on her hands" at this "very genuine feeling" follow-up to her former pop-up ventures. From "a well chosen menu of distinctive dishes with an authentic 'home cooked' vibe", the resulting dishes are "full of spicy flavour without being greasy or heavy". "It's so authentic even Indians can't get enough of it!" / W1B 5PW; www.darjeeling-express.com; @Darjeelingldn; Sun-Thu 11 pm, Fri & Sat midnight.

The Dartmouth Castle W6 £47 | 3 | 4 | 3 |
26 Glenthorne Rd   020 8748 3614   8–2C
This "excellent local pub/restaurant" near Hammersmith Broadway caters with aplomb to everyone from "the giddy lunchtime rush of the nearby office population to the more genteel folk of the 'hood dining and wining in the evening". / W6 0LS; www.thedartmouthcastle.co.uk; @DartmouthCastle; Mon-Wed 10 pm, Thu-Sat 11 pm; closed Sat L.

Darwin Brasserie EC3 £73 2 3 4
1 Sky Garden Walk 033 3772 0020 10–3D
"The view and experience of looking across London are second to none"
when you visit this all-day operation at the top of the Walkie Talkie, where
a wander amongst the Sky Garden's tropical foliage is a talking point before
or after either a business meal or a date. Prices are a sore subject here,
though, with critics advising: "forget the food and just take in the view".
/ EC3M 8AF; skygarden.london/darwin; @SG_Darwin; Sun-Thu 10 pm, Fri & Sat
10.30 pm.

Dastaan KT19 £43 5 4 2
447 Kingston Rd 020 8786 8999 1–4A
"A real diamond-in-the-rough, setting wise – why they picked this location
in a most unexpected part of Ewell isn't obvious, but when you eat here all
is forgotten". "Terrific and authentic Indian flavours are created by two
former top chefs from Gymkhana" and even if "the shabby chic could
be improved" the interior is "lively (in a good way)" and "the superb quality
of food more than compensates". "Simply put: just go there!" / KT19 0DB;
dastaan.co.uk; @Dastaan447; 10.30 pm, Sun 9.30 pm; closed Tue-Fri L, closed Mon;
booking weekdays only.

Daylesford Organic £56 3 2 2
44b Pimlico Rd, SW1 020 7881 8060 6–2D
6-8 Blandford St, W1 020 3696 6500 2–1A
76-82 Sloane Avenue, SW3 awaiting tel 6–2C NEW
208-212 Westbourne Grove, W11 020 7313 8050 7–1B
"Lovely for a breakfast or lunch snack, and with good bread etc to buy
to take home" – Lady Bamford's faux-rustic organic cafés can make a good
choice for a posh brunch, despite toppish prices and historically variable
service. In October 2018, the brand arrives in its spiritual London home,
with a large new 'Farmshop and Café' near chichi Brompton Cross.
/ www.daylesford.com; SW1 & W11 9.30 pm, Mon 7 pm, Sun 4 pm; W1 9 pm,
Sun 6.15 pm; W11 no booking L; SRA-Food Made Good – 3 stars.

Dean Street Townhouse W1 £69 2 3 5
69-71 Dean St 020 7434 1775 4–1D
"Soak up the superb atmosphere and enjoy!" – with a terrace in summer,
and "wonderfully welcoming interior on a cold winter day, with warm fire
and subdued lighting" – this slick operation (attached to a Soho House
group hotel) makes a fantastic Soho rendezvous, for business or pleasure.
The brasserie cooking has historically been a bit forgettable here, but it won
consistent praise this year for its "honest" results. Top Tip: "Refreshing and
dangerously delicious Bloody Marys" means there's "no better way to start
a weekend than with brunch here". / W1D 3SE; www.deanstreettownhouse.com;
@deanstreettownhouse; Mon-Thu midnight, Fri & Sat 1 am, Sun 11 pm.

Defune W1 £84 3 2 1
34 George St 020 7935 8311 3–1A
There are many constants in feedback over the years on this veteran
Japanese in Marylebone – its small fan club swears that it serves
"unquestionably the best sushi in London"; it has "no ambience"; and it's
"very, very expensive". / W1U 7DP; www.defune.com; 11 pm, Sun 10.30 pm.

Dehesa W1 £55 3 2 3
25 Ganton St 020 7494 4170 4–2B
Part of the Salt Yard Group – this "lovely little dining room" off Carnaby
Street has won a reputation for its "excellent quality" Spanish and Italian
tapas. All reports here remain upbeat, but – while the most enthusiastic
feels the cooking "never fails to impress" – since the departure of Ben Tish,
the chain's chef-director, ratings have slipped and the most sceptical regulars
feel the "food has fallen from delicious to mediocre". / W1F 9BP;
www.saltyardgroup.co.uk/dehesa; @SaltYardGroup; 10.45 pm, Sun 9.45 pm.

Delamina £41 442
56-58 Marylebone Lane, W1   020 3026 6810   3–1A
151 Commercial St, E1   020 7078 0770   13–2B
"Fresh Middle Eastern flavours with lots of good spice" are found on the *"fairly short but tempting menu (with lots of vegetable options, but fish and meat too)"* at this Marylebone venue – *"a fantastic new opening"* that inspires rave reviews. Its the second venture from Amir and Limor Chen who run Shoreditch's Strut & Cluck – now re-branded 'Delamina East', and likewise praised (if only slightly less effusively) for its *"consistently excellent and healthy"* Levantine dishes.

The Delaunay WC2 £59 244
55 Aldwych   020 7499 8558   2–2D
"Like The Wolseley, minus the poseurs and food-tourists" – Corbin & King's *"very professionally run"* outpost on Aldwych is *"not as hectic as its sibling"* and boasts *"uncramped surroundings"* and *"classy"* comfy decor that make it particularly *"perfect for business"*, be it at breakfast (*"feels like you're being really spoilt"*), lunch or dinner. It's a natural for *"sophisticated pre-theatre meals"* too. The *"ersatz Mittel-european dishes"* (schnitzel, for instance) are *"satisfying"* to fans, but even some supporters concede *"the menu can be a little pedestrian"*, and a borderline-concerning number of visits were really *"not very inspiring"* food-wise this year. Top Tip: *"marvellous Viennese afternoon tea at £19.75, with all the silverware and trimmings"*. / WC2B 4BB; www.thedelaunay.com; @TheDelaunayRest; midnight, Sun 11 pm; closed Sat & Sun L.

Delfino W1 £57 332
121a Mount St   020 7499 1256   3–3B
"The BEST secret in Mayfair", this *"bustling and buzzing traditional Italian with the most amazing pizzas"* is just a few steps from the Connaught. *"The oven-fired pizza is thin, crispy and excellent"*. / W1K 3NW; www.finos.co.uk; 10 pm; closed Sun.

Delhi Grill N1 £32 332
21 Chapel Mkt   020 7278 8100   9–3D
"You can eat like a king for under £20 and every sauce is slow-cooked, all to family recipes" at this *"astonishingly cheap"* 'dhaba' (roadside canteen) in Islington's Chapel Market. *"In a world of posh Indians, DG cuts through them all!"*. / N1 9EZ; www.delhigrill.com; @delhigrill; Sun-Thu 10.30 pm, Fri & Sat 11 pm; closed Sun L; cash only.

Delicatessen NW3 £64 322
46 Rosslyn Hill   020 7700 5511   9–2A
"The best kosher newcomer in years" is not quite the resounding endorsement it might be given the dire state of London's kosher offerings, but this *"shabby chic"* Hampstead yearling is (mostly) credited to be *"an excellent arrival"* with *"well-prepared and delicious"*, *"kosher-fusion"* dishes (*"Middle Eastern inspired but including North African and central and eastern European influences"*). Service can occasionally hit the wrong note here. / NW3 1NH; delicatessen.company; Sun-Thu, Sat 11 pm; closed Sat L, closed Fri.

La Delizia Limbara SW3 £44 322
63-65 Chelsea Manor St   020 7376 4111   6–3C
This *"great little Italian pizza place"* in a side street off the King's Road is a *"best-in-class for a cheap and cheerful bite"*. There's a *"limited menu, but what it does it does well"*… and has done for yonks. / SW3 5RZ; www.ladelizia.org.uk; @ladelizia; 10 pm, Sun 3.30 pm; no Amex.

Department of Coffee EC1 £10 3 4 3
14-16 Leather Ln 020 7419 6906 10–2A
*"Leave your laptop at home and just enjoy the coffee" – "the best in town",
according to many fans – at the Leather Lane original of this coffee bar
group. "Good cakes, too." / EC1N 7SU; departmentofcoffee.com; @DeptOfCoffee;
closed Mon-Fri D, closed Sat & Sun; no booking.*

Din Tai Fung WC2 NEW
5-6 Henrietta St awaiting tel 5–3D
*Since launching in Taipei in 1972 – selling dumplings as a sideline from
a cooking oil store that was struggling to make ends meet – this soup
dumpling and noodle brand has gone global. Its first foray into the
UK market was due to open at the revamped Centre Point development
in Summer 2018 but will now open in 2019, preceded by this 'second'
outpost in Covent Garden late in 2018; exact opening dates still TBA.
/ WC2E 8PT; 11 pm.*

The Dining Room, The Goring Hotel SW1 £97 3 5 4
15 Beeston Pl 020 7396 9000 2–4B
*For a "quintessential English experience" in London, it's hard to beat this
"wonderful family-owned and managed hotel in the heart of Victoria and its
marvellous dining room". "Perfect, courteous and caring service" is at the
heart of a formula which feels like "a trip back to yesteryear" and which
is "class personified". As such, though not at all corporate, it's "a first-rate
way to wow potential clients (especially Americans!)", backed up by
luxurious traditional cuisine that's "old school and all the better for it".
There's also a "fascinating wine list, with many entries chosen personally
by Mr Goring on his travels". This is also the location for "the most civilised
breakfast in London", and there's a "marvellous, sumptuous afternoon tea
served in the opulent lounge at the Goring: enveloping cosy chairs,
fine china, an extensive selection of teas, sandwiches, scones and the
prettiest of cakes, plus Champagne options. A total treat best saved for
special days". / SW1W 0JW; www.thegoring.com; @TheGoring; 10 pm,
Sun 2.30 pm; closed Sun D; No jeans; booking max 8 may apply.*

Dinings £69 5 3 2
22 Harcourt St, W1 020 7723 0666 9–4A
Walton House, Walton St, SW3 020 7723 0666 6–2C
*"Sublime fish" employed in "lots of new-style sushi" helps win nothing but
adulation for Tomonari Chiba's operation, now split between two sites –
both of which deliver "exquisite" Japanese cuisine. The Marylebone original
suffers from being a "cramped basement", but the new Knightsbridge site
makes a "great addition", with "better decor and a larger kitchen, resulting
in a wider menu and a better dining experience". / dinings.co.uk.*

Dinner, Mandarin Oriental SW1 £125 2 2 2
66 Knightsbridge 020 7201 3833 6–1D
*"Heston Blumenthal would do well to pay attention and create some new
ideas" at this Knightsbridge dining room, where ratings this year are
continuing on their remorseless march south (and whose ongoing inclusion
in William Reed's World's 50 Best awards seems to represent the worst kind
of spineless kowtowing to celebrity). Undoubtedly, there are many loyalists,
who "love the menu that's full of history" (being researched from medieval
recipe books), and who feel Ashley Palmer-Watts and his team deliver
"entertaining", "alternative" cuisine that's "so impressive". There are too
many reporters however, for whom it's becoming an "overpriced nightmare"
– charming "extortionate prices" for "mediocre" or even "dreadful" fare.
Despite its park views, reporters are also increasingly "not sure about the
dining room" either: "all dark wood and posh design looking into the
kitchen, it lacks intimacy" and can seem totally "atmosphere-free". STOP
PRESS – after the fire at the hotel in June 2018, the restaurant remains
closed, with "partial re-opening" in late 2018 a possibility. / SW1X 7LA;
www.dinnerbyheston.com; Mon-Fri 10.15 pm, Sat & Sun 10.30 pm.*

Dip & Flip £34 333
87 Battersea Rise, SW11   no tel   11–2C
115 Tooting High St, SW17   no tel   11–2C
62 The Broadway, SW19   no tel   11–2C
64-68 Atlantic Rd, SW9   no tel   11–2C

"Delicious beef patties served with a bowl of proper gravy to dip them in – perfect!" say aficionados of this unusual twist on the burger bar, with outlets in Battersea, Brixton, Tooting and Wimbledon. "The gravy thing feels so wrong but so right at the same time – sweet potato fries on the side partially assuage that guilt." No booking, but "they'll text you when your table is ready so you can have a drink in a local bar while you wait". / 10 pm, Thu-Sat 11 pm; SW9 & SW17 booking: 8 min.

Dip in Brilliant SW6 NEW £46 333
448 Fulham Rd   020 3771 9443   6–4A

Near Stamford Bridge, this Spring 2018 newcomer is the inspiration of Dipna Anand – daughter of the founder of Southall's famous canteen Brilliant – and this new café on the site of Kishmish (RIP) offers a fast-casual concept (diners can 'dip in and out' in 30 minutes) featuring Punjabi sharing platters, thalis and tandoori dishes. Good if you're on the way to the footie, but not a substitute for a pilgrimage to the original. / SW6 1DL; www.dipinbrilliant.com; @dipnaanand; Mon-Thu 10 pm, Fri 10.30 pm, Sat 11 pm; closed Mon-Sat L, closed Sun.

Dirty Burger £34 222
86 The Broadway, SW19   020 3859 1122   11–2B NEW
Arch 54, 6 South Lambeth Rd, SW8   020 7074 1444   2–4D
13 Bethnal Green Rd, E1   020 7749 4525   13–1B

This hip small chain has established a solid following with its "fun" grill shacks serving "quality" burgers and "generous desserts". "Always good for families, with something for everyone", including "excellent chicken and sides". / www.eatdirtyburger.com; 10 pm-midnight, Fri & Sat 11pm-2 am, Sun 8 pm-11 pm; no bookings.

Dishoom £44 345
22 Kingly St, W1   020 7420 9322   4–2B
12 Upper St Martins Ln, WC2   020 7420 9320   5–3B
The Barkers Building, Derry St, W8   020 7420 9325   6–1A
Stable St, Granary Sq, N1   020 7420 9321   9–3C
7 Boundary St, E2   020 7420 9324   13–1B

"No wonder people queue out the door!" – "it feels like you are actually in Mumbai, even the smells wafting round the room", at these "terrific" and "incredibly busy" outlets, whose "distinctive" interiors generate a "vibrant atmosphere" that's reasonably faithful to the buzz in India's Irani cafés. "The bar areas with good cocktails help make the long and boring wait bearable" and, once seated, servers "are full of fun and energy" (admittedly probably with one eye on "efficiently maximising table turnover"). For most customers, any hassle is "worth it for the absolutely yum-tastic Indian street food" – special shout outs go to the "reinvention of the bacon butty (naan with crispy cured Ginger Pig bacon) which is the perfect breakfast"; and "the black daal and Ruby Murray, which are standout dishes". But declining ratings do support the doubters who feel that "quality has declined following the brand's extraordinary rise in popularity", or that "while it's good enough, the chain definitely doesn't excite like it once did". Even most critics would acknowledge that "the glow hasn't worn off Dishoom yet", however, and if you haven't been already, you should go: it can still provide "a real revelation". / www.dishoom.com; @Dishoom; 11pm, Thu-Sat midnight; breakfast 8, Sat & Sun 9; booking: min 6 at D.

Diwana Bhel-Poori House NW1 £28 **3**|2|1|
121-123 Drummond St   020 7387 5556   9–4C
"Still around after nearly 50 years", this "battered-looking" south Indian
veggie canteen in the 'Little India' stretch behind Euston station is "still
dishing out some of the best dosas, thalis and vegetarian snacks in London"
– and still at a "low, low price". Top Tip: BYO. / NW1 2HL;
www.diwanabph.com; @DiwanaBhelPoori; 11.30 pm, Sun 10 pm; no Amex; may need
10+ to book.

Dokke E1 £42 **3**|4|3|
Ivory House, 50 St Katharine's Way   020 7481 3954   10–3D
Feedback is limited but enthusiastic when it comes to this "small" café
overlooking the water of St Katharine Docks, where healthy options and
brunch are two strengths: "dishes are presented with beautiful artistry and
served by friendly and helpful staff, who are up for a chat but don't
intrude". / E1W 1LA; www.dokke.co.uk; @dokkelondon; Mon-Thu 11 pm, Fri & Sat
midnight; booking max 10 may apply.

Dominique Ansel Bakery London SW1 £17 **3**|2|2|
17-21 Elizabeth St   020 7324 7705   2–4B
Doubts crept in this year regarding the Belgravia outpost of NYC's
trendiest of bakeries. For its cronut-crazed fans, its deluxe delicacies are still
the biz, but for sceptics, the performance here is "nice but not amazing",
or even "losing momentum: after several visits (and numerous trips in NYC),
I'm not rushing back – overrated and, I must say, overpriced". / SW1W 9RP;
www.dominiqueansellondon.com; @DominiqueAnsel; 10 pm; no booking.

The Don EC4 £63 **3**|3|2|
The Courtyard, 20 St Swithin's Lane   020 7626 2606   10–3C
As "a solid choice for business entertaining", this "classy and popular" venue
(which feels "slightly off-the-beaten-track", even though it's right by the Bank
of England) remains one of the City's prime choices thanks to its "reliable,
well-cooked French cuisine" and "huge wine list". / EC4N 8AD;
www.thedonrestaurant.com; @thedonlondon; 10 pm; closed Sat & Sun; No shorts.

The Don Bistro and Bar EC4 £65 **3**|4|4|
21 St Swithin's Ln   020 7626 2606   10–3C
A good City "secret" – cellars that once housed the Sandeman wine and
sherry importers have been converted into a "wonderful tucked-away
location" – perfect for a business meal with no mobile signal. There's
a "good wine list" and it's "very buzzy at lunchtime (quiet some evenings)".
"Good value" for the Square Mile, too. / EC4N 8AD;
www.thedonrestaurant.com/bistro; @TheDonLondon; 10 pm; closed Sat & Sun.

Donostia W1 £56 **4**|4|4|
10 Seymour Pl   020 3620 1845   2–2A
"Perfect, high-quality Spanish food", "well presented by personal and
engaging staff" win only the highest praise for this little but "really lively"
and "fun" pintxos and tapas bar near Marble Arch (which, as well as a
counter by the open kitchen, also has a couple of tables at the back).
"Possibly a bit noisy" is the closest any reporter comes to a criticism. Sibling
to nearby Lurra, it is named after the Basque for San Sebastian, the region's
culinary mecca. / W1H 7ND; www.donostia.co.uk; @DonostiaW1; 10 pm,
Sun 9 pm; closed Mon L; booking max 8 may apply.

Dorchester Grill, Dorchester Hotel W1
£110   3 4 4

53 Park Lane   020 7629 8888   3–3A

Culinary mastermind Alain Ducasse is behind something of a renaissance at this "very elegant dining room" in Mayfair, which had lost its way quite badly a few years ago. With its luxurious decor and "wonderful" modern French cuisine it can be "unbeatable for a special occasion". Hardly surprisingly, it is "not cheap", but this is one of London's grander dining rooms and deserves to be more discovered again. / W1K 1QA; www.thedorchester.com; @TheDorchester; 10.30 pm, Sun 9 pm; No trainers.

Dotori N4
£34   4 3 2

3a Stroud Green Rd   020 7263 3562   9–1D

"Unexpectedly good" Korean and Japanese food, including "wonderful sushi", justifies submitting to the "confined" seating and inevitable wait for a table at this no-bookings outfit near Finsbury Park station. "It might be small, crowded and bustling – but that's exactly how food from the Orient should be served!". / N4 2DQ; www.dotorirestaurant.wix.com/dotorirestaurant; 10.30 pm, Sun 10 pm; closed Tue-Thu, Sun L, closed Mon; no Amex; no booking.

The Dove W6
£51   3 3 5

19 Upper Mall   020 8748 5405   8–2B

History is in the air at this riverside pub, down a cute Hammersmith alley, and with fine views from the small Thames-side terrace. Feedback is enthusiastic about its "fantastic" pub scoff, but the marvellous characterful interior is the big deal here. / W6 9TA; www.fullers.co.uk; @thedovew6; Mon-Thu 11 pm, Fri & Sat midnight, Sun 10.30 pm; closed Sun D.

Dozo
£46   3 2 2

32 Old Compton St, W1   020 7434 3219   5–2A

68 Old Brompton Rd, SW7   020 7225 0505   6–2B **NEW**

"Informal Japanese" which offers "rare good value" in pricey South Kensington, near the former Christie's showroom (there's also a similar heart-of-Soho branch which inspires little feedback). Eating at "sunk-in tables" adds to the ambience.

Dragon Castle SE17
£48   3 3 3

100 Walworth Rd   020 7277 3388   1–3C

"Hong Kong comes to the Elephant & Castle" at this "huge and bustling dim sum paradise". It's "very reliable", and "the new regional dishes are interesting and well executed". Top Tip: "don't miss the prawn & sugarcane lollipops or the turnip cake". / SE17 1JL; www.dragoncastlelondon.com; @Dragoncastle100; 10.30 pm.

Drakes Tabanco W1
£55   2 2 4

3 Windmill St   020 7637 9388   2–1C

Inspired by the sherry taverns of Andalucia, this "warm and accommodating" Fitzrovia tapas bar has "lots of interesting sherries and Spanish wines" and food of "some authenticity". / W1T 2HY; www.drakestabanco.com; @drakestabanco; Mon-Thu 11 pm, Fri & Sat midnight, Sun 10.30 pm; booking max 7 may apply.

The Drapers Arms N1
£53   3 3 4

44 Barnsbury St   020 7619 0348   9–3D

"Ticking the boxes for an excellent neighbourhood local" – this mega-popular Islington gastropub has a "lovely building and location", provides "solid and interesting food at quite sensible prices" and "drinkers are just as welcome as those wanting food" (with "a very good wine list if you're not into pints"). / N1 1ER; www.thedrapersarms.com; @DrapersArms; Mon & Tue, Sun 10 pm, Wed-Sat 11 pm; no Amex.

The Drop N1 NEW
Coal Drops Yard awaiting tel 9–3C
A new wine bar (with outside terrace) from the Hart Bros arrives in October 2018 at canalside retail development Coal Drops Yard (a converted Victorian coal store near King's Cross). / N1C 4AB.

The Drunken Butler EC1 NEW £58 4 3 3
20 Rosebery Avenue 020 7101 4020 10–1A
French cuisine with Persian influences? That's the deal at this Clerkenwell newcomer with open kitchen, the first solo effort from chef Yuma Hashemi (previously of The Chancery), serving morning coffee, and tasting menus of small plates by day and night. Standard critic Fay Maschler delivered a less-than-kind verdict, but our initial feedback is more upbeat: "a real asset to the culinary landscape with imaginative cooking beautifully presented in informal surroundings and a wine list and short cocktail list to match". / EC1R 4SX; www.thedrunkenbutler.com; @SYumaHashemi; Wed-Sat 10 pm; Online only.

The Duck & Rice W1 £55 3 2 4
90 Berwick St 020 3327 7888 4–2C
Chinese-meets-gastropub is the formula under test at this three-year-old venture on Soho's atmospheric Berwick Street Market – the brainchild of serial restaurant creator Alan Yau. The "delightful dishes" and "lovely" contemporary design do go down well with most reporters, but there's little sign just yet that he has another tearaway hit like Wagamama on his hands. / W1F 0QB; www.theduckandrice.com; @theduckandrice; Mon-Thu 11 pm, Fri & Sat 11.30 pm, Sun 10 pm.

Duck & Waffle Local SW1 £50 3 3 3
No 2, St. James's Market, 52 Haymarket 020 3900 4444 4–4D
New spin-off from the City venue, in the new St James's Market development, with its trademark duck-based menu; feedback echoes its sibling – some good, some bad, but no criticisms are grievous and breakfast is similarly recommended. / SW1Y 4RP; duckandwafflelocal.com; @duckwafflelocal; 1 am.

Duck & Waffle EC2 £75 2 2 5
110 Bishopsgate, Heron Tower 020 3640 7310 10–2D
"The lift up is a little scary" (in a good way), but the payoff is the "breathtaking view" from this "trendy-but-tasteful" venue on the 40th floor of the Heron Tower (adjacent to Sushisamba): a natural choice both for a business or romantic occasion. Most – but not all – reporters feel its slightly wacky menu (the restaurant being named for its signature dish) is "well conceived" and – aided by the fact that it's open 24/7 – the place is particularly popular for its "sophisticated and interesting breakfast dishes". / EC2N 4AY; www.duckandwaffle.com; @DuckandWaffle; open 24 hours.

Duck Duck Goose SW9 £41 4 4 3
49 Brixton Station Rd no tel 11–1D
"Amazing to see perfectly cooked Peking ducks and crispy pork belly coming out of a tiny shipping container!" – this "modern Chinese canteen" occupies one of the units at Pop Brixton, and the results are "super tasty!" / SW9 8PQ; www.duckduckgooselondon.com; 10 pm; Fri & Sat 11 pm; closed Sun & Mon.

The Duck Truck E1 £11 5 3 3
Lamb St 07919 160271 13–2C
"The best street food ever" say fans of the "fab, fun, fast and delicious" dishes at this truck, permanently parked alongside Spitalfields Market. Amongst the numerous options: confit duck leg, pulled duck or duck steaks in a brioche bun, and wraps. / E1 6EA; www.theducktruck.com; @TheDuckTruck1; Mon & Tue, Sat & Sun 5 pm, Thu & Fri 6 pm, Wed 4 pm; closed Mon-Sun D.

Ducksoup W1 £61 **4 4 4**

41 Dean St 020 7287 4599 5–2A

A "go-to spot in Soho" serving natural and biodynamic wines by the bottle or glass alongside a hybrid menu of "delectable" Italian-North African dishes "that let the high-quality ingredients sing for themselves". "Super-lively on a busy night" while also "laid back and relaxed", it's a "great place to hang out by yourself or go on a date". Top Tip: "the drinking vinegars [true] are delicious and must be tried". / W1D 4PY; www.ducksoupsoho.co.uk; @ducksoup; 10.30 pm, Sun 5 pm; closed Sun D; may need 3+ to book.

Duddell's SE1 £83 **4 2 4**

6 St Thomas St 020 3957 9932 10–4C

"Best Peking duck ever, other than top restaurants in Beijing!"… "and unbelievably the dim sum was even better!!" – this "great reinvention of the Michelin-starred Hong Kong favourite" occupies an "amazingly converted church" (St Thomas's in London Bridge), and even though its most ardent fans admit that it's "pricey" the "cost isn't insane, and for once the hype is right". Service, though, is "a bit chaotic at times". / SE1 9RY; www.duddells.co/london; @DuddellsLondon; 11 pm, Sun 10.30 pm.

The Duke of Richmond E8 NEW £49

316 Queensbridge Rd 020 7923 3990 14–1A

Chef and restaurateur, Tom Oldroyd, follows up his diminutive debut, Oldroyd in N1, with this much larger venue near London Fields, which opened in June 2018 – a pub and dining room offering a French twist on seasonal British produce; ex-Canton Arms and Winemakers Deptford chef Rory Shannon is in charge of the open fire cooking in the semi-open kitchen. Early press reviews are a tad mixed, but overall positive. / E8 3NH; www.thedukeofrichmond.com; @dukeofrichmond_; Mon-Fri 11 pm, Sat midnight, Sun 10.30 pm; closed Mon-Fri L

Duke of Sussex W4 £52 **2 2 3**

75 South Pde 020 8742 8801 8–1A

This handsome Victorian tavern by Acton Green Common serves "good Anglo-Spanish food in comfortable surroundings at a reasonable price". Perhaps, though, the "menu is too long" – it "looked promising, but only some of the dishes lived up to the billing". / W4 5LF; www.metropolitanpubcompany.com; @thedukew4; 10 pm, Sun 9 pm.

Dum Biryani W1 £53 **3 2 2**

187 Wardour St 020 3638 0974 3–1D

"It's easy to miss this Soho basement" just south of Oxford Street, housing a "really authentic" yearling Indian biryani specialist. Cooked in a heavy pot – the 'dum' – "they are available in two sizes, single or sharing, and are topped with a crisp edible topping". "The simple fit-out of the interior could be improved", though. / W1F 8ZB; dumlondon.com; Sun-Wed 10 pm, Thu-Sat 10.30 pm; may need 5+ to book.

Dynamo £44 **3 2 3**

200-204 Putney Bridge Rd, SW15 020 3761 2952 11–2B
16-18 Ritherdon Rd, SW17 020 8767 3197 11–2C NEW

"The best coffee stop on the way home from laps of Richmond Park!" – you don't have to arrive on two wheels to appreciate the "amazing brunch and even better pizzas" at this Putney cycle-themed café, which has recently branched out into Balham too. / www.the-dynamo.co.uk; @WeAreTheDynamo.

The Dysart Petersham TW10 £75 333

135 Petersham Rd 020 8940 8005 1–4A

"The food is delicious, inventive and carefully sourced" at this upscale Arts & Crafts pub near Richmond Park, where "dining is so romantic with the fairy lights glittering through the leaded windows, log fire and flagstone floors". Irish chef Kenneth Culhane's cooking is "Asian-influenced and nuanced – it's not flashy, but there's a lot of thought in it". / TW10 7AA; www.thedysartarms.co.uk; @dysartpetersham; Wed-Fri 11.30 pm, Sat midnight, Sun 3.30 pm; closed Sun D, closed Mon & Tue.

E Mono NW5 £11 422

285-287 Kentish Town Rd 020 7485 9779 9–2B

"Top kebabs" at "bargain" prices win acclaim for this small Turkish café/takeaway in Kentish Town, named for signage uncovered during its renovation (and originally brought to attention by Giles Coren over five years ago). / NW5 2JS; emono.co.uk.

E&O W11 £55 344

14 Blenheim Cr 020 7229 5454 7–1A

"Still a great fusion restaurant", Will Ricker's pan-Asian tapas and cocktail hang-out in Notting Hill is "buzzing", if no longer thronged with the celebs of yesteryear. "Dependably good food, happy service, silly prices, and always very silly Notting Hill hipsters vogue-ing at the bar!" / W11 1NN; www.rickerrestaurants.com; 11 pm, Sun 10.30 pm; booking max 6 may apply.

The Eagle EC1 £38 334

159 Farringdon Rd 020 7837 1353 10–1A

"The formula has not changed over the years" at the stripped-back pub, near Exmouth Market, that's often hailed as London's first modern-day gastropub. According to its large fan club, it's still "the original and the best", thanks to Mediterranean-inspired cooking from the blackboard that's (almost) as "tasty" as ever; and a "crowded and noisy" setting that's enjoyably rough 'n' ready. / EC1R 3AL; www.theeaglefarringdon.co.uk; @eaglefarringdon; 11 pm, Sun 5 pm; closed Sun D; no Amex; no booking.

Earl Spencer SW18 £55 323

260-262 Merton Rd 020 8870 9244 11–2B

A "superb and friendly gastropub", this "large" Edwardian roadhouse in Southfields rates consistently for its "great beer" and "an ever-changing, better-than-average menu". / SW18 5JL; www.theearlspencer.com; @TheEarlSpencer; Mon & Tue, Sun 10 pm, Wed-Sat 11 pm; Mon-Thu D only, Fri-Sun open L & D.

Eat 17 £55 343

Unit A 77 Fulham Palace Rd, W6 020 8521 5279 8–2C NEW
28-30 Orford Rd, E17 020 8521 5279 1–1D
64-66 Brooksbys Walk, E9 020 8986 6242 14–1C

The "excellent burgers and pub-type grub" at these 'Spar-supermarkets-with-kitchen-attached' in Walthamstow Village and Hackney (and also Bishop's Stortford) make them favourite local hang outs as well as "super places to go for a meal with the kids" (even if non-parents can sometimes find it "family overfriendly!"). Top Tip: the "renowned chicken burger" (and their famous bacon jam, which can be bought by the jar). In late summer 2018 a new branch opened on the opposite side of town, south of Hammersmith Broadway. / www.eat17.co.uk; @eat_17; E17 10 pm, Sun 9 pm, E9 9 pm, Fri & Sat 9.30 pm, Sun 8 pm.

Eat Tokyo £31 3 3 2

16 Old Compton St, W1   020 7439 9887   5–2A
50 Red Lion St, WC1   020 7242 3490   2–1D
27 Catherine St, WC2   020 3489 1700   5–3D
169 King St, W6   020 8741 7916   8–2B
18 Hillgate St, W8   020 7792 9313   7–2B
14 North End Rd, NW11   020 8209 0079   1–1B
628 Finchley Rd, NW11   020 3609 8886   1–1B

"A go-to place for an affordable and tasty Japanese 'hit'" – this superbly consistent, "authentic" (slightly "dingy" looking) chain is "always full of Japanese diners so you know you're onto a good thing". "Prices are not the cheapest-of-the-cheap, but great value for the quality of Japanese food served" including the "real sushi, which bears no resemblance to the factory-produced, over-cooled and formulaic conveyor-belt muck you get elsewhere". "Daily specials and a wide range of lunch Bento boxes mean they're always bustling." / www.eattokyo.co.uk; Mon-Sat 11.30 pm, Sun 10.30 pm.

Eccleston Place by Tart London SW1 NEW £66

3-4 Eccleston Yard   020 7627 2176   2–4B

Jemima Jones and Lucy Carr-Ellison – the duo behind Tart London (the catering company favoured by London's top fashion brands) – are set to open in a very cool site in a new development near Victoria – an old Victorian space featuring the original arched roof and skylights. / SW1W 9AZ; www.eccleston-place.com; @tart_london; Tue-Sat, Mon 10.30 pm, Sun 3.30 pm.

Eco SW4 £38 3 2 3

162 Clapham High St   020 7978 1108   11–2D

Sami Wasif, who helped create the Franco Manca chain, has run this "buzzy" Clapham hangout for over 20 years: "it's nothing hip or über-trendy, just serves really great pizza" (occasionally chaotically). / SW4 1UG; www.ecorestaurants.com; @ecopizzaLDN; Mon-Thu 11 pm, Fri & Sat 11.30 pm, Sun 10.30 pm.

Edera W11 £65 3 4 3

148 Holland Park Ave   020 7221 6090   7–2A

This unusually professional neighbourhood Italian in Holland Park, boasting "attentive service and well-spaced tables", specialises in Sardinian cuisine. "Expensive for a local", it is "perfect for a business lunch or dinner" – and they know how to look after loyal regulars: "we go about 50 times a year and they treat us as family – if there's a hiccup, they're good at putting it right". / W11 4UE; www.edera.co.uk; 11 pm, Sun 10 pm.

Edwins SE1 £57 3 4 4

202-206 Borough High St   020 7403 9913   10–4B

"What a good find – a cosy room over a pub beside Borough tube station", "brimming with atmosphere and goodwill". The modern bistro food is up to scratch, too, whether an "excellent weekend breakfast" or a "lovely meal on a chilly night after Christmas". / SE1 1JX; www.edwinsborough.co.uk; @edwinsborough; 11 pm; closed Sun D.

Eight Over Eight SW3 £56 3 3 4

392 King's Rd   020 7349 9934   6–3B

"Always fun with a great vibe" – Will Ricker's clubby Chelsea haunt near the kink in the King's Road has a large and widespread fanclub thanks to its "always enjoyable" Asian fusion fare and yummy cocktails. / SW3 5UZ; www.rickerrestaurants.com/eight-over-eight; 11 pm, Sun 10.30 pm; closed Mon-Fri L.

F S A

Electric Diner W11 £49 **2 2 3**
191 Portobello Rd   020 7908 9696   7–1B
In the side of one of London's oldest cinemas, this "noisy and cool brasserie"
– "a great space", with comfortable US diner styling – is something of a
Notting Hill classic nowadays; and as such is a prime spot for people-
watching the trustafarian locals who tolerate its "sloppy service and average
food". / W11 2ED; www.electricdiner.com; @ElectricDiner; 10.30 pm.

Ella Canta,
InterContinental London Park Lane W1 £80 **3 4 4**
Park Lane   020 7318 8715   3–4A
The Times's Giles Coren described it as "the worst restaurant he's ever
reviewed", but reporters' feedback (if still a tad limited) is very much more
upbeat on Martha Ortiz's London newcomer, which occupies the
Intercontinental Park Lane's 'second' dining space (as made-over by David
Collins Studio). Its most ardent fans say, "the heart and soul of the very
best Mexico has to offer is brought to lucky London", and even those who
find it "very expensive" say that "it's a fun experience, with great staff and
interesting and unusual food". / W1J 7QY; www.ellacanta.com; @ellacantalondon;
Mon-Thu 1 am, Fri & Sat 2 am, Sun 6 pm; closed Mon L.

Elliot's Café SE1 £55 **4 3 3**
12 Stoney St   020 7403 7436   10–4C
Brett Redman's "relaxed and bohemian" open-fronted venue offers "great
people watching amongst the hubbub of Borough market" and is a "great
place for a cheapish top-quality lunch of excellent tapas-style food" and
a "wonderful list" of natural wines. / SE1 9AD; www.elliotscafe.com; @elliotscafe;
10 pm; closed Sun.

Elystan Street SW3 £107 **3 3 2**
43 Elystan St   020 7628 5005   6–2C
Phil Howard's "exciting", yet "unfussy" food ("at last, a top chef that has the
confidence to cook a beautifully balanced meal and not hide behind another
two-bite tasting menu") "pushes the boundaries, whilst feeling familiar;
and always has fabulous vegetarian options that highlight the joys of the
freshest in-season produce" ("roasted cabbage was my main dish of the
year… and I'm no veggie!"). As a result, a massive fan club "LOVE, LOVE,
LOVE" his Chelsea two-year-old, whose "restrained, light and spacious
decor" and "professional" approach help set up a "thoroughly civilised and
relaxed experience". But even those who consider the cuisine here
"top class" can feel prices are "astronomical", and this "casual" space can
also appear "canteen-like" and far too "noisy" for somewhere in this league.
/ SW3 3NT; www.elystanstreet.com; @elystanstreet; Mon-Thu 10 pm, Fri & Sat
10.30 pm, Sun 9.30 pm.

Ember Yard W1 £54 **3 3 4**
60 Berwick St   020 7439 8057   3–1D
"Delicious tapas from the Salt Yard crew" – as the name suggests,
this smart Soho outfit has a "focus on open-fire cooking", and ratings
bounced back this year, with praise for small plates that are "often special
and surprising". / W1F 8SU; www.emberyard.co.uk; @emberyard; 10 pm,
Sun 9 pm; booking max 13 may apply.

Emilia's Crafted Pasta E1 £46 **4 4 3**
Unit C3 Ivory House, St Katharine Docks   020 7481 2004   10–3D
"Pasta is elevated to an art form" at this inexpensive yearling
in St Katharine Docks, whose "romantic" potential on a sunny day
is boosted by attractive dock-side tables. / E1W 1AT; www.emiliaspasta.com;
@emiliaspasta; 11 pm, Sun 10 pm.

The Empress E9 £50 `3` `3` `4`

130 Lauriston Rd   020 8533 5123   14–2B

This landmark east London gastropub near Victoria Park is an "easy destination for a great night out or a weekend treat... always fun and welcoming". The menu "mixes conventional with more adventurous options". / E9 7LH; www.empresse9.co.uk; @elliottlidstone; 10 pm, Sun 9 pm; closed Mon L; no Amex.

Eneko Basque Kitchen & Bar WC2 £78 `3` `2` `1`

1 Aldwych   020 7300 0300   2–2D

Eneko Atxa's subterranean two-year-old, in the basement of No 1 Aldwych, is, on numerous accounts, something of an "undiscovered gem" thanks to its "interesting Basque cooking", serving "imaginative" dishes that are "expertly cooked and presented". The main sticking point on this site, is the "below-the-streets space" which – when under-patronised – seems "echoey" and "like a bit of a mausoleum". / WC2B 4BZ; www.eneko.london; @OneAldwych; 11 pm, Sun 10 pm.

Enoteca Rosso W8 NEW £69 `2` `2` `2`

276-280 Kensington High St   07384 595191   8–1D

"Basically the interest is on the wine" at this Kensington newcomer, where a "well-priced" all-Italian list is showcased, stacked in triangular shelving, lining the walls. It inspires supportive but mixed feedback: "small plates are interesting and reasonably priced", but "there's a feeling of trying too hard, and not being sure what it wants to be"; still, they are "nice people". / W8 6ND; www.enotecarosso.com; Mon & Tue 9 pm, Fri & Sat 11.30 pm, Wed 10 pm, Thu 11 pm, Sun 5 pm.

Enoteca Turi SW1 £78 `3` `5` `3`

87 Pimlico Rd   020 7730 3663   6–2D

"A good transplant now working seamlessly in its new home" – Giuseppi and Pamela Turi shifted after decades in Putney to a new Pimlico site a couple of years ago, and their new gig is continuing to prove "a superb addition to the SW1 scene". The "very traditional northern Italian food" is "consistently good", the setting is "simple but elegant" and the experience is "amplified by the long-standing family ownership" as the Turis are "super hosts". The big deal gastronomically speaking is the "HUGE" and "outstanding" Italian wine list "with an amazing selection of unusual and delicious vintages" – "worth a visit in its own right" and "made more interesting by the inclusion of Giuseppi's comments". / SW1W 8PH; www.enotecaturi.com; @EnotecaTuri; 11 pm; closed Sun; booking max 8 may apply.

The Enterprise SW3 £54 `2` `3` `4`

35 Walton St   020 7584 3148   6–2C

"A pretty place with pretty customers" is a verdict few would contest on this "smart yet casual" Chelsea haunt – "a fun spot enjoyed by young and old" with a "great ambience and buzz". The food is "sound – with high prices reflecting the location" on gorgeous Walton Street. / SW3 2HU; www.theenterprise.co.uk; 11 pm, Sun 10.30 pm.

L'Escargot W1 £76 `3` `4` `5`

48 Greek St   020 7439 7474   5–2A

"Thoroughly recommended, even after all these years!" – this "truly excellent" Gallic venue in the heart of Soho is marching towards its centennial in good form. A menu of "French classics, always to a high standard" is perfect "comfort food" and "combines with the lovely ambience" of the characterful dining room and "excellent service" to ensure it's "always an enjoyable experience". / W1D 4EF; www.lescargot.co.uk; @LEscargotSoho; 11.30 pm, Sun 6 pm; closed Sun D.

Essence Cuisine EC2 NEW £36 4 3 2
94 Leonard St 020 7729 5678 13–1B
A fully plant-based menu (just about all of it vegan) is the draw at this sparse, health-conscious new Shoreditch venture which looks like (and is partly) a take-out, but which also has a limited amount of seating and a fuller dinner offering. The menu is 100% free of meat, dairy, gluten, and refined sugar and has been developed with US chef Matthew Kenney. Worth a go, especially if you're a raw food fan. / EC2A 4RH; www.essence-cuisine.com; @essence_cuisine; 9 pm, Mon 7 pm; closed Sun; Online only.

Essenza W11 £68 2 3 3
210 Kensington Park Rd 020 7792 1066 7–1A
Mixed and limited feedback on this smart Notting Hill Italian. To fans it's a favourite with top class cooking (speciality black and white truffles) and a romantic interior – to the odd detractor it's not bad, merely "forgettable". / W11 1NR; www.essenza.co.uk; 11.30 pm.

Est India SE1 £39 3 2 3
73-75 Union Street, Flat Iron Square 020 7407 2004 10–4B
"Terrific Indian food with a great range of spices, not just chilli" hits the spot at this modern outfit in a basement space of the Flat Iron Square development. / SE1 1SG; www.estindia.co.uk; @EstIndiaLondon; 11 pm, Sun 10.30 pm.

Estiatorio Milos SW1 £114 3 2 3
1 Regent St 020 7839 2080 4–4D
"A fabulous selection of fresh fish on display to choose from" is the dramatic hallmark of Costas Spiladis's "upscale Greek" in the West End (where you choose your fish and pay by weight). Its most ardent fans feel it "gives Scott's a run for its money", but even some who feel it has "the best fish, with the best fish chefs in town" still say it's "pricey": "bring your bank manager along with you, as they'll need to extend your overdraft after eating here!" / SW1Y 4NR; www.milos.ca/restaurants/london; @Milos_London; midnight.

Evelyns Table at The Blue Posts W1 NEW £74 4 4 4
28 Rupert St no tel 4–3D
"The guys behind The Palomar and The Barbary nailed it again", according to fans of this vibey, clandestine cellar below the characterful (Grade II listed, 275-year-old) Blue Posts pub in Chinatown, whose ground floor is now The Mulwray cocktail bar, and where here, down below, they serve funky, small plates (of Italian inspiration, with an emphasis on Cornish-sourced fish). It's even more cramped than its siblings though, with an 11-seat counter and a couple of tiny tables. / W1D 6DJ; thebluposts.co.uk; Mon-Fri 10 pm, Sat & Sun 9 pm.

Everest Inn SE3 £41 3 2 3
41 Montpelier Vale 020 8852 7872 1–4D
"Great Gurkha curries" – and other Nepalese specialities (the best menu bets) – make this Blackheath curry house an "excellent local", notwithstanding that service can be "hit and miss". / SE3 0TJ; www.everestinnblackheath.co.uk; Mon-Thu 11 pm, Fri & Sat 11.30 pm, Sun 10.30 pm.

The Fallow Deer Cafe TW11 £23 3 4 3
130 High St 020 8943 2578 1–4A
"A great place to bring the family on a Sunday" – this funky Teddington café is arguably the 'burb's top brunch spot. Also featured: Cocktail Fridays (the only regular evening openings) with tapas and sharing plates); and irregular evening supper clubs and events with more ambitious fare. / TW11 8JB; www.thefallowdeer.com; @FallowDeerCafe; Mon-Thu, Sat & Sun 5 pm, Fri 11 pm; closed Mon-Thu, Sat & Sun D.

La Famiglia SW10 £63 2 2 2
7 Langton St   020 7351 0761   6–3B
A datedly glamorous, "bustling" Chelsea trat' that celebrated its half centenary two years ago, and which has over the years welcomed into its delightful back garden the likes of Princess Margaret, Peter Sellers, Brigitte Bardot and Jack Nicholson. One or two diehard fans still think of it as "London's best Italian" and say "nothing changes" here; but ratings support those who feel it's "nowhere near as good as it once was years ago", "expensive" for what it is, and on its worst days, quite "poor". Top Tip: still a favourite option for Chelsea folk with kids in tow. / SW10 0JL; www.lafamiglia.co.uk; @lafamiglia_sw10; 10.30 pm, Sun 9.30 pm.

Fancy Crab W1 £65 2 3 2
92 Wigmore St   020 3096 9484   3–1A
"Excellent crab" is the cornerstone offer at this year-old Marylebone concept, with a menu offering red king crab from the north Pacific in numerous guises, which is "indeed as good as lobster but larger and loads cheaper"; other items are "uneven" and "overpriced", while the venue "feels like a fast-food chain" or a "nightclub, with its noisy tables and music". / W1U 3RD; www.fancycrab.co.uk; @fancycrabuk.

Fannys Kebabs N16 NEW £21
92 Stoke Newington High St   020 3302 5831   1–1C
From Claude Compton and James Morris – the duo behind Claude's Kitchen, Amuse Bouche and Tommy Tucker – this little, new, stripped-down kebab canteen on Stoke Newington High Street, opened in spring 2018 on the back of a storming crowdfunding campaign and sell-out pop-up at the Sun & 13 Cantons in Soho. No survey feedback as yet – on the short menu: 'babs (with wrap, rice or salad), bar snacks and sides. / N16 7NY; www.fannyskebabs.com; @fannyskebabs; Tue-Sat, Mon 10.30 pm, Sun 3.30 pm.

Farang N5 £39 4 3 2
72 Highbury Park   020 7226 1609   9–1D
"Incredibly zingy Thai flavours" – "brilliant spicing and several ingredients that were new to me" – are establishing Seb Holmes's "reasonably priced" pop-up-gone-permanent (in the former premises of San Daniele, RIP) as a "foodie gem in Highbury". A few critics query "what's the fuss? The food's OK but the place is very cramped and nothing to get excited about overall". Much more numerous, though, are those who feel that "if it was located in central London it would have queues out the door every day". / N5 2XE; www.faranglondon.co.uk; @farangLDN; 10.30 pm; closed Tue-Fri L, closed Sun & Mon.

Farmacy W2 £56 2 3 4
74 Westbourne Grove   020 7221 0705   7–1B
"A fantastic vegan restaurant that your non vegan friends and kids will enjoy" is how fans proclaim Camilla Fayed's Californian-inspired Bayswater venture, which – though it does take some flak for the odd "taste-free" meal – particularly wins praise as a favoured brunch spot. / W2 5SH; www.farmacylondon.com; @farmacyuk; 10 pm, Sun 9.30 pm; SRA-Food Made Good – 2 stars.

Fayre Share E9 NEW £47
178-180 Victoria Park Rd   020 3960 7765   14–2C
In Hackney's picturesque Victoria Park village, a new 'family-style' feasting joint where all menu items can be served for 1, 2 or 4 people – in particular it's "ideal for families especially where children don't eat full portions". / E9 7HD; www.fayreshare.co.uk; @FayreShare; 10 pm.

Fenchurch Restaurant, Sky Garden EC3 £91 3️⃣2️⃣4️⃣

20 Fenchurch St 033 3772 0020 10–3D
Perched at the top of the City's 'Walkie-Talkie' tower, this 37th-floor venue has hot competition among London's recent spate of high-rise restaurant openings – but some fan feel "[it has the best views of them all]". The food is "very good", too – "delicious and well executed" – by Dan Fletcher, former head chef at The Square. "Shame it's so expensive", though.
/ EC3M 3BY; skygarden.london/fenchurch-restaurant; @SG_Fenchurch; 10.30 pm; booking max 7 may apply.

Fera at Claridge's, Claridge's Hotel W1 £122 4️⃣4️⃣4️⃣

49 Brook St 020 7107 8888 3–2B
"Seemingly doing just fine post-Simon Rogan" – this "beautiful" Art Deco chamber appears to have shrugged off the loss of the L'Enclume chef in April 2017, and although Matt Starling's ambitious cuisine is maybe a fraction less highly rated, most reports are of meals that are "perfect in every way" (even "if, like me, you were/are a Rogan fan, Fera should remain on your list!"). The "gracious and comfortable space" is "made to impress" (and "lends itself to romance or business"); "caring" service "puts you at your ease"; and where the cooking is concerned (experienced via the à la carte or the five-course and seven-course tasting menus) "you really feel the passion for the ingredients and, although stylish, there's no sacrifice of substance and flavour". Top Tip: "it can seem pricey unless set lunch is selected – £42 for an impeccably prepared three courses".
/ W1K 4HR; www.feraatclaridges.co.uk; @FeraAtClaridges; 10 pm.

Ferdi W1 £78 1️⃣1️⃣2️⃣

30 Shepherd Market 07375 538309 3–4B
"Hope they can get their act together..." This year-old London outpost of a models-and-celebs hangout in Paris's 1er arrondissement (where Kim and Kanye are apparently regulars) has failed to inspire much gastronomic excitement for its international comfort food since landing in Mayfair's cute Shepherd Market. / W1J 7QN; www.ferdi-restaurant.com; @ferdi.london; midnight.

La Ferme £46 3️⃣3️⃣3️⃣

154 Regent's Park Rd, NW1 020 7483 4492 9–3B NEW
102-104 Farringdon Rd, EC1 020 7837 5293 10–1A
"Very French and lovely" – the new NW1 branch of this 'bistronomic-driven' duo of rustic-style outfits serves creative, modern Gallic cuisine; and there's solidly good ratings, too, for the cosy café/deli original, just around the corner from Exmouth Market. (Also to be seen with stalls selling French dishes and produce at numerous London food markets).

Fernandez & Wells £54 3️⃣3️⃣3️⃣

43 Lexington St, W1 020 7734 1546 4–2C
55 Duke St, W1 020 7042 2774 3–2A
1-3 Denmark St, WC2 020 3302 9799 5–1A
Somerset Hs, Strand, WC2 020 7420 9408 2–2D
8 Exhibition Rd, SW7 020 7589 7473 6–2C
A small group of "appealing no-frills cafés with a rustic feel" in sought-after locations, including South Kensington and Somerset House. Already "stalwarts" on the London scene, they are "intimate" places providing "simple tapas with the best ingredients", plus "coffee or a glass of interesting wine"; and there's "no music, which aids conversation".
/ www.fernandezandwells.com; 11 pm, Sun 6 pm; St Anne's Court closed Sun.

Fez Mangal W11 £23 5 3 3
104 Ladbroke Grove   020 7229 3010   7–1A
"Excellent Turkish food at cheap 'n' cheerful prices" used to guarantee
queues at this "friendly" kebab house on Ladbroke Grove – "but now they've
expanded you can always get a table". Top Tip: "BYO – they have no licence
and don't charge corkage, so take a decent bottle of red, spend £15 per
head, and eat like a king". / W11 1PY; www.fezmangal.com; @FezMangal;
11.30 pm; no Amex.

Fiddies Italian Kitchen NW3 £38 3 3 2
13 New College Parade   020 7586 5050   9–2A
The "jolly owner" adds to the "very friendly" style of this "good cheap 'n'
cheerful Italian" in Swiss Cottage. "The food is unpretentious, such as mix-
and-match pasta/pizza with traditional fillings or toppings – nothing more,
but it's good." / NW3 5EP; fiddiesitaliankitchen.com; @FiddiesItalian.

Fields Beneath NW5 £11 3 2 3
52a Prince of Wales Rd   020 7424 8838   9–2B
Beneath Kentish Town station, this well-established and cosy neighbourhood
café "recently went all-vegan" and the change has been a hit – "it still
produces good coffee" and light dishes that are "always delicious".
"It just needs more space!" / NW5 3LN; www.thefieldsbeneath.com; Mon-Fri 4 pm,
Sat & Sun 5 pm; closed Mon-Sun D.

Fifteen N1 £73 2 2 2
15 Westland Place   020 3375 1515   13–1A
Only Jamie O's celebrity justifies the continued inclusion of this obscure
Hoxton venture – in its 2002 heyday the UK's most famous restaurant
by dint of the TV series of the same name. Nowadays, its once-cutting-edge
Hoxton location should put it on the hipster roadmap, yet it inspires few
reports, and such as do crop up continue a perennially lacklustre theme
regarding its Italian fare and service. (It is a non-profit organisation,
but since 2016 no longer trains the cohorts of youngsters that won it fame,
although some do pass through its kitchens as part of a nationwide
scheme). / N1 7LP; www.fifteen.net; @JamiesFifteen; 10.30 pm, Sun 9.30 pm;
booking max 12 may apply.

Finks Salt and Sweet N5 £37 3 4 4
70 Mountgrove Rd   020 7684 7189   9–1D
Straightforward but superior deli/café on a Highbury street corner that's
"fantastic any time of the day" – for the most part brunches, coffee and
cakes are the orders of the day, but there's more substantial fare served
on weekend evenings. / N5 2LT; finks.co.uk; @FinksLondon; Mon-Wed 7 pm, Fri &
Sat 11 pm, Thu 10.30 pm, Sun 5 pm; closed Sun D.

Fischer's W1 £66 3 3 4
50 Marylebone High St   020 7466 5501   2–1A
"Step into old-world Vienna" at Corbin & King's "elegant" re-creation of a
"classic Austrian-themed café" (with menu to match) in Marylebone. Its
strongest features are the "splendid" atmosphere – "cosy, buzzy and oozing
charm" – and "very pleasant service", but its "reliable, if unadventurous
dishes" (schnitzel, veal, etc) received a consistently good rep this year:
"we visit Austria twice a year and when we need an Austrian food fix
we always go here!" Top Tip: "great fun for a cake stop". / W1U 5HN;
www.fischers.co.uk; @FischersLondon; 11 pm, Sun 10.30 pm.

Fish Central EC1 £33 3 2 2
149-155 Central St   020 7253 4970   13–1A
This "unique" and "good value" Clerkenwell chippy scores well for "perfect
fish, cooked simply, plus a decent set of basic wines". / EC1V 8AP;
www.fishcentral.co.uk; @fishcentral1968; Mon-Thu, Sat 10.30 pm, Fri 11 pm;
closed Sun.

FSA RATINGS: FROM 1 POOR — 5 EXCEPTIONAL

Fish in a Tie SW11   £38   3 3 3
105 Falcon Rd   020 7924 1913   11–1C
"Good value" all round has long been the defining characteristic of this long-
serving bistro, near Clapham Junction station. Despite the name, it's not
just a fish and seafood place, with at least as many meat dishes as fish
options featuring on the menu. / SW11 2PF; www.fishinatie.com; 11.30 pm,
Sun 10.30 pm.

Fish Market EC2   £60   3 2 2
16a New St   020 3503 0790   10–2D
This solid performer from D&D London occupies a converted City
warehouse near Liverpool Street. The "tables are slightly crowded", but the
"excellent fish" lives up to its name. / EC2M 4TR;
www.fishmarket-restaurant.co.uk; @FishMarketNS; 10.30 pm; closed Sun.

fish! SE1   £59   3 2 2
Cathedral St   020 7407 3803   10–4C
"Bustling, loud and lively", "glass-enclosed" operation a two-minute step
from foodie Borough Market. Its selection of fish is "a tad pricey",
but generally "beautifully cooked". / SE1 9AL; www.fishkitchen.co.uk;
@fishborough; 9.30 pm, Sun 3 pm.

Fishworks   £69   3 2 2
7-9 Swallow St, W1   020 7734 5813   4–4C
89 Marylebone High St, W1   020 7935 9796   2–1A
"You enter through the front shop full of fresh fish" at these straightforward
seafood bistros just off Piccadilly Circus and in Marylebone (surviving
branches of what was once a national chain). You don't get fireworks,
but you do get "excellent simple fish", "reliably prepared" at "reasonable
prices" and the Swallow Street branch in particular is brilliantly located.
/ www.fishworks.co.uk; W1B 10.30 pm, Fri & Sat 11 pm; W1U 10.30 pm.

Fiume SW8   £56   3 4 3
Circus West Village, Sopwith Way   020 3904 9010   11–1C
"A real asset to Battersea Power Station's restaurant scene" – this 120-
cover D&D London yearling was one of the first to open in the new
development and has a fine Thames-view location with copious outside
tables. So long as you don't go with expectations raised too high by all the
PR about input from star chef Francesco Mazzei, it's "a very enjoyable spot"
with "decent food", "friendly service" and "chic surroundings". "Handy for
riverboat trips going east", too. / SW8 5BN;
www.danddlondon.com/restaurant/fiume; @FiumeLondon; Tue-Sat, Mon 10 pm,
Sun 9 pm; closed Mon L.

The Five Fields SW3   £106   5 5 4
8-9 Blacklands Ter   020 7838 1082   6–2D
"Fabulous on all levels" – Taylor Bonnyman's "utterly exceptional" dining
room, "hidden in the heart of Chelsea" provides "not only a real treat, but a
genuinely interesting gastronomic experience". "Beautifully crafted, creative
food combinations are served with professional yet genuine charm"
in "such a beautiful space". "It's difficult to find any fault" – if you tried hard
you might say that the "decor is a bit 'posh restaurant'". / SW3 2SP;
www.fivefieldsrestaurant.com; @The5Fields; 10 pm; closed Mon-Fri L, closed
Sat & Sun; No trainers.

Five Guys   £19   3 2 2
"Elevating the fast food experience" – this fast-growing US-based chain
provides "a better class of quick burger" (with a good variety of toppings),
plus "fries that are so savoury, and so-tasty milkshakes almost too thick
to suck through a straw!" ("just don't watch the calories…"). On the
downside, "the ambience leaves a lot to be desired: it feels like a less
glamorous McDonalds!" / @FiveGuysUK; 11 pm, Thu-Sat midnight.

500 N19 £53 **4** **3** **2**
782 Holloway Rd 020 7272 3406 9–1C
"Almost invisible from the outside", this 10-year-old local near Archway makes you feel like you're in Italy" and serves "excellent Sardinian/Sicilian food". The name is a tribute to founder chef Mario Magli's favourite Fiat Cinquecento, and a nod to the minuscule proportions of the venue ("whose hard walls can make it noisy"). / N19 3JH; www.500restaurant.co.uk; @500restaurant; 10 pm, Sun 9 pm; Mon-Thu D only, Fri-Sun open L & D.

500 Degrees SE24 £23 **3** **2** **2**
Herne Hill, 153a Dulwich Rd 020 7274 8200 11–2D
"Cheap 'n' cheerful, and very authentic", this Herne Hill two-year-old is an "excellent neighbourhood pizzeria". The name refers to the temperature its wood-fired oven must reach to cook its pizzas: there is nothing else on the menu beyond a quartet of salads. / SE24 \N; www.500degrees.co; @500degreesuk; 11 pm, Sun 10 pm.

Flat Iron £32 **3** **4** **4**
17 Beak St, W1 020 3019 2353 4–2B
17 Henrietta St, WC2 020 3019 4212 5–3C
9 Denmark St, WC2 no tel 5–1A
46 Golborne Rd, W10 no tel 7–1A
47-51 Caledonian Rd, N1 no tel 9–3D **NEW**
77 Curtain Rd, EC2 no tel 13–1B
"If steak 'n' chips is what you want, then it's hard to beat", this "simple, yet very effective" small chain, which is "all about doing just one thing and doing it right": "superbly cooked" meat from a "limited choice" of cuts (majoring in the 'flat iron' itself) plus salad, "no starters or dessert, but a free ice cream cone as you leave". "A simple set up", it inspired "no complaints" this year, even if – with expansion, including a new King's Cross branch – ratings are not quite as exciting as once they were. / www.flatironsteak.co.uk; midnight, Sun 11.30pm; EC2 11 pm; W1F 11 pm, Thu 11.30 pm, Fri & Sat midnight, Sun 10.30 pm; no bookings.

Flat Three W11 £90 **4** **4** **3**
120-122 Holland Park Ave 020 7792 8987 7–2A
The "Nordic-Korean-Japanese fusion cooking" at this experiment-driven, "forage-style restaurant" in Holland Park is a "real surprise" and deserves wider recognition. The "top-quality ingredients" include "excellent fish and seafood", and much of the distinctive flavouring comes from fermentation processes. The venue is a well-designed basement, and there are plenty of vegan options on the tasting menus. / W11 4UA; www.flatthree.london; @infoflat3; 9.30 pm; closed Tue-Thu L, closed Sun & Mon.

Flat White W1 £10 **4** **4** **3**
17 Berwick St 020 7734 0370 4–2D
"London's original artisanal Kiwi coffee shop" still makes "a wonderful place to chill any day of the week" down to its "easy breezy Antipodean vibe", plus "a wide variety of music, ever-charming staff and an eclectic mix of Berwick Street locals!". All this, plus epic brews and "eggs to go with the great caffeine". / W1F 0PT; www.flatwhitesoho.co.uk; @flatwhitesoho; 6 pm; L only; cash only; no booking.

Flesh and Buns WC2 £53 **2** **3** **3**
41 Earlham St 020 7632 9500 5–2C
This "fun and exciting" Soho basement is a Japanese take on the Asian steamed bun phenomenon. Part of the Bone Daddies group, fans say its dishes are "always superbly cooked and presented", but ratings were dragged down this year by a significant minority who reckon it's just "overpriced and quite average". Top Tip: oft-nominated for its brunch. / WC2H 9LX; www.bonedaddies.com/restaurant/flesh-and-buns; @FleshandBuns; 10 pm, Wed-Sat 11 pm, Sun 9.30 pm; booking max 8 may apply.

Flora Indica SW5 £47 **4** **3** **3**
242 Old Brompton Rd   020 7370 4450   6–2A
"Hitting the spot after a few false starts while transforming from Mr Wing (RIP)" – the former long-term occupant of this two-level (ground and basement) Earl's Court venue – this interesting yearling is decked out with distinctive steampunk flourishes to its contemporary curry house decor, and wins praise for food that's "spot on and encourages exploration of new flavours mainly from northern and central India, interpreted in a modern style". / SW5 0DE; flora-indica.com/flora03; @Flora_Indica; midnight.

Flotsam and Jetsam SW17 £24 **3** **2** **3**
4 Bellevue Parade   020 8672 7639   11–2C
This "phenomenally popular" cafe overlooking Wandsworth Common is a "tight ship run by a team of friendly Antipodeans" – "the only downside is that it's just not big enough". "Child and dog-friendly", naturally, it is "coffee heaven" and "great for a quick breakfast with the kids". / SW17 7EQ; www.flotsamandjetsamcafe.co.uk; @_flotsam_jetsam; Mon-Fri 3 pm, Sat & Sun 4 pm; closed Mon-Sun D; no booking.

Flour & Grape SE1 £47 **3** **4** **3**
214 Bermondsey St   020 7407 4682   10–4D
Limited but enthusiastic feedback on this casual spot in Bermondsey (once known as Antico) where the focus is on fresh, handmade pasta and a selection of Italian wines. They also run the gin bar downstairs ('214 Bermondsey'). / SE1 3TQ; www.flourandgrape.com; @flourandgrape; 11 pm, Sun 10 pm; closed Mon; booking max 6 may apply.

FM Mangal SE5 £36 **3** **3** **3**
54 Camberwell Church St   020 7701 6677   1–3C
"Killer charred sumac onions, fabulously tasty grilled flatbreads and brilliant charcoal-grilled meats" win high ratings for this "cheap 'n' cheerful" Turkish grill – "a great neighbourhood gem" in Camberwell. / SE5 8QZ; midnight; no Amex; no booking.

Foley's W1 £47 **4** **4** **3**
23 Foley St   020 3137 1302   2–1B
"Different flavours" from an "original" menu of eclectic inspiration win enthusiastic (if slightly limited) feedback for ex-Palomar chef Mitz Vora's "warm and friendly" Fitzrovia two-year-old (which avoided a repeat of last year's uneven feedback in the current survey). / W1W 6DU; www.foleysrestaurant.co.uk; @foleyslondon; Wed-Sat 11 pm.

Forest Bar & Kitchen E17 NEW £22
149 Forest Rd   020 8281 4428   1–1D
The husband-and-wife team behind Forest Wines just a few doors down launched this neighbourhood wine bar in early 2018, providing a seasonal, modern European menu, complemented by a list of mostly organic and biodynamic vino. No survey reports yet, but looks worth a look when down Walthamstow way. / E17 6HE; forestbarandkitchen.com; @forestbarkitchn; Tue-Sat, Mon 10.30 pm, Sun 3.30 pm.

Forman's E3 £53 **4** **3** **2**
Stour Rd, Fish Island   020 8525 2365   1–1D
Within a famous salmon smokery by the River Lea (a modern building, though the business has been on the site for over a century) – this venue "overlooks the Olympic stadium" (and offers special menus for West Ham home games). Limited feedback on its fish-based menu, but such as exists is all-round very upbeat: "I love it!". / E3 2NT; www.formans.co.uk/restaurant; @formanslondon; Thu-Sat 11 pm, Sun 5 pm; closed Thu & Fri L closed Sun D, closed Mon & Tue & Wed.

Fortnum & Mason,
The Diamond Jubilee Tea Salon W1   £72   3 4 4

181 Piccadilly   020 7734 8040   3–3D

"Nowhere compares to the exquisite setting and experience of Fortnum
& Mason high tea", according to fans of the "delicious sandwiches
(made with interesting breads), excellent selection of teas and best-ever
drinking chocolate" graciously served on the third floor of The Queen's
favourite grocer. "A lovely place for a special occasion – it's become very
expensive, but this doesn't seem to dent the enthusiasm of the hordes
of family groups, ladies-who-lunch and tourists!". "It can be a bit too much
food, but they offer you a doggy bag of the uneaten cakes, jam, scones…"
/ W1A 1ER; www.fortnumandmason.com; @Fortnums; 9.30 pm, Sun 6 pm; closed
Sun D.

The Parlour,
Fortnum & Mason W1   £38   3 3 3

181 Piccadilly   0845 6025694   3–3D

"We treated our god-daughter to a tenth birthday ice cream (her pick
of venue) accompanied by her parents and younger sister: the experience
was wonderful (and delicious)!" This first floor café within the famous
Piccadilly grocers is "a great place to bring the kids for a special teatime
treat", where "they can have fun creating their own yummy concoctions
from the wide choice of flavours and all the extra toppings". "Excellent
coffee" and "delicious" light savouries too ("such as Welsh rarebit, smoked
salmon etc"). / W1A 1ER; www.fortnumandmason.com; 8 pm, Sun 5 pm; closed
Sun D.

45 Jermyn Street SW1   £68   3 4 4

45 Jermyn Street, St. James's   020 7205 4545   3–3D

"Slightly theatrical service" of Beef Wellington and traditional flambé dishes
from trolleys adds to the retro appeal and glamorous atmosphere
of Fortnum & Mason's chic, St James's restaurant (whose cocktail bar,
and witty evoking of a "bygone era", contrasts sharply with the more
'maiden aunt' styling of The Fountain, RIP, which it replaced a couple
of years ago). It's a useful location, nominated for business and breakfast –
often at the same time! / SW1Y 6DN; www.45jermynst.com; @45JermynSt;
11.30 pm, Sun 10.30 pm; closed Sun D.

40 Maltby Street SE1   £68   4 4 3

40 Maltby St   020 7237 9247   10–4D

"Amazing cooking in the tiniest of kitchens" – chef Steve Williams works
with "great seasonal produce" at this cult foodie destination – a wine
warehouse under the railway arches leading to London Bridge station,
with the menu chalked up on a blackboard. "The most adventurous natural
wine list is paired with great cuisine, and the knowledgeable and personable
staff match them if asked." / SE1 3PA; www.40maltbystreet.com;
@40maltbystreet; 9.30 pm; closed Mon, Tue, Wed L, Thu L, Sat D & Sun; no Amex;
no booking.

Forza Win SE15   £48   3 4 3

Unit 4.1, 133 Copeland Rd   020 7732 9012   1–4D

A "bright and airy" warehouse conversion (formerly a cash & carry) is home
to this previously roving set-up – a communal-seating, vibey space, praised
for its "delicious Italian food and very friendly service". / SE15 3SN;
www.forzawin.com; @forzawin; Wed-Sat 11.30 pm, Sun 4 pm; closed Sun D, closed
Mon & Tue.

400 Rabbits £26 3 3 2
143 Evelina Rd, SE15   020 7732 4115   1–4D
30-32 Westow St, SE19   020 8771 6249   1–1D
Crystal Palace 'sodo' pizza spot which has also hopped into Nunhead (just on the border of Peckham) with its second London site – a bright canteen with hard, school-type chairs. No feedback on the original, but the food is well-rated here: wood-fired and with British rye flour sourdough bases.

The Four Seasons £52 5 1 1
11 Gerrard St, W1   020 7287 0900   5–3A NEW
12 Gerrard St, W1   020 7494 0870   5–3A
23 Wardour St, W1   020 7287 9995   5–3A
84 Queensway, W2   020 7229 4320   7–2C
"It's a bit of a dive" with "charmless" service ("you have to queue even if you've booked") but everyone raves about the "divine" duck – "the best in London" – and other "brilliant barbecued meats and roast pork" at these clattery canteens in Chinatown and Bayswater. / www.fs-restaurants.co.uk; 11pm-midnight.

Fox & Grapes SW19 £54 3 3 3
9 Camp Rd   020 8619 1300   11–2A
"Wonderfully situated on the edge of Wimbledon Common", this attractive pub is ideal for recuperating "after a brisk walk" ("perfect for a boozy Sunday lunch"). "Prices are a bit punchy" for grub that's "not high end" but it delivers "high-quality pub food" that's "always decent". / SW19 4UN; www.foxandgrapeswimbledon.co.uk; @thefoxandgrapes; 11 pm, Sun 10.30 pm.

The Fox and Anchor EC1 £53 2 2 3
115 Charterhouse St   020 7250 1300   10–1B
For "good, old-London pub atmosphere and straightforward food", this Victorian institution near Smithfield Market is a perennial, and – as one of the few watering holes licenced from the early hours to serve market traders – is most famous for "a quality traditional breakfast, served with a pint of Guinness". / EC1M 6AA; www.foxandanchor.com; @foxanchor; 9.30 pm, Sun 6 pm.

Foxlow £55 2 2 2
Lower James St, W1   020 7680 2710   4–3C
15-19 Bedford Hill, SW12   020 7680 2700   11–2C
St John St, EC1   020 7014 8070   10–2A
"Excellent steaks and burgers" do win a sizeable band of fans for the Hawksmoor group's budget chain of spin-offs, but – while decent enough – they seem lacklustre for a business associated with such a key brand: detractors don't say they're appalling or anything, just a bit... meh. The Chiswick branch failed to gain traction and shut up shop this year. / www.foxlow.co.uk; @FoxlowTweets; 10 pm, Fri & Sat 10.30 pm, Sun 9 pm; EC1 10.30 pm, Sun 3.30 pm ; EC1 closed Sun D; SRA-Food Made Good – 3 stars.

Franco Manca £30 2 2 2
"Despite the ever-expanding franchise", the pizzas are "solidly enjoyable and a cut above" ("you've just got to love the sourdough bases" and "quality toppings"), according to the hordes of fans of the "buzzing, busy and rather cramped" branches of this crazily expanding chain, which nowadays is the survey's "go-to for a cheap 'n' cheerful family pizza", eclipsing the once-mighty PizzaExpress in the level of interest it generates. There's no hiding its steadily declining ratings, though, with a sentiment that "while it's still usually very reliable, standards have slipped over repeat visits"; for its harshest critics the effect is now "Frankly Manky!". / www.francomanca.co.uk; 10 pm, Wed-Sat 11 pm; no bookings.

Franco's SW1 £74 3|4|4
61 Jermyn St 020 7499 2211 3–3C
"Simultaneously up-to-date and old-school" – one of London's oldest Italians (dating from 1946) makes an ideal business lunch spot in St James's, with a busy, bustling atmosphere that's formal but "not too serious", and with "excellent cooking and friendly service". Perhaps unsurprisingly, it is also rather "expensive". Top Tip: "breakfast is always good here… especially if someone else is paying!". / SW1Y 6LX; www.francoslondon.com; @francoslondon; 10.30 pm, Sun 10 pm; closed Sun.

Franklins SE22 £56 3|2|2
157 Lordship Ln 020 8299 9598 1–4D
"High-quality" traditional British fare has made this pub conversion an East Dulwich fixture over the past two decades; and it now has its own farm shop over the road. "A good find for lunch near Dulwich Picture Gallery". Top Tip: "quality breakfast and a great Sunday lunch too". / SE22 8HX; www.franklinsrestaurant.com; @frankinsse22; 10.30 pm, Sun 10 pm; no Amex.

Frantoio SW10 £68 3|4|4
397 King's Rd 020 7352 4146 6–3B
Now in its 20th year, this World's End trattoria feels "like a private club" thanks to the "consistently warm welcome" extended by its charismatic owner, Bucci. It's a "family favourite" for both "fun and quality", and "if the food is not always quite perfect, the atmosphere and conviviality make up for that!". / SW10 0LR; www.frantoio.co.uk; 11 pm.

Freak Scene W1 NEW £47 5|3|4
54 Frith St 07561 394 497 5–2A
Ex-Nobu head chef Scott Hallsworth and Phar Shaweewan's storming pan-Asian pop-up has found a permanent home in Soho, in the small bar premises that formerly housed the original Barrafina. Early reports suggest it's a worthy successor and award full marks to its super-freaky, tapas-y flavour-bomb dishes of Asian-Latino inspiration, washed down with a selection of cocktails. / W1D 4SL; freakscene.london; @freakscene.

Frederick's N1 £66 3|4|5
106 Camden Passage 020 7359 2888 9–3D
"None of its charm has been lost over the years", say fans of this "romantic" and "spacious" Islington stalwart, where the best spot is "eating on the terrace overlooking the lovely garden". "The cooking is old school, but very enjoyable". / N1 8EG; www.fredericks.co.uk; @fredericks_n1; 11 pm; closed Sun.

Frenchie WC2 £79 3|2|2
18 Henrietta St 020 7836 4422 5–3C
Perhaps the most famous alumnus of Jamie Oliver's Fifteen – Gregory Marchand (aka 'Frenchie') launched his Covent Garden operation a couple of years ago as a London spin-off to his first 'Frenchie', which opened in Paris in 2009. With its shortish menu of "quirky" Gallic dishes, "eclectic" wine list and "fun" (if "noisy") style, it was one of the hits of last year. This year, however, its ratings dipped, and – while fans still praise its "well-crafted and tasty dishes" – there are a few critics to whom it seems "totally overrated". Post-survey in July 2018, Marchand transferred the executive chef of his Parisian group, Dale Sutton, to London, presumably to help pep things up a bit? / WC2E 8QH; www.frenchiecoventgarden.com; @frenchiecoventgarden; 11 pm, Sun 10 pm.

The Frog £71 5 5 4

35 Southampton St, WC2   020 7199 8370   5–3D
45-47 Hoxton Square, N1   020 3813 9832   13–B1

"A new star in London's dining scene!" – Adam Handling's "outstanding" year-old Covent Garden branch is proving just as big a smash hit as his E1 original (which, in mid 2018, moved to a new, 60-cover site on the corner of Hoxton Square, together with a bar and coffee shop). His "clever and delicious" British tapas feature "brilliant taste combinations" yet "without being prissy or overly expensive"; while the "chilled" atmosphere is "that so hard-to-achieve balance of professionalism with perfect relaxation and excitement". Service, too, gets a big thumbs up: "top class and efficient but not obtrusive, and so friendly". See also Belmond Cadogan Hotel. / www.thefrogrestaurant.com; @TheFrogE1.

La Fromagerie £48 3 3 3

2-6 Moxon St, W1   020 7935 0341   3–1A
52 Lamb's Conduit St, WC1   020 7242 1044   2–1D
30 Highbury Park, N5   020 7359 7440   9–2D

"Cheese shop by day, great little bistro by night – highly recommended" is a typically enthusiastic response to this popular and upmarket trio in Marylebone, Bloomsbury and Highbury. The quote is slightly misleading, since all three have pretty serious breakfast and brunch offerings through the day, with "delicious food and some beautiful vegetable combinations". But it is their cheese selection – from the UK, Ireland, France and Italy – that wins them renown. / www.lafromagerie.co.uk; @LaFromagerieUK.

The Frontline Club W2 £60 3 3 4

13 Norfolk Pl   020 7479 8960   7–1D

"Handy in the culinary desert that is Paddington" – this well-appointed venue is the ground floor of a club dedicated to war reporters (expect some eye-catching photo-reportage on the walls). It's a "comfortable setting" for food that's "relatively simple" but "remarkably good in the context of the general quality of restaurants in the vicinity". / W2 1QJ; www.frontlineclub.com; @frontlineclub; 11 pm; closed Sat L, closed Sun; booking max 6 may apply.

Fumo WC2 £61 3 3 3

37 St Martin's Lane   020 3778 0430   5–4C

"A gem right next to the ENO", this two-year-old Italian cicchetti (small plates) venue from the San Carlo group is "a great addition to the theatre district". Most reporters are very happy with the food – "been twice, and both visits produced at least one truly memorable dish". / WC2N 4JS; www.sancarlofumo.co.uk/fumo-london; @sancarlo_fumo; Mon-Thu 11.30 pm, Fri & Sat midnight, Sun 10.30 pm.

Gaby's WC2 £36 3 2 2

30 Charing Cross Rd   020 7836 4233   5–3B

"A staple of Theatreland", this grungy deli by Leicester Square (apparently Jeremy Corbyn's favourite restaurant) "is never going to win any awards for its decor" ("too dismal to qualify even as raffish"). The reason it's treasured by regulars, rich and poor alike, is the "ever-charming Gaby", who has been behind the counter most days since 1965, and his selection of "authentic, unmodernised Middle Eastern food", incorporating "falafel to die for", "very good value salt beef sandwiches" and "highly tasty mixed salad plates". "Thank heavens the aristocratic freeholder hasn't managed to prise it out of its premises yet – go while it's still there!". / WC2H 0DE; midnight, Sun 10 pm; no Amex.

Gallery Mess,
Saatchi Gallery SW3 £53 2️⃣3️⃣3️⃣
Duke of Yorks HQ, Kings Rd   020 7730 8135   6–2D
A "great sunny terrace" for warm weather adds to the appeal of this art-hung space – part of the impressive former barracks housing the Saatchi Gallery and a handy all-day dining (and afternoon tea) venue near Sloane Square. No-one suggests the food here will set the world on fire, however. / SW3 4RY; www.saatchigallery.com/gallerymess; @gallerymess; 11 pm, Sun 6 pm; closed Sun D.

Galley N1 £56 3️⃣3️⃣3️⃣
105-106 Upper St   020 3670 0740   9–3D
"A restaurant for a proper meal on Upper Street" – former Randall & Aubin head chef Marcel Grzyb teamed up with his sister Oriona Robb to create this welcoming yearling: "the cooking won't knock your socks off but everything is nicely done and it is a good, safe choice". / N1 1QN; www.galleylondon.co.uk; @Galleylondon; 11 pm.

Gallipoli £40 2️⃣3️⃣3️⃣
102 Upper St, N1   020 7359 0630   9–3D
120 Upper St, N1   020 7226 8099   9–3D
"Reliably decent Turkish food" and a "friendly, jolly atmosphere" make this pair of Ottoman-themed cafés on Upper Street in Islington a "great standby for birthday celebrations or big groups". / www.cafegallipoli.com; @CafeGallipoli; 11 pm, Fri & Sat midnight.

Galvin at the Athenaeum W1 £66 3️⃣3️⃣2️⃣
Athenaeum Hotel, 116 Piccadilly   020 7640 3333   3–4B
Feedback is positive about the Galvin Bros' year-old revamp of this well-known Art Deco dining room, lauding its "good, mainly British cuisine", civilised location ("lovely on a sunny day, overlooking Green Park") and "high standards" generally. Its ratings are undercut, though, by incidents of "routine" cooking, and a sense that "some of its former quirkiness was lost in the (2016) makeover". Top Tip: "wonderful, luxurious afternoon tea". / W1J 7BJ; www.athenaeumhotel.com; @galvinathenaeum; midnight, Sun 11 pm.

Galvin at Windows,
Park Lane London Hilton Hotel W1 £114 2️⃣3️⃣5️⃣
22 Park Ln   020 7208 4021   3–4A
"Truly spectacular panoramas across Buckingham Palace" (The Queen has, it is said, never forgiven them for building this place) make this 28th-floor dining room a big romantic favourite; and similarly, if on business, "clients can't help but be impressed with the outlook". With its "lovely" cooking and "excellent service" it's hard to fault generally, other than that, predictably, "it's not very competitively priced!" Top Tip: cheapskates can get all the view for the price of a cocktail in the adjoining bar. / W1K 1BE; www.galvinatwindows.com; @GalvinatWindows; Mon-Wed 10 pm, Thu-Sat 10.30 pm, Sun 3 pm; closed Sat L closed Sun D; No trainers; booking max 5 may apply.

Galvin HOP E1 £57 2️⃣2️⃣3️⃣
35 Spital Sq   020 7299 0404   13–2B
"Café A Vin changed into Galvin HOP" a couple of years ago and feedback on the Galvins' posh gastropub near Spitalfields Market (and adjacent to Galvin La Chapelle) is rather limited and mixed. "The food is perhaps a notch lower than the previous incarnation", but attractions include "good steaks", and, as ever, that "you can also sit outside at the front or in the garden, which is nice in good weather". / E1 6DY; www.galvinrestaurants.com/section/62/1/galvinhop; @Galvin_brothers; 10.30 pm, Sun 9.30 pm; booking max 5 may apply.

Galvin La Chapelle E1 £85 **4**|**4**|**5**

35 Spital Sq   020 7299 0400   13–2B

The "exciting and gorgeous" setting (a "spectacular" conversion of a Victorian school chapel) helps create "a certain aura" – fitting both romantic dinners and power lunching – at the Galvin Bros' Spitalfields fixture. Its "fabulous standard" of modern French cuisine and "professional but easy-going service" won it more consistent praise this year as one of the best all-rounders in the City, and, some would say, in town. / E1 6DY; www.galvinlachapelle.com; @galvin_brothers; 10.30 pm, Sun 10 pm; No trainers; booking max 8 may apply.

The Game Bird at The Stafford London SW1 £73 **3**|**5**|**3**

16-18 St James's Place   020 7518 1234   3–4C

"A great addition to this hidden gem of a hotel" in St James's – this "beautiful" dining room affords "lots of space" to diners and inspires nothing but rave reviews (and numerous nominations as a top spot for business entertaining). The "traditional British food with a twist" is "beautifully presented, with bags of taste, and the matching wines are bang on". Top Tip: as the name hints: "it's an excellent choice during the game season". / SW1A 1NJ; thestaffordlondon.com/the-game-bird; @TheGameBirdLON; 10 pm.

Ganapati SE15 £46 **4**|**3**|**3**

38 Holly Grove   020 7277 2928   1–4D

"The home-made parathas, masala dosas and pickles are the stuff of dreams" at this early pioneer of the Peckham food scene – "a favourite for many years". The "delicious South Indian regional food" comes courtesy of Claire Fisher, who was inspired to open the venue after her travels. One or two reporters, though, feel that while it's "a nice neighbourhood restaurant", it "never quite lives up to our high expectations" nowadays. / SE15 5DF; www.ganapatirestaurant.com; 10.30 pm, Sun 10 pm; closed Mon; no Amex.

Garden Cafe at the Garden Museum SE1 £45 **3**|**2**|**3**

5 Lambeth Palace Rd   020 7401 8865   2–4D

"Not just a museum cafe but a proper destination restaurant" – this year-old venue in a copper-and-glass pavilion at Lambeth's Garden Museum is a "really brilliant addition to what is otherwise a rather poorly served corner of London". "Fresh honest flavours are simply but interestingly prepared" by chefs Harry Kaufman (ex-St John Bread & Wine) and George Ryle (ex-Padella and Primeur). / SE1 7LB; www.gardenmuseum.org.uk; @GardenMuseumLDN; Mon, Wed & Thu, Sun 5 pm, Tue, Fri 10 pm, Sat 3.30 pm; closed Mon, Wed & Thu, Sat & Sun D; no Amex; Booking max 12 may apply.

Le Garrick WC2 £55 **3**|**3**|**4**

10-12 Garrick St   020 7240 7649   5–3C

"A far cry from tourist-land on its doorstep!" – this cute little bistro in Covent Garden has "a wonderful and unexpectedly intimate atmosphere" and can be "a brilliant find for pre-/post- theatre" thanks to its "lovely French dishes". / WC2E 9BH; www.legarrick.co.uk; @le_garrick; midnight, Sun 5 pm; closed Sun D.

The Garrison SE1 £51 **3**|**2**|**3**

99 Bermondsey St   020 7089 9355   10–4D

A pioneer of the Bermondsey food scene, this former pub with "quirky, fun decor" "remains a favourite, with an ever-changing menu, beautifully executed". It stays true to its prior calling with "good real ale", and "can get a bit noisy" when full. / SE1 3XB; www.thegarrison.co.uk; @TheGarrisonSE1; midnight, Sun 11 pm.

Gastronhome SW11 £71 543

59 Lavender Hill, London   020 3417 5639   11–2C

"Out-of-the-way Gallic treasure" that's worth the detour to Lavender Hill
(near Clapham Junction), for Damien Fremont's traditional French cuisine
'with a modern touch'. It attracts the highest ratings and fulsome praise this
year, especially for the "sublime" five-course tasting menu. Fremont and his
co-founder, fellow Frenchman Christopher Nespoux, who runs the front
of house, first met working at the Ritz Club 10 years ago. / SW11 \N;
www.gastronhome.co.uk; @gastronhome1; 10:15 pm; closed Mon & Sun; No jeans.

The Gate £54 423

22-24 Seymour Place, W1   020 7724 6656   2–2A
51 Queen Caroline St, W6   020 8748 6932   8–2C
370 St John St, EC1   020 7278 5483   9–3D

Bravos abound for the "superb" dishes ("imaginative and ambitious
conceptions whose flavours make non-vegetarians desist from any pity about
a lack of meat!") at these accomplished veggies, which in recent years have
added outlets in Seymour Village and Sadler's Wells to the "legendary", long-
standing original (just south of Hammersmith Broadway). "However, quality
of service and staff response can be variable" at all branches, and this
is most particularly the case at W1, which needs to "up its game" generally,
not least its cooking, as a number of regulars discern "a big drop
in standards since it opened". / www.thegaterestaurants.com; @gaterestaurant;
10.30 pm; W1 Sun 9.45 pm; W6 Sun 9.30 pm.

Gaucho £89 222

Steaks are "perfectly nice" but prices are "silly" at this glossy, "dimly lit"
Argentinian steak house chain (whose Latino wine list is also a feature) –
perhaps explaining why it went into administration in summer 2018. Under
a rescue package that saw sibling brand Cau shut down, former CEO
Martin Williams (who left in 2014 to set up M Restaurants) is returning
to the helm. As of September 2018, it remains to be seen how many of the
12 London venues will stay open. / www.gauchorestaurants.co.uk; @gauchogroup;
11 pm, Thu-Sat midnight ; EC3 & EC1 closed Sat & Sun, WC2 & EC2 closed
Sat L & Sun.

Gauthier Soho W1 £79 544

21 Romilly St   020 7494 3111   5–3A

"Stepping through that front door (you ring to enter) takes you into a better
world" at Alexis Gauthier's "quirky", converted townhouse in Soho, which
provides "some of the best French cooking in London". "The cuisine achieves
a masterful balance of traditional technique applied to the finest ingredients
– flavour, intensity, plus beautiful presentation"; and the "empathic service"
is "friendly but always professional". The venue's "distinctiveness continues
into the maze of cosy yet elegant rooms" spread "higgledy piggledy" over
a couple of floors, and "with only a few tables in each room", the style
is "peaceful" going on "seductive". Why Michelin took their star away is an
utter mystery. Top Tips – "the eight-course tasting menu is a fabulous foodie
experience; the three-course De Luxe lunch is an absolute steal";
"the devoted vegan tasting menu is superb"; last but not least, "the truffle
risotto is a 'Desert Island Dish'". / W1D 5AF; www.gauthiersoho.co.uk;
@GauthierSoho; 11 pm, Sun 10.30 pm; closed Mon & Sun; booking max 7 may
apply.

Le Gavroche W1 £137 4 5 4
43 Upper Brook St 020 7408 0881 3–2A
"When everywhere else seems forced to bow to fashion and follow the latest trend, Le Gavroche sails serenely on, delighting those who appreciate the true heart and spirit of gastronomy!!" Michel Roux Jr's Mayfair "haute cuisine temple" (here since 1982, founded by his father Albert in Chelsea in 1967) may "in some respects reflect an earlier era of fine dining", with its "fabulous" Gallic cuisine ("superb Omelette Rothschild", "soufflé Suissesse to die for!"...), but that merely reinforces its position as "an absolute favourite" for its massive following, who confirm that "every mouthful is a delight". "Very warm and welcoming staff have absolutely nailed the balance in service, friendliness and knowledge" and – especially for a basement – the very "grown up" dining room is supremely "cosy, luxurious and celebratory". "As well as top notch food, the wine list is spectacular and although there are oligarch-friendly, five-figure bottles, if you look there are some gems for those willing and able to pay more for a special wine". And "the great man's regular presence is one of the special things about Le Gavroche" – "Michel told us some of the history of the restaurant and really made us welcome!" A visit is a second-mortgage job, of course, but there's a "marvellous value set lunch (even if you do have to book it three months in advance)". / W1K 7QR; www.le-gavroche.co.uk; @michelrouxjr; 10 pm; closed Sat L, closed Sun & Mon; Jacket required.

Gaylord W1 £60 3 3 3
79-81 Mortimer St 020 7580 3615 2–1B
This Fitzrovia veteran, "the ultimate traditional Indian", still cooks dishes in a tandoor oven imported in 1966, and believed to be the first in the UK. The menu has been successfully modernised in recent years, with such choices as 'paneer jalfrezi tacos' giving "an Indian twist to the Mexican street-food favourite". / W1W 7SJ; www.gaylordlondon.com; @gaylord_london; 10.45 pm, Sun 10.30 pm.

Gazelle W1 NEW
48 Albemarle St 020 7751 5812 3–3C
Scottish chef Rob Roy Cameron (whose career includes a stint as pastry chef at the legendary El Bulli) runs the first-floor restaurant, while star-mixologist Tony Conigliaro (who started out life at Zetter before moving on to 69 Colebrooke Row and Untitled in Hackney) looks after the second-floor cocktail bar at this ambitious, two-floor Mayfair operation which set up shop in July 2018. / W1S 4DH; www.gazelle-mayfair.com; @GazelleMayfair; Tue-Sat, Mon 10.30 pm, Sun 3.30 pm.

Gazette £53 3 3 3
79 Sherwood Ct, Chatfield Rd, SW11 020 7223 0999 11–1C
100 Balham High St, SW12 020 8772 1232 11–2C
147 Upper Richmond Rd, SW15 020 8789 6996 11–2B
"A banker for those who like traditional Gallic brasserie food", this Gallic trio in Balham, Clapham and Putney provides an "excellent-value set lunch", while the "à la carte covers all the French classics at reasonable prices". / www.gazettebrasserie.co.uk; 11 pm.

Geales W8 £57 2 2 2
2 Farmer St 020 7727 7528 7–2B
"If you want to eat good fish and chips" most reports still commend this pre-War Notting Hill chippie (est 1939), although its more recent Chelsea offshoot shut up shop this year. It doesn't have nearly the following it once did though, and one or two reporters feel it's now "living on the name and nothing else". / W8 7SN; www.geales.com; 10.30 pm, Sun 10 pm; closed Mon L.

Gem N1 £32 **3** **4** **3**
265 Upper St   020 7359 0405   9–2D
Turkish-Kurdish outfit near Angel that offers "exceptionally good value for Upper Street". "No fireworks here, simply decent portions of good food in a friendly place". Top Tip: the "set menu of mixed mezze is an especially good bargain". / N1 2UQ; www.gemrestaurant.org.uk; @Gem_restaurant; Mon-Thu 11 pm, Fri & Sat midnight, Sun 10.30 pm; no Amex.

Genesis E1 NEW
144 Commercial St   020 7375 2963   13–2B
When you turn your back on the family firm, you have to do it in style – in this case, the Santoro brothers moved on from their century-old family meat business and have opened this Shoreditch newcomer: a 100% plant-based restaurant with a globetrotting menu – what they call 'vegan alchemy'... It's GMO-free and organic, too (with Soil Association certification). / E1 6NU; eatgenesis.com; @EatGenesis.

George in the Strand WC2 £53 **3** **3** **3**
213 Strand   020 7353 9638   2–2D
Opposite the Royal Courts of Justice, this traditional but updated historic hostelry is worth remembering for its "unusually interesting pub food", both in the ground floor bar and upstairs 'Pig and Goose' dining room. / WC2R 1AP; www.georgeinthestrand.com; @thegeorgestrand; Mon-Thu 10 pm, Fri & Sat 10.30 pm, Sun 9 pm.

German Gymnasium N1 £72 **2** **1** **4**
1 King's Boulevard   020 7287 8000   9–3C
"The location is stunning (albeit loud when it fills with customers)", but – when evaluating this D&D London operation, housed within a "fantastic 1860s building in King's Cross" – there are just "too many missed opportunities in this grand space". "Because of the sheer size of the place (probably) the service is dreadful, which detracts from the experience", and when it comes to the "not-strictly-German cuisine" then "prices feel way too high" for an offering that's too "uninspired". As a business venue it has its fans, though, and also for the "great brunch menu with free-flowing bubbles". And "the bar's very good" too. / N1C 4BU; www.germangymnasium.com; @TheGermanGym; Tue-Sat, Mon 11 pm, Sun 3 pm; closed Mon L closed Sun D.

Giacomo's NW2 £38 **3** **3** **2**
428 Finchley Rd   020 7794 3603   1–1B
"Cosy local Italian" in Childs Hill that's "friendly", with "reliably good food" that won't break the bank. Family run, it has been established here for 16 years and "never disappoints". / NW2 2HY; www.giacomos.co.uk; 9.30 pm.

Gifto's Lahore Karahi UB1 £27 **3** **2** **2**
162-164 The Broadway   020 8813 8669   1–3A
Something of a local landmark – this large Pakistani diner on one of Southall's main routes makes an affordable choice, with top menu billing going to the "excellent grills". / UB1 1NN; www.gifto.com; @GiftosSouthall; Mon-Fri 11.30 pm, Sat & Sun midnight; booking weekdays only.

The Gilbert Scott NW1 £74 **2** **2** **4**
Euston Rd   020 7278 3888   9–3C
A "magnificent" space, within the "spectacular neo-gothic hotel attached to St Pancras Station" provides a superb backdrop to a meal at Marcus Wareing's "impressive" dining room; and it's a good place to entertain on business ("ideally situated for the Eurostar!"). When it comes to the "very British" food however, results remain mixed: even fans can find it "a shade lacking given the ticket price" and numerous sceptics describe it as "adequate, but totally unmemorable". / NW1 2AR; www.thegilbertscott.co.uk; @Thegilbertscott; 10.30 pm, Sun 9.30 pm; booking max 7 may apply.

Ginger & White £13 3 3 3
2 England's Ln, NW3   020 7722 9944   9–2A
4a-5a, Perrins Ct, NW3   020 7431 9098   9–2A
These "lovely" Antipodean-style cafés in Hampstead and Belsize Park are "worth the sharp elbows to get in". The lattes and all-day breakfasts are highly rated, if a little "pricey" but – be warned – they are "often full of the activewear-clad chattering classes". / www.gingerandwhite.com; 5.30 pm; W1 closed Sun.

Ginza Onodera SW1 £95 4 4 2
15 Bury St   020 7839 1101   3–3D
Aficionados of Japanese cuisine love the "wonderfully fresh and inventive yet traditional" cooking in this large, luxurious operation in a St James's basement (which, for many years, traded as Matsuri, RIP, and is nowadays run by an international chain). It's not an inexpensive option, though, and has a peaceful style that's not everyone's cup of green tea. / SW1Y 6AL; onodera-group.com/uk; @Onodera_London; 10.30 pm, Sun 10 pm.

The Glasshouse TW9 £82 3 3 2
14 Station Pde   020 8940 6777   1–3A
"In the style of sister establishments Chez Bruce and La Trompette", this neighbourhood star in a parade of shops right by Kew Gardens tube station also has a fine record of "superb, well-balanced cooking with great seasonal ingredients". Its ratings sagged quite noticeably this year, though, with numerous reports that performance is "off the boil" of late, and – "with the quality seeming to have dipped" – it can seem "quiet" or "a bit lacking in atmosphere". / TW9 3PZ; www.glasshouserestaurant.co.uk; @The__Glasshouse; 11.30 pm, Sun 3.30 pm; booking max 8 may apply.

Go-Viet SW7 £56 4 4 2
53 Old Brompton Rd   020 7589 6432   6–2C
"Superb Vietnamese food" – "diverse, delicious and really refined" – is on the menu at this yearling from Jeff Tan, the ex-Hakkasan owner of Soho's Viet Food. One cavil: the "very plain surroundings" mean it's "lacking in atmosphere". / SW7 3JS; vietnamfood.co.uk/go-viet; Sun-Thu 10.30 pm, Sat 11 pm; closed Fri.

La Goccia WC2 NEW £52 3 3 5
Floral Court, off Floral St   020 7305 7676   5–3C
"A promising start for one of Petersham Nurseries' new openings in Floral Court" – this is the less pricey of their two new restaurants, serving pizzetti, antipasti, risotti, pasta and so on, which – on early feedback – were consistently well-rated. Well hidden, but in the heart of Covent Garden, it sits on a lovely courtyard, complete with outside tables; see also The Petersham. / WC2E 9DJ; petershamnurseries.com/dine/la-goccia; @PetershamN; Mon-Fri 10 pm, Sat & Sun 9 pm; SRA-Food Made Good – 3 stars.

Goddards At Greenwich SE10 £15 3 4 4
22 King William Walk   020 8305 9612   1–3D
"Traditional pie 'n' mash (but with more choice of pies these days)" and "genuine and friendly counter service" again win very positive (if limited) feedback for this Greenwich fixture (est 1890) – one of London's few surviving pie 'n' mash shops. / SE10 9HU; www.goddardsatgreenwich.co.uk; @GoddardsPieMash; Sun-Thu 7.30 pm, Fri & Sat 8 pm; L & early evening only.

Gökyüzü N4 £32

26-27 Grand Pde, Green Lanes   020 8211 8406   1–1C

"Full of noise and activity", this longstanding Green Lanes BBQ is *"the most popular Turkish eatery in the area"* – *"with queues down the street on Sundays"* – thanks to its *"wonderful selection of food"*: *"sharing platters are plentiful"* (*"doggy bags are happily provided"*) and *"the quality of the grilled meat is excellent"*. There are now spinoffs in Chingford and Walthamstow, with Finchley opening in late 2018. Top Tip: *"Turkish breakfast served till 4pm: fresh honeycomb, bread from the grill, plenty of treats – and unlimited tea"*. / N4 1LG; www.gokyuzurestaurant.co.uk; @Gokyuzulondon; Sun-Thu midnight, Fri & Sat 1 am.

Gold Mine W2 £38

102 Queensway   020 7792 8331   7–2C

"Great roast duck" and other meats shine at this functional Bayswater Cantonese. Aficionados rate it as *"better than its famous neighbour"*, the Four Seasons. / W2 3RR; 11 pm.

Golden Dragon W1 £45

28-29 Gerrard St   020 7734 1073   5–3A

"My go-to place for dim sum", this substantial Chinatown operation looks *"rather touristy"* but pleases the crowd with Cantonese favourites including *"the best roast duck in town"*. It now has an offshoot in the new Bang Bang Oriental food hall in Colindale. / W1 6JW; www.gdlondon.co.uk; Mon-Thu 11.30 pm, Fri & Sat midnight, Sun 11 pm.

Golden Hind W1 £39

73 Marylebone Ln   020 7486 3644   2–1A

"Brilliant, classic, old-style British fish 'n' chips – what more do you need?" That's why folk still seek out this Marylebone institution, founded in 1914. The jury is still out a bit on the new management (which changed a couple of years ago) but most reporters feel this is *"still as good a chippy as you can find in Central London"*. / W1U 2PN; www.goldenhindrestaurant.com; 10 pm; closed Sat L, closed Sun.

Good Earth £60

233 Brompton Rd, SW3   020 7584 3658   6–2C
143-145 The Broadway, NW7   020 8959 7011   1–1B
11 Bellevue Rd, SW17   020 8682 9230   11–2C

"Reliable, good quality, pricey but satisfying" – such virtues have long attracted fans to these *"old favourite"*, family-owned Chinese stalwarts in Knightsbridge, Balham and Mill Hill. Viewed from the other side of the coin, they serve *"satisfactory but unadventurous fare that seems somewhat overpriced and lacks edginess"*. / www.goodearthgroup.co.uk; Mon-Sat 10.45 pm, Sun 10 pm; NW7 11.15 pm, Sun 10.45 pm.

The Good Egg £57

Unit G9 Kingly Court, W1   020 3911 2000   4–2B NEW
93 Church St, N16   020 7682 2120   1–1C

"Exceptional breakfasts and exceptionally welcoming staff" are the two most highly praised features of this Israeli deli in Stokey, which now has a Soho offshoot too. One former fan however, complained of *"corners cut"* of late – hopefully just a blip. / thegoodeggn16.com; @TheGoodEgg_.

Good Neighbour SE5 NEW £39

21 Camberwell Church St   07981 396 180   1–3C

Further gentrification comes to Camberwell in the form of this cute new wine bar – a late spring 2018 newcomer from Aussie chef Paul Williamson (formerly of WC in Clapham and Soho House). There's a menu of Mediterranean-inspired small plates, pizzette, cheese and charcuterie alongside a rotating range of wines. / SE5 8TR; www.goodneighbour.uk.com; @gdneighbourldn.

Goodman £93
24-26 Maddox St, W1   020 7499 3776   3–2C
3 South Quay, E14   020 7531 0300   12–1C
11 Old Jewry, EC2   020 7600 8220   10–2C
"A wide range of both grass-fed and grain-fed steaks from around the globe"
helps fully satisfy the cravings of *"those who like a good steak meal and
decent bottle of red"* at this *"very solid"* group of NYC-style steak-houses,
which – amongst the more expensive multiples – remains the *"best in
town"*. *"It's not a cheap option by any means, but great for a business lunch
or blow-out in the evening". / www.goodmanrestaurants.com; 10.30 pm; W1 closed
Sun, EC2 closed Sat & Sun, E14 closed Sat L & Sun.*

Gordon Ramsay SW3 £169
68-69 Royal Hospital Rd   020 7352 4441   6–3D
"He should concentrate on the cuisine at this price, not his celebrity!" The
world-famous TV chef's original solo HQ in Chelsea continues to divide
opinion and scored even lower overall marks in the survey this year.
Undoubtedly it still has many advocates who feel Matt Abé (who actually
does all the cooking) produces a menu that's *"a total delight for the senses"*,
and that service is *"unbeatable"* (under longstanding *"perfectionist"* maître
d', Jean Claude Breton, plus *"very helpful"* sommelier James Lloyd). Critics,
though, are more vocal than supporters, feeling the *"food needs to move
on"*, or that the ambience (*"limited by the layout of the room"*)
is *"too manufactured and precious to be enjoyable"*. All-in-all, Michelin's
continual failure to recognise the long-term slide here is baffling, and to
continue to award this establishment three stars seems nothing more than
cynical sucking up to the world's biggest culinary media figure. / SW3 4HP;
*www.gordonramsay.com; @GordonRamsay; 10.15 pm; closed Sun & Mon; No jeans;
booking max 9 may apply.*

Gordon's Wine Bar WC2 £41
47 Villiers St   020 7930 1408   5–4D
*With its ancient, dark, candle-lit cellars and the benefit of one of central
London's biggest terraces (adjoining Embankment Gardens), this old wine
bar (dating from the 1890s) is perpetually thronged (mostly by young
professionals), and has seemingly been visited by everyone in London
at some point (even if they may struggle to remember exactly what it was
called). Right by Embankment tube, it's a handy rendezvous, and an
affordable one too, even if the self-service food is very basic (cold cuts,
cheeses, salads and simple hot platters). Queues for service, cramped
seating and a general feeling of scrum are all part of the experience.
/ WC2N 6NE; www.gordonswinebar.com; @GordonsWineBar; 11 pm, Sun 10 pm.*

Gourmet Burger Kitchen £32
*Fans of London's original upmarket burger chain still acclaim the
"best patties around" but this stalwart brand is looking "a little tired and
worn out" nowadays. In summer 2018, its owners Famous Brands
announced they were 'considering their strategic options' after a £2m loss
at the group, although many reporters feel "there's nothing really wrong with
the concept". / www.gbkinfo.com; most branches close 10.30 pm; no booking.*

Gourmet Goat SE1 £9
Borough Market, Unit 27a Rochester Walk   020 8050 1973   10–4C
*Nothing but positive vibes again on this Borough Market stall, which serves
simple East Mediterranean dishes to take away. Top Menu Tips: kid goat
or veal wrap. / SE1 9AH; www.gourmetgoat.co.uk; @gourmet_goat; Mon & Tue
4 pm, Wed & Thu, Sat 5 pm, Fri 6 pm; closed Mon-Thu, Sat D, closed Sun;
no booking; SRA-Food Made Good – 3 stars.*

Goya SW1 £48 **3** **3** **2**
34 Lupus St   020 7976 5309   2–4C
This "reliable tapas bar" in a "desolate stretch of Pimlico" "takes some beating". "Lunch for two including a bottle of wine, sardines, lamb chops, fried potatoes, espresso and service charge for £40 is terrific value" – no wonder "it's always busy". / SW1V 3EB; www.goyarestaurant.co.uk; 10 pm, Sun 9 pm.

Granary Square Brasserie N1 NEW £52 **2** **2** **4**
Granary Square, 1-3 Stable St   020 3940 1000   9–3C
"The fantastic decor and impressive bar greet guests with a 'WOW'" at The Ivy Collection's new opening on the former site of Bruno Loubet's Grain Store (RIP), which also boasts a bar and al-fresco dining terrace. "Unfortunately all this does not translate to the average food offerings" which live up to the DNA of Richard Caring's ever-expanding stable. / N1C 4AA; www.granarysquarebrasserie.com; @granarysqbrasserie; Mon-Thu 12.30 am, Fri & Sat 1.30 am, Sun 11.30 pm; Booking max 12 may apply.

Grand Trunk Road E18 £59 **4** **4** **3**
219 High St   020 8505 1965   1–1D
"Some amazing tastes" reward a visit to this Woodford two-year-old from the ex-manager and ex-head chef of Mayfair's Tamarind – "not your normal Indian, with a menu that showcases dishes from across the subcontinent (Afghanistan, Pakistan, North India and Bangladesh)". Even those who feel the food "is a bit pricey for its location" say "it's very good". / E18 2PB; www.gtrrestaurant.co.uk; @GT_Road; Tue-Thu 10.30 pm; closed Mon, Fri & Sat & Sun.

Granger & Co £53 **2** **2** **3**
237-239 Pavilion Rd, SW1   020 3848 1060   6–2D
175 Westbourne Grove, W11   020 7229 9111   7–1B
Stanley Building, St Pancras Sq, N1   020 3058 2567   9–3C
The Buckley Building, 50 Sekforde St, EC1   020 7251 9032   10–1A
"A great way to start the day!" – "Be prepared to wait" (particularly at the W11 original) if you want to sample the trademark funky brunch of this star Aussie chef's "cool and airy" chain. But while feedback contains lots of adulation for his "light", "fresh" and "innovative" fare, even fans can find it "a real mix in terms of quality" and those who feel it's a case of "hype and trend over taste" say "it's astonishing that people queue in the rain to eat this mediocre-at-best food!" / Mon-Sat 10 pm, Sun 5pm.

The Great Chase EC1 £46 **3** **4** **2**
16 Saint John St   020 7998 0640   9–3D
Chef Radoslaw Nitkowski combines high-welfare, fully halal, British ingredients with non-alcoholic drinks (mocktails, handmade cordials and rare tea) at this innovative, inclusive small restaurant, near Sadlers Wells. It doesn't inspire a huge volume of feedback, but such as exists is very positive. / EC1V 4NT; www.thegreatchase.co.uk; @thegreatchaserestaurant; Wed-Sat 10.30 pm, Sun 5 pm; closed Wed L closed Sun D, closed Mon & Tue.

Great Nepalese NW1 £40 **3** **4** **2**
48 Eversholt St   020 7388 6737   9–3C
"If you want a curry, go Nepalese", say loyal fans of this age-old (over 50 years old) small and inconspicuous-looking outfit, down the side of Euston station, where the Nepalese specials are the way to go. Very limited feedback this year, but of the 'all good' variety. / NW1 1DA; www.great-nepalese.co.uk; 11.30 pm, Sun 10 pm; closed Sun.

Great Queen Street WC2   £55   **3**2 2
32 Great Queen St 020 7242 0622 5–1D
"Still a great option around Covent Garden" – this "quite large" foodie
gastropub (spiritually it's actually more "a restaurant that looks something
like a pub") "keeps things properly seasonal" with a "rustic", "something-for-
everyone" British menu "that emphasises hearty dishes like game or meat
pies". "At times, service can disappear completely, but when it's there
it functions well." / WC2B 5AA; www.greatqueenstreetrestaurant.co.uk;
@greatqueenstreet; 10.30 pm, Mon 11 pm, Sun 3 pm; closed Sun D; no Amex.

The Green EC1   £48   **3**4 3
29 Clerkenwell Grn 020 7490 8010 10–1A
Good ratings all round for this year-old modern gastropub on a corner
by Clerkenwell Green, under the same ownership as The Culpeper, nearby.
Top Tip: "the £15 two-course lunch menu is a steal". / EC1R 0DU;
www.thegreenclerkenwell.com; 10.30 pm.

The Green Café SE10   £19   **3**3 2
285 Greenwich High Rd 020 8305 0799 1–3D
"Spot on for brunch at any time of the day!" – a superior "local caff"
in Greenwich with "good fry-ups" and "lots of healthy options too":
"bespoke English breakfast, great poached egg dishes, super sweet potato
fries, good breads, waffles, fab tea and coffee; oh, and maybe a slice of cake
to take home!" / SE10 8NB; @greencafeLDN; Mon-Fri 5 pm, Sat & Sun 5.30 pm;
closed Mon-Sun D.

Green Cottage NW3   £38   **3**2 2
9 New College Pde 020 7722 5305 9–2A
This veteran Chinese in a Swiss Cottage parade of shops "never fails
to please with its authentic food in generous portions", according to a
regular who has "been going for 40 years". No huge prizes for service here,
though. / NW3 5EP; 11 pm; no Amex.

**The Green Room,
The National Theatre SE1**   £46   2 **3** 2
101 Upper Ground 020 7452 3630 2–3D
Fans of the National Theatre's glass-walled 'neighbourhood diner' feel it's
a "good pre-show venue" with "professional and helpful service" and food
that's "well-prepared, albeit pretty basic". The feeling is quite widespread,
however, that – for such an "interesting site" – the "disappointing menu
could be so much better". / SE1 9PP; www.greenroom.london; @greenroomSE1;
Wed & Thu 11 pm, Fri & Sat midnight, Sun 6 pm.

Greenberry Café NW1   £56   **3**3 4
101 Regents Park Rd 020 7483 3765 9–2B
Limited but positive feedback this year on this cute all-day café on Primrose
Hill's atmospheric main drag – a top local haunt, ideal for lazy breakfasts,
light lunches or coffee and a bun any time of day. / NW1 8UR;
greenberrycafe.co.uk; @Greenberry_Cafe; 10.30 pm; closed Mon D & Sun D;
no Amex.

The Greenhouse W1 £128 3 3 3
27a Hays Mews 020 7499 3331 3–3B

You feel "far from the madding crowd, but in the heart of Mayfair" at this "stylish" haunt "tucked away near Park Lane", where "a pretty entrance through a city garden leads to a calm and well-styled modern interior". It's a "spacious" and luxurious room which is "great for business, but which would also impress a date" (although it can also seem "a bit stiff" for some tastes). Having won gastronomic acclaim (not least two Michelin stars) in recent times with some "exemplary" modern cuisine, Arnaud Bignon moved on in mid-2018, perhaps explaining why ratings in this year's survey were lower across the board. New exec chef Alex Dilling (ex-Hélène Darroze) has promised to shake up the menu, with a focus on British and fresh produce. One constant, however: "one of London's best wine selections, especially if you are able to use your business credit card". / W1J 5NY; www.greenhouserestaurant.co.uk; @greenhouse27a; 10.30 pm; closed Sat L, closed Sun; booking max 12 may apply.

The Greyhound Cafe W1 NEW £59 2 2 3
37 Berners St 020 3026 3798 3–1D

"Lively and busy" first European outpost of a popular Thailand-based chain, which opened its doors in Fitzrovia in early 2018. Despite the odd adulatory newspaper review, our reporters' response is middling: it's "pleasant" (if "noisy") with somewhat fusionesque Thai cooking "of a decent standard" and "slightly chaotic service". / W1T 3NB; www.greyhoundcafe.uk; Mon-Fri 10 pm, Sat & Sun 9 pm.

Ground Coffee Society SW15 £18 3 2 2
79 Lower Richmond Rd 0845 862 9994 11–1B

This 10-year-old Antipodean café (with an in-house roastery) in Putney serves "better coffee than many of the more self-conscious central London coffee shops". It's also a "great family breakfast/ brunch destination", and is "popular with Sunday morning cyclists". / SW15 1ET; www.groundcoffeesociety.com; @groundcoffeesociety; 6 pm; L only; no booking.

Guglee £40 3 3 2
7 New College Pde, NW3 020 7722 8478 9–2A
279 West End Ln, NW6 020 7317 8555 1–1B

"A discovery" for first-timers – this duo of modern Indians in West Hampstead and Swiss Cottage win praise for their street-food-influenced dishes. / www.guglee.co.uk; 11 am.

The Guildford Arms SE10 £52 3 4 3
55 Guildford Grove 020 8691 6293 1–3D

"Not your typical pub food, there's real quality and great staff" at this three-storey Georgian boozer in Greenwich. "Attention to culinary detail" comes thanks to chef Guy Awford, previously of the area's "late, lamented Inside restaurant (RIP)". "Midweek lunch is exceptional value, given the quality". / SE10 8JY; www.theguildfordarms.co.uk; @GuildfordArms_; 10 pm, Sun 9 pm; closed Mon.

The Guinea Grill W1 £75 3 3 4
30 Bruton Pl 020 7409 1728 3–3B

"Old school" grill room adjacent to a tucked-away Mayfair mews pub, whose traditional British pies and steaks have grown something of a renaissance for its profile. A natural favourite for expense-accounters, the relatively grand "back dining room is the best for business", or you can grab one of their award-winning steak 'n' kidney puds in the small and cosy bar at the front. / W1J 6NL; www.theguinea.co.uk; @guineagrill; 11.30 pm, Sun 3.30 pm; closed Sat L & Sun; booking max 8 may apply.

The Gun E14 £71 2|3|4

27 Coldharbour   020 7515 5222   12–1C

A fine position by the Thames, looking over to the O2, is the draw to this 200-year-old, Grade II listed tavern in the depths of Docklands. Since its sale by ETM group to Fuller's, it doesn't attract the attention it once did as a dining destination, but feedback on eating here remains upbeat. / E14 9NS; www.thegundocklands.com; @thegundocklands; 10 pm, Sun 7 pm; closed Sun D.

Gunpowder £38 4|4|3 NEW

One Tower Bridge, 4 Crown Square, SE1   awaiting tel   10–4D NEW
11 Whites Row, E1   020 7426 0542   13–2C

"Home-style Indian tapas" – "beautifully spiced, without overpowering the flavour of the ingredients" and "each plate a unique reinvention of a traditional dish" – lures sizeable queues outside this "cosy, if slightly cramped" two-year-old "tucked away 150m from Spitalfields Market"; a second branch opened in the shiny new One Tower Bridge development at the start of September 2018. Top Menu Tip: "the spicy venison doughnut is inspired". / www.gunpowderlondon.com; @gunpowder_ldn.

Gustoso Ristorante & Enoteca SW1 £48 2|4|3

33 Willow Pl   020 7834 5778   2–4B

"As the years have gone by", this "enjoyable and efficient" Pimlico stalwart, "on a quiet street behind Westminster Cathedral", has won a very loyal following thanks to its "family-style atmosphere, lovely service, and well-chosen wines". Some reports say the food is a little "basic" or "variable", but most accounts describe it as "authentic" and "affordable". / SW1P 1JH; ristorantegustoso.co.uk; @GustosoRist; 10.30 pm, Sun 10 pm.

Gymkhana W1 £70 4|3|4

42 Albemarle St   020 3011 5900   3–3C

"For high-end Indian cuisine, it's still streets ahead" – the Sethi family's epic Mayfair venture, near The Ritz, remains the survey's most-mentioned Indian, marrying "sophisticated interior design" (on an "old-style, colonial" theme), with "superbly original", "well-spiced and complex" cooking that's "so much more interesting than the huge majority of its peers". Service is "charming", but can on occasion be "erratic" too. / W1S 4JH; www.gymkhanalondon.com; @GymkhanaLondon; 10.30 pm; closed Sat & Sun.

Haché £43 3|3|2

95-97 High Holborn, WC1   020 7242 4580   2–1D
329-331 Fulham Rd, SW10   020 7823 3515   6–3B
24 Inverness St, NW1   020 7485 9100   9–3B
37 Bedford Hill, SW12   020 8772 9772   11–2C
153 Clapham High St, SW4   020 7738 8760   11–2D
147-149 Curtain Rd, EC2   020 7739 8396   13–1B

"Even for burgers the French do it better", say fans of this small group with a Gallic-inspired take on American fast food: "steak haché comme il faut, and les frites are also perfect". / www.hacheburgers.com; 10.30 pm, Fri-Sat 11 pm, Sun 10 pm; WC1 9 pm; WC1 Sat & Sun.

Hai Cenato SW1 £55 2|3|2

2 Sir Simon Milton Square, 150 Victoria St   020 3816 9320   2–4B

"It's pizza, Jim, but not as we know it..." say fans of Jason Atherton's large and "buzzy" pizzeria in Victoria's Nova development, who go a bundle on its "unusual toppings on good quality bases" (plus pasta and some other fare). Even some supporters acknowledge that "it's a little pricey" however, and there's quite a significant constituency that says the experience here is "reasonable" but "wouldn't leave you clamouring to return". / SW1H 0HW; haicenato.co.uk; @haicenato; 10 pm, Sun 9.30 pm; booking max 6 may apply.

Hakkasan £99 [4][2][4]

17 Bruton St, W1   020 7907 1888   3–2C
8 Hanway Pl, W1   020 7927 7000   5–1A

"It is everything I would expect not to like: a proven formula, a bit on the expensive side, way too trendy… but in spite of everything I can't get enough of it!" These "dark", "nightclub-style", "very noisy" Chinese/pan-Asians "haven't changed since they opened" (which, in the case of the original, was 17 years ago in 2001, with Mayfair following in 2010). They are "still at the top of their game" with "always zingy and exciting" cuisine and a "chic and moneyed aesthetic" that particularly suits those looking for "a showy-off night out". Service can be "haughty and inconsistent" – no changes there then either… Top Menu Tip: "still a go-to for quality dim sum". / www.hakkasan.com; 12.30 am, Sun 11.15 pm; W1 12.30 am, Thu-Sat 12.45 am, Sun midnight; no trainers, no sportswear.

Ham NW6 NEW £53 [3][2][3]

238 West End Lane   020 7813 0168   1–1B

"A very welcome addition to the otherwise disappointing collection of West Hampstead eateries" is how most reporters and press reviewers judge Aussie chef Matt Osborne's new neighbourhood venture, whose brunch menu in particular "is inventive and varied, from hearty to healthy". That's the majority view anyway: to a minority, its excellence can seem a bit over-egged. / NW6 1LG; www.hamwesthampstead.com/ham; @hamwhampstead/; Wed-Sat 11 pm, Sun 6 pm; closed Mon & Tue.

Ham Yard Restaurant,
Ham Yard Hotel W1 £73 [2][3][4]

1 Ham Yd   020 3642 1007   4–3D

"If you can find this hidden-away gem, it is superbly located for Theatreland" – just a short stroll from Piccadilly Circus, yet seemingly miles away, with "a great courtyard for a summer lunch", and "lovely interior" with "amazing Kit Kemp decor that makes it a particularly great lunch venue". Judged on its food alone, it can be "average" (and somewhat "let the whole meal down"), but is mostly "solid"; and the "sumptuous afternoon tea in the heart of the West End" is terrific – "somewhere to take both Granny and your hipster cousin". / W1D 7DT; www.firmdalehotels.com; @Firmdale_Hotels; 11.30 pm, Sun 10.30 pm.

The Hampshire Hog W6 £51 [3][3][3]

227 King St   020 8748 3391   8–2B

"Attractively decorated rooms, a friendly pub ambience and good food" make it worth remembering this large pub (with big rear garden), near Hammersmith Town Hall. / W6 9JT; www.thehampshirehog.com; @TheHampshireHog; 10 pm, Sun 4 pm; closed Sun D.

Hans Bar & Grill SW1 NEW £78

164 Pavilion Rd   020 7730 7000   6–2D

Just off Sloane Square in chichi Pavilion Road, this svelte new brasserie is run by swanky nearby boutique hotel 11 Cadogan Gardens (a stablemate of luxurious Cliveden House and Chewton Glen). It opened in May 2018, just as the survey was drawing to a close – no reports as yet on its all-day seasonal menu, but in this location, something is very wrong if it doesn't become a hub for the Made in Chelsea crowd. / SW1X 0BP; www.hansbarandgrill.com; @HansBarGrill; 10.30pm.

The Harcourt W1 £59 [3][3][4]

32 Harcourt St   020 3771 8660   7–1D

This swish, five-storey gastropub (Grade II listed) on the fringes of Marylebone "is a beautiful spot in the centre of town, with a cool interior" and serving some "very good" cooking (with Nordic influences). / W1H 4HX; www.theharcourt.com; @the_harcourt; 11 pm, Sun 10.30 pm.

Hare & Tortoise £40 **3** **3** 2
11-13 The Brunswick, WC1 020 7278 9799 2–1D
373 Kensington High St, W14 020 7603 8887 8–1D
156 Chiswick High Rd, W4 020 8747 5966 8–2A
38 Haven Grn, W5 020 8810 7066 1–2A
296-298 Upper Richmond Rd, SW15 020 8394 7666 11–2B
90 New Bridge St, EC4 020 7651 0266 10–2A
*"Tasty food in huge portions" hits the spot at this casual pan-Asian group
with a "good range of dishes to please the whole family". "Consistent levels
of cooking" and "well presented sushi" make it a cut above most chain
rivals at a similar price and something of a quiet success story.*
*/ www.hareandtortoise-restaurants.co.uk; 11 pm; EC4 10.30, Fri 11 pm; EC4 closed
Sun; W14 no bookings.*

The Harlot W4 NEW
210 Chiswick High Rd awaiting tel 8–2A
*Henry Harris and James McCulloch (trading as Harcourt Inns) are on a roll
with their pub-conversion concept; it's just been announced that a fourth
venue is being developed (to join The Coach, The Hero of Maida and Three
Cranes), this time in Chiswick. The last pub of any ambition to open
in downtown Chiswick was Gordon Ramsay's The Devonshire: let's hope they
can do better than that: they certainly have a good start with some
gorgeous premises in the shape of Chiswick's late Victorian police station
(complete with charming back courtyard), which until recently traded
as Carvosso's (RIP). / W4 1PD.*

Harry Morgan's NW8 £42 2 **3** 2
29-31 St John's Wood High St 020 7722 1869 9–3A
*"Excellent salt beef", "lots of versions of chicken soup" and other Jewish deli
classics are the stars of the show at this St John's Wood institution, whose
overall food offer is solid rather than spectacular. "It never changes",
say fans: "we love it!". Top Tip: great all-day breakfast. / NW8 7NH;
www.harryms.co.uk; @morgan_hm; Sun-Thu 9 pm, Fri & Sat 9.30 pm.*

Harry's Bar W1 NEW
30-34 James St awaiting tel 3–1A
*A second addition to Caprice Group's new 'Harry's' brand opens in autumn
2018, with an all-day menu under the same executive chef (Diego Cardoso).
With its Mayfair location and aim to "serve a slice of the 'Dolce Vita' in the
heart of the West End" this is very much known territory for Richard
Caring's luxury group. See also 'Harry's Dolce Vita'. / W1U 1EU;
www.harrys-bar.co.uk.*

Harrys Dolce Vita SW3 NEW £59 **3** **4** **5**
27-31 Basil St 020 3940 1020 6–1D
*Near the back of Harrods, "the latest addition to the Caprice Holdings
group" delights Knightsbridge shoppers and other denizens of SW3 with its
"glamorous" decor and very "traditional" menu of cicchetti, pasta, pizze,
risotti and grills. It inspired the odd gripe ("like a crowded train carriage"),
but more common are raves for its "reasonably priced" fare (for the
location) and slick service ("superb coffee too… the real McCoy, oh, and did
I mention the olive oil!"). A new sibling – Harry's Bar (see also) – opens
in October 2018. / SW3 1BB; www.harrysdolcevita.com; Mon-Fri 10 pm, Sat & Sun
9 pm.*

Harwood Arms SW6   £68   4 3 3
Walham Grove   020 7386 1847   6–3A
"Terrific game dishes" (not least "the best venison specials in the whole
of London") are highlights of the "interesting menu" (culinary oversight
comes from Brett Graham of The Ledbury and Mike Robinson of Berkshire's
Pot Kiln) at this renowned hostelry, lost in the distant backstreets of Fulham,
which finally seized the crown for the first time this year as the survey's No.1
gastropub (from The Anchor & Hope). "This is a pub where the food takes
pride of place and drinking is incidental", but it's a "perfect mix" of the two,
preserving the "informal" approach of a traditional boozer (if with very
limited space for non-diners). / SW6 1QP; www.harwoodarms.com;
@HarwoodArms; Tue-Sat, Mon 9.30 pm, Sun 9 pm; closed Mon L; credit card
required to book.

Hashi SW20   £37   3 3 2
54 Durham Rd   020 8944 1888   11–2A
"Awesome sushi" and other Japanese dishes make this low-key outfit
in suburban Raynes Park a "great local", "consistent year after year".
("Unfortunately they've stopped doing BYO.") / SW20 0TW; 10.30 pm,
Sun 10 pm; closed Tue-Fri L, closed Mon; no Amex.

Hatched (formerly Darwin) SW11 NEW   £69   4 4 2
189 Saint John's Hill   020 7738 0735   11–2C
"What's not to love" about this new Battersea favourite, which inspires
major love from local reporters for its "fine dining done informally and
brought to the local high street". The only quibble is that its interior is "a bit
Spartan", but it provides "superb top-end cooking" ("deconstructed classics,
with some genuine taste sensations") from the open kitchen. / SW11 1TH;
www.hatchedsw11.com; @HatchedSW11; Wed & Thu 9.30 pm, Fri & Sat 10 pm,
Sun 3 pm; closed Wed & Thu L closed Sun D, closed Mon & Tue.

The Havelock Tavern W14   £51   3 2 4
57 Masbro Rd   020 7603 5374   8–1C
This backstreet Olympia gastropub is not the major destination it once was,
but locals agree it's still "at the top after all these years". "They produce
different menus morning and evening, seven days a week – the cooking
is imaginative, tasty and reliably so". "Amazing that they still maintain the
unpretentious, high-quality food at such reasonable prices." / W14 0LS;
www.havelocktavern.com; @HavelockTavern; 10.30 pm, Sun 10 pm.

Haven Bistro N20   £49   3 4 3
1363 High Rd   020 8445 7419   1–1B
"An oasis" in Whetstone and the outer fringes of north London, which locals
reckon is the best bet in the area for "good food and friendly, excellent
service". / N20 9LN; www.haven-bistro.co.uk; 10.30 pm, Sun 10 pm; No shorts.

Hawksmoor £79 ③②②

5a Air St, W1   020 7406 3980   4–4C
11 Langley St, WC2   020 7420 9390   5–2C
3 Yeoman's Row, SW3   020 7590 9290   6–2C
16 Winchester Walk, SE1   020 7234 9940   10–4C
157 Commercial St, E1   020 7426 4850   13–2B
10-12 Basinghall St, EC2   020 7397 8120   10–2C

"Mouth-watering steaks at eye-watering prices" is the harsh-but-fair summary on Huw Gott and Will Beckett's famous and fashionable steakhouse chain. To its enormous cult following: "yes, it's pricey, but – wow! – it's worth it!", thanks to its "melt-in-the-mouth" British-bred meat (some would say "the best in London"), "delicious sides", "impressive cocktail menu", and a "distinctly clubby" style that is, for a fair few expense-accounters, "perfect for business" too. With the inexorable expansion of the brand, though (next stop – NYC – with an opening in mid-2019, not far from Gramercy Park) has come an inexorable and ongoing decline in ratings, with increasing gripes about "hit-and-miss service", an atmosphere that's too "loud and busy", and a feeling that "it's not the Hawksmoor it used to be". / www.thehawksmoor.com; 10.30 pm; W1 & WC2 Fri & Sat 11 pm, Sun 9pm-10 pm; EC2 closed Sat & Sun; SRA-Food Made Good – 3 stars.

Haz £50 ②②②

9 Cutler St, E1   020 7929 7923   10–2D
34 Foster Ln, EC2   020 7600 4172   10–2B
64 Bishopsgate, EC2   020 7628 4522   10–2D
112 Houndsditch, EC3   020 7623 8180   10–2D
6 Mincing Ln, EC3   020 7929 3173   10–3D

"Fabulous smells, reliable cooking and rapid service" make this Turkish group a popular choice for a "self-funded lunch" in the Square Mile. On the downside, they can be "far too noisy for conversation" and sometimes the food is no more than "predictable, going on adequate". / www.hazrestaurant.co.uk; 11.30 pm; EC3 closed Sun.

Heddon Street Kitchen W1 £71 ②②②

3-9 Heddon St   020 7592 1212   4–3B

As "a nice option for a mid-shopping break", Gordon Ramsay's West End outfit off Regent Street improved its previously dire ratings this year, although the experience can still seem "beige". It's best with kids in tow, as under-12s eat free at any time from the menu of Tilly's Treats, designed by junior TV chef Matilda Ramsay ("and the kids love the ice cream parlour too"). / W1B 4BE; www.gordonramsayrestaurants.com/heddon-street-kitc; @heddonstkitchen; midnight, Sat 1 am.

Hedone W4 £129 ④③②

301-303 Chiswick High Rd   020 8747 0377   8–2A

Ex-solicitor, Mikael Jonsson's "idiosyncratic" passion-project in deepest Chiswick continues to inspire controversy amongst its large following. No-one is too fussed that the interior is "clinical, with harsh light": it's the hit to the wallet that elicits grief, with many critics apt to rate the food highly, but still cavil at the "outrageous prices". Its disciples, though, are "captivated" and feel "the enormous bill is entirely fair" given the "stunning" ingredients ("some not seen elsewhere"), and the "mouthwateringly wonderful", "constantly evolving" and "exciting" cuisine ("only on offer as tasting menus, but with each course a surprise and delight"). In their view: "at one Michelin star this restaurant is under-rated" – "the food level sometimes touches a three-star, but is certainly two-star and way better than just the one!" Top Menu Tip: don't miss the bread. / W4 4HH; www.hedonerestaurant.com; @HedoneLondon; 9.30 pm; closed Tue-Thu L, closed Sun & Mon; booking max 7 may apply.

Heirloom N8 £53 333
35 Park Rd   020 8348 3565   9–1C
*"A really cool neighbourhood local" up in Crouch End, with an emphasis
on seasonal cooking and biodynamic wines. Brunch and Sunday roast are
key occasions in its week – at other times a somewhat more ambitious,
modern British menu is served. / N8 8TE; www.heirloomn8.co.uk; @HeirloomN8;
Mon-Wed midnight, Thu-Sat 1.30 am, Sun 11 pm.*

Hélène Darroze,
The Connaught Hotel W1 £147 344
Carlos Pl   020 3147 7200   3–3B
*"The beautiful room… the attentive, enthusiastic and highly competent
staff… the exceptional precision of the cuisine, together with its subtlety" –
Hélène Darroze's "romantic" operation in this most pukka of Mayfair hotels
is a fine example of "refined, effortless and luxurious 'art de la table'"
(including a notably good wine list) and its many advocates feel you "can't
fault the place". Sceptics agree "it's very good… just not worth the mega
prices". / W1K 2AL; www.the-connaught.co.uk; @TheConnaught; 10 pm, Sun 9 pm;
closed Mon & Sun; No trainers.*

Heliot Steak House WC2 £64 333
Cranbourn St   020 7769 8844   5–3B
*"Surprisingly tasty and well-cooked steaks considering it's in a casino" make
it worth remembering this glitzy grill, looking down onto the roulette tables
of the UK's biggest casino (by Leicester Square tube). Top Tip: great pre-
theatre deal. / WC2H 7AJ; www.hippodromecasino.com; @HippodromeLDN; 1 am;
closed Mon-Fri L, closed Sun.*

Helix (Searcys at The Gherkin) EC3 £78 335
30 St Mary Axe   033 0107 0816   10–2D
*"The view – ground-level to zenith – is breathtaking", sitting on the 39th-
floor of this London landmark: "go if you need to impress, especially an out-
of-towner". And – though "security to enter is (understandably) Draconian"
– all-in-all performance defies the usual rules about rooms-with-a-view: it's
"so uplifting to combine great vistas with very competent standards". Until
recent times, entry was restricted to employees within the building, but the
caterers rebranded and relaunched the space (fka 'Searcys at The Gherkin')
in summer 2018, and it's now open to all (including the top-floor 'Iris' bar).
/ EC3A 8EP; searcysatthegherkin.co.uk/helix-restaurant; @SearcysGherkin; 9 pm,
Sun 3 pm; closed Sun D.*

Henrietta Bistro WC2 £62
Henrietta St   020 3794 5314   5–3C
*Ollie Dabbous has now left this dining room inside the new 18-room
Henrietta Hotel (sibling to Grand Pigalle in Paris), and it has been re-
christened from plain 'Henrietta'. New chef Sylvain Roncayrol offers a menu
inspired by SW France, Basque and Corsican cuisine. / WC2E 8NA;
www.henriettahotel.com; 11 pm.*

Hereford Road W2 £50 433
3 Hereford Rd   020 7727 1144   7–1B
*"Excellent" seasonal British cuisine – and "modestly priced" too, especially
given the quality of the ingredients – is complemented by a "thoughtful wine
list" at chef/patron Tom Pemberton's "wonderful neighbourhood restaurant"
in Bayswater. The odd reporter feels "ambience is lacking", but the majority
say "the comfortable modern design and overall atmosphere is really
conducive to a great meal". / W2 4AB; www.herefordroad.org; @3HerefordRoad;
10.30 pm, Sun 10 pm.*

The Hero of Maida W9 £58

55 Shirland Rd   020 7266 9198   1–2B

Formerly popular as The Truscott Arms (RIP) which closed after the owners tussled with the landlords, this revivified boozer opened in spring 2018 as part of the trio of pubs launched by James McCulloch in partnership with the former chef/patron of Racine. It opened too late for significant survey feedback, but one early report was very enthusiastic: "it seems as if Henry Harris has worked his magic", with some excellent dishes reported. / W9 2JD; theheromaidavale.co.uk; @TheHeroofMaida; Mon-Fri 10 pm, Sat & Sun 11 pm.

The Heron W2 £39   **4 3 1**

1 Norfolk Cr   020 7706 9567   9–4A

"Tucked away under a grotty pub" at the foot of a Bayswater block, you don't come here for style points, but "Thai food, like in Thailand". Results took a dip last year, but regulars say it's back on form. / W2 2DN; www.theheronpaddington.com; @theheronpaddington; 11 pm, Sun 10.30 pm.

Hicce N1 **NEW**

Coal Drops Yard   awaiting tel   9–3C

Ramsay protégée and former head chef at Angela Hartnett's Murano, Pip Lacey will open her first restaurant, in King's Cross's hip Coal Drops Yard development, in late October 2018, with friend and business partner (who will be front-of-house) Gordy McIntyre; apparently they have been talking about running a restaurant together for 17 years! The focus will be on traditional techniques (marinating, curing and pickling) and there will (of course) be an open wood fire for cooking. Hicce is pronounced ee-che, by the way. / N1C 4AB; www.hicce.co.uk; @hiccelondon; Mon & Tue 9 pm, Fri & Sat 11.30 pm, Wed 10 pm, Thu 11 pm, Sun 5 pm.

Hide W1 **NEW** £95   **5 4 5**

85 Piccadilly   020 3146 8666   3–4C

"Wow, what a debut!" – this "huge", two-floor (plus basement bar), glass-fronted opening, on which Russian-owned Hedonism wines have reportedly spent £20m, is the most ambitious new project of 2018, occupying a landmark, 250-cover site "with a great view over Green Park", which old hands will remember from days of yore as the home of Fahkreldine (long RIP). On the ground floor ('Hide Below' – price shown) an all-day luxurious brasserie, while this first-floor location is dedicated to even finer dining from a six- or nine-course tasting menu (all-in with wine from about £200, with a lighter three-course option available at lunch). Chef-patron "Ollie Dabbous has done it again" with his "exquisite", "light-with-a-Nordic-touch" cuisine, which "looks fabulous and tastes even better"; and whose "extraordinary attention to detail" matches that of the "stunningly beautiful" interior (which, in an ultra-luxe way, also appears "charming and simple"). At both locations, you can order from the "remarkable wine list", also with the option of dialling up any of the 6,500 wines stocked by Hedonism's Mayfair store (keep a clear head though – their most expensive vintages are over £10k!). "Definitely memorable!" / W1J 8JB; www.hide.co.uk; @hide_restaurant; Mon-Fri 10 pm, Sat & Sun 9 pm.

High Road Brasserie W4 £59   **2 2 2**

162-166 Chiswick High Rd   020 8742 7474   8–2A

"A great place to watch the world go by and for brunch on the weekend" – this Soho House owned hang-out, complete with large outside terrace, continues to be a top breakfasting spot for the glitterati of Chiswick (if that's not a contradiction in terms). / W4 1PR; highroadbrasserie.co.uk; @HRBrasserie; Sun-Thu 11 pm, Fri & Sat midnight; booking max 8 may apply.

High Timber EC4 £70 2 3 3
8 High Timber St   020 7248 1777   10–3B
This "reliable and accommodating" South African-owned wine bar by the
Wobbly Bridge (opposite Tate Modern) has a "limited", "steak-specialist"
menu – "which is good because that means it's freshly cooked". The
"incredible wine cellar downstairs and decent South African list upstairs"
make it a great escape from the City. "The interior is a bit spartan 1980s
but the outdoor terrace on the river is great for a dreamy lunch in the
summer". / EC4V 3PA; www.hightimber.com; @HTimber; 10 pm; closed Sat & Sun.

Hill & Szrok E8 £55 3 3 3
60 Broadway Mkt   020 7254 8805   14–2B
Atmospheric Broadway Market butchers, where, by night, you perch
on stools for a counter-style supper of steaks, grills and a small selection
of wines. A funky set-up, but it's decidedly not cheap, and not everyone goes
a bundle on the experience. / E8 4QJ; www.hillandszrok.co.uk; @hillandszrok;
10.30 pm; no Amex; no booking.

Hispania EC3 £66 3 3 3
72-74 Lombard St   020 7621 0338   10–3C
Nothing but praise this year for the high-quality Spanish cuisine offered
by this characterful two-floor restaurant right by the Bank of England, which
is done out in a distinctive, comfy and plush Iberian style, teetering
agreeably between the formal and informal. / EC3V 9AY;
www.hispanialondon.com; @hispanialondon; Tue-Fri 10 pm, Mon 9.30 pm; closed
Sat & Sun.

Hix W1 £64 1 2 2
66-70 Brewer St   020 7292 3518   4–3C
Fans of Mark Hix's West End flagship hail its "excellent modern British
food" and "terrific ambience and premier Soho location", particularly
recommending it for a "lunchtime business meeting". But overall it inspires
remarkably little feedback these days, far too much of it to the effect that
it's too costly and can be "very disappointing". / W1F 9UP;
www.hixrestaurants.co.uk/restaurant/hix-soho; @HixRestaurants; 11.30 pm,
Sun 10.30 pm.

Hix Oyster & Chop House EC1 £63 3 2 2
36-37 Greenhill Rents, Cowcross St   020 7017 1930   10–1A
"Buried off Smithfield on the way to the tube", Mark Hix's original solo
operation put in a strong all-round performance this year. "Business-friendly,
but without compromising on quality" – "the inventive and seasonal British
menu is worthwhile and there is always a decent bit of steak". Top Tip:
4pm-7pm is Happy Hour for oysters. / EC1M 6BN;
www.hixrestaurants.co.uk/restaurant/hix-oyster-cho; @hixchophouse; 11 pm,
Sun 10 pm; closed Sat L.

Holborn Dining Room WC1 £75 3 3 3
252 High Holborn   020 3747 8633   2–1D
"Pies to die for" are the ace in the Brit-food pack at this "huge dining room"
of a business-friendly hotel on the edge of the City. Chef Calum Franklin
is the "wizard" behind this "savoury pastry mecca", which has its own Pie
Room with a dedicated take-away hatch, along with pie and Wellington
masterclasses. Top Tip: "excellent choice for breakfast, too". / WC1V 7EN;
www.holborndiningroom.com; @HolbornDining; 10.30 pm, Sun 10 pm.

Holly Bush NW3 £50 3 3 5
22 Holly Mount   020 7435 2892   9–1A
This "lovely, cosy, traditional pub" – an "unmodernised" 17th-century, Grade
II listed building in Hampstead – is "relaxed and quiet enough for good
conversation", with "a great atmosphere" and "really good food to match".
"Exceptional Sunday roasts" – "but make sure you sit upstairs". / NW3 6SG;
www.hollybushhampstead.co.uk; @thehollybushpub; 10 pm, Sun 8 pm.

Home SW15 SW15 NEW   £57   3 3 3
146 Upper Richmond Rd   020 8780 0592   11–2B
Limited but upbeat feedback on this new neighbourhood café, bar and restaurant on the former site of BIBO (RIP) in Putney, not far from East Putney tube – run by three friends who met at west London Charlotte's Group, and serving a similarly easygoing mix of cocktails and modern bistro dishes. | SW15 2SW; www.homesw15.com; @homesw15; Mon-Fri 10 pm, Sat & Sun 9 pm.

Homeslice   £37   3 3 3
52 Wells St, W1   020 3151 7488   2–1B
13 Neal's Yd, WC2   020 7836 4604   5–2C
101 Wood Lane White City, W12   020 3034 0381   1–2B
374-378 Old St, EC1   020 3151 1121   13–1B
69-71 Queen St, EC4   020 3034 0381   10–2C
"Huge tasty pizzas" with a "very thin crust and unusual toppings" have attracted a strong following for this stripped-down concept. (The group is owned by the late Terry Wogan's sons and has a branch in his old stamping-ground, the BBC's former home at White City.) | www.homeslicepizza.co.uk; @homesliceLDN; 11 pm, EC1 & W1 Sun 10 pm; no booking.

Honest Burgers   £28   3 3 3
"A lot of chains could learn an awful lot from Honest Burgers" which is pipped to the crown of London's best burger only narrowly by a couple of smaller groups (Patty & Bun and Bleecker). "Gloriously juicy" and "scrumptious" patties are served "with lovely buns" and – not to be forgotten – "the legendary, addictive rosemary fries to die for" (included in the price). All this plus "really helpful staff and a lively, industrial-chic vibe" make it a massive ongoing hit. "They even do gluten-free burger buns!". "No wonder it's tough times at Byron…" | www.honestburgers.co.uk; @honestburgers; 10 pm-11 pm; SW9 closed Mon D; EC3 closed Sat & Sun; no booking; SRA-Food Made Good – 1 star.

Honey & Co W1   £47   4 4 3
25a Warren St   020 7388 6175   2–1B
"It's hard to get a table… and a tight fit if you do", but Sarit Packer and Itamar Srulovich's deceptively ordinary looking little Warren Street café punches well above its weight with its "amazingly friendly" service, and "exotic" and "sumptuous" Middle Eastern dishes – "a rare combination of simplicity and outstanding realisation". "A gem for any meal between breakfast (al fresco!) and late dinner." | W1T 5JZ; www.honeyandco.co.uk; @Honeyandco; Sun-Thu midnight, Fri & Sat 1 am; closed Sun; no Amex.

Honey & Smoke W1   £50   4 3 2
216 Great Portland St   020 7388 6175   2–1B
"Delicious, copious and very original Middle Eastern cuisine" inspires nothing but praise for Honey & Co's bigger sibling, south of Great Portland Street tube – a modern take on the grill house – even if ratings support those who feel "it's not quite as excellent as when it first opened". "Shame the decor is so unwelcoming", too – "it looks like a converted office" and can seem "awkward and uncomfortable", especially in comparison with the "café intimacy" of its stablemate. | W1W 5QW; www.honeyandco.co.uk/smoke; @Honeyandco; 11.30 pm; closed Sun & Mon.

Hood SW2   £50   4 3 3
67 Streatham Hill   020 3601 3320   11–2D
"A small-but-changing menu of high-quality dishes using fresh, local and seasonal produce, a great selection of beers and ales plus English wines (and interesting soft drinks)" is served "promptly but without being rushed" at this "fabulous local" in Streatham. | SW2 4TX; www.hoodrestaurants.com; @HoodStreatham; Sun-Thu midnight, Fri & Sat 1 am.

Hoppers £61   4 2 2
49 Frith St, W1 no tel 5–2A
77 Wigmore St, W1 020 3319 8110 3–1A
"Fabulous spiced dishes" based around hoppers (Sri Lankan rice pancakes) offer "a completely different experience of Indian (or akin to Indian anyway) food" at the Sethi family's "so original" and "fun" street-food cafés, in Soho and Marylebone. But while fans still find the formula "amazing... even with the wait", ratings slid badly this year due to the number of reporters who found it "didn't live up to the hype", citing issues including "pushy" or "overly swift" service and a sense it's "just a bit too pleased with its own vibe". Soho is walk-in only, except for ticketed events every other Sunday.

The Horseshoe NW3 £53   3 3 4
28 Heath St 020 7431 7206 9–2A
This "buzzy" gastropub has a "hipper atmosphere than most in Hampstead". The "good honest local food" is a "reliable bet" to accompany "great beer" from the in-house Camden Town Brewery – founded downstairs in the cellar and now brewed nearby. / NW3 6TE; www.thehorseshoehampstead.com; @TheHorseShoeCTB; 10 pm, Fri & Sat 10.30pm, Sun 9.30 pm.

Hot Stuff SW8 £28   3 5 2
19-23 Wilcox Rd 020 7720 1480 11–1D
"A simple menu of vibrant and fresh-tasting curries" is a joy at this "favourite local Indian": a "very charming" and "reasonably priced" family business in the characterful stretch of Vauxhall's Little Portugal that featured in the movie 'My Beautiful Laundrette'. / SW8 2XA; www.welovehotstuff.com; Mon-Thu, Sat, Fri 10 pm; closed Mon-Thu, Sat L, closed Sun; no Amex; no booking.

House of Ho W1 £62   3 4 4
1 Percy St 020 7323 9130 2–1C
Vietnam meets Japan at this "buzzy" outfit in an "attractive townhouse off Charlotte Street" in Fitzrovia. Chef Ian Pengelly's "delicious and mostly authentic food" combines with "attentive service" for "a wonderful experience that's hard not to enjoy". / W1T 1DB; www.houseofho.co.uk; @HouseOfHo; 11 pm; closed Sun.

House Restaurant, National Theatre SE1 £56   2 3 2
National Theatre, South Bank 020 7452 3600 2–3D
An "ideal pre-theatre venue", the National's "pleasant" dining room focuses wisely on a "small, tight menu" that satisfies most reporters – and "surprises" some. "The standard of cooking varies, but the service is always excellent": "they'll get you to your seat at the theatre in time!". / SE1 9PX; house.nationaltheatre.org.uk; @NT_House; 10.30 pm, Sun 10 pm; D only (L served on matinee days), closed Sun.

Hovarda W1 NEW £68   2 3 4
36-40 Rupert St 020 3019 3460 4–3D
"Lovely place... shame about the ridiculous portion-sizes given the price": this good-looking winter 2017 opening, just south of Shaftesbury Avenue, is the brainchild of the folks behind Marylebone's Yosma, serving an 'Aegean-inspired' (i.e. Turkish/Greek) menu, but even those who find the "food's good, sometimes brilliant" can still on occasion feel it's "overpriced". / W1D 6DR; www.hovarda.london; Sun-Thu 11 pm, Fri & Sat 11.30 pm.

Hubbard & Bell, Hoxton Hotel WC1 £57   3 3 3
199-206 High Holborn 020 7661 3030 2–1D
"A very cool place, at its best at breakfast and late at night" – this chilled hang-out in a chichi Soho House hotel (actually in Holborn, despite the name) serves superior burgers, and other "good, down-to-earth dishes". / WC1V 7BD; www.hubbardandbell.com; @HubbardandBell; Tue-Thu 9.30 pm, Fri & Sat 10 pm.

Humble Grape £53 3 4 4
Theberton St, N1 020 3904 4480 9–3D
2 Battersea Rise, SW11 020 3620 2202 11–2C
8 Devonshire Row, EC2 020 3887 9287 10–2D NEW
I Saint Bride's Passage, EC4 020 7583 0688 10–2A
"Unpretentious, relaxed and with a wide choice of wines and small plates" –
with the latter *"nicely judged to complement wines"* – plus *"enthusiastic and
knowledgeable service"* win particular praise for the Battersea original
of this small group, and also its EC4 spin-off *"hidden away and
almost under the crypt of St Bride's Church"*. Last year, a further outlet also
opened in Islington (no reports yet), and in 2018 a new City branch opened
near Liverpool Street. Top Tip: *"Monday nights is the time to go as wine
is sold at retail price"*. / www.humblegrape.co.uk; @humblegrape.

Hunan SW1 £94 5 2 1
51 Pimlico Rd 020 7730 5712 6–2D
"Truly one-of-a-kind" – the Peng family's Pimlico stalwart *"continues
to surprise and tantalise with its amazing"* cooking and is an *"all-time
favourite"* for many reporters, as well as regularly topping the
list of London's best Chinese restaurants. *"Don't ask for the menu"* –
"let Mr Peng or his son Michael decide what you should be served with" –
a never-ending stream of tapas-sized dishes (if you don't like one, you won't
go hungry as plenty more will arrive). Typically results are *"brilliant"*,
and there's a *"huge wine list that's amazingly well-suited to spicy food"*.
/ SW1W 8NE; www.hunanlondon.com; 11 pm; closed Sun.

Hush W1 £86 2 2 2
8 Lancashire Ct 020 7659 1500 3–2B
"The best location", a courtyard off Bond Street where *"you can sit when
the weather is warm"*, makes this bar and brasserie (co-founded by Roger
Moore's son Geoffrey Moore) a *"perennial favourite"* of the Mayfair crowd
as it approaches its 20th anniversary. There's a *"nice atmosphere about the
place and it works equally well for business as it does for fun"*. *"The food
is lovely but so it should be at these prices – although if you're shopping
in Mayfair you can probably afford it!"*. Branches in Holborn and St Paul's
have both closed down in recent years. / W1S 1EY; www.hush.co.uk; 11 pm;
closed Sun; booking max 12 may apply.

**Hutong,
The Shard SE1** £100 2 2 4
31 St Thomas St 020 3011 1257 10–4C
"On the 33rd-floor the views over London are spectacular" as you'd expect
of this dramatically-located dining room – the Shard's most commented-on
destination – which won more consistent praise this year for its *"exciting and
delicious"* Chinese cuisine under chef Sifu Fei Wang. On the downside, it can
still be *"let down a little by the service"*, but there's only really one major
complaint here: that it's still *"grossly overpriced"*. / SE1 9RY; www.hutong.co.uk;
@HutongShard; 10.30 pm; No shorts.

Ibérica £53 2 2 3
Zig Zag Building, 70 Victoria St, SW1 020 7636 8650 2–4B
195 Great Portland St, W1 020 7636 8650 2–1B
12 Cabot Sq, E14 020 7636 8650 12–1C
89 Turnmill St, EC1 020 7636 8650 10–1A
"A decent Spanish option (but it won't blow your mind)" – these *"welcoming
and buzzy tapas bars"* remain *"the kind of places one can linger with
friends in true Hispanic style"* (but perhaps lack the pizzazz of the brand's
early days), providing *"cheerful"* (but *"uneven"*) service, and *"reasonably
priced"* (but slightly *"formulaic"*) cuisine. / 11pm, SW1 Sun 10.30 pm;
W1 closed Sun D.

Icco Pizza £18 5 2 1
46 Goodge St, W1   020 7580 9688   2–1C
21a Camden High St, NW1   020 7380 0020   9–3B NEW

"Zero frills… unless you count the oil and spice shaker!" do nothing to dent the adulation for these utilitarian "pit stops" with "bare stainless steel tables and collection from the counter". Fans say its "hot, fresh, thin-based pizza" is "about the best you can get at any price anywhere", and "with a Margherita at £4 and not much more for other options, it is easy to see why there are queues out the door on busy lunchtimes". / www.icco.co.uk; @ICCO_pizza.

Ichi Buns W1 NEW £43 3 2 3
24 Wardour St   020 3937 5888   5–3A

"Great Japanese-style decor" adds pizzazz to this energetically designed three-floor newcomer in Chinatown, complete with clubby basement (with DJs). Feedback is still quite limited, but its menu of ramen, Japanese spring rolls and wagyu beef burgers was mostly highly rated. / W1D 6QJ; www.ichibuns.co.uk; @ichibuns; Mon & Tue 11 pm, Wed & Thu midnight, Fri & Sat 2 am, Sun 10.30 pm.

Ida W10 £47 3 2 3
167 Fifth Ave   020 8969 9853   1–2B

"Tucked away in an unfashionable corner near the Queen's Park Estate", this "genuine neighbourhood Italian" is "usually booked out by an eclectic mix of locals". "Basically this is a pasta restaurant" and – even if results are not show-stoppers – offers "well-priced, sensibly portioned home cuisine"; meanwhile, the welcome is "very friendly" (even if sometimes "the level of service could use an upgrade"), and the interior full of "rustic charm". / W10 4DT; www.idarestaurant.co.uk; 11 pm; closed Mon-Sat L, closed Sun; no Amex.

Ikoyi SW1 £60 4 3 2
1 St James's Market   020 3583 4660   4–4D

"Posh and West African food? I didn't think they went together" – but the "strikingly original fusion" of modern techniques and Nigerian culinary traditional has produced some of "the most interesting cooking in London" at this year-old venue in a new development behind Piccadilly Circus. "An amalgam of an African chef (Iré Hassan-Odukale) and a Heston Blumenthal chef (Canadian-Chinese Jeremy Chan, ex-Fat Duck)", it is housed in a "Scandi-chic interior". "One of the most memorable meals of the year", "it all felt new to me!" / SW1Y 4AH; www.ikoyilondon.com; closed Sun.

Il Guscio N5 £51 3 4 3
231 Blackstock Rd   020 7354 1400   9–1D

"My local Italian and I love it!" – this tightly packed Highbury fixture serves "really tasty pizza" as well other affordable Sardinian-inspired dishes. All this plus "friendly service, and it's child-friendly too!" / N5 2LL; www.ilgusciohighbury.co.uk; Sun-Thu 10.30 pm, Fri & Sat 11 pm; closed Mon-Fri L.

In Parma W1 £40 4 3 2
10 Charlotte Place   020 8127 4277   2–1C

"I hate to admit it, but the cappelletti in brodo" ("pasta filled with Parmesan cheese and beef, slowly cooked for a couple of days and served in a rich capon broth, all of which really is exceptional") "might even be better than my mother's!!" – This Fitzrovia Italian (run by the Food Roots company, and sibling to Hoxton's Via Emilia) offers "authentic Parmesan dishes, prepared by authentic Parmesans", with an emphasis on charcuterie and cheeses from Parma, and with "good Lambrusco served in traditional crockery" (by the bowl) being something of a hallmark. "The restaurant itself is long and narrow and would be a bit of a squeeze when busy, but service is pleasant and prices reasonable. Recommended." / W1T 1SH; www.in-parma.com; 11 pm, Sun 10.30 pm.

India Club,
Strand Continental Hotel WC2   £32   2 2 2
143 Strand   020 7836 4880   2–2D
"The climb up the stairs never fails to get the taste buds revving" on arrival
at this "1940s time-warp" curry house, close to the Indian High
Commission in the Strand. Recently saved from redevelopment, this "iconic"
venue with its "mismatched Formica-topped tables" is "still one of the
best and cheapest Indians in London". Top Tip: "BYO, or buy good-value
beer at the hotel bar". / WC2R IJA; www.strand-continental.co.uk;
@hostelstrandcon; 10.50 pm; booking max 6 may apply.

Indian Accent W1   £91   5 4 4
16 Albemarle St   020 7629 9802   3–3C
"Quite simply, stunning – the best sub-continental cuisine you can get
anywhere outside the subcontinent!" This "addictive" newcomer (a spin-off
from one of India's top restaurants, in New Delhi, with an NYC sibling)
occupies the same site (and is under the same ownership) as its predecessor
Chor Bizarre (RIP) and has made an "astonishingly good" debut with
"very refined and skilful" fusion cuisine (blue cheese naan, for instance)
that's already achieved nigh on the highest ratings in town – "slick service"
and svelte decor: "it's a real joy to eat here". / W1S 4HW;
indianaccent.com/london; @Indian_Accent; Sun-Thu 10 pm, Fri & Sat 10.30 pm.

Indian Moment SW11   £42   3 3 2
44 Battersea Rise   020 7223 6575   11–2C
This local-favourite curry house near Clapham Junction is a "good and
accessible option for all palates" – even if it "tries too hard not to be of the
after-pub variety". "The move around the corner from Northcote Road
to Battersea Rise hasn't reduced its popularity, but the new dining room can
get cramped and extremely noisy". / SW11 1EE; www.indianmoment.co.uk;
@indianmoment; midnight, Sun 10 pm.

Indian Ocean SW17   £36   3 4 2
214 Trinity Rd   020 8672 7740   11–2C
This "wonderfully friendly local curry house" with a long-established fanbase
by Wandsworth Common is "quite the best Indian restaurant in the area".
"Its menu is a bit different from the standard, and well executed."
/ SW17 7HP; www.indianoceanrestaurant.com; 11 pm, Sat 11.30 pm; closed
Mon-Fri L

Indian Rasoi N2   £36   3 3 2
7 Denmark Terrace   020 8883 9093   1–1B
"Don't be fooled by the off-putting exterior" of this intimate Muswell Hill
Indian, which specialises in Mughal-era cuisine. Inside you'll find "rich, tasty
food with some offbeat options" – "really good, authentic grub". / N2 9HG;
www.indian-rasoi.co.uk; 11 pm, Sun 10.30 pm; no Amex.

Indian Zing W6   £54   4 3 2
236 King St   020 8748 5959   8–2B
"Wonderful Indian cuisine with unusual and delicious use of spices" has
generated a big name and following for Manoj Vasaikar's "varied and
interesting" nouvelle Indian, a short walk from Ravenscourt Park. On the
downside, its premises – while attractive – are "tightly packed" and "can be
quite noisy". / W6 0RS; www.indian-zing.co.uk; @IndianZing; 10.30 pm, Sun 10 pm.

Inko Nito W1 NEW £50
55 Broadwick St 020 3959 2650 4–2B
From the folks behind Zuma and Roka, comes a kind of Roka-lite aiming to capture the millennial crowd with this cheaper newcomer in Soho (designed by a Californian agency, and whose sibling is already open in downtown LA). As at Roka, charcoal-grill cooking on the robata (here with Korean influences) is centre stage, but prices are lower than at its swankier stablemates. Too few reviews for a rating as yet, although one early reporter does think it's "very cool". / W1F 9QS; www.inkonitorestaurant.com/london-soho; 11.30 pm, Sun 10 pm.

Ippudo London £46 3 2 3
31a Villiers St, WC2 020 3667 1877 5–4D NEW
1 Crossrail Pl, E14 020 3326 9485 12–1C
"A genuine import from Japan"; lovers of "decent, authentic noodles" give the thumbs-up to the "authentic" ramen served at the three London branches of this chain originating in Fukuoka, with venues in Holborn, Embankment and Canary Wharf. One aficionado insists they're actually "better than their Japanese outlets (although twice the price!)". / @IppudoLondon; WC2 10.30 pm; E14 9.30 pm, Sun 8.30 pm; no bookings.

Isabel W1 £77 2 4 5
26 Albemarle St 020 3096 9292 3–3C
Juan Santa Cruz's gorgeous, gold-and-ebony Mayfair yearling (on the former site of Sumosan, RIP) draws a smart, Eurotrashy crowd and is undoubtedly "beautiful, and great for people watching". "You don't mind a high-end price tag, if the food measures up" too, but whereas some fans describe "such amazing and different flavours from the tapas-style menu" there is a high proportion for whom results are "just uneventful and unexciting". / W1S 4HQ; isabelw1.london; 2.30 am, Sun 11.30 pm.

Ishtar W1 £51 3 3 2
10-12 Crawford St 020 7224 2446 2–1A
The "high-quality Turkish cooking" at this "very welcoming" Marylebone fixture has been "remarkably consistent for a few years now". Top Tip: "exceptional grilled lamb cutlets". / W1U 6AZ; www.ishtarrestaurant.com; 10 pm, Sun 9 pm.

The Ivy WC2 £76 2 3 4
1-5 West St 020 7836 4751 5–3B
"I know it's not the celeb haunt it used to be and is now a bit touristy, but they still make you feel like a king" is still a widely held view on this epic "Theatreland classic" (the original in what's an increasingly sizeable national chain); and for its many fans a visit here is still a "warm, life-affirming experience". However, it feels to some regulars like the appeal is becoming "all about the room" and its "glamorous" decor, amidst growing unease that Richard Caring's group is just "milking it" nowadays – ratings slid across the board this year, and its comfort food cuisine "is as it always was, nothing special… just now even more expensive!". / WC2H 9NQ; www.the-ivy.co.uk; @TheIvyWestSt; Mon-Wed 11.30 pm, Thu-Sat midnight, Sun 10.30 pm; No shorts; booking max 6 may apply.

The Ivy Café £59 1 2 3
96 Marylebone Ln, W1 020 3301 0400 2–1A
120 St John's Wood High St, NW8 020 3096 9444 9–3A
75 High St, SW19 020 3096 9333 11–2B
9 Hill St, TW9 020 3146 7733 1–4A
"A dilution of the Ivy name" – the cheaper, more bistro-esque 'Café' sub-brand is "a woeful imitation of the original" that's "all style and has nothing else to recommend it". Even many of those recommending breakfast – its best feature – say the results are "very predictable", and later in the day you get "standard pub grub-type food at fine dining prices" served by "brittle" and "amateur" staff. "Avoid at all costs!" / 11 pm, Fri & Sat 11.30 pm, Sun 10.30 pm; SW19 11 pm, Sun 10.30 pm; midnight.

Ivy Grills & Brasseries £59 2️⃣2️⃣4️⃣
26-28 Broadwick St, W1   020 3301 1166   4–1C
1 Henrietta St, WC2   020 3301 0200   5–3D
197 King's Rd, SW3   020 3301 0300   6–3C
96 Kensington High St, W8   020 3301 0500   6–1A
One Tower Bridge, 1 Tower Bridge, SE1   020 3146 7722   10–4D
69 Old Broad St, EC2   020 3146 7744   10–2D **NEW**

*"On a nice day in the garden, there couldn't be a better way to have lunch!"
(or an "amazing brunch") than at the Chelsea Garden branch of Richard
Caring's bold brand-extension – "easily the best of the Ivy offshoots". But
even fans concede that "service could be better" and that "you don't come
here for the food": "it's all about that warm, buzzy atmosphere in glorious
surroundings (outside in summer you'll swear you are in the South of France,
watching the Provencal rosé making its way around the beautifully dressed
ladies-who-lunch!)" The other branches offer a similar trade-off, with the
outlets in Kensington and by Tower Bridge ("incredible views from the picture
windows") both scoring well for ambience, although their "comfort food"
offerings are even more "memorably mediocre" than in SW3. 'Ivy in the
Park' which is to open in Canary Wharf is the most recently announced
arrival in the group (at 50 Canada Square Park). On the overall concept,
reporters are split. For a majority "although the spin-offs are not to be
compared with the original Ivy, their name does help give a certain dignity
to the experience". For a significant number though, "the brand is being
trashed" with these "pretentious, unimaginative, chichi and average"
imitations: "Obviously I understand the idea is to shamelessly exploit and
monetise The Ivy name, but this is taking it too far!!" / ivycollection.com.*

Jackson & Rye £54 2️⃣2️⃣2️⃣
56 Wardour St, W1   020 7437 8338   4–2D
219-221 Chiswick High Rd, W4   020 8747 1156   8–2A
Hotham House, 1 Heron Sq, TW9   020 8948 6951   1–4A
*This trio of US-style diners attracts mixed reports, with the Richmond
branch receiving the highest praise for a "great view of the Thames". The
food is "perfectly acceptable" to some, "tasteless and insipid" to others,
but there's general agreement that "breakfast is the best option".
/ www.jacksonrye.com; @JacksonRye; 11 pm, Sun 10.30 pm; EC2 closed Sat & Sun.*

Jacob the Angel WC2 £9 3️⃣3️⃣3️⃣
16a Neal's Yard   no tel   5–2C
*Zoë and Layo Paskin (the siblings behind The Palomar and The Barbary) run
this tiny coffee house (just 10 covers) in Seven Dials. A few in-the-know rate
it for a quick brunch, superior bun or coffee, but don't go expecting magic.
/ WC2H 9DP; www.jacobtheangel.co.uk; 5 pm; closed Mon-Sun D; no booking.*

Jaffna House SW17 £30 3️⃣2️⃣2️⃣
90 Tooting High St   020 8672 7786   11–2C
*This "no-nonsense", "authentic, family-run caff" in Tooting split opinion this
year. Most reporters still approve its "wide variety of unusual Sri Lankan
specialities and incredibly good value thali selection" all at "cheap prices"
in "a rather 1980s time-warp dining room". Others though are more
cautious: "tipped as one of the better south Indians in Tooting but very
cramped and nothing out-of-the-ordinary in my experience". / SW17 0RN;
11.30 pm.*

Jamavar W1 £83 3 4 3
8 Mount St 020 7499 1800 3–3B
"Having been to Jamavar in Bangalore, I tried their London restaurant and
was most impressed" – Leela Palace's "plush", colonial-style yearling
("I'm not sure the decor is very PC!") is "a great addition to Mayfair" and
wins ecstatic praise from many reporters for its "super slick service" and
"fabulous and spicy" dishes that "strike a balance between the traditional
spicing and flavours of Indian cuisine, but with high-end presentation and
gastronomic flourishes!" No hiding, however, that it was a blow when they
lost founding chef Rohit Ghai in January 2018, with ratings in this year's
survey at laudable levels, but miles away from the giddy heights achieved
in year one. / W1K 3NF; www.jamavarrestaurants.com; @JamavarLondon;
closed Sun.

James Cochran EC3 EC3 £68
19 Bevis Marks, Liverpool St 020 3302 0310 10–2D
James Cochran has left his eponymous City venture which retains the right
to trade under his name. (He has now re-appeared in Islington, with the
opening of 1251, a few doors along from his short lived Upper Street
venture). This venue, serving the small plates Cochran developed, recorded
some high marks this year. That said, there were also those who, perhaps
unsurprisingly, have discerned "a lack of buzz or passion" about the place
in recent times and, in the circumstances it seems best to leave a re-rating
till next year. / EC3A 7BJ; www.jcochran.restaurant; @jcochranchef; Wed-Sat 10 pm,
Sun 4.30 pm; closed Sat L & Sun.

Jamies Italian £53 1 1 1
"Just because it says Jamie Oliver on the door does not mean it is going
to be good", and for the last six years his beleaguered chain has received
a dire scorecard in the Harden's survey – "awful, just awful" – no wonder
the TV chef had to rescue it with his own, very deep, pockets this year. With
these well-publicised financial problems, media fooderati like Marina
O'Loughlin in The Sunday Times have finally woken from their long slumber
and begun to comment on the fact that the emperor isn't wearing any
clothes (bringing new meaning to the name 'Naked Chef'!): what on earth
took them so long? / www.jamiesitalian.com; @JamiesItalianUK; 11.30 pm,
Sun 10.30 pm; booking: min 6.

Jashan N8 £33 4 4 2
19 Turnpike Ln 020 8340 9880 1–1C
"It looks like your average curry house, but is anything but" – this "low-key
favourite" provides "superlative dishes and cooking amid bog-standard decor
in remote Turnpike Lane" and "is so cheap too!". / N8 0EP; www.jashan.co.uk;
10.15 pm, Fri & Sat 10.30 pm; closed Mon-Sun L; no Amex; may need 6+ to book.

Jean-Georges at The Connaught W1 £98 3 3 3
The Connaught, Carlos Place 020 7107 8861 3–3B
Mixed and limited feedback on this stellar NYC's chef, Jean-Georges
Vongerichten's latest London foray, which occupies a light-filled conservatory
at the side of this blue-blooded Mayfair hotel. Ratings are not bad for its
eclectic menu – from caviar and wagyu beef to pizza and cod 'n' chips –
but although results can be "really lovely", it's darn expensive and no-one
is that blown away. One stand-out feature though – "superb afternoon tea".
/ W1K 2AL; www.the-connaught.co.uk/mayfair-restaurants/jean-georges;
@TheConnaught; 11 pm.

Jidori £23 3 3 2
15 Catherine St, WC2 020 7686 5634 5–3D
89 Kingsland High St, E8 020 7686 5634 14–1A
Well-reputed (slightly hyped) Dalston yakitori café (run by Natalie Lee-Joe
& Brett Redman) which wins solid (if not spectacular) ratings for its
Japanese small plates. They must be doing something right, as they opened
a 50-cover Covent Garden sibling in February 2018, praised in early reports
for its "good food and friendly staff".

Jikoni W1 £68 [4][4][4]
21 Blandford St 020 70341988 2–1A
Ravinder Bhogal's "magic touch with flavour" helps create "wonderful and interesting dishes" at her Marylebone yearling (whose cuisine reflects the chef-patron's mixed heritage with flavours from East Africa, the Middle East, Asia and Britain). With its "informal service" and "cosy" style it's "a perfect venue for culinary exploration". / W1U 3DJ; www.jikonilondon.com; @JikoniLondon; Wed-Fri, Tue, Sat 10.30 pm; closed Tue, Sat L, closed Sun & Mon.

Jin Kichi NW3 £47 [5][4][3]
73 Heath St 020 7794 6158 9–1A
"Like walking through a portal into Tokyo" – this "really tiny" Japanese stalwart is "one of the few Hampstead restaurants worth going to" (note: "you'll need to book"). "The stuff on the grill/ BBQ (including yakitori meat skewers) is to die for", and "the sushi remains excellent", while "a recent revamp has not dulled its charm". "Sit and watch the superb food being prepared right under your nose – amazing!". / NW3 6UG; www.jinkichi.com; 10.30 pm, Sun 10 pm; closed Mon.

Jinjuu W1 £61 [4][3][4]
16 Kingly St 020 8181 8887 4–2B
Korean-American TV chef Judy Joo "puts a fun – and delicious – twist on Korean food" at her "hidden gem" – a "lively and noisy" basement off Carnaby Street. Attractions include some of "the best Korean fried chicken in town and the rest of the food is damn good too", but some feel that it's "way too small to have a DJ" – you've been warned! / W1B 5PS; www.jinjuu.com; @JinjuuSoho; Mon-Wed midnight, Thu-Sat 1.30 am, Sun 11 pm.

Joanna's SE19 £47 [3][5][4]
56 Westow Hill 020 8670 4052 1–4D
"A great local", this American-inspired venue in Crystal Palace has been run by two generations of the Ellner family and "celebrated its 40th anniversary this year with an excellent retro menu". "Really reliable for every occasion", from breakfast through to "taking the in-laws out for dinner". / SE19 1RX; www.joannas.uk.com; @Joannas_1978; 10 pm, Sun 9 pm.

Joe Allen WC2 £55 [2][3][4]
2 Burleigh St 020 7836 0651 5–3D
"Well done!" – "The move from Exeter Street to nearby Burleigh Street looks to have paid off" for this famous and "fun" Covent Garden veteran, forced to relocate a year ago. "The iconic Joe Allen atmosphere has been almost totally recreated, with the help of most of the original fixtures and fittings from the old place". "Service has moved up a notch or two" and while "the food can still be a bit hit 'n' miss", it's actually rated as much more consistently dependable now. Top Menu Tip: the "hidden off-the-menu burger" is still the top menu choice. / WC2E 7PX; www.joeallen.co.uk; @JoeAllenWC2; 11 pm, Sun 10.30 pm.

Joe Public SW4 £15 [3][4][2]
4 The Pavement 020 7622 4676 11–2D
"If all you want is a quick, bite-sized tasty pizza and a glass of vino, pop in here!" – to this quirky, small, handily-located outlet (in a converted WC) by Clapham Common. / SW4 7AA; www.joepublicpizza.com; @JoepublicSW4; midnight, Sun 11 pm; no booking.

Jolene N16 NEW
20 Newington Green 020 3887 2309 1–1C
On the former Newington Green site of Dandy (RIP), a new bakery (and evening restaurant) from the founders of Primeur and Westerns Laundry, Jeremie Cometto-Lingenheim and David Gingell. Rare and ancient grains [you can say that sort of thing with a straight face nowadays! Ed] feature in the bread and cakes, milled and baked daily on site. / N16 9PU; www.jolenen16.com.

Jollibee SW5 NEW
180-182 Earls Court Rd   awaiting tel   6–2A
Fried chicken and spaghetti with sweet hot dog sauce may not sound that interesting, but when the first European branch of Filipino fast food chain Jollibee opened in Milan in early 2018, people queued for HOURS to try it. Jollibee has been 'bringing chicken joy' for over 40 years in over 750 locations – and now it's our turn with this opening, in October 2018, on the former Earl's Court Wagamama site. / SW5 9QG; www.jollibee.com.ph/international; @Jollibee.

Jolly Gardeners SW18   £52   3 3 3
214 Garratt Ln   020 8870 8417   11–2B
An Earlsfield gastroboozer with a dining room in a "bright extension at the back", with a "good menu", from former MasterChef winner Dhruv Baker. Top Tip: "go later in the week for more interesting food". / SW18 4EA; www.thejollygardeners.com; @Jollygardensw15; 9.30 pm.

Jones & Sons N16   £51   3 3 3
Stamford Works, 3 Gillett St   020 7241 1211   14–1A
"A weekly-changing, perfectly executed modern British menu", with plenty of steak and fish options, wins praise for this open-plan venture near Dalston station. "I'm always surprised it's not full but maybe all the local hipsters have gone vegan?" / N16 8JH; www.jonesandsonsdalston.com; @JonesSons; Mon-Thu midnight, Fri & Sat 1 am, Sun 7 pm; booking max 7 may apply.

The Jones Family Kitchen SW1 NEW
7-8 Eccleston Yard   020 7739 1740   2–4B
This June 2018 opening near Victoria Coach Station, from the folks behind the Jones Family Project in Shoreditch, majors in steaks, with meat sourced from The Ginger Pig. Early reports suggest it's a useful newcomer in a still-underprovided area. / SW1W 9AZ; www.jonesfamilyproject.co.uk; @JonesShoreditch; Tue-Sat, Mon 10.30 pm, Sun 3.30 pm.

The Jones Family Project EC2   £58   3 4 4
78 Great Eastern St   020 7739 1740   13–1B
Charcoal-grilled steaks and other meaty fare are the menu mainstays at this Shoreditch basement (with cocktail bar above), and were again solidly well-rated this year. / EC2A 3JL; www.jonesfamilyproject.co.uk; @JonesShoreditch; midnight, Sun 6 pm.

José SE1   £52   5 4 5
104 Bermondsey St   020 7403 4902   10–4D
"Pretty much as good as it gets for high-end tapas, and fantastic Spanish wines" – José Pizarro's "genius" Bermondsey original is "a rare combination of delicious food" ("new twists on classic dishes" which are "exceptional in their simplicity and quality"), "plus careful service and a joyful atmosphere"… "if you can squeeze in, it's always impossibly busy". / SE1 3UB; www.josepizarro.com; @Jose_Pizarro; 10.15 pm, Sun 5.15 pm; closed Sun D; no booking.

José Pizarro EC2   £59   3 2 2
Broadgate Circle   020 7256 5333   13–2B
This three-year-old tapas joint in Broadgate Circle consistently rates quite well and is often deafeningly busy, but in this more corporate environment has never generated the wider interest surrounding Pizarro's original venue in Bermondsey. / EC2M 2QS; www.josepizarro.com/jose-pizarro-broadgate; @JP_Broadgate; 10.30 pm; closed Sun.

Joy King Lau WC2 £39 3 2 2
3 Leicester St   020 7437 1132   5–3A

"Old-school Cantonese" over three floors just off Leicester Square with "legendary soft shell crab and brilliant dim sum", "fabulous, flavoursome morsels that arrive hot and steaming at your table". It's "not at all glamorous, but once you start eating you won't notice!" and it's "always super busy and crowded, so you have to queue – but it's soooo worth it". / WC2H 7BL; www.joykinglau.com; 11.30 pm, Sun 10.30 pm.

Jugemu W1 £40 5 2 3
3 Winnett St   020 7734 0518   4–2D

"If you know your Japanese food and you don't want high-end dining with all the associated costs, then flock here! Flock and wait for one of the precious tables" at this little Soho izakaya presided over by chef Yuya Kikuchi (the best bet is to sit at the bar and watch him in action). Stellar sushi is the star turn here, although there are other menu options. Communication is "more or less without English" and "service is fine… if you have a clue what is going on". / W1D 6JY; jugemu-uk.crayonsite.com; 10 pm, Sun 9 pm.

The Jugged Hare EC1 £63 4 2 2
49 Chiswell St   020 7614 0134   13–2A

"Fabulous olde English food" – "game, pies, Scotch eggs, jugged hares, trotters" – "in a bustling modern setting" gives this gastropub near the Barbican a real edge. "We put up with the noise and over-stretched service for the sheer variety of game in season", and "their own-brand beer is too damn good!". / EC1Y 4SA; www.thejuggedhare.com; @thejuggedhare; Mon-Wed 11 pm, Thu-Sat midnight; closed Sun.

Julie's W11 £55
135 Portland Rd   020 7229 8331   7–2A

'Coming Soon 2018' is the message on the website of this once-famous, old Holland Park classic – a famously sexy 1970s subterranean tangle of rooms, where rock stars once partied hard, and where Princess Anne's first hubbie, Captain Mark Phillips, had his stag night back in the day. Apparently, it's been just-about-to-reopen ever since it closed for a refurb in spring 2016 – we continue to maintain a listing in the hope rather than the expectation that this is correct. / W11 4LW; www.juliesrestaurant.com; 11 pm.

K10 £32 3 3 2
3 Appold St, EC2   020 7539 9209   13–2B
Minster Ct, Mincing Ln, EC3   020 3019 2510   10–3D
15 Queen St, EC4   020 3019 9130   10–2C NEW
78 Fetter Lane, EC4   020 3019 9140   10–2A NEW

A "lunchtime sushi favourite" in the City – the Mincing Lane branch boasts Europe's longest 'kaiten' conveyor belt of sushi, sashimi and other Japanese dishes. This and the Broadgate restaurant are only open for weekday lunch, but the chain has takeaway and delivery options in the evening. New branches opened this year in Queen Street and Fetter Lane. / www.k10.com; 3 pm; Appold 9 pm; Closed D, closed Sat & Sun; no booking at L.

Kaffeine £13 3 5 4
15 Eastcastle St, W1   020 7580 6755   3–1D
66 Great Titchfield St, W1   020 7580 6755   3–1C

"Some of the best coffee shops anywhere!" – this Aussie/Kiwi-owned duo are "fabulous independents" ranking in London's very top tier, with their "delicious sarnies and salads" and addictive coffees from a regularly changing selection of suppliers. "Great vibe at both locations" too. / kaffeine.co.uk/Eastcastle; @kaffeinelondon; 6 pm, Sun 5 pm; no bookings.

Kahani SW1 NEW
1 Wilbraham Place   020 7730 7634   6–2D
*This September 2018 opening took over the 90-cover site, opposite
Cadogan Hall, that was formerly Canvas (RIP). It's the brainchild of chef
Peter Joseph (raised in Tamil Nadu, and ex-executive chef of Mayfair's
Tamarind) and offers modern Indian cuisine, with British influences.
/ SW1X 9AE; www.kahanilondon.com; 10.30 pm.*

Kai Mayfair W1   £121   2 2 2
65 South Audley St   020 7493 8988   3–3A
*Not every Chinese restaurant features bottles of Chateau Pétrus on its wine
list at over £8,000, and Bernard Yeoh's swish, contemporary Mayfair
institution remains one of London's most ambitious Asian venues. Practically
all reports agree on the high pedigree of its cuisine, but even fans can
acknowledge some dishes seem very fully priced. / W1K 2QU;
www.kaimayfair.co.uk; @kaimayfair; 10.45 pm; closed Sun.*

Kaifeng NW4   £70   3 2 2
51 Church Rd   020 8203 7888   1–1B
*The value equation often features in reports on this well-known Chinese
stalwart in Hendon, acclaimed by fans for "wonderful kosher food that's
worth paying a bit extra for". Coeliacs (also catered for) feel the same way
"although pricey, it's the only place I can get a decent Chinese meal that
doesn't compromise on taste". Those without special dietary requirements,
though, merely find it "very overpriced". In case you're wondering, it's named
after the eastern city where Jewish merchants on the Silk Road settled more
than a thousand years ago. / NW4 4DU; www.kaifeng.co.uk; @KaifengKosher;
10 pm; closed Fri & Sat.*

Kanada-Ya   £29   5 3 3
3 Panton St, SW1   020 7930 3511   5–4A
64 St Giles High St, WC2   020 7240 0232   5–1B
35 Upper St, N1   020 7288 2787   9–3D NEW
*"The best ramen in London" ("the pork broth is wonderful – there's nought
better on a cold day, when it really hits the spot") scores nothing but high
praise for this small Japanese noodle chain with bars in Soho, Covent
Garden and now also in Islington. Top tip – look for the "Burford eggs done
just enough with a slightly runny yolk" and "don't miss the truffle ramen,
which is absolutely the best!" / 10.30 pm; WC2 no bookings.*

Kaosarn   £28   4 2 3
110 St Johns Hill, SW11   020 7223 7888   11–2C
181 Tooting High St, SW17   020 8672 8811   11–2C NEW
Brixton Village, Coldharbour Ln, SW9   020 7095 8922   11–2D
*These "cheap 'n' cheerful" family-run outfits in Brixton, Battersea and now
Tooting serve "really tasty Thai food", although "they seem to want you
in and out very quickly!" "Love that you can BYO". / SW9 10 pm, Sun 9 pm;
SW11 closed Mon L.*

Kappacasein SE16   £9   4 3 3
1 Voyager Industrial Estate   07837 756852   12–2A
*"Some of the best cheese toasties in London, plus fantastic raclette" won
renown for Bill Oglethorpe's Borough Market venture – for years a stall
in the market and since 2017 with permanent shop premises in nearby
Stoney Street. / SE16 4RP; www.kappacasein.com; @kappacasein; closed Sat D,
closed Mon-Fri & Sun; cash only; no booking.*

Kashmir SW15 £43 **4** **3** 2
18-20 Lacy Rd 07477 533 888 11–2B

"An upscale addition to Putney's diverse Indian dining scene, Kashmir is the restaurant we locals didn't know we needed!" – "a distinct cut above a typical local cuzza", with "genuinely delightful" service and regional Kashmiri dishes (as well as more usual options) that are "sensitively-spiced and freshly-cooked, with good depth of flavour". / SW15 1NL; www.kashmirrestaurants.co.uk; @KashmirRestUK; Mon, Wed & Thu, Tue, Sun 10.30 pm, Fri & Sat 11 pm; closed Tue L.

Kaspar's Seafood and Grill,
The Savoy Hotel WC2 £92 **3** **3** **4**
100 The Strand 020 7420 2111 5–3D

This "beautiful Art Deco dining room" – known for decades as The Savoy River Restaurant – puts "the emphasis on fish and seafood" with a "very good range" realised proficiently and "welcoming" service too. Numerous "wonderful experiences" are reported, and it's a good venue for business entertaining too. Top Tip: "perfect breakfast". / WC2R 0EU; www.kaspars.co.uk; @TheSavoyLondon; 11 pm.

Kateh W9 £70 **3** 2 **3**
5 Warwick Pl 020 7289 3393 9–4A

This "lovely neighbourhood Persian" in Little Venice serves "interesting and delicious" modern interpretations of classic dishes with traditional Iranian hospitality. It can be a squeeze and "the acoustics are terrible – but it's worth it". / W9 2PX; www.katehrestaurant.co.uk; @RestaurantKateh; 11 pm; closed Mon-Fri L.

Kazan £53 **3** **4** **3**
77 Wilton Rd, SW1 020 7233 8298 2–4B
93-94 Wilton Rd, SW1 020 7233 7100 2–4B

A "local gem" a short walk from Victoria station – this "professional and unpretentious" Ottoman-themed outfit (with a smaller offshoot opposite) "sets out to provide well-cooked Turkish food to its neighbourhood, and does it very well". "A real unexpected pleasure – quality ingredients, treated simply and with the lightest of touches". / www.kazan-restaurant.com; 10 pm, Fri & Sat 10.30 pm, Sun 9.30 pm.

Kazu W1 NEW £55
64 Charlotte St 020 3848 5777 2–1C

No reports yet on this early 2018 opening – a 'contemporary Japanese' in fairly traditional style on Fitzrovia's 'restaurant row', majoring in sushi. It has a good pedigree, with a head chef formerly of Chisou (Dham Kodituwakku). / W1T 4QD; kazurestaurants.com; @KazuRestaurants; Mon-Fri 10 pm, Sat & Sun 9 pm.

The Keeper's House,
Royal Academy W1 £66 2 2 **3**
Royal Academy of Arts, Burlington House, 020 7300 5881 3–3D

Tucked away in the basement of the massively expanded Royal Academy, this "quiet" and elegant venue (with bar, garden and dining room) is undoubtedly "useful if visiting an exhibition". Fans acclaim the modern British cooking here, too, but the odd doubter continues to feel that it "needs to do better" on the food front. / W1J 0BD; www.royalacademy.org.uk/keepers-house; @TheKeepersHouse; 11.30; closed Sun.

Ken Lo's Memories SW1 £60 2 2 2
65-69 Ebury St 020 7730 7734 2–4B

The late Ken Lo's Belgravia operation was a pioneer of high-quality Oriental cuisine. It retains a loyal fan base, but while some regulars judge it "tried and trusted… not the cheapest but superb", others fear it is becoming "a shadow of its former self". / SW1W 0NZ; www.memoriesofchina.co.uk; 11 pm, Sun 10.30 pm.

Kennington Tandoori SE11 £54 **3 3 3**
313 Kennington Rd 020 7735 9247 1–3C
*For "curries a cut above the average" – and the chance to spot MPs from
nearby Westminster – this Indian local in Kennington "is a vote winner".
There's a "buzzing ambience", with "the owner a convivial ringmaster". Top
Tip: "avoid cricket days as it is very near The Oval!". / SE11 4QE;
www.kenningtontandoori.com; @TheKTLondon; Mon-Thu 12.30 am, Fri 1 am;
no Amex.*

Kensington Place W8 £60 **3 2 2**
201-209 Kensington Church St 020 7727 3184 7–2B
*Top dog in the London dining scene 25 years ago – and nowadays
specialising in fish as part of the D&D London stable – this extensively
glazed, "very noisy" venue just off Notting Hill Gate "can be patchy, but hits
the spot exactly when on form", with "lovely fresh seafood", "cooked
to perfection". / W8 7LX; www.kensingtonplace-restaurant.co.uk;
@KPRestaurantW8; 10 pm; closed Mon L, closed Sun.*

Kensington Square Kitchen W8 £47 **4 4 3**
9 Kensington Sq 020 7938 2598 6–1A
*"The perfect spot for breakfast/brunch" – a cute little café (also with
basement seating) in Kensington's oldest square, providing "delicious coffee,
cakes, soups and salads and a nice neighbourhood feel". / W8 5EP;
www.kensingtonsquarekitchen.co.uk; @KSKRestaurant; 4.30 pm, Sun 4 pm; closed
Mon-Sun D; no Amex.*

The Kensington Wine Rooms W8 £57 **2 3 3**
127-129 Kensington Church St 020 7727 8142 7–2B
*"Lots of interesting and different wines by the glass" ("some you would not
normally come across") is the star feature at this modern wine bar
(with stablemates in Fulham and Hammersmith), just off Notting Hill Gate.
Most (if not quite all) reports say "the food is pretty good too". / W8 7LP;
www.greatwinesbytheglass.com; @wine_rooms; Mon-Wed 11 pm, Thu-Sat midnight.*

Kerbisher & Malt £26 **3 2 2**
164 Shepherd's Bush Rd, W6 020 3556 0228 8–1C
50 Abbeville Rd, SW4 020 3417 4350 11–2D
*This contemporary take on an "old-style fish-and-chip shop" has won a solid
following over the past seven years, first in Brook Green and more recently
in Clapham (outposts in Ealing and East Sheen have come and gone).
Ethical sourcing is given due prominence, and the results are "good fresh
fish, perfectly cooked" in a "clean" environment ("a bit draughty in winter")
and giving "reliable value for money". / www.kerbisher.co.uk; 10-10.30 pm, Sun &
Mon 9-9.30 pm; W6 closed Mon; no booking.*

Kerridges Bar & Grill SW1 NEW £80
Whitehall Place 020 7321 3244 2–3D
*Hand & Flowers chef and TV star, Tom Kerridge, launched in the capital
in September 2018, taking over the magnificent chamber at this five-star
hotel between Trafalgar Square and Embankment that was formerly
Massimo (RIP), and which has had a makeover care of design agency The
Studio. Head chef Nick Beardshaw creates, so we are told, 'refined British
comfort food and reborn classics' in a brasserie-style format which aims
to dispel the stultifying grandeur of its former occupant. / SW1A 2BD;
www.kerridgesbarandgrill.co.uk; @kerridgesbandg; Fri-Sun, Mon-Thu 10 pm.*

Kettners W1 NEW £65 3 3 5
29 Romilly St 020 7734 6112 5–2A
"An old treasure given the Nick Jones treatment... welcome back!" –
this resurrected Soho landmark gets the thumbs-up from most who have
visited after its swish revamp care of the Soho House group, certainly for its
"handsome looks" (including the gorgeous bar). Its "initially underwhelming-
looking" brasserie menu can "deliver real joy", even if overall ratings for the
cooking are rather more middling. / W1D 5HP; www.kettners.com; 1 am,
Sun midnight.

Khan's W2 £26 2 2 2
13-15 Westbourne Grove 020 7727 5420 7–1C
Big and busy curry house institution on Westbourne Grove, known for the
distinctive palm-tree pillars in its main dining room. Its 70+ main courses
number "all the standard dishes" – results are "solid if not perhaps great"
but come at a cost that's "extremely cheap". Founded more than 40 years
ago, it has been alcohol-free for the past 19 (no-alcohol Cobra beer is on
the menu). / W2 4UA; www.khansrestaurant.com; @KhansRestaurant; Mon-Thu,
Sat & Sun, Fri 11 pm.

Kiku W1 £69 3 3 2
17 Half Moon St 020 7499 4208 3–4B
Stalwart Mayfair Japanese near Shepherd Market, where a small but
dedicated fan club continue to acclaim high quality, traditional cooking.
/ W1J 7BE; www.kikurestaurant.co.uk; 11 pm, Sun 10.30 pm; closed Sun L.

Kiln W1 £33 4 3 4
58 Brewer St no tel 4–3C
"Sit at the bar and watch with glee as dishes come towards you..." –
Ben Chapman's Soho sensation instantly carved a massive reputation with
its "unique menu (great for spice lovers)" that "nails Thai tastes very well",
with an "original but unpretentious" selection of "excellent, hearty, modern"
Thai creations ("charcoal grills, plus a speciality daily noodle dish").
Conditions are "crammed-in" and "loud", but frickin' funky. / W1F 9TL;
www.kilnsoho.com; 11 pm; closed Sun.

Kimchee WC1 £38 2 2 2
71 High Holborn 020 7430 0956 2–1D
These "busy" Korean BBQ joints – a Holborn original and in the new
Pancras Square development (tel 020 3907 8474) – offer a range of grilled
dishes, signature hot pickles and Korean cocktails in modern settings.
Reports are "slightly variable" but most feel the food is "enjoyable".
/ WC1V 6EA; www.kimchee.uk.com; @KIMCHEErest; 10.30 pm.

Kintan £35 3 2 2
21 Great Castle St, W1 020 3890 1212 3–1C
34-36 High Holborn, WC1 020 7242 8076 10–2A
This Japanese tabletop BBQ is a "great place for a fun night out" in Holborn
(there's also a new branch at Oxford Circus), cooking your own meat from
a "good, reasonably priced set dinner selection". It is part of a Tokyo-based
group with branches in eight countries.

Kipferl N1 £45 3 2 3
20 Camden Passage 020 77041 555 9–3D
"Great coffee and breakfast" are the crowd-pleasers at this Viennese café
in Islington – "but it's more than a coffee house, it's a good restaurant too",
say fans. "Try the dumplings and schnitzel". A second branch in Ladbroke
Grove (at 95 Golborne Rd, tel 020 8969 5852) is more like a 'Heurigen' –
an Austrian wine bar. / N1 8ED; www.kipferl.co.uk; @KipferlCafe; 10.30 pm,
Sun 10 pm; closed Mon; booking weekdays only.

Kiraku W5 £41 **4**2**2**
8 Station Pde   020 8992 2848   1–3A
This low-profile Japanese canteen near Ealing Common tube station wins
perennial high scores for its high-quality and good-value cooking – and has
a loyal following from Japanese expats in the area. / W5 3LD;
www.kiraku.co.uk; @kirakulondon; Tue-Thu 3 pm, Fri-Sun 11 pm; closed Tue-Thu D,
closed Mon; no Amex.

Kiru SW3 £52 **3**3**3**
2 Elystan St   020 7584 9999   6–2D
"The food is always excellent and staff lovely" at this two-year-old
contemporary take on Japanese fine dining, by Chelsea Green. The kitchen
is run by Taiji Maruyama, a third-generation sushi chef with a nine-year stint
at Nobu under his toque. / SW3 \N; www.kirurestaurant.com; @KiruRestaurant;
10 pm, Fri & Sat 10.30 pm.

Kitchen Table at Bubbledogs W1 £166 **5**3**3**
70 Charlotte St   020 7637 7770   2–1C
"The most memorable meal ever, for all the right reasons!" – James
Knappett's multi-course set meal, prepared in front of just 20 diners sitting
around a horseshoe bar in Fitzrovia, is a "fun and fascinating spectacle",
producing "utterly astonishing", "truly superb food". "Kinda expensive... but
very, very worthwhile to visit once for the experience". Arrival is equally
unusual, through the hotdog-and-Champagne bar that shares the premises
(see also Bubbledogs). STOP PRESS: On October 1 2018, Michelin surprised
everyone by awarding Kitchen Table two stars – one of their better awards
of recent times. / W1T 4QG; www.kitchentablelondon.co.uk; @bubbledogsKT;
seatings only at 6 pm & 7.30 pm; closed Wed-Sat L, closed Mon & Tue & Sun.

Kitchen W8 W8 £72 **4**4**3**
11-13 Abingdon Rd   020 7937 0120   6–1A
"An upmarket neighbourhood restaurant, in an upmarket part of town" –
this "unpretentious" sidestreet fixture, just off High Street Ken', has a
deserved reputation for "always good and sometimes exceptional cuisine"
aided by input from star chef Phil Howard (who has an interest in it).
If there's a weakness, it's an ambience that fans find "lovely" but which
critics feel is "a touch limp" – perhaps its August 2018 revamp will add
va va voom. Top Tip: "the set lunch menu is great value". / W8 6AH;
www.kitchenw8.com; @KitchenW8; Sun-Thu 9.30 pm, Fri & Sat 10 pm; booking
max 6 may apply.

Kitty Fisher's W1 £75 **2**3**3**
10 Shepherd Mkt   020 3302 1661   3–4B
A tsunami of press hype around its launch set the bar high for this
"cute and cosy" little venture set in the "interesting and lively locale"
of Shepherd Market, and now in its third year of operation. Fans do still
applaud its "consistently good" British dishes and "warm and welcoming"
service, but it can also seem "a touch disappointing for such a legend!",
and cynics cite food "lacking oomph" as a sign that it's now "probably
past its peak". / W1J 7QF; www.kittyfishers.com; @kittyfishers; 11 pm, Sun 9 pm;
closed Sun.

The Kitty Hawk EC2 £49 **3**3**3**
11, 13 & 14 South Place   020 3319 9199   13–2A
Large, year-old city venue just around the corner from Finsbury Circus; no-
one claims it rivals the Goodmans and Hawksmoors of the world but
it provides a "very comfortable" (if slightly City-anonymous) modern
environment and surprises are generally on the upside: "was expecting little
but had an excellent steak and interesting starters". / EC2M 7EB;
www.thekittyhawk.co.uk; @KittyHawkLdn; Mon & Tue, Fri 11 pm, Wed & Thu
midnight; closed Sat & Sun.

Knife SW4 £57 554
160 Clapham Park Rd 020 7627 6505 11–2D
"Fantastic meat" – led by "truly excellent steaks (ethically sourced from the Lake District) – has made this tiny, "noisy" two-year-old steakhouse on the Clapham-Brixton border one of the hottest dining tickets in South London. "The Sunday lunches are legendary: homemade bread with butter, then a board of mini Yorkshire puds with unctuous dipping gravy. And that's even before the main course, where beef is best – superlatively rare". All is "served with real charm and enthusiasm" by "attentive staff who remember you when you return". / SW4 7DE; knifrestaurant.co.uk; @KnifeLondon; Wed-Sat 10 pm, Sun 4.30 pm; closed Wed-Sat L closed Sun D, closed Mon & Tue.

Koji SW6 £84 334
58 New King's Rd 020 7731 2520 11–1B
"Fantastic food and some of the best cocktails" fuels a fervent Fulham fanclub for Pat & Mark Barnett's "Asian-fusion" sushi, ceviche and robata haunt, near Parsons Green, whose "layout is nightclubby without being overbearing". / SW6 4LS; www.koji.restaurant; @koji_restaurant; D only, Sun open L & D.

Kolossi Grill EC1 £38 232
56-60 Rosebery Ave 020 7278 5758 10–1A
"Welcoming service" in particular has helped make this prehistoric taverna a popular fixture off Exmouth Market for more than 50 years, and old-timers say "nothing has changed" over the years ("although one brother retired", apparently). But if "it's a wonder this place survives, look at the price of the set lunch" – £7 for three courses! (which fans insist is "always reliable and great value"). / EC1R 4RR; www.kolossigrill.com; 11 pm; closed Sat L, closed Sun.

Koya £40 443
50 Frith St, W1 020 7434 4463 5–2A
Bloomberg Arcade, Queen Victoria St, EC2 no tel 10–3C
"Authentic, fresh udon" bring a real and very affordable taste of Japan to Soho and now to the City's new Bloomberg Arcade. Quite different from the ramen that has proliferated recently in London, udon are soft, fat wheat noodles that can be eaten hot or cold – "great value for money" and "their specials change constantly and are fantastic too. / www.koyabar.co.uk; W1 10.30 pm, Thu-Sat 11 pm, Sun 10 pm; no booking.

Kricket W1 £48 444
12 Denman St 020 7734 5612 4–3C
"A strong modern twist on Indian flavours and good vibes all round" make Rik Campbell and Will Bowlby's "hustling and fast-paced" Soho dive ("it's not a place to linger") a worthy success to their phenomenal Brixton original (in a shipping container) – "one of the most successful switches from street food to a central London restaurant in recent times, while still keeping everything well-priced". Let's hope they keep up the good work with their expansion this year, with a permanent Brixton branch, plus a new White City spin-off, which opened at TV Centre in late September 2018. / W1D 7HH; www.kricket.co.uk; @kricketlondon; 10 pm; closed Sun.

Kudu SE15 NEW £50 333
119 Queen's Rd 020 3950 0226 1–4D
This somewhat South African-influenced newcomer (it's primarily trendy modern British small plates) created by chef Patrick Williams and front-of-house Amy Corbin (daughter of restaurant royalty, Chris Corbin) inspires a mix of opinions. Fans are in the majority and say "it's superb to enjoy food of this standard in the heart of Peckham", but one or two detractors feel culinary results are either "not that great" or "a bit pricey". / SE15 2EZ; www.kudu-restaurant.com; @KuduRestaurant; Mon-Fri 10 pm, Sat & Sun 9 pm.

Kulu Kulu £34 **3** 2 1
76 Brewer St, W1 020 7734 7316 4–3C
51-53 Shelton St, WC2 020 7240 5687 5–2C
39 Thurloe Pl, SW7 020 7589 2225 6–2C
*"Fab for a quick and dirty sushi fix", this Soho and South Kensington duo
offer "good value Japanese food". "Everything passes by on a conveyor
in front of you", which makes them "non-intimidating for those not familiar
with sushi and its variations". / 10 pm, SW7 10.30 pm; closed Sun; no Amex;
no booking.*

Kurobuta £60 **3** 2 2
312 King's Rd, SW3 020 7920 6442 6–3C
17-20 Kendal St, W2 020 7920 6444 7–1D
*The "mish-mash of very tasty plates" can still win praise these "fun",
Japanese-inspired izakayas in Chelsea and Marble Arch. The odd fear
is raised that "it's gone really downhill" since it was sold by founder, Aussie
chef Scott Hallsworth, in 2017, particularly at the W2 branch, but the
ratings in SW3 are pretty consistent. / www.kurobuta-london.com;
@KurobutaLondon; 10.30 pm; SW3 closed Mon-Thu L*

Kurumaya EC4 £37 **4** 3 3
76-77 Watling St 020 7236 0236 10–2B
*"Been going here years and love their sushi", say fans of this well-established
operation near St Paul's, which has "a conveyor belt bar upstairs and
a restaurant downstairs" – "the best value for money Japanese in the area,
and the quality is always very good". / EC4M 9BJ; www.kurumaya.co.uk;
@Kurumaya76; 9.30 pm; closed Sat & Sun.*

Kutir SW3 NEW
10 Lincoln St awaiting tel 6–2D
*Ex-Jamavar chef Rohit Ghai is to launch his first solo site in November
2018, on the elegant Chelsea townhouse site that for many years housed
Vineet Bhatia's excellent nouvelle Indian. As well as an à la carte option,
the cuisine here will feature a tasting menu inspired by Indian hunting
expeditions. / SW3 2TS; kutir.co.uk.*

Kym's by Andrew Wong EC4 NEW
Bloomberg Arcade Queen Victoria St awaiting tel 10–3C
*This much-heralded venture from chef Andrew Wong opened at Bloomberg's
new European HQ in the City in September 2018. (For restaurant history
anoraks, Kym's was the name of Andrew's parents' Pimlico restaurant
of almost three decades' standing, which he renamed A Wong in 2012;
it was also one of the first ever establishments visited and reviewed for
Harden's London Restaurants 1992, our very first print edition). The new
venture sits alongside 10 other restaurants (including Koya, Caravan and
Vinoteca) in the new Bloomberg Arcade. / EC4N 8AR; www.kymsrestaurant.com;
@kymsrestaurant; Mon-Fri 10 pm, Sat & Sun 9 pm.*

Kyseri W1 NEW £57
64 Grafton Way 020 7383 3717 2–1B
*From Selin Kiazim and Laura Christie, the talented duo behind Shoreditch's
Oklava, this small (35 cover) May 2018 newcomer, near Warren Street,
showcases the cuisine of central Anatolia. It opened too late for survey
feedback, but early press reviews compliment its interesting and unusual
cooking and selection of wines from the eastern Mediterranean. / W1T 5DN;
www.kyseri.co.uk; @kyseri_ldn; closed Sun & Mon.*

The Ladbroke Arms W11 £54 **3****3****3**

54 Ladbroke Rd 020 7727 6648 7–2B

"It has the feel of a pub", but this posh hostelry at the Holland Park end of Ladbroke Grove is very genteel as boozers go. It's a very consistent all-rounder, with "extremely friendly service" and "a weekly changing menu of fresh and reliable fare" that's "affordable" too. "Fun, even when crowded", its welcoming nature includes dog-owners and their pets. / W11 3NW; www.ladbrokearms.com; @ladbrokearms; Sun-Thu 11 pm, Fri & Sat midnight; no booking after 8 pm.

Lady Mildmay N1 £38 **3****4****3**

92 Mildmay Park 020 7241 6238 1–1C

"A better-than-average gastropub" on the corner of Newington Green, "whose properly-prepared dishes are at a level of skill which is increasingly rare in pub restaurants". Top Tip: "secret weekday lunch treat – a choice of three or four dishes from only £6!" / N1 4PR; www.ladymildmay.com; @theladymildmaypub; 11 pm; may need 6+ to book.

Lahore Kebab House E1 £28 **4****2****1**

2-10 Umberston St 020 7481 9737 12–1A

"Kebabs and chops to die for" mean this big and famously grungy East End canteen is "still a standard bearer" for down-to-earth "full-flavoured, spicy, meaty Pakistani scoff that's always satisfying" and "at the same ultra-reasonable price-level it's maintained for the last 20 years". A Streatham offshoot never achieved traction, and has now closed. / E1 1PY; www.lahore-kebabhouse.com; 10 pm.

Lahpet E1 NEW £50 **3****3****3**

58 Bethnal Green Rd 020 3883 5629 13–1C

If you fancy trying a still-under-represented cuisine, the latest iteration of this Burmese canteen (originally a Maltby Street stall, and then at a London Fields site which closed in March 2018) has a stylish new home in Shoreditch and "showcases some great and original dishes". Top Tip: "the Tea Leaf salad is spot on". / E1 6JW; www.lahpet.co.uk; @Lahpet.

Lamberts SW12 £56 **5****5****5**

2 Station Parade 020 8675 2233 11–2C

"A culinary beacon in Balham" that's been "consistently excellent for 15 years" – Joe Lambert's "outstanding local independent" provides "very seasonal" cooking of a kind that "stays current without slipping into faddishness". "The ambience is somewhat Scandi-cool" but livened up by the "engaging and lovely staff". Top Menu Tip: "outstanding Sunday roasts". / SW12 9AZ; www.lambertsrestaurant.com; @lamberts_balham; 10 pm, Sun 4 pm; closed Tue-Fri L closed Sun D, closed Mon; no Amex.

The Landmark, Winter Garden NW1 £78 **2****4****5**

222 Marylebone Rd 020 7631 8000 9–4A

With its palm trees and soaring, glass-roofed atrium, it's not hard to see why this beautiful and "very relaxing" space features in lists of London's most Instagrammable locations. Its other top features include a luxurious Sunday brunch buffet with 'bottomless' champagne, and plush afternoon tea. / NW1 6JQ; www.landmarklondon.co.uk; @landmarklondon; 10.15 pm; No trainers; booking max 12 may apply.

Langan's Brasserie W1 £67 2 2 4
Stratton St 020 7491 8822 3–3C
"Why change a winning formula" is the view of the many fans who
"just love" this famous brasserie near The Ritz (many of whom are old
enough to remember when it was opened by Peter Langan, in partnership
with Michael Caine, in 1976): they say, *"it's not the best, nor the coolest,
nor the fanciest, but my favourite, with a brilliant atmosphere"*. The only
dispute relates to its *"retro"*, *"classic"* cuisine, which fans feel is *"always
predictable (in a good way)"* and which critics dismiss as *"churned out and
very average"*. It's particularly recommended as being *"great for business"*.
/ W1J 8LB; www.langansrestaurants.co.uk; @langanslondon; Mon-Thu 11 pm, Fri &
Sat 11.30 pm; closed Sun.

Palm Court,
The Langham W1 £75 3 3 4
1c Portland Place 020 7636 1000 2–1B
*"The wonderful mirrors and damask decor and the pianist playing all make
for an event"* in the *"very civilised"* lounge of this *"pukka five-star*, opposite
Broadcasting House, which claims to be the birthplace of the sacred
national ritual of afternoon tea. Options include a children's tea
in conjunction with Hamley's (which includes a 'free' teddy bear): *"we adults
looked on enviously as the kids received jigsaw-cut sandwiches (as many
as they wanted) and beautifully constructed small scones, cakes... although
the adult tea was also made with marvellous attention to detail!"* / W1B 1JA;
www.palm-court.co.uk; @Langham_London; Sun-Thu 10.30 pm, Sat 11 pm;
No trainers.

Lantana Cafe £46 3 3 3
13-14 Charlotte Pl, W1 020 7323 6601 2–1C
45 Middle Yd, Camden Lock Pl, NW1 020 7428 0421 9–2B
Ground Floor West, 44-46 Southwark St, SE1 no tel 10–4B
Unit 2, 1 Oliver's Yd, 55 City Rd, EC1 020 7253 5273 13–1A
"Cool vibes, friendly service and an interesting menu" make this 10-year-old
trio of Aussie-style cafés *"favourites for brunch"* in Fitzrovia, Shoreditch and
London Bridge. / lantanacafe.co.uk; @lantanacafe/; EC1 9.30 pm, Sat & Sun 3 pm;
W1 3.30 pm, Sat & Sun 5 pm; NW1 5.30 pm; NW1 closed Sun; W1 no booking
Sat & Sun.

Lardo £54 2 2 2
158 Sandringham Rd, E8 020 3021 0747 14–1B
197-201 Richmond Rd, E8 020 8533 8229 14–1B
The Arthaus building near London Fields houses the original of these
East London pizza-stops, the spin-off 'Bebe' branch being in nearby
Hackney Downs. Neither inspired much interest this year amongst reporters
compared with previously: such as there was said the pizza is *"creditable"*
but can seem *"expensive"*. / 10.30 pm, Sun 9.30 pm.

The Laughing Heart E2 £64 2 2 3
277 Hackney Rd 020 7686 9535 14–2A
As *"a wine lover's choice"* in particular, Charlie Mellor's stylish Hackney wine
bar (above his trendy wine store), complete with brick walls, open kitchen
and funky small plates menu has won a following. Feedback remains a mite
variable though, with one return visitor commenting: *"after a couple
of excellent visits just after it opened, the shine seems to have gone off
somewhat"*. / E2 8NA; thelaughingheartlondon.com; closed Mon-Sat L, closed Sun.

Launceston Place W8   £84   **3** **4** **4**

1a Launceston Pl   020 7937 6912   6–1B

*This "tucked-away townhouse in Kensington" has "a unique set-up" that
makes for a "romantic" ambience and – with its "attentive but unobtrusive
service" – is "ideal for a relaxed, long, blow-out meal". Foodwise it's "had its
ups-and-downs as chefs have changed over the last several years", but since
Ben Murphy took over the stoves in early 2017, most reporters feel the
"the food is back on fantastic form" with "wonderful innovative dishes from
this wunderkind new chef": "the little extras such as the lovely amuses
bouches and petits fours lift the meal and make it a real treat". One or two
reporters, though, feel it still has a way to go: "there are some wonderful
flavour combinations: if the kitchen only had the level and consistency
of execution to keep up with these, this place could trouble the Michelin
inspectors for a visit". / W8 5RL; www.launcestonplace-restaurant.co.uk;
@LauncestonPlace; 10 pm, Sun 9.30 pm; closed Mon & Tue L.*

Laurent at Cafe Royal W1 NEW

Hotel Café Royal, 68 Regent St   020 7406 3310   4–4C

*Branded for French chef Laurent Tourondel (known for his ventures
in Miami, Charlotte and New York) – this May 2018 opening adds an open
kitchen, grill and sushi bar to the mezzanine level of the Café Royal.
/ W1B 4DY; www.hotelcaferoyal.com/laurent-at-cafe-royal; @HotelCafeRoyal.*

The Ledbury W11   £156   **5** **4** **4**

127 Ledbury Rd   020 7792 9090   7–1B

*"Phenomenal on all levels"; Brett Graham's "unfailingly impressive" Notting
Hill favourite only narrowly misses 5/5 in all categories and, for very many
discerning foodies, this is "the best restaurant in London", delivering food
that's "sheer artistry": "original, brilliantly executed, and with a passion that
shines through". Notwithstanding an interior that's "serene and upmarket,
with comfortably spaced tables", the overall effect is one of "relaxed
confidence throughout" and "less formal than other top-level
establishments": and it's "so refreshing for a venue of this calibre to have
such fun, friendly staff". "The free take-home compost is a nice touch."
/ W11 2AQ; www.theledbury.com; @theledbury; 9.45 pm; closed Mon & Tue L;
booking max 6 may apply.*

Lemonia NW1   £49   **1** **4** **5**

89 Regent's Park Rd   020 7586 7454   9–3B

*"Always packed to the rafters" and "buzzing, buzzing, buzzing" –
this "busy cheerful hub of Primrose Hill" – a sprawling mega-taverna –
has been a "warm and comforting" north London phenomenon for about
as long as most folks remember. Even many fans accept the food is "tired
and boring" yet "still we all love it and come back every chance we get!"
The secret to its enduring (to a few sceptics "mysterious") success is that
"Tony and the staff have been here for decades and a genuinely warm
welcome is assured". "Our newborn son had his first restaurant experience
here, followed thirty four years later by our newborn grandson's. The whole
restaurant recently joined in with Happy Birthday to a 104 year old! This
is a family run restaurant with a loyal family clientele." / NW1 8UY;
www.lemonia.co.uk; @Lemonia_Greek; 10.30 pm, Sun 10 pm; closed Sun D;
no Amex.*

Leroy EC2 NEW   £50   3 4 3
18 Phipp St   020 7739 4443   13–1B
The team from Hackney hit Ellory (RIP) have shaken up the letters in its
name in order to baptise this new venture (drawn, according to urban
legend, by Shoreditch rents which are now cheaper than in so-very-now E8).
Occupying slightly offbeat, triangular-shaped premises opposite Oklava,
"the focus is on wine and accompanying small plates" as well as some more
substantial fare. Early reports are positive, praising "fab food and
knowledgeable staff", but – noting that "it's not sure if it's a restaurant or a
wine bar" – fall short of the gushing rapture it's inspired amongst nearly all
newspaper critics. / EC2A 4NP; www.leroyshoreditch.com; @leroyshoreditch;
10.30 pm; closed Mon L, closed Sun; Credit card deposit required to book.

Levan SE15 NEW
3-4 Blenheim Grove   awaiting tel   1–4D
An all-day (from breakfast) restaurant and wine bar in Peckham opening
in October 2018, from the team behind Brixton's Salon, featuring an offbeat
wine selection and contemporary European cuisine in a casual bistro style.
/ SE15 4QL; levanlondon.co.uk; 10 pm, Sun 4 pm.

The Lido Café,
Brockwell Lido SE24   £42   3 2 4
Dulwich Rd   020 7737 8183   11–2D
"OK, it helps if it's a good day, but this is always an amazing location" –
the all-day café, attached to Brixton's characterful old lido. It's a top brunch
destination – "perfect refuelling after a swim, and I'd make a diversion for
the scrambled eggs on toast!" / SE20 0PA; www.thelidocafe.co.uk; @thelidocafe;
10 pm, Sun 9 pm; closed Sun D; no Amex; booking max 8 may apply.

The Light House SW19   £54   3 3 3
75-77 Ridgway   020 8944 6338   11–2B
This well-thought-of independent in Wimbledon, now entering its 20th year,
is capable of producing "really outstanding food". Scores could
be significantly higher but the kitchen is let down by inconsistency. "The food
varies between a 5 and a 1, which means you're slightly apprehensive
before you go!". / SW19 4ST; www.lighthousewimbledon.com; Sun-Thu 11 pm, Fri &
Sat midnight; closed Sun D.

The Lighterman N1   £60   3 3 4
3 Granary Square   020 3846 3400   9–3C
"An unbeatable location by the water in Granary Square, with lovely terrace
tables for fine weather" and a "scenic, glass-walled dining room" wins a very
large following for this "three-storey pub overlooking Regents Canal". On the
downside, it's "very busy and noisy", but "service is efficient and personable
despite what seem to be unrelenting crowds and the food's surprisingly
good". / N1C 4BH; www.thelighterman.co.uk; @TheLightermanKX; Mon-Thu
10.30 pm, Fri & Sat 11 pm, Sun 9.30 pm.

Lima   £80   3 3 2
31 Rathbone Pl, W1   020 3002 2640   2–1C
14 Garrick St, WC2   020 7240 5778   5–3C
"Imaginative and different" dishes, "beautifully presented" (not to mention
"highly recommended pisco sours") have produced a big culinary reputation
for this Peruvian duo in Fitzrovia and Covent Garden ("Floral by Lima") and
"not just for the novelty factor". On the downside, they can seem
"too expensive". / www.limalondongroup.com/fitzrovia; @lima_london; 10.30 pm,
Sun 9.30 pm; Mon L closed.

Lina Stores W1 **NEW** £36 **5** **3** **3**
51 Greek St 020 3929 0068 5–2A
"For what it is, this small spin-off from the well-known Italian deli is a great way to dine casually, including at the bar" – Soho institution, Lina Stores (est 1944) has opened this nearby, snappily decorated, no-reservations pit-stop, with a 12-seater kitchen counter and 50 covers over two floors. Early reports praise its "exceptional, cheap 'n' cheerful food" – the pasta is the star – and to say that the newspaper reviewers have gushed would be an understatement. / W1D 4EH; www.linastores.co.uk; @Linastores; closed Sun.

Linden Stores N1 **NEW** £36 **4** **3** **3**
220 Saint Paul's Rd 020 7226 0728 9–2D
"A brilliant new restaurant in the old Prawn on the Lawn site" (RIP) – this little spot near Highbury & Islington tube from Laura Christie (one half of Oklava) and Chris Boustead (one half of pop-up Boustead & Bidois) provides "interesting dishes (mostly small plates)" on a British tapas theme, with "friendly and professional service" and "a downstairs that's very cosy". / N1 2LL; Wed-Sat 11 pm; closed Wed-Fri L, closed Mon & Tue & Sun; Online only.

Lisboa Pâtisserie W10 £8 **3** **2** **4**
57 Golborne Rd 020 8968 5242 7–1A
"It feels like Lisbon with the bustle and blue tiles" when you visit this long-established North Kensington café. Expect excellent coffee and "great cakes at keen prices" including "the best pastéis de natas outside (or possibly inside) Portugal". / W10 5NR; 7.30 pm, Sun 7 pm; L & early evening only; no booking.

The Little Bay NW6 £33 **3** **3** **4**
228 Belsize Rd 020 7372 4699 1–2B
For the cash-strapped romantic, this long-serving budget bistro off Kilburn High Road hits the right note with its intimate booths and balconies, while "under £15 for two courses represents excellent value". "I hadn't visited for ages, but nothing seems to have changed and the profiteroles were just as delicious as I remember!" / NW6 4BT; www.littlebaykilburn.co.uk; Sun-Thu 11 pm, Fri & Sat midnight.

Little Bird £59 **3** **2** **4**
1 Station Parade, W4 020 3145 0894 1–3A
1 Battersea Rise, SW11 020 7324 7714 11–2C
"Sumptuous sofas", "incredible cocktails", and "enjoyable Asian/European food in generous portions" win fans for Lorraine Angliss's (Annie's, Rock & Rose) neighbourhood haunts, "hidden away beside Chiswick station" and also in Battersea. / www.littlebirdrestaurants.com; @LittleBirdW4.

Little Social W1 £79 **4** **2** **3**
5 Pollen St 020 7870 3730 3–2C
A better year for Jason Atherton's even more informal 'Social' (opposite his Pollen Street Mayfair flagship), where ratings have leapt for the "excellent, unusual, 100% more-ish food" served in a "gorgeous, cosseted ambience". Top Tip: "pre-theatre menu is an absolute bargain". / W1S 1NE; www.littlesocial.co.uk; @_littlesocial; 10.30 pm; closed Sun; booking max 6 may apply.

Little Taperia SW17 £43 **3** **2** **2**
143 Tooting High St 020 8682 3303 11–2C
"From the first taste you know that they know what they're doing" at this Hispanic three-year-old in Tooting: "a fun destination with a short list of unusual and delicious tapas". / SW17 \N; www.thelittletaperia.co.uk; @littletaperia; Mon-Fri 4 pm, Sat & Sun 4.30 pm; may need 6+ to book.

Llerena N1 NEW £38 442
167 Upper St 020 7704 9977 9–2D
Opening at the start of 2018, this Islington tapas bar is related to one of Spain's top producers of jamón ibérico (Jamón y Salud, from Extremadura) and initial feedback is enthusiastic – "a stand out for its product quality and, equally, value for money". / N1 1US; www.jamonysalud.co.uk; 11 pm, Sun 10.30 pm.

Llewelyn's SE24 £54 322
293-295 Railton Rd 020 7733 6676 11–2D
"Just the kind of restaurant you want down your street" – this all-day yearling in a former Victorian dining room opposite Herne Hill station can deliver "wonderfully judged, honest modern British food". It's by no means perfect – one or two reporters have been disappointed with the cooking, "tables are close together" and "it gets noisy when it's crowded" – but the response is mostly upbeat (and it's kid-friendly too). / SE24 0JP; www.llewelyns-restaurant.co.uk; @llewelynslondon; 9.30 pm; closed Mon; booking max 8 may apply.

Lluna N10 £47 323
462 Muswell Hill Broadway 020 8442 2662 1–1B
This "perfect neighbourhood local" – a modern Spanish bar/restaurant on Muswell Hill's Broadway – serves a "fascinating mix of outstanding tapas dishes". It's popular in the area, and "has now expanded so you can get in at peak times". / N10 1BS; lalluna.co.uk; @lallunalondon; Sun-Thu 10.30 pm, Fri & Sat 11 pm.

LOBOS Meat & Tapas SE1 £50 432
14 Borough High St 020 7407 5361 10–4C
"Full of energy and zest" – the "amazing" meat-based tapas cooking wins raves for this Spanish operation, concertina-ed under a railway viaduct on the edge of Borough Market, while service is "smiling and extremely friendly". It has "a great vibe about it", but on the downside is "very squished". / SE1 9QG; www.lobostapas.co.uk; @LobosTapas; Wed-Sun 11 pm; booking max 8 may apply.

Locanda Locatelli, Hyatt Regency W1 £85 343
8 Seymour St 020 7935 9088 2–2A
"Always a winner" – Giorgio Locatelli's Marylebone HQ maintains a big following thanks to its "expensive but good" cuisine, fine selection of Italian wines, and "impeccable service". When it comes to the "luxurious" interior, its dim-lit and moody styling is starting to look "a little dated" to quite a few reporters, but even so the overall effect is described as "oddly agreeable" or "romantic". / W1H 7JZ; www.locandalocatelli.com; 10.30 pm; booking max 8 may apply.

Loch Fyne £51 –33
For "consistent quality fish dishes" (and they do a good line in seafood too, particularly oysters), this national chain with its consistently "pleasant" branches "executes its staples very well". "Go off-piste, and perhaps results are more mixed" (but serious gripes are few and far between). / www.lochfyne-restaurants.com; 10 pm, WC2 Mon-Sat 10.30 pm.

Lokhandwala W1 NEW £63 333
93 Charlotte St 020 7637 7599 2–1B
"Off-the-beaten-track" Fitzrovia Indian offering, amongst other items, a range of vegan Ayurvedic shots and smoothies. Not all reporters gave it full marks, but for the most part there's praise for its "cosy interior (inspired, apparently, by an 18th century love story), fab cocktails, and originally presented (eg dosa hats) tapas dishes". / W1T 4PY; www.lokhandwala.co.uk; @lokhandwala_uk; Sun-Wed 10.30 pm, Thu-Sat 11.30 pm; closed Sun-Wed-Sat L; Credit card deposit required to book.

London Grind SE1 £43 4 4 4
2 London Bridge   020 7378 1928   10–3C
With its "origin coffees from the best roastery", this breakfast-to-cocktail-
hour café in a stripped-down old bank above Borough Market
"has inevitably become a free office space for freelancers". There "a good
mix of on-trend, healthy and wholesome food" to keep them going,
then "great espresso martinis" to wind down with. Top Tips – "handy for
a breakfast meeting"; and "£5 cocktails on Mondays are a complete
winner". / SE1 9RA; www.londongrind.com; @LondonGrind; Mon-Thu midnight, Fri &
Sat 1 am, Sun 7 pm.

London House SW11 £61 2 2 2
7-9 Battersea Sq   020 7592 8545   11–1C
Gordon Ramsay's Battersea venture pitches itself as a family-friendly
('kids eat free') neighbourhood local, and attracts large groups for
celebratory meals. It scored some hits this year ("we had 15 folks faultlessly
looked after") but those reporting misses were more vocal: "totally
overpriced…", "all the atmosphere of a rail station waiting room…",
"…if this is the best Gordon Ramsay can do with his spin-offs, not sure how
he is keeping in business!" / SW11 3RA;
www.gordonramsayrestaurants.com/london-house; @londonhouse; 11 pm, Sun 9 pm.

London Shell Co. W2 £65 4 4 5
Sheldon Square   07818 666005   7–1C
"Food tastes all the better when afloat" and fans of this "utterly delightful"
canal boat, moored in the Paddington Central development, say it's
"a must do!" – not just on account of the novel setting, but also the
"knowledgeable staff", and "truly fresh fish and shellfish" which
is exceptionally well-prepared. / W2 6EP; www.londonshellco.com;
@LondonShellCo; 10.30 pm, Sun 3.30 pm; closed Sun D, closed Mon.

Londrino SE1 NEW £54 2 3 3
36 Snowsfields   020 3911 4949   10–4C
Leandro Carreira has been associated with a fair few London hits (Viajante,
Koya, Lyle's) and opened his first solo venture a few streets south of The
Shard in November 2017. The cuisine makes a culinary nod to his native
Portugal, but no more than a nod: the style is primarily experimental and
cheffy, and results are very variable with reviews ranging from "not only
stunning visually, but with exceptional flavour" to "up itself, lacking
generosity" and "disappointing". / SE1 3SU; www.londrino.co.uk; @londrinolondon;
11 pm, Sun 3 pm; closed Sun D, closed Mon.

Lorne SW1 £60 4 5 3
76 Wilton Rd   020 3327 0210   2–4B
"It arrived in a wave of critical approval and it well deserves all the praise
it has received!" – Katie Exton and Peter Hall "have done an incredible job"
with this "fantastic, relatively new addition to Pimlico" in the "tricky locale"
near Victoria station. A "lovely little neighbourhood spot", "the kitchen
produces exquisite food using market-fresh produce" from a "concise,
regularly-changing menu of inventive food that's not overly fussy" but
"executed delightfully, often with an unexpected twist". "Front of house
is the co-owner Katie, who will guide you through the excellent wine list: her
wine knowledge is superb and her advice sensible and unpretentious".
(The restaurant was closed for a significant chunk of 2018 due to flooding,
but has now reopened.) / SW1V 1DE; www.lornerestaurant.co.uk; 9.30 pm; closed
Mon L, closed Sun.

Louie Louie SE17 £41 3 2 3
347 Walworth Rd 020 7450 3223 1–3C
"A welcome addition to SE17" – this popular two-year-old is a refuge from "the pollution and noise of Walworth Road" and scores well with its "fun" combination of "tasty" small plates from guest chefs, cocktails and local beers, and the soundtrack of vintage vinyl. The odd fan, though, can feel "they take advantage of being one of the only kids on the block" hereabouts, with sometimes "disinterested service". / SE17 2AL; louielouie.london; @LouieLouie_Ldn; 4.30 pm.

Luca EC1 £80 3 3 4
88 St John St 020 3859 3000 10–1A
"It's a joy to dine" at this "lovely" Clerkenwell yearling – a "really cool" space with bar at the front and "buzzy" conservatory restaurant to the rear. It's actually a sibling to the legendary Clove Club, although the culinary style is more traditional here, with the aim to produce Italian cuisine from British produce. Results evidence some "serious cooking" producing "consistently good" results, although fair to say it's not as earth-shattering as its stablemate and can seem a tad "pricey". Top Menu Tip: "delicious Parmesan fries". / EC1M 4EH; luca.restaurant; @LucaRestaurant; 11 pm, Sun 10 pm.

Luce e Limoni WC1 £59 4 4 3
91-93 Gray's Inn Rd 020 7242 3382 10–1A
"Proper, high-quality Italian cooking" backed up by an "excellent Sicilian wine list" earn consistently high ratings for Fabrizio Zafarana's "spacious and charming restaurant" on the edge of Bloomsbury. "Fabrizio is a very special host" – "it's a brilliant place for a proper catch-up meal". Top Tip: "order in advance for the best chocolate mousse in the land, made without gelatine". / WC1X 8TX; www.luceelimoni.com; @Luce_e_Limoni; Mon-Thu 10 pm, Fri & Sat 11 pm; closed Sat L, closed Sun.

Luciano's SE12 £52 4 3 2
131 Burnt Ash Rd 020 8852 3186 1–4D
This "great Italian" in Lee is both family-run and family-friendly, and has won high scores for its cooking this year – "what more could you want from a neighbourhood pizza and pasta restaurant?" / SE12 \N; www.lucianoslondon.co.uk; @LucianosLondon; 10.30 pm, Sun 10 pm.

Lucio SW3 £75 3 2 2
257 Fulham Rd 020 7823 3007 6–3B
"Fab Tuscan food" ("unsurpassable homemade pasta") inspires fans of this family-run Chelsea Italian. Service can be "erratic" but regulars say if you get to know the owner it's "terrific". Top Tip: "the set lunch is fantastic value". / SW3 6HY; www.luciorestaurant.com; 10.45 pm.

Lupins SE1 £48 4 4 3
66 Union St 020 3617 8819 10–4B
"Booking is essential – otherwise, be prepared to wait!" – if you want to sample Lucy Pedder and Natasha Cooke's "tiny small-plates restaurant", "in the Flat Iron complex near London Bridge" and "handy for Tate Modern and Borough Market". It's set over two floors: "a large café on the ground floor" and a "lovely", "atticy" upstairs. "The all-women staff and owners have really gotten their act together" – "friendly service enhances the whole experience" and the "unusual tapas-style dishes" are "really great sharing food with some sublime flavours"; "writing my review has reminded me to go back immediately!" / SE1 1TD; www.lupinslondon.com; 10.15 pm, Sun 8.45 pm; closed Mon D & Sun D.

Lupita £43 **3 3 2**
13-15 Villiers St, WC2   020 7930 5355   5–4D
7 Kensington High St, W8   020 3696 2930   6–1A
60-62 Commercial Street, Spitalfields, E1   020 3141 6000   13–2C
"Proper enchiladas" and "amazing guacamole made at the table" are typical of the "authentic, not Tex Mex" approach at these colourful and "very friendly" budget Mexican joints in Kensington, by the side of Charing Cross station, and on the edge of the City. They also serve "good cocktails" (but the wine list is "very limited").

Lure NW5 £37 **3 5 3**
56 Chetwynd Rd   020 7267 0163   9–1B
"Beautifully battered fish, great chips and a good selection of seasonal specials" make Aussie Philip Kendall's Dartmouth Park outfit more than just a top chippy – "it's a perfect local restaurant". "Lovely staff", "child-friendly", and the short list of desserts is "always worth the extra course". / NW5 1DJ; www.lurefishkitchen.co.uk; @Lurefishkitchen; Wed-Sat 10 pm, Sun 9.30 pm; closed Wed-Fri L, closed Mon & Tue; booking weekends only.

Lurra W1 £56 **3 4 4**
9 Seymour Place   020 7724 4545   2–2A
"An oasis from the noise of Oxford Street" – this two-floor corner Spanish grill-house in Seymour Village is, on practically all accounts, "a wonderful tribute to Basque cuisine" – particularly its "awesome Galician steak" – and "paired with an excellent wine list". Even fans however can find the small menu selection, focussed on 2-3 main options, "too limited". Top Tip: "their courtyard is an overlooked gem in London, especially in the warmer months and on a Sunday when it's quieter". / W1H 5BA; www.lurra.co.uk; @LurraW1; 10.30 pm, Sun 3.30 pm; closed Mon L closed Sun D.

**Lutyens Grill,
The Ned EC2** £90 **3 4 4**
27 Poultry   020 3828 2000   10–2C
"Quieter than the other restaurants in the building" – The Ned's steakhouse is to be found at the edge of the ground floor of the old Midland Bank HQ. Originally members-only, it's been open to all since February 2018, and its "elegant" panelled interior makes it a "perfect location for a business lunch". Most of the well-realised menu is devoted to steaks – mostly from the UK, but also with a selection from the US – and (as well as a few fish and seafood choices) there's also the option of Beef Wellington carved at the table. / EC2R 8AJ; www.thened.com; @TheNedLondon; 11 pm, Sun 5 pm; closed Sat L closed Sun D.

Lyle's E1 £83 **4 2 2**
The Tea Building, 56 Shoreditch High St   020 3011 5911   13–1B
"Don't be put off by the hipster canteen vibe" say fans of James Lowe's venerated Shoreditch foodie-mecca, offering "always-original" small plates and "a small but really interesting wine list". But ratings here no longer scale the absolute pinnacles they once did, dragged down by a minority who find the place "too impressed by itself" for an achievement level that's good, but no more. / E1 6JJ; www.lyleslondon.com; @lyleslondon; 11 pm; closed Sat L & Sun.

M Restaurants £85 222
Zig Zag Building, Victoria St, SW1 020 3327 7776 2–4B
Brewery Wharf, London Rd, TW1 020 3327 7776 1–4A
2-3 Threadneedle Walk, EC2 020 3327 7770 10–2C
With their "clubby", "dark" decor, Martin Williams's Vegas-esque
steakhouses can "feel like they're trying too hard to be cool". For more
reporters, though, they are "an expensive but guilty pleasure" with
"perfectly executed steak". Change may be afoot, because, as of September
2018, Williams is no-longer the 'ex-Gaucho CEO', but has returned back
to that post to turn around the chain he headed for many years. Where this
will leave this project remains to be seen. Top Tip: "excellent deal with free-
flowing Prosecco". / www.mrestaurants.co.uk; @mrestaurants_; midnight; EC2 closed
Sat L & Sun, SW1 closed Sun.

Ma Goa SW15 £44 443
242-244 Upper Richmond Rd 020 8780 1767 11–2B
"A dependable Putney stalwart now back on top form", this family-run
operation serves "outstanding home cooking, Goan-style" and remains
a major hit with locals, some of whom have been coming for 20 or more
years. A refurb has seen the dining room modernised and reduced in size
with a wine shop added next door. / SW15 6TG; www.magoaputney.co.uk;
@magoarestaurant; 10.30 pm, Fri & Sat 11 pm, Sun 10pm.

Mac & Wild £54 324
65 Great Titchfield St, W1 020 7637 0510 3–1C
9a Devonshire Square, EC2 020 7637 0510 10–2D
"Venison cooked in a variety of ways" sits alongside Scottish shorthorn beef,
oysters and salmon at this "passionate but unpretentious" Fitzrovia three-
year-old, which also has a sibling at Devonshire Square, near Liverpool
Street. Owner Andy Waugh's Scottish family estate is the source for much
of the produce.

Macellaio RC £54 333
6 Store St, WC1 awaiting tel 2–1C NEW
84 Old Brompton Rd, SW7 020 7589 5834 6–2B
Arch 24, 229 Union St, SE1 07467 307682 10–4B
124 Northcote Rd, SW11 020 3848 4800 11–2C
38-40 Exmouth Market, EC1 020 3696 8220 10–1A
"Meat! More meat! And more meat!" is the order of the day
(notwithstanding a few pasta options, and Sicilian tuna in the Exmouth
Market branch) from the menu of Roberto Costa's Italian steakhouse group,
which showcases "amazing cuts of beef" from Piedmont's Fassone breed
of cattle, and where the arrival of the food is dramatised by the "stabbing
of a steak knife into the table". "The wine list has some interesting choices"
too, and some affordable ones at that. In summer 2018 it announced its
fifth opening, in Bloomsbury. / www.macellaiorc.com; @macellaiorc; 11 pm.

Machiya SW1 £44 422
5 Panton St 020 7925 0333 5–4A
High-quality Japanese dishes and patisserie win strong ratings for this little
two-year-old near Leicester Square, from Aaron Burgess-Smith and Tony
Lam (the duo behind Kanada-Ya on the same street). It's named after the
stacked wooden town houses in Kyoto, but the setting is the weakest part
of the offering. / SW1Y 4DL; machi-ya.co.uk; @MachiyaLondon; 10.30 pm, Fri &
Sat 11 pm, Sun 10 pm.

Made in Italy £47 **3**1**2**
50 James St, W1   020 7224 0182   3–1A
249 King's Rd, SW3   020 7352 1880   6–3C
141 The Broadway, SW19   020 8540 4330   11–2B
"Pitch-perfect pizza" with a "terrific charred flavour" emerges by the metre from the ovens at this expanding southwest London group. Occasionally "abysmal" service needs sorting out, however – "it can be really slow if they're busy". / www.madeinitalygroup.co.uk; @MADEINITALYgrp; SW3 11.30 pm; W1 11.30 pm, Sun 10.30 pm; SW19 11 pm; SW3 closed Mon L.

Made of Dough SE15 £32 **4**4**3**
182 Bellenden Rd   020 7064 5288   1–4D
"From a small shop come the most divine pizzas – yes, even beating Franco Manca's original (i.e. Brixton) branch" – that's the bold claim made by fans of this year-old pop-up-turned permanent in Peckham (which also operates out of a container at Pop Brixton). / SE15 4BW; www.madeofdough.co.uk; @MadeOfDoughLDN; Mon-Thu 11 pm, Fri & Sat midnight, Sun 10 pm; no booking.

Madhu's UB1 £41 **4**5**3**
39 South Rd   020 8574 1897   1–3A
One of Southall's best-known Indian stalwarts – the Anand family's acclaimed central curry house has helped found a successful empire, providing catering for events at many of the capital's top venues. Those who make the pilgrimage say the food's "such good value" and "service is top-notch". / UB1 1SW; www.madhus.co.uk; Tue-Thu 3 pm, Fri-Sun 11 pm; closed Tue, Sat L & Sun L; no booking.

Maggie Jones's W8 £61 **2**2**4**
6 Old Court Pl   020 7937 6462   6–1A
Limited feedback this year on this "romantic" stalwart near Kensington Palace (named after the pseudonym Princess Margaret used to use when booking here). Such as there is supports the view that the main reason to visit is the date-potential of the charming, faux-rustic decor, rather than the indifferently rated Anglo-French bistro fare. / W8 4PL; www.maggie-jones.co.uk; 11 pm, Sun 10.30 pm; closed Mon-Sat & Sun.

Magpie W1 £72 **4**4**3**
10 Heddon St   020 3903 9096   4–3B
Just off Regent Street, the year-old West End outpost of Hackney superstar Pidgin has taken a little bit of time to settle down, and part of its original concept – the trolley service of British 'dim sum' – went by the wayside in early 2018. Now in a more conventional 'small plates' mode, at its best, it's a repeat of the "all-round brilliance" of its sibling – "really fun" and with "outstanding food you will want to go back for again and again". / W1B 4BX; www.magpie-london.com; @mgpldn; 10.30 pm, Sun 3 pm; closed Sun D.

Maguro W9 £57 **4**4**2**
5 Lanark Pl   020 7289 4353   9–4A
This "great little Japanese" near Little Venice is highly rated for its "tasty" dishes from a small but well thought-out menu. It's "tiny" and popular – "so be sure to book". / W9 1BT; www.maguro-restaurant.com; 11 pm, Sun 10.30 pm; no Amex.

Maison Bab WC2 NEW
4 Mercer Walk   020 7439 9222   5–2C
A second venture from the team behind Soho's highly popular Le Bab – this latest addition to Covent Garden's new Mercers Walk development opened in September 2018. The brainchild of Stephen Tozer and Ed Brunet, the 40-cover restaurant (plus takeaway) serves the same style of modern kebabs and mezze that made its sister site such a success, but has the added benefit of a ten-seater chef's table. / WC2; www.eatlebab.com; @eatlebab; Mon-Thu 10 pm, Fri & Sat 10.30 pm.

Maison Bertaux W1 £8 444
28 Greek St   020 7437 6007   5–2A
*A "Soho institution that should be experienced" – this French teahouse
(est 1871) offers "wondrous pâtisserie and very good tea (in teapots) in the
most charming, if somewhat ramshackle, surroundings". It's a "window
on Soho", so "just sit with a delicious cake and watch the world go by".*
/ W1D 5DQ; www.maisonbertaux.com; @Maison_Bertaux; 11 pm, Sun 9.30 pm.

Malabar W8 £46 333
27 Uxbridge St   020 7727 8800   7–2B
*"A long-time favourite", this stalwart Notting Hill curry house "always
delivers", even after more than 30 years, and offers a "nice mix of unusual
as well as usual menu items". Ratings have tumbled from previous highs this
year – perhaps just partly a reflection of the "sharp increase in competition
and quality among modern Indian restaurants". / W8 7TQ;
www.malabar-restaurant.co.uk; 10 pm, Sun 9 pm.*

Malabar Junction WC1 £42 343
107 Gt Russell St   020 7580 5230   2–1C
*The "excellent South Indian menu" at this Bloomsbury stalwart includes
"interesting Keralese fish specialities that distinguish it from the average
curry house". The "modern colonial" décor and "especially graceful service"
add to the appeal (though not everybody likes the art). "Very handy for the
British Museum and a good alternative to the underwhelming chain options
in Charlotte Street". / WC1B 3NA; www.malabarjunction.com; 11 pm.*

MAM W11 £41 433
16 All Saints Rd   020 7792 2665   7–1B
*Pronounced 'mum' and meaning fermentation in Vietnamese – Colin Tu's
BBQ yearling on what used to be Notting Hill's edgy frontier is well-rated
as "a great new local". / W11 1HH; mamlondon.com; 11 pm; closed Mon-Fri L.*

Mamarosa EC2 NEW
Shoreditch Village, Holywell Lane   awaiting tel   13–1B
*A London version of Barcelona's Italian celeb-magnet is slated to open at the
Shoreditch Village development this year. It will open adjacent to the
citizenM boutique hotel just off Shoreditch High Street (the original is part
of Barcelona's 5-star W hotel). / EC2; 12.30 am, Sun midnight.*

Mamma Dough £40 333
40 Ladywell Rd, SE13   awaiting tel   1–4D NEW
179 Queen's Rd, SE15   020 7635 3470   1–4D
76-78 Honor Oak Pk, SE23   020 8699 5196   1–4D
354 Coldharbour Ln, SW9   020 7095 1491   11–2D
*"Well-priced sourdough pizzas" served in "very basic but functional"
surroundings have established a foothold in South London for this group
(Brixton, Peckham, Honor Oak Park and most recently Ladywell). Fans
appreciate the "small menu which makes it easy to order"; the drinks
list features local craft beer, coffee roasted in Shoreditch and ginger beer
brewed on site. / www.mammadough.co.uk; SE23 10 pm, SW9 11 pm,
SE15 10.30 pm; Mon-Thu closed L.*

Mandarin Kitchen W2 £40 432
14-16 Queensway   020 7727 9012   7–2C
*"The best lobster noodles in London (if not the world)" is the famous
signature dish of this "reliable old favourite" Chinese, opposite Queensway
tube. Other standout seafood dishes include crab and razor clams. It's
always full and the decor – though improved in recent years – isn't hugely
inspiring, so don't come with a view to linger among elegant surroundings –
"eat and leave for somewhere more salubrious!" / W2 3RX;
mandarinkitchen.co.uk; 11.15 pm.*

Mangal I E8 £27 **5** **3** **2**
10 Arcola St 020 7275 8981 14–1A

"The best shish kebabs" – "juicy", "melt-in-the-mouth tender" – all cooked in "the marble-clad pit in the middle of the room" are "the genuine article" and have won renown for this Turkish grill in Dalston. And it's "good value" too, aided by the fact that you can BYO. "After 20 years I still go here every week, and it never fails to impress!" / E8 2DJ; www.mangal1.com; @Mangalone; Mon-Fri midnight, Sat & Sun 1 am; cash only; no booking.

Manicomio £75 **2** **2** **3**
85 Duke of York Sq, SW3 020 7730 3366 6–2D
6 Gutter Ln, EC2 020 7726 5010 10–2B

"If there were such a term as Rustic Italian Fine Dining", it could be used to describe the style of these "delightful" modern Italians, located in Chelsea ("a lovely oasis just off the King's Road with outside seating"); and the City ("good for impressing business visitors"). Both locations provide "a seasonal menu with quality ingredients" that's "beautifully presented" but cost is an issue – the food seems "generally pricey for what it is". / www.manicomio.co.uk; SW3 10 pm, Sun 4 pm; EC2 10 pm; EC2 closed Sat & Sun.

Manna NW3 £56 **2** **2** **2**
4 Erskine Rd 020 7722 8028 9–3B

This "vegetarian and vegan place of pilgrimage" on Primrose Hill, which has logged 50 years to make it Britain's longest-serving veggie, is now "so old it's fashionable again". "The menu is enticing and quantities are vast", but when it comes to realisation, it's perennially a case of hit and miss here. / NW3 3AJ; www.mannav.com; @mannacuisine; 10 pm, Sun 7 pm; closed Mon.

Manuka Kitchen SW6 £53 **3** **4** **3**
510 Fulham Rd 020 7736 7588 6–4A

"They make an effort" at this nifty NZ-inspired bar/café near Fulham Broadway – a key local brunch spot with "interesting dishes and charming service". Kick off an evening in their gin bar '510 Below'. / SW6 5NJ; www.manukakitchen.com; @manukakitchen; Mon-Thu midnight, Fri & Sat 1 am, Sun 11 pm; closed Sun D; booking max 8 may apply.

Mãos E2 NEW £200 **5** **4** **4**
Redchurch St no tel 13–1C

"The best food I've eaten this year!" – early reporters award the highest ratings to mould-breaking chef Nuno Mendes's "fantastic" latest project: a 16-seater that opened without fanfare in April 2018, but which is one of the most culinarily interesting arrivals of recent times. "Hidden away, up a secret staircase in Redchurch Street", it's part of Shoreditch's funky Blue Mountain School ('an interdisciplinary space dedicated to nurturing engagements and interactions between diverse practices'… and also selling really expensive stuff). This new venture is a revival of sorts of Mendes's Loft Project fine dining supper club, and it inspires ne'er a word of protest regarding the price tag – just first impressions of "an all-round excellent experience, from meeting Nuno and his brigade in the kitchen and eating snacks, to sitting down at a communal table and being served course after course of exceptional, innovative food. There is an impressive wine room too" and all-in-all it offers "a superb night out as well as a great concept". / E2 7DJ; www.maos.dinesuperb.com; Tue-Sat, Mon 10.30 pm, Sun 3.30 pm.

Mar I Terra SE1 £42 **2** **2** **2**
14 Gambia St 020 7928 7628 10–4A

"Fair value" for "authentic" scoff is to be had at this pub-turned-tapas-bar in a side street between Tate Modern and Southwark tube, which "feels like an old friend" for its many regulars, although "the experience you get slightly depends on how well you get on with the owner" (who is mostly "amiable", but on a bad day, "grumpy"). / SE1 0XH; www.mariterra.co.uk; Sun-Thu 11 pm, Fri & Sat midnight; closed Sat L & Sun.

Marcella SE8 £43 3 3 2
165a Deptford High St   020 3903 6561   1–3D
"Another great place in burgeoning Deptford" – this "neighbourhood-style Mediterranean bistro on the increasingly-hip High Street" is a year-old sibling to Peckham's Artusi. "It's simple in style, but the food is very well executed". / SE8 3NU; www.marcella.london; @MarcellaDeptfrd; Mon-Thu 10 pm, Fri & Sat 10.30 pm; closed Mon L, closed Sun; may need 6+ to book.

Marcus,
The Berkeley SW1 £122 3 4 3
Wilton Pl   020 7235 1200   6–1D
Marcus Wareing's "quietly luxurious" Belgravia dining room is one of London's best-known temples of gastronomy and for its very many fans it fully lives up to that reputation with its "balanced, precise and beautifully presented cuisine", "discreet and attentive service", and its "spacious and elegant" quarters ("if you want to seal a business deal, then just wow them with dinner in this place, which strikes that delicate balance between formal and relaxed!"). Not absolutely everyone is wowed though – in particular, the prices can seem plain "silly". STOP PRESS: Those not wowed now includes the Michelin Man who demoted Marcus from two stars to one in October 2018. / SW1X 7RL; www.marcusrestaurant.com; @marcusbelgravia; 10 pm; closed Sun; No trainers; booking max 6 may apply.

Margot WC2 £57 4 5 4
45 Great Queen St   020 3409 4777   5–2D
"Very suave service" ("the staff make the meal into an occasion") adds to the polish of Pablo de Tarso and Nicolas Jaouën's "elegant" and "quite formal" ("white tablecloths, etc") Italian: one of the better options in Covent Garden "to make an evening feel special before or after a show". "Very accomplished" cooking completes the picture, although arguably "more traditional dishes work best". Top Menu Tip: "particularly excellent osso bucco". / WC2B 5AA; www.margotrestaurant.com; @MargotLDN; 11 pm, Sun 10 pm.

Market Hall Fulham SW6 NEW £22
472 Fulham Rd   020 3773 9350   6–4A
The first in a series of 'Market Halls' pitched up in Fulham Broadway's old ticket hall in 2018, transforming the fabulous space into a street food fest, with nine different, regularly changing, kitchens, which currently include Super Tacos (from Breddo's), sourdough pizzas from Yard Sale, Butchies' free-range fried chicken and hot drinks from Press Coffee. Other Market Halls will follow in Victoria (November 2018, in the former Pacha nightclub building) and London's West End (TBC). / SW6 1BY; www.markethalls.co.uk; @markethalls.

The Marksman E2 £65 4 3 4
254 Hackney Rd   020 7739 7393   14–2A
"Just an East End boozer it's not" – this converted public house and dining rooms a short walk from Columbia Road has "an airy, modern and confident first-floor dining room, with food to make you smile and make you think". "It's nothing over-fancy, nothing over-priced" – "taking dishes beyond what one would describe as pub grub", although there's "no better place for a relaxed Sunday lunch". / E2 7SJ; www.marksmanpublichouse.com; @marksman_pub; 10 pm, Sun 9 pm; closed Mon-Thu L.

Maroush £54   3 2 2
I) 21 Edgware Rd, W2   020 7723 0773   7–1D
II) 38 Beauchamp Pl, SW3   020 7581 5434   6–1C
V) 3-4 Vere St, W1   020 7493 5050   3–1B
VI) 68 Edgware Rd, W2   020 7224 9339   7–1D
- Garden) 1 Connaught St, W2   020 7262 0222   7–1D
"The good-quality Lebanese food never disappoints" at this high-profile chain that has prospered for more than 30 years. *"It's very easy to fill up on the starters, which are always delicious"* – and more *"affordable"* than the mains. For live music and belly dancing, head to the original Edgware Road venue. Top Tip: café sections at I and II offer an excellent menu of wraps at bargain prices. / www.maroush.com; most branches close between 12.30 am-5 am.

Masala Zone £43   3 3 4
"Very interesting Indian food for a chain", *"professional service"* and a *"lovely atmosphere"* have carved a strong reputation for these well-established street-food cafés. *"Prices seem to be creeping up"* however, and even those who praise its *"fresh flavours"* feel it's *"not quite as good value as in the past"*. / www.masalazone.com; @masalazone; 11 pm, Sun 10.30 pm; W1U 9 pm, Sun 4 pm; booking: min 8.

MASH Steakhouse W1 £84   3 3 2
77 Brewer St   020 7734 2608   4–3C
A stone's throw from Piccadilly Circus (next to Brasserie Zédel) this American-style steakhouse is praised by fans for its *"delicious food and courteous service"*. Supporters similarly find the setting *"wonderfully relaxed and luxurious"*, but it's a massive space, and – to a minority – *"great steak is let down by the ambience of the huge dining hall"*. / W1F 9ZN; www.mashsteak.co.uk; @mashsteaklondon; 10.30 pm; closed Sun L.

Masters Super Fish SE1 £27   3 2 1
191 Waterloo Rd   020 7928 6924   10–4A
This classic chippie with table service near Waterloo station (popular with taxi drivers) may serve *"only fish 'n' chips – but it's VERY GOOD fish 'n' chips!"* – in *"large portions and with crisp batter"*. / SE1 8UX; masterssuperfish.com; 10.30 pm; closed Mon L, closed Sun; no Amex; no booking, Fri D.

Matsuba TW9 £46   3 3 2
10 Red Lion St   020 8605 3513   1–4A
Nothing but good feedback this year on this *"excellent"* Korean-run Japanese on the fringes of Richmond town centre – a low-key, café-style place, whose sushi gets top billing. / TW9 1RW; www.matsuba-restaurant.com; @matsuba; 10.30 pm, Sun 10 pm; closed Sun.

Max's Sandwich Shop N4 £33   4 4 3
19 Crouch Hill   no tel   1–1C
Who knew sarnies could be so exciting? Max Halley's *"fun and noisy"* Crouch Hill café puts others to shame with its paper parcels of enticing stuffed-focaccia creations, washed down with some good beers. / N4 4AP; www.maxssandwichshop.com; @lunchluncheon; Wed & Thu 11 pm, Fri & Sat midnight, Sun 6 pm; closed Wed-Fri L, closed Mon & Tue; no Amex, no booking.

Mayfair Pizza Company W1 £52   3 3 3
4 Lancashire Ct   020 7629 2889   3–2B
"Pizza isn't my favourite, but the truffled one here tastes better than it smells… and it smells great!" – this fun pizza stop (nowadays incorporated into the 'Mews of Mayfair' empire, to which it's a neighbour) is worth knowing about for a light, relatively affordable bite, off Bond Street. / W1S 1EY; www.mayfairpizzaco.com; @mayfairpizzaco; Wed-Sat 8.30 pm, Sun 1.30 pm.

maze W1 £85 1 2 1

10-13 Grosvenor Sq   020 7107 0000   3–2A

Ratings have declined yet further this year for Gordon Ramsay's Mayfair venue, a star under long-gone founding chef Jason Atherton 10 years ago. Even fans damn it with faint praise: "food better than you expect" – "quite good, but a bit 'hotelly'". Critics don't hold back: "appalling"; "woeful food – had to send three dishes back" and "eye-watering prices". / W1K 6JP; www.gordonramsayrestaurants.com; @mazerestaurant; 9.30 pm; No trainers; booking max 9 may apply.

maze Grill W1 £76 1 2 2

10-13 Grosvenor Sq   020 7495 2211   3–2A

If it were not one of the restaurants that propelled Gordon Ramsay to fame (and also its erstwhile chef, Jason Atherton) – and if it wasn't at the heart of a posh postcode – we would have long ago dropped this hotel grill room in Mayfair: it attracts precious little feedback nowadays, all of it disappointing. / W1K 6JP; www.gordonramsay.com; @mazegrill; 11 pm; No shorts.

maze Grill SW10 £54 3 3 2

11 Park Wk   020 7255 9299   6–3B

The decor can seem "dreary" – a complaint that has dogged this Chelsea site ever since its heady days as 'Aubergine' (long RIP) – but this three-year-old spin-off from Gordon Ramsay's Mayfair grill puts in a better showing than the original: "dreamy burgers" and "outstanding beef" both win praise (if, as at the original, on fairly limited feedback). / SW10 0AJ; www.gordonramsay.com/mazegrill/park-walk; @GordonRamsayGRP; Mon-Thu 10 pm, Fri & Sat 11 pm, Sun 9 pm.

Mazi W8 £64 3 4 3

12-14 Hillgate St   020 7229 3794   7–2B

"Imaginative deconstructed modern Greek cooking" brings locals back to this "cramped and always crowded" taverna in the backstreets of Hillgate Village, near Notting Hill Gate tube (whose small garden is open in summer). "Once you know your way around the menu the food is excellent and at a reasonable price – the uninitiated will find it expensive." Top Tip: "fried feta and caper meringue should be a classic". / W8 7SR; www.mazi.co.uk; @mazinottinghill; Sun & Mon 10 pm, Tue-Sat 10.30 pm; closed Sun & Mon L.

MEATLiquor £37 3 2 4

74 Welbeck St, W1   020 7224 4239   3–1B
6 St Chad's Place, WC1   020 7837 0444   9–3C
17 Queensway, W2   020 7229 0172   7–2C
133b Upper St, N1   020 3711 0104   9–3D
37 Lordship Lane, SE22   020 3066 0008   1–4D
74 Northcote Rd, SW11   awaiting tel   11–2C **NEW**
Brixton Market, SW9   020 7924 9001   11–1D **NEW**

"The chilli cheeseburger and Dead Hippie are burger masterpieces", proclaim fans of this grungy, in-yer-face chain – still the go-to place for a superlative "filthy" burger ("don't go in your best jeans unless you want a dry cleaning bill afterwards"). The "delicious alcoholic milkshakes and fried onions the size of frisbees" also go down well. A new Battersea branch is opening in autumn 2018. / meatliquor.com; @MEATLiquor; W1 midnight (Fri & Sat 2 am), N1 11 pm, SE22 midnight, Sun 10.30 pm-11.30 pm; booking: min 6.

MEATmarket WC2 £27 3 2 2
Jubilee Market Hall, I Tavistock Ct 020 7836 2139 5–3D
"Sitting above the indoor market at Covent Garden adds to the greasy-spoon vibe" of this central spin-off from the MEATliquor chain – "a good spot for a quick burger fix when out-and-about for the day in town". There's "not a worry about calories in sight" – just "burgers at their best, an excellent choice of sides (e.g. chilli cheese fries, monkey fingers and jalapeno poppaz) that add a bit of fire to the proceedings; and the milkshakes are a must-try!" / WC2E 8BD; www.themeatmarket.co.uk; @MEATmarketUK; Mon-Thu 11 pm, Fri & Sat midnight, Sun 10 pm; no Amex; no booking.

MEATmission N1 £31 3 3 4
14-15 Hoxton Market 020 7739 8212 13–1B
"Wow, what a burger (and great hot dogs too)", say fans of the trademarked 'Dead Hippie' and other mostly meaty treats at the MEATliquor group's Hoxton outlet. / N1 6HG; www.meatmission.com; @MEATmission; midnight, Sun 11 pm.

Mediterraneo W11 £65 3 3 3
37 Kensington Park Rd 020 7792 3131 7–1A
"A long-standing favourite" (including of actor Richard E Grant) in Notting Hill, lauded by a small but devoted fan club for its "excellent traditional Italian cooking" – "we go with the grandparents and kids at the weekend and everyone comes out happy!" / W11 2EU; www.mediterraneo-restaurant.co.uk; 11.30pm, Sun 10.30 pm; booking max 10 may apply.

Medlar SW10 £81 4 4 3
438 King's Rd 020 7349 1900 6–3B
"In an otherwise rather barren part of Chelsea", this low-profile, but immensely popular, fixture is "a great neighbourhood restaurant that's worth a journey if it's not in your neighbourhood". "Why did it lose its Michelin star" a couple of years ago? – we just don't know, as Joe Mercier-Nairne's "refined" cuisine is "very accomplished" and often "memorable"; service is "professional" and "exceptionally friendly"; and "the extent and variety of the wine list is a constant surprise, with recommendations that are spot-on every time". The weakest link is a dining room that some say is "not the most elegant", but others value its "intimate" feel. / SW10 0LJ; www.medlarrestaurant.co.uk; @MedlarChelsea; 9 pm.

Mei Ume,
Four Seasons Hotel EC3 £108 3 3 4
10 Trinity Square 020 3297 3799 10–3D
"A great new restaurant addition to Four Seasons Hotel" that opened alongside the better-known Dame de Pic, which – unusually – combines dishes of Chinese and Japanese inspiration (and has one chef for each cuisine). All reports rate the food highly, but no surprises that it's no great bargain: "I went on a deal and it was absolutely delicious… not sure I'd have paid the actual price for it though!" / EC3N 4AJ; www.meiume.com; @FSTenTrinity; 10 pm; closed Sun.

Melange £50 3 2 2
45 Topsfield Parade, Tottenham Lane, N8 020 8341 1681 9–1C
240 Haverstock Hill, NW3 020 3759 6310 9–2A **NEW**
'A taste of France & Italy… in a versatile industry-vintage interior' is the promise of this modern bistro in Crouch End, which inspires limited but positive feedback. It must be doing something right, however, as this year it's spread its wings to take over the prominent Belsize Park site that was most recently The Truscott Arms (and which some still remember as the Weng Wah House, long RIP).

Mele e Pere W1 £54 3 4 3
46 Brewer St 020 7096 2096 4–3C
"A funky and friendly Italian in Soho that's the total opposite of all the Italian chain eateries in the area". "Staff are a joy (if sometimes overworked)" and put "real care into providing good portions of very tasty food". Top Tip: "terrific vermouth cocktails at the welcoming bar". / W1F 9TF; www.meleepere.co.uk; @meleEpere; 11 pm, Sun 10 pm.

Menier Chocolate Factory SE1 £56 2 3 3
51-53 Southwark St 020 7234 9610 10–4B
Book early for the meal-with-ticket deal at this theatre-restaurant in a converted Victorian chocolate factory opposite Borough Market: "they are such good value that they sell out early and are hard to come by". If you miss the deal, think again: there are "plenty of more attractive pre-theatre options nearby". / SE1 1RU; www.menierchocolatefactory.com; @MenChocFactory; Mon-Thu 12.30 am, Fri 1 am; closed Mon & Sun D.

Meraki W1 £62 3 2 4
80-82 Gt Titchfield St 020 7305 7686 3–1C
This "beautiful" yearling is Arjun and Peter Waney's stab at bringing their magic (Roka, Zuma, The Arts Club) to contemporary Greek cuisine, in the 100-cover Fitzrovia premises that some may remember as Efes (long RIP). Promising but a work-in-progress seems a fair summary of feedback: the vibe is "lively", and the food can be "exceptional", but reports often note it's "very expensive" and the "charming but slightly haphazard service" can "be a bit too keen on the up-sell". / W1W 7QT; www.meraki-restaurant.com; @meraki_lon; Mon-Thu 11 pm, Fri & Sat 11.30 pm, Sun 6 pm.

Mercato Metropolitano SE1 £25 5 3 3
42 Newington Causeway 020 7403 0930 1–3C
"Everyone makes their own choice and meets in the middle to eat" at this "fun" experience – a converted 45,000 square foot paper factory, which is nowadays a covered foodie market, with 25-30 stalls drawing from cuisines from all over the globe. Owned by Italian businessman Andrea Rasca (who owns two other similar centres in Italy), it has brought some much-needed life to the area north of Elephant & Castle since 2016 and is "changing and improving all the time; it's now complete with its own micro-brewery" and mushroom farm. "Perfect for a larger group of friends & family when you don't know how many of them will show up". New arrivals this year include Abel – a stall from ex-head chef of Barrafina Drury Lane, Javier Duarte Campos. STOP PRESS: a second location, Mercato Mayfair, will open in early 2019 in a Grade 1 former church just off Oxford Street. / SE1 6DR; www.mercatometropolitano.co.uk; @mercatometropol; 11 pm, Sun 10 pm.

The Mercer EC2 £63 2 2 2
34 Threadneedle St 020 7628 0001 10–2C
"Decent British cooking, competently done" keeps trade ticking over at this converted banking hall over two floors in Threadneedle Street. "Definitely a businessperson's restaurant", it also provides an "exceptional breakfast". / EC2R 8AY; www.themercer.co.uk; @TheMercerLondon; 9.30 pm; closed Sat & Sun.

Merchants Tavern EC2 £61 3 3 4
36 Charlotte Rd 020 7060 5335 13–1B
"A wonderful combination of low-key style, effortlessly friendly service, and exceptionally well-crafted food" draw fans to Angela Hartnett's "buzzy", "unstuffy" and spacious pub in Shoreditch (converted from a former warehouse). A minority, though, are less wowed: it's "decent, but there's no racing of the pulse". / EC2A 3PG; www.merchantstavern.co.uk; @merchantstavern; 11 pm, Sun 9 pm.

Le Mercury N1 £34 2️⃣2️⃣3️⃣
154-155 Upper St   020 7354 4088   9–2D
"A gem of its type" – this traditional candle-lit Islington bistro "changes surprisingly little over the years" and "you still can't beat it for value-for-money in North London". "Portions are generous and having the same price for all starters and mains makes paying as a group so much easier!"
/ N1 1QY; www.lemercury.co.uk; 1 am; Mon-Thu D only, Fri-Sun open L & D.

Mere W1 £89 4️⃣4️⃣3️⃣
74 Charlotte St   020 7268 6565   2–1B
"Monica Galetti's attention to detail shines through" and helps inspire a "stand-out total experience" at the Fitzrovia yearling that she runs with her husband David (formerly the sommelier at Le Gavroche): you start with "amazing cocktails" in the ground floor bar, and then move on to the "welcoming" downstairs restaurant. Alongside the à la carte options, it features "a very memorable tasting menu" ("exquisite flavours and textures, all perfectly cooked" and with a veggie option), and marries them with wine from the "superb" and "well-matched wine list". If there's a quibble, it's that "portions can be very small for the price". La Patronne "takes the time to visit each table"; and the "friendly and professional" service led by her hubbie adds a lot to the experience. And although "tables are perhaps a little close together", reporters generally like this "intimate" and "good-looking space". / W1T 4QH; www.mere-restaurant.com; @mererestaurant; Jacket & tie required.

Meson don Felipe SE1 £42 2️⃣2️⃣3️⃣
53 The Cut   020 7928 3237   10–4A
This "fun" tapas veteran sits a minute's walk from the Old and Young Vic theatres, and is always "cramped and crowded" ("you need to arrive early to get a table"). "A very good Spanish wine list" helps buoy the "great atmosphere", and for everyone who feels the food's average or "past its sell-by", there are others who still think it's "terrific". / SE1 8LF; www.mesondonfelipe.com; 10 pm; closed Sun; no Amex; no booking after 8 pm.

Mews of Mayfair W1 £70 3️⃣2️⃣3️⃣
10 Lancashire Court, New Bond St   020 7518 9388   3–2B
A super-cute location – a cobbled alleyway, just off Bond Street – sets an upbeat tone to this hidden-away haunt which comprises both a bar and brasserie. Historically the former has seemed more reliable than the latter, but – while it attracts curiously few reports – such feedback as we have is all-round positive. / W1S 1EY; www.mewsofmayfair.com; @mewsofmayfair; 11 pm, Sun 4 pm; closed Sun D.

Meza £37 3️⃣3️⃣2️⃣
34 Trinity Rd, SW17   07722 111299   11–2C
70 Mitcham Rd, SW17   020 8672 2131   11–2C
"Very fresh, bright tastes and efficient service" are the stand-out qualities in this "jolly" little pair of Lebanese cafés in Tooting and Clapham ("the Trinity Road branch buzzes a bit more than the one on Tooting Broadway"). Top Tip: "complex fried chicken livers".
/ www.mezarestaurant.co.uk; @MezaRestaurants; 11 pm, Fri & Sat 11.30 pm.

La Mia Mamma SW3 🆕 £61
257 King's Rd   020 7351 2417   6–3C
'Food like mamma used to make' is the promise of this May 2018 opening in Chelsea, where 20 matriarchs a year are shipped over to create a rotating roster of residencies, with each chef hailing from a different region of Italy. / SW3 5EL; www.lamiamamma.co.uk; @LaMiaMamma_.

Michael Nadra £60 `4` `3` `2`
6-8 Elliott Rd, W4 020 8742 0766 8–2A
42 Gloucester Ave, NW1 020 7722 2800 9–3B
Michael Nadra makes "a talented and charming chef/patron" and his duo of neighbourhood restaurants – in Chiswick and Camden Town (right next to the Regent's Canal) – both provide a "welcoming" venue and "surprisingly good value for sophisticated modern French cooking". On the downside, both inhabit awkward sites – NW1 is "cavernous" and slightly "remote", while W4 is low-ceilinged and tightly packed.
/ www.restaurant-michaelnadra.co.uk; @michaelnadra; W4 10 pm, Fri-Sat 10.30 pm, NW1 10.30 pm, Sun 9 pm; NW1 closed Mon, W4 closed Sun D.

Mien Tay £37 `3` `2` `2`
45 Fulham High St, SW6 020 7731 0670 11–1B **NEW**
180 Lavender Hill, SW11 020 7350 0721 11–1C
122 Kingsland Rd, E2 020 7729 3074 14–2A
"Authentic, hot and spicy Vietnamese food never disappoints" at this quartet of neighbourhood restaurants in Battersea, Fulham, Shoreditch and now Wood Green. "Fabulous fresh dishes at amazing prices" can mean that they're "crowded and noisy, even on a weekday night – no wonder some of the waiters can seem grumpy..." / mientay.co.uk; @Mien_Tay; 11 pm, Sun 10 pm; E2 Sun 10.30 pm.

Mildreds £46 `3` `2` `2`
45 Lexington St, W1 020 7494 1634 4–2C
200 Pentonville Rd, N1 020 7278 9422 9–3D
9 Jamestown Rd, NW1 020 7482 4200 9–3B
Upper Dalston Sq, E8 020 8017 1815 14–1A
"Good value vegetarian food" offering "excellent quality and choices" (including gluten-free and vegan) have driven the expansion of this 30-year-old veggie outfit from Soho into Camden, Dalston and King's Cross. The Soho original is "cramped but likeable", while the newer outposts are more "light and airy". / @mildredslondon.

Milk SW12 £16 `4` `3` `3`
20 Bedford Hill 020 8772 9085 11–2C
"Delicious food... as long as you don't mind queuing on weekends" continues to win many votes for this Antipodean café which is world famous down Balham way as a "fabulous breakfast and brunch" destination.
/ SW12 9RG; www.milk.london; @milkcoffeeldn; Mon-Wed 5 pm, Thu-Sat 10 pm, Sun 6 pm; closed Mon-Wed D; no booking.

Min Jiang,
The Royal Garden Hotel W8 £81 `4` `4` `5`
2-24 Kensington High St 020 7361 1988 6–1A
"Exquisite Beijing duck" and "divine dim sum" are twin culinary highlights of this "top-class" Chinese, which occupies a "beautiful and comfortable" dining room on the eighth floor of Kensington's Royal Garden Hotel. "The rare and privileged views across the park to Kensington Palace takes this place to another level", though – "request a window seat!" / W8 4PT; www.minjiang.co.uk; @minjianglondon; 10 pm.

Minnow SW4 £54 `3` `3` `3`
21 The Pavement 020 7720 4105 11–2D
"A strong new arrival in SW4" – "inventive modern British cooking" is "served by friendly, informal but informative, staff in a space which is larger than it appears from outside" at Jake Boyce's year-old venture, tipped for its good brunch. / SW4 0HY; minnowclapham.co.uk; @minnowclapham; Sun & Mon 5 pm, Wed & Thu 10 pm, Fri & Sat 11 pm, Tue 6 pm.

Mint Leaf £73 3 2 3

Suffolk Pl, Haymarket, SW1   020 7930 9020   2–2C
Angel Ct, Lothbury, EC2   020 7600 0992   10–2C
This "swanky" operation – whose slick contemporary decor has
an "international feel" – serves "very different, very original Indian/Asian
fusion food" and "excellent cocktails" at its two venues, off Trafalgar Square
and near Bank. / www.mintleafrestaurant.com; 10.45 pm; SW1 closed
Sat L & Sun D, EC2 closed Sat & Sun.

Mirch Masala SW17 £26 4 2 1

213 Upper Tooting Rd   020 8767 8638   11–2D
"Amazing flavours at amazing prices" means it's always packed at this
Pakistani canteen in Tooting – "now apparently gaining fame as Sadiq
Khan's favourite restaurant". "It wins hands-down on value for money,
especially with the BYO policy". Order the "wonderful slow-cooked meat
specials or excellent veggie options". / SW17 7TG;
www.mirchmasalarestaurant.co.uk; midnight; cash only; no booking.

Mirror Room WC1 £80 3 3 4

Rosewood London, 252 High Holborn   020 3747 8620   2–1D
Pastry chef, Mark Perkins, takes inspiration from Cubism and Pop Art for
the "beautiful afternoon tea" at this descriptively-named chamber within this
plush Holborn hotel. It's "an interesting room" and the "exceptional cakes
and pastries are truly a work of art… and taste great too!". / WC1V 7EN;
www.rosewoodhotels.com; @RosewoodLondon; 11 pm, Sun 10.30 pm.

The Modern Pantry EC1 £65 2 2 2

47-48 St Johns Sq   020 7553 9210   10–1A
Aussie fusion chef Anna Hansen's 10-year-old Clerkenwell flagship
(the offshoot in Finsbury Square is no more) is a "perennially brilliant brunch
spot" with "interesting food and great service… hence its popularity,
especially on weekends". "Love the sugar-cured prawn, spring onion and
sambal omelette" – a dish that has entered folklore. But some diners are
not convinced, dismissing the food as merely "trendy" or "mediocre and
disappointing". / EC1V 4JJ; www.themodernpantry.co.uk; @themodernpantry;
10 pm.

Moksha KT3 £35 5 4 3

Kingston Rd   020 894 92211   1–4A
"First class Indian food" wins high esteem for experienced restaurateurs,
Arjun Singh Rawat and Rajeev Danga's top tier North Indian two-year old,
although, by dint of its New Malden location, feedback is still limited: more
reports please! / KT3 3RJ; www.moksharestaurant.uk; @Mokshanewmalden; Mon &
Tue 9 pm, Fri & Sat 11.30 pm, Wed 10 pm, Thu 11 pm, Sun 5 pm.

Momo W1 £76 3 3 3

25 Heddon St   020 7434 4040   4–3B
Mourad Mazouz's "atmospheric" and clubby party scene first brought
glamour to Moroccan cuisine – and the fast crowd to Mayfair's Heddon
Street – back in the 1990s. "Tagines presented bubbling to your table" are
a highlight on a menu also featuring grills, couscous and some fusion-esque
North African starters (e.g. foie gras with pomegranate molasses, Scottish
beef tartare with Batata harra foam). Kick off an evening with cocktails
in the vibey basement bar. / W1B 4BH; www.momoresto.com; @momoresto;
1 am, Sun midnight; credit card required to book.

Mon Plaisir Restaurant WC2　　　£53　　3 3 4
19-21 Monmouth St　020 7836 7243　5–2B
"Long may it survive!"; fans *"never tire"* of this *"well-established favourite"* of 70 years' standing – an *"evergreen, authentic buzzing bistro"* near Seven Dials, whose *"charmingly eccentric"*, much-extended premises have *"a unique, unmistakably Gallic atmosphere"*. The odd critic feels that its *"old-fashioned French"* cuisine has *"seen better days"*, but the vast majority feel it's *"no bad thing that it's predictable"*, praising results as *"delicious"* and *"sensibly priced"* (and loving the *"fabulous cheese trolley"*). Top Tip: *"great pre/post theatre deals"*. / WC2H 9DD; www.monplaisir.co.uk; @MonPlaisir4; 11 pm; closed Sun.

Mona Lisa SW10　　　£39　　3 3 2
417 King's Rd　020 7376 5447　6–3B
"No pretensions but amazing value and large portions" of *"inexpensive, honest comfort food"* make this Italian-run greasy spoon on the King's Road a useful option in pricey Chelsea (*"workers' caff by day, restaurant by night"*). Top Tip: where else can you still find a three-course set menu for £9.95? / SW10 0LR; monalisarestaurant.co.uk; 11 pm, Sun 5.30 pm; closed Sun D; no Amex.

Monkey Temple W12　　　£33　　3 4 2
92 Askew Rd　020 8743 4597　8–1B
In ever-more chichi 'Askew Village' (aka deepest Shepherd's Bush) this *"excellent"* local curry house is a top option for a very decent curry: *"nowt fancy, but reliable"* and with *"lovely service"*. / W12 9BL; monkeytempleonline.co.uk; 10.30 pm; closed Mon L; no Amex.

Monmouth Coffee Company　　　£7　　3 4 4
27 Monmouth St, WC2　020 7232 3010　5–2B
2 Park St, SE1　020 7232 3010　10–4C
"The best coffee on the planet" (*"a fabulous diverse array complemented by very knowledgeable and friendly staff"*) ensure that these *"caffeine-lovers' paradises"* remain the survey's No.1 chain of coffee houses and are *"consistently so rammed"*. Foodwise, there's just *"a small range of good pastries, brownies and shortbreads"*, but at the mega-popular Borough Market branch you can *"nibble on jam and butter on crusty white bread, while people watching"*. / www.monmouthcoffee.co.uk; WC2 6:30 pm; SE1 6 pm; SE16 Sat 1.30 pm; WC2 & SE1 closed Sun; no Amex; no booking.

Monty's Deli N1　　　£36　　4 4 3
225-227 Hoxton St　020 7729 5737　14–1B
This *"great Jewish restaurant on the fringes of Hoxton"* is touted by fans as *"hands-down the best place to get deli food in London"*. Founders Mark Ogus and Owen Barratt crowdfunded the move to a permanent site after perfecting their 'Jewish soul food' classics on a market stall. *"The attention to detail is fantastic: the pickles are tiny and piquant, the spicing spot on, the potato latkes shatter crisply"*. Top Tip: *"perfect soft and fatty salt beef and pastrami"*. In summer 2018, having smashed a Crowdcube fundraiser target, they have plans to expand into a national chain starting with another three London sites: the first to be in the new Victoria Market Halls development. / N1; montys-deli.com; @MontysDeli; 10 pm, Sun 4 pm; closed Sun D, closed Mon.

Morito £44 4 3 4

195 Hackney Rd, E2 020 7613 0754 14–2A
32 Exmouth Mkt, EC1 020 7278 7007 10–1A

"An utterly brilliant tapas café, where you perch on stools, in the window or at the bar; staff are relaxed and chatty, and the food is expertly cooked, delicious and really good value". That's the low-down on Moro's first spin off, a few doors down from the mothership, on Exmouth Market. Since last year it has a "more comfortable Hackney Road version" (near Columbia Road flower market). "Lovely Mediterranean-inspired dishes here too, plus a great spacious setting", "very buzzy counter-style dining" and "you can book any time". Top Menu Tips – "yummy aubergine fritters" ("I don't know how they get them that crispy and tasty"); and a "scrumptious North African/Mediterranean twist on brunch". / EC1 11 pm, Sun 4 pm; E2 10.30 pm, Sun 9 pm; EC1 closed Sun D; no booking.

Moro EC1 £61 4 3 3

34-36 Exmouth Mkt 020 7833 8336 10–1A

"I've been coming for 20 years – it's yet to disappoint". Samuel & Samantha Clark's "unpretentious" ("no cheffery") Exmouth Market landmark still turns out "memorable Spanish and North African dishes, with a terrific selection of Spanish and Portuguese wines and sherries". Indeed, for its vast fan club, "the only limitation is the noise: it's not great for conversation" given how "echoey" the room can become. All this said, a small band of long-term fans do sound a warning note, feeling "the food has become a bit more variable in quality and interest" in recent years. It's still a minority view though – most reporters are just "grateful not to live nearby: otherwise I'd never go anywhere else…" / EC1R 4QE; www.moro.co.uk; @RestaurantMoro; 10.30 pm, Sun 9.30 pm; closed Sun D.

Motcombs SW1 £56 2 3 3

26 Motcomb St 020 7235 6382 6–1D

Like many of its patrons, this stalwart wine bar (upstairs) and restaurant (downstairs) has long been 'part of the furniture' in the ever-more-chichi heart of Belgravia. It's perennially been accused of somewhat "uninspired" fare, but – now under new ownership – fans feel that "even if the inimitable Mr Lawless has finally sold up, it remains good value in a top postcode". / SW1X 8JU; www.motcombs.co.uk; @Motcombs; 10 pm; closed Sun D.

Mother SW11 £44 2 2 3

2 Archers Lane, Battersea Power Station 020 7622 4386 11–1C

This dark and moodily decorated yearling – London's branch of Copenhagen's 'Italian pizza without all the nonsense' concept – occupies a railway arch at Battersea Power Station's Circus West Village. Opinion is divided on the all-important question of the pizza: "average" vying with "good value and tasty". / SW11 8AB; www.motherrestaurant.co.uk; @mother_ldn; Sun-Thu 11 pm, Fri & Sat midnight.

Mr Bao SE15 £35 4 3 3

293 Rye Ln 020 7635 0325 1–4D

Frank Yeung's "friendly and small Peckham cafe serves delectable Taiwanese street food, in particular heavenly steamed buns". In February 2018 he opened a Tooting spin-off Daddy Bao – see also. / SE15 4UA; www.mrbao.co.uk; @MrBaoUK; 11 pm; closed Sun & Mon.

Mr Chow SW1 £88 2 3 3

151 Knightsbridge 020 7589 7347 6–1D

All reporters have nice things to say about the cuisine at this datedly glamorous A-lister, near 1 Hyde Park, whose heyday was in the 1960s and 1970s. It can, however, seem "insanely expensive for what is just some nice Chinese food". / SW1X 7PA; www.mrchow.com; @mrchow; midnight; closed Mon L.

Munal Tandoori SW15   £27   3 4 2
393 Upper Richmond Road, Putney   020 8876 3083   11–2A
"Just a great local curry" on the edge of Putney – this Nepalese has been a handy stop on the South Circular for more than 25 years. Regulars praise its *"really tasty food and generous portions"* – *"it can't be beaten for a really inexpensive meal!"* / SW15 \N; Mon-Thu 11 pm, Sat midnight, Sun 10.30 pm; closed Mon-Thu L, closed Fri.

Murano W1   £99   4 5 3
20-22 Queen St   020 7495 1127   3–3B
Angela Hartnett's *"superb"* Mayfair flagship has taken Pip Lacey's 2017 departure in its stride, and although its ratings dipped fractionally year-on-year, many reporters still feel Oscar Holgado's *"Italian-oriented cuisine must be amongst the best in town"*. When it comes to the interior, the harsh view is that these *"un-flashy"* premises *"on a quiet street"* are *"a little dull"*, but the more common verdict is that its *"restrained and elegant"* style *"oozes class and calm"* and that *"the warm welcome and graceful professional service gets any visit off to a flying start"*. / W1J 5PP; www.muranolondon.com; @muranolondon; 11 pm; closed Sun; credit card required to book.

Mustard W6   £45   3 3 3
98-100 Shepherd's Bush Rd   020 3019 1175   8–1C
"A pleasant oasis in the desert of Shepherd's Bush Road" – this smart brasserie north of Brook Green is *"a great local"*, offering *"food that's perfectly fine, comfortable surroundings and willing service"*. / W6 7PD; www.mustardrestaurants.co.uk; @mustarddining; 10 pm, Sun 5 pm; closed Mon & Sun D.

Namaaste Kitchen NW1   £44   4 3 2
64 Parkway   020 7485 5977   9–3B
"Creative and intelligent" cooking wins nothing but high praise for this contemporary update of the traditional curry house, in Camden Town. It has a sister venue, Salaam Namaste, in Bloomsbury. / NW1 7AH; www.namaastekitchen.co.uk; @NamaasteKitchen; midnight, Sun 6 pm.

Nanashi EC2   £62   3 3 2
14 Rivington St   020 7686 0010   13–2B
"First class sushi, complemented by some decent hot dishes" win a repeat thumbs-up for this Japanese yearling in Shoreditch. *"The tuna sushi burger is worth a try, but the main show is the other fish"*. / EC2A 3DU; www.nanashi.co.uk; Tue, Wed 10.30 pm, Thu-Sat 11 pm; closed Sun & Mon.

Nanban SW9   £44   4 2 3
Coldharbour Ln   020 7346 0098   11–2D
"Different and great flavours" are to be discovered at former MasterChef winner Tim Anderson's *"fun"* fixture, where he cooks up his own distinctive and very alternative 'Japanese Soul Food' (incorporating eclectic ingredients from nearby Brixton Market). / SW9 8LF; www.nanban.co.uk; @NanbanLondon; Mon-Thu 11 pm, Sat midnight, Sun 10.30 pm.

The Narrow E14   £57   2 2 4
44 Narrow St   020 7592 7950   12–1B
The *"fantastic river location and views"* at Gordon Ramsay's Limehouse pub have never in all the many years he's owned it been matched by its kitchen. No-one says its dire nowadays, but feedback on the *"standard gastropub food"* is very middling – a *"very average offering from Ramsay, this"*. / E14 8DP; www.gordonramsayrestaurants.com/the-narrow; @thenarrow; Mon-Thu 12.30 am, Fri 1 am.

Native SE1 NEW £56
32 Southwark St   07943 934 375   10–4C
In its former home – "an unassuming corner of Neal's Yard" – Ivan Tisdall-Downes and Imogen Davis's on-trend venture (100% Brit produce, zero waste and, quote, 'profound respect for the natural environment') was thriving. Their lease fell through in mid-2018, but every cloud has a silver lining, as the old gaff was "rather worn and plain" and this new home is bigger, with 60 covers. A daily changing menu with a focus on game remains a feature, as do the 'Chef's Wasting Snacks' (canapés making use of leftovers others would chuck out, e.g. fish skins, potato peelings... better than it sounds anyway). It opened too late for a survey rating, but there's no reason to think its "small, exquisite, wow of a menu" and "enthusiastic and patient service" will not transfer well. / SE1 1TU; www.eatnative.co.uk; @eatnativeuk; closed Sun & Mon.

Naughty Piglets SW2 £57 5 5 3
28 Brixton Water Ln   020 7274 7796   11–2D
"Truly the best conceptual-type restaurant I've been to in ages" – Joe and Margaux Sharratt's small French-accented outfit in a Brixton side street charms all comers with its "expert cuisine (with innovative combinations such as Devon crab, peanut and pickled cabbage)" and "love of doing it right". Opened to acclaim three years ago – and now with a sister venue at Andrew Lloyd Webber's The Other Palace theatre in Victoria – it shows no sign of flagging. Top Tip: "sit at the bar to watch the talented chefs in action". / SW2 1PE; www.naughtypiglets.co.uk; 10 pm; closed Mon-Wed L, closed Sun.

Nautilus NW6 £35 4 3 1
27-29 Fortune Green Rd   020 7435 2532   1–1B
"Fish 'n' chips the way it should be!" – this classic West Hampstead chippy is reckoned by fans to be "still the best in the northwest". Nobody disputes that the fish is "fantastic", "but the restaurant needs redoing" (as it has done for decades) – "much better for take-away". Top Tip: choose matzo meal over batter. / NW6 1DU; 11 pm; closed Sun; no Amex.

Navarro's W1 £39 3 3 3
67 Charlotte St   020 7637 7713   2–1C
This "fantastic, traditional-style tapas restaurant" in Fitzrovia was founded in 1985, well before the contemporary tapas boom. Family-run, "humble" and "down-to-earth" – it may lack the pizzazz of its more modern Iberian competitors, but is "very good value". / W1T 4PH; www.navarros.co.uk; @SpanishEchelon; 10 pm; closed Sat L, closed Sun.

Needoo E1 £25 4 2 2
87 New Rd   020 7247 0648   13–2D
There are more famous Pakistani BYO destinations in E1, but the small-but-devoted fan club of this sizeable Whitechapel grill-house extol its "terrific curries and great value for money". / E1 1HH; www.needoogrill.co.uk; @NeedooGrill; 11.30 pm.

Neo Bistro W1 £58 4 4 3
11 Woodstock St   020 7499 9427   3–1B
"In a slightly barren part of town" – just behind Bond Street tube – this "little gem" opened in summer 2017, with two young chefs (Alex Harper, ex-Harwood Arms and Mark Jarvis, ex-Anglo) inspired by the modern Parisian bistro movement. It's a "great concept" with accomplished cuisine ("a showcase of ingredients and technique"), "accommodating service" and "a thoughtful wine list". / W1C 2JF; www.neobistro.co.uk; @neo_bistro; 9.45 pm.

Neptune,
The Principal WC1 NEW   **£86**
The Principal London, 8 Russell Square   020 7520 1806   2–1D
*The setting: a dramatic late-Victorian pile (fka Hotel Russell) on the eastern
flank of Russell Square which has finally received the bold revamp it's been
crying out for, for decades. No expense has been spared, and this seafood
temple is a superb new space. It opened just as our 2018 survey was
drawing to a close, and though we had one enthusiastic report, more muted
press reviews suggest the level of achievement of the cuisine overseen by ex-
Richmond-chef, Brett Redman is very fully priced. You can always poke your
head around the door on a visit to one of the hotel's other venues: afternoon
tea parlour Palm Court, Fitz's cocktail bar or Burr & Co coffeehouse.*
/ WC1B 5BE; neptune.london; @Principal_Hotel; Mon-Fri 10 pm, Sat & Sun 9 pm.

Niche EC1   **£55**   2 3 2
197-199 Rosebery Avenue   020 7837 5048   9–3D
*Only limited feedback and only reasonable ratings for this compact
contemporary bistro near Sadler's Wells Theatre: London's first 100%
gluten-free restaurant (motto: 'gluten-free, but you wouldn't know it'). Still,
if that's your dietary ticket it has evident attractions, and they must be doing
something right, as July 2018 saw them close to refurbish, and launch
a new crowdsourcing campaign for a second opening, pencilled in for Ealing.*
/ EC1R 4TJ; www.nichefoodanddrink.com; @Nichefooddrink; 11 pm, Sun 10 pm.

The Ninth London W1   **£78**   4 3 2
22 Charlotte St   020 3019 0880   2–1C
*"It's all about the food" – you could call it "casual Michelin" – at Jun
Tanaka's Fitzrovia HQ, which provides a "relaxed", "buzzing" (and quite
"romantic") environment in which to enjoy his "innovative" and sometimes
"amazing" culinary creations. Quibbles? – "it's quite a difficult menu to get
your mind around" ("we were told it was small plates but were still asked
to choose separate courses each"); and "although it's a pretty space it can
feel a bit cramped".* / W1T 2NB; www.theninthlondon.com; @theninthlondon;
Mon-Wed 10 pm, Thu-Sat 10.30 pm; closed Sun.

No 29 Power Station West SW8   **£56**   2 1 4
Circus West, Battersea Power Station   020 3857 9872   11–1C
*"Delicious brunch in a large airy room overlooking the river" is one draw
to Darwin & Wallace's latest venue, in Battersea Power Station's Circus
West Village – a bar/brasserie with a fine riverside location and small
outside terrace. One bugbear: "service is friendly but can be haphazard".*
/ SW8 5BP; www.no29powerstationwest.co.uk; @batterseapwrstn; Sun-Thu midnight,
Fri & Sat 1 am; SRA-Food Made Good – 3 stars.

Noble Rot WC1   **£74**   3 4 4
51 Lamb's Conduit St   020 7242 8963   2–1D
*An oenophile's dream – Mark Andrew and Daniel Keeling's "jolly"
Bloomsbury two-year-old is, for the second year running, in strong contention
as "London's best wine option, bar none". "Old-fashioned (in a good way)",
it occupies the endearingly "dingy" '70s site that for many years traded
as Vats (RIP) and "aside from being a bit noisy, the place itself is wonderfully
atmospheric". "Staff are friendly with an expert knowledge of the wines"
and the list itself is "extensive, but even for the non-connoisseur
or financially constrained customer there are quite a lot of bottles coming
in at less than £30". The "well-crafted" food is "much-more-than-
serviceable" too – a selection of "very tasty and reasonably priced small
plates".* / WC1N 3NB; www.noblerot.co.uk; @noblerotbar; 10 pm; closed Sun.

Nobu,
Metropolitan Hotel W1 £100 322
19 Old Park Ln 020 7447 4747 3–4A

"The food is just as good as it always was" (if no longer as trailblazing) at this Japanese-South American fusion concept, a global operation that exploded onto the London scene 21 years ago in this minimalist (some would say boring), first-floor space, overlooking Hyde Park. "Not the destination it used to be for spotting a celeb", that's not without its benefits ("there's no problem getting a table") and though as "expensive" as it's always been (and with so-so service), it can "still impress". / W1K 1LB; www.noburestaurants.com; @NobuOldParkLane; Mon-Wed 10.30 pm, Thu-Sat 11 pm, Sun 10 pm.

Nobu Berkeley W1 £104 322
15 Berkeley St 020 7290 9222 3–3C

More "brash and boisterous" than its (older) Park Lane sibling, this Mayfair venue continues to attract a steady stream of positive reviews for its "sublime sushi" and other Japanese fusion-wizardry. For how long can they keep milking the franchise as hard as they do, though? – this place seems to become ever-more "wildly overpriced" by the year. / W1J 8DY; www.noburestaurants.com; @NobuBerkeleyST; Mon-Wed 11 pm, Thu-Sat midnight, Sun 9.45 pm; closed Sun L

Nobu Shoreditch EC2 £110 323
10-50 Willow St 020 3818 3790 13–1B

"I can't believe there's a Nobu in Shoreditch!" – there is indeed, a 240-seater in the basement (with small courtyard garden attached) of London's first hotel from the Japanese-American superbrand, serving all "the usual fare" ("consistently great sushi", "top-notch black cod", etc) "with a couple of Shoreditch specials". Some fans reckon it's "better than the others in the stable", especially its "buzzy, loud 'cool' dining room", but like its siblings it can seem well "overpriced": "loved it, but there were too many City-types spending the bosses' money!" / EC2A 4BH; www.nobuhotelshoreditch.com; @NobuShoreditch; Sun & Mon 10.45 pm, Tue-Sat midnight.

Noizé W1 £78 454
39 Whitfield St 020 7323 1310 2–1C

A particularly "excellent choice of wines both by the glass and the bottle" and "seamless and friendly service" are features of this quite small (36-seat) and agreeably "unfussily decorated" Fitzrovia newcomer (on the former site of Dabbous, RIP) – no surprises, perhaps, as its patron Mathieu Germond is a former co-owner and manager of nearby Pied à Terre. When it comes to the chef Ed Dutton's "imaginative" modern French cuisine, all reports agree results are "excellent" going on "exceptional". (There's also a basement bar). / W1T 2SF; www.noize-restaurant.co.uk; @NoizeRestaurant; 10.30 pm; closed Sat L, closed Sun & Mon.

Noor Jahan £48 333
2a Bina Gdns, SW5 020 7373 6522 6–2B
26 Sussex Pl, W2 020 7402 2332 7–1D

An "old favourite" – this "reliable workhorse" on the Earl's Court / South Ken' borders is a proper, "old-fashioned Indian" and has everything you'd expect from a "great neighbourhood curry house", including a "loyal clientele and staff that have been there forever". There's "nothing extravagant about it, but that's its charm" and it's always "impressively busy". (It has a similar, but lesser-known Bayswater spin-off.) / W2 11.30 pm, Sun 11 pm; SW5 11.30 pm.

Nopi W1 £74 4 3 3

21-22 Warwick St   020 7494 9584   4–3B

The "awesome food" at influential writer-chef Yotam Ottolenghi's Soho flagship is "a treat to the tastebuds" – and his Middle Eastern small plates even make "eating out feel healthy for once". When it comes to the atmosphere, most diners experience a "happy buzz" but it's "too loud" and "busy" for some tastes. Top Tip: "delightful at breakfast". / W1B 5NE; www.nopi-restaurant.com; @ottolenghi; 10.30 pm, Sun 4 pm; closed Sun D.

Nordic Bakery W1 £13 3 2 2

14a Golden Sq   020 3230 1077   4–3C

"Good coffee, excellent Nordic-based rye-bread sandwiches and the famous cinnamon buns" have made this café a fixture in Golden Square, Soho, for more than a decade. Its expansion plans seem to have hit the rocks, however, with the sudden closure of three satellite spin-offs all in the past year. / W1F 9JG; www.nordicbakery.com; 8 pm, Sat & Sun 7 pm; L & early evening only; no Amex; no booking.

The Norfolk Arms WC1 £49 2 3 3

28 Leigh St   020 7388 3937   9–4C

This King's Cross gastroboozer with an "extensive tapas menu" is a "bright, lively spot in a part of town that's otherwise a little sparse for restaurants". Food that generally exceeds expectations and "relaxed staff" make this a "good place for a party" – and there are private dining rooms upstairs. / WC1H 9EP; www.norfolkarms.co.uk; 10.30 pm, Mon 11 pm, Sun 3 pm; no Amex.

North China W3 £44 3 4 2

305 Uxbridge Rd   020 8992 9183   8–1A

"Still the stand-out Chinese" in Acton (and fans would say beyond) – this neighbourhood stalwart can pleasantly surprise with the quality of its cooking, and "the maitre d' Laurence remembers you even if you haven't been for years!". "We went three times in six days on a recent visit to town!" / W3 9QU; www.northchina.co.uk; Sun-Thu 11 pm, Fri & Sat 11.30 pm.

North Sea Fish WC1 £45 3 3 2

7-8 Leigh St   020 7387 5892   9–4C

A "great institution" – this "very traditional" family-run Bloomsbury chippy is one of the best around the West End, and a safe bet for "good fresh fish, grilled or battered, with proper crisp chips". "You don't come here for the ambience" – it's "had a facelift" but "never really changes… thank goodness!". / WC1H 9EW; www.northseafishrestaurant.co.uk; 10 pm; closed Sun L; no Amex.

The Northall, Corinthia Hotel WC2 £103 3 2 3

10a Northumberland Ave   020 7321 3100   2–3C

Overshadowed by the opening of Kerridge's Bar & Grill, opinions were more split this year on the hotel's plush 'other' dining room – an "elegant" ("slightly cavernous") space with orange leather seating and "well-spaced tables". Practically all reports are of "excellent", "traditional" cooking, but one former fan felt it "had become more noticeably overpriced since the last visit" and to another sceptic: "the food's OK, but I'm not sure how much the hotel values the place other than for serving in-house guests". / WC2N 5AE; www.thenorthall.co.uk; @CorinthiaLondon; 11 pm.

Northbank EC4 £60 3 2 3

One Paul's Walk   020 7329 9299   10–3B

"It's the location that's the 'icing on the cake' – with the Thames, Tate Modern, and picture windows so that you can see it all" – at this City bar/café, beside the Wobbly Bridge. Even if it can seem "a bit pricey", the food – with "a focus on Cornwall and fish" – tries harder than that of many well-situated destinations. / EC4V 3QH; www.northbankrestaurant.co.uk; @NorthbankLondon; 10 pm; closed Sun.

Novikov (Asian restaurant) W1 £96 3 2 4
50a Berkeley St 020 7399 4330 3–3C
*For a "perfect, fun buzzy time", this glam Russian-owned pan-Asian near
Berkeley Square is a perennial smash hit with a glossy, very Mayfair crowd.
Its mix of sushi, dim sum, charcoal grill dishes and noodles is dependably
delectable, but if you are at all budget-conscious, spare yourself the stress
induced by the bill and head elsewhere. / W1J 8HA; www.novikovrestaurant.co.uk;
@NovikovLondon; midnight.*

Novikov (Italian restaurant) W1 £110 1 2 2
50a Berkeley St 020 7399 4330 3–3C
*A few fans – all of whom seem to have put 'Investment Banker' in the
occupation field of the survey form – feel the food is "first rate" in the
Italian section of Russian restaurateur Arkady Novikov's Eurotrashy Mayfair
hang-out. Those not blessed with a career in the money factories are more
apt to feel the experience is "appalling all-round", with particular antipathy
to the Sputnik-high prices – "bare-faced robbery!". / W1J 8HA;
www.novikovrestaurant.co.uk; @NovikovLondon; Mon-Wed midnight, Thu-Sat
12.45 am, Sun 11 pm.*

Nuala EC1 NEW £57 4 3 4
70-74 City Rd 020 3904 0462 13–1A
*"Cool surroundings and diners… as befits the location" set the tone at this
"interesting" (if sometimes "noisy and frantic") newcomer, just south
of Silicon Roundabout, where cooking over open flames is the order of the
day. Even a reporter who found results "interesting in conception but lumpy
in execution", found their visit "enjoyable", and most reports are
of "well presented dishes with good flavours". / EC1 2BJ; www.nualalondon.com;
@nualalondon; Mon-Fri 10 pm, Sat & Sun 9 pm.*

Nuovi Sapori SW6 £50 3 3 4
295 New King's Rd 020 7736 3363 11–1B
*"An old favourite" – this "welcoming neighbourhood trattoria" near Parsons
Green offers a "conventional Italian menu" alongside "cheerful service and
atmosphere that ensure that it's always busy". / SW6 4RE;
www.nuovisaporilondon.co.uk; 11 pm; closed Sun; booking max 6 may apply.*

Nusr-Et Steakhouse,
The Park Tower Knightsbridge SW1 NEW
101 Knightsbridge awaiting tel 6–1D
*Former incumbent on this site, One-O-One (sadly RIP), was of rare quality,
but its closure wasn't too hard to fathom, given the hollow ambience that
has always dogged this prime Knightsbridge site. Being too low-key shouldn't
be a problem for long, however, with the announcement that in late 2018
the site's new occupant will be the London home of Turkish-butcher-turned-
Instagram-sensation, Salt Bae – real name Nusret Gökçe – a new
stablemate to outposts in Miami and New York, as well as in the Middle
East. / SW1X 7RN; www.nusr-et.com.tr/en/home.aspx; Tue-Sat, Mon 10.30 pm,
Sun 3.30 pm.*

Nutbourne SW11 £59 2 2 3
29 Ransomes Dock, 35-37 Parkgate Rd 020 7350 0555 6–4C
*"There's always an interesting menu" at the Gladwin brothers' farm-to-table
Battersea venture (named after the family farm and vineyard
in West Sussex) in the riverside venue that for many years was Ransome's
Dock (long RIP). The food's execution can vary, though – what is "excellent"
in some cases only rates as "underwhelming to adequate" in others,
and service is "slightly vague". / SW11 4NP; www.nutbourne-restaurant.com;
@NutbourneSW11; 11 pm, Sun 5 pm; closed Sun D, closed Mon.*

O'ver SE1 £51 **4 3 3**

44-46 Southwark St   020 7378 9933   10–4C

This superior pizzeria near Borough Market lists pure seawater as a key ingredient in its dough. Boss Tommaso Mastromatteo is a teacher at the Associazione Verace Pizza Napoletana, which promotes and protects true Neapolitan pizza. / SE1 1UN; www.overuk.com; Wed-Sat 11 pm.

Oak £57 **3 3 4**

243 Goldhawk Rd, W12   020 8741 7700   8–1B
137 Westbourne Park Rd, W2   020 7221 3355   7–1B

"Excellent pizzas" and a vibey interior contribute to the impressive magnetism of this appealing Notting Hill pub-conversion. It has a similar (but bigger and more "comfy") Shepherd's Bush sibling, near the bottom of the Askew Road. / W12 10.30pm, Fri & Sat 11 pm Sun 9.30pm; W2 10.30pm, Fri & Sat 11 pm, Sun 10 pm.

Oblix SE1 £102 **2 2 3**

Level 32, The Shard, 31 St. Thomas St   020 7268 6700   10–4C

"A table by the window overlooking the Thames and St Paul's, a glass of Champagne: ultimate romance!" – that's the impression left on some fans of this sky-high brasserie from Rainer Becker (of Zuma and Roka fame). That "the food is great, too" can seem like something of an afterthought, but on most accounts it does live up, even if prices are as steep as The Shard's glass sides! You can book for either the 'West' or 'East' sections – the former's selection of grills from the Josper (plus flatbreads, salads, and so on) is more extensive than the latter's. / SE1 9RY; www.oblixrestaurant.com; @OblixRestaurant; 11 pm; booking max 6 may apply.

Odette's NW1 £70 **4 3 3**

130 Regents Park Rd   020 7586 8569   9–3B

"Surprisingly good after so many years" – star Welsh chef Bryn Williams's intimate 40-year-old Primrose Hill fixture (10 under his ownership) "has a loyal following" and under this stewardship delivers ambitious British cuisine that's "never less than delicious". / NW1 8XL; www.odettesprimrosehill.com; @Odettes_rest; 10 pm, Sun 3 pm; closed Sun D, closed Mon; no Amex.

Ognisko Restaurant SW7 £50 **3 4 5**

55 Prince's Gate, Exhibition Rd   020 7589 0101   6–1C

The "superb" setting of this "big and airy room" – plus "a lovely terrace at the back for those warm summer days" – sets up a "special" atmosphere at this former émigrés club, occupying a wonderfully "elegant", if romantically faded, building in South Kensington. The "flavourful and varied Polish cuisine" is arguably "better than in Poland" and "you will not leave hungry"; but at least as great an attraction is the "impressive range of vodkas" and "a great long wine list including some lively, rarely seen eastern European vintages". "Ideal for the Royal Albert Hall." / SW7 2PN; www.ogniskorestaurant.co.uk; @OgniskoRest; 9 pm, Sun 3 pm; closed Mon L; No trainers.

Oka £53 **3 2 2**

Kingly Court, 1 Kingly Court, W1   020 7734 3556   4–2B
251 King's Rd, SW3   020 7349 8725   6–3C
71 Regents Park Rd, NW1   020 7483 2072   9–3B

"Amazing sushi" and a "fantastic range of hot dishes" enable these "great value" Japanese cafés to stand out in the marketplace. They are "ridiculously small", though – "you might not get a table". / www.okarestaurant.co.uk; 10.30 pm.

Oklava EC2 £56 443
74 Luke St 020 7729 3032 13–1B
"Dishes bursting with flavour" from a "lively", "Turkish-with-a-twist" menu,
win nothing but the highest regard for Selin Kiazim and Laura Christie's
"intimate little place" in Shoreditch (across the road from Leroy).
"We especially enjoyed watching an (almost) entirely female brigade
of cooks working so co-operatively and well together – it feels like a really
intelligently thought-through restaurant, full of people who are passionate
about the food". Top Menu Tips – "really memorable pomegranate sauce
lamb", "fantastic kebabs" and "don't miss out on ordering a pide, too". See
also Kyseri. / EC2A 4PY; www.oklava.co.uk; @oklava_ldn; midnight; booking max 6
may apply.

Oldroyd N1 £52 332
344 Upper St 020 8617 9010 9–3D
That it's "very cramped" and "cheek by jowl" is the main accusation made
against Tom Oldroyd's "tiny" Islington two-year-old ("basically a house made
into a restaurant, where upstairs is quieter and lighter"). "As you head
up the rickety staircase and cross the wonky floorboards, a hint of doubt
may cross your mind – don't let it!", say fans, applauding the
"unpretentious", "individual" and "full-flavoured" food from "a limited but
well-put-together menu". That said, ratings were "off the boil" compared
with last year – perhaps the pressure of opening the Duke of Richmond
(see also)? / N1 0PD; www.oldroydlondon.com; @oldroydlondon; Mon-Thu 11 pm,
Fri & Sat 11.30 pm, Sun 10 pm; booking max 4 may apply.

Oliveto SW1 £60 421
49 Elizabeth St 020 7730 0074 2–4A
This popular Sardinian has provided "exceptional pasta, pizza, tuna and
sweets" to the denizens of Belgravia for many years – and at reasonable
prices for the locale. Any complaints? "It needs a makeover". / SW1W 9PP;
www.olivorestaurants.com/oliveto; 10.30 pm, Sat 11 pm; booking max 7 may apply.

Olivo SW1 £75 332
21 Eccleston St 020 7730 2505 2–4B
"Still the go-to Belgravia Italian" – the "consistent" and "friendly" flagship
of Mauro Sanna's upmarket local Sardinian group has been a fixture of the
area for over 20 years and inspires more-than-local acclaim for its deft,
"light and fresh" cooking alongside "some truly delicious wines" on a
Sardinian list. / SW1W 9LX; www.olivorestaurants.com; 10.30 pm; closed
Sat L & Sun L.

Olivocarne SW1 £80 322
61 Elizabeth St 020 7730 7997 2–4A
"Reliably good Sardinian cooking" and "a warm welcome" greet you at this
smart Belgravia outfit specialising in meat. A relatively recent addition
to Mauro Sanna's established Olivo group, it is "slightly more upmarket than
its sister restaurants". / SW1W 9PP; www.olivorestaurants.com; 11 pm,
Sun 10.30 pm.

Olivomare SW1 £79 331
10 Lower Belgrave St 020 7730 9022 2–4B
A "delightful Sardinian take on seafood and fresh fish" is the successful
focus of this Belgravia venue – part of Mauro Sanna's Olivo group – whose
"honest and low key" style makes it an enduring and popular destination.
But while "the food speaks for itself", the interior "feels rather cramped and
clinical". / SW1W 0LJ; www.olivorestaurants.com; @OlivoGroup; 11 pm,
Sun 10.30 pm; booking max 10 may apply.

Olle W1 £46 ② ② ②
86-88 Shaftesbury Avenue 020 7287 1979 5–3A
Limited and somewhat up-and-down reports on this two-floor Chinatown-fringe yearling, featuring traditional Korean BBQ at the table – feedback veers from total enthusiasm to the view that it is "generally disappointing". / W1D 6NH; www.ollelondon.com; 10.30 pm, Sun 10 pm.

Olley's SE24 £39 ③ ③ ②
65-69 Norwood Rd 020 8671 8259 11–2D
"The batter is light and complements the fish well" at this thirty-year-old venue opposite Brockwell Park, themed 1980s-style with Olde Worlde flourishes. There are cheaper chippies to be found, but regulars say it "never fails to provide excellent, well-cooked fish 'n' chips". / SE24 9AA; www.olleys.info; Tue-Sun, Mon 9.30 pm; closed Mon L; no Amex.

Olympic,
Olympic Studios SW13 £49 ② ② ③
117-123 Church Rd 020 8912 5161 11–1A
Attracting "everyone from mamas with buggies to white-haired seniors", this all-day brasserie – the ground floor of a legendary former recording studios, which is nowadays an independent local cinema and chichi members' club – has become a major social hub in Barnes. But while it's "lively and buzzy" and stylish, the food offering is "just OK", and service is "slow". / SW13 9HL; www.olympiccinema.co.uk; @Olympic_Cinema; Tue, Sat 10 pm, Wed-Fri 11 pm, Mon 9 pm.

Olympus Fish N3 £34 ③ ③ ②
140-144 Ballards Ln 020 8371 8666 1–1B
"Super-fresh fish" "cooked on a charcoal grill", "served sizzling hot", "with plump and plentiful chips" and "in copious portions" make this "truly excellent" Turkish-run outfit in Finchley one of north London's top chippies. One or two reporters, though, fear it may be starting to "rest on its laurels". / N3 2PA; www.olympusrestaurant.co.uk; @Olympus_London; 11 pm.

Omars Place SW1 NEW £61 ④ ④ ④
13 Cambridge St 07881 777227 2–4B
Down a side street near Victoria station, Egyptian restaurateur Omar Shabaan has teamed up with well-known Mallorcan chef Vicente Fortea to launch this well-designed Pimlico venue – a stylishly converted former pub serving Mediterranean small plates and wine. On limited feedback to date, results are excellent. / SW1V 4PR; www.omarsplace.co.uk; @omarspldn.

On The Bab £36 ③ ② ②
39 Marylebone Ln, W1 020 7935 2000 2–1A
36 Wellington St, WC2 020 7240 8825 5–3D
305 Old St, EC1 020 7683 0361 13–1B
9 Ludgate Broadway, EC4 020 7248 8777 10–2A
This K-pop styled, Korean street-food group has a "short and very tasty menu" of "freshly cooked and great value bites". The minimalist and buzzy outlets across central London "continue to shine": in particular the WC2 branch is "a good option in Covent Garden". / onthebab.co.uk; @onthebab; EC1 & WC2 10.30 pm, Sun 10 pm; W1 & EC4 4 pm; EC4 closed Sat & Sun; W1 closed Sun.

On the Dak WC2 NEW £13 ⑤ ③ ①
1 Monmouth St 020 7836 5619 5–2C
"It's best to eat out" ("you just have to accept the tiny interior with three tables if you eat in") at Linda Lee's (of On the Bab and Mee Market) latest creation – a simple café/take-away on the fringes of Covent Garden, serving "stunning" Korean-fried chicken. / WC2H 9DA; www.onthedak.co.uk; @OnTheDakLDN; 10 pm, Sun 9 pm.

One Canada Square E14   £62   2 3 2

1 Canada Square   020 7559 5199   12–1C

In the lobby of Canary Wharf's top landmark, this is "a business restaurant primarily, so I don't really rate the atmosphere" ("it's too bland for anything else"). "However, it works perfectly for a meeting: breakfast and lunch menus are well thought out and the food well put together". For its purpose "definitely one of the best restaurants in the Wharf". / E14 5AB; www.onecanadasquarerestaurant.com; @OneCanadaSquare; 10.45 pm; closed Sun.

108 Brasserie W1   £61   3 3 3

108 Marylebone Ln   020 7969 3900   2–1A

"Useful for the area" – this very "pleasant" and attractive hotel dining room at the top of Marylebone Lane, wins all-round praise for its brasserie fare, much of it from the Josper grill. / W1U 2QE; www.108brasserie.com; @108Marylebone; 10.30pm.

108 Garage W10   £60   2 2 2

108 Golborne Rd   020 8969 3769   7–1A

Fans still hail its "totally original cuisine" ("a total surprise to the point of mind-blowing!") at this "relaxed and laid back" venue at the top end of Portobello Market, but its ratings took a nosedive this year, reflecting the strains of expansion to Southam Street (see also) and the corresponding change of chef from Chris Denny to Greg Clarke. To the fair few who reported a bad trip, the venture can now seem "overhyped and over here, with clever food but no fireworks and too expensive to justify the clamour". Perhaps with Southam Street's opening behind them, it may now be on the up? / W10 5PS; www.108garage.com; 10 pm, Sun 3 pm; closed Sun D, closed Mon.

101 Thai Kitchen W6   £37   4 3 2

352 King St   020 8746 6888   8–2B

"It's like being in Thailand" – serving "real Thai fare in a real Thai setting" – according to cognoscenti of this basic and grungy caff, around the corner from Stamford Brook tube: food journos and bloggers in particular go absolutely nuts for this place. / W6 0RX; Sun-Thu 10.30 pm, Fri & Sat 11 pm; no Amex.

Les 110 de Taillevent W1   £72   3 2 3

16 Cavendish Square   020 3141 6016   3–1B

"If you have the money, the great indulgence of wines that are rarely served by the glass" ("where else can you buy a £500 bottle of wine in a 250ml measure") can be satiated at this London outpost of the famous Parisian venue, which occupies a converted banking hall behind Oxford Street's John Lewis – a dignified space, but one whose "small tables" make it feel more like a brasserie than a fine-dining destination. Arguably, "the wonderful wine list has put the food unfairly in the shadows", as some of the "modern French-style dishes show great skill", but – that said – while "the set lunch is excellent value, other prices seem to have crept up of late". / W1G 9DD; www.les-110-taillevent-london.com; @110London; 10.30 pm, Sun 3.30 pm; closed Sat L & Sun.

100 Wardour Street W1   £69

100 Wardour St   020 7314 4000   4–2D

To a bizarre extent, this large D&D London venue in central Soho – home in its day to the legendary Marquee Club, and nowadays featuring entertainment with DJs, cocktails and dinner – inspires practically zero feedback. Top Tip: such commentary as we have is for what is perhaps its best feature: Saturday brunch (£25 for two courses, plus £20 for bottomless Prosecco). / W1F 0TN; www.100wardourst.com; @100WardourSt; Tue, Wed 2 am, Thu-Sat 3 am; closed Tue-Sat L, closed Sun & Mon.

1 Lombard Street EC3 £78 2 2 3
1 Lombard St   020 7929 6611   10–3C
"With its large domed roof", "good buzz and business-like feel", Soren Jessen's converted banking hall near Bank has changed little over the years. It's "perfectly located" for Square Mile expense-accounters (who seem to make up about 99.9% of its custom), "the food is fine but nothing special", "it's spacious enough on the larger tables for confidential conversations" and does a good breakfast. / EC3V 9AA; www.1lombardstreet.com; @1LombardStreet; 10 pm; closed Sat & Sun; booking max 10 may apply.

Opera Tavern WC2 £53 3 3 3
23 Catherine St   020 7836 3680   5–3D
"Superior" Hispanic-inspired plates have created a major reputation over the years for this "great tapas-stop close to Covent Garden" – a "sociable" ("at times noisy") converted, two-floor pub. It was sold by its original founders Salt Yard Group in late summer 2018 to Urban Pubs and Bars – we've left the rating as is for the time being. / WC2B 5JS; www.saltyardgroup.co.uk/opera-tavern; @saltyardgroup; Mon-Wed 11 pm, Thu-Sat 11.30 pm, Sun 10 pm.

Opso W1 £59 3 4 3
10 Paddington St   020 7487 5088   2–1A
"Put aside your preconceptions of Greek food" say fans of this "buzzy and fun" Marylebone corner café, serving Greek-with-a-twist cuisine that won't break the bank, from breakfast on. / W1U 5QL; www.opso.co.uk; @OPSO_london; Mon-Thu 10 pm, Fri & Sat 11 pm, Sun 9 pm; closed Sun D.

The Orange SW1 £60 3 3 3
37 Pimlico Rd   020 7881 9844   6–2D
This "fun pub" on a pretty Pimlico square combines "traditional ambience with modern, clean premises", and there's "always something interesting on the menu", ranging from roasts to wood-fired pizza. / SW1W 8NE; www.theorange.co.uk; @theorangesw1; Mon-Thu 11.30 pm, Fri & Sat midnight, Sun 10.30 pm.

Orange Pekoe SW13 £35 3 3 4
3 White Hart Ln   020 8876 6070   11–1A
"About 30 different types of brew" further boost the civilised tone at this "always crowded" but "very pleasant" tea shop, on the fringe of Barnes, which serves "light lunches" ("interesting salads") and "sublime cakes". / SW13 0PX; www.orangepekoeteas.com; @OrangePekoeTeas; 5 pm; closed Mon-Sun D.

The Orange Tree N20 £45 3 2 3
7 Totteridge Village   020 8343 7031   1–1B
Up Totteridge way, this is the top gastropub in the village: "always buzzy" (if sometimes "very noisy") and where the modernised pub grub is consistently well rated. / N20 8NX; www.theorangetreetotteridge.co.uk; @orangetreepub; Mon-Thu 11 pm, Fri & Sat 11.30 pm, Sun 10.30 pm.

Orée £18 3 2 3
275-277 Fulham Rd, SW10   020 3813 9724   6–3B
65 King's Rd, SW3   020 3740 4588   6–3D
147 Kensington High St, W8   020 3883 7568   6–1A
"Fabulous breads and pastries" (as well as "better coffee than some of the favourites") bring a taste of 'the boulangeries and patisseries of rural France' to the three west London sites operated by this outfit from Nantes. / www.oree.co.uk; @oreeboulangerie.

Ormer Mayfair W1 £100 3 2 2

Half Moon St 020 7016 5601 3–4B

Somewhat more mixed feedback this year on Shaun Rankin's "smart" two-year-old tenure at this Mayfair dining room. For the most part, reports continue to extol his "extremely original and exciting cuisine" (even if it's "seriously expensive"), but service can hit the wrong note, and the "rather hotel-y" basement setting "could be more cheery". / W1J 7BH; www.ormermayfair.com; @ormermayfair; 10.30 pm; closed Sun & Mon; No shorts.

Oro Di Napoli W5 £34 4 3 2

6 The Quadrant, Little Ealing Lane 020 3632 5580 1–3A

The "top-notch Neapolitan wood-fired pizza" – "beautiful, thin-crusted delights" – from this "small but perfectly formed neighbourhood joint" in South Ealing rivals those of nearby Santa Maria, "and that's saying something!". / W5 4EE; www.lorodinapoli.co.uk; 11 pm.

Orrery W1 £90 2 3 3

55 Marylebone High St 020 7616 8000 2–1A

D&D London's "pleasant light room above the Conran shop in Marylebone" has a "fantastic airy atmosphere" with attractive views, and its ambience is only limited by its "slightly corridor-like" proportions. "Dining on the roof terrace in the summer is an added bonus" too, and as a business venue it can be ideal. Fans say its Gallic cuisine is "first rate" too, although overall ratings are more middling, perhaps because it's "priced accordingly". / W1U 5RB; www.orrery-restaurant.co.uk; @The_Orrery; Sun-Thu 10 pm, Fri & Sat 10.30 pm; booking max 8 may apply.

Oscar Wilde Lounge at Cafe Royal W1 £82 3 3 5

68 Regent St 020 7406 3333 4–4C

"The most wonderful room is a beautiful backdrop to a superb afternoon tea" (the only meal the room currently supplies) in this gilded chamber (the original 'Café Royal Grill' dating back to 1865), whose "sumptuously elaborate" rococo decor is one of the finest historic restaurant spaces in town: "wonderful sandwiches, scones, cakes and pastries… and the pianist was the icing on the cake!" The hotel are permanently rumbling about re-launching the space and returning it to its former glory, so change may be afoot. / W1B 1N; www.hotelcaferoyal.com/oscarwildebar; @HotelCafeRoyal; L & afternoon tea only.

Oslo Court NW8 £66 3 5 4

Charlbert St 020 7722 8795 9–3A

"An excellent throwback, which shows that the 1970's can't have been all bad!" – this "golden oldie" ("hard to find under an apartment block" north of Regent's Park) is "unashamedly trapped in a bygone era" and everyone adores it (especially its devoted following of silver- and white-haired north Londoners). The "large menu" of retro fare is "always well-cooked", comes in "very ample portions" and is served by "the friendliest and most efficient, caring waiters on the planet" (with a special shout out to Neil, the "entertaining man in charge of the sweet trolley"; reason to visit in itself for its magnificent selection of "ridiculously indulgent desserts"). "This is not dinner, but a night out!" – "go before it disappears!" / NW8 7EN; www.oslocourtrestaurant.co.uk; 11 pm; closed Sun; No jeans.

Osteria,
Barbican Centre EC2 £57 1 1 2

Level 2 Silk St   020 7588 3008   10–1B

The main restaurant at the Barbican arts centre is "handy for a pre-theatre supper" – ("ask for a window seat when booking") – but on its current level of performance "not a destination in its own right". A reboot by caterer Searcys with an Italian menu by chef Anthony Demetre (late of Soho's Arbutus, RIP) has failed to turn the tide, with too many complaints about the food ("style over substance") and service ("our main course never arrived, so we sat hungry through a three-hour play!"). / EC2Y 8DS; osterialondon.co.uk; @osterialondon; Wed & Thu 11 pm, Fri & Sat midnight, Sun 6 pm; closed Sun.

Osteria Antica Bologna SW11 £51 3 3 2

23 Northcote Rd   020 7978 4771   11–2C

This "great neighbourhood Italian" near Clapham Junction has ticked all the boxes for "amazing pasta and allotment-fresh vegetables" for two decades. "The focus is on beautifully cooked, classic dishes rather than food presentation or stylish décor". / SW11 1NG; www.osteria.co.uk; @OsteriaAntica; Mon-Wed 11 pm, Thu-Sat 11.30 pm, Sun 10 pm.

Osteria Basilico W11 £63 4 2 2

29 Kensington Park Rd   020 7727 9957   7–1A

"An all-time family favourite", this long-running Notting Hill trat is "a lovely little place, always full and lively", with "divine pizza and pasta, excellent antipasti and wonderful home-baked bread", it's "as authentic as Italian cooking gets in London". "Make friends with the manager or the service can be snooty". / W11 2EU; www.osteriabasilico.co.uk; 11.30 pm, Sun 10.30 pm; no booking, Sat L.

Osteria Dell'Angolo SW1 £64 2 2 2

47 Marsham St   020 3268 1077   2–4C

"Efficient" and "reasonably priced for Westminster", this "large" and peaceful venue serves "mainstream Italian food, all of it cooked perfectly well" – although it's "difficult to rave over any dish". Especially "useful for conference-goers at the Emmanuel Centre" nearby. / SW1P 3DR; www.osteriadellangolo.co.uk; @Osteria_Angolo; 10.30 pm; closed Sat L, closed Sun.

Osteria Tufo N4 £49 3 2 2

67 Fonthill Rd   020 7272 2911   9–1D

This intimate Finsbury Park local, where proprietor Paola greets each customer, has a sensibly "limited menu" of "interesting" Neapolitan home cooking (no pizza) – "but what they do, they do well". / N4 3HZ; www.osteriatufo.co.uk; @osteriatufo; Tue-Fri 10 pm, Mon 9.30 pm; closed Mon & Sun L; no Amex.

The Other Naughty Piglet SW1 £60 4 3 2

12 Palace St   020 7592 0322   2–4B

Andrew Lloyd Webber's import, last year, of Brixton's Naughty Piglets team to the "airy" space above his Other Palace Theatre was one of last year's better openings, and fabulous for still-dire Victoria. Its "bright-tasting" small plates are "on-trend" and "perfectly executed" and there's some "superb" wines ("Lord Lloyd Webber's bin ends at the back of the wine list make an interesting read!"). / SW1E 5JA; www.theothernaughtypiglet.co.uk; Tue-Thu 9 pm; closed Mon, Fri & Sat & Sun; booking max 10 may apply.

Otto's WC1   £72   **4 4 4**

182 Gray's Inn Rd   020 7713 0107   2–1D

"Immune to trends and setting its own agenda" – visiting this "old-fashioned" Bloomsbury parlour is a little "like stepping back a generation". "Wonderful, old-fashioned, French, classic cuisine" is served in a "delightful" dining room, overseen with "charming professionalism" by the owner Otto ("invariably there") who is "amusing and fun". Top Menu Tips – "everyone raves (rightly) about the pressed duck and Poularde de Bresse, but Otto also does the best Steak Tartare in the UK (made at the table with Otto's inevitable theatrical flourish)". / WC1X 8EW; www.ottos-restaurant.com; 9.30 pm; closed Sat L, closed Sun & Mon.

Ottolenghi   £57   **3 2 2**

13 Motcomb St, SW1   020 7823 2707   6–1D
63 Ledbury Rd, W11   020 7727 1121   7–1B
287 Upper St, N1   020 7288 1454   9–2D
50 Artillery Pas, E1   020 7247 1999   10–2D

"Drool over the pastries" and the "exquisite" salads ("so many unusual combinations and lovely flavours, it's hard to make a decision") at Yotam Ottolenghi's "always popular", but "rather stark" cafés ("overcrowded with shared tables and yummy mummies with prams"). At its best, "the food's so fresh and creatively different, you feel you are dining on something superbly healthy", but ratings overall slipped this year, with a number of regulars noting that "while it's an excellent concept, execution's not as consistent as it should be". / www.ottolenghi.co.uk; N1 10.30 pm, Sun 7 pm; W11 & SW1 8 pm, Sat 7 pm, Sun 6 pm; E1 10.30 pm, Sun 6 pm; N1 closed Sun D; Holland St takeaway only; W11 & SW1 no booking.

Outlaw's at The Capital SW3   £97   **4 4 2**

22-24 Basil St   020 7591 1202   6–1D

With its "perfectly prepared and delicately flavoured dishes", Nathan Outlaw's Knightsbridge outpost lives up to his renown for "truly excellent and creative fish cuisine" and ranks amongst the UK's best in that respect. The location, near the back of Harrods, is a "small" hotel dining room that has for decades divided opinion: to fans "smart" and "sophisticated", but to others "lacking some character"; although the "excellent service" from the current team helps boost its appeal. Chef Andrew Sawyer succeeded Tom Brown (who left to found Cornerstone) in late 2017, and though a small minority of reporters feel "the food has gone downhill" as a result, ratings here actually strengthened across the board this year. / SW3 1AT; www.capitalhotel.co.uk; @OUTLAWSinLondon; 10 pm; closed Sun; credit card required to book.

Oval Restaurant SW1 NEW   £81

11 Knightsbridge   020 3668 6530   6–1D

Limited but all-round very positive feedback on this small (26 covers) oval-shaped dining room, which is part of a swish hotel right by Hyde Park Corner (which older folk will recall as Pizza on the Park). With its gold-and-light-pink colour scheme and ostrich leather walls, it's a glam location in which to enjoy some luxurious Italian cuisine (available à la carte, or with the option of five- or six-course tasting menus). / SW1X 7LY; www.thewellesley.co.uk/oval-restaurant; @WellesleyLondon; 10:30pm.

Oxo Tower, Restaurant SE1   £92   **1 1 1**

Barge House St   020 7803 3888   10–3A

"Same as usual – fantastic view, but grotty food at the price". The story remains the same at this South Bank landmark whose dubious achievement is invariably appearing at or near the top of the survey's lists of both most disappointing and most overpriced restaurants in London. / SE1 9PH; www.harveynichols.com/restaurant/the-oxo-tower; @OxoTowerWharf; 11 pm, Sun 10 pm; booking max 8 may apply; SRA-Food Made Good – 2 stars.

Oxo Tower, Brasserie SE1 £75 1 1 2
Barge House St   020 7803 3888   10–3A
"Fabulous views and the buzzy (perhaps too noisy) atmosphere" lure diners to the cheaper section of this South Bank landmark. But for the sky-high price they exact for its humdrum brasserie fare and so-so service, it's a perennially disappointing and overpriced experience; try to get someone else to pay… / SE1 9PH; www.harveynichols.com/restaurants/oxo-tower-london; Thu-Sat, Wed 9 pm; may need 2+ to book; SRA-Food Made Good – 2 stars.

The Oystermen WC2 £58 4 4 3
32 Henrietta St   020 7240 4417   5–3D
"A jewel of a find" – this "tiny", "cupboard-sized" yearling in Covent Garden receives a resounding "bravo!" from reporters for its "fun" style, "charming service" and "fabulous" seafood ("oysters are the speciality, but there's a good range of other fish dishes"). Top Tip: 'Bubbles 'n' Oysters Happy Hour – "I called in after reading a review in Harden's newsletter, and was amazed at the quality of the oysters with a glass of bubbly for £10!" STOP PRESS: just as we went to press, the Oystermen expanded into the space next door, giving them 50 covers, a walk-in-only raw bar and a bigger open kitchen. / WC2E 8NA; oystermen.co.uk; @theoystermen.

Ozone Coffee Roasters EC2 £28 3 3 4
11 Leonard St   020 7490 1039   13–1A
Fabulous aromas from the large roasting machines in the basement hit you as you enter this hip haven for caffeine-lovers – a perfect hipster combination of cool Kiwi and chilled Shoreditch vibes, and one delivering superlative brews and dependable brunch fare. / EC2A 4AQ; ozonecoffee.co.uk; @ozonecoffeeuk; Sun-Thu 10.30 pm, Fri & Sat 11 pm; may need 8+ to book.

P Franco E5 £48 4 2 4
107 Lower Clapton Rd   020 8533 4660   14–1B
In any other 'hood, this engaging Clapton bottle shop (focused on funky 'natural' vintages) with communal central table – and serving some eclectic but interesting small dishes – would be a handy, loveable find. Sitting as it does at the very epicentre of the East End's fooderati community, it is front page news, as exemplified by its being website Eater's bizarre choice as 'London Restaurant of the Year 2017'. In September 2018 it took on a new chef for at least a 6-month residency: Anna Tobias. / E5 0NP; www.pfranco.co.uk; @pfranco_e5; Thu-Sat 10 pm, Sun 9 pm; closed Mon-Wed, Thu-Sat D only, Sun L & D; no Amex; no booking.

Padella SE1 £28 5 4 3
6 Southwark St   no tel   10–4C
"A true and glorious phenomenon… you just need to arrive very early to beat the queues!" – Tim Siadatan and Jordan Frieda's Borough Market two-year-old is the ultimate budget option in the capital thanks to serving "perfect pasta" ("the best in London"), "served quickly" and at a supremely "affordable" price, in a setting that's "cramped" but "buzzy" and "fun". And "now with a virtual queuing system in the evening, you can head off for a drink instead of waiting outside!" / SE1 1TQ; www.padella.co; @padella_pasta; 10 pm; no booking.

Paladar SE1 NEW £58
4-5 London Rd 020 7186 5555 10–4A
A stylish new restaurant, wine bar and bodega, not far from Elephant & Castle, showcasing flavours from across South America. (The name means palate in Spanish and Portuguese, and in Cuba a 'paladar' is also a privately-run restaurant with character.) Founder Charles Tyler was behind Bermondsey's once-pathbreaking Champor Champor, while chef Jose Rubio-Guevara hails from Colombia via Miami and draws on various Latino inspirations (as do the cocktails, wines and cigars). Too little feedback for a rating as yet, but for one early reporter it's already a favourite. / SE1 6JZ; www.paladarlondon.com; @paladarlondon; Tue-Sat, Mon 10.30 pm, Sun 3.30 pm.

Palatino EC1 £59 **4 3 3**
71 Central St 020 3481 5300 10–1B
"The simplicity of the dishes belies the amazing flavours that come off the plates", according to the many fans of Stevie Parle's popular yearling, where "authentic pasta" is the highlight of its Roman-inspired menu. Arguably "being part of an office space detracts from the atmosphere" but most reporters find its setting "calm and spacious". Top Menu Tip: "divine cacio e pepe". / EC1V 8AB; palatino.london; @PalatinoLondon; 10 pm; closed Mon-Sat & Sun.

The Palmerston SE22 £57 **3 3 3**
91 Lordship Ln 020 8693 1629 1–4D
This "high class" gastropub in East Dulwich is "informal but top notch", with "consistently high-class cooking". "It's a proper restaurant operation... but in a pub." / SE22 8EP; www.thepalmerston.co.uk; @thepalmerston; 11 pm; closed Sun; no Amex.

The Palomar W1 £73 **4 3 3**
34 Rupert St 020 7439 8777 4–3D
"It is frustratingly difficult to plan to eat" at this Tel Aviv-comes-to-Theatreland venture, given its humongous popularity and limited ability to book (only possible in the relatively un-funky dining room). The main action is "sitting at the counter watching the chefs (a riot!)" and its "great range of Middle Eastern / Mediterranean tapas" delivers "small plates zinging with flavour and invention". With its "fabulous buzz", fans say "you can't say you've eaten in London till you've tried here", but there's the odd niggle too – "noisy", "cramped" and "chaotic" conditions (to fans part of the charm), and a staff attitude that can sometimes "verge on arrogant". / W1D 6DN; www.thepalomar.co.uk; @palomarsoho; 11 pm, Sun 9 pm; closed Sun L.

Pappa Ciccia £36 **3 4 3**
105 Munster Rd, SW6 020 7384 1884 11–1B
41 Fulham High St, SW6 020 7736 0900 11–1B
"Good, generous-sized pizzas", and a "lively" and "cheerful" atmosphere keep business ticking over at this family-owned local trio in Fulham and Putney. They are "excellent value", too, helped by BYO on beer and wine at a flat £4.50 per head. / www.pappaciccia.com; SW6 5RQ 11 pm, Sat & Sun 11.30 pm; SW6 3JJ 11 pm.

Parabola, Design Museum W8 £60
224-238 Kensington High St 020 7940 8795 6–1A
The food and drink operation at the new Design Museum in Kensington opened with high hopes, with Rowley Leigh at the stoves; but he quickly left, and then, following the demise of Prescott & Conran in the summer of 2018, its been taken over by caterer Searcys. The food now (e.g. 'Bassett Stilton and broccoli tart; Loch Duart salmon fillet with crushed Jersey royals') sounds less ambitious than it was under Leigh, but we've maintained the listing and left the restaurant un-rated pending feedback. / W8 6AG; www.parabola.london; @ParabolaLondon; 9.45 pm; closed Mon-Sun D.

Paradise by Way of Kensal Green W10   £53   3 2 4
19 Kilburn Lane   020 8969 0098   1–2B
One of London's hardiest evergreen destinations – this huge and vibey
Kensal Green tavern has been a magnet for cool twenty- and
thirtysomethings for as long as anyone can remember (and was one of the
first 'gastropubs' as such to hit the capital). The interior is gorgeous, and the
menu much more "interesting" than it needs to be. / W10 4AE;
www.theparadise.co.uk; @weloveparadise; 10 pm, Sun 4 pm; closed weekday L;
no Amex.

Paradise Hampstead NW3   £41   3 5 4
49 South End Rd   020 7794 6314   9–2A
"Always packed with locals" who come for the "huge portions from a menu
that never changes", this "mainstay" Hampstead Heath curry house is now
run by the founder's son, but the "exceptional" welcome and service "are as
warm as ever". / NW3 2QB; www.paradisehampstead.co.uk; Wed & Thu 11 pm,
Fri & Sat midnight, Sun 6 pm.

El Parador NW1   £40   4 4 3
245 Eversholt St   020 7387 2789   9–3C
High marks for the "wonderful", authentic tapas at this busy Hispanic,
near Mornington Crescent. "Why can't the ambience match the food?"
query some; but on summer days its garden provides a lovely location.
/ NW1 1BA; www.elparadorlondon.com; 11 pm, Fri & Sat 11.30 pm, Sun 9.30 pm;
closed Sat L & Sun L; no Amex.

Park Chinois W1   £131   2 2 3
17 Berkeley St   020 3327 8888   3–3C
With its "sexy", "1920s-Shanghai" interior, Alan Yau's "opulent" Mayfair
blow-out offers a "decadent" combination of "delicious" Chinese cuisine and
regular entertainment in a "vibey" setting that's definitely "different".
Sceptics dismiss it as a "ridiculously OTT" display "for people with more
money than taste", but for most reporters the only downside is that
"Dick Turpin turns up at the same time as the bill!" / W1S 4NF;
www.parkchinois.com; @ParkChinois; 2 am, Sun midnight; No jeans.

Park Terrace Restaurant,
Royal Garden Hotel W8   £59   3 3 4
2-24 Kensington High St   020 7361 0602   6–1A
This "comfortable and well-spaced" hotel dining room with "views over
Kensington Gardens" maintains a low profile despite its mightily handy
location off High Street Kensington. Worth remembering as a "reliable"
standby, it mainly scores highly for its "amazing kids' afternoon tea" –
"such good value" and with "plenty of space for naughty children". / W8 4PT;
www.parkterracerestaurant.co.uk; 10.30 pm.

Parlour Kensal NW10   £50   3 3 4
5 Regent St   020 8969 2184   1–2B
Chilled Kensal Rise pub conversion that continues to inspire nothing but
praise for its "good value and quality food and friendly service". Its top dish
historically has been 'cow pie', but its appeal isn't limited to meat-eaters:
"the vegan breakfast is great – they've really thought about it and created
a real feast". / NW10 5LG; www.parlourkensal.com; @ParlourUK; 10.30 pm;
closed Mon.

Parsons WC2 NEW   £65   4 3 3
39 Endell St   020 3422 0221   5–2C
"Living up to the hype despite the narrow space" – this new opening from
the folks behind The 10 Cases (just across the road) is one of the
most applauded arrivals of the past year and "a great addition to Covent
Garden". "A short menu of the freshest fish and seafood" is served
"with good wines and no faff" in a "refreshingly unpretentious",
but "stylishly simple" white-tiled environment, and results are "sparkling".
/ WC2H 9BA; www.parsonslondon.co.uk; closed Sun.

Passione e Tradizione N15 £37 3 3 2
451 West Green Rd   020 8245 9491   1–1C
"A real gem in the hinterland between Wood Green and Tottenham",
this "industrial-chic, trendy and hard-surfaced" Italian yearling is a sister
to Mustapha Mouflih's highly rated Anima e Cuore in Kentish Town.
"Yes, the pizza is brilliant" but there is also "exceptional homemade pasta"
and chalkboard specials (although "don't get me wrong, quality ingredients
are used, but not all the combinations are totally convincing"). Top Tip:
"incredible homemade ice cream, which they now sell at the newly opened
deli opposite". / N15 3PL; spinach.london; 11 pm; closed Mon & Tue L.

Passo EC1 NEW £50 2 2 2
80 City Rd   020 3883 9377   13–1A
Mixed reviews for this big, all-day Italian newcomer by Old Street tube –
a large, modern unit where they've spent a packet on the design. Some
do praise its "imaginative" fare and say it's a good place to take business
associates, but there's also a feeling that "the food doesn't live up to the
prices and comes in small portions": "this is expense account grub for global
biz travellers who truly believe 'Silicon Roundabout' is a really cool place".
/ EC1Y 2AS; www.passorestaurant.com; Tue-Thu 8.30 pm, Fri 9 pm, Sat 9.30 pm,
Sun 7 pm.

Pasta Remoli N4 £39 3 3 3
7 Clifton Terrace   020 7263 2948   9–1D
That "the pasta is great" and that "it's an easy choice with kids" are twin
strengths of this café in Finsbury Park. Top Tip: "good value for pre-theatre"
(the Park Theatre being next door). / N4 3JP; www.pastaremoli.co.uk;
@PastaRemoli; 11 pm, Sun 10.30 pm.

Pastaio W1 £44 3 2 3
19 Ganton St   no tel   4–2B
As "a pasta pit-stop", Stevie Parle's "buzzy and canteen-like" Soho yearling
("well-located in Kingly Court) wins a fair amount of praise as a "good-
value-for-money" option around shopping or before a movie. On the
downside, some who were "hoping for big things" given Parle's reputation
felt it fell short – in particular, "amateurish" service can take the gloss off
the experience. / W1F 7BU; www.pastaio.london; @pastaiolondon; Sun-Thu
10.30 pm, Fri & Sat 11 pm.

El Pastór SE1 £44 4 3 5
7a Stoney St   no tel   10–4C
"Top tortillas. Amen!"… "Divine tacos"… "Wish I didn't have to share with
my friend, as I could have happily hoovered the lot" – the Hart Bros'
"cool and vibey" taqueria has become one of Borough Market's top
destinations. "Great Mexican drinks", too, including 17 mezcals, but you
can't book. / SE1 9AA; www.tacoselpastor.co.uk; @Tacos_El_Pastor; Mon-Wed
11 pm, Thu-Sat midnight; no booking.

Patara £68 3 3 3
15 Greek St, W1   020 7437 1071   5–2A
7 Maddox St, W1   020 7499 6008   4–2A
181 Fulham Rd, SW3   020 7351 5692   6–2C
9 Beauchamp Pl, SW3   020 7581 8820   6–1C
82 Hampstead High St, NW3   020 7431 5902   9–2B
18 High St, SW19   020 3931 6157   11–2B
"A small chain with a big reputation that's well deserved", say fans of this
long-standing, "friendly and courteous" Thai group, praised for its "well-
flavoured food". Ratings went into reverse this year, however, due to those
who find it "a bit pricey", or "making too many concessions to western
palates". Top Tip: "exceptional lunch deal". / www.pataralondon.com;
@PataraLondon; 10.30 pm, Thu-Sat 11 pm; Greek St closed Sun L.

Paternoster Chop House EC4 £61 2 2 2
1 Warwick Court 020 7029 9400 10–2B
Overlooking St Paul's from the fringes of the Square Mile's Paternoster Square development, this D&D London operation caters mainly for City expense-accounters. It's best known as the location for TV show First Dates, but for romance look elsewhere – "the tables are too close together" and the food's "expensive and average". / EC4M 7DX; www.paternosterchophouse.co.uk; @paternoster1; 10.30 pm, Sun 3.30 pm; closed Sun D; booking max 12 may apply.

Patogh W1 £17 4 3 2
8 Crawford Pl 020 7262 4015 7–1D
"Persian perfection" – "honest and straightforward" dishes offer "wonderful quality for the money" at this tiny dining room off Edgware Road. "Like I imagine being in a café in Iran" … with the addition of BYO booze! / W1H 5NE; www.patoghlondon.com; 11 pm; cash only.

Patty and Bun £28 4 3 3
18 Old Compton St, W1 020 7287 1818 5–2A
54 James St, W1 020 7487 3188 3–1A
14 Pembridge Rd, W11 020 7229 2228 7–2B
19 Borough High St, SE1 020 7407 7994 10–4C **NEW**
36 Redchurch St, E2 020 7613 3335 13–1C
2 Arthaus Building, 205 Richmond Rd, E8 020 8525 8250 14–1B
22-23 Liverpool St, EC2 020 7621 1331 10–2D
8 Brown's Buildings, Saint Mary Axe, EC3 020 3846 3222 10–2D
"People waiting outside in the rain for a table speaks volumes" for this expanding chain (the latest branches are in TV Centre and Borough High Street), which "really fulfils the craving for a juicy, tasty burger" (and is the equal-highest rated in town in that department). Other elements of the formula are, however, "nothing fancy". Top Menu Tip: "the Lambshank Redemption is unparalleled in the hugely contested world of burgers". / www.pattyandbun.co.uk; @pattyandbunjoe; 10 pm-11.30 pm, Sun 9 pm-10pm.

Pavilion Cafe & Bakery E9 £9 4 2 4
Victoria Park, Old Ford Rd 020 8980 0030 14–2C
A quaint structure in "a beautiful position on the lake" – "the cafe on the water at Victoria Park is a wonderful setting" with food that's "surprisingly excellent" – "not just exceptional English breakfast fare but also Sri Lankan and vegan options"; "superlative coffee and pastries, too". / E9 7DE; www.pavilionbakery.com; @pavilionbakery; Mon-Fri 5 pm, Sat & Sun 6 pm; closed Mon-Fri D; no Amex; no booking.

The Pear Tree W6 £49 3 3 4
14 Margravine Rd 020 7381 1787 8–2C
"Awesome and very friendly" little Victorian pub, just behind Charing Cross Hospital, with a charming, small interior – the food, from a limited menu, "is lovely too". / W6 8HJ; www.thepeartreefulham.com; 10.30 pm; Mon-Thu D only, Fri-Sun open L & D.

Pearl Liang W2 £48 4 3 3
8 Sheldon Square 020 7289 7000 7–1C
An "uninspiring location" – a Paddington Basin basement – has not held back this large and attractively decorated Cantonese: nowadays very well-established and "always very crowded", especially at weekends, for its "amazing dim sum", of a quality "really quite different to the majority of Chinese restaurants". Top Tip: "lobster noodles also brilliant". / W2 6EZ; www.pearlliang.co.uk; @PearlLiangUK; Mon-Thu 11 pm, Fri & Sat 11.30 pm, Sun 10.30 pm.

Peckham Bazaar SE15 £51 433
119 Consort Rd 020 7732 2525 1–4D
Whether it's labelled "pan-Balkan" or "the best Greek-ish cooking
in London", this "delightful and informal converted neighbourhood pub"
"does charcoal-grilled food that's just a bit different from (and better than)
the competition", and is "worth the trek" to furthest Peckham. There are
also "unusual and surprisingly good wines" from the region. / SE15 3RU;
www.peckhambazaar.com; @PeckhamBazaar; Sun-Thu 10.30 pm; closed Mon,
Tue-Fri D only, Sat & Sun open L & D; no Amex.

Peckham Levels SE15 NEW £16
95a Rye Lane 020 3793 7783 1–4D
This six-year project was created by the same team as Pop Brixton
in response to a consultation by Southwark Council about what to do with
Peckham's under-used multi storey car park. Levels five and six are home
to street food traders such as Nandine (Kurdish mezze), Canard (confit
duck as street food), Drums & Flats (chicken wings), Other Side Fried (fried
chicken) and the splendidly named PickyWops (vegan pizza) – early
feedback from reporters says it's worth a visit. / SE15 4TG;
www.peckhamlevels.org; @peckhamlevels; Mon & Tue 9 pm, Fri & Sat 11.30 pm,
Wed 10 pm, Thu 11 pm, Sun 5 pm; closed Sun D.

E Pellicci E2 £16 355
332 Bethnal Green Rd 020 7739 4873 13–1D
"It never changes and that's the point" of a visit to visiting this well-
preserved (hipster-free) greasy spoon in Bethnal Green, whose listed,
Art Deco interior (much used in filming TV dramas) is a fine period piece.
That "there's always a special welcome" confirms its position in the hearts
of its fans as "one of the best places in London for breakfast" of the
traditional variety. / E2 0AG; epellicci.com; closed Mon-Sat D, closed Sun; cash only;
no booking.

Pentolina W14 £52 443
71 Blythe Rd 020 3010 0091 8–1C
"Michele in the kitchen cooks up a dream and Heidi looks after the front
of house beautifully" at this "very charming" backstreet Olympia favourite.
The result is "delightful and delicious Italian food" from a "short seasonal
menu" served in a "lovely and low-key" setting that makes it a "perfect
local", and one that folks travel for. / W14 0HP; www.pentolinarestaurant.co.uk;
10 pm; closed Sun & Mon; no Amex.

Percy & Founders W1 £60 333
1 Pearson Square, Fitzroy Place 020 3761 0200 2–1B
On the ground floor of a Fitzrovia development (on the site of the old
Middlesex Hospital), this spacious, tucked-away bar/brasserie with terrace
offers a convenient and tranquil rendezvous in the West End. Top Tip:
"love their bottomless Prosecco brunch". / W1W 7EY;
www.percyandfounders.co.uk; @PercyFounders; Wed & Thu 11 pm, Fri & Sat
midnight, Sun 6 pm; closed Sun D.

Perilla N16 £62 333
1-3 Green Lanes 07467 067393 1–1C
"I cannot believe that somewhere like Perilla opened on Newington Green –
what a fantastic addition to the local area!" Ben Marks and Matt Emerson's
yearling, "with its "huge picture windows overlooking the green",
"high ceilings, open aspect and well-spaced tables" serves some
"astoundingly tasty dishes, using interesting earthy ingredients" and there's
"a great local feel to the place". Not everyone who lives nearby is wowed,
though: "I wanted to like this place, but found it too cool-for-skool"… "it was
too quirky and elaborate and felt like a 'concept'" rather than a satisfying
night of food". / N16 9BS; www.perilladining.co.uk; @perilladining; 10 pm,
Sun 8.30 pm; closed Mon-Fri L.

Pescatori W1 £75 2 2 2
57 Charlotte St 020 7580 3289 2–1C
Some reporters accuse it of being too "unimaginative", but this traditional-ish West End Italian still wins an impressive number of nominations for the very "competent" quality of its fish cuisine, and "pleasant" style generally. Top Tip: "their free-flowing Prosecco deal makes this an excellent choice for a meet-up with the girls!" / W1T 4PD; www.pescatori.co.uk; @PescatoriLondon; 10.30 pm, Sun 3 pm; closed Sat L & Sun.

The Petersham WC2 £84 3 3 5
Floral Court, off Floral St 020 7305 7676 5–3C
"Enchanting decor" – very "calming and relaxing", considering it's so central – is a major highpoint of this ambitious newcomer from the Boglione family, which is part of a very attractive new development in Covent Garden. It repeats a lot of the DNA of their original venture – Richmond's famously romantic, shabby chic Petersham Nurseries – although the punchy prices for its "refined and elegant" dishes have so far inspired less controversy here. / WC2E 9DJ; petershamnurseries.com; @PetershamN; midnight; SRA-Food Made Good – 3 stars.

Petersham Nurseries Cafe TW10 £78 2 2 5
Church Lane (signposted 'St Peter's Church') 020 8940 5230 1–4A
"It's just fab eating great food in a greenhouse in summer or on a blue-sky winter's day", say fans of this "unique and magical" destination (part of a garden centre near Ham Common), which famously "oozes Bohemian charm" and is a top "romantic" trysting spot. Even those who feel its modern British cuisine is "very good" however, concede that it's "probably not as good as it was a few years ago" (when Skye Gyngell was at the stoves, and pioneering the use of edible flowers) and more cynical souls ponder whether "seating you amongst the potted plants on rickety furniture lets them get away with the high prices and mediocre service". It now has a sibling in Covent Garden (see also). / TW10 7AB; www.petershamnurseries.com; 10.30 pm, Sun 9.30 pm; L only, closed Mon; SRA-Food Made Good – 3 stars.

The Petersham Restaurant TW10 £67 2 2 5
Nightingale Lane 020 8003 3602 1–4A
"The view from the restaurant is one of the best in London" – "the best tables are near the window" where you can enjoy the "splendid setting overlooking the Thames" – from the traditional dining room of this old-fashioned and "romantic" Richmond hotel. Fans (often silver-haired) acclaim its cuisine as "a safe bet", but a number of meals this year also ended up feeling "pricey" or "perfunctory". / TW10 6UZ; petershamhotel.co.uk/restaurant; @thepetersham; 9.30 pm, Sun 9 pm.

Petit Ma Cuisine TW9 £50 2 2 2
8 Station Approach 020 8332 1923 1–3A
This textbook, 1950s-style "cramped" French bistro – gingham tablecloths, Toulouse-Lautrec posters and a menu of classics – is promoted by fans as a "lovely find close to Kew Gardens". "The food's decent, but prices are on the toppy side". / TW9 3QB; www.macuisinebistrot.co.uk; 10 pm, Fri & Sat 10.30 pm; no Amex.

Petit Pois Bistro N1 £57 4 2 3
9 Hoxton Square 020 7613 3689 13–1B
"The quality is very high but the prices are not", say fans of this two-year-old Gallic bistro on Hoxton Square – "a real, cute gem" serving "lovely French fare" in a "trendy but cosy" space (and also with a small outside seating area). / N1 6NU; www.petitpoisbistro.com; @petitpoisbistro; 9.30 pm.

The Petite Coree NW6 £42 **4** **3** **2**
98 West End Lane   020 7624 9209   1–1B
"Excellent Korean/modern European fusion cooking" ensures that this "genuinely friendly" (and good value) little bistro has become a fixture on the West Hampstead culinary scene. Chef Jae worked at Nobu and Hélène Darroze (The Connaught); his wife Yeon runs the front of house. / NW6 2LU; www.thepetitecoree.com; @thepetitecoree; 9.30 pm; booking max 6 may apply.

La Petite Maison W1 £97 **3** **2** **3**
54 Brook's Mews   020 7495 4774   3–2B
"Always top of its game and up there with the best" is how we've customarily reviewed this glam Mayfair haunt, just around the corner from Claridges, which perennially attracts a Côte d'Azur-style crowd with its sunny, gorgeously light sharing plates and easygoing "busy and buzzy" glamour. Its ratings took a bit of a dip this year, however – it's always been "a bit too expensive" but hitherto no-one has seemed to mind. / W1K 4EG; www.lpmlondon.co.uk; @lpmlondon; 10.30 pm, Sun 9.30 pm; closed Mon.

Pétrus SW1 £118 **4** **4** **4**
1 Kinnerton St   020 7592 1609   6–1D
With its "stunning" cuisine, "wine list that reads like War & Peace", "caring and attentive" staff and "beautiful" interior (arranged around a glass-walled wine vault), this luxurious Knightsbridge dining room is the only restaurant in Gordon Ramsay's stable that lives up to his name nowadays, and on practically all reports is "a joy to visit". Let's hope new chef Russell Bateman, who joined in summer 2018, can keep up the good work. / SW1X 8EA; www.gordonramsayrestaurants.com; @petrus; 10.30 pm, Sun 9.30 pm; closed Sun; No trainers.

Peyotito W11 £56 **3** **3** **2**
31 Kensington Park Rd   020 7043 1400   7–1A
"Top-notch authentic Mexican small or sharing plates", plus "great tequila and mezcal cocktails" can add up to a "fun, noisy night out" at this two-year-old in the heart of Notting Hill, notwithstanding its "haphazard service and very cramped interior". "Low-key when empty" – maybe go "later in the evening". / W11 2EU; www.peyotitorestaurant.com; @peyotitolondon; midnight, Fri & Sat 1 am, Sun 10.30 pm.

Pham Sushi EC1 £41 **4** **2** **3**
159 Whitecross St   020 7251 6336   13–2A
"Great sushi and sashimi", "at reasonable prices", are the draw at this "authentic" Japanese spot near the Barbican. "Flawless food without the pretentiousness of some high-end Japanese" – no wonder it's "always packed"./_ EC1Y 8JL; www.phamsushi.com; @phamsushi; 10 pm; closed Sat L, closed Sun. / EC1Y 8JL; www.phamsushi.com; @phamsushi; 10 pm; closed Sat L, closed Sun.

Phat Phuc SW3 £30 **4** **3** **1**
Chelsea Courtyard, 151 Sydney St   020 7351 3843   6–3C
"For a simple bowl of fragrant steaming noodles", reporters give a big thumbs up to this basic, hilariously-named joint, in a courtyard near Chelsea Farmers Market – about as close as you can get to street food in SW3! / SW3 6NT; www.phatphucnoodlebar.co.uk; @Phat_PhucNoodle.

Pho £43 **3** **2** **2**
"Solid and tasty Vietnamese dishes are served in a flash" at this street food chain; fans feel they've really "nailed the concept" of "fresh", "very decent" scoff in a "cheap 'n' cheerful" setting, all at a "great price". / www.phocafe.co.uk; 10 pm-11pm, Sun 6.30 pm-10 pm; EC1 closed Sat L & Sun; no booking.

Pho & Bun W1 £46 3 3 2
76 Shaftesbury Ave   020 7287 3528   5–3A

This straightforward Vietnamese pitstop for pho and steamed buns, on the edge of Chinatown, by all accounts offers "very good food and value for money". / W1D 6ND; vieteat.co.uk/pho-bun; @phoandbun; Sun-Thu 10.30 pm, Fri & Sat 11 pm; booking max 8 may apply.

Phoenix Palace NW1 £57 3 3 3
5-9 Glentworth St   020 7486 3515   2–1A

This spacious, classic Cantonese refectory near Baker Street scores well for "fun, good food and great service", while fans claim it does the "best dim sum in London". There's a "large and varied menu, with lots of interesting dishes" and a very "70s vibe". / NW1 5PG; www.phoenixpalace.co.uk; 11.30 pm, Sun 10.30 pm.

Picture £67 3 3 2
110 Great Portland St, W1   020 7637 7892   2–1B
19 New Cavendish St, W1   020 7935 0058   2–1A

"Simply presented but expertly prepared taste combinations that just make you want to come back" from a "limited-but-seasonal menu" are at the root of the success of this "relaxed and reliable" duo of Fitzrovia and Marylebone favourites. The chief gripe is that in each case "the interior lacks atmosphere", but no-one thinks the situation is grievous. / 10.30 pm; closed Sun.

Pidgin E8 £72 5 5 3
52 Wilton Way   020 7254 8311   14–1B

"Breathtakingly inventive and excellently executed" cooking ("best described as modern British with a substantial Asian influence") has won renown out of all proportion to the "extremely small" size of this Hackney two-year-old, which has a better claim to culinary fame than most East End ventures. "How they keep up such high standards with a weekly changing tasting menu is astonishing" ("although we have eaten there more than six times in the last couple of years, I cannot think of any single dish that has ever been repeated"). "And it still feels like a cosy neighbourhood restaurant", although on the downside "tables are very small and crammed too close together". / E8 1BG; www.pidginlondon.com; @PidginLondon; Wed-Sun 11 pm; closed Wed & Thu L, closed Mon & Tue.

Piebury Corner £20 3 3 3
3 Caledonian Rd, N1   020 7700 5441   9–3C
209-211 Holloway Rd, N7   020 7700 5441   9–2D

"A nice stop on the road to the Emirates" – this popular 'pie deli' has won a certain notoriety with its range of pies, whose names make most sense if you follow The Gunners; also with a more conventional, less Arsenal-centric caff selling traditional scran in King's Cross. / N7 9 pm, N1 11 pm; N7 closed Mon-Wed & Sun D, N1 closed Sun D.

Pied À Terre W1 £112 4 4 4
34 Charlotte St   020 7636 1178   2–1C

"David Moore's gastronomic home has stood the test of time through many chefs that have gone on to star elsewhere". All reports on this "world-class" Fitzrovia townhouse agree that – with the help of Asimakis Chaniotis at the stoves (since October 2017) – "it is amazing how standards have been maintained" with "creative cuisine that's delicious but not fussy". "Friendly guidance from the knowledgeable and engaging sommelier" is another plus in navigating an "exceptional" wine list, with "interesting and well-priced vintages from unusual places". Gripes about the ambience were largely absent this year, with typical feedback describing it as "always elegant, always stylish". Top Tip: "the space at the front of the restaurant is more crowded – ask for the back room when booking". / W1T 2NH; www.pied-a-terre.co.uk; @PiedaTerreUK; 11 pm; closed Sat L, closed Sun; booking max 7 may apply.

Pig & Butcher N1 £52 4 4 4

80 Liverpool Rd 020 7226 8304 9–3D

"For carnivores and beer lovers", this attractively located Islington gastroboozer butchers its own meat on site, so "always produces the best cuts, excellently cooked". There's a good selection of craft ales too, "but really it's more a restaurant than a pub", and manages to "attract, train and keep very friendly and knowledgeable waiting staff". / N1 0QD; www.thepigandbutcher.co.uk; @pigandbutcher; 11 pm; Mon-Thu D only, Fri-Sun open L & D.

Pilpel £11 3 3 2

38 Brushfield Street, London, E1 020 7247 0146 13–2B

60 Alie St, E1 020 7952 2139 10–2D

Old Spitalfields Mkt, E1 020 7375 2282 13–2B

146 Fleet St, EC4 020 7583 2030 10–2A

Paternoster Sq, EC4 020 7248 9281 10–2B

"Pittas of pleasure" – "Mediterranean/Israeli street food of the best type (vegetarian, fresh and bursting with taste)" – keep office workers healthy and happy at these City-based "pitstops". "No wonder there's always a queue at lunchtime." / www.pilpel.co.uk; EC4 4 pm; E1 6 pm; Brushfield St & Alie St 9pm, Fri 4pm, Sun 6pm; Paternoster Sq 9 pm, Fri 4 pm; EC4 branches closed Sat & Sun; no booking.

Pique Nique SE1 £60 3 3 3

32 Tanner St 020 7403 9549 10–4D

"Poulet de Bresse in all its glory" from the spit roast helps earn a big thumbs-up for this "fun sibling to neighbouring Casse-Croute", which opened last year. "Ebullient service and a winning, laid-back atmosphere" complete the picture. / SE1 3LD; pique-nique.co.uk; @piquenique32; 11 pm, Sun 6 pm.

El Pirata W1 £42 2 2 4

5-6 Down St 020 7491 3810 3–4B

As "a reasonable option in overpriced Mayfair", this very atmospheric, "if crowded and noisy" tapas-haunt is "well above-average" and "has a huge following". However, even many reporters who view it through rose-tinted specs would acknowledge "it needs to innovate and generally improve its offering". / W1J 7AQ; www.elpirata.co.uk; @elpirataw1; 10.30 pm; closed Sat L & Sun.

Pisqu W1 £56 3 2 3

23 Rathbone Place 020 7436 6123 5–1A

"Very different" cuisine from the Amazon and the Andes has carved a niche for this Peruvian yearling off Charlotte Street in Fitzrovia. "A good addition to the London dining scene, with an interesting menu" and cocktails. / W1T 1HZ; www.pisqulondon.com; @PisquLondon; Sun-Thu 11 pm, Fri & Sat midnight.

Pitt Cue Co EC2 £59 4 2 2

1 The Ave, Devonshire Sq 020 7324 7770 10–2D

"Dish after dish that will delight any carnivore worth the name" emerges from the grill or smoker at Tom Adams's American-inspired operation near Liverpool Street. "Loyalists and purist fans of 'old' Pitt Cue in Soho lament the sterile, corporate feel of the new location, but the food is still some of the best BBQ in London", thanks to "utter fanaticism about the core ingredients, combined with wonderful skill in the kitchen". / EC2 \N; www.pittcue.co.uk; @PittCueCo; Mon-Fri 11 pm, Sat 10.30 pm; closed Sat L, closed Sun.

Pizarro SE1 £60 `3` `2` `3`

194 Bermondsey St   020 7256 5333   10–4D

José Pizarro's contemporary Spanish restaurant never quite matches the drama (or ratings) of his original venture – the nearby tapas bar sibling, José, on the other side of Bermondsey Street. Service here can be "a bit hit and miss", but in other respects it is a "highly competent" operation with a "warm" atmosphere and "authentic" cuisine from "a relatively short menu". / SE1 3TQ; www.josepizarro.com; @Jose_Pizarro; 10.30 pm, Sun 9.30 pm.

Pizza da Valter SW17 £43 `3` `2` `2`

7 Bellevue Rd   020 8355 7032   11–2C

"Good pasta, sides and mains as well as great pizza" win applause for this "very good local pizzeria", attractively situated by Wandsworth Common. / SW17 7EG.

Pizza East £56 `4` `3` `4`

310 Portobello Rd, W10   020 8969 4500   7–1A
79 Highgate Rd, NW5   020 3310 2000   9–1B
56 Shoreditch High St, E1   020 7729 1888   13–1B

"A really interesting take on the pizza genre" (with a focus on "original", often hearty, toppings) combined with an exciting hipster vibe ensure this successful Soho House-owned group remains "extremely popular and always busy". "Prices are reasonable too" and for such a style-conscious scene, gripes about service are notable by their absence. / www.pizzaeast.com; @PizzaEast; E1 midnight, .

Pizza Metro SW11 £47 `3` `2` `2`

64 Battersea Rise   020 7228 3812   11–2C

"Great pizza" is sold 'al metro' (it was the first place in town to serve it by length) "or as a traditional round" at this Neapolitan in Battersea, which was quite a destination back in the day. The second branch in Notting Hill closed down this year. / SW11 1EQ; www.pizzametropizza.com; @pizzametropizza; 10.30 pm, Mon 11 pm, Sun 3 pm; no Amex.

Pizza Pilgrims £40 `3` `3` `3`

102 Berwick St, W1   07780 667258   4–1D
11-12 Dean St, W1   020 7287 8964   4–1D
Kingly Ct, Carnaby St, W1   020 7287 2200   4–2B
23 Garrick St, WC2   020 3019 1881   5–3C
12 Hertsmere Rd, E14   020 3019 8020   12–1C
136 Shoreditch High St, E1   020 3019 7620   13–1B
15 Exmouth Mkt, EC1   020 7287 8964   10–1A
Swingers Crazy Golf, Saint Mary Axe, EC3   no tel   10–2D

From a tiny van named Conchetta to a bricks 'n' mortar chain – the Elliot brothers deliver a pizza hit that's still "a step-up from standard fare" at their expanding group, but its ratings are becoming more mainstream than during their heady earlier days. / pizzapilgrims.co.uk; @pizzapilgrims; 10.30pm, Sun 9.30 pm; WC2 11 pm, Sun 10 pm; Dean St booking: min 8.

PizzaExpress £49 ②②②

*"There is a lot more competition in the chain pizza market these days";
and while this long-enduring (est 1965) feature of every high street still has
a very large fan club, it is steadily losing support. Some of this may be that
"it is inevitably a much less distinctive presence nowadays" and huge
numbers of reporters do still see it as a "safe bet" (and most particularly
"an easy choice for a meal out with a five-year old"). More rivalry doesn't
really explain its steadily bombing ratings however – in particular the
evaporation of the once-excellent ambience at its branches since Hony
Capital took charge. In this regard, cynicism seems justified: "my favourite
branch has been ruined by the greedy private equity owners cramming
in small tables so that the atmosphere is as delightful as rush hour on the
underground. Such a pity – as it was so good for so many years". "Generous
discounting" has also seemingly become a permanent factor – "without one
of their plentiful voucher deals, it can seem distinctly overpriced".*
/ www.pizzaexpress.co.uk; 11.30 pm - midnight; most City branches closed all or part
of weekend; no booking at most branches.

Pizzeria Pappagone N4 £35 ③④③
131 Stroud Green Rd 020 7263 2114 9–1D
*"Very crowded and lively", twenty-year-old Finsbury Park stalwart featuring
pizza from a wood-fired oven. "It's not for the sensitive – you will love it or
overlook it as it's noisy"… adding to its appeal as a kid-friendly option!*
/ N4 3PX; www.pizzeriapappagone.co.uk; @pizza_pappagone; midnight.

Pizzicotto W8 £54 ④④③
267 Kensington High St 020 7602 6777 8–1D
*"So much better than the chain alternatives" – this smart three-year-old
pizzeria directly opposite the new Design Museum in Kensington
"specialises in on-site-produced pizzas… and what pizzas they are,
the tastiest ever!". An offshoot of the family-run Il Portico five doors away,
it shares the same "friendly service".* / W8 6NA; www.pizzicotto.co.uk;
@pizzicottow8; Mon-Thu 11 pm, Fri & Sat midnight, Sun 10.30 pm.

Plaquemine Lock N1 £46 ③③③
139 Graham St 020 7688 1488 9–3D
*This "surprising re-invention of a 'lost boozer'" done out with a "bright and
colourful interior" brings "fascinating Louisiana cuisine" to Angel, right
on the Regent's Canal. Opened a year ago by Jacob Kenedy (Bocca di Lupo,
Gelupo and Vico), it manages to "keep the feel of a great local" while being
"quite niche". Top Tip: "really first-class grilled oysters".* / N1 8LB;
plaqlock.com; 10 pm, Sun 9 pm.

Plateau E14 £74 ②③③
4th Floor, Canada Sq 020 7715 7100 12–1C
*A brilliant view, from a location convenient for Canary Wharf worker-bees,
is the pull to this "reliable" business-friendly outfit from D&D London.
Opinion is split on the food: some praise "Jeremy Trehout's French classicism
overlaid with British-European modernism" while others find it "boring" and
"expensive". Top Tip: "stick to the bar and grill and you can be in/out in an
hour at a reasonable price".* / E14 5ER; www.plateau-restaurant.co.uk;
@plateaulondon; 11 pm; closed Sat L & Sun.

Plot SW17 £40 ④④④
Broadway Market, Tooting High St 020 8767 2639 11–2C
*"Yummy" food from a short but "ever-changing menu" at this two-year-old
pioneer has helped put Tooting Market on the foodie map. The focus is on
British small plates, and it's seasonal in more ways than one, so "you'll need
to wear warm clothes" in winter because "it's under cover but still outside…".*
/ SW17 0RL; plotkitchen.com; @plot_kitchen; midnight; closed Tue, Wed L, closed
Sun & Mon.

The Plough SW14 £45 2️⃣3️⃣4️⃣

42 Christ Church Rd   020 8876 7833   11–1A

This 18th-century inn with a big outside terrace inhabits a leafy and lovely East Sheen conservation area, and also trades well on its proximity to Richmond Park. It wins praise from most (if not quite all) reporters for its "good, honest pub food". / SW14 \N; www.theplough.com; Mon-Thu 9.30 pm, Fri & Sat 10 pm, Sun 9 pm.

**Plum + Spilt Milk,
Great Northern Hotel N1** £73 2️⃣3️⃣3️⃣

King's Cross St Pancras Station, Pancras Rd   020 3388 0818   9–3C

"Smart" railway-hotel brasserie at King's Cross (named after the livery used by the Flying Scotsman's dining carriages) that can provide "surprisingly good quality meals and attentive service". A "lovely place for lunch" – "not too businessy" – it wins particular recommendations for its "tasty and well-executed breakfast". The worst folks say about the place? – "pleasant enough but mystifyingly pricey". / N1C 4TB; plumandspiltmilk.com; @PlumSpiltMilk; 10.30 pm, Mon 11 pm, Sun 3 pm.

Pollen Street Social W1 £101 3️⃣3️⃣3️⃣

8-10 Pollen St   020 7290 7600   3–2C

"Well deserving its accolades" – Jason Atherton's smooth Mayfair HQ combines "consistently great quality cuisine" (in particular the "wonderful tasting menu") with an "impressively relaxed atmosphere" and "cool design" and is truly dazzling to its large and enthusiastic fan club. On the downside, "deep pockets are needed", and the service can be "slightly erratic" (although is generally "excellent"). / W1S 1NQ; www.pollenstreetsocial.com; @PollenStSocial; 10.30 pm; closed Sun; booking max 7 may apply.

Polpetto W1 £51 3️⃣3️⃣2️⃣

11 Berwick St   020 7439 8627   4–2D

Russell Norman's 'bacaro' in the middle of Soho (behind what used to be called Raymond's Revue Bar) won solid ratings this year for its menu of Venetian small plates: "The food always has an extra something beyond Polpo and the price is about the same". / W1F 0PL; www.polpetto.co.uk; @polpettoW1; 11 pm, Sun 10.30 pm; booking L only.

Polpo £52 2️⃣2️⃣2️⃣

41 Beak St, W1   020 7734 4479   4–2B
6 Maiden Ln, WC2   020 7836 8448   5–3D
Duke Of York Sq, SW3   020 7730 8900   6–2D
126-128 Notting Hill Gate, W11   020 7229 3283   7–2B
2-3 Cowcross St, EC1   020 7250 0034   10–1A

Russell Norman's "buzzy and very casual" cicchetti cafés still have a large fan club who applaud "very tasty, tapas-style fare", "drinkable wine served in tumblers" and a "friendly atmosphere". But the feeling that it "was once original, but has now been bypassed and needs updating" captures the mood of a fair few who "expected more" of the "hit 'n' miss service" and "uninspired food". / www.polpo.co.uk; 10 pm-11.30 pm, EC1 Sun 4 pm; EC1 closed D Sun; no bookings.

Pomona's W2 £56 3️⃣4️⃣4️⃣

47 Hereford Rd   020 7229 1503   7–1B

La-La Land comes to W2 at this brightly converted pub, with garden – nowadays a haven of immunity-boosting, locally-sourced, charcoal-grilled, seasonal fare – "a top neighbourhood option", ideal for breakfast (including with kids in tow). It takes some flak, though, for "meagre portions priced at Notting Hill-banker levels". / W2 5AH; www.pomonas.co.uk; @PomonasLondon; Tue-Thu 10 pm, Fri & Sat 10.30 pm, Sun 9 pm; closed Mon.

Le Pont de la Tour SE1 £76 [2][2][2]
36d Shad Thames   020 7403 8403   10–4D
"A blissful location by Thames" with "stunning views of Tower Bridge" and outside tables in summer has always been the 'crown jewel' feature of D&D London's Thames-side flagship (where, back in the day, Tony Blair memorably entertained Bill Clinton). A relaunch a couple of years ago seemed to stem its slide into obscurity, but its ratings sank again this year, with punishing pricing leaving it feeling "quite underwhelming" not helped by "very conventional" cooking and service that's "nothing like what it used to be". The wine list is "not as good as it was" either – perhaps why it receives surprisingly few expense-accounter nominations nowadays. / SE1 2YE; www.lepontdelatour.co.uk; @lepontdelatour; 10.30 pm, Sun 9.30 pm; No trainers.

Popeseye £63 [3][2][2]
108 Blythe Rd, W14   020 7610 4578   8–1C
36 Highgate Hill, N19   020 3601 3830   9–1B
"Unassuming and purist" – this characterful-going-on-grotty Olympia steakhouse is little changed since opening in 1994, and serves nothing but grass-fed beef from northeast Scotland (the name comes from a thin cut of Scottish rump). The steak's very competent but some feel the plonk is better: "it's beloved of wine merchants with good reason – lots of clever bin ends". A branch in Highgate managed separately by the owners' son opened in 2015 (no recent feedback), but the Putney outpost closed earlier this year. / www.popeseye.com; W14 11.30 pm; SW15 11 pm; N19 10.30 pm, Sun 9 pm; W14 & SW15 closed Sun; N19 closed Mon.

Popolo EC2 £52 [5][4][3]
26 Rivington St   020 7729 4299   13–1B
"Phenomenal dishes" – not least "the best pasta on the planet" – win praise from the small but very dedicated fan club of Jonathan Lawson's "friendly" little Shoreditch yearling. If you sit at the downstairs counter rather than in the small upstairs, it's "a fantastic opportunity to see the chefs working from close up". / EC2A 3DU; popoloshoreditch.com; @popolo_EC2; 2 am, Sun midnight; no booking.

Poppies £43 [3][2][3]
59 Old Compton St, W1   020 7482 2977   4–2D
30 Hawley Cr, NW1   020 7267 0440   9–2B
6-8 Hanbury St, E1   020 7247 0892   13–2C
Founder Pat "Pops" Newland, who started working in the East End fish trade at the age of 11, has decorated these venues (Soho, Spitalfields and Camden Town) in 1950s memorabilia, so "it feels like Poppies has been around since London's rock'n'roll days". It's not as bad as it sounds – you get "proper fish and chips": "all the classics are here, together with some welcome additions (seafood platter, lemon sole)", but "most importantly, the chips are great!". / 11 pm, Fri & Sat 11.30 pm, Sun 10.30 pm.

La Porchetta Pizzeria £41 [2][3][2]
33 Boswell St, WC1   020 7242 2434   2–1D
147 Stroud Green Rd, N4   020 7281 2892   9–1D
74-77 Chalk Farm Rd, NW1   020 7267 6822   9–2B
84-86 Rosebery Ave, EC1   020 7837 6060   10–1A
"Pizza without the attitude" – in "large delicious portions" – along with an "exceptionally family-friendly" approach and "cheap" prices keep regulars flocking to these old-school comfort-food Italians in north London. Founded in 1990, the chain now has four branches. / www.laporchetta.net; N1, NW1 & EC1 11pm, Fri & Sat midnight, Sun 10 pm; N4 11 pm, Sun 10 pm; WC1 11 pm, Fri midnight; WC1 closed Sat & Sun; NW1, N1 & N4 closed Mon-Fri L; EC1 closed Sat L; no Amex.

Il Portico W8 £60 3 5 4
277 Kensington High St   020 7602 6262   8–1D
"One of the last, good, old-fashioned Italians, churning out those dishes we love" – this "always reliable, family run Italian" has "a formula that's worked for decades, so why change?". There's a "wonderful manager, James" (the original owner's son), and "you're always welcomed like a long-lost friend". But "it's not an institution living on past glories": "the food is without pretence" but "with some newer dishes to maintain interest". / W8 6NA; www.ilportico.co.uk; 11 pm; closed Sun.

Portland W1 £84 4 3 2
113 Great Portland St   020 7436 3261   2–1B
Will Lander & Daniel Morgenthau's "stark and simple" Fitzrovia three-year-old shot to fame on opening, thanks to its "clever" cuisine (for which it was quickly awarded a Michelin star); its "super choice of perfectly conditioned fine wines by the glass"; and sure-footed service that "combines professionalism with warmth and enthusiasm". Even those who feel "it's dropped off a little since its debut" feel "it's still a restaurant to go to if you like to try something new", and on most accounts a meal here remains "an exciting prospect". / W1W 6QQ; www.portlandrestaurant.co.uk; Wed & Thu 11 pm, Fri & Sat midnight, Sun 6 pm; closed Sun.

Portobello Ristorante Pizzeria W11 £54 3 4 4
7 Ladbroke Rd   020 7221 1373   7–2B
"An excellent covered terrace for summer days and evenings" is a major plus point for this "fantastic and genuine local" just off Notting Hill Gate, whose "management really make the place buzz". It serves a range of "good Italian food, especially seafood and great pizzas". / W11 3PA; www.portobellolondon.co.uk; 10 pm, Fri & Sat 11 pm, Sun 10 pm.

The Portrait, National Portrait Gallery WC2 £67 2 3 4
St Martin's Place   020 7306 0055   5–4B
"Great vistas over centuries-old London rooftops to Parliament" lend a frisson to a visit to this top-floor dining room, which remains a highly popular West End destination. Even if the "pleasant", "unadventurous" food is arguably "nothing to write home about" the "other elements make up for it". Top Tip: good afternoon tea ("it looks as if Nelson could step off his pedestal and join you – who could blame him with all the goodies on offer…") / WC2H 0HE; www.npg.org.uk/visit/shop-eat-drink/restaurant.php; @NPGLondon; Sun-Wed 3 pm, Thu-Sat 8 pm; closed Sun-Wed D.

Potli W6 £44 4 4 3
319-321 King St   020 8741 4328   8–2B
"Not your stereotypical curry house – the focus is on street food, with a menu that dares to be different and pulls it off superbly" at this "fun" and very popular Indian near Ravenscourt Park. For one or two sceptics, though, it's "good but hyped" – "other than the outstanding service, it wasn't as good as some of its local rivals". / W6 9NH; www.potli.co.uk; @Potlirestaurant; Sun-Thu 10 pm, Fri & Sat 10.30 pm.

La Poule au Pot SW1 £62 2 2 5
231 Ebury St   020 7730 7763   6–2D
"Soft lighting, snug and hidden tables" and "the whole full-on Frenchiness of it all" imbue this "dated (but that's part of the joy)" Pimlico classic with a "dark and seductive ambience" that for many years won it the survey's nomination as London's top spot for a date (and it still ranks at No. 2). "The solid French regional food has always been unspectacular" ("it's not why you come") while ultimately how much you enjoy the experience often comes down to how well you hit it off with the "colourful", very Gallic staff. / SW1W 8UT; www.pouleaupot.co.uk; 10 pm; closed Mon-Sat & Sun.

Prawn on the Lawn N1   £61   **3** 3 2
292-294 St Paul's Rd   020 3302 8668   9–2D
"Top-quality fish, simply cooked" and "served tapas-style" in an "informal setting" make this fishmonger/seafood bar on Highbury Corner (with a sibling in Padstow) a "great neighbourhood place". "Can be busy and cramped, but the food is very good." / N1 2LY; prawnonthelawn.com; @PrawnOnTheLawn; 11 pm; closed Sun & Mon; no Amex.

Primeur N5   £55   **3** 3 3
116 Petherton Rd   020 7226 5271   1–1C
Sharing plates and unusual wines draw a steady crowd to this "lovely" if "busy" Highbury local, where seating is at communal tables in a 1920s former car garage. / N5 2RT; www.primeurN5.co.uk; @Primeurs1; 10.30 pm, Sun 5 pm; closed Mon, Tue L, Wed L, Thu L & Sun D; booking max 7 may apply.

The Princess Victoria W12   £48   **3** 3 3
217 Uxbridge Rd   020 8749 4466   8–1B
"Back from the brink, with good, reasonably priced food and an outstanding wine list… especially for a pub in W12" – this huge gin palace (with fine, traditional interior) on the main drag out of Shepherd's Bush has survived turbulent times (due to a change of ownership) and is now back on form. / W12 9DH; www.princessvictoria.co.uk; @threecheerspubs; Mon-Thu 11 pm, Fri & Sat midnight, Sun 10.30 pm.

Princi W1   £37   **3** 2 2
135 Wardour St   020 7478 8888   4–1D
This "busy coffee shop with wonderful cakes" is the Soho outpost of a smart Milanese bakery, with self-service from the counter from breakfast until late at night, providing upmarket fast food, including pizzas. / W1F 0UT; www.princi.com; midnight, Sun 10 pm; no booking.

Prix Fixe W1   £44   **3** 2 2
39 Dean St   020 7734 5976   5–2A
"Traditional French dishes with well-integrated flavours", a "classic bistro atmosphere" and "remarkably good value" add up to a "reliable experience" at this Soho sibling to Pierre Victoire. The set lunch menu also offers an "unusually large choice". / W1D 4PU; www.prixfixe.net; @prixfixelondon; Sun-Thu 10 pm, Fri & Sat 10.30 pm.

The Promenade at The Dorchester W1   £132   2 **4** 4
The Dorchester Hotel, 53 Park Lane   020 7629 8888   3–3A
The "marvellous" afternoon tea in the "beautiful setting" of this grand Mayfair hotel's opulent lounge – rumoured to be as long as Nelson's Column is tall – is "a wonderful experience" – "expensive", no doubt, "but at the same time excellent value". / W1K 1QA; www.dorchestercollection.com/en/london/the-dorchester/restaurant-bars/afternoon-tea; @TheDorchester; 10.30 pm; No shorts.

Provender E11   £41   **3** 4 4
17 High St   020 8530 3050   1–1D
Veteran Francophile restaurateur Max Renzland's "superb, neighbourhood bistro gem" is a particularly good discovery in furthest Wanstead, with "proper, traditional French cooking" that's "not flashy, over the top or over-priced" and a "relaxing and delightful atmosphere". It's "better than many restaurants I know in France… and I live there!". / E11 2AA; www.provenderlondon.co.uk; @ProvenderBistro; 10.30 pm; booking max 10 may apply.

The Providores and Tapa Room W1   £73   **4** **4** **3**
109 Marylebone High St   020 7935 6175   2–1A
*"Peter Gordon, the father of fusion food, still produces delicious food with
great flair" – "superbly executed and with vibrant flavours" – at his
Marylebone venue. There's a strong taste of his native New Zealand led
by "exceptional Kiwi wines". It's quite a "cramped" place though, and some
recommend "choose the bustling, atmospheric ground floor, not upstairs".
/ W1U 4RX; www.theprovidores.co.uk; @theprovidores; Mon-Thu 9 pm, Fri & Sat
9.30 pm, Sun 2.30 pm; SRA-Food Made Good – 2 stars.*

Prufrock Coffee EC1   £13   **3** **2** **2**
23-25 Leather Ln   020 7242 0467   10–2A
*A haven for City caffeine junkies for nearly 10 years, this busy café near
Chancery Lane also provides good-value lunch and snacks, including
"wonderful cheese scones". / EC1N 7TE; www.prufrockcoffee.com;
@PrufrockCoffee; Mon-Fri 6 pm, Sat & Sun 5 pm; L only; no Amex.*

The Punchbowl W1   £61   **3** **4** **3**
41 Farm St   020 7493 6841   3–3A
*"Great pies and good crunchy vegetables" combine with "romantic booths"
at this "lovely pub" in Mayfair. It's "over 300 years old" and has more
recent history, under the former ownership of Madonna's ex, film director
Guy Ritchie. / W1J 5RP; www.punchbowllondon.com; @ThePunchBowlLDN; 11 pm,
Sun 10.30 pm; closed Sun D.*

Punjab WC2   £41   **3** **4** **3**
80 Neal St   020 7836 9787   5–2C
*"Long-established, traditional Indian" north of Covent Garden that's "always
a pleasure". Founded in 1946 and now in the fourth generation
of ownership by the same family, part of their successful formula
is "very competitive prices". / WC2H 9PA; www.punjab.co.uk; 11 pm, Sun 10 pm;
booking max 8 may apply.*

Pure Indian Cooking SW6   £50   **4** **4** **2**
67 Fulham High St   020 7736 2521   11–1B
*"Delicious and inventive Indian dishes" – "really fresh and interesting" –
ensure that this unassuming little venue just off the Fulham Palace Road
stands out from the curry house crowd. Chef and proprietor Shilpa
Dandekar used to work for Raymond Blanc. / SW6 3JJ;
www.pureindiancooking.com; @PureCooking; 10 pm, Sun 9.30 pm.*

Purezza NW1 NEW   £45   **3** **3** **2**
43 Parkway   020 3884 0078   9–3B
*"A welcome addition to Camden's burgeoning vegan scene" – the UK's
first vegan pizzeria hit Brighton in 2015 and this "lively" London offshoot
opened in March 2018, featuring sourdough, hemp or gluten-free bases,
plus a smattering of other dishes. In case you were wondering, the 'artisan
Mozzarella' is made from fermented brown rice milk. / NW1 7PN;
www.purezza.co.uk; @purezzauk; Mon-Fri 10 pm, Sat & Sun 9 pm.*

Quaglino's SW1   £76   **2** **3** **4**
16 Bury St   020 7930 6767   3–3D
*D&D London's "spectacular" Mayfair basement – dating from the 1920s
but revamped in glam style by Sir Terence Conran in 1993 – put in a much
better showing this year: the criticism of recent years was notable by its
absence, and instead it generally "exceeded expectations" as a "buzzing
and fun venue" with "delicious cocktails", lively entertainment and "OK"
food. Even so, "in the evening, the very loud music and the McMafia
clientele can combine to be a little oppressive!" / SW1Y 6AJ;
www.quaglinos-restaurant.co.uk; @quaglinos; Sun-Thu 10.30 pm, Fri & Sat 11 pm;
closed Sun; No trainers.*

The Quality Chop House EC1   £68   3 3 3
94 Farringdon Rd   020 7278 1452   10–1A
"The wooden booths are lovely for privacy if not for comfort" (their hard benches, while "iconic", are "not really designed to be sat on for two hours or so"), at Will Lander & Daniel Morgenthau's "snug" but "bum-numbing" Grade II listed 'Working Class Caterer' (est 1869), which has been a foodie favourite since it became a trailblazer for modern British cuisine in the early '90s (and more recently its re-re-launch in 2012). Its meat-heavy menu is "innovative but not showy" and "consistently good" if a little pricey. Recent innovations include an adjacent café and wine shop. / EC1R 3EA; thequalitychophouse.com; @QualityChop; 10 pm, Sun 4 pm; closed Sun D.

Quantus W4   £56   3 5 3
38 Devonshire Rd   020 8994 0488   8–2A
Featuring "good, Latin-influenced cuisine from a small menu", this "unpretentious" local is "one of the best in Chiswick". The experience is "made more special by owner Leo Pacarada and his staff, who could not be more obliging", and it "holds its own despite being opposite La Trompette!". / W4 2HD; www.quantus-london.com; Sun-Thu 10 pm, Fri & Sat 10.30 pm; closed Mon L, Tue L & Sun.

Quartieri NW6   £44   4 3 3
300 Kilburn High Rd   020 7625 8822   1–2B
"Traditional and new-style pizza with great flavours" from the wood-fired oven wins a consistent thumbs-up for this year-old, small-but-stylish Neapolitan-owned haunt in Kilburn. / NW6 2DB; www.quartieri.co.uk; @quartierilondon; 11 pm.

Le Querce SE23   £43   3 3 2
66-68 Brockley Rise   020 8690 3761   1–4D
"Divine home-made pasta" and other "good Sardinian food" has made Antonello Serra's "welcoming", family-run (and "very family-friendly") neighbourhood Italian a beacon in Brockley for more than a decade. But ratings are still on the wane here, year-on-year, with some regulars expressing caution: "it's a sad thing when you find fault in something you love, but I've had two disappointing meals in a row of late – pasta was still excellent, everything else seemed rather basic". / SE23 1LN; www.lequerce.co.uk; Tue-Sun, Mon 9.30 pm; closed Mon & Tue L.

Quilon SW1   £69   5 5 2
41 Buckingham Gate   020 7821 1899   2–4B
Sriram Aylur's "amazingly light and delicate Keralan cuisine" is twinned with "impeccable service" at the Taj Group's formidably good Indian, which "maintains the great standards it's set for the last decade or so" (and which was the highest rated posh Indian in the survey this year). Even fans acknowledge the space looks "drab", which "takes away the feeling of a special occasion", "but hey, you don't eat the decor". / SW1E 6AF; www.quilon.co.uk; @thequilon; 11 pm, Sun 10.30 pm.

Quirinale SW1   £66   3 4 3
North Ct, 1 Gt Peter St   020 7222 7080   2–4C
One of the top culinary attractions in striking distance of the Palace of Westminster (with a clientele incorporating many MPs and senior civil servants) – this "restrained Italian" in a basement is "discreet and quiet" and serves "classic food to a high standard", alongside "an interesting and accessible wine list". / SW1P 3LL; www.quirinale.co.uk; @quirinaleresto; 10.30 pm; closed Sat L, closed Sun.

Quo Vadis W1 £60 **4** **4** **5**
26-29 Dean St   020 7437 9585   4–1D
This "special" Soho veteran "continues to delight and surprise", under the Hart Bros, whose sure-handed stewardship of the property is in stark contrast to when it lost its way in the Marco Pierre White years. Despite a reformatting a year ago which left its premises "somewhat truncated" (to make space for a branch of Barrafina) the dining room remains "totally charming". "When chef Jeremy Lee is at his best there is no comparison for simple excellence" and his "perfectly poised, thoughtful and considered" seasonal British comfort food is provided with "originality and flair" to create a culinary experience that's "reliable without ever being predictable"… "and you also get the best martini in town". Top Tip: breakfast: "Jeremy's golden eggs, exquisite bread, gently roasted tomatoes…there is no better way to start the day". / W1D 3LL; www.quovadissoho.co.uk; @QuoVadisSoho; 10.30 pm; closed Sun.

Rabbit SW3 £54 **3** **2** **3**
172 King's Rd   020 3750 0172   6–3C
The Gladwin brothers' "fun", faux-rustique, four-year-old haunt on the King's Road still wins a lot of praise for its "inventive and tasty", farm-to-table "British tapas". There's a minority, though, who "go with high expectations (we were told it was amazing)", but leave finding it "overrated and overpriced". / SW3 4UP; www.rabbit-restaurant.com; @RabbitResto; 10 pm, Sun 5 pm; closed Mon L & Sun D.

Rabot 1745 SE1 £63 **2** **2** **2**
2-4 Bedale St   020 7378 8226   10–4C
The "quirky menu" of "unique cocoa-based cuisine" at this Borough Market venue was developed at a historic St Lucia cocoa plantation owned by Hotel Chocolat, and is rated a middling success. The big deal here? – "They serve amazing hot chocolate… well worth the calories!" It's also "a lovely place for an informal coffee", or "after work it turns into a bar, so you can have cocktails". / SE1 9AL; www.rabot1745.com; @rabot1745; 9.30 pm; closed Sun & Mon.

Radici N1 £62 **2** **2** **1**
30 Almeida St   020 7354 4777   9–3D
"Very disappointing all round" is too often the verdict on this D&D London yearling (formerly the Almeida, RIP), where Francesco Mazzei is the figurehead for the Italian cuisine. Fans do praise it as "great for pre/post theatre" (the Almeida theatre is over the road) with "great pizza and zucchini fries" and other southern Italian fare, but numerous reporters "went expecting great things", but found "limited and not particularly well-executed" cooking, served "in a barn-like place with zero atmosphere and lacklustre service". / N1 1AD; www.radici.uk; @radici_n1; 10.30 pm, Sun 9 pm; closed Mon L.

Ragam W1 £31 **4** **3** **2**
57 Cleveland St   020 7636 9098   2–1B
"Year after year Ragam churns out delicious south Indian food, with lots of excellent vegetarian options" ("perfect dosas") – "it's not fancy but it's full of flavour and never fails!". The ambience at this basement near the Telecom Tower "doesn't get much better (despite two refurbs!), but the service is friendly" and everything comes "at a very reasonable price". / W1T 4JN; www.ragamindian.co.uk; 11 pm.

Rail House Café SW1 £60 2️⃣2️⃣2️⃣
Sir Simon Milton Sq   020 3906 7950   2–4B
This "cool-looking venue" in Victoria's new Nova development has
a "good all-round menu with lots of tasty choices", and makes "a worthy
addition to the Riding House Café group". But the middling ratings indicate
that Adam White's team are still struggling to meet the demands of a 300-
cover operation on two floors. Top Tip: a good choice for brunch.
/ SW1H 0HW; www.railhouse.cafe; @railhouse_cafe; closed Mon-Sat & Sun.

Rainforest Café W1 £61 1️⃣3️⃣3️⃣
20-24 Shaftesbury Ave   020 7434 3111   4–3D
"You're not here for the food, but for the sake of keeping young children
busy", say reports on this Piccadilly Circus fixture, complete with animatronic
animals and indoor rain storms. "The food's average and overpriced,
the decor's tired… but the kids love it and ask to go time and time
again…" / W1V 7EU; www.therainforestcafe.co.uk; @RainforestCafe; Sun-Wed
10 pm, Thu-Sat 8.30 pm; credit card required to book.

Rambla W1 £52 4️⃣3️⃣3️⃣
64 Dean St   020 7734 8428   5–2A
"Big flavours (and decent-sized portions too)" help inspire only positive
reviews for Victor Garvey's "superb new Catalan venture" in Soho, which
delivers "accomplished" cooking and "excellent value for money". This said,
numerous newspaper reviewers have gushed about the place bigtime,
and there is the odd caution that "although it's above average, it's not quite
as exceptional as some well-known critics might wish you to believe".
/ W1D 4QG; www.ramblalondon.com; @ramblasoho.

Randall & Aubin W1 £60 3️⃣3️⃣4️⃣
14-16 Brewer St   020 7287 4447   4–2D
"So long as you don't mind sharing a table with strangers" – this "always-
fun" Soho "institution" makes a perfect way to punctuate an evening. With
its "great buzz and very nice vibe, it's always full of energy", and "warm and
friendly" staff deliver "outstanding fresh seafood, especially the big plateaux
de fruits de mer", plus "sumptuous natives, fish 'n' chips, fish soup and
lobster po'boy, all of 'em delicious". / W1F 0SG; www.randallandaubin.com;
@randallandaubin; Mon-Thu 11 pm, Fri & Sat midnight, Sun 10 pm; booking L only.

Randy's Wing Bar E15 £35 3️⃣3️⃣3️⃣
Queen Elizabeth Olympic Park   020 8555 5971   14–1C
"Very good wings, beers and cocktails" are the payoff to a trip to this unit
in Hackney Wick's Here East development: feedback is limited but upbeat.
/ E15 2GW; www.randyswingbar.co.uk; @randyswingbar; 11 pm, Sun 10.30 pm;
closed Sun D.

Raoul's Café W9 £42 3️⃣2️⃣4️⃣
13 Clifton Rd   020 7289 7313   9–4A
"Very consistent in term of food, atmosphere (and slightly unmotivated
service!)" – this popular and long-established café near Little Venice
is known for its "great breakfast and brunch selection" and charming
outside tables. Its other spin-offs (including in Notting Hill) are no more.
/ W9 1SZ; www.raoulsgourmet.com; 9 pm; no booking L.

Rasa £35 3|3|2

6 Dering St, W1 020 7629 1346 3–2B
55 Stoke Newington Church St, N16 020 7249 0344 1–1C
56 Stoke Newington Church St, N16 020 7249 1340 1–1C

"It's easy to over-eat" at these basic cafés, whose still-quite-unusual Keralan menu is "still good after all these years" ("at the price it can seem quite amazing!") and "much better than 'normal' north Indians for veggies". The Stokie original is nowadays less popular than its "handy-to-know-about" offshoot "in the little patch near Oxford Circus bereft of decent options". / www.rasarestaurants.com; N16 & Travancore N16 10.45 pm, Fri & Sat 11.30 pm, W1 11 pm, Sun 9 pm; WC1 closed L, Sun L&D, N16 closed Mon-Fri L, Travancore closed L.

Ravi Shankar NW1 £30 3|2|2

132-135 Drummond St 020 7388 6458 9–4C

The "unbelievable value" lunchtime and weekend buffet makes this longstanding South Indian veggie a "great choice" among the Little India curry canteens near Euston station. "A bit rough around the edges", perhaps, but that is compensated by "quick and cheery service". / NW1 2HL; www.ravishankarbhelpoori.com; 10.30 pm; closed Mon-Sun L.

Red Farm WC2 NEW

9 Russell St 020 3883 9093 5–3D

A fun spin on Chinese cuisine – with an Instagramable dim sum prawn dish that looks like the ghosts in Pacman – this canteen-style import from NYC (where it's famous) has quietly arrived on a three storey site in Covent Garden with very little publicity, and a recreation of its no bookings policy. In an initial September 2018 review, The Evening Standard's Fay Maschler suggests prices are a little "ballsy", 'specially as Chinatown is only a stroll away. / WC2B 5HZ; redfarmldn.com.

Red Fort W1 £75 3|2|2

77 Dean St 020 7437 2525 4–1D

This once-famous Soho stalwart, modernised after a fire a few years back, is, in style, a "sort-of-posh Indian, midway between your local curry house and an upmarket place like Benares" (and the overall effect of its minimal, contemporary decor strikes some customers as a bit "dismal"). For its regulars "it's been going forever and never lets its standards slip" but more sceptical folk can just find the cooking "rather disappointing" nowadays. / W1D 3SH; redfort.co.uk; @redfortlondon; 11.30 pm; closed Sat L, closed Sun; No shorts.

The Red Lion & Sun N6 £52 3|2|3

25 North Rd 020 8340 1780 9–1B

This "great gastropub" in a leafy corner of Highgate "serves good, imaginative food at reasonable prices", catering for all tastes from classic Sunday roast to vegetarian and vegan. There's an "excellent wine list", "open fires", and "dogs are welcome". / N6 4BE; www.theredlionandsun.com; @redlionandsun; 10 pm.

The Red Pepper W9 £50 3|2|2

8 Formosa St 020 7266 2708 9–4A

This "tiny pizza place in Little Venice" is a popular and "friendly" local institution that is now entering its 25th year. Known for its "excellent wood-fired pizza", it also specialises in unusual dishes from Sardinia and southern Italy. / W9 1EE; www.theredpepperrestaurant.co.uk; Sun-Thu 10.30 pm, Sat, Fri 11 pm; closed Mon-Fri L; no Amex.

Red Rooster EC2 £68 2 2 **3**

45 Curtain Rd   020 3146 4545   13–1B

"The food is decent (the whole fried chicken with a sparkler looks impressive when it comes out) but doesn't live up to the hype" is the overall verdict on Ethiopian-Swedish chef, Marcus Samuelsson's soul-food-via-Scandinavia yearling: the London sibling to the hugely popular Harlem original, at the foot of Shoreditch's Curtain hotel. It has "a clubby (very noisy) vibe and nice live music". / EC2A 4PJ; www.thecurtain.com; @RoosterHarlem; 2 am, Sun midnight; closed Sun D.

Regency Cafe SW1 £16 **3** **4** **5**

17-19 Regency St   020 7821 6596   2–4C

"I am always surprised why this great caff is never included in your guide!!" – "If you like honest-to-goodness British grub, then join the queues for a proper fry-up" at this "brilliant", "cheap 'n' cheerful" dive "caught in a 1960's time warp", whose "full English can't be beaten". "With its beautiful tiled exterior and no nonsense service this is surely the platonic ideal of a Greasy Spoon": "the portions are large, the service is hectic, the seats are basic, and the food is incredible". "A real SW1 institution": "everyone goes – locals from the posh flats, and the council flats, taxi drivers, MPs, Channel 4 media executives, Scotland Yard detectives, über-stylish Burberry types and civil servants. We all eat here and love it!" / SW1P 4BY; regencycafe.co.uk; Mon-Fri 7.15 pm, Sat 12 pm; closed Sat D, closed Sun.

Le Relais de Venise L'Entrecôte £47 **3** **3** 2

120 Marylebone Ln, W1   020 7486 0878   2–1A
50 Dean St, W1   020 3475 4202   5–3A
5 Throgmorton St, EC2   020 7638 6325   10–2C

"The simplest menu" – the only items are "great steak-frites" accompanied by their "legendary secret sauce" (though you do get a choice of dessert) – makes for a "winning formula" at the three London branches of this international French-based chain. "If steak and chips tick your boxes, this will too!". "Time it wrong, and you'll have to queue". / www.relaisdevenise.com; 10.45 pm-11 pm, Sun 9 pm-10.30 pm; EC2 closed Sat & Sun; no booking.

Restaurant Ours SW3 £82 2 2 **3**

264 Brompton Rd   020 7100 2200   6–2C

As a bar, there's much to recommend this Eurotrash-friendly South Kensington two-year-old (complete with indoor foliage and fairy lights), whose current incarnation is a couple of years old. Since Tom Sellers departed this year, its food ratings have actually started to scrape off rock-bottom – whether it's that the food has improved, or folks' high expectations are now just a bit more realistic is unclear. / SW3 2AS; www.restaurant-ours.com; @restaurant_ours; midnight, Fri & Sat 1.30 am; closed Mon & Sun.

Reubens W1 £57 2 2 2

79 Baker St   020 7486 0035   2–1A

This age-old deli in Marylebone is one of the longest running kosher options in the West End. "Salt beef still tops the bill", and other dishes are dependably OK, in both the café upstairs and downstairs restaurant. / W1U 6RG; www.reubensrestaurant.co.uk; 11 pm; closed Fri D & Sat; no Amex.

The Rib Man E1 £8 **5** **3**–

Brick Lane, Brick Lane Market   no tel   13–2C

"Unbelievably tasty ribs, worth crossing London for" and perfect pulled pork, again score high ratings for street-food star Mark Gevaux, who is to be found on Sundays on Brick Lane (and outside West Ham for home games). Delight your friends with a gift of his trademark 'Holy F**k' hot sauce. / E1 6HR; www.theribman.co.uk; @theribman; closed Sun D, closed Mon-Fri & Sat; no booking.

Rib Room, Jumeirah Carlton Tower SW1 £100   2 2 **3**
Cadogan Pl   020 7858 7250   6–1D

*Lost in the Gucci-clad international black hole that is the upper end
of Sloane Street, this luxurious dining room (relaunched in late 2017) has
long been known for its steaks and prime beef. Feedback was limited,
but conformed to the age-old theme here: good but ferociously pricey.
/ SW1X 9PY; www.theribroom.co.uk; @RibRoomSW1; 10.30 pm; closed Sun.*

Riccardo's SW3   £51   2 2 2
126 Fulham Rd   020 7370 6656   6–3B

*This "little slice of Italy with a sunny terrace" in Chelsea "attracts a loyal
clientele" despite a widespread feeling that it's nowadays "tired" and
"without flair". But those who are more forgiving feel it's a "real antidote
to the Italian-themed chains" with "always a great welcome" perhaps from
the man himself: "people say the food's hit and miss, but stick to the staples
and all will be well". / SW3 6HU; www.riccardos.it; @ricardoslondon; 10 pm.*

Rick Stein SW14   £64   2 2 **3**
Tideway Yard, 125 Mortlake High St   020 8878 9462   11–1A

*"I love Rick's TV programmes, but his Barnes restaurant is a bit of a rip
off". The Stein empire "could have tried a bit harder" with their first London
outpost, which even some fans say is "no better than its previous incarnation
(The Depot)". You do get "lovely views of the river" from its charming
riverside location, near Barnes Bridge; and the food rating is middling not
terrible; but "foodwise, this place couldn't be more different from the
original in Padstow". / SW14 8SN; www.rickstein.com/eat-with-us/barnes;
@SteinBarnes; 9.30 pm; SRA-Food Made Good – 1 star.*

Riding House Café W1   £58   2 2 **3**
43-51 Great Titchfield St   020 7927 0840   3–1C

*"Fun" Fitzrovia all-day brasserie, with vaguely Manhattan-esque undertones,
where breakfast and weekend brunch are the favoured times for a visit,
although it's also tipped by creative types as a good place for a business
meal. But be warned: one person's "buzzy" can be another's "fiendishly
noisy". / W1W 7PQ; www.ridinghousecafe.co.uk; Mon-Thu 11.30 pm, Fri & Sat
midnight, Sun 10.30 pm.*

The Rising Sun NW7   £59   **3 3 3**
137 Marsh Ln   020 8959 1357   1–1B

*Run by Luca and Matteo Delnevo from Parma ("who pride themselves
on friendly service and great food"), this lovely old pub (circa 1600) in Mill
Hill provides "delicious" Italian cooking that's "by far the best gastroboozer
grub for miles". It's "exceptionally child-friendly" too and "can be very busy
at weekends, so book ahead". / NW7 4EY; www.therisingsunmillhill.com;
@therisingsunpub; Sun-Wed 10 pm, Thu-Sat 10.30 pm; closed Mon L.*

Ristorante Frescobaldi W1   £82   **3** 4 **3**
15 New Burlington Pl   020 3693 3435   4–2A

*The "stunning, consistently good Italian food" at this three-year-old Mayfair
venture is accompanied by a wine list that reflects its ownership by a 700-
year-old Florentine banking and wine dynasty. It is certainly expensive,
but "I don't fully understand why it's not busier". / W1S 5HX;
www.frescobaldirestaurants.com; @frescobaldi_uk; Mon-Wed midnight, Thu-Sat
1.30 am, Sun 11 pm.*

The Ritz, Palm Court W1   £107   2 4 **5**
150 Piccadilly   020 7493 8181   3–4C

*"As a location, it's synonymous with afternoon tea", and "although it is very
expensive" on practically all accounts this "gold standard" experience
provides a "fantastic occasion" that's "worth it", with a drool-worthy
selection of pastries, sandwiches, scones and cakes that "live up to the
sumptuous surroundings", plus a choice of 18 different brews. Various
Champagne and 'Celebration' packages are available. / W1J 9BR;
www.theritzlondon.com; @theritzlondon; Jacket & tie required.*

The Ritz W1 £132 **3 4 5**

150 Piccadilly 020 7493 8181 3–4C

"One of the best rooms in London, if not in the world!" –
this "most beautiful" Louis XVI chamber provides a "glorious" riot
of bronze, marble, painted ceiling and mirrors. From the kitchen overseen
by John Williams, the "traditional Anglo-French dishes served from splendid
silver carts" provide "an utterly magnificent and delightfully plutocratic
experience… if sadly with prices to match". "Service treats you like royalty",
and "for a romantic evening, you can't beat it" (especially, for older
lovebirds, if combined with the evenings of music and dance). / W1J 9BR;
www.theritzlondon.com; @theritzlondon; 10 pm; Jacket & tie required; SRA-Food
Made Good – 3 stars.

Riva SW13 £64 **3 3 2**

169 Church Rd 020 8748 0434 11–1A

Tucked away in a row of Barnes shopfronts, this "soigné" North Italian
is "unchanged in 20 years", during which Andreas Riva has built a devoted
following, particularly amongst in-the-know foodies, with cooking that's
"consistently superb, simply presented and concentrating on quality
ingredients". It can feel a bit cliquey, though: "the proprietor seems to take
pride in ignoring you unless you're a regular – or a celebrity". / SW13 9HR;
10 pm, Sun 9 pm; closed Sat L.

Rivea, Bulgari Hotel SW7 £88 **3 4 3**

171 Knightsbridge 020 7151 1025 6–1C

One of French superchef Alain Ducasse's luxury London hotel venues
(the others being in the Dorchester) – this luxurious Knightsbridge basement
presents his take on the cuisine of the French and Italian Riviera. While
there is fulsome praise for some "delightful food" including "among the
best desserts in London", some reporters expect to find more than merely
"a reasonable all-rounder". / SW7 1DW; www.bulgarihotels.com; @bulgarihotels;
10.30 pm; booking max 7 may apply.

The River Café W6 £97 **3 4 4**

Thames Wharf, Rainville Rd 020 7386 4200 8–2C

"An amazing place that's still full on a midweek winter evening after
30 years" – Hammersmith's world famous, riverside Italian shows no sign
of running out of steam: "it still feels fresh and contemporary", "Ruthie
Rogers herself is still there doing some of the cooking", and it remains
a standard-bearer for "the simplicity and clarity" of its Tuscan cuisine. The
perennial elephant in the room here is "wallet-busting" prices, which
regularly win this W6 legend the survey's booby prize as London's
Most Overpriced Restaurant. Even so, most reporters are inclined to be
forgiving: they "love the place despite the absurd cost", particularly those
who appreciate "the very best, carefully sourced ingredients"; who adore the
"helpful staff"; or who acclaim "the glorious outside terrace in summer",
which "can't be matched". A sizeable minority though "know all the
arguments as to why the place is worth it… but don't agree". A prime gripe
for those who feel the most taken for a ride is the "crazy bills you get for
sitting in what's basically a big canteen": while fans applaud this egalitarian
set-up as "a perfect mix between formality and informality", the less
charitable find it "noisy" and "crammed in" ("my chair was frequently
banged into by waiters squeezing past"). / W6 9HA; www.rivercafe.co.uk;
@RiverCafeLondon; Mon-Fri 9 pm, Sat 9.30 pm, Sun 3 pm; closed Sun D.

Rivington Grill SE10 £55 | 2 | 2 | 2 |
178 Greenwich High Rd 020 8293 9270 1–3D
The brand that time forgot! – this Caprice Group venue is the sole survivor of a chain concept that went nowhere (and where the Rivington Street original has now gone). In direly provided Greenwich though, it's a case of 'the one eyed man is king' – "it's fairly standard fare, but I liked the ambience and it may be your best bet if you're in SE10!"; good for "a relaxed brunch". / SE10 8NN; www.rivingtongrill.co.uk; 11 pm, Sun 10 pm; closed Mon, Tue L & Wed L.

Roast SE1 £70 | 2 | 2 | 3 |
Stoney St 0845 034 7300 10–4C
This Borough Market showcase for traditional British food enjoys a "great location" (incorporating a glass portico that was originally part of the Royal Opera House) with "wonderful views north to the City, east to the (bottom of the) Shard, and over the market itself". But every report of exceptional results ("best pork-and-crackling sandwich"; "amazing Chateaubriand") is matched by gripes about "very average" fare ("burnt Yorkshire pudding"; "the meat may be of a good quality but the cooking is not!"). It's also "on the expensive side". Top Tips: "excellent breakfast option – very filling"; "nab a window seat". / SE1 1TL; www.roast-restaurant.com; @roastrestaurant; 10.45 pm, Sun 6.30 pm; closed Sun D.

Rocca Di Papa £43 | 3 | 4 | 4 |
73 Old Brompton Rd, SW7 020 7225 3413 6–2B
75-79 Dulwich Village, SE21 020 8299 6333 1–4D
"Buzzy", "cheap 'n' cheerful" Italians in South Kensington and Dulwich Village that provide "lively service", "delicious, freshly made food" and "good pizzas with unusual toppings". "They love children and are relaxed about noise and mess", and there are "plenty of staff so you're not kept waiting". / www.roccarestaurants.com; SW7 11.30 pm; SE21 11 pm.

Rochelle Canteen E2 £64 | 2 | 2 | 4 |
Rochelle School, Arnold Circus 020 7729 5677 13–1C
The bike sheds of a former school near Spitalfields – converted by Melanie Arnold and Margot Henderson (wife of St John's Fergus) – are "a relaxed and leafy garden space, and romantic too" – "perfect for a summer lunch". It remains a favourite East End destination for those in the know on account of its simple, short menu of quality British fare but – coincidental with their opening at the ICA – ratings waned here this year, with more middling feedback and the odd "unsatisfactory meal". / E2 7ES; www.arnoldandhenderson.com; Thu-Sat 9 pm; closed Mon-Sun D; no Amex.

Rochelle Canteen at the ICA SW1 £45 | 4 | 4 | 3 |
The Mall 020 7930 8619 2–3C
"I didn't think they'd do it in the arid ICA... but it's a triumph... Melanie and Margot, we love you!". Melanie Arnold and Margot Henderson have pulled off the successful opening of an offshoot to their Boho Spitalfields venture in this "rather odd space" – a cultural centre near the start of The Mall – which, while "cramped and lacking comfort", is "laid back" and pepped up by "cheerful service". The main event though is the "simple, hearty but utterly delicious English food cooked with care and passion" – "just right, no-frills perfection!" / SW1Y 5AH; www.ica.art/visit/caf-bar; 11 pm; closed Mon.

Roganic W1 £93 5 4 2

5-7 Blandford St   020 3370 6260   2–1A

Simon Rogan's 2011 pop-up has been resurrected as a permanent fixture, replacing L'Autre Pied (RIP) – the most recent inhabitant of this "odd" ("cramped" and "slightly bleak") Marylebone site – and offering either short (eight-course) or standard (over 12 courses) tasting menus. "Sometimes you want simple, delicious food, sometimes you want refinement and sophistication, and sometimes you want a meal that pushes things even further: this is a mix of sophistication and pushing-things-further, from single mouthfuls to fuller, complex, flavour-packed dishes", with "stunning presentation (every dish is a work of art) and divine tastes". Even so, there are one or two who feel that "while it's inventive and good, it's also overpriced with miniscule portions and you leave wondering what you've had". Top Menu Tip: the easiest way to dip your toe in the water here is the £35, short business tasting menu. / W1U 3DB; www.simonrogan.co.uk; @simon_rogan; 9.15 pm; closed Sun & Mon.

Rök £57 3 4 3

149 Upper St, N1   no tel   9–3D
26 Curtain Rd, EC2   020 7377 2152   13–2B

"Stripped-down ambience" and a "simple menu of interesting Nordic dishes" (many of them smoked, brined or fermented) hit the spot at this accomplished Scandi-inspired duo in Shoreditch and Islington. (There were plans for a Soho branch too, but these seem to have been backburnered for the time being). STOP PRESS: it was announced the original Shoreditch branch will close in early October 2018. / N1 midnight, EC2 11 pm, Fri & Sat 1 am; EC2 closed Sun.

Roka £85 4 3 3

30 North Audley St, W1   020 7305 5644   3–2A
37 Charlotte St, W1   020 7580 6464   2–1C
Aldwych House, 71-91 Aldwych, WC2   020 7294 7636   2–2D
Unit 4, Park Pavilion, 40 Canada Sq, E14   020 7636 5228   12–1C

"I love sitting at the counter with my partner, drinking the cocktails and sake, and having the most brilliant food!" – These "chilled" (if "noisy" and "buzzy") operations hail from the same stable as Zuma, and have carved a formidable following thanks to a Japanese-inspired array of "clean tasting" fusion dishes, sushi and robata grills, full of "vibrant flavour". "It all adds up to a wonderful experience, but with a bill to match!". Top Tips – "fantastic weekend brunch menu with booze included!" at all branches; and "rocking basement bar" at the Charlotte Street original. / www.rokarestaurant.com; 11.30 pm, Sun 10.30 pm; E14 11pm, Sun 8.30 pm; WC2 11 pm, Sun 8 pm; booking: max 5 online.

Romulo Café W8 £59 3 3 3

343 Kensington High St   020 3141 6390   8–1D

"You don't find many Filipino restaurants in the UK" and this two-year-old outpost of a restaurant group based in the Philippines aims to change all that. "First timers should like it" on account of its novelty; old hands may find it "a little pricier than other representatives of the cuisine… I guess you're paying for the Kensington price tag, and for food that's beautifully presented and delicious". / W8 6NW; www.romulocafe.co.uk; @romulolondon; 10 pm; closed Sun.

Rosas £46 3 2 2

The "cheap and tasty Thai food" at this fast-growing chain "hits a decent standard despite its many branches" and its delivered by "friendly, speedy staff" making them "a good stand-by option". Founders Saiphin and Alex Moore, who opened the original branch in 2008, have recently sold a majority stake to US investors TriSpan. / rosasthaicafe.com; @RosasThaiCafe; 10.30 pm, Fri & Sat 11 pm; E15 9 pm, Sat 10 pm, Sun 6 pm; W1F & W1D Sun 10 pm; ; E1, SW1 & SW9 6+ to book, W1 4+ to book.

The Rosendale SE21 £52 343

65 Rosendale Rd 020 8761 9008 1–4D

"Simple food but well executed (great burgers, pizzas and Sunday lunch)"
has helped win a following for this fine Victorian coaching inn
in West Dulwich (which has an enclosed garden for the kids). / SE21 8EZ;
www.therosendale.co.uk; @threecheerspubs; 10.30 pm; no Amex.

Rossopomodoro £46 222

John Lewis, 300 Oxford St, W1 020 7495 8409 3–1B
50-52 Monmouth St, WC2 020 7240 9095 5–3B
214 Fulham Rd, SW10 020 7352 7677 6–3B
1 Rufus St, N1 020 7739 1899 13–1B
10 Jamestown Rd, NW1 020 7424 9900 9–3B
46 Garrett Ln, SW18 020 8877 9903 11–2B

"Good Neapolitan cuisine including nice pizzas" in *"huge portions (with a
useful kids' menu)"* is *"a pleasant surprise"* for most who report on this
global chain, which actually originates in Naples itself. Feedback is not all
bouquets though – ratings are undercut by one or two reports of *"mediocre"*
(eg *"stodgy"*) dishes. / www.rossopomodoro.co.uk; 11 pm, Fri & Sat 11.30 pm,
Sun 10 pm.

Roti Chai W1 £46 333

3 Portman Mews South 020 7408 0101 3–1A

"A menu inspired by street hawkers and roadside cafés" produces
"delicious" and *"authentic"*-tasting street food at this highly popular,
contemporary Indian operation, near Selfridges. The formula is essentially
the same in the ground floor café or basement restaurant, and in general
folks *"are not sure that eating downstairs is worth the extra"*. / W1H 6HS;
www.rotichai.com; @rotichai; 9 pm; booking D only.

Roti King,
Ian Hamilton House NW1 £17 521

40 Doric Way 020 7387 2518 9–3C

*"Brought up in Singapore so the roti with curry sauce was a trip down
memory lane!"* – this *"crazy busy"* basement dive near Euston serves
a *"good representation of Malaysian kopitiam (coffee shop)/hawker cuisine"*.
"The large number of SE Asian students" and *"bargain prices"* result
in *"significant queues and the need to share the tightly packed tables"* –
which is *"annoying… until the food arrives and all is forgiven!"* / NW1 1LH;
www.rotiking.in; 10.30 pm; closed Sun; no booking.

Rotorino E8 £49 243

434 Kingsland Rd 020 7249 9081 14–1A

Inspired by southern Italy, Stevie Parle's slick-looking venue is still capable
of producing hit dishes (*"gnudi worth the trip to Dalston"*) but a couple
of poor reports this year makes it hard to give it an unqualified
recommendation. / E8 4AA; www.rotorino.com; @Rotorino; 11 pm, Sun 9 pm.

Rotunda Bar & Restaurant,
Kings Place N1 £55 334

90 York Way 020 7014 2840 9–3C

A wonderful waterside location, and *"smart and buzzy"* interior place this
canal-side dining room very much at the upper end of your typical arts
centre venue, as does its 'farm to fork' ethos with meat sourced from its
own Northumberland farm. Results here – generally good – can sometimes
be *"run of the mill"*, but may see a boost from a significant summer 2018
refurb to mark its 10th year. Changes include an open-to view kitchen
(relocated from the lower level of the building), a large meat-ageing cabinet,
chef's counter heaters, enabling the terrace to be used all-year-round.
/ N1 9AG; www.rotundabarandrestaurant.co.uk; @rotundalondon; 11 pm; closed Sun.

Roux at Parliament Square, RICS SW1
£91 🖥 5 4 3

12 Great George St   020 7334 3737   2–3C

"The food is executed with such skill" at this "superb" Roux-branded operation – "a calm haven away from the Parliament Square traffic", which shines all the brighter "in the culinary wastelands of Westminster". "Warm and comforting decor from the recent revamp" softens the "very 'establishment'" decor, while service "strikes the perfect balance between being polite and informative, but willing to have a laugh". Top Tip: "at £40 the set lunch may sound expensive but this is top class cuisine at a reasonable price". / SW1P 3AD; www.rouxatparliamentsquare.co.uk; @RouxAPS; Mon-Fri 9 pm; closed Sat & Sun; No trainers.

Roux at the Landau, The Langham W1
£92 4 4 4

1c Portland Pl   020 7965 0165   2–1B

"All round 10/10!" – The re-launched Roux-branded operation in this "elegant" and "beautiful" dining room, a stone's throw from Broadcasting House, jumped up several gears this year, as a lift in ratings coincided with its February 2018 re-launch in a new more "relaxed and simple" guise, incorporating a new, central dining counter and adopting a luxurious, 'no-tablecloths' style. "Not one thing is amiss" when it comes to the "exceptional" modern French cuisine (which now takes a more ingredient-led approach), service is exemplary, and the overall experience is "one of pure indulgence" (especially for a romantic occasion). / W1B 1JA; www.rouxatthelandau.com; @Langham_Hotel; 10.30 pm, Sun 11.30 am; closed Sun D, closed Mon; No trainers.

ROVI W1 NEW
£63

59-65 Wells St   020 3963 8270   3–1D

This light and bright July 2018 opening from Yotam Ottolenghi is, er, Ottolenghi-like in its culinary character: that is to say firmly rooted in eastern Mediterranean cuisine; but here with a spin that's even more veg-centred, and also now with a focus on fermentation and cooking over fire. The eco-friendly, waste-reducing, Fitzrovia site is initially open for lunch and dinner, but breakfast will follow. / W1A 3AE; www.ottolenghi.co.uk/rovi; @rovi_restaurant; 10.15 pm, Sun 3.30 pm; closed Sun D.

Rowley's SW1
£74 2 2 2

113 Jermyn St   020 7930 2707   4–4D

A St James's veteran from 1976, this British steakhouse inhabits some of the early premises of the Wall's meat empire (on this site from 1836). Results here have been perennially uneven over the years, and not even the promise of unlimited fries (which accompany items like Entrecôte and Chateaubriand) stopped some meals this year from seeming disappointing or overpriced. / SW1Y 6HJ; www.rowleys.co.uk; @Rowleys_steak; 10.30 pm.

Rox Burger SE13
£28 4 3 3

82 Lee High Rd   020 3372 4631   1–4D

"A great choices of amazing, fresh burgers" plus a selection of craft beers make it worth discovering this "very casual" Lewisham venture; "it's pretty small but they also do take away". / SE13 5PT; www.roxburger.com; @RoxburgerUK; 10 pm; closed Mon-Fri L.

Royal China £56 3 1 2
24-26 Baker St, W1   020 7487 4688   2–1A
805 Fulham Rd, SW6   020 7731 0081   11–1B
13 Queensway, W2   020 7221 2535   7–2C
30 Westferry Circus, E14   020 7719 0888   12–1B

"The only reason you would go is for the sooooo very yummy dim sum" nowadays, say loyal fans of this *"super-busy and slightly chaotic"* Cantonese chain, with its hallmark black-and-gold, lacquered decor. It *"remains the benchmark"* for many Londoners, but the *"brisk (read brusque) service"* seems increasingly *"careless (my food arrived cold)"* and the *"very dated and fairly grotty environment"* seems ever-more *"tired"*. The *"cavernous"* Bayswater branch is best – but *"you can't book at weekends, so it's first-come-first-served chaos with families and buggies"*. / www.royalchinagroup.co.uk; 11 pm, Sun 10 pm; W1 Fri & Sat 11.30 pm; no booking Sat & Sun L.

Royal China Club W1 £68 4 2 2
38-42 Baker St   020 7486 3898   2–1A

The flagship of what many consider *"the best Chinese restaurant group in London"* – the China Club HQ offers *"luxury twists on traditional dishes"*, results in *"superb food, whether it's dim sum for brunch or seafood and classic Cantonese in the evening"*. It reopened in early August 2018 after a four-month refurb and expansion into the adjacent corner site – hopefully this will please reporters who had recommended *"a facelift"* (the rating above is for the former decor). / W1U 7AJ; www.royalchinagroup.co.uk; @RoyalChinaGroup; 1 am, Sun midnight; booking weekdays only.

Rucoletta EC2 £48 3 2 1
6 Foster Lane   020 7600 7776   10–2B

This *"hidden gem"* in a backstreet near St Paul's is an *"old school"*, *"cheap 'n' cheerful Italian serving mama's cooking in the City"*. *"The basic premises are quite crowded, but the simple food's excellent"*. / EC2V 6HH; www.rucoletta.co.uk; @RucolettaLondon; 9.30 pm, Thu & Fri 10 pm; closed Sat D & Sun; no Amex.

Rugoletta £53 3 3 2
308 Ballards Ln, N12   020 8445 6742   1–1B
59 Church Ln, N2   020 8815 1743   1–1B

These *"excellent, cheap and reliable family Italians"* in Barnet and East Finchley are popular in the area – so you *"must book Friday and Saturday evenings"*. They are *"cramped"*, but *"don't seem to mind noisy children"*. / www.la-rugoletta.com; 10.30 pm; N12 Fri & Sat 11 pm; N2 closed Sun.

Rules WC2 £78 2 3 5
35 Maiden Ln   020 7836 5314   5–3D

"Like stepping into a time warp" – London's oldest restaurant (in these Covent Garden premises since 1798) is a magnificent period piece, complete with a gorgeous panelled interior. Inevitably it's *"very touristy"* although many Londoners also harbour a very soft spot for the old place. That said, its *"old-school British cooking"* has been better in living memory and many reporters continue to find *"prices are high for rather indifferent food"*: *"our American friends were happy, but we were not impressed and the steak 'n' kidney pudding was not as good as we remembered!"* Top Tip: *"unbeatable game in season"*. / WC2E 7LB; www.rules.co.uk; 11.30 pm, Sun 10.30 pm; No shorts.

Ruya W1 NEW
30 Upper Grosvenor St   020 3848 6710   3–3A

On swanky Park Lane, this June 2018 debut is another example of the growing number of Middle East-based restaurant empires (here Dubai) opening in prime London sites. Restaurateur Umut Özkanca and chef Colin Clague promise a fine dining take on Middle Eastern food with a nod to Özkanca's native Turkey. / W1K 7PH; ruyalondon.com; Mon & Tue 9 pm, Fri & Sat 11.30 pm, Wed 10 pm, Thu 11 pm, Sun 5 pm.

Sabor W1 £60 4 4 4

35 Heddon St   020 3319 8130   4–3A

Ex-Barrafina executive head chef, Nieves Barragán Mohacho and José Etura's yearling off Regent's Street, comprises both a downstairs floor with tapas counter and a "wonderfully buzzy" upstairs room with shared tables, which revolves around the open kitchen's asador (wood-fired oven). Both come recommended, with reporters "blown away" by the "delightful service", "outstanding" food and upstairs the "fabulous experience of cooking right in front of your eyes". But while fans predictably say "move over Barrafina", ratings have a way to go yet to rival their former employer. Top Menu Tip: "finally, suckling pig just like you get in Spain" from the asador. / W1B 4BP; www.saborrestaurants.co.uk; @sabor_ldn; 10.30 pm, Sun 6 pm; closed Mon.

Le Sacré-Coeur N1 £42 2 3 3

18 Theberton St   020 7354 2618   9–3D

"You could almost be in Paris" at this "astonishingly good-value bistro" off Upper Street – "quite the Islington institution". It has a "wide menu at an attractive fixed price, served by jolly staff who are very well led". / N1 0QX; www.lesacrecoeur.co.uk; @LeSacreCoeurUK; Sun-Thu 10.30 pm, Fri & Sat 11.30 pm.

Sacro Cuore £38 5 3 2

10 Crouch End Hill, N8   020 8348 8487   1–1C NEW
45 Chamberlayne Rd, NW10   020 8960 8558   1–2B

"The best pizza outside Italy!" (their authentic Neapolitan-style bases are "to die for") is more than enough to inspire rave reviews for this north London pair, which serve nothing else beyond a few starters and desserts. Kensal Rise came first but it could well be the case that "the Crouch End branch is even better than the original!". / www.sacrocuore.co.uk; @SacroCuorePizza.

Sagar £36 4 3 2

17a Percy St, W1   020 7631 3319   3–1D
31 Catherine St, WC2   020 7836 6377   5–3D
157 King St, W6   020 8741 8563   8–2C

"Delicious, well-spiced, memorable" – "and really cheap!" – South Indian vegetarian food ("with most dishes also available as vegan") wins high ratings for this well-established small chain of low-key cafés, located in Covent Garden, Tottenham Court Road, Hammersmith and Harrow. / www.sagarveg.co.uk; W1 10.45 pm-11pm, Sun 10 pm.

Sagardi EC2 £70 2 3 3

Cordy House, 95 Curtain Rd   020 3802 0478   13–1B

"A bit pricey but worth the splurge", say fans of this "relaxed" Basque pintxos bar and charcoal grill in Shoreditch, who praise the "fantastic, beautifully cooked" dishes (the speciality is Galician Txuleton beef). No matter the quality, others just can't get their head around the bill here: "it would have been a fine meal, but we were sold a steak that was really overpriced by a factor of 2x". / EC2A 3AH; www.sagardi.co.uk; @Sagardi_UK; 11 pm.

Sager + Wilde £60 2 2 3

193 Hackney Rd, E2   020 8127 7330   14–2A
250 Paradise Row, E2   020 7613 0478   14–2B

Hackney oenophiles make a beeline for these this ambitious pair – "I love the wine list!". The Paradise Row venue, in a railway arch with a large terrace, features an Italian menu, while the Hackney Road wine bar serves snacks and charcuterie. In either case the food avoids criticism, but the liquid refreshment is the main event.

Saigon Saigon W6 £36   2 3 3
313-317 King St 020 8748 6887 8–2B
"Always packed", this well established Hammersmith Vietnamese
is "all round OK" at "a great price" (if arguably "nothing to get overly
excited about"). There's an "extensive menu" and the "comforting and
deeply flavoured pho" is always a good bet. / W6 9NH; www.saigon-saigon.co.uk;
@saigonsaigonuk; 11 pm, Sun 10 pm.

St John Bread & Wine E1 £66   3 3 3
94-96 Commercial St 020 7251 0848 13–2C
"You can't beat a great bacon sarnie and a range of other delicious
breakfast specials" at this long-established spin-off from Smithfield's St John,
near Spitalfields Market. At other times this utilitarian canteen serves its
"very good, if sometimes overly quirky" offal-centric British menu alongside
a "wine list full of vintages you've never heard of, but which are always
enjoyable". / E1 6LZ; www.stjohngroup.uk.com/spitalfields; @sjrestaurant; Sun &
Mon 10 pm, Tue-Sat 11 pm.

St John Smithfield EC1 £67   5 4 3
26 St John St 020 7251 0848 10–1B
"Still managing to excel itself on a regular basis" – Trevor Gulliver and
Fergus Henderson's white-walled temple near Smithfield Market coined the
concept of 'nose-to-tail' eating with its "incredibly stimulating menu"
featuring "all sorts of offal and cuts of meat not usually available
elsewhere"; and there's "still nothing quite like it" after over two decades
in operation. "Friendly and efficient service helps soften the austere interior"
and "if you want honest, seasonal British food with soul and heart" arguably
"there is no better place". "We recently ate bone marrow, tripe, and pig's
tongue, then watched longingly as a grouse pie was delivered to a
neighbouring table". "Splendid wine" too. Top Tip: the bar and its simpler
menu is a good way to dip your toe in the water. / EC1M 4AY;
stjohnrestaurant.com/a/restaurants/smithfield; @SJRestaurant; 11 pm, Sun 4 pm;
closed Sat L closed Sun D.

St Johns N19 £55   3 4 5
91 Junction Rd 020 7272 1587 9–1C
"Still the top gastropub for miles around" – this Archway boozer is a
"brilliant" spot throughout, both in the characterful bar, but particularly
in the "spacious" and extremely atmospheric rear dining room (originally
built as a ballroom). On the menu – "excellent" modern British food,
provided by staff who are "cheerful even when rushed off their feet".
/ N19 5QU; www.stjohnstavern.com; @stjohnstavern; 10.30 pm, Sun 9.30 pm;
Mon-Thu D only, Fri-Sun open L & D; no Amex; booking max 12 may apply.

St Moritz W1 £55   3 3 4
161 Wardour St 020 7734 3324 4–1C
"Like being transported to Switzerland for the evening!" – this "unique"
chalet-style, Swiss-themed "institution" in Soho may sound too kitsch to be
taken seriously, but scores have been consistently strong here over many
years: "the fondues are amazing", and the overall effect on a cold winter's
night is "heavenly". / W1F 8WJ; www.stmoritz-restaurant.co.uk; Mon-Thu
11.30 pm, Fri & Sat midnight, Sun 10.30 pm.

Sakagura W1 £53   3 4 2
8 Heddon St 020 3405 7230 4–3B
An "enjoyable take on Japanese" – this 'steak and sake bar' in the Heddon
Street foodie enclave off Regent Street invites customers to 'cook their own'
meat (including "excellent wagyu beef"), fish and vegetables over a tabletop BBQ or hot lava stone. There are also "exceptional sake choices", along
with sake cocktails, shochu and Japanese craft beers. From the team behind
Shoryu Ramen and the Japan Centre. / W1B 4BU; www.sakaguralondon.com;
@sakaguraldn; Mon-Wed 11 pm, Thu-Sat midnight; closed Sun.

Sake No Hana SW1   £78   3️⃣3️⃣3️⃣
23 St James's St   020 7925 8988   3–4D
Set in a very 1960s Modernist building next to The Economist,
this ambitious Japanese in St James's is part of the all-conquering Hakkasan
Group, but its up-and-down performance over the years means it's never
achieved the high profile of its siblings. This said, "the food has moved up a
level" in the last couple of years, and the place is nowadays achieving
consistently good ratings all-round. / SW1A 1HA; www.sakenohana.com;
@sakenohana; Mon-Thu 11 pm, Fri & Sat 11.30 pm; closed Sun.

Sakonis   £28   3️⃣2️⃣1️⃣
127-129 Ealing Rd, HA0   020 8903 9601   1–1A
330 Uxbridge Rd, HA5   020 8903 9601   1–1A
"Probably the best-value buffet in London" (served through breakfast and
lunch) draws fans of veggie Indian fare from far and wide to this mainstay
of Wembley's Ealing Road (which at other times sells a less interesting fast-
foodish menu incorporating street food, pizza and Indo-Chinese dishes).
There's also been a sibling in Hatch End since September 2017.

Salaam Namaste WC1   £46   3️⃣2️⃣2️⃣
68 Millman St   020 7405 3697   2–1D
It's worth remembering this central but affordable Bloomsbury Indian –
'specialising in modern and healthy cooking' – which scores consistently solid
all-round ratings. / WC1N 3EF; www.salaam-namaste.co.uk; @SalaamNamasteUK;
Tue-Thu 3 pm, Fri-Sun 11 pm.

Sale e Pepe SW1   £67   3️⃣2️⃣3️⃣
9-15 Pavilion Rd   020 7235 0098   6–1D
Age-old trattoria near Harrods and Harvey Nichols that's "lots of fun" to a
crowd who, in some cases, have been coming for decades. Don't let the
"dated interior" put you off – the cuisine can be of a "very high standard".
/ SW1X 0HD; www.saleepepe.co.uk; @salepepe_it.

Salloos SW1   £67   3️⃣2️⃣2️⃣
62-64 Kinnerton St   020 7235 4444   6–1D
"Very good, very authentic home-cooked Pakistani food" sums up the appeal
of this veteran, tucked away in a Belgravia mews. It has always been
"expensive", as might be deduced from its location a short stroll from
Knightsbridge. Top tip – legendary lamb chops. / SW1X 8ER; www.salloos.co.uk;
11 pm; closed Mon-Sat & Sun; may need 5+ to book.

Salon Brixton SW9   £56   5️⃣4️⃣3️⃣
18 Market Row   020 7501 9152   11–2D
"Capable and unshowy modern British cooking, using all sorts of influences"
(plus de rigeur pickling and preserving) from a "very seasonal", if "limited"
menu scores the highest praise for Nicholas Balfe's "fun" and "buzzy"
fixture in Brixton Market – "one of those places where you want to eat
everything on the menu" and with "a (mostly natural) wine list that's
interesting, too". Top Tip: "superb vegetarian dishes". Balfe and his team are
opening a bistro Levan in Peckham in October 2018. / SW9 8LD;
www.salonbrixton.co.uk; @Salon_Brixton; 9.15 pm.

Le Salon Privé TW1   £52   3️⃣4️⃣3️⃣
43 Crown Rd   020 8892 0602   1–4A
Notably smart with its white tablecloths and stained-glass windows,
this three-year-old St Margarets bistro is a hit with local diners for its
"beautifully prepared" French classics, "friendly service and good ambience".
"The new vegetarian menu is a definite winner", and for rugby fans,
it's "ideal when going to Twickers!". / TW1 3EJ; lesalonprive.net; @lesalon_tweet;
11 pm, Sun 10 pm.

Salt Yard W1 £52 **4** **3** **3**

54 Goodge St 020 7637 0657 2–1B

"Delights such as octopus with saffron mayo" are amongst the "very appealing small plates" inspired by Spain and Italy that put Simon Mullins's "friendly and informal" bar in Fitzrovia at the vanguard of London's "upmarket tapas" trend. Even if it no longer makes culinary waves as it did, ratings are back to a five-year high this year. Any complaints? – as ever, it's "cramped and crowded". / W1T 4NA; www.saltyard.co.uk; @SaltYardGroup; Sun-Thu 10.30 pm, Sat, Fri 11 pm; ; booking max 8 may apply.

Salut N1 £69 **3** **2** **2**

412 Essex Rd 020 3441 8808 9–3D

"Beautifully presented, interesting and well-cooked" modern dishes of a high level of ambition justify the trip to this Canonbury two-year-old at the 'wrong' end of the Essex Road. But is loses some points for "close tables", "small portions" and "high prices given the location". / N1 3PJ; www.salut-london.co.uk; @Salut_London; Tue-Sun 11 pm; closed Tue-Thu L, closed Mon.

Sam's Riverside, Riverside Studios W6 NEW

101 Queen Caroline St awaiting tel 8–2C

Restaurateur Sam Harrison – who owned neighbourhood favourites Sam's Brasserie in Chiswick and Harrison's in Balham, until both sites were sold to Foxlow in 2015 – has announced plans to open a new restaurant and bar in February 2019 as part of the rebuilt Riverside Studios. Facing the Thames with views of Hammersmith Bridge, the all-day 90-cover brasserie will have an outdoor terrace and private dining room, and will provide W6 with a long-needed cheaper alternative to another river café five minutes walk away… / W6 9BN; www.samsriversidelondon.com; @samsriversideW6.

San Carlo SW1 NEW £64

2 Regent Street Saint James's 020 3778 0768 4–4D

The glam San Carlo group's latest London fixture – and the first to carry the main brand rather than the less formal 'Cicchetti' name – is a large, 130-cover operation (most recently Norte, RIP) which opened in May 2018 on the lower half of Regent Street, plushly decked out with lots of linen, leather, marble and panelling. / SW1Y 4AU; sancarlo.co.uk/restaurants/san-carlo-london; @SanCarlo_Group.

San Carlo Cicchetti £59 **3** **3** **4**

215 Piccadilly, W1 020 7494 9435 4–4C
30 Wellington St, WC2 020 7240 6339 5–3D

"Glitzy interiors (and customers!)" are a hallmark of these "fun and buzzy" Venetian brasseries (part of an increasingly sizeable national chain, based in Manchester). Although the locations are "a little touristic" – particularly the large branch near Piccadilly Circus – the "feel is genuinely North Italian", the food is "good for the price" , service is "warm" and "the overall experience is very good". / www.sancarlocicchetti.co.uk; @SanCarlo_Group; W1 11.30 pm; WC2 midnight; M1 11 pm, Sun 10 pm.

San Pietro W8 NEW £50 **3** **3** **3**

7 Stratford Rd 020 7938 1805 6–1A

"A good addition to the area" – this Italian newcomer has adopted the tucked-away Kensington mews site that was for ages Chez Patrick (RIP), and although "they've spent a fortune on doing it up" bears some comparison to its predecessor: it's still "rather cramped" ("they generally seat you upstairs nowadays"); and the food (majoring in fish and pizza like its sibling Portobello Ristorante) is "good but a little pricey". / W8 6RF; www.san-pietro.co.uk; Mon & Tue 9 pm, Fri & Sat 11.30 pm, Wed 10 pm, Thu 11 pm, Sun 5 pm.

The Sands End SW6 £54 3 3 4
135 Stephendale Rd 020 7731 7823 11–1B
Prince Harry brought Meghan Markle for lunch before their engagement to this backstreet Fulham gastro-boozer owned by one of his pals: a "great local spot", which fans say is "fantastically hospitable" and with consistently highly rated nosh too. / SW6 2PR; www.thesandsend.co.uk; @thesandsend; 11 pm.

Santa Maria £41 4 3 2
160 New Cavendish St, W1 020 7436 9963 2–1B **NEW**
92-94 Waterford Rd, SW6 020 7384 2844 6–4A
15 St Mary's Rd, W5 020 8579 1462 1–3A
"The best pizza in London" is a claim that's regularly made for the "tight on space, and always crowded" Ealing original of this small group (which "has expanded into the Red Lion pub next door") – "the ingredients are painstakingly sourced and the attention to detail on the dough is second to none!" With the chain expanding constantly however (they've just opened in Fitzrovia), overall marks support those who feel "the pizzas are good… perhaps not as good as the reputation". / www.santamariapizzeria.com; @SantaMariaPizza.

Santa Maria del Sur SW8 £54 3 4 3
129 Queenstown Rd 020 7622 2088 11–1C
"One of best steaks I've had in London", reports a satisfied customer of this "off the beaten track" Argentinian steakhouse with a strong following down Battersea way. There's also a list of exclusively South American wines. / SW8 3RH; www.santamariadelsur.co.uk; @StaMariadelSur; 10 pm.

Santini SW1 £82 2 2 2
29 Ebury St 020 7730 4094 2–4B
Frank Sinatra was among the notables who flocked to this sleek Belgravia Italian in its 80s heyday. Nowadays run by the founder Gino's daughter Laura, It still delivers an "imaginative menu" with Venetian specialities, a "pleasant atmosphere" and "good service", but even diehard supporters complain that it's "pricey" and sceptics say it's "gone over the hill". / SW1W 0NZ; www.santini-restaurant.com; @santinirest; 10.45 pm.

Santo Remedio SE1 £63 3 2 3
152 Tooley St 020 7403 3021 10–4D
"More-ish small Mexican dishes" feature at this hip new Bermondsey street food venture founded by Edson Diaz-Fuentes (ex-Wahaca) and his wife Natalie after a Kickstarter campaign (their short lived Shoreditch site closed in 2016 after property problems). Early reports are promising: "if you enjoy Mexican food, this is the place to come". Top Tip: "hot guacamole with crickets was interesting and delicious". / SE1 2TU; www.santoremedio.co.uk; @santoremediouk; 10.30 pm; closed Sun.

Santore EC1 £51 3 3 2
59-61 Exmouth Mkt 020 7812 1488 10–1A
"An antidote to Mediterranean chain restaurants", this "quite noisy" family-run Neapolitan in Exmouth Market excels for "the consistent quality of the pizzas". "We're not talking haute cuisine – just simple food, well done". Top Tip: "try the half-and-half pizza/calzone for something a bit different and very tasty". / EC1R 4QL; www.santorerestaurant.london; @Santore_london; 10 pm.

Sanxia Renjia £37 **3** **3** **2**
29 Goodge St, W1 020 7636 5886 2–1B
36 Deptford Broadway, SE8 020 8692 9633 1–3D
"If you can get over the location the food is wonderful" say fans of this
Chinese in "up-and-coming Deptford", blessed this year with an admiring
review of its fiery Sichuanese cooking by critic Jay Rayner. But while generally
upbeat, reporters don't go quite so overboard as The Observer's man did
(and the sole reporter who tried its Goodge Street sibling was
least impressed of all: "I was looking forward to hot, numbing food but what
came out was bland and under-seasoned, even if the staff were friendly and
decor, etc was fine").

Sapling E8 NEW £55
378 Kingsland Rd 020 7870 1259 14–2A
A new wine-focused restaurant and larder on Dalston's main drag from
restaurateur Bob Ritchie and sommelier Dan Whine (ace name for
a sommelier, huh?). The weekly changing list of around 36 wines, including
a number of grower Champagnes and other notable sparkling wines,
is sustainable, organic, biodynamic or low-intervention, available by the glass
and complemented by food from chef Jon Beeharry. Too little feedback for
a rating as yet, but one early report says it's all-round brilliant (as does the
Evening Standard's David Sexton). / E8 4AA; www.sapling-dalston.com;
@saplingdalston; Mon-Fri 10 pm, Sat & Sun 9 pm.

Saponara N1 £27 **4** **3** **3**
23 Prebend St 020 7226 2771 9–3D
"Tucked away off Upper Street", this genuine "small" deli/restaurant
"has 'Italy' sprayed all over it" – "a busy and popular" spot, featuring
"lots of regional ingredients", and with "great fresh pasta" and "consistently
fantastic pizza you can take away too". / N1 8PF; saponarapizzeria.co.uk;
Wed-Sat 10 pm, Tue 4.30 pm; closed Tue D, closed Sun & Mon.

Sapori Sardi SW6 £56 **3** **3** **2**
786 Fulham Rd 020 7731 0755 11–1B
"Simple, well-prepared dishes" and "a real Sardinian feel" continue
to inspire the small but enthusiastic fan club of this neighbourhood Italian
in Fulham. / SW6 5SL; www.saporisardi.co; @saporisardi; 10.30 pm, Sun 9.30 pm;
no Amex.

Saravanaa Bhavan HA0 £41 **4** **3** **2**
531-533 High Rd 020 8900 8526 1–1A
A "huge range of exceptional dosas" are the highlight of the menu at this
Wembley branch of a South Indian-based veggie chain, billed as the world's
biggest. "Great value" too, but note – "it's aimed at Indians, so not Anglo
curry". / HA0 2DJ; ww12.saravanabhavanuk.com; Sun-Thu 10.30 pm, Fri & Sat
11 pm.

Sardine N1 £58 **4** **4** **3**
15 Micawber St 020 7490 0144 13–1A
Aptly named, this "small but perfectly formed" two-year-old, near Old Street
station, is a "real find" on account of ex-Rotorino chef, Alex Jackson's very
accomplished southern French-inspired cooking – "thoughtful, without being
over-prepared and foam-ridden". "Intriguing wine list", too. / N1 7TB;
www.sardine.london; @sardinelondon; 10 pm.

Sargeants Mess EC3 NEW £56
Tower of London   020 3166 6949   10–3D
Mark Sargeant's starry name helped draw attention to this May 2018 opening under Tower Bridge, with an outside terrace looking onto the wall of the Tower of London (a venture between caterers CH&Co and Historic Royal Palaces). Stylewise, the menu seems somewhat 'wrapped up in the Union Jack' – eg cod 'n' chips, toad in the hole, treacle tart – but early press and online reviews suggest an all-too-traditional rendering of our nation's culinary classics. / EC3N 4AB; www.sargeantsmess.com; @SargeantsMess.

Sarracino NW6 £43 **3 3** 2
186 Broadhurst Gdns   020 7372 5889   1–1B
"Good pizzas" are the top recommendation at this "cheap 'n' cheerful" West Hampstead stalwart trattoria of long standing. / NW6 3AY; www.sarracinorestaurant.com; closed weekday L.

Sartoria W1 £77 **3 3 3**
20 Savile Row   020 7534 7000   4–3A
"Ideal for a business lunch" – D&D London's "large" and posh Italian (overseen by Francesco Mazzei) is widely seen as "a safe bet", with its combination of "well-spread out tables", "rather formal service" and "a reliable, good quality of food". The flipside of this assessment however is that it can also seem "very Mayfair but nothing special" and "overpriced for what it delivers". / W1S 3PR; www.sartoria-restaurant.co.uk; @SartoriaRest; 11 pm; closed Sat L & Sun.

Savoir Faire WC1 £47 **3 4** 2
42 New Oxford St   020 7436 0707   5–1C
"Don't be put off by the funny looks" of this muralled Gallic corner-bistro (family run on this site since 1995) – "it's really good" if you're looking for a good value meal in the environs of the British Museum. / WC1A 1EP; www.savoir.co.uk; 10.30 pm.

The Savoy Hotel, Savoy Grill WC2 £101 2 2 2
Strand   020 7592 1600   5–3D
For decades this "atmospheric" and "impressive", "panelled chamber" just off the foyer of the Strand's famous Art Deco landmark was London's power dining scene par excellence; and with its "old-fashioned" style and menu of "solid, traditional British staples" it remains a strong business favourite to this day. Under Gordon Ramsay's management of the last 15 years, however, its performance has always been up-and-down, and this year's was one of the weakest yet, with complaints about "average food" that's "not good value for money" and a "dingy" overall ambience. / WC2R 0EU; www.gordonramsayrestaurants.com; @savoygrill; midnight, Sun 11 pm.

The Savoy Hotel, Thames Foyer WC2 £97 2 **3 4**
The Savoy, The Strand   020 7420 2111   5–3D
For an "excellent tea in beautiful, opulent surroundings", this landmark hotel's "peaceful" lounge (set beneath a glass dome, and complete with pianist) is a "super location" providing a "classic" experience. We have no accounts of a full meal here (but prices on the all-day menu seem a tad fierce: eg £21 for a club sandwich with fries). / WC2R \N; www.fairmont.com/savoy-london; @fairmonthotels; 11 pm.

Scalini SW3 £86 **3 3 3**
1-3 Walton St   020 7225 2301   6–2C
"If you're looking for a rock-solid, traditional Italian restaurant, then look no further", say devotees of this "loud but great fun" outfit just "a stone's throw from Harrods". There's a "fabulous atmosphere" and the menu, which is "just what you would expect", is "executed with complete assurance". / SW3 2JD; www.scalinilondon.co.uk; 11 pm; No shorts.

Scarlett Green W1 NEW £62
4 Noel St   020 7723 3301   4–1C
A new opening spot from The Daisy Green Collection (Daisy Green, Timmy Green, Beans Green) on the former site of Timberyard in Soho, serving bottomless brunch and an extensive Aussie wine list. It opened in late May 2018 after the conclusion of our survey. / W1F 8JB; www.daisygreenfood.com; @daisygreenfood; midnight, Sun 10.30 pm.

Schmaltz Truck EC2 NEW £10   5 3 3
Exchange Square   no tel   13–2B
"An unmissable food experience in Broadgate" – this "amazingly decorated", "state-of-the-art" food truck (complete with funky floral design) offers "restaurant grade, stylish fast-food" from a "high quality all-chicken menu of sandwiches (using a whole breast), soups and a burger". It's "exceptional value" and "the execution of the concept is outstanding": rolls are made teardrop-shaped, better to fit the chicken breasts. The birds themselves are all French Label Rouge, and seared and roasted with the skin on. / EC2M 2QA; www.schmaltzlondon.com; @schmaltzlondon; closed Mon-Fri D, closed Sat & Sun.

Scott's W1 £85   4 4 5
20 Mount St   020 7495 7309   3–3A
"You feel like you are somebody on walking in and the gloss stays with you for a while after you leave" at Richard Caring's "legendary" Mayfair veteran (007's favourite lunch spot), whose "classically elegant" interior "oozes class", and where "every table looks like they're famous". On the menu – "sensational", "classic fish dishes" and "some of the best seafood in London" – indeed, only Sheekeys keeps it from being voted London's best in that department (although, unlike its stablemate, here "tables are far-enough apart for business"). All this "glam, glam, glam" comes with a slight edge though: in particular, the "very professional" service "can come with an attitude that matches the A-list clientele". / W1K 2HE; www.scotts-restaurant.com; 10.30 pm, Sun 10 pm; booking max 6 may apply.

Scully SW1 NEW £62   5 5 3
Saint James's Market   020 3911 6840   4–4D
"A breath of fresh air in the stuffy world of gastronomic London" – this stupendous first solo venture from former Nopi head chef Ramael Scully opened in St James's Market in early 2018 creating 'out there' fusion fare which reflects his heritage… which is Chinese/Indian/Irish/Balinese! He's assembled "a joyful, creative, team of people who care and love food" and results are "exceptional in every sense": "innovative food that's a simple and pure joy" and "staff who make a visit a very special occasion". / SW1Y 4QU; www.scullyrestaurant.com; @scully_ldn; Tue-Thu 8.30 pm, Fri 9 pm, Sat 9.30 pm, Sun 7 pm.

Sea Containers, Mondrian London SE1 £69   1 2 2
20 Upper Ground   020 3747 1063   10–3A
"Way overpriced" – this "noisy" nautical-themed dining room on the South Bank near Blackfriars Bridge has "amazing views of the river" (if from ground-floor level) but the "silly, confusing menu" of sharing plates is simply "not appropriate for a high-end hotel". The "bottomless fizz" and "burgers-and-brunch catering that masquerades as dining" are clues that it's "probably focused on the tourist wallet". / SE1 9PD; www.seacontainersrestaurant.com; @MondrianLDN; 11 pm.

Sea Garden & Grill SW17 NEW £40 444
Broadway Market, 29 Tooting High St   020 8682 2995   11–2C
"Fabulous new fish restaurant in Tooting Market" with a "delicious and fresh" selection of seafood dishes, run with charm by antiques dealer, Jimmy Luttman. The set-up is very similar to that at Plot (see also) – you eat at communal tables in the covered market, or the counter with open kitchen beyond. / SW17 0RJ; www.seagardenandgrill.co.uk; @theseagardenuk; Tue-Thu 10 pm, Fri & Sat 11 pm; closed Tue-Fri L, closed Sun & Mon.

Seafresh SW1 £50 322
80-81 Wilton Rd   020 7828 0747   2–4B
This veteran Pimlico fish restaurant is "always reliable and satisfying". There are few frills, but it has "become much more upmarket" with "delicious grilled fish" – "although the set menu haddock or cod and chips remains popular", "especially with taxi drivers". "The main problem is getting a table – it's so popular with large parties of visiting tourists". / SW1V 1DL; www.seafresh-dining.com; @SeafreshLondon; 10.30 pm; closed Sun.

Searcys St Pancras Grand NW1 £57 213
The Concourse   020 7870 9900   9–3C
The "beautiful Art Deco setting" of this modern railway dining room raises expectations which are all too often "disappointed" by the meal. There's a real sense of an opportunity missed, with Searcys performance and "poor service" too reminiscent of the bad old days of British Rail. / NW1 2QP; www.searcys.co.uk; @SearcyStPancras; 10 pm, Sun 7.15 pm.

The Sea Shell NW1 £55 322
49 Lisson Grove   020 7224 9000   9–4A
"An institution for decades" – this famous "fish and chippery" in Lisson Grove traces its origins back almost a century and took its current name in 1964 (but don't go expecting period decor – the interior's not unpleasant but anodyne). "Eat in or take away, generous portions and freshly cooked". / NW1 6UH; www.seashellrestaurant.co.uk; @SeashellRestaur; 10.30 pm; closed Sun.

Season Kitchen N4 £49 332
53 Stroud Green Rd   020 7263 5500   9–1D
"Superlative seasonal veg" but also "great steaks" top the bill at this Finsbury Park fixture. There's a "small, changing menu" of "interesting dishes", many of which you can order in either 'starter' or 'main-course' size, and "you just know they have a passion for fine cooking". / N4 3EF; www.seasonkitchen.co.uk; @seasonkitchen; Sun-Thu 10 pm, Fri & Sat 10.30 pm; D only.

Sen Viet WC1 £20 432
119 King's Cross Rd   020 7278 2881   9–3D
"Good food in a bit of a culinary desert" makes it worth knowing about this "useful Vietnamese pit-stop" in the thinly provided southern fringes of King's Cross, which offers "freshly cooked, decent spicing and excellent value for money". / WC1X 9NH; senviet.uk; 11 pm.

Señor Ceviche W1 £51 333
Kingly Ct   020 7842 8540   4–2B
An "interesting attempt at Peruvian food" in Soho's thronging Kingly Court that's consistently well-rated. It's a lively spot too, if "cramped and extremely noisy". / W1B 5PW; www.senor-ceviche.com; @SenorCevicheLDN; 11 pm, Sun 10 pm; booking max 6 may apply.

Serge et Le Phoque W1 £38 2 3 3

The Mandrake Hotel, 20-21 Newman St 020 3146 8880 3–1D
There's a stark contrast between the vast number of newspaper column
inches generated by Charles Pelletier and Frédéric Peneau's dining room
in this year-old Fitzrovia boutique-hotel dining room (whose Hong Kong
sibling has a Michelin star) and the low level of reporter interest it inspires.
Moreover such feedback as we have is very mixed. / W1T 1PG;
www.themandrake.com; Tue-Fri 10.30 pm, Sun & Mon ; closed Sun & Mon
D, closed Sat.

Seven Park Place SW1 £112 4 4 3

7-8 Park Pl 020 7316 1620 3–4C
Chef William Drabble maintains a low profile but his "expert cuisine"
inspires a small but smitten fan club for this under-the-radar dining room
in a swish St James's hotel – a "cosy room with enough room between tables
for privacy". "He remains in the kitchen, where he belongs, and remains
my favourite chef!" / SW1A 1LS; www.stjameshotelandclub.com; @SevenParkPlace;
10 pm; closed Sun & Mon.

Sexy Fish W1 £98 1 1 2

1-4 Berkeley Sq 020 3764 2000 3–3B
"Crammed with people taking selfies, dodgy looking businessmen and
hapless, concierge-victim tourists", Richard Caring's "bling bling" Mayfair
venture is a bad case of "too much spent on the decor and not enough
concentration on the food"; and with its huge prices and "appalling service
(unless you're spending £000's)" it can end up feeling like "a horrendous
ripoff and an all round horrible experience". More upbeat reporters do find
its luxurious seafood format "memorable… just best enjoyed at someone
else's expense!". Top Tip: "the best ambience is at lunch, at dinner
it changes quite dramatically… not in the most positive way". / W1J 6BR;
www.sexyfish.com; @sexyfishlondon; 11 pm, Sun 10 pm; booking max 6 may apply.

Shackfuyu W1 £46 4 3 3

14a, Old Compton St 020 7734 7492 5–2A
"Perfect Westernised Japanese food" – Bone Daddies's Soho sister has
a "hip atmosphere and great staff", and provides an object lesson
in "how to do fusion cuisine". "The tasting menu is a bargain at £30 as it
includes all their signature dishes". Top Tip: "Kinako French toast with
Matcha is a delight" – "how can bread and ice cream be this good?".
/ W1D 4TH; www.bonedaddies.com/restaurant/shackfuyu; @shackfuyu; 10.30 pm;
no booking.

Shahi Pakwaan N2 £31 5 4 3

25 Aylmer ParadeAylmer Rd 020 8341 1111 1–1B
"Authentic Hyderabadi cooking and attentive service" has helped this "great
local" – a year-old shop conversion in East Finchley – "build up a very good
reputation in a short time" and it's consistently rated for its excellent value.
/ N2 0PE; www.shahipakwaan.co.uk; Mon-Thu, Sat, Fri 11 pm, Sun 10 pm; closed
Fri L.

Shake Shack £29 **3****2****2**

Nova, 172 Victoria St, SW1 01923 555188 2–4B
80 New Oxford St, WC1 01925 555171 5–1B
24 The Market, WC2 020 3598 1360 5–3D
Boxpark Wembley, Olympic Way, HA9 no tel 1–1A **NEW**
The Street, Westfield Stratford, E20 01923 555167 14–1D
45 Cannon St, EC4 01923 886211 10–3B **NEW**

NYC star-restaurateur Danny Meyer's global operation was founded as a hot-dog cart in a New York park in 2001 and has found success in London as elsewhere. "Admittedly the burgers are pretty good", but ratings support those who feel "they are not that amazing versus others" and likewise that "there's nothing in the decor to make you want to hang around". Recent openings include Cannon Street and a new outlet is scheduled at Boxpark Wembley in late 2018. / WC2 & E14 11 pm, Sun 9 pm-10.30 pm; E20 9.30 pm, Fri & Sat 11 pm.

Shampers W1 £47 **3****4****4**

4 Kingly St 020 7437 1692 4–2B

"Still doing it right after 30 years" – "this reliable old friend ain't bust so they haven't fixed it". "They don't make them like this any more!", but if you want to see what a wine bar looked like in the 1970s, this "lively and fun" Soho venue perfectly fits the bill. It helps that "the owner, Simon, takes a personal interest", and presides over "an extensive list of wines, many of them by the glass"; plus "a varied and well-cooked menu". / W1B 5PE; www.shampers.net; @shampers_soho; 11 pm; closed Sun.

The Shed W8 £58 **3****4****3**

122 Palace Gardens Ter 020 7229 4024 7–2B

"Unusual, intriguing and packed to the gunnels" – the Gladwin family's quirky, rustic farm-to-fork outfit just off Notting Hill Gate – on a small site which old-timers still recall as The Ark (long, RIP) – can be "noisy", but the British seasonal tapas is "of good quality" and service is "good-humoured". / W8 4RT; www.theshed-restaurant.com; @theshed_resto; 10.30 pm; closed Mon L & Sun.

J Sheekey WC2 £81 **3****4****4**

28-34 St Martin's Ct 020 7240 2565 5–3B

"A proper, old-school London tradition that never fails" – Richard Caring's "beautiful and iconic" Theatreland classic (est 1896) remains both the survey's No 1 most-talked-about destination and also its top choice for fish. You approach its intriguing etched-glass façade via a Dickensian alley, off St Martin's Lane, and once inside navigate a succession of "charming", "old-fashioned small rooms" presided over by "slick" and "professional" staff. There's "a great buzz" – almost "too noisy" – and even if "tables are a little close for a private conversation" it is "particularly enjoyable for late, relaxing dinners after a show". When it comes to the "traditional" cuisine, "they are not trying to reinvent the wheel" – "dishes are not particularly delicate, creative or ambitious, but they are generous", "not overly mucked-about-with", and "showcase the quality of the produce on the plate". The wide-ranging menu of "fish and seafood galore" delivers "all you could want from the oceans!", but it's the down-to-earth "brilliant, warming, rich and comforting fish pie" that's actually its best-known option. Ratings were higher here five years ago, and the venue's ongoing "expansion has not helped standards". That said its level of achievement has remained incredibly impressive and on virtually all accounts "it's a cherished, special place". / WC2N 4AL; www.j-sheekey.co.uk; @JSheekeyRest; 11.30 pm, Sun 10 pm; booking max 6 may apply.

J Sheekey Atlantic Bar WC2 £68 3 3 4
28-34 St Martin's Ct 020 7240 2565 5–3B
"Classic small plates" of "fantastic quality seafood", "served in a 1930's-style atmosphere" have evolved a separate, highly popular identity for Sheekey's "bustling" and "beautiful" adjacent bar, which fans say is "better than the restaurant!" and whose relatively "informal" approach is particularly "great for pre-/post-theatre". Its ratings don't hit the heights they once did however, with the odd gripe that "while the welcome was warm, the food was nothing to write home about". / WC2N 4AL; www.j-sheekey.co.uk; @JSheekeyRest; midnight, Sun 10.30 pm; booking max 3 may apply.

Shepherd's SW1 £57 3 3 4
Marsham Ct, Marsham St 020 7834 9552 2–4C
"Perfect for a business lunch… and not just for politicians" – this resurrected traditional dining room is a well-known politico troughing spot, with well-spaced tables and old-school decor. One or two reporters feel "it's not up to the mark of previous years", but typically feedback is full of praise for its "charming staff" and "wonderful British dishes at reasonable prices". / SW1P 4LA; www.shepherdsrestaurant.co.uk; @shepherdsLondon; 10.30 pm; closed Sat & Sun.

Shikumen,
Dorsett Hotel W12 £55 4 3 2
58 Shepherd's Bush Grn 020 8749 9978 8–1C
"Excellent dim sum and Peking duck" backed up by a "laudably original menu" and "beautiful presentation" make this slick operation overlooking grimy Shepherd's Bush Green a culinary standout in West London. The setting, in an upmarket modern hotel, is also "unexpectedly smart for SheBu". / W12 5AA; www.shikumen.co.uk; @ShikumenUK; 10.30 pm.

Shilpa W6 £34 4 2 1
206 King St 020 8741 3127 8–2B
"Skilfully blended flavours in sensational dishes" ("delicious vegetarian" and "dazzling seafood") come as a total surprise at this utterly nondescript looking Keralan café, in an anonymous row of restaurants near Hammersmith town hall. "No 'two-pot' cooking here – clear use of fresh herbs and spices". It's also "extraordinarily good value". Any gripes? Well, the room is pretty "downbeat" and "you may have to wait while they churn out the take-aways". / W6 0RA; www.shilparestaurant.co.uk; Sun-Wed 11 pm, Thu-Sat midnight.

Shoryu Ramen £48 3 3 2
9 Regent St, SW1 no tel 4–4D
3 Denman St, W1 no tel 4–3C
5 Kingly Ct, W1 no tel 4–2B
Broadgate Circle, EC2 no tel 13–2B
"Tasty (and filling) noodle dishes and decent quality sashimi" draw a steady crowd to these Japanese pit stops: a "good option in busy, trendy areas", even if "space is cramped" and "you might have to queue". / 11 pm-midnight, Sun 9.30 pm-10 pm; E14 9 pm, Sun 6 pm; no booking (except Kingly Ct).

Shu Xiangge Chinatown W1 NEW
10 Gerrard St 07552 388888 5–1C
If you crave authenticity and offal in equal portions, this new 2018 opening on Chinatown's main drag (sibling to an existing operation in Holborn) looks like it may be the place for you. A traditional Sichuan hot pot specialist, choose from over 80 ingredients – from assorted types of tripe, aorta and brain to wagyu beef and seafood. / W1D 5PD; www.chinatown.co.uk/en/restaurant/shu-xiangge; @chinatownlondon; Tue-Thu 10 pm, Fri & Sat 10.30 pm, Mon 9.30 pm, Sun 9 pm.

The Sichuan EC1 £57 3 2 2
14 City Rd 020 7588 5489 13–2A
"Reliably tasty Sichuanese food" makes it worth remembering this Sichuan
two-year-old, near the entrance to the Honourable Artillery Company.
/ EC1Y 2AA; www.thesichuan.co.uk; Sun-Thu 10.30 pm, Fri & Sat 11 pm.

Sichuan Folk E1 £45 4 3 2
32 Hanbury St 020 7247 4735 13–2C
"The hot pots are exceptional… some of which are very hot!", according
to fans of this *"great Sichuanese"*. *"It's not the most attractive restaurant,
but the food makes a trip well worth it!"* / E1 6QR; www.sichuan-folk.co.uk;
10.30 pm; no Amex.

Signor Sassi SW1 £65 2 3 3
14 Knightsbridge Green 020 7584 2277 6–1D
"You get what it says on the tin" according to fans of this classic trattoria
of many years standing near Harrods (nowadays part of the glossy San
Carlo group) who acclaim its *"great atmosphere"* and for whom it's often
a long-term favourite. Alongside strong praise, a couple of off-reports
dragged down ratings this year – hopefully just a blip. / SW1X 7QL;
www.signorsassi.co.uk; @SignorSassi; 11.30 pm.

Silk Road SE5 £23 5 2 1
49 Camberwell Church St 020 7703 4832 1–3C
This *"amazing Uighur canteen in the depths of Camberhell"* serves
"incredible" food with *"punchy flavours and interesting textures"* from
China's northwestern Xinjiang province – *"homemade noodles, dumplings,
stews, & lamb skewers"* – *"without any fanfare"*. It's *"cash-only (and very
cheap)"*, *"noisy"*, with *"communal benches and abrupt service"* – *"so don't
go for a quiet romantic evening"*. Top Tip: *"lamb and fat chunks is mind-
blowing"*. / SE5 8TR; 11 pm; closed Mon-Sun L; cash only; no booking.

Simpson's in the Strand WC2 £76 2 2 3
100 Strand 020 7420 2111 5–3D
"The revamp seems to have done them good" at this legendary temple
of traditional British cuisine (with origins back to 1828) –
and most famously roast beef – which finally seems to be re-emerging after
many, many years in the doldrums. Yes, it can still appear all too touristy
and expensive, but *"the iconic building still has a lot of atmosphere"*, and its
"olde English staples" receive very much more consistent praise since its
refurb – *"it is one of the rare places in London where you can get traditional
carvery on a trolley which tastes good!"* Perhaps in keeping with the story
of renewal, new chef Adrian Martin (who previously oversaw Annabel's and
Harry's Bar) took over as chef from William Hemming in August 2018.
/ WC2 0EW; www.simpsonsinthestrand.co.uk; @simpsons1828; 11 pm, Sun 8 pm;
No trainers.

Simpson's Tavern EC3 £41 1 3 5
38 1/2 Ball Ct, Cornhill 020 7626 9985 10–2C
"Olde English tradition lives on" at this ancient chophouse down
a picturesque alleyway: a City institution dating from 1757. *"It could be a
museum of the British restaurant"* with its *"engaging service that treats you
like one of the boys"*, Dickensian interior and *"authentic period food"*,
including daily roasts and house special 'stewed cheese'. / EC3V 9DR;
www.simpsonstavern.co.uk; @SimpsonsTavern; Tue-Fri, Mon 3.30 pm; closed Tue-Fri,
Mon D, closed Sat & Sun.

Sinabro SW11 £64 4 4 3
28 Battersea Rise 020 3302 3120 11–2C
Little Battersea Rise bistro (20 covers) which receives outstanding ratings
from locals for its deftly executed modern British cooking and appealing
style. / SW11 1EE; www.sinabro.co.uk; @SinabroLondon; Tue-Thu 10 pm, Fri & Sat
10.30 pm; closed Tue-Thu L, closed Sun & Mon.

Singapore Garden NW6 £49 3 3 2
83a Fairfax Rd   020 7624 8233   9–2A
"Utterly reliable and (even more welcome) reasonably priced", this "always packed" pan-Asian veteran in an anonymous Swiss Cottage shopping parade offers a mix of Chinese, Malaysian and Singaporean dishes. Giles Coren of The Times heads its list of admirers. / NW6 4DY; www.singaporegarden.co.uk; @SingaporeGarden; Sun-Thu 11 pm, Fri & Sat 11.30 pm.

Singburi Royal Thai Café E11 £23 4 3 3
593 Leytonstone High Rd   020 8281 4801   1–1D
"A brill' little Leytonstone local" that "feels like sitting in someone's front room". "No thrills, just great Thai food and BYO to boot!". / E11 4PA; @SingburiThaiCaf; 10.30 pm, Sun 10 pm; closed Tue-Sun L, closed Mon; cash only.

Six Portland Road W11 £58 4 5 3
6 Portland Rd   020 7229 3130   7–2A
"An exceptional local" – this "small" modern bistro in Holland Park attracts folks from neighbouring postcodes and beyond with its "most delicious" Gallic-influenced dishes (from an ex-Terroir team) and "an interesting wine list with some unusual choices". One or two reporters discern "a lack of ambience", but for most people it's a "cosy" place with particularly "charming" service. / W11 4LA; www.sixportlandroad.com; @SixPortlandRoad; 10 pm; closed Mon & Sun D.

Sketch, Lecture Room W1 £148 3 3 4
9 Conduit St   020 7659 4500   4–2A
First timers can "look around in disbelief at the over-the-top decor" on the first floor of this huge Mayfair palazzo (and that's before the call of nature takes them to the 'Swarovski Crystal Bathrooms'), and it is a "most opulent" and "seductive" setting in which to enjoy ambitious cuisine overseen by überchef Pierre Gagnaire. It's ratings took a dive this year however, as its vertiginous prices can seem as overblown as the interior design (it doesn't help that "sadly it looks like the Gourmet Rapide lunch has been guillotined"). / W1S 2XG; www.sketch.uk.com; @sketchlondon; 10 pm; closed Tue-Thu L, closed Sun & Mon; No trainers; booking max 6 may apply.

Sketch, Gallery W1 £90 1 2 3
9 Conduit St   020 7659 4500   4–2A
The "pure opulence" of this Mayfair hangout for the art and fashion crowd – with David Shrigley's "camp and ridiculous", pink-walled contemporary baroque decor – makes it many fashionista's "favourite, special place". Foodwise, it's "all very nice... but not really, at that price". Top Tip: the whole point of a meal is the chance to visit the egg-shaped toilet pods. / W1S 2XG; www.sketch.uk.com; @sketchlondon; 11 pm, Sun 8 pm; booking max 6 may apply.

Skewd Kitchen EN4 £47 3 3 3
12 Cockfosters Parade   020 8449 7771   1–1C
"We eat out a lot, but finding this nearly on our doorstep made my year!" – a typically enthusiastic report on this popular modern Turkish grill in Cockfosters. / EN4 0BX; www.skewdkitchen.com; @SkewdKitchen; Mon & Tue 11 pm, Wed & Thu midnight, Fri & Sat 2 am, Sun 10.30 pm.

Skylon, South Bank Centre SE1 £76 2 2 4
Belvedere Rd   020 7654 7800   2–3D
"Fabulous view of the Thames through huge glass windows is so romantic after a stroll along the river" in the signature dining room at the Southbank Centre. Its cooking (mostly) avoided criticism this year, but even some fans acknowledge that while "the food's fine, but it's the setting that makes the place". (See also Skylon Grill.) / SE1 8XX; www.skylon-restaurant.co.uk; @skylonsouthbank; Tue-Thu 11 pm, Fri-Sun midnight; closed Sun D; No trainers.

Skylon Grill SE1 £70 2 2 **4**
Belvedere Rd   020 7654 7800   2–3D
"Thank goodness for the view" – the "saving grace" at this riverside grill in the South Bank arts centre, sibling to its D&D London stablemate next door. For most reporters, the food is little better than "average" – "not so much dialling as texting it in these days. Such a shame as the space is so wonderful!". / SE1 8XX; www.skylon-restaurant.co.uk; @skylonsouthbank; 10.30 pm, Sun 4 pm; closed Sun D.

Smith & Wollensky WC2 £102 2 2 2
The Adelphi Building, 1-11 John Adam St   020 7321 6007   5–4D
"Much maligned", say fans (often expense-accounters) of this outpost near the Strand of the famous NYC steakhouse chain, for whom its "confident cocktails", "stunning list of American wines" and "USDA cuts cooked to order make it a meat-lover's paradise – request a private booth and let the deal-making juices flow". The colossal ticket price however remains a major turnoff to sceptics, who say: "the steaks are ridiculously overpriced, and the wine list is designed only for oligarchs… who wouldn't be seen dead here in any case!" / WC2N 6HT; www.smithandwollensky.co.uk; @sandwollenskyuk; Mon-Thu 10.30 pm, Fri & Sat 11 pm, Sun 3.30 pm; closed Sun D; booking max 12 may apply.

Smith's Wapping E1 £71 **4 4 5**
22 Wapping High St   020 7488 3456   12–1A
"If you nab a window table, you get great views" of the Thames, Tower Bridge and City at this "clean-lined, sharp and professional" fish brasserie at the foot of a Wapping development (sibling to a long-standing original, in Ongar). A superb all-rounder, it deserves to be (even) better known given its mix of "expertly prepared" fish ("fresh ingredients handled with a light touch and the confidence not to over-egg things"), "very accommodating and unobtrusive service" and "impressive" location. / E1W 1NJ; www.smithsrestaurants.com; @smithswapping; Mon-Fri 10 pm, Sat 10.30 pm, Sun 5.30 pm; closed Sun D; No trainers.

Smiths of Smithfield, Top Floor EC1 £77 **3** 2 **3**
67-77 Charterhouse St   020 7251 7950   10–1A
"Superb views over Smithfield meat market, St Paul's and the Square Mile" can still make a trip to this spacious top-floor restaurant special. Once upon a time it was one of the top business lunch destinations for City types but achieves no such recommendations nowadays. But while it's "not quite as good as it used to be in its heyday, it still serves up some delicious steak". / EC1M 6HJ; www.smithsofsmithfield.co.uk; @thisissmiths; 10.30 pm, Sun 9.30 pm; closed Sat L & Sun; booking max 10 may apply.

Smiths of Smithfield, Dining Room EC1 £76 2 2 2
67-77 Charterhouse St   020 7251 7950   10–1A
This first-floor dining room of the large (but nowadays somewhat overlooked) Smithfield venue by the meat market was one of the 1990s fave raves. As "a safe choice for an informal business lunch" it still has its fans, but even some supporters acknowledge the food "is tasty without being amazing" and harsher critics dismiss the cooking as too "colourless". / EC1M 6HJ; www.smithsofsmithfield.co.uk; @thisissmiths; 10 pm; closed Sat L & Sun; booking max 12 may apply.

Smoke & Salt SW9 £41 5 4 3
53 Brixton Station Rd 07421 327556 11–1D
"Surely this is as much fun as you can have in a shipping container?" –
this year-old occupant of the 20-seat unit at Pop Brixton that formerly
housed Kricket (now permanent in Soho) focuses for its culinary inspirations
on preserving, fermenting and smoking and is *"well worth the trip
to Brixton"*. All reporters acclaim the *"inventive flavour combinations,
perfectly seasoned with fabulous style, and served up by Remi from the tiny
kitchen, plus charming bonhomie from Aaron front of house"*. One issue for
some customers – the background music isn't always in the background…
/ SW9 8PQ; www.smokeandsalt.com; @SmokeandSaltLDN; 10 pm, Sun 3 pm; closed
Mon-Fri L closed Sun D; may need 4+ to book.

Smokehouse Islington N1 £55 3 3 2
63-69 Canonbury Rd 020 7354 1144 9–2D
"Particularly good for special cuts of meat cooked to order" – a Canonbury
gastropub (with garden) specialising in grills as part of a modern British
menu, and *"great for a winter Sunday Roast"*. / N1 2RG;
www.smokehouseislington.co.uk; @smokehouseN1; 10 pm, Sun 9 pm; closed
weekday L.

Smokestak E1 £49 4 3 3
35 Sclater St 020 3873 1733 13–1C
"Incredible, slow-cooked, smoked meats" makes David Carter's moodily
designed grill-house, just off Brick Lane – arranged around a 2m width
of glowing charcoal, complete with grilling paraphernalia and dudish chefs –
a mecca for meat hungry hipsters. *"Good beer and cocktail selection"* too.
/ E1 6LB; www.smokestak.co.uk; @smokestakUK; 11 pm, Sun 9.30 pm.

Smoking Goat E1 £49 4 3 4
64 Shoreditch High St no tel 13–1B
*"Having lived in Bangkok for 7 years I am a tough critic of Asian food,
but these guys get it right every time!"* – Ben Chapman's *"vibey and totally
unique"* Thai BBQ mecca in Shoreditch delivers *"such original, authentic and
inventive flavour pairings and deeply satisfying plates of meat and fish"* and
it *"feels buzzing and exciting as soon as you step through the doors"*.
(The Soho branch closed last year). / E1 6JJ; www.smokinggoatsoho.com;
@SmokingGoatBar; Wed-Sat 11.30 pm, Sun 4 pm.

Snaps & Rye W10 £59 3 4 3
93 Golborne Rd 020 8964 3004 7–1A
"The daytime sandwiches are the prettiest creations" and the *"dinner
menus are incredible, with delicious seafood and beautiful flavours"*, say fans
of this Danish Diner in North Kensington, whose *"fairly recent refurbishment
has made it even cosier"*; tipped for brunch. / W10 5NL; www.snapsandrye.com;
@snapsandrye; Tue, Wed, Sun 5 pm, Thu-Sat 11 pm; closed Tue, Wed, Sun D,
closed Mon.

Snooty Fox N5 £40 3 2 3
75 Grosvenor Avenue 020 7354 9532 9–2D
"Busy but very friendly pub" near Canonbury station with a fine selection
of real ales, and whose food is well-rated, in particular roasts and burgers.
/ N5 2NN.

Social Eating House W1 £80 3 3 4
58-59 Poland St 020 7993 3251 4–1C
"It feels like it's where it's all happening … I LOVE IT!" – so say the many
fans of Jason Atherton's Soho operation – who believe it *"has it all…
buzzing atmosphere, superb cuisine – food you really want to eat!"* –
wondrous cocktail bar upstairs, and staff who buzz professionally too"*. Its
ratings were undercut this year however by a number of reporters who felt
that *"the food is good, but you do pay a lot for it"*. Top Tip: *"excellent set
lunch deal"*. / W1F 7NR; www.socialeatinghouse.com; @socialeathouse; 10.45 pm;
closed Sun.

Social Wine & Tapas W1   £60   4 4 3
39 James St   020 7993 3257   3–1A
*"Perfect sharing plates", "lovely staff" and a "wonderful evening
atmosphere – like being on the Continent" – have made this three-year-old
bar, restaurant and wine shop near Selfridges a "welcome addition" to Jason
Atherton's stable of Socials. On the downside, "it can work out expensive".
/ W1U 1EB; www.socialwineandtapas.com; @socialwinetapas; 11 pm, Sun 9 pm;
closed Sun; credit card required to book.*

Soif SW11   £59   3 3 3
27 Battersea Rise   020 7223 1112   11–2C
*There's "always something different and exciting to try" at this "bustling,
buzzy and slightly cramped" modern bistro in Battersea serving "tasty"
small plates and with a "brilliant focus on bio/organic/orange wines that not
many other places do" (it's part of Les Caves de Pyrène, which helped put
natural wines on the dining map). / SW11 1HG; www.soif.co; @Soif_SW11;
11 pm, Sun 4 pm; closed Mon-Wed L closed Sun D.*

Som Saa E1   £52   5 4 4
43a Commercial St   020 7324 7790   13–2C
*"Taste explosions abound" – "a variety of flavours, with inventiveness and
fun as well as staying true to authentic Thai cooking" – at this hip
Spitalfields two-year-old, which also features "a spacious bar with very good
cocktails". For many reporters, "it's simply the best Thai food I've had
in London" ("Thai food is a favourite of mine, I've tried lots of places over
the last 36 years, and this beats 'em all!") / E1 6BD; www.somsaa.com;
@somsaa_london; 10.30 pm, Mon 10 pm; closed Mon L, closed Sun; may need
4+ to book.*

Sông Quê E2   £35   3 3 2
134 Kingsland Rd   020 7613 3222   14–2A
*"Excellent pho, and a great buzzy atmosphere typical of the area" maintain
the appeal of this long-established "cheap 'n' cheerful" Vietnamese canteen,
on Shoreditch's busy Kingsland Road. / E2 8DY; www.songque.co.uk; 11 pm,
Sun 10.30 pm; no Amex.*

Sonny's Kitchen SW13   £56   3 3 2
94 Church Rd   020 8748 0393   11–1A
*Rebecca Mascarenhas's long-serving "Barnes institution" (nowadays part-
owned by top chef Phil Howard of Elystan Street) is, say fans, "back on
form", and while ratings may still be adrift of the glory days here,
most reporters feel its "consistently good" cooking and "always friendly
service" equip it as a place "worthy of special occasions as well as regular
lunch dates". / SW13 0DQ; www.sonnyskitchen.co.uk; @sonnyskitchen; Mon-Fri
10 pm, Sat 10.30 pm; closed Sun; booking max 5 may apply.*

Sophies Steakhouse   £63   2 2 2
42-44 Great Windmill St, W1   020 7836 8836   4–3D
311-313 Fulham Rd, SW10   020 7352 0088   6–3B
*"For steaks and burgers, entertaining the kids, and before a match
at Stamford Bridge", the original Fulham Road branch of this steak house
duo is still "buzzing and reliable, with good, well-cooked steaks".
By contrast its new Soho outlet inspires very mixed feedback – some praise
for "a good varied menu with lovely smokey flavours", but also those who
feel it's become "VERY expensive…", "seems to have lost its way…",
"wouldn't hurry back". / www.sophiessteakhouse.com; SW10 11.45 pm,
Sun 10.45 pm; WC2 12.45 am, Sun 10.45 pm; no booking.*

Sorella SW4 £51 **4** **3** **3**
148 Clapham Manor St 020 7720 4662 11–1D

An "excellent new Italian, with pasta to die for" – Irish chef Robin Gill's year-old relaunch of his popular The Manor, around the corner from his Clapham HQ The Dairy, takes culinary inspiration from the Amalfi coast. Reports are generally outstanding, and credit it with being a "worthy successor" on the site and "a valuable addition to the locality". There's a strong undercurrent though from those who were "left feeling rather underwhelmed" however – they say it's OK but "not as good as it thinks it is". Top Tip: "go à la carte, the bigger portions are more suited to the cuisine than grazing on the tasting menu". / SW4 6BX; www.sorellarestaurant.co.uk; @SorellaClapham; Mon & Tue 9 pm, Fri & Sat 11.30 pm, Wed 10 pm, Thu 11 pm, Sun 5 pm.

Southam Street W10 £63 **3** **2** **3**
36 Golborne Rd 020 3903 3591 7–1A

In the un-lovely shadow of the Trellick Tower, this ambitious newcomer occupies a stylishly converted three-floor Victorian boozer, whose latest former incarnation was as West Thirty Six (RIP). The second venture from Luca Longobardi and Chris Denney of 2017's smash hit '108 Garage', it's inspired surprisingly little press attention (perhaps because of its obscure-whatever-the-trendies-may-tell-you setting), but such feedback as we have is upbeat praising its "Asian-inspired" cuisine as "fresh, light and really great". The first floor Raw Bar serves Nikkei (a fusion of Peruvian and Japanese cuisines) while the second floor houses a private members' Tequila and Mezcal bar. / W10 5PR; www.southamstreet.com; @southamstreet; Tue-Thu midnight, Fri & Sat 1 am, Sun 4 pm; closed Tue-Thu L closed Sun D, closed Mon.

Soutine NW8 NEW
60 Saint Johns Wood High St awaiting tel 9–3A

Corbin & King's latest opening takes over the prime St John's Wood site vacated as part of the retrenchment of the Carluccio's chain. An opening some time in 2019 is expected, with such limited details as are available (for example Jeremy King's comment that it will be "Colbert meets Fischer's") suggesting a continental grand café style reminiscent of the group's other ventures. / NW8 7SH; Wed-Sat midnight.

Sparrow SE13 £44 **4** **5** **3**
Rennell St 020 8318 6941 1–4D

"A gem in Lewisham" – and perhaps the area's first proper neighbourhood restaurant – this yearling quickly hit the sweet spot with locals for "creative cuisine built on solid foundations" and "something that's a little different too". "Delightful" chefs Terry Blake and Yohini Nandakumar have impressive track records (St John, Bao, Merchant's Tavern, Pollen Street Social, The Square), and have put together a menu of "quirky and original sharing plates" with Sri Lankan influences. / SE13 7HD; sparrowlondon.co.uk; @sparrowlondon.

The Spread Eagle E9 NEW £31 **3** **3** **3**
224 Homerton High St 020 8985 0400 14–1C

"Vegan delight" is to be found at London's first 100%-vegan pub, occupying a prime spot in east Homerton. In most respects it feels just like any old fun gastropub, but even the drinks and cocktails are vegan! while the Latino-slanted fare is from the folk behind Club Mexicana; "fantastic!" / E9 6AS; www.thespreadeaglelondon.co.uk; @SpreadEagleLDN.

Spring Restaurant WC2   £85   3 3 4
New Wing, Lancaster Pl   020 3011 0115   2–2D
*Within gorgeous Somerset House, this "elegant and light-filled dining room"
makes "an exceptionally civilised place to eat", and Skye Gyngell's "enticing"
menu of "delicate, seasonal and delicious" dishes, plus "charming service"
contribute to an "airy, fresh and delightful" experience that better fulfilled its
promise this year as "one of the most impressive restaurants in this part
of London". In particular it's a romantic favourite: "I recommended it to
my son for an early date, and now he's marrying the lady concerned!"
/ WC2R 1LA; www.springrestaurant.co.uk; @Spring_Rest; 11 pm, Sun 10.30 pm;
closed Sun D; credit card required to book.*

The Square W1   £131   3 3 2
6-10 Bruton St   020 7495 7100   3–2C
*"Yet another new chef and change of design"… yet this twice relaunched
Mayfair temple of gastronomy (both times by recent buyer, Marlon Abela)
nowadays bears a not-so-different set of strengths and weaknesses from its
original self. Chef (since November 2017) Clement Leroy "maintains the
highest standards" and fans feel it "deserves to reclaim its position as one
of London's top tables" (although you can quibble as to whether the cuisine
is quite as good as under Phil Howard). Despite attempts to pep up the
room, it retains a "slightly downbeat ambience", but this doesn't put off the
expense accounters for whom it's always been a favourite, drawn in part
by its ever-formidable wine list. / W1J 6PU; www.squarerestaurant.com;
@square_rest; Mon-Thu 10 pm, Fri & Sat 10.30 pm; closed Sun; booking max 8 may
apply.*

Sri Suwoon SW1   £34   4 4 3
44 Hugh St   020 7828 0321   2–4B
*"A backstreet Pimlico gem just off the main thoroughfare in Victoria" –
this "brilliant neighbourhood Thai" wins raves from locals for its "authentic
specialities with just the right amount of spice". "Service is charming and
the room delightful". ("I recently revisited with two friends extremely
knowledgeable about Thai food and they raved on about it!"). / SW1V 4EP;
www.srisuwoon.com; @sri_suwoon; 11 pm; closed Mon & Tue, Sat L, closed Sun.*

St Leonards EC2 NEW   £70
70 Leonard St   020 7613 5346   13–1B
*Formerly the site of Eyre Brothers (sadly RIP) then very briefly the very
short-lived 70 Leonard St (not so sadly RIP) – now this Shoreditch venue has
been taken over by Jackson Boxer (of Brunswick House/LASSCO fame) and
Andrew Clarke and given a very Shoreditch makeover (lots of polished
concrete), plus an ice bar for raw fish and shellfish and open-hearth cooking
for meat and vegetables. Early press reviews ("cutting edge", "vivid",
"concentrated", "musky", "smokey acidity", "almost-too-pungent")
suggest the cuisine's certainly not boring, and arguably an expression
of "mad genius". / EC2A 4QX; stleonards.london; @stleonardsEC2.*

St Luke's Kitchen, Library WC2   £64   2 3 3
112 Saint Martin's Lane   020 3302 7912   5–4C
*Limited feedback this year on this "quirky" venue – "a slightly offbeat mix
of clubbiness and restaurant" in a boutique-guesthouse near the Coliseum,
whose cuisine is "of the fusion variety". Such as there is though praises it as
"a perfectly decent choice for a pre-theatre supper". / WC2N 4BD;
www.lib-rary.com; @LibraryLondon; 1 am; closed Sun; No trainers.*

Stecca SW10   £76
14 Hollywood Rd   020 7460 2322   6–3B
*All reports acknowledge the high quality of the cooking at this Chelsea
yearling, in a posh sidestreet near the Chelsea & Westminster Hospital
(with small rear garden). Its "high prices" though are another common
theme in feedback. / SW10 9HY; www.stecca.co.uk; Sun-Wed 10 pm, Thu-Sat
10.30 pm.*

Stem W1 NEW £61 4 4 3
5 Princes St 020 7629 9283 4–1A
Mark Jarvis, chef-patron of Anglo in Farringdon and Neo Bistro off Oxford Street, launched this smallish (35-cover) Mayfair newcomer in May 2018 just as the survey was closing. Early feedback is positive about the ambitious, seasonal British cuisine, from chef Sam Ashton-Booth (former head chef of Anglo) with options including a five-course tasting menu (with matching wine flight available) as well as à la carte and an express lunch. / W1J 0DW; www.stem-byneo.co.uk; @stemrestaurant; Tue-Sat, Mon 10.30 pm, Sun 3.30 pm; closed Mon L closed Sun D.

Stick & Bowl W8 £24 3 3 1
31 Kensington High St 020 7937 2778 6–1A
For Chinese chow as cheap as chips and chock full of flavour, this small, 1950s-style dive on posh Kensington High Street is just the ticket – it's not a foodie fave rave, but a 'good-nosh-for-not-a-lot-of-dosh' kind of joint. / W8 5NP; 10.45 pm; cash only; no booking.

Sticks'n'Sushi £59 3 2 2
3 Sir Simon Milton Sq, Victoria St, SW1 020 3141 8810 2–4B
11 Henrietta St, WC2 020 3141 8810 5–3D
113-115 King's Rd, SW3 awaiting tel 6–3C NEW
Nelson Rd, SE10 020 3141 8220 1–3D
58 Wimbledon Hill Rd, SW19 020 3141 8800 11–2B
Crossrail Pl, E14 020 3141 8230 12–1C
"Scandinavian sushi... sounds odd, but it works!" This Danish chain has proved a perhaps-unlikely hit, praised as "a concept that pays off" with enjoyably "fresh" and "eclectic" food and a "lively" style. "It has gotten much more expensive" however in recent times, and ratings have dipped accordingly. At the start of October 2018 they opened their biggest site yet on Chelsea's King's Road. / www.sticksnsushi.com; @sticksnsushi_UK; 10 pm, Wed-Sat 11 pm.

Sticky Mango at RSJ SE1 £47 2 3 2
33 Coin St 020 7803 9733 10–4A
A change of direction has seen this 30-year stalwart near the South Bank Arts Centre modify its name (from RSJ) and adopt an "Asian-influenced menu". To some extent, it's a case of 'plus ça change' – "the key attraction here has always been its list of Loire wines and proximity to the Festival Hall – changing the cuisine hasn't affected either" (nor the ambience, which has always teetered on the "lousy"). When it comes to the cooking views divide – what is "tasty" fare at "sensible prices" to fans is, to foes, "slightly bland and lacking kick". / SE1 9NR; www.stickymango.co.uk; @stickymangoldn; 10.30 pm; closed Sun.

Stockwell Continental SW8 NEW £43 3 3 3
169 South Lambeth Rd 020 3019 0757 11–1D
On the Stockwell site that was once popular as Rebatos (long RIP): this new venture hails from the same family as the renowned Canton Arms nearby, but in this case – a departure for this gastropub group – the focus is on Italian cooking, with a café (coffee, pastries, pizza) in the space that once was the tapas bar here, and more substantial fare in the rear restaurant. One early report captures it well: "not quite on a par with the other members of the Anchor & Hope stable yet. But the Roman style pizzas are a nice change from the heavier Neapolitans favoured by most. And the cured meats and antipasti are all good. The menu has been cleverly designed, which inevitably leads to raised eyebrows when the final bill arrives. This could become a local institution... but it's not quite there yet". / SW8 1XW; www.stockwellcontinental.com.

Story SE1   £154   3 3 3

199 Tooley St   020 7183 2117   10–4D

"Superb innovation" delivers a series of "sensational dishes" say devotees
of Tom Sellers's acclaimed culinary temple, near Tower Bridge, where
between eight and eleven courses of his experimental cuisine are delivered
according to the evening's 'story' (with a four-course format at lunch).
However, opinions diverged on the experience this year with doubters who
"don't understand the hype" and who find the concept "confused",
"misjudged", or "so expensive". As the survey was concluding it emerged
from a big refurb in May 2018, perhaps heralding a more consistent return
to form? / SE1 2UE; www.restaurantstory.co.uk; @Rest_Story; 9.15 pm; closed
Mon & Sun.

The Straight & Narrow E14   £55   2 3 3

Mosaic Building, 45 Narrow St   020 3745 8345   12–1B

Live music while you eat is a regular feature at this two-year-old piano bar
at the foot of a new development in Limehouse. Feedback is a bit up-and-
down but basically supportive: "better than expected, if a little
overpriced"… "struggling to find its identity as it keeps reinventing itself….
despite which it's a great, relaxed place for Sunday lunch and mid week
dinner". / E14 8DN; www.thestraightandnarrow.co.uk; @straightNpiano; 10 pm,
Sun 9 pm.

Street Pizza EC4 NEW   £45

10 Bread St   020 3030 4050   10–2B

'Bottomless' pizza (ie eat as much as you like for £15) plus a copious drinks
menu is the concept for the latest brand in the Gordon Ramsay stable,
which opened quietly on the ground floor of Bread Street Kitchen in the
City's One New Change development by St Paul's. Too little feedback for
a rating – online reviews are hit 'n' miss. / EC4M 9AJ;
www.gordonramsayrestaurants.com/street-pizza; @GRStreetPizza; Mon-Wed midnight,
Thu-Sat 3 am, Sun 10 pm.

Street XO W1   £98   2 2 2

15 Old Burlington St   020 3096 7555   4–3A

Superstar Spanish chef David Muñoz's nightclubby Mayfair yearling attracts
only very limited feedback, and it remains mixed. Fans of the Hispanic-Asian
fusion cuisine that he has concocted to great acclaim (and three Michelin
stars) in Madrid say the "exceptional" cooking here is "seriously
underrated". But they are not huge in number, and set against this is the
view that it is "tasty and well-presented but overpriced". / W1X IRL;
www.streetxo.com; @StreetXO_London; Mon-Wed 11 pm, Thu-Sat midnight,
Sun 9.30 pm; closed Mon L.

Sub Cult EC2   £14   5 3 2

Container, Finsbury Avenue Sq   no tel   13–2A

Gourmet US deli-style sub rolls score full marks from addicts of Ben
Chancellor and Gaz Phillips's four-year-old street food brand, which, as well
as weekend operations at Brockley and Maltby Street markets, can be found
during the week (from 8pm to 4pm) at their container in Broadgate.
/ EC2M 2PP; www.sub-cult.co.uk; @SubCultSubs; Mon, Wed & Thu, Sun 5 pm, Tue, Fri
10 pm, Sat 3.30 pm.

Sukho Fine Thai Cuisine SW6   £52   5 5 3

855 Fulham Rd   020 7371 7600   11–1B

"The best Thai food in southwest London" – and arguably the entire capital
– is found at this "lovely" if "always busy" (hence "very crowded") Fulham
shop conversion. Fans travel across town attracted by its "really interesting
and delicious menu" and service that's "charming and courteous".
/ SW6 5HJ; www.sukhogroups.com; 9.30 pm, Sun 4 pm.

Suksan SW10 £49 3 3 2
7 Park Walk   020 7351 9881   6–3B
"Admirable consistency" is a virtue of this "reliable neighbourhood gem"
on a Chelsea corner. Fans say it's "as good as its sibling" Sukho Fine Thai
Cuisine in Fulham, but its ratings have a little way to go to match its stellar
relative. / SW10 0AJ; www.sukhogroups.com; 10.45 pm, Sun 9.45 pm.

Sumak N8 £39 4 4 2
141 Tottenham Lane   020 8341 6261   1–1C
"Seriously tasty Turkish cuisine" – "a real cut above" and "very well priced"
– wins high ratings for this popular Crouch End fixture. "The welcome
is warm, service is efficient, and the decor is typically Turkish (murals and
slightly glitzy floor tiles)". / N8 9BJ; www.sumakrestaurants.co.uk; midnight,
Sun 11.30 pm.

The Summerhouse W9 £71 2 2 5
60 Blomfield Rd   020 7286 6752   9–4A
"On a summer day you forget you're in the middle of the city" at this
canalside spot in lovely Little Venice. Fans say its fish and seafood likewise
"warrants a journey", but it can also feel very "expensive", and too many
reporters say "it's all about the location" nowadays, citing "very average"
cooking and "disappointing service" too. / W9 2PA; www.thesummerhouse.co;
@FRGSummerhouse; midnight, Sun 11.30 pm; no Amex.

Sumosan Twiga SW1 £69 2 2 3
165 Sloane St   020 3096 0222   6–1D
"When I heard the restaurant was a fusion of Japanese and Italian, I was
sceptical!" – a perhaps natural reaction to this Belgravia outpost of the 20-
year-old, Moscow-based, luxury dining empire. Originally located in Mayfair
– where the style was purely Japanese-fusion – when it relocated to Sloane
Street a couple of years ago, it both acquired the 'Twiga' suffix to its name,
and also an Italian menu (presented side-by-side). Like its predecessors
on this tricky site (Monte's, Pengelley), this glossy operation inspires little
feedback as a result of a location whose primary passing trade is designer-
clad Eurotrash; and predictably it is sometimes dismissed as "overpriced"
and mediocre all-round; but some reporters do declare themselves "really
surprised and pleased with the culinary results". Top Tip: dip your toe in the
water with a visit to its glam second-floor cocktail bar. / SW1X 9QB;
www.sumosan.com; @sumosantwiga.

Sunday N1 £31 4 2 3
169 Hemingford Rd   020 7607 3868   9–2D
"Ridiculously good breakfasts and brunch" draw big queues to this popular
café, on the fringes of Islington ("if you ask how long until you're seated,
be prepared for a stony stare"). / N1 1DA; @sundaybarnsbury; 10.30 pm; closed
Mon, Tue D, Wed D & Sun D; no Amex.

Supawan N1 £45 4 4 2
38 Caledonian Rd   020 7278 2888   9–3D
"A fabulous spot near Kings Cross" offering "a busy, buzzy different take
on Thai cooking". "The food takes prominence" – "real care is evident in its
preparation, avoiding run-of-the-mill dishes so common elsewhere". / N1 9DT;
www.supawan.co.uk; closed Sun.

Super Tuscan E1 £51 3 4 3
8a Artillery Passage   020 7247 8717   13–2B
This "vibrant but understated Italian" hidden down an alley in the City
is "run by two Anglo-Italian brothers who clearly have a passion for
authentic food". It's "buzzy and cramped, with honest cooking using high-
quality ingredients", which are "imported weekly from small
specialist providers in Italy". / E1 7LJ; www.supertuscan.co.uk; 10 pm, Sun 4 pm;
closed Sat & Sun.

Sushi Atelier W1   £31   5 3 3
114 Great Portland St   020 7636 4455   2–1B
*"Sit at the counter for the full experience" at this traditional-ish Japanese
yearling in Fitzrovia – a new departure for the owners of the small
(and well-rated) Chisou group – consistently receiving excellent ratings for its
"delicious sushi and sashimi". / W1W 6PH; www.sushiatelier.co.uk;
@sushiatelierlondon; 5 pm.*

Sushi Bar Atari-Ya   £46   5 2 1
20 James St, W1   020 7491 1178   3–1A
1 Station Pde, W5   020 8896 3175   1–3A
75 Fairfax Rd, NW6   020 7328 5338   9–2A
*Though centrally made, the sushi is some of "the best and best-priced
in London" ("not surprising as they supply many of the top restos") at this
small collection of cafés, run by a Japanese food importer. "Don't expect
any ambience to write home about" – decor is "very basic" – while service
is "fine without being personable". Branches in N12 and W3 closed this
year, which also saw the group rebrand from plain 'Atari-Ya'.
/ www.sushibaratariya.co.uk; W1 8 pm, NW6 & W5 9.30 pm, W9 9 pm, N12 &
W3 6.30 pm, Sat & Sun 7 pm; NW6 closed Mon, W5 closed Mon & Tue.*

Sushi Bar Makoto W4   £48   4 3 1
57 Turnham Green Terrace   020 8987 3180   8–2A
*"An excellent range of inexpensive sushi and sashimi is served in an
unpretentious setting", at this "cheerful local sushi-café", in the foodie
parade of shops near Turnham Green station. / W4 1RP;
www.sushibarmakoto.co.uk; 10 pm, Sun 9 pm.*

Sushi Masa NW2   £40   3 4 3
33b Walm Lane   020 8459 2971   1–1A
*"A worthy successor to Sushi Say" – this "good neighbourhood Japanese
restaurant with a tatami mat booth at the back" is doing "something not
easy to achieve" by (almost) filling the boots left by its predecessor.
/ NW2 5SH; 10.30 pm, Sun 9 pm.*

Sushi Tetsu EC1   £89   5 5 3
12 Jerusalem Pas   020 3217 0090   10–1A
*"Like dining in Japan!" – Toru Takahashi is "the real deal" and provides
an "intimate master sushi experience" at his "special" Clerkenwell 7-seater,
which "is without doubt the best sushi in London at this price point"
(and which some would argue invites comparison with The Araki, which
charges about 4x the price here). The only fly in the ointment is the
"ridiculous booking process" – it's just "so hard to get a seat". / EC1V 4JP;
www.sushitetsu.co.uk; @SushiTetsuUK; Tue-Fri 10 pm, Sat 9.30 pm; closed Tue-Sat L,
closed Sun & Mon.*

Sushisamba   £96   2 2 3
Opera Terrace, 35 The Market, WC2   020 3053 0000   5–3D
Heron Tower, 110 Bishopsgate, EC2   020 3640 7330   10–2D
*What's not to like at this "fabulous" 39th floor pan-Asian in the Heron
Tower (reached by western Europe's fastest lifts!) – the interior
is "very cool", "the views are to die for" and "the food just sings – punchy
flavours of sweet, sour, salty deliciousness". The answer, unfortunately,
is "slow and disorganised service" and "prices even higher than the
skyscraper it's based in" which leave far too many reporters nowadays
(including former fans) accusing it of "style over substance". Its long-awaited
new Covent Garden sibling – occupying the dramatic site that has seen
many chains come and go (most recently Brasserie Blanc) finally opens
in November 2018. / 1.30 am, Wed-Sat 2 am.*

Sutton and Sons £35 **4** **3** **2**
90 Stoke Newington High St, N16   020 7249 6444   1–1C
356 Essex Rd, N1   020 7359 1210   14–1A
240 Graham Rd, E8   020 3643 2017   14–1B
"Yummy" fresh fish and "crispy fat chips" all in "great value, generous portions" win raves – if from a small fanclub – for these "classy" chippies in Stokey, Hackney Central and Islington. October 2018 marks a first, with the launch of London's first vegan chippie at the Hackney Central branch (which is itself moving down the road to 218 Graham Road). / www.suttonandsons.co.uk; @sutton_and_sons; 10 pm, Fri & Sat 10.30 pm; E8 Fri 10 pm; no bookings.

The Swan W4 £52 **3** **4** **4**
1 Evershed Walk, 119 Acton Ln   020 8994 8262   8–1A
"Everything you could want from a pub" is to be found at this "quasi-rustic", panelled tavern, hidden away in a backstreet on the Chiswick / Acton borders: "unexpectedly sophisticated food" ("from a Mediterranean/Italian menu that delivers the classics as well as seasonal-inspired dishes"), "seamless, jolly yet gentle service", "terrific beer, wine and gin… and you get hydrangeas in the kid-friendly garden!" / W4 5HH; www.theswanchiswick.co.uk; @SwanPubChiswick; Sun-Thu 10.30 pm, Sat, Fri 11 pm; closed weekday L.

The Swan at the Globe SE1 £60 **3** **2** **4**
21 New Globe Walk   020 7928 9444   10–3B
The faux-Elizabethan tavern connected to Shakespeare's Globe theatre on the first floor has "great views over the river to St Paul's" and food – by chef Allan Pickett – that is "imaginative, seasonal, locally sourced and well executed without being pretentious". Top Tip: "gentleman's afternoon tea (beef sliders, Scotch egg and a tankard of beer instead of bubbles) is outstanding". / SE1 9DT; www.swanlondon.co.uk; @swanabout; Tue-Fri 10 pm, Sat 9.30 pm.

Sweet Thursday N1 £43 **3** **2** **3**
95 Southgate Rd   020 7226 1727   14–1A
You'll find a "friendly welcome" (and a good choice of wines) at this "very child-friendly" local pizza parlour and bottle shop in gentrified De Beauvoir Town. / N1 3JS; www.sweetthursday.co.uk; @Pizza_and_Wine; 11 pm, Sun 10.30 pm.

Sweetings EC4 £76 **3** **2** **4**
39 Queen Victoria St   020 7248 3062   10–3B
"A throwback to 100 years ago" – this "unique", "magnificently unchanged" Victorian relic is "an old school experience of the best sort" and a revered haunt for its pinstriped clientele attracted by "some of the finest fish and seafood". "Sitting at the bar is lovely and you get great attention from the waiting staff", or sit down at the back to a full meal of "black velvet in a tankard, followed by oysters and then lovely fish (perfectly cooked), with splendid jam sponge". That prices are slightly "outrageous" has always been part of the package. Except for private parties, it's always been a weekday lunch-only venue, but in September 2018, they seem to be experimenting with the odd evening service. / EC4N 4SA; www.sweetingsrestaurant.co.uk; @SweetingsLondon; closed Mon-Fri D, closed Sat & Sun; no booking.

Taberna Etrusca EC4 £58 **3** **2** **3**
9 -11 Bow Churchyard   020 7248 5552   10–2C
Limited but positive praise this year for the cooking at this long-established and traditional City Italian. It particularly comes into its own in summer, when you can eat on its al fresco patio and fully enjoy its quiet location, just off Bow Churchyard. / EC4M 9DQ; www.etruscarestaurants.com; Tue-Fri 10 pm, Mon 3.30 pm; closed Mon D, closed Sat & Sun.

The Table SE1 £48 3 2 2
83 Southwark St   020 7401 2760   10–4B
"After a bit of culture on the Southbank", this café-style contemporary haunt is a "go-to for a Saturday or Sunday brunch" – "prices are pretty fair, and they actually care about their vegan options". / SE1 0HX; www.thetablecafe.com; @thetablecafe; 10.30 pm; closed Mon D, Sat D & Sun D; booking weekdays only.

Table Du Marche N2 £55 3 3 2
111 High Rd   020 8883 5750   1–1B
"Onion soup, complete with toast, cheese & plenty of onions" typifies the "tasty" and "reasonably priced" Gallic fare at this "reliable" bistro two-year-old in East Finchley. Top Tip: "excellent value lunchtime prix fixe". / N2 8AG; www.tabledumarche.co.uk; @TableDuMarche; 11 pm, Sun 10.30 pm.

TAKA W1 £59 3 3 3
18 Shepherd Market   020 3637 7677   3–4B
Limited but positive all-round feedback on this small Mayfair newcomer which aims to bring affordably priced Japanese cooking to Shepherd Market, with a selection of robata and sushi (probably the way to go) dishes. / W1J 7QH; www.takalondon.com; @takamayfair; Mon-Thu 10.30 pm, Fri & Sat 10.45 pm; closed Sun.

Takahashi SW19 £48 5 5 3
228 Merton Rd   020 8540 3041   11–2B
"An unbelievably good neighbourhood find!" – "some of the best Japanese food ever!" and wonderfully "caring service" can be discovered "in a tiny room at this unlikely location": a deeply suburban parade near South Wimbledon tube station. The "sublime" and "mouth-watering" cuisine – "Japanese with a Mediterranean twist" – is freshly prepared by chef-proprietor Taka, formerly of Nobu. / SW19 1N; www.takahashi-restaurant.co.uk; @takahashi_sw19; 10 pm, Fri & Sat 10.30 pm, Sun 9 pm.

Tamarind W1 £91 4 4 3
20 Queen St   020 7629 3561   3–3B
"A consistent pleasure", this Mayfair pioneer of Indian fine dining (in 2001 the first Indian to bag a Michelin star) closed for six months in early 2018 for a complete revamp – and not before time, with reporters critical of the "passé fit-out". The October relaunch promises a 'private club atmosphere' with 'lighter' dishes and sharing plates under new head chefs Karunesh Khanna (ex-Amaya) and Manav Tuli (ex-Chutney Mary). / W1J 5PR; www.tamarindrestaurant.com; @TamarindMayfair; 10.30 pm, Sun 10 pm; closed Sat L; No trainers.

Tamarind Kitchen W1 £54 3 4 4
167-169 Wardour St   020 7287 4243   4–1C
"Great Indian with food with a real vibe in the heart of Soho" earns plaudits for this offshoot of Mayfair's upscale Tamarind, albeit at more "mid-level prices". The pedigree shows, though, in its "complex spices and luxurious setting". / W1F 8WR; tamarindkitchen.co.uk; Sun-Thu 11 pm, Fri & Sat 11.30 pm.

Tamp Coffee W4 £42 3 4 4
1 Devonshire Rd   no tel   8–2A
"A bizarre combination of (superb) flat whites and empañadas… it somehow works!" – say devotees of this coffee bar on Chiswick's "lovely Devonshire Road". This "quality coffee joint" has "great snacks" and "plenty of papers to while away a Saturday morning". / W4 1N; www.tampcoffee.co.uk; @tampcoffee; L only; booking max 6 may apply.

Tandoor Chop House WC2 £49 4 4 3
Adelaide St   020 3096 0359   5–4C
"Wow, every dish on the menu is a treat" at this year-old modern culinary mashup backed by Ennismore Capital, which combines the trad British chophouse with northern Indian techniques and spicing, in an atmospheric, wood-panelled space, just behind St Martin in the Fields. / WC2N 4HW; tandoorchophouse.com; @tandoorchop; 11 pm, Sun 10.30 pm; booking max 6 may apply.

Tapas Brindisa £59 3 3 2
18-20 Rupert St, W1   020 7478 8758   4–3D
46 Broadwick St, W1   020 7534 1690   4–2B
18-20 Southwark St, SE1   020 7357 8880   10–4C
"Arrive early to avoid the queue", especially if you visit the *"very busy"* original Borough Market branch of this well-known and *"consistently good"* tapas chain, which *"rarely drops the ball and is a safe bet for a swift and enjoyable meal"*. Of the other branches, the South Kensington one is very pleasantly located near the tube with extensive pavement seating: *"go on a summer's day and sit outside, watching the world pass by"*. / www.brindisakitchens.com; @Brindisa; 11 pm-11.30 pm, EC2 12.30 am, Morada Sun 4 pm; Morada closed Sun D; SE1 no booking.

Taqueria W11 £42 3 3 3
141-145 Westbourne Grove   020 7229 4734   7–1B
For a vivacious, *"cheap 'n' cheerful"* bite, this buzzy, well-established Mexican cantina on the border where Notting Hill meets Bayswater is a popular choice, with practically all reporters impressed by its authentic tacos, Latino beers and cocktails. / W11 2RS; www.taqueria.co.uk; @TaqueriaUK; 11 pm, Fri & Sat 11.30 pm, Sun 10.30 pm; no Amex.

Tarantella Ristorante Pizzeria W4 £50 3 3 3
4 Elliot Rd   020 8987 8877   8–2A
"Tiny family-run Italian near Turnham Green station" – *"nothing flash"* but a popular *"cheap 'n' cheerful"* local that's *"a cut above the average"* with *"great value"*, *"simple"* home cooking (*"great homemade pasta"*), plus *"friendly"* service: *"feels like you're on hols in Italia!"* / W4 1PE; Mon-Fri 10.45pm, Sat & Sun 10.45 pm.

Taro £36 3 2 2
61 Brewer St, W1   020 7734 5826   4–3C
193 Balham High Rd, SW12   020 8675 5187   11–2C
44a Cannon St, EC4   020 7236 0399   10–3B
"Fast, efficient, delicious and great value" – what more could you want from a Japanese canteen? The Soho original, now in its 20th year, is *"always packed"*. These days there are also branches in the City and Balham. / www.tarorestaurants.co.uk; W1F 10.30 pm, Fri & Sat 11 pm, Sun 9.30 pm; W1D 10.30 pm, Fri & Sat 10.45 pm, Sun 9.30 pm, Mon 10 pm; no Amex; Brewer St only small bookings.

Tas £45 2 2 2
"Quick and cheerful", with *"tasty Turkish food"*, this chain has a strong presence on the South Bank, and its branch adjacent to Shakespeare's Globe is especially popular (see Tas Pide). Regulars say the operation is *"reliable and reasonable"* – even if it has over the years *"lost some of its allure"*. / www.tasrestaurant.com; 11.30 pm, Sun 10.30 pm; EC4 Sat 5 pm; 72 Borough High St 6 pm, Sat & Sun 4 pm; EC4 closed Sat D & Sun, cafe SE1 closed D.

Tas Pide SE1 £37 233
20-22 New Globe Walk   020 7928 3300   10–3B

"A reliable quick meal before the Globe – never fails!" This spin-off from the Tas chain (named for its speciality of Turkish pizza, 'pide') has a cosy Anatolian interior and, although there are "no surprises here" foodwise, its "quick and cheerful" and provides "great affordable food, in a super location with friendly staff who are patient and kind with children!" / SE1 9DR; www.tasrestaurants.co.uk; @TasRestaurants; 11.30 pm, Sun 10.30 pm.

Tate Britain,
Whistler Restaurant SW1 £64 234
Millbank   020 7887 8825   2–4C

"The joy of a wine list (an impressive worldwide selection at not-unreasonable prices) curated by Hamish Anderson, continues to be the star of the show here" in this "wonderful room" whose "murals by Rex Whistler are well worth a visit in their own right". The other aspects of the experience – not least its British fare – have traditionally played second fiddle here, but won higher ratings this year, with regulars judging both food and service to be "better than in the past". / SW1 4RG; www.tate.org.uk/visit/tate-britain/rex-whistler-restaurant; @Tate; closed Mon-Sun D; booking D only.

Tate Modern,
Kitchen & Bar,
Level 6 SE1 £58 223
Level 6 Boiler House, Bankside   020 7887 8888   10–3B

"You come for the view, which does not disappoint" ("stunning") at Tate Modern's original upper-level perch on the South Bank of the Thames. Gastronomically, though, its seasonal British fare is something of a missed opportunity: admittedly "better than expected", but nevertheless "unexciting", from a "limited menu" and "not in the same league as the Rex Whistler" (at Tate Britain). / SE1 9TG; www.tate.org.uk; @TateFood; 9 pm; Sun-Thu L only, Fri & Sat open L & D.

Taylor St Baristas £12 333
"Superb coffee and great cakes" make this small chain a "go-to" choice for a caffeine hit in the City or Mayfair. Service can be "slightly slow" but "being hipster central it's probably uncool to criticise". / www.taylor-st.com; most branches close 5 pm-5.30 pm, WC2 7 pm, Wed-Fri 9 pm; Old Broad ST, Clifton St, W1, E14 closed Sat & Sun; New St closed Sat; TW9 closed Sun.

Tayyabs E1 £28 422
83 Fieldgate St   020 7247 6400   10–2D

"Embrace the chaos and suck down those chops!" – this "noisy and rambunctious neighborhood joint with 500 seats" has become "an East End institution" to rival the older Lahore. "The queues are tough" but "it's worth the wait and the hassle for fabulous Pakistani food at ridiculously cheap prices". "For Cobra, shop up the street at the Tesco Metro as they are BYO". / E1 1JU; www.tayyabs.co.uk; @1tayyabs; 11.30 pm.

Tell Your Friends SW6 NEW £48
175 New King's Rd   020 7731 6404   11–1B

Sisters Lucy and Tiffany Watson – best known for featuring in Made in Chelsea – are behind this vegan, spring-2018 newcomer (which is actually located in Parson's Green, not Chelsea). The aim: to 'demystify veganism and showcase how tasty it can be'. / SW6 4SW; www.tellyourfriendsldn.com.

temper £48 2 2 4
25 Broadwick St, W1 020 3879 3834 4–1C
5 Mercers Walk, WC2 020 3004 6669 5–2C **NEW**
Angel Court, EC2 020 3004 6984 10–2C
"The theatre of the fire pits" ("grab a table at the counter to see your food cooking, and to strike up a conversation with the chefs") helps inspire fans of the "extraordinary culinary style" of Neil Rankin's "loud", "subterranean temple to everything carnivorous" in Soho, which has a spin off in the City ("in a quiet alley by Bank") and now also in Covent Garden (where most of the cooking is in a wood-fired oven, and where they also do pizza). The verdict on the food however, is becoming increasingly mixed – to fans the smoked BBQ fare is "brilliant and creative", featuring "dishes unlike anywhere else", but the proportion of sceptics who find the food "bland", or "over-salted" or "very over-hyped" is growing. / temperrestaurant.com; @temperldn.

The 10 Cases WC2 £54 3 4 3
16 Endell St 020 7836 6801 5–2C
A "wonderful left-field wine list" – "a rapidly varying selection" of "different and uncommon vintages" at "sensible prices" – is what makes this highly appealing wine bar "a dark haven of happiness in the tourist wastelands of Covent Garden". There's solid support too for the "straightforward, well presented tapas" to accompany it. / WC2H 9BD; www.the10cases.co.uk; @10cases; 11 pm; closed Sun.

10 Greek Street W1 £58 4 4 3
10 Greek St 020 7734 4677 5–2A
"Lovely…", "fun…", "affordable…", "…a delight!" – this "cramped" modern wine bar in Soho is "a place to go back again and again" with its "stunning and original", "locally sourced" food and its "handwritten Wine Journal with interesting entries and very reasonable mark ups". "Love sitting by the bar to watch the chefs, but does get a little smokey at times!" / W1D 4DH; www.10greekstreet.com; @10GreekStreet; 11 pm, Sun 9 pm; closed Sun; booking L only.

Tendido Cero SW5 £52 3 3 4
174 Old Brompton Rd 020 7370 3685 6–2B
"If you want Spanish tapas, it doesn't get much better" than at this self-styled "designer tapas" and wine bar in South Kensington. It's "very noisy" when packed, which is often, but fans reckon it has "recovered from a dip a couple of years back" and now has "better tapas than you get in Spain". A warning: "be prepared for a big bill if you really go to town". / SW5 0BA; www.cambiodetercio.co.uk; @CambiodTercio; 11 pm.

Terroirs £53 3 2 3
5 William IV St, WC2 020 7036 0660 5–4C
38 Lordship Lane, SE22 020 8693 9021 1–4D **NEW**
With its "outstanding range and quality of wines" (many of them funky, if "slightly hit-and-miss" 'biodynamique' vintages); "limited-but-quirky menu" of rustic French fare (charcuterie, cheese, eel salad, smoked cod roe), all at "decent prices", this well-known dive of nearly ten years standing, near Charing Cross station, "feels like a trusty friend" to very many reporters. "Perhaps one was more excited a few years back when places like these were less common" but its ratings have softened in recent years – "dishes can be a little inconsistent" and the very "Gallic" service "has gone backwards". Still it's "always buzzing". In October 2017, owners Cave des Pyrène rebranded its East Dulwich offshoot ToastED under the same name. / terroirswinebar.com; @TerroirsWineBar.

Texture W1 £118 5 3 3

34 Portman St 020 7224 0028 2–2A

"Unbelievable… everything was magnificent!" – Aggi Sverrisson's "more-than-First Class" but comparatively low-profile venture (now over ten years old) is a showcase for his truly "superb" Scandi-inspired cooking (with a focus on top-quality seafood and meat, but also with a vegan option). And there's an outstanding wine selection too. In a year that has seen him put his 28/50 chain up for sale, his focus on this, his flagship, earned him the highest food scores in the survey, bar none! "Service is occasionally hit and miss but mostly good". Top Tip: don't miss the fish tasting menu here. / W1H 7BY; www.texture-restaurant.co.uk; @TextureLondon; 11 pm; closed Tue, Wed L, closed Sun & Mon.

Thali SW5 £48 4 4 3

166 Old Brompton Rd 020 7373 2626 6–2B

"Why does this restaurant seem to fly under the radar?" – A "classy" contemporary Indian café on the fringes of South Kensington, decorated with Bollywood posters, which serves "lovingly prepared, fresh and aromatic dishes" (based on recipes sourced from the owner's relatives). "It should be better known". / SW5 0BA; @ThaliLondon; Sun-Thu 11 pm, Fri & Sat 11.30 pm.

Theo Randall W1 £90 4 4 2

InterContinental Hotel, 1 Hamilton Pl 020 7318 8747 3–4A

The home of some of "the best Italian food going" is how fans recommend this ex-River Café head chef's luxurious dining room, just off a hotel foyer by Hyde Park Corner, which also benefits from an "enormous and interesting wine list" (although the latter "can bring tears to your wallet"). The space lacks natural light, but the revamp a couple of years ago has made it more "charming". / W1J 7QY; www.theorandall.com; @theorandall; 11 pm; closed Sat L & Sun.

Theo's SE5 £39 3 3 2

2 Grove Ln 020 3026 4224 1–3C

"Excellent charred crusts from a thin sourdough and really interesting well-sourced toppings" inspire love for this "great neighbourhood pizzeria" in Camberwell, often praised for its "excellent value for money"; it also has a "lovely garden area at the back". / SE5 \N; www.theospizzeria.com; @theospizzaldn; Tue-Thu, Sun 10.30 pm, Fri & Sat 11 pm, Mon 10 pm; no Amex; may need 6+ to book.

Theos Simple Italian SW5 £69 3 3 2

34 - 44 Barkston Gardens, Kensington 020 7370 9130 6–2A

"A real mixed bag" – Theo Randall goes casual at his branded spin-off in a low-profile Earl's Court hotel. Reports generally are positive regarding the pizza and "top pasta", but more complex dishes can be "marred by some heavy-handed treatment" and – while "staff are friendly" – "the decor is incongruous and the space feels very like the hotel restaurant that it is". / SW5 0EW; www.theossimpleitalian.co.uk; @TRSimpleItalian; 10.30 pm.

34 Mayfair W1 £79 2 2 3

34 Grosvenor Sq 020 3350 3434 3–3A

Plush New York-style grill near the former US Embassy, from Richard Caring's stable, that's "perfect for a business lunch over good food" if you're willing to pay top Mayfair dollar. But ratings are down this year amid signs of resistance to such pricing: "expense accounters (and victims of hotel concierges) seem to be the mainstays". / W1K 2HD; www.34-restaurant.co.uk; @34_restaurant; 11.30 pm, Sun 10.30 pm.

The Thomas Cubitt SW1 £68 **3 4 4**
44 Elizabeth St   020 7730 6060   2–4A
"A very busy, popular local in Belgravia, with excellent food and atmosphere, particularly in the first floor dining room", which – with its linen and light decor is "more decent restaurant than good gastropub"; "genuine smiling service" too. / SW1W 9PA; www.thethomascubitt.co.uk; @TheThomasCubitt; 10 pm, Sun 9.30 pm.

Three Cranes EC4 NEW £57
28 Garlick Hill   020 3455 7437   10–2C
Historic, heart-of-the-city tavern (with two serviced apartments) that's part of the well-publicised collaboration of Henry Harris (formerly chef-patron of Racine) and founder of Harcourt Inns, James McCulloch. It's been less PR'd than the other ventures, but early reports cite "simple French food, under the guidance of Henry Harris that make this small City pub near Mansion House a very good place". / EC4V 2BA; www.threecranescity.co.uk; @threecranesldn; Mon & Tue 9 pm, Fri & Sat 11.30 pm, Wed 10 pm, Thu 11 pm, Sun 5 pm.

tibits £42 **3 2 3**
12-14 Heddon St, W1   020 7758 4110   4–3B
124 Southwark St, SE1   020 7202 8370   10–4B
This Swiss self-service vegetarian concept, with a flagship off Regent Street and a "welcome" branch near Tate Modern, serves "freshly prepared, global" dishes which you pay for per 100g. By West End standards, they offer "great value for money" for "lunch or dinner in relaxed surroundings" – "I've taken meat eaters and they're converted!". / www.tibits.co.uk; @tibits_uk.

Timmy Green SW1 £67 **3 3 3**
Nova Victoria, 11 Sir Simon Milton Square   020 3019 7404   2–4B
For "a delicious Aussie breakfast in Victoria", many reporters recommend this big (150 cover) "cheap 'n' cheerful" haunt in the huge Nova development: part of the 'Daisy Green' brasserie chain. At other times, the focus is on steaks and other grills from the Josper, plus craft beers and cocktails. / SW1E 5BH; www.daisygreenfood.com/venues/timmy-green; 11 pm, Sun 10 pm.

TING SE1 £98 **2 2 4**
Level 35, 31 St Thomas St   020 7234 8108   10–4C
The Shangri-La's luxuriously appointed eyrie on the 35th floor of the Shard (named after a Chinese word for 'living room'), does win praise for its gastronomic potential, but most reports focus almost exclusively on its "excellent views" over London, 128 metres below. The other features rating mention – other than the vertiginous nature of the bill – are the memorable afternoon teas (choose from British or Oriental tea menus). / SE1 9RY; www.ting-shangri-la.com; @ShangriLaShard; 11 pm; No trainers; credit card required to book.

Tish NW3 NEW
196 Haverstock Hill   020 7431 3828   9–2A
Property Developer, David Levin has apparently always dreamed of opening a kosher eatery and is behind this 160 cover venture – a July 2018 opening, billed as London's 'largest and finest' Kosher restaurant – an all-day brasserie in Belsize Park. Its early days – first rumbles on the bush telegraph so far suggest the fit-out is splendid, and that the cooking is still a work in progress. / NW3 2AG; www.tish.london; @tish_london; Tue-Thu 10 pm, Fri & Sat 10.30 pm, Sun 9.30 pm.

Titu W1 NEW   £61   4 5 4
1A Shepherd St   020 7493 8746   3–4B
Limited but hugely positive initial feedback on ex-Novikov Kiwi chef, Jeff Tyler's tiny (15-seater) newcomer in Mayfair's picturesque Shepherds Market. "It's a lovely and fun little operation, where service is by two charming young ladies who knew the food well". On the menu: handmade, non-traditional gyoza and a range of colourful Asian-inspired salads and snacks, all of which are praised for being very well-crafted. / W1J 7HJ; www.titurestaurant.com; @titulondon.

Toffs N10   £40   3 4 3
38 Muswell Hill Broadway   020 8883 8656   1–1B
"Dependably excellent" Greek Cypriot chippie in Muswell Hill, whose big fanclub extends across neighbouring postcodes and beyond – a stalwart operation, which serves "scrumptious" fish, chips and Greek salads in "portions verging on the ridiculously large". The grilled fish is particularly popular, but "battered rock and haddock are to die for", too. / N10 3RT; www.toffsfish.co.uk; @toffsfish; 10 pm; closed Sun.

Tokimeite W1   £109   3 2 2
23 Conduit St   020 3826 4411   3–2C
It has impeccable credentials – it's backed by Japan's largest agricultural co-op, ZeN-Noh, and overseen by two of Japan's more famous chefs – but this Mayfair two-year-old inspires precious little feedback. Such as there is says the food's really "quite good" but that the overall formula doesn't quite hang together – "maybe they're not quite sure what sort of restaurant this should be. Is it all about its wagyu, or is it a kappo kaiseki place [a multi-course meal, where the selection is left to the chef]… or is it just one of those bland Mayfair places for hedgies to spend obscene amounts of money…?" / W1S 2XS; www.tokimeite.com; @tokimeitelondon; 10.30 pm; closed Sun.

Tokyo Diner WC2   £24   3 3 3
2 Newport Place   020 7287 8777   5–3B
"A huge choice of classic Japanese fast food" at "very reasonable prices for central London" make this diner a real "go-to" in Chinatown. The tastes are "authentic – just like in a Tokyo eatery", although "portions are larger". There's a "buzzy atmosphere and cheerful but slightly haphazard service". Top tip – "bento boxes definitely recommended". / WC2H 7JJ; www.tokyodiner.com; 11.30 pm; closed Tue-Sun L, closed Mon; no Amex; no booking.

Tom Simmons SE1   £60   3 2 2
2 Still Walk   020 3848 2100   10–4D
"A welcome addition to the growing Tower Bridge development" – this year-old London debut of Pembrokeshire-born chef Tom Simmons (who appeared on MasterChef – The Professionals) brings a focus on Welsh ingredients to the capital and wins praise for its "good produce, well put together", and "sensible prices". Teething issues have included gripes about staff training, and some feel "the décor could do with an uplift" but its "excellent position makes it a good choice for a business lunch" (or eating around a show at the new Bridge Theatre). Hopefully a financial restructuring (which took place in mid summer 2018) will provide the necessary headroom to develop the site further. / SE1 2UP; tom-simmons.co.uk; @TomSimmons_TB; 11 pm; closed Sun & Mon.

Tommi's Burger Joint   £29   3 3 3
30 Thayer St, W1   020 7224 3828   3–1A
37 Berwick St, W1   020 7494 9086   4–2D
342 Kings Rd, SW3   020 7349 0691   6–3C
"Smoky little room (in a good way), fast service, brilliant condiments and amazing burgers" – "at a decent price" – is the offer at the Soho and Marylebone outlets of Icelander Tómas Tómasson's international chain. Top Tip: "awesome sweet potato fries". / www.burgerjoint.co.uk; @BurgerJointUk; 10.30 pm, Sun 9 pm; booking: min 5.

Tomoe SW15 £37 **4** **2** **1**
292 Upper Richmond Rd   020 3730 7884   11–2B
The "superb fresh sushi and sashimi" at this "tucked-away little place" in Putney is some of "the best no-frills Japanese food in town". "The number of Japanese customers shouts volumes" about a kitchen that has carried on where its predecessor on the site, Cho-San (RIP), left off – in the same "far-from-uplifting surroundings". / SW15 \N; 9.30 pm.

Toms Kitchen £67 **2** **2** **2**
27 Cale St, SW3   020 7349 0202   6–2C
11 Westferry Circus, E14   020 3011 1555   12–1C
1 Commodity Quay, E1   020 3011 5433   10–3D
These "smart" casual dining venues in Chelsea and Canary Wharf win most acclaim for their "top breakfasts" and the Somerset House outlet has "a fabulous location on the river (outside in summer)". The food is "decent" but gives no particular hints of much connection with chef Tom Aikens, who founded the group. / www.tomskitchen.co.uk; @TomsKitchens; SW3 10.30 pm, Sun 9.30 pm; WC2 10 pm; E14 9.30 pm; E1 10.30 pm; SE1 6 pm; B1 10.30 pm, Sun 5 pm; WC2, E14, B1 & E1 closed Sun D.

Tonkotsu £43 **4** **3** **3**
Selfridges, 400 Oxford St, W1   020 7437 0071   3–1A
63 Dean St, W1   020 7437 0071   5–2A
7 Blenheim Cr, W11   020 7221 8300   7–1A
4 Canvey St, SE1   020 7928 2228   10–4B
Battersea Power Station Arches, SW8   020 7720 7695   11–1C **NEW**
Unit 1, Endeavour Square, E20   020 8534 6809   14–1D **NEW**
382 Mare St, E8   020 8533 1840   14–1B
Arch 334, 1a Dunston St, E8   020 7254 2478   14–2A
"The broth is so incredibly thick and creamy, and this combined with the very generous servings makes for a very good quick eat" at these cramped ramen-pit stops serving "noodles… more noodles… and some side dishes for those not wanting noodles". "As it's just a place for sustenance, you go with the flow, but staff are friendly and helpful". / www.tonkotsu.co.uk; @TonkotsuSoho; 10 pm-11 pm; Selfridges 30 mins before store closing; no bookings.

Tosa W6 £39 **3** **3** **2**
332 King St   020 8748 0002   8–2B
"Yakitori – charcoal-grilled chicken skewers – are the real draw" at this "brilliant local" Japanese in Stamford Brook, but it has an "interesting menu" generally, which includes noodles, sashimi and sushi, and makes for "fun casual dining". / W6 0RR; 11 pm, Sun 10.30 pm.

Tozi SW1 £50 **3** **4** **3**
8 Gillingham St   020 7769 9771   2–4B
"A must-try if you like Italian" – this "cheerful but noisy" specialist in Venetian cicchetti (small plates) attached to a hotel near Victoria station serves up "a lively dining experience with interesting and original dishes". / SW1V 1HN; www.tozirestaurant.co.uk; @ToziRestaurant; Tue-Thu 10 pm, Fri & Sat 10.30 pm, Mon 9.30 pm, Sun 9 pm.

The Trafalgar Dining Rooms SW1 **NEW** £65 **3** **3** **3**
Spring Gardens   020 7870 2901   2–3C
Positive ratings (although limited feedback as yet) on the new Mediterranean-influenced restaurant and cocktail bar in the stylishly revamped foyer of the Trafalgar Hotel, whose best perches look right out onto Trafalgar Square. Don't forget to check out The Rooftop (see also) while you're there. / SW1A 2TS; www.trafalgardiningrooms.com; @DiningroomSW1; Sun-Thu 11 pm, Fri & Sat midnight.

The Tramshed EC2   £60   3|2|3

32 Rivington St   020 7749 0478   13–1B

"A stuffed Damien Hirst cow dominates the dining room" at Mark Hix's big, Britart-decorated Victorian tramshed conversion in Shoreditch. Six years on from the excitement of its launch, the large space can seem "quiet", but by most accounts it's still "always a total pleasure" – if perhaps a slightly "overpriced" one – with its menu of "good steaks and impressive whole roast chicken (served upright, claws intact)". / EC2A 3LX; www.hixrestaurants.co.uk/restaurant/tramshed; @the_tramshed; 10.30 pm, Sun 4 pm.

Trangallan N16   £47   4|4|3

61 Newington Grn   020 7359 4988   1–1C

"Inventive dishes that you won't find in other tapas places" distinguish this "excellent" (if "pricey") Newington Green Spaniard with Galician specialities. / N16 9PX; www.trangallan.com; @trangallan_n16; Sat, Mon-Fri 11 pm, Sun 10 pm; closed Mon; no Amex; No trainers.

Tratra E2   £64

2-4 Boundary St   020 7729 1051   13–1B

Limited and somewhat cautious feedback on Stéphane Reynaud's first venture outside of France, in the basement of the Conran family's stylish boutique hotel (the only bit of the Prescott & Conran empire they decided to buy back from the administrator). We've left a rating until we have more reports. / E2 7DD; boundary.london; @BoundaryLDN.

Tredwell's WC2   £60   2|2|2

4 Upper St Martin's Ln   020 3764 0840   5–3B

Marcus Wareing's multi-level Theatreland diner doesn't sit within any easily-defined niche and continues to split opinions. At its best this is a versatile, "buzzy and fun" destination ("especially if you can grab a booth"), suited to many occasions; and fans of its "interesting, varied menu, with amazing flavours" just "can't wait to go back". Sceptics though, feel the food is "less inspired than expected from a Marcus Wareing venue", with "a total bill that's too much for an ultimately unsatisfying experience". Top Tip: often nominated as a kid-friendly choice. / WC2H 9NY; www.tredwells.com; @tredwells; Mon-Thu 10 pm, Fri & Sat 11 pm, Sun 9 pm.

Treves & Hyde E1   £54   3|4|3

15-17 Leman St   020 3621 8900   10–2D

At the foot of a new aparthotel near Aldgate East tube, this year-old venture comprises a coffee shop and terrace downstairs, and a restaurant and bar upstairs, which – under seasoned chef George Tannock – tries harder than you might expect in this location: "a welcome, local, go-to business lunch place, with an excellent and varied menu and staff who are efficient but welcoming". / E1 8EN; trevesandhyde.com; @trevesandhyde; 10.30 pm, Sun 6 pm.

Tried & True SW15   £23   3|3|3

279 Upper Richmond Rd   020 8789 0410   11–2A

"A good local vibe", "very helpful staff" and "very good breakfasts" are key selling points of this Kiwi café in Putney. / SW15 \N; www.triedandtruecafe.co.uk; @tried_true_cafe; Mon-Fri 4 pm, Sat & Sun 4.30 pm; closed Mon-Sun D.

Trinity SW4   £75   5|5|4

4 The Polygon   020 7622 1199   11–2D

"Since getting a (long-overdue) Michelin star the team have upped their game" yet further, at Adam Byatt's ever-more outstanding Clapham trailblazer – "a very slick operation", with an attractive position near Clapham Common. "In many respects it rivals Chez Bruce with the added advantages of more table space and less lead time for a table!" "Exemplary cuisine combines the familiar with interesting novelties without being outlandish or showing off". "You are made to feel very welcome" by the "unusually well-informed staff" and the setting is "delightfully calm and relaxing". See also Upstairs at Trinity. / SW4 0JG; www.trinityrestaurant.co.uk; @TrinityLondon; 10 pm, Sun 9 pm; closed Mon L & Sun D.

Trinity Upstairs SW4 £50 5 4 4
4 The Polygon 020 3745 7227 11–2D
"Upstairs should be cloned for every city in the world" according to fans
of Adam Byatt's more relaxed alternative to the main dining space below –
"an informal venue" (arguably *"more vibey than downstairs"*) with *"an open
kitchen plus about 30 covers on high stools and narrow tables"*; and looked
after by *"hard working staff"*. *"Adventurous regularly changing menus"*
(often featuring guest chefs) use a small plates format, and results are *"truly
exciting"*. / SW4 0JG; www.trinityrestaurant.co.uk; @trinityupstairs; 10 pm.

Trishna W1 £83 4 2 2
15-17 Blandford St 020 7935 5624 2–1A
The Sethi family's original London venture – this *"low-key"*-looking, ten-year-
old recreation of a famous Mumbai venue in Marylebone is beginning
to show its age a little. Fans still tout its *"exquisitely prepared and not over-
spiced cuisine"*, as *"the best in fine-end Indian dining"* and on a par with its
now more high-profile sibling, Gymkhana. But ratings here slid noticeably
across the board in this year's survey amidst gripes about *"rather sporadic
service"* and food that's *"starting to feel a mite unexciting nowadays"*.
Is their empire finally showing growing pains? / W1U 3DG;
www.trishnalondon.com; @TrishnaLondon; 10 pm.

La Trompette W4 £82 5 5 3
5-7 Devonshire Rd 020 8747 1836 8–2A
"The kind of restaurant that sets the gold standard" – this *"classy and
understated"* neighbourhood star has an obscure location in a Chiswick
sidestreet and echoes the *"unshowy"* excellence of its stablemate Chez
Bruce, *"delivering the goods year on year"*. *"Novel, vibrant and exciting
cooking still thrills and surprises"* and service likewise *"is outstanding –
you never feel like a waiter is looking over your shoulder but the staff are
attentive to everything"*. The persnickety feel that the interior is maybe
a mite *"clinical"*, but most reporters feel *"the surroundings are lovely"*,
"all very relaxed", cosseted by *"the hum of happy diners"*. / W4 2EU;
www.latrompette.co.uk; @LaTrompetteUK; 10.30 pm, Sun 9.30 pm.

Trullo N1 £60 3 3 3
300-302 St Paul's Rd 020 7226 2733 9–2D
*"It's best to book ahead at this ever-popular pit-stop, just off Highbury
Corner"* – a *"fantastic, generous and fairly priced neighbourhood Italian"*,
which was the survey's most commented-on destination in North London
this year. *"It's probably the sheer simplicity of the decor and apparently
happy waiting staff – coupled with a chatty clientele who appreciate the
carefully curated ingredients – which make it such a consistent pleasure
to visit"*. *"Despite the squashed and clattery interior it manages to dish
up really well judged Italian cooking"* – *"simple classic dishes"*
(*"not standard fare pasta and pizza"*) – *"and an utterly enjoyable evening"*.
/ N1 2LH; www.trullorestaurant.com; @Trullo_LDN; 10 pm, Sun 2.30 am; closed
Sun D; no Amex.

Tsunami SW4 £48 5 2 3
5-7 Voltaire Rd 020 7978 1610 11–1D
"A real gem" – *"extraordinary"* – this Clapham fixture has for many,
many years produced some of *"the best Japanese you can get at a really
reasonable price"*: in fact locals feel *"to be honest, it's far better than the
very expensive well-known Japanese restaurants in Central London"*. It also
mixes up *"some of the most innovative cocktails in town"*. The catch:
*"it's always packed so the service lets it down... but that means nothing
when you taste the food"*. *"Pity the Fitzrovia branch closed"* – but do try
Yama Momo in East Dulwich. / SW4 6DQ; www.tsunamirestaurant.co.uk; 11 pm,
Fri-Sun midnight; closed Sat L & Sun; no Amex.

Tuyo E2 £57 3 3 3
129a Pritchard's Rd   020 7739 2540   14–2B
You look out from big windows at this bright contemporary café in the environs of Hackney's busy Broadway Market, where an ex-Salt Yard chef provides an eclectic menu of Mediterranean tapas, plus wine and cocktails. The food is well-rated and prices are not punishing. / E2 9AP; www.tuyo.london; @Tuyocafebistro; Sun-Thu 10.30 pm, Fri & Sat 11 pm.

1251 N1 NEW
107 Upper St   no tel   9–3D
James Cochran has launched again in Islington, on the site of Chinese Laundry (RIP), just months after his James Cochran N1 closed (it has been retrospectively called a pop-up). He is also no longer cooking at the EC1 restaurant that bears his name (see also). The food here is "modern British, taking inspiration from James's Scottish and Vincentian roots" and will also feature "Asian influences". / N1 1QN; www.1251.co.uk.

28 Church Row NW3 £53 4 4 4
28 Church Row   020 7993 2062   9–2A
"Head down a modest staircase into a warm informal space with an open kitchen to watch" at one of Hampstead's most exciting openings of recent times (for those with long memories, "the old Cellier Du Midi premises transformed by a local couple who like to meet their customers"). On the menu "amazing contemporary tapas, with some of the more substantial offerings a meal in themselves: the pig's cheek, for example". "You can't book" and "evenings can be busy, so be prepared to wait at the pub opposite and they'll phone you when ready". / NW3 6UP; www.28churchrow.com; @28churchrow.com; 10.30 pm, Sun 9.30 pm; closed Mon-Fri L.

28-50 £68 2 2 3
15-17 Marylebone Ln, W1   020 7486 7922   3–1A
17-19 Maddox St, W1   020 7495 1505   4–2A
140 Fetter Ln, EC4   020 7242 8877   10–2A
"Superb wines (many sold in smaller, affordable, measures)" still win praise for Agnar Sverrisson's business-friendly wine bar group of bar/bistros. The food ("simple dishes" like burgers, plus cheese and charcuterie) has always been a case of "no fireworks but good value" but slipping ratings across the board this year coincided with news in June 2018 that the business is up for sale. With Fetter Lane sold off, the future for the (more successful) Marylebone and Mayfair branches is up for grabs. / www.2850.co.uk; @2850Restaurant; 9.30 pm-10.30 pm; EC4 closed Sat & Sun, W1S closed Sun.

24 The Oval SW9 NEW
24 Clapham Rd   020 7735 6111   11–1D
Now open in Oval, a May 2018 newcomer from Matt Wells, (co-owner of The Dairy, Clapham) and his business partner from SW4 steakhouse Knife, Andrew Bradford. Unlike the tapas-y format which won The Dairy renown, it's full-sized plates of Modern British cuisine here which is winning upbeat initial press reviews. / SW9 0JG; www.24theoval.co.uk; @24theoval.

Twist W1 £64 4 5 4
42 Crawford St   020 7723 3377   2–1A
"Eduardo Tuccillo's relative newcomer [it's three years old] is well-hidden in the depths of Marylebone" on a site that some reporters "date themselves" by recalling in its days as Garbos (long RIP). As with its long-departed predecessor, the "minimalist interior" is a fraction "bare and noisy", but all reports acknowledge it as "a real winner". "Plates are designed for sharing tapas style" and "if you are a proper foodie, you will love his phenomenally creative Italo-Spanish cooking with some Asian-fusion to surprise as well". "It's in my neighbourhood but I've only just discovered it: glad I did!" / W1H 1JW; www.twistkitchen.co.uk; @twistkitchen; closed Sun.

Two Brothers N3 £34 3 2 2

297-303 Regent's Park Rd 020 8346 0469 1–1B

"Authentic, high-quality fish 'n' chips" win consistently high marks for this traditional Finsbury chippy, whose high standards have made it a popular local favourite for 25 years. / N3 1DP; www.twobrothers.co.uk; 10 pm; closed Mon.

Two Lights E2 NEW

28-30 Kingsland Rd awaiting tel 13–1B

From The Clove Club: the team have set up former head chef Chase Lovecky in his own restaurant, which opened in September 2018 just up the road from the mothership. We're told to expect 'a neighbourhood spot, serving modern American food', and with his track record (at momofuku in NYC and Jean Georges) it will hopefully be anything but boring. / E2 8DA; www.twolights.restaurant; 10.30 pm, Mon 11 pm, Sun 3 pm.

2 Veneti W1 £55 3 3 3

10 Wigmore St 020 7637 0789 3–1B

"Excellent Venetian food" is the point of difference at this "very welcoming" and "consistently good" Italian near the Wigmore Hall – a "popular (and sometimes noisy) spot for those who lunch". "The only place I've found bigoli" (a regional pasta). / W1U 2RD; www.2veneti.com; @2Veneti; 10.30 pm, Sat 11 pm; closed Sat L & Sun.

Uli W11 £47 3 4 4

5 Ladbroke Rd 020 3141 5878 7–2B

"It's a surprise to find such an outstanding restaurant in such an unlikely place", say fans of Michael Lim's resurrected pan-Asian, nowadays on the more obscure fringes of Notting Hill (previously near the Portobello Road). With its "wonderful" Asian cuisine, fans feel "it's just as good as it was in All Saints Road", and even if ratings are still a tad off their historic highs, it's widely seen as "a fab addition to W11's culinary choices". / W11 3PA; www.ulilondon.com; @ulilondon; midnight, Sun 11 pm; D only, closed Sun.

Umu W1 £120 2 3 3

14-16 Bruton Pl 020 7499 8881 3–2C

"Japanese cuisine at its finest (the quality of ingredients, especially fish, is simply amazing!)" inspires respect for Marlon Abela's much-vaunted venture dedicated to Kyoto-style kaiseki cuisine, tucked away in a delightful Mayfair mews and whose sleek styling is "not typically Japanese… in a good way". Ever since it opened in 2004, it has taken flak for being "grossly overpriced", but the reason its ratings were dragged down this year related to a couple of unusually disappointing reports. / W1J 6LX; www.umurestaurant.com; 10.30 pm; closed Sun; No trainers; booking max 14 may apply.

Union Street Café SE1 £62 3 2 3

47-51 Great Suffolk St 020 7592 7977 10–4B

More positive, if limited feedback this year on this Gordon Ramsay group casual Italian in Borough: reporters award solid ratings to food that was "decent to excellent" if perhaps "not cheap" (offsetting which, there are "often good value special deals"). / SE1 0BS; www.gordonramsayrestaurants.com/union-street-cafe; @unionstreetcafe; Mon-Fri 10.30 pm, Sat midnight, Sun 5 pm; closed Sun D.

Unwined SW17 £26 3 4 4

21-23 Tooting High St 020 3583 9136 11–2C

"Ever-changing, themed menus" ("very global!") add pizzazz to this "delightful wine bar in the middle of Tooting market" – "a great find where guest chefs have a 6-week residency and diners squeeze round a communal table. The food's really interesting and it always leads to a fun night out". / SW17 0SN; agrapenightin.co.uk; @UnwinedSW17; Wed-Sat 11 pm, Tue 10 pm, Sun 5.30 pm; closed Tue L closed Sun D, closed Mon.

Le Vacherin W4 £64 3 3 3
76-77 South Parade 020 8742 2121 8–1A
"You'd think you were in a modern version of a Belle Epoque Parisian bistro" at this "classic French" outfit by Acton Green. "It specialises in delicious dishes made with Vacherin cheese – but there's much more to choose from". After 15 years, a major refurb is planned for early 2019. / W4 5LF; www.levacherin.co.uk; @Le_Vacherin; 10.30 pm, Sun 9 pm; closed Mon L.

Vagabond Wines £41 2 2 3
77 Buckingham Palace Rd, SW1 020 7630 7693 2–4B NEW
25 Charlotte St, W1 020 3441 9210 2–1C
18-22 Vanston Place, SW6 020 7381 1717 6–4A NEW
4 Northcote Rd, SW11 020 7738 0540 11–2C NEW
"A great concept" for wine-tasting accompanied by sharing plates of charcuterie makes this chain of six bars "fun, too" ("once you've worked out how it all works!"). "Buy an Oyster-style card, top it up and sample a wide variety of different wines until you find one you just have to fill your glass with. Then repeat". On the downside, "it's easy to spend a fortune as none of the wines are cheap". The latest to open, in Battersea Power Station, is also producing its own wine on the premises. / www.vagabondwines.co.uk; @VagabondWines.

Vanilla Black EC4 £65 4 3 3
17-18 Tooks Ct 020 7242 2622 10–2A
"Beautifully presented meat-free food" – arguably "the most adventurous vegetarian cuisine in London" (and at "incredible prices given it's so central") – inspired numerous rave reviews and much more consistently upbeat feedback this year for this ambitious operation near Chancery Lane. / EC4A 1LB; www.vanillablack.co.uk; @vanillablack1; 10 pm; closed Sun; no Amex.

Vasco & Piero's Pavilion W1 £61 3 3 2
15 Poland St 020 7437 8774 4–1C
"A truly Italian venue in central London" – this "old-fashioned" Umbrian stalwart of half a century standing has a "wonderfully understated" style, and delights its regulars with its "delicious cooking" ("superb pasta") and very characterful service. Fun fact – Gordon Brown had his engagement party here. / W1F 8QE; www.vascosfood.com; @Vasco_and_Piero; 10 pm; closed Sat L, closed Sun.

Veeraswamy W1 £80 4 4 4
Victory Hs, 99-101 Regent St 020 7734 1401 4–4B
"A venerable institution that you have to visit at least once" – London's oldest Indian (est 1926) is still one of its best, having received a "calm, spacious and classy" contemporary revamp a few years ago (at the hands of its current owners, the Chutney Mary group) and serving "imaginative Indian dishes" with "original flavours". "There are probably better Indian restaurants in the West End, but for an overall experience, this takes some beating!" / W1B 4RS; www.veeraswamy.com; @theveeraswamy; Wed-Sun 9.30 pm; booking max 12 may apply.

Verdi's E1 £44 3 4 3
237 Mile End Rd 020 7423 9563 14–2B
"Welcoming service" and "authentic Italian food" inspired by the owner's origins in Parma (Giuseppe Verdi is the city's most famous son) make this trattoria a welcome addition to Stepney Green – "the atmosphere makes it seem long-standing". "The pizzas are worth a special mention". / E1 4AA; www.gverdi.uk; @verdislondon; Mon-Wed 5 pm, Thu-Sat 10 pm, Sun 6 pm.

Vermuteria N1 NEW

Coal Drops Yard   awaiting tel   9–3C

Anthony Demetre (he of Wild Honey and formerly Arbutus) has been announced as the latest incumbent of the Coal Drops Yard development in King's Cross. His bar and cafe will be an all-day take on the vermouth bars of Spain and Italy (vermuterias); over 50 different vermouths will be available. / N1C 4AB.

Via Emilia N1 NEW   £33

37a Hoxton Square   020 7613 0508   13–1B

From the Food Roots company (and sibling to Fitzrovia's In Parma), this late 2017 opening in Hoxton Square obsesses over its north Italian sourcing, with home-made pasta the particular draw, served alongside charcuterie and cheeses from Parma. / N1 6NN; www.via—emilia.com; 11 pm, Sun 10.30 pm.

Il Vicolo SW1   £55   3 3 2

3-4 Crown Passage   020 7839 3960   3–4D

This "wonderful family-run restaurant" with "lovey owners" is a rarity for the heart of St James's – hidden away down an alleyway and popular for its "friendly staff and consistently good Italian food", which – considering the pukka location – is "surprisingly well priced". / SW1Y 6PP; www.ilvicolorestaurant.co.uk; 10 pm; closed Sat L & Sun.

The Victoria SW14   £53   2 2 3

10 West Temple Sheen   020 8876 4238   11–2A

"A popular Sheen gastropub near Richmond Park" with a "charming and stylish" interior, plus "a recently refurbished conservatory and play area for children". Critics feel the food is "rather ordinary" by comparison with its past best, but most reports say it's "always reliable". / SW14 7RT; victoriasheen.co.uk; @TheVictoria_Pub; 10 pm, Sun 9 pm; no Amex.

Viet Food W1   £32   3 2 2

34-36 Wardour St   020 7494 4555   5–3A

"Just like eating in Asia", say fans of this "informal Vietnamese street food" warehouse-style operation in Chinatown from former Hakkasan chef Jeff Tan. "Fresh and tasty – and good value for money". / W1D 6QT; www.vietnamfood.co.uk; Sun-Thu 10.30 pm, Fri & Sat 11 pm.

Viet Grill E2   £45   3 2 2

58 Kingsland Rd   020 7739 6686   14–2A

Long hailed as one of the better options on Kingsland Road's 'pho mile' – this "cheap 'n' cheerful" Vietnamese café only inspired limited feedback this year, but all of it positive. / E2 8DP; www.vietnamesekitchen.co.uk; @CayTreVietGrill; Tue-Fri, Mon 3.30 pm.

Vijay NW6   £35   4 4 1

49 Willesden Ln   020 7328 1087   1–1B

Its decor is "old-looking" – and has been that way for about the last 30 years – but this "perennial favourite" in Kilburn continues to inspire an impressively "eclectic following (from humble local tradesmen to ladies in diamonds walking out of their limos)" with its "delicate yet pungent and flavourful South Indian dishes", and at "cheap" prices too. Top Tip: pay corkage to BYO. / NW6 7RF; www.vijayrestaurant.co.uk; Sun-Thu 10.45 pm, Fri & Sat 11.45 pm; no booking.

Villa Bianca NW3   £68   2 2 2

1 Perrins Ct   020 7435 3131   9–2A

"Old-style Italian" whose popularity is underpinned by its gorgeous central Hampstead location and comfortable, retro decor. Fans acclaim it as a "top-end" destination of some accomplishment: those with less rose-tinted glasses say "it's a nice place to sit, but with overpriced and variable food that's no better than a tourist venue in Italy itself". / NW3 1QS; www.villabiancanw3.com; @VillaBiancaNW3; 11.30 pm, Sun 10.30 pm.

Villa Di Geggiano W4   £65   **3** **4** **3**
66-68 Chiswick High Rd   020 3384 9442   8–2B
That it "tries hard" and "is a bit overdone on the decor" ("interesting art"
on the walls) is mainly seen as a positive for this "lovely" and "upscale"
Chiswick venture, operated by a 500-year-old Chianti dynasty as a showcase
for Tuscan cuisine and wine. The cooking is consistently well-rated and the
wine list includes "bottles from their own estate at exceptional prices".
There's a 50-seater terrace for al fresco summer dining. / W4 1SY;
www.villadigeggiano.co.uk; @villadigeggiano; 10.30 pm; closed Mon.

The Vincent Rooms,
Westminster Kingsway College SW1 £38   **3** **2** **2**
76 Vincent Sq   020 7802 8391   2–4C
"Kingsway College catering students staff this modern brasserie" in a quiet
and leafy Westminster square, where customers are effectively 'guinea pigs'
for training purposes. The "classic fare" is often (not always) "fully up to
commercial standards" – but "service, by waiters learning their trade,
can be terrible – yet the very reasonable prices make you forgive them!".
/ SW1P 2PD; www.westking.ac.uk/about-us/vincent-rooms-restaurant;
@thevincentrooms; Mon, Fri 3 pm, Tue-Thu 9 pm; closed Mon & Fri D, closed
Sat & Sun; no Amex.

Vinoteca   £60   **2** **2** **3**
15 Seymour Pl, W1   020 7724 7288   2–2A
18 Devonshire Rd, W4   020 3701 8822   8–2A
One Pancras Sq, N1   020 3793 7210   9–3C
7 St John St, EC1   020 7253 8786   10–1B
Bloomberg Arcade, EC2   020 3150 1292   10–3C **NEW**
"No surprise that the focus is on the wine" – "a huge and varied list,
with loads of wines by the glass" and "many you've never heard of to
challenge your taste buds" – at these "modern/industrial" bars, of which the
King's Cross and new Bloomberg branches attract most comment
(Soho closed this year). "Don't forget the food though". "It may play second
fiddle" but is "simple and satisfying". / www.vinoteca.co.uk; 11 pm, W1H &
W4 Sun 4 pm; W1F 10.45 pm, Sun 9.30 pm; EC1 closed Sun; W1H & W4 closed
Sun D.

Vivat Bacchus   £60   **3** **4** **2**
4 Hay's Ln, SE1   020 7234 0891   10–4C
47 Farringdon St, EC4   020 7353 2648   10–2A
"An eclectic and fascinating cellar, especially the South African options"
(perhaps "the best selection of Saffer vintages in town") "scores alpha plus
plus for the wines" at this very popular and "noisy" wine bar duo,
and "amazingly knowledgeable and helpful staff" help with your
deliberations. Though not the point, "the food is pretty good too" with steak
the top choice. / www.vivatbacchus.co.uk; 10.30 pm; closed Sun.

VIVI WC1
Centre Point   awaiting tel   5–1A
As part of the renovation of the Centre Point complex, caterers rhubarb
(Sky Garden, Saatchi Gallery, Royal Albert Hall) are poised to open this new
venue in autumn 2018 on the bridge link overlooking the square, featuring
four separate dining areas, and with a comforting British menu: from
chicken Kiev and fries to VIVI arctic roll. / WC1A 1DD; www.rhubarb.co.uk;
@VIVIRestaurant; 9.30 pm.

VQ £48 [2][3][3]
St Giles Hotel, Great Russell St, WC1   020 7636 5888   5–1A
325 Fulham Rd, SW10   020 7376 7224   6–3B
24 Pembridge Rd, W11   020 3745 7224   7–2B
9 Aldgate High St, EC3   020 3301 7224   10–2D

"Open 24/7" – the stalwart SW10 original "has been there forever, and is still the same old reliable standby at all hours": "it's a simple menu, but what they do, they do well". In recent years it's spawned a number of spin offs – WC1 in particular "has a large turnover and is reasonably priced". / www.vingtquatre.co.uk; @vqrestaurants; open 24 hours, W11 1 am, Thu-Sat 3 am, Sun midnight; booking: max 6 online.

Vrisaki N22 £42 [3][3][3]
73 Middleton Rd   020 8889 8760   1–1C

"The food just keeps coming" at this veteran Bounds Green taverna and take-away, when you go for the famous mezze special: "I've never had a bad meal and my guests ask, 'when are we going back again?'". / N22 8LZ; vrisakirestaurant.com; @vrisakiuk; 11 pm; closed Sun & Mon; no Amex.

Wagamama £42 [1][1][2]
Fans still say "you can't go wrong for a quick noodle fix", but overall ratings are starting to crater at these ubiquitous, communal pan-Asian canteens, where "the food has gone downhill", "the quality of ingredients seems to be dropping" and service can now be very "disjointed". On the plus side "they love kids, and kids love it". / www.wagamama.com; 10 pm - 11.30 pm; EC2 Sat 9 pm; EC4 closed Sat & Sun; EC2 closed Sun; no booking.

Wahaca £39 [2][3][3]
For a "flavourful and fun", "dependable and quick" meal, fans of Thomasina Miers' group of street food cantinas still feel it's "one of the best chains around", citing its "decent Mexican eats" and "fab cocktails" (and that it's "great with kids", if "a bit yummy mummy at the weekends"). But while ratings for its "friendly and prompt" service and energetic vibe have proved surprisingly enduring over the years, its food score dipped this year, with some regulars noting it has felt "a tad off-the-boil" of late. / www.wahaca.com; 11 pm, Sun 10.30 pm; W12, Charlotte St, SW19 Sun 10 pm; no booking or need 6+ to book.

Wahlburgers WC2 NEW
James St   awaiting tel   5–2D

If you're a Mark Wahlberg fan (aka Dirk Diggler in Boogie Nights) you only have to wait till late 2018 to visit the first of his 20 or so burger joints to be located in the UK. This first one will be opposite Covent Garden tube, with the major draw of video screens to allow 'live' FaceTime-style, video conversations with the great man himself. / WC2E; www.wahlburgersrestaurant.com; @Wahlburgers; Sun-Thu 11 pm, Fri & Sat midnight

The Wallace,
The Wallace Collection W1 £58 [2][2][5]
Hertford Hs, Manchester Sq   020 7563 9505   3–1A

The beautiful glass-ceilinged atrium of the Wallace Collection museum in Marylebone provides the "perfect atmosphere for tea – very civilised and respectable". "The café's food (from caterer Peyton & Byrne) is hit and miss, service not brilliant but the space is really impressive". "Always does the trick for a business meeting – so much better than sitting in a coffee shop". / W1U 3BN; www.peytonandbyrne.co.uk; 10.30 pm, Sun 4 pm; Sun-Thu closed D; no Amex; booking max 10 may apply.

Wander N16 NEW £48 [4][3][3]
214 Stoke Newington High St   020 7249 7283   1–1C

"Interesting Aussie dishes" are the reason to discover this casual small café-style venture – a Spring 2018 opening in Stokey from Australian-born chef Alexis Noble. / N16 7HU; www.wanderrestaurant.com; Tue-Thu 8.30 pm, Fri 9 pm, Sat 9.30 pm, Sun 7 pm.

Waterloo Bar & Kitchen SE1 £53 **3** **2** **2**
131 Waterloo Rd 020 7928 5086 10–4A
"It looks like a pretty uninspiring venue", but this busy brasserie near the
Old Vic is a useful amenity – the "international menu (from crispy duck
to Toulouse sausage)" can be "surprisingly good", comes "at reasonable
prices" and "is served with flexibility and a smile!" / SE1 8UR;
www.barandkitchen.co.uk; @BarKitchen; 11 pm, Sun 10 pm.

The Waterway W9 £52 **2** **2** **3**
54 Formosa St 020 7266 3557 9–4A
"Great views over the canal" make this Little Venice venue – a funked-up
former pub with a big terrace – an "easy-go-to local". Comments on the
modern pub grub? – "nice", "solid"… / W9 2JU; www.thewaterway.co.uk;
@thewaterway_; 10 pm, Sun 2.30 am.

Wellbourne W12 🆕 £43 **3** **3** **2**
201 Wood Lane 020 3417 4865 1–2B
This "just-opened, all-day brasserie in White City" (within the ever-more
lively environs of the old Beeb commercial HQ) is a functional space whose
associations with a well-known Bristol restaurant (and even a branch
in Spain) might not be instantly apparent. Useful to know about though,
with very competent staples produced by a duo of former Dabbous chefs.
/ W12 7TU; www.wellbourne.restaurant; @WellbourneWCP; 10 pm, Sun 5 pm; closed
Sun D.

The Wells Tavern NW3 £56 **3** **3** **4**
30 Well Walk 020 7794 3785 9–1A
"The ideal gastropub for after a walk on the Heath" – Hampstead's
most popular pub (owned by Beth Coventry, Fay Maschler's sister) is one
of the area's most consistent attractions, offering "a range of classic dishes
alongside a well-thought-out wine list", plus "efficient and friendly service"
and "a great buzz". Top Tip: "go, if possible, for the bright and airy room
upstairs – it's more relaxed and spacious, and a perfect place to eat".
/ NW3 1BX; thewellshampstead.london; @WellsHampstead; 10 pm, Sun 9.30 pm.

Westerns Laundry N5 £57 **3** **3** **3**
34 Drayton Park 020 7700 3700 9–2D
"You feel cool just knowing about this place!" – "a packed and unbelievably
noisy room just off the Holloway Road", which – on its launch in 2017 –
scored some of the best newspaper critic reviews of the year. With its
"edgy and friendly" approach and "urban, industrial-style decor",
it's indisputably "a great addition to Drayton Park" but "after all the hype"
numerous reporters felt anticlimactic: "nothing really bad" but "flavours
didn't always work together" and "while small plates are fashionable, these
aren't small, they're tiny!" Tons of praise is recorded too though – "take your
friends and dine on sharing plates, whose powerful and memorable tastes
are so good you'll want to scoff them all and not share!" Top Tip:
"It's best as a foursome as couples may be squashed on the long sharing
tables". / N5 1PB; www.westernslaundry.com; @WesternsLaundry; 10.30 pm,
Sun 5 pm.

The Wet Fish Café NW6 £50 **2** **3** **4**
242 West End Lane 020 7443 9222 1–1B
"A little corner of originality in a city plagued by uniformity" – that, to date,
has been the upbeat verdict on this all-day West Hampstead bistro (named
in honour of the 1930s fishmonger whose interior it inherited) still hailed
by the majority as "a dream local delivering equally well for coffee, brunch
and dinner". Its ratings suffered however this year on the back of several
downbeat reports: "very disappointing, with a more standard and boring
menu – I went back three times to check!" / NW6 1LG;
www.thewetfishcafe.co.uk; @thewetfishcafe; 10 pm; no Amex; booking D only.

White Bear SE11 £34 **3** **3** **3**
138 Kennington Park Rd   020 7490 3535   11–1D
"A proper restaurant has recently been added to this formerly rather depressing Kennington pub, now part of the Young's chain, and with an enterprising small theatre upstairs". *"Excellent for British staples: liver and bacon, Shepherd's pie, Cumberland sausage, fish 'n' chips, …"* / SE11 4DJ; www.whitebearkennington.co.uk; Mon-Thu 11.30 pm; closed Fri & Sat & Sun.

The White Onion SW19 £68 **3** **4** **2**
67 High St   020 8947 8278   11–2B
An offshoot of Eric and Sarah Guignard's highly rated and long-established French Table in neighbouring Surbiton, this accomplished three-year-old has proved *"a great addition to the Wimbledon restaurant scene",* with *"complex"* Gallic cuisine, *"executed to a very high standard"* and *"swift service".* / SW19 5EE; www.thewhiteonion.co.uk; @thewhiteonionSW; Tue-Thu 10 pm, Fri & Sat 10.30 pm, Sun 2.30 pm; closed Tue-Thu L closed Sun D, closed Mon.

The Wigmore, The Langham W1 £50 **4** **4** **4**
15 Langham Place, Regent St   020 7965 0198   2–1B
"Good food, good crowd, great value!" – Michel Roux's gastropub yearling makes a brilliant find near Oxford Circus, with a polished and plush (but still pub-like) interior, whose beautiful design reflects the fact that it's been carved from a corner of the luxurious Langham Hotel (of which it is part). Reports are notably upbeat on its its roster of superior pub grub, and it has *"a lovely ambience, especially in winter".* / W1B 3DE; www.the-wigmore.co.uk; @Langham_London; 9.30 pm, Sun 5 pm.

Wild Honey W1 £79 **3** **3** **3**
12 St George St   020 7758 9160   3–2C
"For dinner, it's warm and inviting", while during its busier lunchtime service, Anthony Demetre's *"very comfortable"* and *"slightly retro"* Mayfair venue is a favoured business entertaining spot. *"The food is delightful (the signature rabbit dish is heavenly)"* and it's also known for its *"interesting and varied wine list".* Top Tip: *"the fixed price lunch is excellent value for money".* / W1S 2FB; www.wildhoneyrestaurant.co.uk; @whrestaurant; 9.30 pm; closed Sun.

The Wilmington EC1 £54 **3** **2** **3**
69 Rosebery Avenue   020 7837 1384   10–1A
Worth knowing about near Sadler's Wells – an *"extremely busy"* Clerkenwell corner pub, well-rated in all reports for its *"reliably good food: from top burgers, to well-thought-out veggie options".* / EC1R 4RL; www.wilmingtonclerkenwell.com; @wilmingtonec1; Mon-Thu 10 pm, Fri & Sat 10.30 pm, Sun 9 pm.

Wiltons SW1 £95 **4** **5** **4**
55 Jermyn St   020 7629 9955   3–3C
"Don't forget your jacket if you're joining the peers of the realm at this classic on Jermyn Street, which has been doing things the way they should be done for more than 270 years (!)", with *"reassuringly unchanging, courteous-old school service"* that *"make you feel like a regular, even if you only visit annually".* The *"superb quality of the fare is without parallel"* from an *"old-fashioned, utterly untrendy menu"* which particularly shines with *"British seafood at its finest",* but is also strong in game. *"Of course it's definitely overpriced, but cheaper than joining a club and on that basis worth every pound!"* / SW1Y 6LX; www.wiltons.co.uk; @wiltons1742; 10.30 pm; closed Sat L, closed Sun; Jacket required.

The Windmill W1 £52 223
6-8 Mill St   020 7491 8050   4–2A

Not a vintage year for this classic, "slightly shabby" Mayfair boozer famous for "first-class pies, and well-kept beer to boot". Fans do still applaud "excellent English cooking", but a number of regulars filed disappointing reports: "standards dropping off…"; "didn't live up to the hype…"; "the fire alarm in the kitchen went off they burnt the pie so badly!" / W1S 2AZ; www.windmillmayfair.co.uk; @windmillpubW1; 10 pm, Sun 5 pm; closed Sat D & Sun.

The Wine Library EC3 £40 235
43 Trinity Sq   020 7481 0415   10–3D

"It's the amazingly wide variety of wines sold at very good value prices" (ie retail) that justifies killing an afternoon in this ancient and atmospheric cellar near Tower Hill – the food, is of "good quality" but of low ambition ("pâtés, quiches, bread rolls, etc"). "If only the seats were more comfortable I would come more often!" / EC3N 4DJ; www.winelibrary.co.uk; 7.30 pm; closed Mon D, Sat & Sun.

The Wolseley W1 £63 235
160 Piccadilly   020 7499 6996   3–3C

"Still the best place to take friends from abroad…", "Still the best place for a business power breakfast…", "Still the absolute best buzz in London!" – Corbin & King's Grand Café near the Ritz is still at the centre of metropolitan life: a "highly tuned, effective and bustling brasserie" where the "fabulous room" means it "always feels like a glamorous treat"; and where the "interesting crowd" typically includes a few famous faces. Its "comprehensive menu" of comfort food (with some Mittel-european specials) is "not out-of-this-world" and has never aimed to be, but is generally "well executed and presented". That said, laurel-resting is an ever-present danger here, and there were one or two more "underwhelming" meals reported this year. Likewise, while on most accounts "everything is so slick", there have also been a few more reports recently of "mixed" and/or "brusque" service. Top Tip: "a good traditional afternoon tea, which (unlike so many places nowadays) doesn't cost the earth". / W1J 9EB; www.thewolseley.com; @TheWolseleyRest; midnight, Sun 11 pm.

Wong Kei W1 £32 321
41-43 Wardour St   020 7437 8408   5–3A

"Always an experience… so long as you are prepared for shared tables and bordering-on-rude staff" – this "functional" multi-storey Chinatown canteen "is the perfect place for a quick, filling, tasty meal amidst a chaotic, bustling backdrop" and as you can get "unlimited free tea" and "a massive plate of food for under a tenner – you can't go wrong!". "OK it's not for the lingering, romantic tete-a-tete… so what?" / W1D 6PY; www.wongkeilondon.com; 11.30 pm, Sun 10.30 pm; cash only.

Wright Brothers £64 443
13 Kingly St, W1   020 7434 3611   4–2B
56 Old Brompton Rd, SW7   020 7581 0131   6–2B
11 Stoney St, SE1   020 7403 9554   10–4C
Battersea Power Station, SW11   020 7324 7734   11–1C
8 Lamb St, E1   020 7377 8706   10–2D

"An amazing selection of oysters" and other "wonderfully inventive fish and shellfish dishes" (in particular, "blackboard specials are usually excellent") have made these bustling fish bistros one of the capital's most popular chains amongst foodies, and – though relatively new – they have "an old-fashioned style, feeling like they've been there for years (in a good way…)". "The latest addition in Battersea Power Station and overlooking the Thames may be the best yet!" / SE1 10 pm, Sat 11 pm; W1 11 pm, Sun 10 pm; E1 10.30 pm, Sun 9 pm; SW7 10.30 pm, Sun 9.30 pm; booking: max 8.

Wulf & Lamb SW1 NEW £49 3 2 2
243 Pavilion Rd   020 3948 5999   6–2D
Vegan newcomer in a hyper-cute backstreet off Sloane Square with a former Vanilla Black chef in the kitchen. Feedback is limited and a bit mixed: the food by-and-large escapes criticism, but on one visit "the ordering system didn't seem very user-friendly". Teething troubles? / SW1X 0BP; www.wulfandlamb.com; @wulfandlamb; 10 pm, Sun 9 pm; no booking.

Xi'an Impression N7 £25 4 2 2
117 Benwell Rd   020 3441 0191   9–2D
"Out-of-this-world food" from Xi'an (the terminus of the Silk Road in central China) – "noodle-based with some street food additions, all delicious" – attracts a steady stream of Chinese diners who "pack out" this "hole-in-the-wall place literally next to the Arsenal stadium". Spurs fans will be relieved to learn that a larger sibling, Xi'an Biang Biang Noodles, opened near Spitalfields in July 2018. / N7 \N; www.xianimpression.co.uk; @xianimpression; 10 pm.

XU W1 £60 4 3 4
30 Rupert St   020 3319 8147   4–3D
From the team and backers behind the brilliant Bao, this "stylishly fitted-out" yearling "is a happy surprise on the edge of Chinatown", and has been smashing it since day one. "The beautiful interior gives a real air of opulence akin to 1930s, Art Deco-style, Taiwanese tea parlours in days gone by" (complete with Mahjong table); and the "excellent (Taiwanese) food, is very different to other restaurants serving 'Chinese' food" ("not every dish is a bullseye, but most are delicious and all interesting"). Top Menu Tip: shou pa chicken ("the chickeniest chicken ever"). / W1D 6DL; xulondon.com; @XU_london; Mon-Thu 11 pm; closed Fri & Sat & Sun.

Yalla Yalla £46 3 2 2
1 Green's Ct, W1   020 7287 7663   4–2D
12 Winsley St, W1   020 7637 4748   3–1C
Pair of Lebanese street food cafés that are "small, busy but worth queuing for!" in central London. "The original hidden in Soho is still the best", but the good-value menu of "fresh" dishes at its Fitzrovia sibling is identical. (The Greenwich branch has bitten the dust). / www.yalla-yalla.co.uk; Green's Court 11 pm, Sun 10 pm; Winsley Street 11.30 pm, Sat 11 pm; W1 closed Sun; booking min 10.

Yama Momo SE22 £53 3 3 3
72 Lordship Ln   020 8299 1007   1–4D
"Consistently delicious sushi" and other "great Japanese dishes" plus "a lovely ambience and a great cocktail list" all rate well at this East Dulwich offshoot of Clapham's popular Pacific-fusion outfit, Tsunami. "Sit at the bar and watch the chefs at work". / SE22 8HF; www.yamamomo.co.uk; @YamamomoRest; 10.30 pm; closed weekday L.

Yamabahce W1 NEW £41 2 2 2
26 James St   020 3905 3139   3–1A
Serial entrepreneur Alan Yau is having another crack at a Turkish pide (flatbread) concept with this white-tiled café with large central oven in a cute enclave off Oxford Street (which opened in late 2017). Early feedback is limited and not impressive – is this going to go the same way as his 2016 attempt, Babaji Pide which started well, but has now gone down the tubes? / W1U 1EN; www.yamabahce.com; may need 6+ to book.

Yard Sale Pizza £38 **5** **3** **3**
54 Blackstock Rd, N4   020 7226 2651   9–1D
622 High Road Leytonstone, E11   020 8539 5333   1–1D **NEW**
Hoe St, E17   020 8509 0888   1–1D
105 Lower Clapton Rd, E5   020 3602 9090   14–1B
"Some of the pizzas would horrify an Italian" – "try the lamb kebab-style!".
"They're definitely not authentic, but they're consistently superb", say the
growing legion of fans of this hip and "very self-aware" East London group,
which opened a new Leytonstone branch this year (and also dug a toehold
into West London in the new Market Halls development on Fulham
Broadway). / 11 pm, Sun 10 pm; closed Mon-Thu L.

Yashin W8 £87 **4** **2** **2**
1a Argyll Rd   020 7938 1536   6–1A
'Pre-seasoned sushi' (you're not supposed to add any extra soya sauce, so as
to emphasise the taste of the fish) is a speciality at this stylish modern
Japanese off High Street Kensington, which opened in 2010 with high
ambitions. Despite its "unique" approach and high level of achievement –
fans feel its outstanding sushi is "simply the best in town" – it maintains
a strangely low profile. Ditto its 'Ocean' sibling on the Old Brompton Road
(not listed), where such feedback as we have says its "expensive but good".
/ W8 7DB; www.yashinsushi.com; @Yashinsushi; 9.30 pm; booking max 7 may apply.

Yauatcha £81 **4** **3** **4**
Broadwick Hs, 15-17 Broadwick St, W1   020 7494 8888   4–1C
Broadgate Circle, EC2   020 3817 9888   13–2B
"Dim sum are top class – beautifully presented and all of them delicious" –
at this slick, "fun" and hugely popular Chinese-inspired duo (originally
created by Hakkasan and Wagamama founder, Alan Yau), whose stylish
looks are "verging on bling, but well done". Both branches score highly,
although the well-established Soho original still has the edge over the
relatively new Broadgate Circle branch. "Great cocktails" too – "their tea
is also exquisite". Top Tip: cool terrace in EC2. / W1 10 pm, Fri & Sat
10.30 pm; EC2 11.30 pm; EC2 closed Sun.

The Yellow House SE16 £46 **3** **4** **3**
126 Lower Rd   020 7231 8777   12–2A
Good all-round ratings again this year for this informal haunt – one of the
few decent options near Surrey Quays station. On the menu: wood-fired
pizza, plus a selection of burgers, steaks and other grills. / SE16 2UE;
www.theyellowhouse.eu; @theyellowhousejazz; Wed-Sat, Tue 9 pm, Sun 3 pm; closed
Mon, Tue-Sat D only, Sun open L & D.

Yen WC2 **NEW** £90 **4** **4** **4**
190 Strand, 5 Arundel St   07825 647 930   2–2D
"Vast" and high-ceilinged newcomer, south of Aldwych, from the Japan-
based fashion group Onward, whose stark styling (featuring lots of wood)
is at odds with the more prosaic offerings typically found in the slightly
featureless environs of The Temple. On all accounts its wide-ranging menu
(sushi and sashimi, wagyu beef steaks, soba noodle dishes, tempura …) are
"very good" and some would say exceptional: "my Japanese friends say this
is London's best authentic Japanese restaurant". / WC2R 3DX;
www.yen-london.co.uk; @YenRestaurant; Tue-Thu 8.30 pm, Fri 9 pm, Sat 9.30 pm,
Sun 7 pm.

Yi-Ban E16 £52 **2** **2** **3**
London Regatta Centre, Royal Albert Dock   020 7473 6699   12–1D
"Views of City Airport and the Albert Dock are perhaps the best feature
of this obscurely-situated Docklands Chinese", overlooking the water. Fans
"love this place" and say its "dim sum is second to none", but others feel
"the food quality has become average at best". / E16 2QT; www.yi-ban.co.uk;
11 pm, Sun 10.30 pm.

Yipin China N1 £45 4 2 2
70-72 Liverpool Rd 020 7354 3388 9–3D
It's "hard to beat the quality of food" at this functional Sichuan/Hunanese canteen near Angel, which raises the bar for "deep, savoury, deliciousness". Top Tip: "superb cold starters: lotus root is amazing". / N1 0QD; www.yipinchina.co.uk; 11 pm; cash only.

Yming W1 £50 3 4 2
35-36 Greek St 020 7734 2721 5–2A
"Ever-helpful" service is "delightful as ever at this bright Soho stalwart" – a "quiet oasis" just beyond Chinatown's northern borders, where a very strong following of loyal regulars "will come back and back for another renewal of old acquaintance" with maitre d' William and owner Christine. Foodwise, results are "very reliable" and "very reasonably priced". / W1D 5DL; www.yminglondon.com; 11.45 pm; closed Sun.

York & Albany NW1 £59 1 1 2
127-129 Parkway 020 7592 1227 9–3B
This substantial Georgian tavern where Camden Town meets Regent's Park is part of Gordon Ramsay's empire, and has disappointed most reporters this year. The owner is famous for his tongue-lashings, and here he gets it back in spades. "Worst meal this year: terrible roast beef, terrible service" – "Ramsay should get his own house in order!" / NW1 7PS; www.gordonramsayrestaurants.com/york-and-a; @yorkandalbany; 10.30 pm, Sun 9 pm.

Yoshi Sushi W6 £38 3 4 2
210 King St 020 8748 5058 8–2B
In an anonymous row of shops near Ravenscourt Park tube, this grungy looking Korean/Japanese stalwart never inspires a huge amount of feedback. Those who discover it are delighted however, acclaiming its "delicious sushi, and other fantastic-value yet high quality and flavoursome food". / W6 0RA; www.yoshisushi.co.uk; 10.30 pm; closed Sun L.

Yoshino W1 £48 4 4 2
3 Piccadilly Pl 020 7287 6622 4–4C
On a quiet alleyway near Piccadilly Circus, this typically low-key (but "welcoming") Japanese, has been an insider's secret for more than two decades, with a simple counter downstairs and table service up. Practically all diners agree it's on good form again now, "after many years of changing chefs and menus". / W1J 0DB; www.yoshino.net; @Yoshino_London; Wed-Sat, Tue 9 pm, Sun 3 pm; closed Sun.

Yum Bun EC2 £19 5 4 2
Dinerama, 19 Great Eastern St 07919 408 221 13–2B
"Best buns in London no contest" – even "better than Bao!" – claim fans of Lisa Meyer's Chinese-inspired steamed buns and dumplings (most popularly stuffed with slow-roasted pork belly), which started as a stall in 2010 on Broadway Market, and are now to be found at The Kitchens, Spitalfields Market, as well as various Street Feast locations. / EC2A 3EJ; www.yumbun.com; @yumbun; Mon & Tue, Sun 5 pm, Wed-Fri 8 pm, Sat 6 pm; closed Mon D, Tue D, Wed D, Sat L & Sun; no booking.

Zafferano SW1 £99 3 3 3
15 Lowndes St 020 7235 5800 6–1D
"Still one of the top Italians in town", say fans of this well-known Belgravian, whose heyday was twenty years ago under founding chef Giorgio Locatelli. But while it's still "always busy and buzzy", survey feedback is much more muted nowadays, and – though it avoids damning critiques – sceptics consider it "dull and completely overpriced". / SW1X 9EY; www.zafferanorestaurant.com; 11 pm, Sun 10.30 pm.

Zaffrani N1 £48 **3**|2|2
47 Cross St 020 7226 5522 9–3D
Not a huge amount to say about this feature of Islington's main drag other
than that it's consistently nominated as "a good local Indian". / N1 2BB;
www.zaffrani.co.uk; 10.30 pm.

Zaibatsu SE10 £30 **4**|4|2
96 Trafalgar Rd 020 8858 9317 1–3D
"Marvellous Japanese food" including "amazing and well-priced sushi"
brings a constant buzz to this "deceptively unimpressive-looking restaurant"
in Greenwich, with "scruffy Formica-topped tables". "BYO, no corkage".
/ SE10 9UW; www.zaibatsufusion.co.uk; @ong_teck; 11 pm; closed Mon; cash only.

Zaika of Kensington W8 £65 **4**|3|3
1 Kensington High St 020 7795 6533 6–1A
"Fine dining at its best from the sub-continent" means this "roomy former
banking hall" beside the Kensington Gardens Hotel is a firm "favourite
Indian" for many diners – especially since ratings have recovered well after
a dip last year. / W8 5NP; www.zaikaofkensington.com; @ZaikaLondon; 10.30 pm,
Sun 9.30 pm; closed Mon L; credit card required to book.

Zela WC2 🆕
The Strand 020 8089 3981 2–2D
Q: What do Cristiano Ronaldo, Enrique Iglesias, Rafael Nadal and NBC
basketball star Pau Gasol have in common? A: This restaurant, and its sibling
in Ibiza, plus an international chain of restaurants under the name Tatel.
Who knew? This London opening promises sushi and sashimi made with
spanking fresh Mediterranean ingredients by chef Ricardo Sanz of Madrid's
Kabuki. / WC2R 1HA; zelarestaurants.com.

Zelman Meats £62 **4**|3|3
Harvey Nichols, 109-125 Knightsbridge, SW1 020 7201 8625 6–1D
2 St Anne's Ct, W1 020 7437 0566 4–1D
"BBQ in excelsis!" – Misha Zelman's budget (well, by comparison to his
Goodman's group, anyway) small chain of funky steakhouses inspires
nothing but high praise for its "flawless" steaks from a "short-but-interesting
menu of cuts", and "vibrant atmosphere". Despite such consistently positive
feedback however, its new branch near the Old Bill proved short lived and
closed in July 2018. / W1 10.30 pm, Sun 8 pm; SW1 10 pm, Sun 7 pm;
N4 midnight; W1 closed Mon L, N4 closed Mon-Fri L.

Zeret SE5 £30 **4**|4|3
216-218 Camberwell Rd 020 7701 8587 1–3C
"Hidden in an estate in Camberwell!" – it's worth discovering this "fabulous
Ethiopian": a well-established, family-run operation of nearly 15 years
standing, decked out with a simple, modern interior. / SE5 0ED;
www.zeretkitchen.com; Sun-Thu 11 pm, Fri & Sat midnight; no Amex.

Zero Degrees SE3 £45 **3**|3|3
29-31 Montpelier Vale 020 8852 5619 1–4D
Since it launched in 2000, this early-wave microbrewery café (where you eat
dwarfed by large steel brewing vessels) has made a fun venue for a pizza
or bowl of moules frites down Blackheath way. It inspires limited feedback,
but all of it positive. / SE3 0TJ; www.zerodegrees.co.uk; @Zerodegreesbeer;
10.30 pm.

**Zest,
JW3 NW3** £60 **3**|3|2
341-351 Finchley Rd 020 7433 8955 1–1B
This "much-loved eatery" in West Hampstead's JW3 Jewish community
centre channels the flavours of contemporary Tel Aviv. "London is very short
of decent kosher restaurants... and the food here isn't bad at all".
/ NW3 6ET; www.zestatjw3.co.uk; @ZESTatJW3; Sun-Thu 10.30 pm; closed
Fri & Sat.

Zheng SW3 £61 **4**3**2**

4 Sydney St   020 7352 9890   6–2C

"Very good use of spicing and heat" helps distinguish the "very good Malaysian/Chinese cooking'" at this "smart" but "fun" Chelsea yearling, which is making a good go of the tricky site that has seen restaurants come and go over the years, most recently in the form of Brasserie Gustave (RIP). / SW3 6PP; www.zhengchelsea.co.uk; 11.30 pm, Sun 10 pm; closed Tue L.

Zia Lucia N7 £35 **4**3**3**

157 Holloway Rd   020 7700 3708   9–2D

"The best charcoal base ever" is just one of the four dough choices on offer (including gluten-free, all slow-fermented for 48 hours) at this "brilliant" and "welcoming" pizzeria on Holloway Road. Its popularity means "door-side queuing, but we've learned to live with it". Top Tip: "charcoal-based Andrea Pirlo (mozzarella, gorgonzola, apple, truffle and olive sauce)". / N7 8LX; www.zialucia.com; @zialuciapizza; 10.30 pm; closed Mon.

Ziani's SW3 £62 **2**4**2**

45 Radnor Walk   020 7351 5297   6–3C

This archetypal, "very friendly" local trattoria off the King's Road is an "old favourite" of the well-heeled Chelsea crowd, and knows just how to look after them. "It's like eating in your living room!" – "a little cramped", but that's all part of the fun. / SW3 4BP; www.ziani.co.uk; 11 pm, Sun 10 pm.

Zoilo W1 £64 **3**3**3**

9 Duke St   020 7486 9699   3–1A

"Unusual but brilliant little Argentinian tapas restaurant tucked away near Selfridges". "After a day's shopping, retire to this calm oasis and you'll be transported to Buenos Aires" (well nearly). / W1U 3EG; www.zoilo.co.uk; @Zoilo_London; Tue-Fri 10 pm, Mon 3.30 pm; closed Sun.

Zuma SW7 £82 **5**3**4**

5 Raphael St   020 7584 1010   6–1C

"It takes flak for being too showy", and "can be a little over-run by glam types", but "the foundations of this fun Knightsbridge scene are as appealing as ever – fantastic, innovative cuisine, welcoming service and a wonderful, vibrant atmosphere". The Japanese-fusion dishes deliver "brilliant flavours": "superb sashimi and black cod (although all the fish is amazing)" to "steak mains to die for". "It's been a favourite for over a decade now and still feels fresh". / SW7 1DL; www.zumarestaurant.com; 10.45 pm, Sun 10.15 pm; booking max 8 may apply.

AREA OVERVIEWS

CENTRAL

Soho, Covent Garden & Bloomsbury
(Parts of W1, all WC2 and WC1)

£190+	Aulis London	*British, Modern*	5 5 4
£110+	L'Atelier de Joel Robuchon	*French*	2 2 2
£100+	The Northall	*British, Modern*	3 2 3
	Savoy Grill	*British, Traditional*	2 2 2
	Smith & Wollensky	*Steaks & grills*	2 2 2
£90+	Kaspar's Seafood	*Fish & seafood*	3 3 4
	The Savoy Hotel	*Afternoon tea*	2 3 4
	Sushisamba	*Japanese*	2 2 3
	Yen	*"*	4 4 4
£80+	Bob Bob Ricard	*British, Modern*	3 3 5
	Mirror Room	*"*	3 3 4
	The Petersham	*"*	3 3 5
	Social Eating House	*"*	3 3 4
	Spring Restaurant	*"*	3 3 4
	Neptune, The Principal	*Fish & seafood*	– – –
	J Sheekey	*"*	3 4 4
	Asia de Cuba	*Fusion*	2 2 3
	MASH Steakhouse	*Steaks & grills*	3 3 2
	Oscar Wilde Lounge	*Afternoon tea*	3 3 5
	Lima Floral	*Peruvian*	3 3 2
	Yauatcha	*Chinese*	4 3 4
	Roka, Aldwych House	*Japanese*	4 3 3
£70+	Christophers	*American*	2 2 3
	Balthazar	*British, Modern*	2 2 4
	Frog by Adam Handling	*"*	5 5 4
	Ham Yard Restaurant	*"*	2 3 4
	The Ivy	*"*	2 3 4
	Noble Rot	*"*	3 4 4
	Holborn Dining Room	*British, Traditional*	3 3 3
	Rules	*"*	2 3 5
	Simpson's in the Strand	*"*	2 2 3
	Clos Maggiore	*French*	3 3 5
	L'Escargot	*"*	3 4 5
	Frenchie	*"*	3 2 2
	Gauthier Soho	*"*	5 4 4
	Otto's	*"*	4 4 4
	Evelyns Table	*Italian*	4 4 4
	Nopi	*Mediterranean*	4 3 3
	Eneko	*Spanish*	3 2 1
	Hawksmoor	*Steaks & grills*	3 2 2
	Cecconi's Pizza Bar	*Pizza*	2 2 3
	The Palomar	*Middle Eastern*	4 3 3
	Red Fort	*Indian*	3 2 2

£60+	Big Easy	*American*	2	2	3
	Scarlett Green	*Australian*	–	–	–
	Bryn Williams, Somerset Hs	*British, Modern*	4	4	3
	Dean Street Townhouse	"	2	3	5
	Ducksoup	"	4	4	4
	Heliot Steak House	"	3	3	3
	Hix	"	1	2	2
	Kettners	"	3	3	5
	The Portrait	"	2	3	4
	Quo Vadis	"	4	4	5
	St Luke's Kitchen	"	2	3	3
	Tredwell's	"	2	2	2
	Parsons	*Fish & seafood*	4	3	3
	Randall & Aubin	"	3	3	4
	J Sheekey Atlantic Bar	"	3	3	4
	Wright Brothers	"	4	4	3
	Café Monico	*French*	2	3	4
	Henrietta	"	–	–	–
	Bocca Di Lupo	*Italian*	4	4	3
	Café Murano	"	2	3	2
	Fumo	"	3	3	3
	Vasco & Pieros Pavilion	"	3	3	2
	100 Wardour Street	*Mediterranean*	–	–	–
	Aqua Nueva	*Spanish*	3	2	4
	Cigala	"	3	2	2
	Sophie's Steakhouse	*Steaks & grills*	2	2	2
	Zelman Meats	"	4	3	3
	Rainforest Café	*Burgers, etc*	1	3	3
	Hovarda	*Turkish*	2	3	4
	Hoppers	*Indian, Southern*	4	2	2
	aqua kyoto	*Japanese*	3	3	4
	Chotto Matte	"	3	2	4
	Jinjuu	*Korean*	4	3	4
	Patara Soho	*Thai*	3	3	3
	XU	*Taiwanese*	4	3	4
£50+	Bodeans	*American*	3	2	3
	Hubbard & Bell	"	3	3	3
	Jackson & Rye	"	2	2	2
	Joe Allen	"	2	3	4
	Andrew Edmunds	*British, Modern*	3	4	5
	Boyds Grill & Wine Bar	"	3	3	3
	Great Queen Street	"	3	2	2
	The Ivy Market Grill	"	2	2	4
	10 Greek Street	"	4	4	3
	Terroirs	"	3	2	3
	Cork & Bottle	*British, Traditional*	2	3	4
	George in the Strand	"	3	3	3
	The Ivy Soho Brasserie	"	2	2	4
	The Delaunay	*East & Cent. European*	2	4	4
	Bonnie Gull Seafood Shack	*Fish & seafood*	5	3	3
	The Oystermen	"	4	4	3
	Antidote Wine Bar	*French*	2	2	3
	Blanchette	"	2	2	3
	Bon Vivant	"	3	3	3
	Cigalon	"	4	4	4

Le Garrick	"		3 3 4
Mon Plaisir Restaurant	"		3 3 4
The Good Egg	Fusion		3 3 3
The 10 Cases	International		3 4 3
Da Mario	Italian		3 4 3
Dehesa	"		3 2 3
La Goccia	"		3 3 5
Luce e Limoni	"		4 4 3
Margot	"		4 5 4
Mele e Pere	"		3 4 3
Polpetto	"		3 3 2
Polpo	"		2 2 2
San Carlo Cicchetti	"		3 3 4
Barrafina	Spanish		5 5 5
Ember Yard	"		3 3 4
Morada Brindisa Asador	"		3 3 2
Opera Tavern	"		3 3 3
Rambla	"		4 3 3
Foxlow	Steaks & grills		2 2 2
Macellaio RC	"		3 3 3
St Moritz	Swiss		3 3 4
Dalloway Terrace	Afternoon tea		3 2 4
Burger & Lobster	Burgers, etc		3 3 3
Fernandez & Wells	Sandwiches, cakes, etc		3 3 3
Bodeans	BBQ		3 2 3
Cantina Laredo	Mexican/TexMex		2 2 2
Casita Andina	Peruvian		3 3 3
Ceviche Soho	"		5 3 4
Señor Ceviche	"		3 3 3
The Barbary	North African		5 5 4
Barshu	Chinese		4 2 2
The Duck & Rice	"		3 2 4
The Four Seasons	"		5 1 1
Yming	"		3 4 2
Darjeeling Express	Indian		5 3 3
Dum Biryani	"		3 2 2
Tamarind Kitchen	"		3 4 4
Flesh and Buns	Japanese		2 3 3
Inko Nito	"		– – –
Oka, Kingly Court	"		3 2 2
Sticks'n'Sushi	"		3 2 2
£40+	Breakfast Club	American	3 3 3
	Coopers Restaurant & Bar	British, Modern	2 3 3
	The Norfolk Arms	"	2 3 3
	Shampers	"	3 4 4
	VQ, St Giles Hotel	"	2 3 3
	Claw Carnaby	Fish & seafood	3 3 2
	Brasserie Zédel	French	1 3 5
	Prix Fixe	"	3 2 2
	Relais de Venise	"	3 3 2
	Savoir Faire	"	3 4 2
	La Fromagerie Bloomsbury	International	3 3 3
	Gordons Wine Bar	"	2 1 5
	Casa Tua	Italian	4 3 3
	Ciao Bella	"	2 3 4

Pastaio	"	3	2	3
La Porchetta Pizzeria	"	2	3	2
Blacklock	Steaks & grills	4	4	4
Mildreds	Vegetarian	3	2	2
Haché	Burgers, etc	3	3	2
The Chipping Forecast	Fish & chips	3	2	2
North Sea Fish	"	3	3	2
Poppies	"	3	2	3
Pizza Pilgrims	Pizza	3	3	3
Rossopomodoro	"	2	2	2
temper Covent Garden	"	2	2	4
Bea's Cake Boutique	Sandwiches, cakes, etc	3	3	3
Chick 'n' Sours	Chicken	4	3	3
temper Soho	BBQ	2	2	4
Breddos Tacos	Mexican/TexMex	3	3	3
Corazón	"	2	4	3
Lupita	"	3	3	2
Yalla Yalla	Lebanese	3	2	2
Le Bab	Turkish	4	3	3
Golden Dragon	Chinese	3	2	2
Dishoom	Indian	3	4	5
Kricket	"	4	4	4
Malabar Junction	"	3	4	3
Punjab	"	3	4	3
Salaam Namaste	"	3	2	2
Tandoor Chop House	"	4	4	3
Bone Daddies	Japanese	3	3	4
Dozo	"	3	2	2
Ichi Buns	"	3	2	3
Ippudo London	"	3	2	3
Jugemu	"	5	2	3
Koya-Bar	"	4	4	3
Shoryu Ramen	"	3	3	2
Tonkotsu	"	4	3	3
Olle	Korean	2	2	2
Freak Scene	Pan-Asian	5	3	4
Hare & Tortoise	"	3	3	2
Cây Tre	Vietnamese	3	2	2
Pho & Bun	"	3	3	2
£35+ Lina Stores	Italian	5	3	3
Princi	"	3	2	2
MEATliquor	Burgers, etc	3	2	4
Homeslice	Pizza	3	3	3
Gabys	Israeli	3	2	2
Joy King Lau	Chinese	3	2	2
Cinnamon Bazaar	Indian	3	3	3
Sagar	"	4	3	2
Kintan	Japanese	3	2	2
Taro	"	3	2	2
Kimchee	Korean	2	2	2
On The Bab	"	3	2	2
Bao	Taiwanese	4	3	3
£30+ Café in the Crypt	British, Traditional	2	1	4
Bar Italia	Italian	3	3	5

263

	Name	Cuisine			
	Flat Iron	Steaks & grills	3	4	4
	Chilli Cool	Chinese	4	2	1
	Wong Kei	"	3	2	1
	Beijing Dumpling	Chinese, Dim sum	4	3	2
	India Club	Indian	2	2	2
	Eat Tokyo	Japanese	3	3	2
	Kulu Kulu	"	3	2	1
	C&R Café	Malaysian	4	2	2
	Kiln	Thai	4	3	4
	Viet Food	Vietnamese	3	2	2
£25+	MEATmarket	Burgers, etc	3	2	2
	Patty and Bun Soho	"	4	3	3
	Shake Shack	"	3	2	2
	Tommi's Burger Joint	"	3	3	3
	Kanada-Ya	Japanese	5	3	3
£20+	Jidori	Japanese	3	3	2
	Sen Viet	"	4	3	2
	Tokyo Diner	"	3	3	3
	Bibimbap Soho	Korean	3	2	2
£10+	Nordic Bakery	Scandinavian	3	2	2
	Bageriet	Sandwiches, cakes, etc	4	3	3
	Flat White	"	4	4	3
	Bun House	Chinese	4	4	4
	On the Dak	Korean	5	3	1
£5+	Jacob the Angel	British, Modern	3	3	3
	Maison Bertaux	Afternoon tea	4	4	4
	Monmouth Coffee Company	Sandwiches, cakes, etc	3	4	4

Mayfair & St James's (Parts of W1 and SW1)

	Name	Cuisine			
£380+	The Araki	Japanese	5	5	3
£140+	Hélène Darroze	French	3	4	4
	Sketch (Lecture Rm)	"	3	3	4
£130+	The Ritz	British, Traditional	3	4	5
	Alain Ducasse	French	2	2	3
	Le Gavroche	"	4	5	4
	The Square	"	3	3	2
	The Promenade	Afternoon tea	2	4	4
	Park Chinois	Chinese	2	2	3
£120+	Fera at Claridge's	British, Modern	4	4	4
	The Greenhouse	French	3	3	3
	Cut, 45 Park Lane	Steaks & grills	3	2	2
	Kai Mayfair	Chinese	2	2	2
	Umu	Japanese	2	3	3
£110+	Dorchester Grill	British, Modern	3	4	4
	Estiatorio Milos	Fish & seafood	3	2	3

	Galvin at Windows	*French*	2	3	5
	Seven Park Place	"	4	4	3
	Novikov	*Italian*	1	2	2
	Benares	*Indian*	3	2	3
£100+	Alyn Williams	*British, Modern*	5	5	3
	Ormer Mayfair	"	3	2	2
	Pollen Street Social	"	3	3	3
	Corrigans Mayfair	*British, Traditional*	3	3	3
	Ritz (Palm Court)	*Afternoon tea*	2	4	5
	Nobu, Metropolitan Hotel	*Japanese*	3	2	2
	Nobu Berkeley	"	3	2	2
	Tokimeite	"	3	2	2
£90+	Hide	*British, Modern*	5	4	5
	Wiltons	*British, Traditional*	4	5	4
	Sexy Fish	*Fish & seafood*	1	1	2
	La Petite Maison	*French*	3	2	3
	Sketch (Gallery)	"	1	2	3
	Beck at Browns	*Italian*	3	4	4
	Bocconcino	"	3	2	2
	Murano	"	4	5	3
	Theo Randall	"	4	4	2
	Street XO	*Spanish*	2	2	2
	Goodman	*Steaks & grills*	3	3	2
	Hakkasan Mayfair	*Chinese*	4	2	4
	Indian Accent	*Indian*	5	4	4
	Tamarind	"	4	4	3
	Ginza Onodera	*Japanese*	4	4	2
	JG at The Connaught	*Pan-Asian*	3	3	3
	Novikov	"	3	2	4
£80+	Hush	*British, Modern*	2	2	2
	Butlers Restaurant	*British, Traditional*	2	4	3
	Babel House	*Fish & seafood*	–	–	–
	Bentleys	"	3	4	3
	Scotts	"	4	4	5
	maze	*French*	1	2	1
	Chucs Dover Street	*Italian*	3	3	3
	Ristorante Frescobaldi	"	3	4	3
	Ella Canta	*Mexican/TexMex*	3	4	4
	Coya	*Peruvian*	3	2	3
	China Tang	*Chinese*	4	4	4
	Chutney Mary	*Indian*	4	4	4
	Jamavar	"	3	4	3
	Veeraswamy	"	4	4	4
	Roka	*Japanese*	4	3	3
£70+	The Avenue	*American*	2	2	2
	Colony Grill Room	"	2	3	4
	Bonhams Restaurant	*British, Modern*	5	5	2
	Le Caprice	"	2	4	4
	Heddon Street Kitchen	"	2	2	2
	Kitty Fisher's	"	2	3	3
	Little Social	"	4	2	3
	Magpie	"	4	4	3

Mews of Mayfair	"		3 2 3
Quaglinos	"		2 3 4
Wild Honey	"		3 3 3
English Tea Rm (Browns)	British, Traditional		3 4 4
The Game Bird	"		3 5 3
Black Roe	Fish & seafood		3 2 3
Boulestin	French		2 3 2
Ferdi	"		1 1 2
The American Bar	International		2 5 3
Isabel	"		2 4 5
Cecconis	Italian		2 2 3
Francos	"		3 4 4
Sartoria	"		3 3 3
Aquavit	Scandinavian		2 2 2
The Guinea Grill	Steaks & grills		3 3 4
Hawksmoor	"		3 2 2
maze Grill	"		1 2 2
Rowleys	"		2 2 2
34 Mayfair	"		2 2 3
Diamond Jub' Salon	Afternoon tea		3 4 4
Momo	Moroccan		3 3 3
Gymkhana	Indian		4 3 4
Mint Leaf	"		3 2 3
Sake No Hana	Japanese		3 3 3
£60+	Bellamys	British, Modern	3 4 4
	Galvin at the Athenaeum	"	3 3 2
	The Keeper's House	"	2 2 3
	Langans Brasserie	"	2 2 4
	The Punchbowl	"	3 4 3
	Stem	"	4 4 3
	The Wolseley	"	2 3 5
	Fishworks	Fish & seafood	3 2 2
	The Balcon	French	2 3 3
	Boudin Blanc	"	3 2 3
	28-50	"	2 2 3
	Café Murano	Italian	2 3 2
	Sabor	Spanish	4 4 4
	Ikoyi	West African	4 3 2
	Bombay Bustle	Indian	4 4 3
	Chisou	Japanese	4 3 2
	Kiku	"	3 3 2
	Titu	Pan-Asian	4 5 4
	Patara Mayfair	Thai	3 3 3
£50+	Duck & Waffle Local	British, Modern	3 3 3
	The Windmill	British, Traditional	2 2 3
	Neo Bistro	French	4 4 3
	Al Duca	Italian	2 2 2
	San Carlo Cicchetti	"	3 3 4
	Il Vicolo	"	3 3 2
	Burger & Lobster	Burgers, etc	3 3 3
	Delfino	Pizza	3 3 2
	Mayfair Pizza Company	"	3 3 3
	Fernandez & Wells	Sandwiches, cakes, etc	3 3 3
	Sakagura	Japanese	3 4 2

	TAKA	*"*	3	3	3

£40+	L'Artiste Musclé	*French*	2	2	5
	El Pirata	*Spanish*	2	2	4
	tibits	*Vegetarian*	3	2	3
	Shoryu Ramen	*Japanese*	3	3	2
	Yoshino	*"*	4	4	2

£35+	The Parlour	*Ice cream*	3	3	3
	Rasa	*Indian, Southern*	3	3	2

Fitzrovia & Marylebone (Part of W1)

£160+	Kitchen Table at Bubbledogs	*Fusion*	5	3	3

£110+	Pied À Terre	*French*	4	4	4
	Texture	*Scandinavian*	5	3	3
	Beast	*Steaks & grills*	1	2	2

£90+	The Chiltern Firehouse	*American*	1	1	3
	Roganic	*British, Modern*	5	4	2
	Roux at the Landau	*"*	4	4	4
	Orrery	*French*	2	3	3
	Hakkasan	*Chinese*	4	2	4

£80+	Clipstone	*British, Modern*	3	3	2
	Portland	*"*	4	3	2
	Clarette	*French*	3	3	3
	Mere	*International*	4	4	3
	Locanda Locatelli	*Italian*	3	4	3
	Lima Fitzrovia	*Peruvian*	3	3	2
	Trishna	*Indian*	4	2	2
	Defune	*Japanese*	3	2	1
	Roka	*"*	4	3	3

£70+	The Berners Tavern	*British, Modern*	2	3	5
	Pescatori	*Fish & seafood*	2	2	2
	Noizé	*French*	4	5	4
	Les 110 de Taillevent	*"*	3	2	3
	Providores (Tapa Room)	*Fusion*	4	4	3
	Caffè Caldesi	*Italian*	3	3	2
	The Ninth London	*Mediterranean*	4	3	2
	Palm Court, The Langham	*Afternoon tea*	3	3	4

£60+	108 Brasserie	*British, Modern*	3	3	3
	Percy & Founders	*"*	3	3	3
	Picture	*"*	3	3	2
	Vinoteca Seymour Place	*"*	2	2	3
	Fischer's	*East & Cent. European*	3	3	4
	Fancy Crab	*Fish & seafood*	2	3	2
	Fishworks	*"*	3	2	2
	28-50	*French*	2	2	3
	Twist	*Fusion*	4	5	4
	Meraki	*Greek*	3	2	4

	Bernardi's	Italian	3	3	3
	Blandford Comptoir	Mediterranean	3	3	3
	ROVI	"	–	–	–
	Social Wine & Tapas	Spanish	4	4	3
	Zoilo	Argentinian	3	3	3
	The Bright Courtyard	Chinese	4	2	2
	Royal China Club	"	4	2	2
	Gaylord	Indian	3	3	3
	Jikoni	"	4	4	4
	Lokhandwala	"	3	3	3
	Hoppers	Indian, Southern	4	2	2
	Dinings	Japanese	5	3	2
	House of Ho	Vietnamese	3	4	4
£50+	Bubbledogs	American	3	4	4
	Caravan	British, Modern	3	3	3
	Daylesford Organic	"	3	2	2
	The Ivy Café	"	1	2	3
	The Wigmore, The Langham	British, Traditional	4	4	4
	Bonnie Gull	Fish & seafood	5	3	3
	The Wallace	French	2	2	5
	Carousel	Fusion	4	3	4
	Opso	Greek	3	4	3
	Briciole	Italian	3	2	2
	2 Veneti	"	3	3	3
	Riding House Café	Mediterranean	2	2	3
	The Harcourt	Scandinavian	3	3	4
	Mac & Wild	Scottish	3	2	4
	Barrica	Spanish	3	3	2
	Donostia	"	4	4	4
	Drakes Tabanco	"	2	2	4
	Ibérica	"	2	2	3
	Lurra	"	3	4	4
	Salt Yard	"	4	3	3
	Boxcar Butcher & Grill	Steaks & grills	4	4	3
	The Gate	Vegetarian	4	2	3
	Burger & Lobster	Burgers, etc	3	3	3
	Pisqu	Peruvian	3	2	3
	Reubens	Kosher	2	2	2
	Maroush	Lebanese	3	2	2
	Honey & Smoke	Middle Eastern	4	3	2
	Ishtar	Turkish	3	3	2
	Kyseri	"	–	–	–
	Royal China	Chinese	3	1	2
	Kazu	Japanese	–	–	–
	The Greyhound Cafe	Thai	2	2	3
£40+	Lantana Café	Australian	3	3	3
	Foley's	International	4	4	3
	La Fromagerie Café	"	3	3	3
	In Parma	Italian	4	3	2
	Made in Italy James St	"	3	1	2
	Rossopomodoro, John Lewis	"	2	2	2
	Vagabond Wines	Mediterranean	2	2	3
	Relais de Venise	Steaks & grills	3	3	2
	Santa Maria	Pizza	4	3	2

	Yalla Yalla	*Lebanese*	**3** 2 2
	Delamina	*Middle Eastern*	**4** 4 2
	Honey & Co	*"*	**4** 4 3
	Yamabahce	*Turkish*	2 2 2
	Roti Chai	*Indian*	**3** **3** **3**
	Bone Daddies	*Japanese*	**3** **3** **4**
	Sushi Bar Atari-Ya	*"*	**5** 2 1
	Tonkotsu, Selfridges	*"*	**4** **3** **3**
£35+	Serge et Le Phoque	*French*	2 **3** **3**
	Navarros	*Spanish*	**3** **3** **3**
	MEATLiquor	*Burgers, etc*	**3** 2 **4**
	Golden Hind	*Fish & chips*	**3** **3** 2
	Buongiorno e Buonasera	*Pizza*	– – –
	Homeslice	*"*	**3** **3** **3**
	Workshop Coffee	*Sandwiches, cakes, etc*	**3** **3** **3**
	Chik'n	*Chicken*	**3** 2 2
	Sanxia Renjia	*Chinese*	**3** **3** 2
	Chettinad	*Indian*	**4** 2 2
	Sagar	*"*	**4** **3** 2
	Kintan	*Japanese*	**3** 2 2
	On The Bab Express	*Korean*	**3** 2 2
	Bao Fitzrovia	*Taiwanese*	**4** **3** **3**
£30+	Ragam	*Indian*	**4** **3** 2
	Sushi Atelier	*Japanese*	**5** **3** **3**
£25+	Patty and Bun	*Burgers, etc*	**4** **3** **3**
	Tommi's Burger Joint	*"*	**3** **3** **3**
£20+	Bibimbap Soho	*Korean*	**3** 2 2
£15+	Icco Pizza	*Italian*	**5** 2 1
	Patogh	*Middle Eastern*	**4** **3** 2
£10+	Kaffeine	*Sandwiches, cakes, etc*	**3** **5** **4**

Belgravia, Pimlico, Victoria & Westminster (SW1, except St James's)

£130+	Celeste, The Lanesborough	*French*	2 2 **4**
£120+	Marcus, The Berkeley	*British, Modern*	**3** **4** **3**
	Dinner, Mandarin Oriental	*British, Traditional*	2 2 2
£110+	Pétrus	*French*	**4** **4** **4**
£100+	Ametsa	*Spanish*	**3** **4** 2
	Rib Room	*Steaks & grills*	2 2 **3**
	The Collins Room	*Afternoon tea*	2 **3** **4**
£90+	Roux at Parliament Square	*British, Modern*	**5** **4** **3**
	The Dining Room	*British, Traditional*	**3** **5** **4**
	Zafferano	*Italian*	**3** **3** **3**

269

	Hunan	*Chinese*	5 2 1
£80+	Kerridges Bar & Grill	*British, Modern*	– – –
	Chucs Harrods	*Italian*	3 3 3
	Olivocarne	*"*	3 2 2
	Oval Restaurant	*"*	– – –
	Santini	*"*	2 2 2
	M Restaurant	*Steaks & grills*	2 2 2
	Mr Chow	*Chinese*	2 3 3
	Amaya	*Indian*	4 2 3
	The Cinnamon Club	*"*	3 2 3
£70+	Hans Bar & Grill	*British, Modern*	– – –
	Olivomare	*Fish & seafood*	3 3 1
	Il Convivio	*Italian*	3 3 3
	Enoteca Turi	*"*	3 5 3
	Olivo	*"*	3 3 2
£60+	Timmy Green	*Australian*	3 3 3
	The Alfred Tennyson	*British, Modern*	2 2 3
	The Botanist	*"*	2 2 2
	45 Jermyn Street	*"*	3 4 4
	Lorne	*"*	4 5 3
	The Orange	*"*	3 3 3
	The Other Naughty Piglet	*"*	4 3 2
	Rail House Café	*"*	2 2 2
	Scully	*"*	5 5 3
	Tate Britain	*"*	2 3 4
	The Thomas Cubitt	*"*	3 4 4
	Bar Boulud	*French*	3 2 3
	Colbert	*"*	1 1 3
	La Poule au Pot	*"*	2 2 5
	Cambridge Street Kitchen	*International*	2 3 3
	Caraffini	*Italian*	3 5 4
	Osteria DellAngolo	*"*	2 2 2
	Quirinale	*"*	3 4 3
	Sale e Pepe	*"*	3 2 3
	San Carlo	*"*	– – –
	Signor Sassi	*"*	2 3 3
	Omars Place	*Mediterranean*	4 4 4
	Trafalgar Dining Rooms	*"*	3 3 3
	Eccleston Place by Tart	*Organic*	– – –
	Boisdale of Belgravia	*Scottish*	2 2 3
	Zelman Meats	*Steaks & grills*	4 3 3
	Oliveto	*Pizza*	4 2 1
	Ken Los Memories	*Chinese*	2 2 2
	Quilon	*Indian, Southern*	5 5 2
	Sumosan Twiga	*Japanese*	2 2 3
	Salloos	*Pakistani*	3 2 2
£50+	Granger & Co	*Australian*	2 2 3
	Aster Restaurant	*British, Modern*	3 2 3
	Daylesford Organic	*"*	3 2 2
	Shepherds	*British, Traditional*	3 3 4
	Motcombs	*International*	2 3 3
	Cacio & Pepe	*Italian*	3 3 2

	Hai Cenato	"	**2**	3	2
	Ottolenghi	"	**3**	2	2
	Tozi	"	**3**	4	3
	About Thyme	Spanish	**2**	3	3
	Ibérica, Zig Zag Building	"	**2**	2	3
	Burger & Lobster	Burgers, etc	**3**	3	3
	Seafresh	Fish & chips	**3**	2	2
	Abd El Wahab	Lebanese	**3**	3	3
	Kazan	Turkish	**3**	4	3
	Sticks'n'Sushi	Japanese	**3**	2	2
£40+	Rochelle Canteen at the ICA	British, Modern	**4**	4	3
	Gustoso	Italian	**2**	4	3
	Vagabond Wines	Mediterranean	**2**	2	3
	Goya	Spanish	**3**	3	2
	Wulf & Lamb	Vegetarian	**3**	2	2
	Cyprus Mangal	Turkish	**3**	3	2
	A Wong	Chinese	**5**	5	3
	Bone Daddies, Nova	Japanese	**3**	3	4
	Machiya	"	**4**	2	2
£35+	The Vincent Rooms	British, Modern	**3**	2	2
£30+	Sri Suwoon	Thai	**4**	4	3
£25+	Shake Shack	Burgers, etc	**3**	2	2
	Kanada-Ya	Japanese	**5**	3	3
£20+	Bleecker Burger	Burgers, etc	**5**	2	2
£15+	Regency Cafe	British, Traditional	**3**	4	5
	Dominique Ansel Bakery	Sandwiches, cakes, etc	**3**	2	2

WEST

Chelsea, South Kensington, Kensington, Earl's Court & Fulham (SW3, SW5, SW6, SW7, SW10 & W8)

£160+	Gordon Ramsay	French	2	2	2
£130+	Bibendum	French	3	3	4
£100+	Elystan Street	British, Modern	3	3	2
	The Five Fields	"	5	5	4
£90+	Outlaw's at The Capital	Fish & seafood	4	4	2
£80+	Launceston Place	British, Modern	3	4	4
	Medlar	"	4	4	3
	Restaurant Ours	"	2	2	3
	Rivea, Bulgari Hotel	International	3	4	3
	Daphnes	Italian	2	2	2
	Scalini	"	3	3	3
	Min Jiang	Chinese	4	4	5
	Koji	Japanese	3	3	4
	Yashin	"	4	2	2
	Zuma	"	5	3	4
£70+	Bluebird	British, Modern	2	3	3
	Clarkes	"	4	5	4
	Kitchen W8	"	4	4	3
	Le Colombier	French	3	5	4
	Lucio	Italian	3	2	2
	Manicomio	"	2	2	3
	Stecca	"	–	–	–
	Cambio de Tercio	Spanish	4	3	3
	Hawksmoor Knightsbridge	Steaks & grills	3	2	2
£60+	Big Easy	American	2	2	3
	The Abingdon	British, Modern	3	3	4
	Brinkleys	"	2	2	3
	Claude's Kitchen	"	3	3	4
	The Cross Keys	"	3	4	4
	Harwood Arms	"	4	3	3
	Parabola, Design Museum	"	–	–	–
	Toms Kitchen	"	2	2	2
	Maggie Joness	British, Traditional	2	2	4
	Kensington Place	Fish & seafood	3	2	2
	Wright Brothers	"	4	4	3
	Belvedere Restaurant	French	3	3	5
	Mazi	Greek	3	4	3
	Enoteca Rosso	Italian	2	2	2
	La Famiglia	"	2	2	2
	Frantoio	"	3	4	4
	La Mia Mamma	"	–	–	–
	Il Portico	"	3	5	4
	Theos Simple Italian	"	3	3	2

Zianis	"	2 4 2
Sophies Steakhouse	Steaks & grills	2 2 2
Chicama	Peruvian	4 2 4
Good Earth	Chinese	2 2 2
Bombay Brasserie	Indian	4 3 3
Zaika of Kensington	Indian, Southern	4 3 3
Chisou	Japanese	4 3 2
Dinings	"	5 3 2
Kurobuta	"	3 2 2
Zheng	Malaysian	4 3 2
Patara	Thai	3 3 3

£50+			
	Bodeans	American	3 2 3
	The Builders Arms	British, Modern	2 2 4
	Daylesford Organic	"	3 2 2
	The Enterprise	"	2 3 4
	The Ivy Chelsea Garden	"	2 2 4
	Manuka Kitchen	"	3 4 3
	maze Grill	"	3 3 2
	Park Terrace Restaurant	"	3 3 4
	Rabbit	"	3 2 3
	The Sands End	"	3 3 4
	The Shed	"	3 4 3
	Bumpkin	British, Traditional	2 2 3
	Bibendum Oyster Bar	Fish & seafood	3 3 3
	Bistro Mirey	Fusion	4 4 3
	The Admiral Codrington	International	3 3 4
	Gallery Mess	"	2 3 3
	The Kensington Wine Rooms	"	2 3 3
	Aglio e Olio	Italian	3 3 2
	Harrys Dolce Vita	"	3 4 5
	Nuovi Sapori	"	3 3 4
	Polpo	"	2 2 2
	Riccardos	"	2 2 2
	San Pietro	"	3 3 3
	Sapori Sardi	"	3 3 2
	The Atlas	Mediterranean	4 4 4
	Ognisko Restaurant	Polish	3 4 5
	Casa Brindisa	Spanish	3 3 2
	Tendido Cero	"	3 3 4
	Macellaio RC	Steaks & grills	3 3 3
	Geales	Fish & chips	2 2 2
	Pizzicotto	Pizza	4 4 3
	Fernandez & Wells	Sandwiches, cakes, etc	3 3 3
	Maroush	Lebanese	3 2 2
	Royal China	Chinese	3 1 2
	Romulo Café	Filipino	3 3 3
	Pure Indian Cooking	Indian	4 4 2
	Akira at Japan House	Japanese	– – –
	Kiru	"	3 3 3
	Oka	"	3 2 2
	Sticks'n'Sushi	"	3 2 2
	Eight Over Eight	Pan-Asian	3 3 4
	Sukho Fine Thai Cuisine	Thai	5 5 3
	Go-Viet	Vietnamese	4 4 2

			Ratings		
£40+	Kensington Square Kitchen	British, Modern	4	4	3
	VQ	"	2	3	3
	Ardiciocca	Italian	–	–	–
	Chelsea Cellar	"	4	4	4
	Da Mario	"	3	3	3
	Made in Italy	"	3	1	2
	Vagabond Wines	Mediterranean	2	2	3
	Daquise	Polish	2	2	2
	Haché	Steaks & grills	3	3	2
	Tell Your Friends	Vegetarian	–	–	–
	La Delizia Limbara	Pizza	3	2	2
	Rocca Di Papa	"	3	4	4
	Rossopomodoro	"	2	2	2
	Santa Maria	"	4	3	2
	Lupita West	Mexican/TexMex	3	3	2
	Dip in Brilliant	Indian	3	3	3
	Dishoom	"	3	4	5
	Flora Indica	"	4	3	3
	Malabar	"	3	3	3
	Noor Jahan	"	3	3	3
	Thali	"	4	4	3
	Bone Daddies, Whole Foods	Japanese	3	3	4
	Dozo	"	3	2	2
	Suksan	Thai	3	3	2
£35+	Churchill Arms	British, Traditional	3	2	5
	Mona Lisa	International	3	3	2
	Pappa Ciccia	Italian	3	4	3
	Best Mangal	Turkish	4	3	3
	Addies Thai Café	Thai	3	3	3
	Mien Tay	Vietnamese	3	2	2
£30+	Ceru	Mediterranean	4	3	2
	Eat Tokyo	Japanese	3	3	2
	Kulu Kulu	"	3	2	1
	Phat Phuc	Vietnamese	4	3	1
£25+	Tommi's Burger Joint	Burgers, etc	3	3	3
£20+	Market Hall Fulham	International	–	–	–
	Stick & Bowl	Chinese	3	3	1
£15+	Oree	Sandwiches, cakes, etc	3	2	3

Notting Hill, Holland Park, Bayswater, North Kensington & Maida Vale (W2, W9, W10, W11)

£150+	The Ledbury	*British, Modern*	5	4	4
£110+	Core by Clare Smyth	*British, Modern*	5	5	4
£90+	Flat Three	*Japanese*	4	4	3
£80+	Chucs Serpentine	*Italian*	3	3	3
	Casa Cruz	*South American*	1	1	3
£70+	The Summerhouse	*Fish & seafood*	2	2	5
	Angelus	*French*	3	4	2
	Assaggi	*Italian*	3	4	2
	Kateh	*Persian*	3	2	3
£60+	The Frontline Club	*British, Modern*	3	3	4
	108 Garage	"	2	2	2
	London Shell Co.	*Fish & seafood*	4	4	5
	Assaggi Bar & Pizzeria	*Italian*	4	3	2
	Edera	"	3	4	3
	Essenza	"	2	3	3
	Mediterraneo	"	3	3	3
	Osteria Basilico	"	4	2	2
	Kurobuta	*Japanese*	3	2	2
	Southam Street	"	3	2	3
£50+	Pomona's	*American*	3	4	4
	Granger & Co	*Australian*	2	2	3
	Daylesford Organic	*British, Modern*	3	2	2
	The Hero of Maida	"	–	–	–
	Julies	"	–	–	–
	The Ladbroke Arms	"	3	3	3
	Paradise by way of Kensal Gn	"	3	2	4
	Six Portland Road	"	4	5	3
	The Waterway	"	2	2	3
	Hereford Road	*British, Traditional*	4	3	3
	Snaps & Rye	*Danish*	3	4	3
	Cepages	*French*	4	3	4
	The Cow	*Irish*	3	3	5
	The Oak	*Italian*	3	3	4
	Ottolenghi	"	3	2	2
	Polpo	"	2	2	2
	Portobello Ristorante	"	3	4	4
	Farmacy	*Vegetarian*	2	3	4
	Pizza East Portobello	*Pizza*	4	3	4
	The Red Pepper	"	3	2	2
	Cocotte	*Chicken*	4	4	3
	Peyotito	*Mexican/TexMex*	3	3	2
	Andina Picanteria	*Peruvian*	3	3	3
	Maroush	*Lebanese*	3	2	2
	The Four Seasons	*Chinese*	5	1	1
	Royal China	"	3	1	2
	Maguro	*Japanese*	4	4	2
	E&O	*Pan-Asian*	3	4	4

£40+	Electric Diner	*American*	2 2 3
	VQ	*British, Modern*	2 3 3
	Bucket	*Fish & seafood*	– – –
	The Chipping Forecast	*"*	3 2 2
	Ida	*Italian*	3 2 3
	Raoul's Café	*Mediterranean*	3 2 4
	Taqueria	*Mexican/TexMex*	3 3 3
	The Cedar Restaurant	*Lebanese*	3 3 2
	Mandarin Kitchen	*Chinese*	4 3 2
	Pearl Liang	*"*	4 3 3
	Bombay Palace	*Indian*	4 3 2
	Noor Jahan	*"*	3 3 3
	Tonkotsu	*Japanese*	4 3 3
	Uli	*Pan-Asian*	3 4 4
	MAM	*Vietnamese*	4 3 3
£35+	MEATliquor	*Burgers, etc*	3 2 4
	Gold Mine	*Chinese*	4 2 2
	The Heron	*Thai*	4 3 1
£30+	Flat Iron	*Steaks & grills*	3 4 4
	C&R Café	*Malaysian*	4 2 2
£25+	Patty and Bun	*Burgers, etc*	4 3 3
	Alounak	*Persian*	3 3 3
	Khans	*Indian*	2 2 2
£20+	Fez Mangal	*Turkish*	5 3 3
£5+	Lisboa Pâtisserie	*Sandwiches, cakes, etc*	3 2 4

Hammersmith, Shepherd's Bush, Olympia, Chiswick, Brentford & Ealing (W4, W5, W6, W12, W13, W14, TW8)

Price	Name	Cuisine			
£120+	Hedone	British, Modern	4	3	2
£90+	The River Café	Italian	3	4	4
£80+	La Trompette	French	5	5	3
£60+	Vinoteca	British, Modern	2	2	3
	Michael Nadra	French	4	3	2
	Le Vacherin	"	3	3	3
	Villa Di Geggiano	Italian	3	4	3
	Popeseye	Steaks & grills	3	2	2
	The Bird in Hand	Pizza	3	2	3
£50+	Jackson & Rye Chiswick	American	2	2	2
	The Anglesea Arms	British, Modern	4	4	4
	The Brackenbury	"	4	4	4
	Brackenbury Wine Rooms	"	2	2	3
	Charlotte's W5	"	3	3	3
	City Barge	"	3	3	3
	The Colton Arms	"	2	3	4
	The Dove	"	3	3	5
	Duke of Sussex	"	2	2	3
	Eat 17 Hammersmith	"	3	4	3
	The Havelock Tavern	"	3	2	4
	High Road Brasserie	"	2	2	2
	The Hampshire Hog	British, Traditional	3	3	3
	Albertine	French	4	4	5
	The Andover Arms	International	2	3	4
	Annies	"	2	3	4
	L'Amorosa	Italian	4	4	3
	Cibo	"	4	5	3
	The Oak W12	"	3	3	4
	Pentolina	"	4	4	3
	Tarantella	"	3	3	3
	The Swan	Mediterranean	3	4	4
	The Gate	Vegetarian	4	2	3
	Quantus	South American	3	5	3
	Shikumen, Dorsett Hotel	Chinese	4	3	2
	Brilliant	Indian	4	4	3
	Indian Zing	"	4	3	2
	Little Bird Chiswick	Pan-Asian	3	2	4
£40+	Bluebird Café White City	British, Modern	–	–	–
	The Dartmouth Castle	"	3	4	3
	Mustard	"	3	3	3
	The Pear Tree	"	3	3	4
	The Princess Victoria	"	3	3	3
	Wellbourne	"	3	3	2
	Cumberland Arms	Mediterranean	3	3	3
	Santa Maria	Pizza	4	3	2
	Tamp Coffee	Sandwiches, cakes, etc	3	4	4
	Chez Abir	Lebanese	3	4	2

	North China	Chinese	3 4 2
	Madhus	Indian	4 5 3
	Potli	"	4 4 3
	Kiraku	Japanese	4 2 2
	Sushi Bar Atari-Ya	"	5 2 1
	Sushi Bar Makoto	"	4 3 1
	Hare & Tortoise	Pan-Asian	3 3 2
£35+	Homeslice	Pizza	3 3 3
	Angie's Little Food Shop	Sandwiches, cakes, etc	3 3 3
	Adams Café	Moroccan	3 5 3
	Best Mangal	Turkish	4 3 3
	Anarkali	Indian	3 4 3
	Sagar	"	4 3 2
	Tosa	Japanese	3 3 2
	Yoshi Sushi	"	3 4 2
	101 Thai Kitchen	Thai	4 3 2
	Saigon Saigon	Vietnamese	2 3 3
£30+	Oro Di Napoli	Pizza	4 3 2
	Monkey Temple	Indian	3 4 2
	Shilpa	Indian, Southern	4 2 1
	Eat Tokyo	Japanese	3 3 2
£25+	Kerbisher & Malt	Fish & chips	3 2 2
	Alounak	Persian	3 3 3
	Gifto's	Indian	3 2 2
£20+	Abu Zaad	Syrian	3 3 2
£5+	Bears Ice Cream	Ice cream	3 3 3

NORTH

Hampstead, West Hampstead, St John's Wood, Regent's Park, Kilburn & Camden Town (NW postcodes)

£70+					
	Landmark (Winter Gdn)	*British, Modern*	2	4	5
	Odettes	"	4	3	3
	The Gilbert Scott	*British, Traditional*	2	2	4
	Kaifeng	*Chinese*	3	2	2

£60+					
	The Booking Office	*British, Modern*	2	2	4
	Bradleys	"	2	2	2
	L'Aventure	*French*	3	4	5
	Michael Nadra	"	4	3	2
	Oslo Court	"	3	5	4
	Bull & Last	*International*	3	3	3
	Villa Bianca	*Italian*	2	2	2
	Zest, JW3	*Kosher*	3	3	2
	Crocker's Folly	*Lebanese*	3	2	4
	Delicatessen	*Middle Eastern*	3	2	2
	Good Earth	*Chinese*	2	2	2
	Patara	*Thai*	3	3	3

£50+					
	The Clifton	*British, Modern*	3	3	5
	Ham	"	3	2	3
	The Horseshoe	"	3	3	4
	The Ivy Café	"	1	2	3
	Parlour Kensal	"	3	3	4
	Searcys St Pancras Grand	"	2	1	3
	The Wells Tavern	"	3	3	4
	The Wet Fish Café	"	2	3	4
	Holly Bush	*British, Traditional*	3	3	5
	York & Albany	"	1	1	2
	La Collina	*Italian*	3	3	2
	Melange	"	3	2	2
	The Rising Sun	"	3	3	3
	28 Church Row	*Spanish*	4	4	4
	Ceremony	*Vegetarian*	3	4	3
	Manna	"	2	2	2
	The Sea Shell	*Fish & chips*	3	2	2
	Pizza East	*Pizza*	4	3	4
	Greenberry Café	*Sandwiches, cakes, etc*	3	3	4
	Phoenix Palace	*Chinese*	3	3	3
	Oka	*Japanese*	3	2	2

£40+					
	Lantana Cafe	*Australian*	3	3	3
	L'Absinthe	*French*	2	3	3
	Authentique	"	–	–	–
	La Cage Imaginaire	"	2	3	4
	La Ferme	"	3	3	3
	Carob Tree	*Greek*	3	4	2
	Lemonia	"	1	4	5
	Anima e Cuore	*Italian*	5	3	1
	La Porchetta Pizzeria	"	2	3	2

279

Name	Cuisine			
Quartieri	"	4	3	3
Sarracino	"	3	3	2
El Parador	Spanish	4	4	3
Beef & Brew	Steaks & grills	3	4	3
Haché	"	3	3	2
Mildreds	Vegetarian	3	2	2
Purezza	"	3	3	2
Harry Morgans	Burgers, etc	2	3	2
Poppies Camden	Fish & chips	3	2	3
L'Artista	Pizza	3	5	3
Rossopomodoro	"	2	2	2
The Cedar Restaurant	Lebanese	3	3	2
Skewd Kitchen	Turkish	3	3	3
Great Nepalese	Indian	3	4	2
Guglee	"	3	3	2
Namaaste Kitchen	"	4	3	2
Paradise Hampstead	"	3	5	4
Saravanaa Bhavan	"	4	3	2
Jin Kichi	Japanese	5	4	3
Sushi Bar Atari-Ya	"	5	2	1
Sushi Masa	"	3	4	3
The Petite Coree	Korean	4	3	2
Singapore Garden	Malaysian	3	3	2
£35+				
Lure	Fish & seafood	3	5	3
Fiddies Italian Kitchen	Italian	3	3	2
Giacomos	"	3	3	2
Nautilus	Fish & chips	4	3	1
L'Antica Pizzeria	Pizza	4	5	3
Sacro Cuore	"	5	3	2
Green Cottage	Chinese	3	2	2
Bonoo	Indian	4	4	3
Vijay	"	4	4	1
Anjanaas	Indian, Southern	4	4	3
Asakusa	Japanese	5	2	2
Bang Bang Oriental	Pan-Asian	3	2	3
£30+				
The Little Bay	Mediterranean	3	3	4
Kenwood (Brew House)	Sandwiches, cakes, etc	2	2	3
Chai Thali	Indian	3	3	3
Ravi Shankar	"	3	2	2
Eat Tokyo	Japanese	3	3	2
£25+				
Shake Shack	Burgers, etc	3	2	2
Ali Baba	Egyptian	3	2	2
Chutneys	Indian	3	2	2
Diwana Bhel-Poori House	"	3	2	1
Sakonis	"	3	2	1
£20+				
L'Antica Pizzeria da Michele	Pizza	–	–	–
Ariana II	Afghani	3	3	2
£15+				
Icco Pizza	Pizza	5	2	1
Roti King	Malaysian	5	2	1

£10+			
Fields Beneath	*Vegetarian*	3 2 3
Ginger & White	*Sandwiches, cakes, etc*	3 3 3
E Mono	*Turkish*	4 2 2

Hoxton, Islington, Highgate, Crouch End, Stoke Newington, Finsbury Park, Muswell Hill & Finchley (N postcodes)

£70+			
Cub	*British, Modern*	4 4 3
Fifteen	"	2 2 2
The Frog Hoxton	"	5 5 4
Plum + Spilt Milk	"	2 3 3
German Gymnasium	*East & Cent. European*	2 1 4

£60+			
Fredericks	*British, Modern*	3 4 5
The Lighterman	"	3 3 4
Perilla	"	3 3 3
Prawn on the Lawn	*Fish & seafood*	3 3 2
Bellanger	*French*	2 2 3
Salut	*International*	3 2 2
Radici	*Italian*	2 2 1
Trullo	"	3 3 3
Vinoteca	*Mediterranean*	2 2 3
Popeseye	*Steaks & grills*	3 2 2

£50+			
Granger & Co	*Australian*	2 2 3
The Bull	*British, Modern*	3 4 4
Caravan King's Cross	"	3 3 3
The Drapers Arms	"	3 3 4
Granary Square Brasserie	"	2 2 4
Heirloom	"	3 3 3
Humble Grape	"	3 4 4
Jones & Sons	"	3 3 3
Oldroyd	"	3 3 2
Pig & Butcher	"	4 4 4
The Red Lion & Sun	"	3 2 3
Rotunda Bar & Restaurant	"	3 3 4
Westerns Laundry	"	3 3 3
St Johns	*British, Traditional*	3 4 5
Galley	*Fish & seafood*	3 3 3
Bistro Aix	*French*	2 2 3
Petit Pois Bistro	"	4 2 3
Sardine	"	4 4 3
Table Du Marche	"	3 3 2
The Good Egg	*Fusion*	3 3 3
Banners	*International*	3 2 4
Primeur	"	3 3 3
500	*Italian*	4 3 2
Il Guscio	"	3 4 3
Melange	"	3 2 2
Ottolenghi	"	3 2 2
Rugoletta	"	3 3 2
Rök	*Scandinavian*	3 4 3
Barrafina	*Spanish*	5 5 5

Café del Parc	"	4	5	3
Camino King's Cross	"	3	3	2
Smokehouse Islington	Steaks & grills	3	3	2
Cocotte	Chicken	4	4	3
Bodean's	BBQ	3	2	3
£40+				
Breakfast Club Angel	American	3	3	3
Wander	Australian	4	3	3
Bergen House	British, Modern	–	–	–
Chriskitch	"	4	3	3
Haven Bistro	"	3	4	3
Season Kitchen	"	3	3	2
Snooty Fox	British, Traditional	3	2	3
Kipferl	East & Cent. European	3	2	3
Le Sacré-Coeur	French	2	3	3
Vrisaki	Greek	3	3	3
Aleion	International	3	3	3
Andi's	"	3	3	4
La Fromagerie	"	3	3	3
The Orange Tree	"	3	2	3
Osteria Tufo	Italian	3	2	2
La Porchetta Pizzeria	"	2	3	2
Alcedo	Mediterranean	3	4	3
Bar Esteban	Spanish	3	3	3
Lluna	"	3	2	3
Trangallan	"	4	4	3
Beef & Brew	Steaks & grills	3	4	3
Mildreds	Vegetarian	3	2	2
Toffs	Fish & chips	3	4	3
Rossopomodoro	Pizza	2	2	2
Sweet Thursday	"	3	2	3
Chick 'n' Sours	Chicken	4	3	3
Plaquemine Lock	Cajun/creole	3	3	3
Black Axe Mangal	Turkish	4	3	2
Gallipoli	"	2	3	3
Yipin China	Chinese	4	2	2
Dishoom	Indian	3	4	5
Zaffrani	"	3	2	2
Supawan	Thai	4	4	2
£35+				
Linden Stores	British, Modern	4	3	3
Passione e Tradizione	Italian	3	3	2
Pasta Remoli	"	3	3	3
Pizzeria Pappagone	"	3	4	3
Lady Mildmay	Mediterranean	3	4	3
Llerena	Spanish	4	4	2
MEATLiquor Islington	Burgers, etc	3	2	4
Sutton and Sons	Fish & chips	4	3	2
Sacro Cuore	Pizza	5	3	2
Yard Sale Pizza	"	5	3	3
Zia Lucia	"	4	3	3
Finks Salt and Sweet	Sandwiches, cakes, etc	3	4	4
Monty's Deli	"	4	4	3
Sumak	Turkish	4	4	2
Indian Rasoi	Indian	3	3	2
Rasa	Indian, Southern	3	3	2

	Farang	*Thai*	**4**	**3**	**2**
£30+	Sunday	*Australian*	**4**	2	**3**
	Two Brothers	*Fish & seafood*	**3**	2	2
	Le Mercury	*French*	2	2	**3**
	Via Emilia	*Italian*	–	–	–
	Flat Iron	*Steaks & grills*	**3**	**4**	**4**
	Cut + Grind	*Burgers, etc*	**4**	**3**	2
	MEATmission	*"*	**3**	**3**	**4**
	Olympus Fish	*Fish & chips*	**3**	**3**	2
	Max's Sandwich Shop	*Sandwiches, cakes, etc*	**4**	**4**	**3**
	Gem	*Turkish*	**3**	**4**	**3**
	Gökyüzü	*"*	2	2	2
	Delhi Grill	*Indian*	**3**	**3**	2
	Jashan	*"*	**4**	**4**	2
	Shahi Pakwaan	*"*	**5**	**4**	**3**
	Dotori	*Korean*	**4**	**3**	2
£25+	Saponara	*Italian*	**4**	**3**	**3**
	Afghan Kitchen	*Afghani*	**4**	2	2
	Xi'an Impression	*Chinese*	**4**	2	2
	Kanada-Ya	*Japanese*	**5**	**3**	**3**
£20+	Piebury Corner	*British, Traditional*	**3**	**3**	**3**
	Fannys Kebabs	*Turkish*	–	–	–
	CôBa	*Vietnamese*	**4**	**3**	2

SOUTH

South Bank (SE1)

£150+	Story	*British, Modern*	3	3	3
£100+	Aqua Shard	*British, Modern*	1	1	3
	Oblix	"	2	2	3
	Hutong, The Shard	*Chinese*	2	2	4
£90+	Oxo Tower (Rest')	*British, Modern*	1	1	1
	TING	*International*	2	2	4
£80+	Duddell's	*Chinese, Dim sum*	4	2	4
£70+	Oxo Tower (Brass')	*British, Modern*	1	1	2
	Le Pont de la Tour	"	2	2	2
	Skylon, South Bank Centre	"	2	2	4
	Skylon Grill	"	2	2	4
	Butlers Wharf Chop House	*British, Traditional*	3	2	4
	Roast	"	2	2	3
	Hawksmoor	*Steaks & grills*	3	2	2
	Baluchi	*Indian*	3	2	4
£60+	40 Maltby Street	*British, Modern*	4	4	3
	Sea Containers	"	1	2	2
	The Swan at the Globe	"	3	2	4
	Tom Simmons	"	3	2	2
	Union Street Café	"	3	2	3
	Applebees Fish	*Fish & seafood*	4	2	2
	Wright Brothers	"	4	4	3
	Arthur Hooper's	*International*	4	4	3
	Vivat Bacchus	"	3	4	2
	Pizarro	*Spanish*	3	2	3
	The Coal Shed	*Steaks & grills*	3	3	3
	Pique Nique	*Chicken*	3	3	3
	Santo Remedio	*Mexican/TexMex*	3	2	3
	Rabot 1745	*Afro-Caribbean*	2	2	2
	Bala Baya	*Middle Eastern*	4	2	2
£50+	The Anchor & Hope	*British, Modern*	4	3	3
	Caravan Bankside	"	3	3	3
	Edwins	"	3	4	4
	Elliot's Café	"	4	3	3
	The Garrison	"	3	2	3
	House Restaurant	"	2	3	2
	The Ivy Tower Bridge	"	2	2	4
	Menier Chocolate Factory	"	2	3	3
	Tate Modern (Level 7)	"	2	2	3
	Waterloo Bar & Kitchen	"	3	2	2
	fish!	*Fish & seafood*	3	2	2
	Native	"	–	–	–
	Casse-Croute	*French*	4	4	4
	Capricci	*Italian*	3	3	2
	Baltic	*Polish*	3	4	3

Bar Douro	Portuguese	4 4 3
Londrino	"	2 3 3
Camino Bankside	Spanish	3 3 2
José	"	5 4 5
LOBOS Meat & Tapas	"	4 3 2
Tapas Brindisa	"	3 3 2
Macellaio RC	Steaks & grills	3 3 3
O'ver	Pizza	4 3 3
Chimis	Argentinian	– – –
Paladar	South American	– – –
Arabica Bar and Kitchen	Lebanese	3 3 3
Champor-Champor	Thai	3 3 3
£40+	Lantana London Bridge	Australian	3 3 3
	Blueprint Café	British, Modern	2 2 4
	The Garden Cafe	"	3 2 3
	The Green Room	"	2 3 2
	Lupins	"	4 4 3
	The Table	"	3 2 2
	Boro Bistro	French	3 3 3
	Flour & Grape	Italian	3 4 3
	Mar I Terra	Spanish	2 2 2
	Meson don Felipe	"	2 2 3
	tibits	Vegetarian	3 2 3
	London Grind	Sandwiches, cakes, etc	4 4 4
	El Pastór	Mexican/TexMex	4 3 5
	Tonkotsu Bankside	Japanese	4 3 3
	Sticky Mango at RSJ	Pan-Asian	2 3 2
£35+	Tas Pide	Turkish	2 3 3
	Est India	Indian	3 2 3
	Gunpowder	"	4 4 3
£25+	Mercato Metropolitano	Italian	5 3 3
	Padella	"	5 4 3
	Patty and Bun	Burgers, etc	4 3 3
	Masters Super Fish	Fish & chips	3 2 1
£5+	Monmouth Coffee Company	Sandwiches, cakes, etc	3 4 4
	Gourmet Goat	Middle Eastern	4 2 2

Greenwich, Lewisham, Dulwich & Blackheath (All SE postcodes, except SE1)

£60+	Brasserie Toulouse-Lautrec	French	3 3 3
	Craft London	Pizza	3 4 2
£50+	The Camberwell Arms	British, Modern	5 3 3
	Franklins	"	3 2 2
	The Guildford Arms	"	3 4 3
	Llewelyn's	"	3 2 2
	The Palmerston	"	3 3 3
	Rivington Grill	"	2 2 2
	The Rosendale	"	3 4 3

			FSA		
	Terroirs	"	3	2	3
	Peckham Bazaar	Greek	4	3	3
	Brookmill	International	3	3	3
	Con Gusto	Italian	3	4	4
	Luciano's	"	4	3	2
	Coal Rooms	Steaks & grills	4	3	3
	Kudu	South African	3	3	3
	Babur	Indian	5	5	4
	Kennington Tandoori	"	3	3	3
	Sticks'n'Sushi	Japanese	3	2	2
	Yama Momo	"	3	3	3
£40+	The Crooked Well	British, Modern	3	2	3
	The Lido Café	"	3	2	4
	Louie Louie	"	3	2	3
	Sparrow	"	4	5	3
	Joannas	International	3	5	4
	The Yellow House	"	3	4	3
	Artusi	Italian	4	3	3
	Forza Win	"	3	4	3
	Le Querce	"	3	3	2
	Marcella	Mediterranean	3	3	2
	Mamma Dough	Pizza	3	3	3
	Rocca Di Papa	"	3	4	4
	Zero Degrees	"	3	3	3
	Dragon Castle	Chinese	3	3	3
	Everest Inn	Indian	3	2	3
	Ganapati	"	4	3	3
	The Begging Bowl	Thai	4	2	2
	Bánh Bánh	Vietnamese	3	4	3
£35+	Babette	British, Modern	3	3	4
	Black Prince	"	3	3	2
	Catford Constitutional Club	"	3	4	4
	Good Neighbour	Mediterranean	–	–	–
	MEATliquor ED	Burgers, etc	3	2	4
	Olleys	Fish & chips	3	3	2
	Theo's	Pizza	3	3	2
	FM Mangal	Turkish	3	3	3
	Sanxia Renjia	Chinese	3	3	2
	Mr Bao	Taiwanese	4	3	3
£30+	White Bear	British, Traditional	3	3	3
	Made of Dough	Pizza	4	4	3
	Zeret	Ethiopian	4	4	3
	Zaibatsu	Japanese	4	4	2
£25+	Rox Burger	Burgers, etc	4	3	3
	400 Rabbits	Pizza	3	3	2
£20+	500 Degrees	Pizza	3	2	2
	Silk Road	Chinese	5	2	1
£15+	Goddards At Greenwich	British, Traditional	3	4	4
	Peckham Levels	International	–	–	–
	The Green Café	Vegetarian	3	3	2

	Café East	*Vietnamese*	**5** 2 2
£5+	Kappacasein	*Sandwiches, cakes, etc*	**4** **3** **3**

Battersea, Brixton, Clapham, Wandsworth Barnes, Putney & Wimbledon
(All SW postcodes south of the river)

£80+	Chez Bruce	*British, Modern*	**5** **5** **4**
£70+	Trinity	*British, Modern*	**5** **5** **4**
	Gastronhome	*French*	**5** **4** **3**
£60+	Hatched	*British, Modern*	**4** **4** 2
	Rick Stein	*Fish & seafood*	2 2 **3**
	Wright Brothers	*"*	**4** **4** **3**
	Sinabro	*French*	**4** **4** **3**
	The White Onion	*"*	**3** **4** 2
	London House	*International*	2 2 2
	Riva	*Italian*	**3** **3** 2
	Good Earth	*Chinese*	2 2 2
	Patara	*Thai*	**3** **3** **3**
£50+	Bodeans	*American*	**3** 2 **3**
	Bistro Union	*British, Modern*	**3** **3** **3**
	Brunswick House Café	*"*	**3** **3** **5**
	Cannizaro House	*"*	1 1 **4**
	Counter Culture	*"*	**3** **4** 2
	The Dairy	*"*	**4** **4** **4**
	Earl Spencer	*"*	**3** 2 **3**
	Home SW15	*"*	**3** **3** **3**
	Hood	*"*	**4** **3** **3**
	Humble Grape	*"*	**3** **4** **4**
	The Ivy Café	*"*	1 2 **3**
	Lamberts	*"*	**5** **5** **5**
	Minnow	*"*	**3** **3** **3**
	No 29 Power Station West	*"*	2 1 **4**
	Nutbourne	*"*	2 2 **3**
	Salon Brixton	*"*	**5** **4** **3**
	Sonnys Kitchen	*"*	**3** **3** 2
	Trinity Upstairs	*"*	**5** **4** **4**
	The Victoria	*"*	2 2 **3**
	Canton Arms	*British, Traditional*	**4** **3** **4**
	Fox & Grapes	*"*	**3** **3** **3**
	Jolly Gardeners	*"*	**3** **3** **3**
	Augustine Kitchen	*French*	**3** **4** **3**
	Bistro Vadouvan	*"*	**4** **4** **3**
	Gazette	*"*	**3** **3** **3**
	Soif	*"*	**3** **3** **3**
	Annies	*International*	2 **3** **4**
	The Light House	*"*	**3** **3** **3**
	Fiume	*Italian*	**3** **4** **3**
	Osteria Antica Bologna	*"*	**3** **3** 2
	Sorella	*"*	**4** **3** **3**

	Foxlow	Steaks & grills	2	2	2
	Knife	"	5	5	4
	Macellaio RC	"	3	3	3
	Naughty Piglets	"	5	5	3
	Addomme	Pizza	4	3	2
	Santa Maria del Sur	Argentinian	3	4	3
	Chokhi Dhani London	Indian	4	4	3
	Cinnamon Kitchen	"	4	3	3
	Sticks'n'Sushi	Japanese	3	2	2
	Little Bird Battersea	Pan-Asian	3	2	4
£40+	The Brown Dog	British, Modern	3	3	3
	Olympic Caf'	"	2	2	3
	Plot	"	4	4	4
	The Plough	"	2	3	4
	Smoke & Salt	"	5	4	3
	Sea Garden & Grill	Fish & seafood	4	4	4
	Made in Italy	Italian	3	1	2
	Pizza Metro	"	3	2	2
	Stockwell Continental	"	3	3	3
	Vagabond Wines	Mediterranean	2	2	3
	Boqueria	Spanish	4	3	3
	Little Taperia	"	3	2	2
	Arlo's	Steaks & grills	3	2	2
	Haché	Burgers, etc	3	3	2
	Bradys	Fish & chips	3	4	3
	Al Forno	Pizza	2	3	4
	Dynamo	"	3	2	3
	Mamma Dough	"	3	3	3
	Mother	"	2	2	3
	Pizza da Valter	"	3	2	2
	Rossopomodoro	"	2	2	2
	Duck Duck Goose	Chinese	4	4	3
	Indian Moment	Indian	3	3	2
	Kashmir	"	4	3	2
	Ma Goa	"	4	4	3
	Nanban	Japanese	4	2	3
	Takahashi	"	5	5	3
	Tonkotsu Battersea	"	4	3	3
	Tsunami	"	5	2	3
	Hare & Tortoise	Pan-Asian	3	3	2
	Bánh Bánh	Vietnamese	3	4	3
	Daddy Bao	Taiwanese	4	3	3
£35+	Fish in a Tie	Mediterranean	3	3	3
	Meatliquor	Burgers, etc	3	2	4
	Eco	Pizza	3	2	3
	Orange Pekoe	Sandwiches, cakes, etc	3	3	4
	Meza	Lebanese	3	3	2
	Indian Ocean	Indian	3	4	2
	Hashi	Japanese	3	3	2
	Taro	"	3	2	2
	Tomoe	"	4	2	1
	Mien Tay	Vietnamese	3	2	2

£30+	Dip & Flip	*Burgers, etc*	3	3	3
	Dirty Burger	"	2	2	2
	Chicken Shop	*Chicken*	2	2	2
	Booma	*Indian*	4	3	2
	Chit Chaat Chai	"	3	3	3
	Jaffna House	*Indian, Southern*	3	2	2
£25+	Unwined	*British, Modern*	3	4	4
	Kerbisher & Malt	*Fish & chips*	3	2	2
	Hot Stuff	*Indian*	3	5	2
	Munal Tandoori	"	3	4	2
	Mirch Masala	*Pakistani*	4	2	1
	Awesome Thai	*Thai*	3	4	2
	Kaosarn	"	4	2	3
£20+	Flotsam and Jetsam	*Australian*	3	2	3
	Tried & True	*British, Modern*	3	3	3
	Cut The Mustard	*Sandwiches, cakes, etc*	3	3	3
£15+	Joe Public	*Pizza*	3	4	2
	Ground Coffee Society	*Sandwiches, cakes, etc*	3	2	2
	Milk	"	4	3	3

Outer western suburbs
Kew, Richmond, Twickenham, Teddington

£80+	The Glasshouse	*British, Modern*	3	3	2
	M Bar & Grill Twickenham	*Steaks & grills*	2	2	2
£70+	The Dysart Petersham	*British, Modern*	3	3	3
	Petersham Nurseries Cafe	"	2	2	5
£60+	The Bingham	*British, Modern*	3	4	5
	The Petersham Restaurant	"	2	2	5
	Al Boccon di'vino	*Italian*	4	4	5
£50+	Jackson & Rye Richmond	*American*	2	2	2
	The Ivy Café	*British, Modern*	1	2	3
	Petit Ma Cuisine	*French*	2	2	2
	Le Salon Privé	"	3	4	3
	A Cena	*Italian*	3	2	3
	Bacco	"	2	2	2
£40+	La Buvette	*French*	3	2	3
	Dastaan	*Indian*	5	4	2
	Matsuba	*Japanese*	3	3	2
£35+	Moksha	*Indian*	5	4	3
£20+	The Fallow Deer Cafe	*International*	3	4	3

EAST

Smithfield & Farringdon (EC1)

£140+	The Clove Club	British, Modern	4 3 3
£100+	Club Gascon	French	4 4 4
£80+	Luca	Italian	3 3 4
	Sushi Tetsu	Japanese	5 5 3
£70+	Bleeding Heart Restaurant	French	3 3 5
	Smiths (Top Floor)	Steaks & grills	3 2 3
	Smiths (Dining Rm)	"	2 2 2
£60+	Anglo	British, Modern	5 4 2
	The Jugged Hare	"	4 2 2
	The Modern Pantry	"	2 2 2
	Vinoteca	"	2 2 3
	The Quality Chop House	British, Traditional	3 3 3
	St John Smithfield	"	5 4 3
	Moro	Spanish	4 3 3
	Hix Oyster & Chop House	Steaks & grills	3 2 2
£50+	Bodeans	American	3 2 3
	Granger & Co	Australian	2 2 3
	Bird of Smithfield	British, Modern	3 3 3
	Caravan	"	3 3 3
	The Coach	"	4 3 3
	The Wilmington	"	3 2 3
	The Fox and Anchor	British, Traditional	2 2 3
	Café du Marché	French	3 3 5
	Comptoir Gascon	"	2 2 2
	The Drunken Butler	"	4 3 3
	Niche	International	2 3 2
	Apulia	Italian	3 3 2
	Palatino	"	4 3 3
	Passo	"	2 2 2
	Polpo	"	2 2 2
	Ibérica	Spanish	2 2 3
	Foxlow	Steaks & grills	2 2 2
	Macellaio RC	"	3 3 3
	The Gate	Vegetarian	4 2 3
	Burger & Lobster	Burgers, etc	3 3 3
	Santore	Pizza	3 3 2
	Nuala	BBQ	4 3 4
	Ceviche Old St	Peruvian	5 3 4
	Berber & Q Shawarma Bar	Middle Eastern	4 3 3
	The Sichuan	Chinese	3 2 2
£40+	Lantana Café	Australian	3 3 3
	The Great Chase	British, Modern	3 4 2
	The Green	"	3 4 3
	La Ferme London	French	3 3 3
	La Porchetta Pizzeria	Italian	2 3 2

Price	Name	Cuisine			
	Morito	Spanish	4	3	4
	Pizza Pilgrims	Pizza	3	3	3
	Breddos Tacos	Mexican/TexMex	3	3	3
	Bone Daddies, The Bower	Japanese	3	3	4
	Pham Sushi	"	4	2	3
	Cây Tre	Vietnamese	3	2	2
£35+	Kolossi Grill	Greek	2	3	2
	The Eagle	Mediterranean	3	3	4
	Homeslice	Pizza	3	3	3
	Workshop Coffee	Sandwiches, cakes, etc	3	3	3
	On The Bab	Korean	3	2	2
£30+	Fish Central	Fish & seafood	3	2	2
	Bowling Bird	International	4	4	3
£25+	Bean & Wheat	Sandwiches, cakes, etc	4	3	3
£10+	Department of Coffee	Sandwiches, cakes, etc	3	4	3
	Prufrock Coffee	"	3	2	2

The City (EC2, EC3, EC4)

Price	Name	Cuisine			
£110+	La Dame de Pic London	French	4	3	2
	Nobu Shoreditch	Japanese	3	2	3
£100+	Mei Ume	Japanese	3	3	4
£90+	City Social	British, Modern	3	3	3
	Fenchurch Restaurant	"	3	2	4
	Angler, South Place Hotel	Fish & seafood	4	3	3
	Coq dArgent	French	2	3	3
	Goodman City	Steaks & grills	3	3	2
	Lutyens Grill, The Ned	"	3	4	4
	Sushisamba	Japanese	2	2	3
£80+	M Restaurant	Steaks & grills	2	2	2
	Coya	Peruvian	3	2	3
	Yauatcha City	Chinese	4	3	4
£70+	Darwin Brasserie	British, Modern	2	3	4
	Duck & Waffle	"	2	2	5
	Helix	"	3	3	5
	High Timber	"	2	3	3
	1 Lombard Street	"	2	2	3
	St Leonards	"	–	–	–
	Sweetings	Fish & seafood	3	2	4
	Cecconi's at The Ned	Italian	2	2	3
	Manicomio	"	2	2	3
	Boisdale of Bishopsgate	Scottish	3	2	3
	Sagardi	Spanish	2	3	3
	Barbecoa	Steaks & grills	2	2	2
	Hawksmoor	"	3	2	2
	Mint Leaf Lounge	Indian	3	2	3

£60+				
The Botanist	British, Modern	2	2	2
Bread Street Kitchen	"	2	2	3
The Don	"	3	3	2
Sign of The Don	"	3	4	4
James Cochran EC3	"	–	–	–
The Mercer	"	2	2	2
Merchants Tavern	"	3	3	4
Northbank	"	3	2	3
Vinoteca City	"	2	2	3
Paternoster Chop House	British, Traditional	2	2	2
Fish Market	Fish & seafood	3	2	2
Cabotte	French	4	5	4
28-50	"	2	2	3
Vivat Bacchus	International	3	4	2
Caravaggio	Italian	3	2	2
Hispania	Spanish	3	3	3
The Tramshed	Steaks & grills	3	2	3
Vanilla Black	Vegetarian	4	3	3
Red Rooster	Chicken	2	2	3
Cinnamon Kitchen	Indian	4	3	3
Nanashi	Japanese	3	3	2

£50+				
Bodeans	American	3	2	3
Pitt Cue Co	"	4	2	2
The Anthologist	British, Modern	2	3	3
Caravan	"	3	3	3
Humble Grape	"	3	4	4
The Ivy City Garden	"	2	2	4
Leroy	"	3	4	3
Sargeants Mess	"	–	–	–
Osteria, Barbican Centre	Italian	1	1	2
Popolo	"	5	4	3
Taberna Etrusca	"	3	2	3
Rök	Scandinavian	3	4	3
Mac & Wild	Scottish	3	2	4
Camino Monument	Spanish	3	3	2
José Pizarro	"	3	2	2
Aviary	Steaks & grills	2	2	3
The Jones Family Project	"	3	4	4
Three Cranes	"	–	–	–
Burger & Lobster	Burgers, etc	3	3	3
Haz	Turkish	2	2	2
Oklava	"	4	4	3
Brigadiers	Indian	5	4	4

£40+				
Café Below	British, Modern	3	2	2
Coppa Club Tower Bridge	"	2	3	4
The Kitty Hawk	"	3	3	3
VQ	"	2	3	3
Simpsons Tavern	British, Traditional	1	3	5
The Wine Library	International	2	3	5
Rucoletta	Italian	3	2	1
Blacklock	Steaks & grills	4	4	4
Relais de Venise	"	3	3	2
Haché	Burgers, etc	3	3	2
Pizza Pilgrims	Pizza	3	3	3

	Street Pizza	"	–	–	–
	temper City	BBQ	2	2	4
	Koya	Japanese	4	4	3
	Shoryu Ramen	"	3	3	2
	Hare & Tortoise	Pan-Asian	3	3	2
£35+	Essence Cuisine	Vegetarian	4	3	2
	Homeslice	Pizza	3	3	3
	Kurumaya	Japanese	4	3	3
	Taro	"	3	2	2
	On The Bab	Korean	3	2	2
£30+	Flat Iron	Steaks & grills	3	4	4
	K10	Japanese	3	3	2
£25+	Patty and Bun	Burgers, etc	4	3	3
	Shake Shack	"	3	2	2
	Ozone Coffee Roasters	Sandwiches, cakes, etc	3	3	4
£20+	Bleecker Burger	Burgers, etc	5	2	2
	Butchies	Chicken	3	2	2
	Bibimbap	Korean	3	2	2
£15+	Yum Bun	Japanese	5	4	2
£10+	Sub Cult	Sandwiches, cakes, etc	5	3	2
	Schmaltz Truck	Chicken	5	3	3
	Pilpel	Middle Eastern	3	3	2
	City Càphê	Vietnamese	3	3	2

East End & Docklands (All E postcodes)

£200+	Mãos	Portuguese	5	4	4
£90+	Goodman	Steaks & grills	3	3	2
£80+	Lyle's	British, Modern	4	2	2
	Galvin La Chapelle	French	4	4	5
	Roka	Japanese	4	3	3
£70+	The Gun	British, Modern	2	3	4
	Pidgin	"	5	5	3
	Smith's Wapping	"	4	4	5
	Plateau	French	2	3	3
	Bokan	International	3	3	3
	Canto Corvino	Italian	3	2	3
	Cecconi's Shoreditch	"	2	2	3
	Hawksmoor	Steaks & grills	3	2	2
£60+	Big Easy	American	2	2	3
	Bistrotheque	British, Modern	3	2	4
	Brat	"	5	4	4
	One Canada Square	"	2	3	2
	Rochelle Canteen	"	2	2	4

	Sager + Wilde	"		2 2 3
	Toms Kitchen	"		2 2 2
	The Marksman	British, Traditional		4 3 4
	St John Bread & Wine	"		3 3 3
	Wright Brothers	Fish & seafood		4 4 3
	Tratra	French		– – –
	The Laughing Heart	International		2 2 3
	Il Bordello	Italian		3 4 4
	Brawn	Mediterranean		4 3 3
	Boisdale of Canary Wharf	Scottish		2 2 3
	Buen Ayre	Argentinian		4 3 2
£50+	The Culpeper	British, Modern		3 3 4
	Eat 17	"		3 4 3
	The Empress	"		3 3 4
	Galvin HOP	"		2 2 3
	The Narrow	"		2 2 4
	Sapling	"		– – –
	The Straight & Narrow	"		2 3 3
	Treves & Hyde	"		3 4 3
	Bumpkin	British, Traditional		2 2 3
	Formans	Fish & seafood		4 3 2
	Blanchette East	French		2 2 3
	Chez Elles	"		4 4 5
	Eat 17	International		3 4 3
	Lardo	Italian		2 2 2
	Super Tuscan	"		3 4 3
	Tuyo	Mediterranean		3 3 3
	Bravas	Spanish		3 4 4
	Ibérica	"		2 2 3
	Hill & Szrok	Steaks & grills		3 3 3
	Burger & Lobster	Burgers, etc		3 3 3
	Pizza East	Pizza		4 3 4
	Andina	Peruvian		3 3 3
	Ottolenghi	Israeli		3 2 2
	Haz	Turkish		2 2 2
	Lahpet	Burmese		3 3 3
	Royal China	Chinese		3 1 2
	Yi-Ban	"		2 2 3
	Café Spice Namaste	Indian		4 4 3
	Grand Trunk Road	"		4 4 3
	Sticks'n'Sushi	Japanese		3 2 2
	Som Saa	Thai		5 4 4
£40+	Breakfast Club	American		3 3 3
	Duke of Richmond	British, Modern		– – –
	Fayre Share	"		– – –
	P Franco	"		4 2 4
	L'Ami Malo	French		5 4 4
	Provender	"		3 4 4
	Blixen	International		3 3 3
	Dokke	"		3 4 3
	Emilias Crafted Pasta	Italian		4 4 3
	Rotorino	"		2 4 3
	Verdi's	"		3 4 3
	Morito	Spanish		4 3 4

	Restaurant	Cuisine			
	Mildreds	*Vegetarian*	3	2	2
	Poppies	*Fish & chips*	3	2	3
	Pizza Pilgrims	*Pizza*	3	3	3
	Chick 'n' Sours	*Chicken*	4	3	3
	Smokestak	*BBQ*	4	3	3
	Lupita	*Mexican/TexMex*	3	3	2
	Berber & Q	*Middle Eastern*	5	3	5
	Delamina East	*"*	4	4	2
	Sichuan Folk	*Chinese*	4	3	2
	Dishoom	*Indian*	3	4	5
	Ippudo London	*Japanese*	3	2	3
	Tonkotsu	*"*	4	3	3
	Smoking Goat	*Thai*	4	3	4
	Viet Grill	*Vietnamese*	3	2	2
£35+	Sutton and Sons	*Vegetarian*	4	3	2
	Ark Fish	*Fish & chips*	3	4	2
	Yard Sale Pizza	*Pizza*	5	3	3
	Randy's Wing Bar	*Chicken*	3	3	3
	Amber	*Middle Eastern*	–	–	–
	Gunpowder	*Indian*	4	4	3
	Mien Tay	*Vietnamese*	3	2	2
	Sông Quê	*"*	3	3	2
	Bao Bar	*Taiwanese*	4	3	3
£30+	The Spread Eagle	*Vegetarian*	3	3	3
	Dirty Burger Shoreditch	*Burgers, etc*	2	2	2
£25+	Patty and Bun	*Burgers, etc*	4	3	3
	Shake Shack	*"*	3	2	2
	Mangal 1	*Turkish*	5	3	2
	Lahore Kebab House	*Pakistani*	4	2	1
	Needoo	*"*	4	2	2
	Tayyabs	*"*	4	2	2
£20+	Forest Bar & Kitchen	*Mediterranean*	–	–	–
	Bleecker Burger	*Burgers, etc*	5	2	2
	Crate	*Pizza*	4	3	4
	Jidori	*Japanese*	3	3	2
	Singburi Royal Thai Café	*Thai*	4	3	3
£15+	Campania & Jones	*Italian*	4	3	4
	E Pellicci	*"*	3	5	5
£10+	The Duck Truck	*Burgers, etc*	5	3	3
	Pilpel	*Middle Eastern*	3	3	2
£5+	The Rib Man	*Burgers, etc*	5	3	–
	Brick Lane Beigel Bake	*Sandwiches, cakes, etc*	3	1	1
	Pavilion Cafe & Bakery	*"*	4	2	4

MAPS

MAP 1 – LONDON OVERVIEW

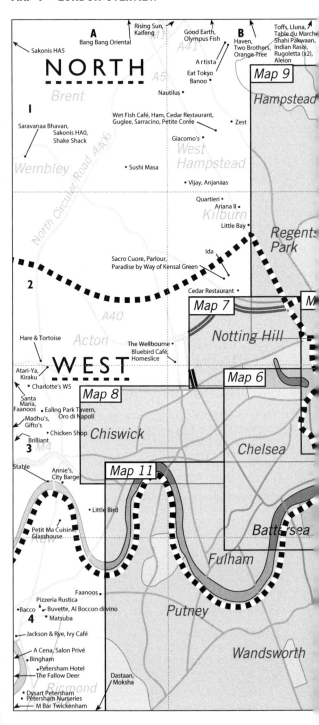

A

Bang Bang Oriental

Rising Sun, Kaifeng

Good Earth, Olympus Fish

B

Haven, Two Brothers, Orange Tree

Toffs, Lluna, Table du Marche, Shahi Pakwaan, Indian Rasoi, Rugoletta (x2), Aleion

Sakonis HA5

NORTH

Artista

Eat Tokyo
Banoo •

Brent

A5

Map 9

Hampstead

1

Nautilus •

Saravanaa Bhavan, Sakonis HA0, Shake Shack

Wet Fish Café, Ham, Cedar Restaurant, Guglee, Sarracino, Petite Corée

• Zest

Wembley

North Circular Road A406

Giacomo's •

West Hampstead

• Sushi Masa

• Vijay, Anjanaas

Quartieri •

Ariana II •

Kilburn

Little Bay •

Regents Park

Sacro Cuore, Parlour, Paradise by Way of Kensal Green

Ida •

Cedar Restaurant •

Map 7

M

2

A40

Acton

Notting Hill

Hare & Tortoise

The Wellbourne •
Bluebird Café, Homeslice

WEST

Map 6

Atari-Ya, Kiraku

• Charlotte's W5

Map 8

Santa Maria, Faanoos

• Ealing Park Tavern, Oro di Napoli

Chiswick

Chelsea

Madhu's, Gifto's

• Chicken Shop

Brilliant

M4

3

Stable

Annie's, City Barge

Map 11

• Little Bird

Battersea

Petit Ma Cuisine, Glasshouse

Kew

Fulham

Faanoos •

Pizzeria Rustica

• Bacco

• Buvette, Al Boccon divino

Putney

4

• Matsuba

Jackson & Rye, Ivy Café

A Cena, Salon Privé

• Bingham

Wandsworth

• Petersham Hotel
The Fallow Deer

• Dysart Petersham
• Petersham Nurseries

Dastaan, Moksha

M Bar Twickenham

Richmond

MAP I – LONDON OVERVIEW

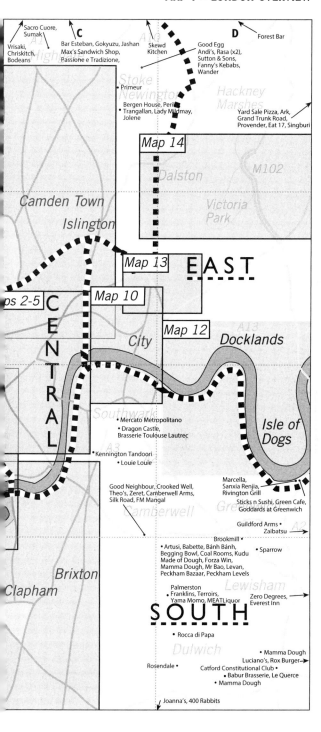

MAP 2 – WEST END OVERVIEW

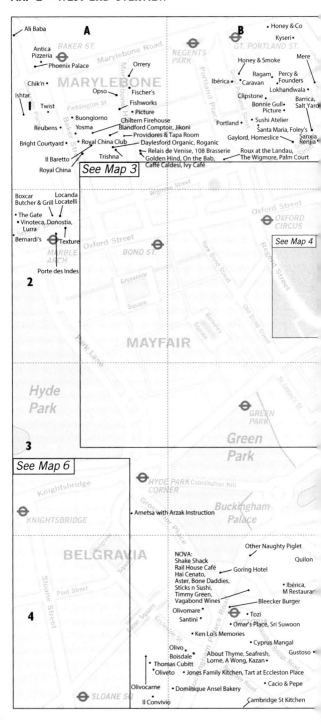

Ali Baba

A

BAKER ST.

Antica
Pizzeria
• Phoenix Palace

Marylebone Road

Orrery

Chik'n •

MARYLEBONE

Ishtar

Opso

Paddington St

Twist

Fischer's

Fishworks

• Picture

Reubens •

Buongiorno
• Yosma
Chiltern Firehouse
Blandford Comptoir, Jikoni

Bright Courtyard •

• Royal China Club
Providores & Tapa Room

Il Baretto

Daylesford Organic, Roganic

Trishna

Royal China

See Map 3

Relais de Venise, 108 Brasserie
Golden Hind, On the Bab,
Caffé Caldesi, Ivy Café

B

• Honey & Co

Kyseri •

REGENTS
PARK

GT. PORTLAND ST.

Honey & Smoke

Mere

Ragam
Ibérica • Caravan

Percy &
Founders
Lokhandwala

Clipstone •
Bonnie Gull
Picture •

Barrica,
Salt Yard

Portland •
Sushi Atelier

Santa Maria, Foley's

Gaylord, Homeslice

Sanxia
Renjia

Roux at the Landau,
The Wigmore, Palm Court

Boxcar
Butcher & Grill

Locanda
Locatelli

• The Gate
• Vinoteca, Donostia,
Lurra
Bernardi's

Oxford Street

OXFORD
CIRCUS

Texture

Oxford Street

BOND ST.

See Map 4

MARBLE
ARCH

Porte des Indes

Grosvenor

Square

2

MAYFAIR

Hyde
Park

GREEN
PARK

3

Green
Park

See Map 6

Knightsbridge

HYDE PARK Constitution Hill
CORNER

KNIGHTSBRIDGE

Ametsa with Arzak Instruction

Buckingham
Palace

BELGRAVIA

Other Naughty Piglet

NOVA:
Shake Shack
Rail House Café
Hai Cenato,
Aster, Bone Daddies,
Sticks n Sushi,
Timmy Green,
Vagabond Wines

Goring Hotel

Quilon

• Ibérica,
M Restaurant

Bleecker Burger

Olivomare •

Santini •

• Tozi

• Omar's Place, Sri Suwoon

4

• Ken Lo's Memories

• Cyprus Mangal

Olivo •
Boisdale •
• Thomas Cubitt
• Oliveto

About Thyme, Seafresh,
Lorne, A Wong, Kazan •

Gustoso •

• Jones Family Kitchen, Tart at Eccleston Place

Olivocarne •

• Dominique Ansel Bakery

• Cacio & Pepe

SLOANE SQ.

Il Convivio

Cambridge St Kitchen

MAP 2 – WEST END OVERVIEW

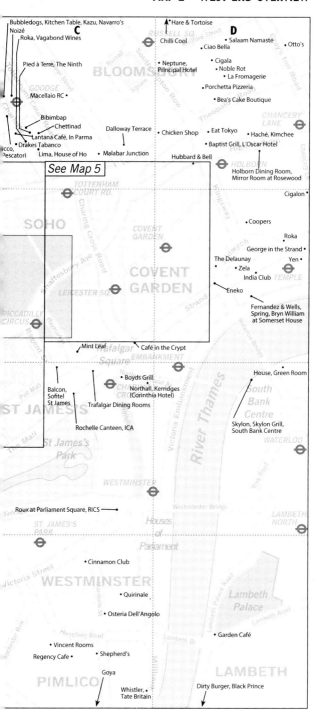

Bubbledogs, Kitchen Table, Kazu, Navarro's
Noizé
Roka, Vagabond Wines

Pied à Terre, The Ninth

Hare & Tortoise
Chilli Cool
Ciao Bella
Salaam Namaste
Otto's

Neptune,
Principal Hotel
Cigala
Noble Rot
La Fromagerie
Porchetta Pizzeria
Bea's Cake Boutique

BLOOMSBURY

GOODGE
Macellaio RC •

CHANCERY
LANE

Bibimbap
Chettinad
Lantana Café, In Parma
icco, • Drakes Tabanco
Pescatori
Lima, House of Ho

Dalloway Terrace

Chicken Shop
Eat Tokyo
Haché, Kimchee
Baptist Grill, L'Oscar Hotel

Malabar Junction

Hubbard & Bell

HOLBORN
Holborn Dining Room,
Mirror Room at Rosewood

See Map 5

TOTTENHAM
COURT RD.

Cigalon •

SOHO

COVENT
GARDEN

Coopers

Roka

George in the Strand •

The Delaunay
Zela
India Club
Yen •

TEMPLE

COVENT
GARDEN

LEICESTER SQ.

Eneko

PICCADILLY
CIRCUS

Fernandez & Wells,
Spring, Bryn William
at Somerset House

Mint Leaf
Café in the Crypt

Trafalgar
Square

EMBANKMENT

House, Green Room

Balcon,
Sofitel
St James

ST JAMES'S

Boyds Grill,
Northall, Kerridges
(Corinthia Hotel)

Trafalgar Dining Rooms

Rochelle Canteen, ICA

South
Bank
Centre

Skylon, Skylon Grill,
South Bank Centre

WATERLOO

The Mall

St James's
Park

WESTMINSTER

River Thames

Roux at Parliament Square, RICS

ST JAMES'S
PARK

Houses

of

Parliament

LAMBETH
NORTH

Cinnamon Club

WESTMINSTER

Quirinale

Osteria Dell'Angolo

Lambeth
Palace

Vincent Rooms
Regency Cafe •
Shepherd's

Garden Café

Goya

PIMLICO

Whistler,
Tate Britain

Dirty Burger, Black Prince

LAMBETH

MAP 3 – MAYFAIR, ST. JAMES'S & WEST SOHO

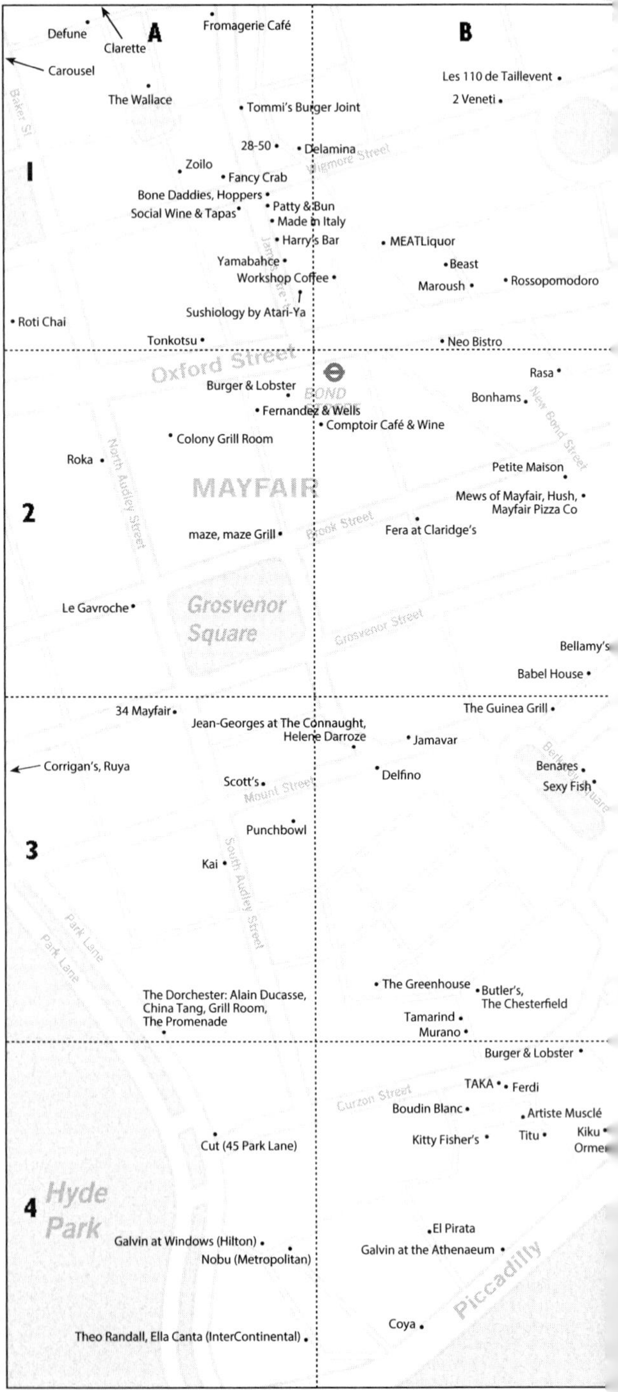

A

B

Defune

Clarette

Fromagerie Café

Carousel

Les 110 de Taillevent

2 Veneti

The Wallace

Tommi's Burger Joint

Baker St

28-50

Delamina

Wigmore Street

Zoilo

Fancy Crab

1

Bone Daddies, Hoppers

Social Wine & Tapas

Patty & Bun

Made in Italy

Harry's Bar

MEATLiquor

Yamabahce

Beast

Workshop Coffee

Maroush

Rossopomodoro

Roti Chai

Sushiology by Atari-Ya

Tonkotsu

Neo Bistro

Oxford Street

BOND

Rasa

Burger & Lobster

Bonhams

Fernandez & Wells

Comptoir Café & Wine

Colony Grill Room

Roka

New Bond Street

Petite Maison

MAYFAIR

Mews of Mayfair, Hush,

Mayfair Pizza Co

2

North Audley Street

Brook Street

maze, maze Grill

Fera at Claridge's

Le Gavroche

Grosvenor

Square

Grosvenor Street

Bellamy's

Babel House

34 Mayfair

Jean-Georges at The Connaught,

Helene Darroze

The Guinea Grill

Jamavar

Corrigan's, Ruya

Scott's

Mount Street

Delfino

Benares

Sexy Fish

3

South Audley Street

Punchbowl

Kai

Park Lane

Park Lane

The Dorchester: Alain Ducasse,

China Tang, Grill Room,

The Promenade

The Greenhouse

Butler's,

The Chesterfield

Tamarind

Murano

Burger & Lobster

Curzon Street

TAKA

Ferdi

Boudin Blanc

Artiste Musclé

Kitty Fisher's

Titu

Kiku

Ormer

Cut (45 Park Lane)

Hyde

Park

4

El Pirata

Galvin at Windows (Hilton)

Galvin at the Athenaeum

Nobu (Metropolitan)

Piccadilly

Theo Randall, Ella Canta (InterContinental)

Coya

MAP 3 – MAYFAIR, ST. JAMES'S & WEST SOHO

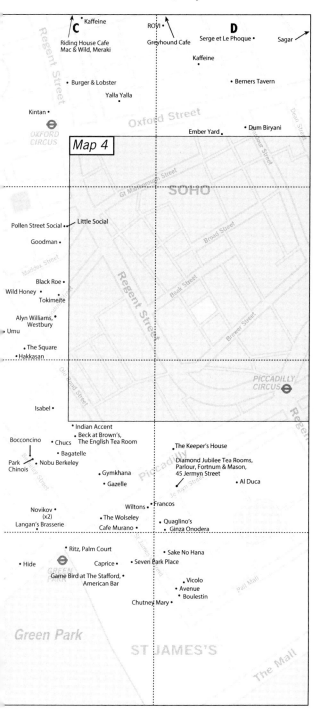

C • Kaffeine

ROVI •

D

Riding House Cafe
Mac & Wild, Meraki

Greyhound Cafe

Serge et Le Phoque •

Sagar

Kaffeine •

• Burger & Lobster

• Berners Tavern

Yalla Yalla •

Kintan •

Oxford Street

OXFORD
CIRCUS

Ember Yard •

• Dum Biryani

Map 4

SOHO

Gt Marlborough Street

Pollen Street Social • — Little Social

Goodman •

Broad Street

Regent Street

Black Street

Brewer Street

Black Roe •

Wild Honey •

Tokimeite •

Alyn Williams, •
Westbury

Umu •

• The Square

• Hakkasan

PICCADILLY
CIRCUS

Isabel •

• Indian Accent

• Beck at Brown's,
The English Tea Room

Bocconcino •

• Chucs

• The Keeper's House

• Bagatelle

Diamond Jubilee Tea Rooms,
Parlour, Fortnum & Mason,
45 Jermyn Street

Park
Chinois

• Nobu Berkeley

• Gymkhana

• Gazelle

• Al Duca

Novikov •
(x2)

Langan's Brasserie •

Wiltons • • Francos

• The Wolseley

Cafe Murano •

• Quaglino's

• Ginza Onodera

• Ritz, Palm Court

• Sake No Hana

• Hide

Caprice •

• Seven Park Place

GREEN
PARK

Game Bird at The Stafford, •
American Bar

• Vicolo

• Avenue

• Boulestin

Chutney Mary •

Green Park

ST JAMES'S

The Mall

MAP 4 – WEST SOHO & PICCADILLY

⊖ OXFORD CIRCUS

A **B**

1

Chisou, Stem

Aqua Nueva, Aqua Kyoto

Antidote

2

Patara

Bombay Bustle

Sketch: Lecture Room, Gallery

28-50

The Windmill

Ristorante Frescobaldi

Tapas Brindisa

Inko Nito

Pastaio

Claw Carnaby

Dehesa

Dishoom, Jinjuu

Polpo

Wright Brothers

Kingly Court: Darjeeling Express, Shoryu Ramen, Señor Ceviche, Oka, Pizza Pilgrims, Le Bab, Good Egg

Shampers

Flat Iron

3

The Araki

Sartoria

Nopi

Street XO

Sabor

Magpie

tibits

Sakagura

Momo

Heddon St Kitchen

4

Cecconi's

Veeraswamy

Bentley's

MAP 4 – WEST SOHO & PICCADILLY

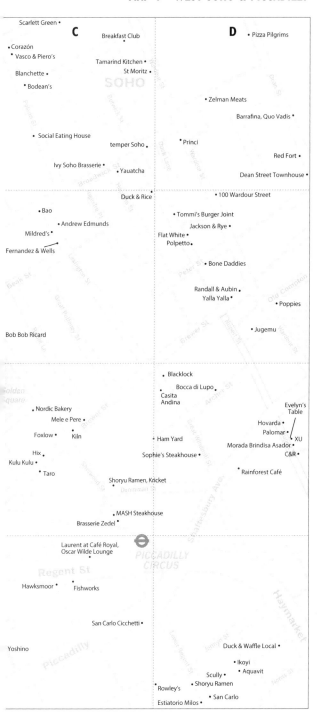

C

D

Scarlett Green •

Breakfast Club •

• Pizza Pilgrims

• Corazón

• Vasco & Piero's

Tamarind Kitchen •

St Moritz •

Blanchette •

SOHO

• Bodean's

• Zelman Meats

Barrafina, Quo Vadis •

• Social Eating House

temper Soho •

• Princi

Red Fort •

Ivy Soho Brasserie •

• Yauatcha

Dean Street Townhouse •

Duck & Rice •

• 100 Wardour Street

• Bao

• Tommi's Burger Joint

• Andrew Edmunds

Jackson & Rye •

Mildred's •

Flat White •

Polpetto •

Fernandez & Wells

• Bone Daddies

Randall & Aubin •

Yalla Yalla •

• Poppies

Bob Bob Ricard

• Jugemu

• Blacklock

Bocca di Lupo •

Casita

Andina

Evelyn's

Table

• Nordic Bakery

Mele e Pere •

Hovarda •

Palomar •

Foxlow •

Kiln

• XU

Ham Yard •

Morada Brindisa Asador •

Hix •

Sophie's Steakhouse •

C&R •

Kulu Kulu •

• Rainforest Café

• Taro

Shoryu Ramen, Kricket •

• MASH Steakhouse

Brasserie Zedel •

Laurent at Café Royal,
Oscar Wilde Lounge

PICCADILLY
CIRCUS

Regent St

Hawksmoor •

Fishworks

San Carlo Cicchetti •

Yoshino

Duck & Waffle Local •

• Ikoyi

• Aquavit

Scully •

• Rowley's

• Shoryu Ramen

• San Carlo

Estiatorio Milos •

Piccadilly

MAP 5 — EAST SOHO, CHINATOWN & COVENT GARDEN

MAP 5 – EAST SOHO, CHINATOWN & COVENT GARDEN

C

Shu Xiangge •

Savoir Faire

High Holborn

Drury Lane

D

Great Queen Street •

Gt. Queen St

• Da Mario

• Punjab
• On The Dak

Parsons • • The 10 Cases
• Kulu Kulu

• The Barbary, Homeslice,
Jacob & the Angel

Endell Street

• Margot

• Barrafina, Drury Lane

Flesh & Buns •

Shelton Street

by Chloe •

• Hawksmoor

COVENT GARDEN

Royal Opera House

Long Acre

• Maison Bab,
temper Covent Garden

Ⓤ • Wahlburgers

Bow Street

COVENT GARDEN

Eat Tokyo, Sagar •
Bodean's, Opera Tavern •
Balthazar • Jidori •
Red Farm •
Sushisamba • Café Murano (x2),
On The Bab
Christopher's, San Carlo Cicchetti

• Bageriet

Cantina Laredo

Lima Floral •

The Petersham,
La Goccia •
Clos Maggiore •

Covent Garden Market

Shake Shack • • MEATmarket

Frog by Adam Handling •

Joe Allen •

Garrick St

• Le Garrick

izza Pilgrims

Din Tai Fung • • Ivy Market Grill

• Oystermen

Cora Pearl • • Sticks 'n' Sushi

Henrietta • Polpo
Flat Iron, Frenchie • Rules •

Big Easy •

Simpsons-in-the-Strand •

Bedford St

Savoy Grill, Kaspar's,
Thames Foyer (Savoy Hotel) •

Asia de Cuba

• Cinnamon Bazaar

Strand

• Fumo

• Lao Café

Smith & Wollensky •

• Saint Luke's Kitchen, Library

Coliseum

William IV Street

• Barrafina • Terroirs

• Tandoor Chop House

• Lupita

Victoria Emb.

• Ippudo

• Gordon's Wine Bar

MAP 6 – KNIGHTSBRIDGE, CHELSEA & SOUTH KENSINGTON

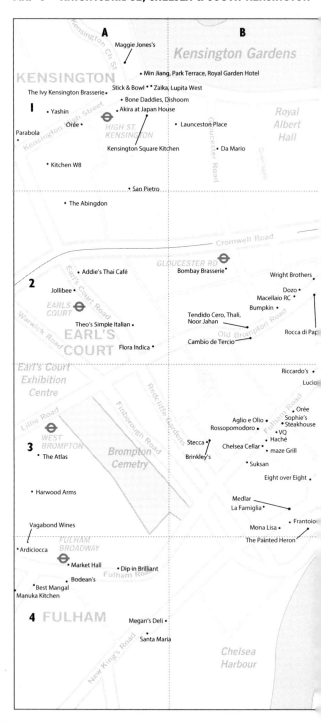

A

Maggie Jones's

Kensington Gardens

KENSINGTON

• Min Jiang, Park Terrace, Royal Garden Hotel

Stick & Bowl • • Zaika, Lupita West

The Ivy Kensington Brasserie •

• Bone Daddies, Dishoom

B

• Akira at Japan House

1

• Yashin

Orée •

Royal Albert Hall

HIGH ST. KENSINGTON

Parabola
•

• Launceston Place

Kensington Square Kitchen

• Da Mario

• Kitchen W8

• San Pietro

• The Abingdon

Cromwell Road

GLOUCESTER RD

• Addie's Thai Café

Bombay Brasserie •

Wright Brothers •

Jollibee •

2

Dozo •
Macellaio RC •

EARLS COURT

Bumpkin •

Theo's Simple Italian •

Tendido Cero, Thali,
Noor Jahan •

Old Brompton Road

Rocca di Pap

EARL'S COURT

Flora Indica •

Cambio de Tercio

Riccardo's •

Earl's Court Exhibition Centre

Lucio

• Orée

Aglio e Olio •

Sophie's
• Steakhouse

Rossopomodoro •

• VQ

WEST BROMPTON

Stecca •

• Haché

Brompton Cemetery

Chelsea Cellar •

• maze Grill

3

• The Atlas

Brinkley's •

• Suksan

Eight over Eight •

• Harwood Arms

Medlar •

La Famiglia •

Vagabond Wines

• Frantoio

Mona Lisa •

• Ardiciocca

FULHAM BROADWAY

The Painted Heron

• Market Hall

• Dip in Brilliant

• Bodean's

Fulham Road

• Best Mangal
Manuka Kitchen

4 FULHAM

Megan's Deli •

• Santa Maria

Chelsea Harbour

New King's Road

MAP 6 – KNIGHTSBRIDGE, CHELSEA & SOUTH KENSINGTON

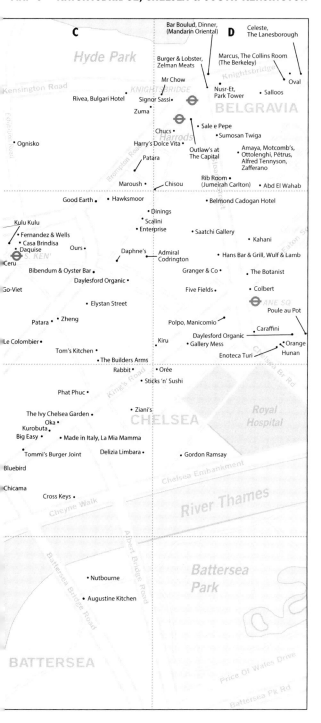

C

Hyde Park

Kensington Road

Bar Boulud, Dinner,
(Mandarin Oriental)

D

Celeste,
The Lanesborough

Burger & Lobster,
Zelman Meats

Marcus, The Collins Room
(The Berkeley)

Mr Chow

Knightsbridge

KNIGHTSBRIDGE

Nusr-Et,
Park Tower

Oval

Rivea, Bulgari Hotel

Signor Sassi

Salloos

Zuma

BELGRAVIA

Ogniska

Chucs

Sale e Pepe

Harry's Dolce Vita

Sumosan Twiga

Patara

Outlaw's at
The Capital

Amaya, Motcomb's,
Ottolenghi, Pétrus,
Alfred Tennyson,
Zafferano

Maroush

Chisou

Rib Room
(Jumeirah Carlton)

Abd El Wahab

Good Earth

Hawksmoor

Belmond Cadogan Hotel

Kulu Kulu

Dinings

Scalini

Fernandez & Wells

Enterprise

Casa Brindisa

Saatchi Gallery

Kahani

Daquise

Ours

Daphne's

Hans Bar & Grill, Wulf & Lamb

Ceru

Admiral
Codrington

S. KEN'

Bibendum & Oyster Bar

Granger & Co

The Botanist

Daylesford Organic

Go-Viet

Five Fields

Colbert

Elystan Street

SLOANE SQ

Poule au Pot

Patara

Zheng

Polpo, Manicomio

Caraffini

Le Colombier

Daylesford Organic

Kiru

Gallery Mess

Orange

Tom's Kitchen

Enoteca Turi

Hunan

The Builders Arms

Rabbit

Orée

King's Road

Sticks 'n' Sushi

Phat Phuc

Royal
Hospital

Ziani's

The Ivy Chelsea Garden

CHELSEA

Oka

Kurobuta

Big Easy

Made in Italy, La Mia Mamma

Tommi's Burger Joint

Delizia Limbara

Gordon Ramsay

Bluebird

Chelsea Embankment

Chicama

Cross Keys

Cheyne Walk

River Thames

Albert Bridge Road

Battersea
Park

Nutbourne

Augustine Kitchen

Battersea Bridge Road

BATTERSEA

Price Of Wales Drive

Battersea Pk Rd

MAP 7 – NOTTING HILL & BAYSWATER

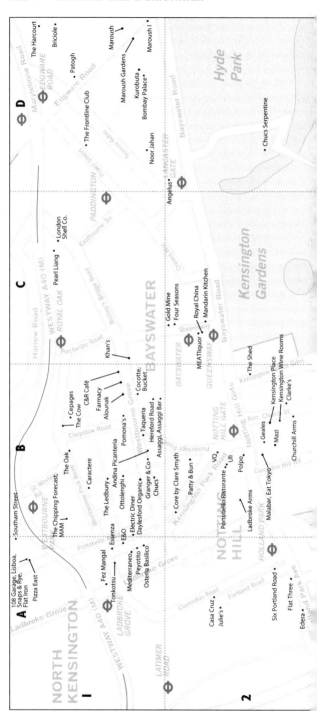

NORTH KENSINGTON

The Harcourt
Briciole
Maroush

EDGWARE ROAD
Patogh
Maroush Gardens
Maroush I
Kurobuta
Bombay Palace
Noor Jahan

The Frontline Club

Hyde Park

Chucs Serpentine

Angelus

London Shell Co.
Pearl Liang

Eastbourne Ter

PADDINGTON

WESTWAY A40 (M)
ROYAL OAK

Harrow Road

BAYSWATER

Kensington Gardens

Gold Mine
Four Seasons
Royal China
Mandarin Kitchen

MEATliquor
BAYSWATER

QUEENSWAY

The Shed

The Oak
Khan's

Cepages
The Cow
C&R Café
Farmacy
Alounak
Cocotte, Bucket
Hereford Road
Taqueria
Assaggi, Assaggi Bar

Chepstow Road

Caractere

The Ledbury
Andina Picantería
Ottolenghi
Electric Diner
Daylesford Organic
Granger & Co
Chucs

Pomona's

Core by Clare Smyth

Patty & Bun
VQ
Portobello Ristorante
Uli
Polpo

Kensington Place
Kensington Wine Rooms
Clarke's
Geales
Mazi
Churchill Arms

NOTTING HILL GATE

108 Garage, Lisboa, Snaps & Rye, Flat Iron
Pizza East
Fez Mangal
Tonkotsu
Mediterraneo
Peyotito
Osteria Basilico

Essenza
EБO
MAM
The Chipping Forecast

Southam Street
WESTBOURNE

LADBROKE GROVE
WESTWAY A40 (M)

Ladbroke Arms
Malabar, Eat Tokyo

NOTTING HILL

Casa Cruz
Julie's

Six Portland Road
Flat Three
Edera

Clarendon Road
Portland Road

HOLLAND PARK

LATIMER ROAD

MAP 8 – HAMMERSMITH & CHISWICK

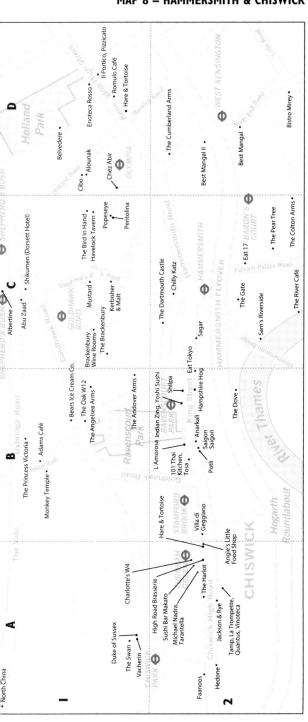

MAP 9 – HAMPSTEAD, CAMDEN TOWN & ISLINGTON

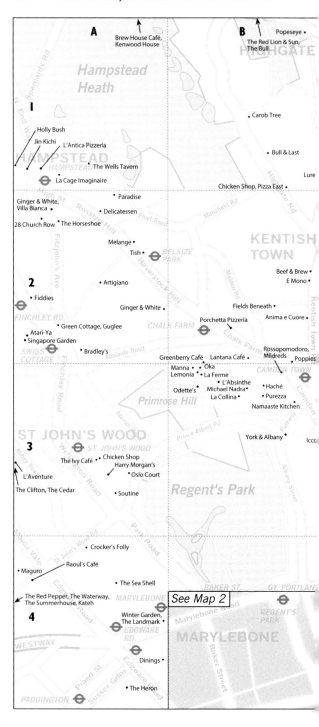

A

Brew House Café, Kenwood House

B

Popeseye •
The Red Lion & Sun,
The Bull

HIGHGATE

Hampstead Heath

1

• Carob Tree

• Holly Bush

Jin Kichi •
• L'Antica Pizzeria

HAMPSTEAD

• Bull & Last

HAMPSTEAD
The Wells Tavern

Lure

La Cage Imaginaire

Chicken Shop, Pizza East

• Paradise

Ginger & White,
Villa Bianca •

• Delicatessen

28 Church Row • The Horseshoe

KENTISH
TOWN

Melange •

Tish • BELSIZE
PARK

2

• Artigiano

Beef & Brew •

E Mono •

• Fiddies

Ginger & White •

Fields Beneath •

FINCHLEY RD.

Porchetta Pizzeria

Anima e Cuore •

CHALK FARM

• Green Cottage, Guglee

Rossopomodoro,
Mildreds

• Atari-Ya
• Singapore Garden

Greenberry Café Lantana Café •

Poppies

SWISS
COTTAGE

• Bradley's

Manna • • Oka

CAMDEN TOWN

Lemonia • • La Ferme

• L'Absinthe

Odette's • Michael Nadra
La Collina •

• Haché

• Purezza

Namaaste Kitchen

Primrose Hill

ST JOHN'S WOOD

Prince Albert Rd

York & Albany •

Iccc

3

ST. JOHN'S WOOD

The Ivy Café • • Chicken Shop
Harry Morgan's

L'Aventure

• Oslo Court

The Clifton, The Cedar

• Soutine

Regent's Park

• Crocker's Folly

Raoul's Café

• Maguro

• The Sea Shell

The Red Pepper, The Waterway,
The Summerhouse, Kateh

MARYLEBONE

See Map 2

GT PORTLAN

BAKER ST.

REGENT'S
PARK

Winter Garden,
The Landmark •

4

EDGWARE
RD.

MARYLEBONE

WESTWAY

Dinings •

• The Heron

PADDINGTON

MAP 9 – HAMPSTEAD, CAMDEN TOWN & ISLINGTON

MAP 10 – THE CITY

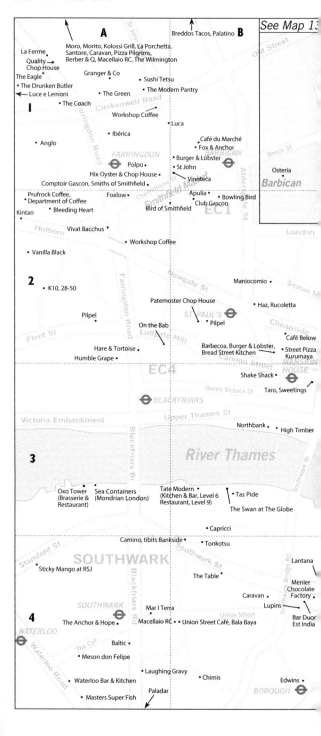

See Map 13

A

B

Breddos Tacos, Palatino

Old Street

La Ferme
Quality
Chop House
The Eagle
The Drunken Butler
Luce e Lemoni

Moro, Morito, Kolossi Grill, La Porchetta,
Santore, Caravan, Pizza Pilgrims,
Berber & Q, Macellaio RC, The Wilmington

Granger & Co

Sushi Tetsu

The Modern Pantry

The Green

The Coach

Clerkenwell Road

Workshop Coffee

Luca

Café du Marché

Ibérica

Fox & Anchor

Anglo

FARRINGDON

BARBICAN

Beech St

Burger & Lobster

St John

Osteria

Polpo

Hix Oyster & Chop House

Aldersgate St

Barbican

Comptoir Gascon, Smiths of Smithfield

Vinoteca

Smithfield Market

London

Prufrock Coffee,
Department of Coffee

Foxlow

Apulia

Bowling Bird

Kintan

Bleeding Heart

Bird of Smithfield

Club Gascon

EC1

Holborn

Vivat Bacchus

Workshop Coffee

Vanilla Black

Newgate St

Maniocomio

Gresham St

2

K10, 28-50

Paternoster Chop House

Haz, Rucoletta

Pilpel

ST PAUL'S

Cheapside

Pilpel

Café Below

Fleet St

Ludgate Hill

On the Bab

Street Pizza

Hare & Tortoise

Barbecoa, Burger & Lobster,
Bread Street Kitchen

Kurumaya

Humble Grape

Cannon Street

MANSION
HOUSE

EC4

Shake Shack

Queen Victoria St

Taro, Sweetings

BLACKFRIARS

Upper Thames St

Northbank

High Timber

Victoria Embankment

Blackfriars Br

River Thames

Southwark Br

3

Oxo Tower
(Brasserie &
Restaurant)

Sea Containers
(Mondrian London)

Tate Modern
(Kitchen & Bar, Level 6
Restaurant, Level 9)

Tas Pide

The Swan at The Globe

Capricci

Camino, tibits Bankside

Tonkotsu

Stamford St

SOUTHWARK

Southwark St

Lantana

Sticky Mango at RSJ

Blackfriars Rd

The Table

Menier
Chocolate
Factory

Caravan

SOUTHWARK

Lupins

Mar I Terra

Union Street

Bar Duor
Est India

WATERLOO

4

The Anchor & Hope

Macellaio RC

Union Street Café, Bala Baya

Waterloo Rd

Baltic

The Cut

Meson don Felipe

Waterloo Bar & Kitchen

Laughing Gravy

Chimis

Edwins

Masters Super Fish

Paladar

BOROUGH

MAP 10 – THE CITY

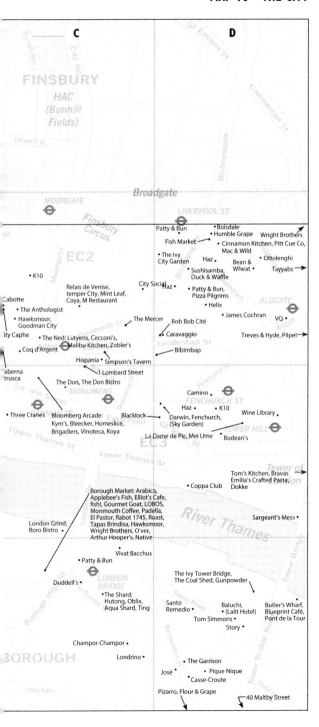

MAP 11 – SOUTH LONDON (& FULHAM)

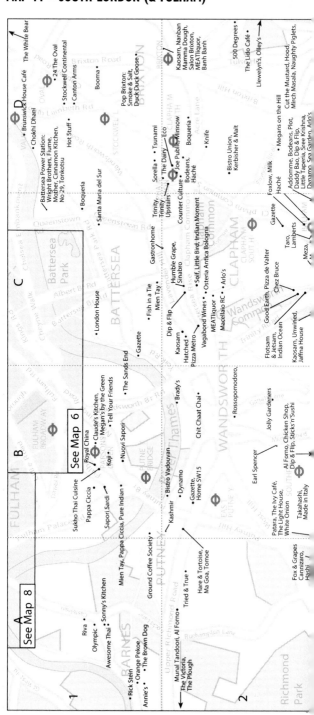

MAP 12 – EAST END & DOCKLANDS

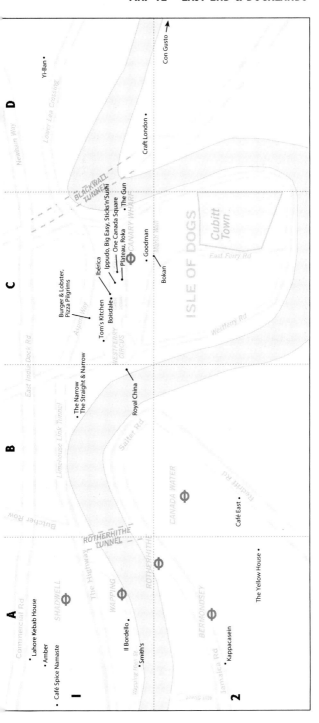

MAP 13 – SHOREDITCH & BETHNAL GREEN

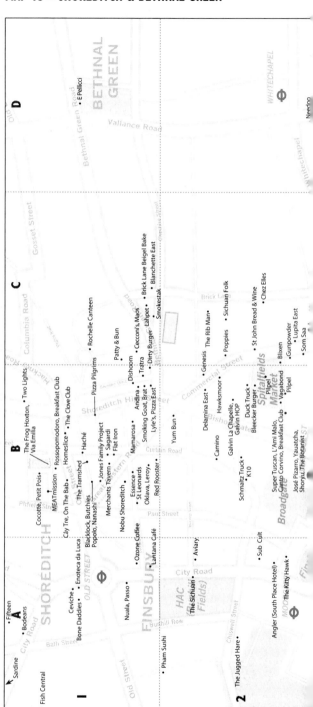

MAP 14 – EAST LONDON

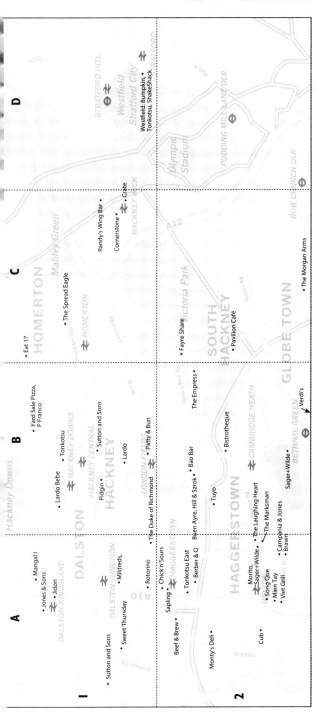